# THE
# GOVERNING
# OF MEN

# AUSTIN RANNEY

The University of Wisconsin

# THE GOVERNING OF MEN

**FOURTH EDITION**

The Dryden Press
Hinsdale, Illinois

**To Betsy, with love**

# PREFACE

This is the fourth edition of a book first published in 1958 and revised previously in 1966 and 1971. It differs considerably from the first three editions, and for good reasons.

For one, in the four years since the third edition—to say nothing of the seventeen years since the first—political events have marched at a vertiginous pace, and many old verities have been replaced by new understandings, questions, and doubts. The world of 1971 was a world of Nixon-Agnew, Heath, Brandt, and Pompidou; of détente with the Soviet Union and apparently implacable hostility to the People's Republic of China; of Vietnam and college campuses racked with protest. The world of 1975 is a world of Ford-Rockefeller, Wilson, Schmidt, and Giscard d'Estaing; of history's first resignation by a President of the United States; of increasing détente with China as well as with the Soviet Union; of oil shortages and escalating inflation; of quiet campuses, crowded libraries and laboratories, and worry about getting jobs. Inevitably, then, we have already forgotten much of what most compelled our attention in 1971; and much of what most concerns us today we little noticed four years ago.

For another, not only have political events marched but some of the ways in which political scientists interpret and explain them have changed as well, as Chapter 1 portrays.

Consequently, while the book's basic structure remains essentially the same, I have revised its order of presentation in order to set forth more clearly the systems-analysis framework which provides its main categories. I have also made considerable changes in the book's contents. These changes reflect not only the recent changes in political science but also the fact that studying how people are governed in the mid-1970s takes place in a very different atmosphere from that of the 1950s or 1960s. Politics and government, to be sure, are among the oldest and most universal of human activities and institutions. Many of the greatest minds in history have pondered their nature and possibilities and have enriched us with their reflections. But today the study of governing has acquired a new and terrible urgency. By the calendar it was not so long ago that most people, at least in the "advanced" nations of the West and particularly in the United States, were confident that their political systems were the best yet devised. Perhaps they are not yet perfect, we felt, but they are perfectible; and if used wisely they are fully capable of achieving our highest goals of individual freedom, social justice, racial and sexual equality, and international peace. Moreover, we assumed that they constitute proper models for the new and backward nations, and when we spoke of "developing nations" we meant nations in the process of becoming more like ours.

But now we are not so sure. Political conflict in the United States and in every other Western nation seems to grow uglier every year. Some blacks say that our most cherished institutions—our courts, our leaders, indeed our whole political system—are all devices to perpetuate white racism. Some young people say that middle America and all its political institutions add up to an Establishment intent on forcing middle-aged, middle-class materialism and hypocrisy on a new generation seeking a better, more meaningful way of life. Some persons of all ages and races insist that the true result of our great material wealth is not a life of richness and satisfaction, but a world of foul air, stinking streams, dead lakes, urban blight, and noise. Now we have learned that a Vice President of the United States took petty graft throughout his term of office, that a President of the United States used the great powers of his office to obstruct justice, and that both were forced to resign as the only alternative to impeachment. And if all this were not enough, over us all, black and white, men and women, young and middle-aged alike, hovers the shadow of The Bomb and thermonuclear World War III.

Physical scientists and ecologists tell us that *homo sapiens* now possesses the technical means either to destroy all life or to build a new life of undreamed richness. How we can get people to make the right choices, they tell us, is a *political* question. And so it is. For amid all the doubts and uncertainties about the future one thing is clear: the most crucial choices humanity makes will emerge from political conflict and be implemented by government action.

Most American colleges and universities and an ever-growing number in other nations recognize the crucial role of politics for the human future by giving the study of political systems prominent places in their curriculums. In most American schools the study of these matters is primarily, although not exclusively, the province of departments variously called "political science" or "government" or "politics." Each such department perennially faces the pedagogical problem of introducing students to this vast, complex, and challenging subject. Two approaches are most commonly used. The first is the detailed study of American government. The second, which may be called the "principles-of-political-science" approach, seeks to identify the properties universal to the governing processes in all human societies and to understand the nature and consequences of the major variations in these processes among different societies.

For a number of years I have taught an introductory undergraduate course using the second approach. My experiences have sensitized me to certain problems arising from its use, and the successive editions of present book represent my changing judgments on how to deal with them.

During the 1950s and early 1960s the main problem seemed to be that of giving students some sense of the relevance of politics and government to their own personal lives, and for many students it remains a major need. Often students begin with the belief that politics is a rather dirty game played by other people and that government is something remote from the really important personal concerns of life. For them I have tried to take as my points of departure certain situations that all students have experienced and have tried to show, step by step, how these situations affect and are affected by what happens in such apparently remote places as United Nations headquarters, Washington, London, Paris, Moscow, Peking—and even in the students' own state capitols and city halls. I have drawn most of my illustrations from current political conflicts in an effort to emphasize the concrete activities and interrelations of real human beings underlying such necessary but highly abstract terms as *demands, supports, conversion processes, culture, socialization,* and the like.

In the mid-1970s, however, many beginning students of political science have no doubt that the subject matter of this discipline is highly relevant to their lives. Some, indeed, feel that what is irrelevant is the matter in which political science treats its materials. "Drop all this scientific pseudo-objectivity," some say, "and talk about the evils of racism, sexism, poverty, and war, about the power structure that sustains them, and about how we should destroy them." However, an accurate understanding of how and why political systems work as they do and produce the policy outputs they do is a necessary, although not sufficient, condition for any effective effort to change those policy outputs and make it a better world. In its present state the contribution political science is best qualified to make is to provide such understanding; and in a general way that is what I have always tried to do in this book.

That is also why I think it important to make students aware of the intellectual processes underlying the facts and conclusions presented by political science. If teachers seek to "give students the facts," they certainly must set forth the facts they consider significant and the explanations of them they consider valid. If teachers also wish to "teach students to think." they must tell students something about the processes by which scholars in the discipline have gathered the facts and drawn conclusions about them. I believe that the first of these two objectives should have the main priority in an introductory course and textbook in political science and that such courses and books should devote most of their space to describing what political scientists have learned. But I also believe that the second objective should receive some attention as well, and that such a course and book should say something about the nature and problems of contemporary political science (as in Chap. 1) and about the particular analytical framework within which the facts of politics and government are described and explained (as in Chaps. 2, 3, 12, and 13).

Like the author of any textbook, I am indebted to many colleagues and friends. I realize that whatever merit—but none of whatever errors—it may have owes much to their help, and I am grateful for the opportunity traditionally provided by the preface to make public my thanks to those to whom I am most deeply in debt. In addition to general thanks to the authors of the many works cited in the text for the insights and information they have provided, I wish to make the following particular acknowledgments of help directly received and valued: to Elizabeth M. Ranney, who read the entire manuscript and commented on it with an architect's understanding of order and a wife's sympathy and encouragement; to my good friends and generous colleagues, Chancellor Jack W. Peltason of the University of Illinois, Urbana-Champaign, and Professor Charles B. Hagan of the University of Houston, each of whom not only read and improved a number of chapters but in the process greatly contributed to my education; to these colleagues who cheerfully read and perceptively criticized particular chapters—Professors Valentine Jobst III, Benjamin B. Johnston, Charles M. Kneier, Philip Monypenny, and Clyde F. Snider, all of the University of Illinois, Charles S. Hyneman of Indiana University, Gillian Dean of Vanderbilt University, Evron M. Kirkpatrick of the American Political Science Association, Jeane J. Kirkpatrick of Georgetown University, Joseph G. LaPalombara of Yale University, Warren E. Miller of the Center for Political Studies of the University of Michigan, James N. Murray of the University of Iowa, Richard L. Park of the University of Michigan, Fred R. von der Mehden of Rice University, Professors Charles W. Anderson, Bernard C. Cohen, Jack Dennis, Leon D. Epstein, David Fellman, and M. Crawford Young, all of the University of Wisconsin, and the late and mourned Sigmund Neumann of Wesleyan University. Finally, my thanks go to Joseph A. Ranney III of the University of Chicago and the United States Army, who rendered great help at various stages in the preparation of both the second and third editions.

Austin Ranney
Madison, Wisconsin
March 1975

# CONTENTS

Contents

Contents

Contents

# I

# POLITICAL SCIENCE: DISCIPLINE AND PROFESSION

# 1

# INSIDE
# POLITICAL
# SCIENCE

The first edition of this book was written in the mid-1950s, and it then seemed appropriate to begin the introductory chapter this way:

> In the course of the hearings in the school-segregation cases before a federal district court in 1953, the attorney for the National Association for the Advancement of Colored People (NAACP), Thurgood Marshall, brought to the stand a number of "expert witnesses"—psychologists, sociologists, professors of education, and the like—to testify on the effects of segregation on Negro children. When he called an associate professor of political science, however, the defendants' counsel objected, on the ground that a political scientist is not qualified to answer the kinds of questions being asked. The following colloquy took place between the judge and Mr. Marshall:
>
> *Judge Parker:* Are you going to offer any more witnesses along this line?
> *Mr. Marshall:* No, sir. The other witnesses are *real* scientists.
> *Judge Parker:* Well, I'll take it for what it's worth. Go ahead.[1]
>
> In a conference at Northwestern University in 1954 on the current state of political science, another political scientist confessed that "the day when children will say 'political scientist' when asked what they want to be when they grow up is remote indeed."[2]

---

[1] Transcript of Record in *Briggs v. Board of Trustees* (the South Carolina segregation case), October Term, 1953, p. 103, emphasis in the original.
[2] Willmoore Kendall, "Social Determinants of American Political Science," Address at Northwestern University, Evanston, Illinois, April 27, 1954, mimeographed.

In the two decades following these rather disparaging (defensive?) comments, the public image and the self-image of political scientists have changed considerably. The membership of the American Political Science Association (APSA) rose from 5,500 in 1955 to more than 16,000 in 1974. The annual number of college students receiving bachelor's degrees in political science increased from a few more than 6,000 in 1958 to 25,000 in 1970. And the number of people receiving Ph.D. degrees in political science grew from 170 in 1958 to 466 in 1970.[3] The National Science Foundation, established by Congress in 1950 to encourage and fund basic research and education in the sciences, now includes and supports political science as one of the "behavioral and social sciences."[4] The APSA's 1973 biographical directory lists such distinguished nonacademic members as Birch Bayh, David Broder, Ralph J. Bunche, McGeorge Bundy, and Hubert H. Humphrey. Newspaper columnists, television commentators, and party politicians now regularly refer to members of the profession as "political scientists" rather than as "political economists" or "historians" (as was common in the early 1950s). And no less an authority than Richard M. Nixon, while denying that there is any "science in politics," nevertheless ascribed the Democratic party's success in the 1964 elections partly to its ability to mobilize the support of so many political scientists; for, Nixon said, political scientists are "tremendously potent people" in political affairs.[5]

The purpose of this chapter is to take the reader on a brief backstage tour of contemporary political science's main professional concerns, methods, and disputes. But first a word about why such a chapter seems in order.

This book is intended to be an introduction to political science mainly in the sense of summarizing and explaining some of the principal conclusions that political scientists have reached about the nature of politics and government in the modern world. Twenty-three of its twenty-four chapters are devoted to such material. But it is important that readers of an introductory survey of any scholarly discipline also learn something about the discipline itself. They should have some idea of the kinds of questions it asks and how it goes about answering them, so that they will have some basis for determining the kind and level of its practitioners' expertise. Such understanding will help them to appreciate what the discipline can and cannot accomplish and what use, if any, society can make of it in dealing with social problems.

The purpose of this chapter, then, is to provide readers with at least a preliminary and general version of such information about political science. We may begin

---

[3] The degree figures are from the U.S. Office of Education, as reported in Heinz Eulau and James G. March (eds.), *Political Science* (Englewood Cliffs, N.J.: Prentice-Hall, Inc., 1969), pp. 68–70. This volume was prepared by a panel of political scientists as part of a general survey of behavioral and social sciences sponsored by the National Academy of Sciences and the Social Science Research Council. It presents concisely the most recent authoritative information on the state of the discipline and the profession and covers in greater detail many matters touched on in this chapter. Also recommended is Frank J. Sorauf, *Political Science: An Informal Overview* (Columbus, O.: Charles E. Merrill Books, Inc., 1965).

[4] According to the National Science Foundation, the others are cultural and physical anthropology, archaeology, demography, economics, geography, linguistics, psychology, sociology, and the history and philosophy of science.

[5] *New York Times,* November 11, 1964, p. 26

by noting that political science, particularly in the United States since the end of World War II, has undergone several periods of intense self-examination and soul searching and that it has been more self-critical in these years than at any time since it emerged as a separate discipline in the late nineteenth century.[6] The learned journals have printed many articles, many books have been written, many professional conferences have been held, and many committees have been formed—all for the purpose of reexamining the scope and methods of political science, of describing and trying to account for the discipline's deficiencies, and usually of offering proposals for improvement.

One consequence of this ferment has been to make it clear that political scientists are widely and sometimes sharply divided among themselves on several questions about the proper direction of their discipline. In our survey of the current state of political science, we shall note some areas of agreement and also describe some principal issues on which they are disagreed and the major points of view expressed on each issue.

## THE SCOPE OF POLITICAL SCIENCE

The categories most generally used to describe the nature of contemporary political science are its scope (the kinds of subject matter with which it deals and the kinds of questions that it asks) and its methods (the techniques political scientists use to answer the questions they raise). As we shall see, there is some disagreement among political scientists about the proper scope of the discipline and a great deal of controversy about the methods that should be used. Let us first consider questions of scope.

### THE EMERGENCE OF POLITICAL SCIENCE[7]

People have pondered and written about the actual and ideal roles of politics and government in human society at least since the time of Socrates in the fifth century B.C.; and the writings of such giants as Plato, Aristotle, St. Thomas Aquinas, Niccolò Machiavelli, Thomas Hobbes, John Locke, and Jean Jacques Rousseau are still studied by students of political science in courses labeled "political theory" or "the history of political ideas." Political science in the modern sense, however, did not emerge as a distinct discipline and academic subject until the late nineteenth century, at first mainly in American colleges and universities. As we shall see, it still has not achieved distinct academic status in the universities of many nations. In the United States it

---

[6] The three main official reassessments before Eulau and March, *Political Science*, occurred in 1914, 1923, and 1930; they are described with bibliographical notes in *Goals for Political Science: The Report of the Committee for the Advancement of Teaching, American Political Science Association* (New York: William Sloane Associates, 1951), pp. 6–14.

[7] The histories of people's philosophizing about politics are too numerous to be mentioned here. An illuminating account of empirical analyses of politics in ancient times is William Anderson, *Man's Quest for Political Knowledge: The Study and Teaching of Politics in Ancient Times* (Minneapolis, Minn.: University of Minnesota Press, 1964). For the early development of political science in the United States, see Anna Haddow, *Political Science in American Colleges and Universities, 1636–1900* (New York: Appleton-Century-Crofts, 1939).

won its academic independence from other disciplines and acquired its present title mainly as a result of two developments.

*Separation of Politics from Other Subjects*

Socrates, Plato, Aristotle, and the other masters of political literature before the nineteenth century were not concerned—as many present-day political scientists are—with identifying the purely "political" or "governmental" in human affairs for the purpose of concentrating their studies on such matters. They were concerned not only with the place of people in society but also with the place of humanity in the universe, and they wrote about what we have come to call "ethics," "history," "economics," "religion," "psychology," "education," and so on, as well as about politics and government. They never raised the question whether or not it might be profitable to distinguish these various aspects of humanity in the universe and, through division of labor, to establish a specialty in each. Although these writers were, in a sense, "political scientists" and "political philosophers," each was also, in modern terminology, a "historian," an "economist," a "psychologist," an "ethical philosopher," and so on.

By the eighteenth century politics and government, like law and political economy, were being taught in English, American, and European universities and colleges only—if at all—as branches of moral philosophy; for the principles of right public conduct were considered merely an aspect of right conduct in general, and the whole purpose of higher education was to instruct pupils in the principles of right conduct. The one exception was Uppsala University in Sweden, which in the early seventeenth century established a chair of "statecraft and eloquence," apparently for the purpose of giving instruction in politics and government as a subject separate from others. The Uppsala example, however, was not followed—even in Sweden— until well into the nineteenth century.[8]

In the late eighteenth and early nineteenth centuries many areas of study began to win academic status independent from moral philosophy. Among the first to be differentiated were the studies of law and political economy. Neither, however, contributed much to the development of the specialized study of politics and government. The newly independent law schools were concerned only with questions of what the law was (see Chap. 18) and dealt little or not at all with the institutions and processes that made the law. "Political economy" was the ancestor of economics, rather than of political science; the term denoted the processes of acquiring wealth in a whole society, as opposed to "domestic economy," the processes in the individual family and household. Political economy had little concern with the policy-making and enforcement processes of government. As far as the latter were considered at all, they were treated as aspects of history.

The study of history began to achieve academic independence in the early 1800s and by the middle of the century was well established as a separate discipline. During that same period, however, the growing intensity of the constitutional crisis in the

[8] See William A. Robson, *The University Teaching of Social Sciences: Political Science* (Leiden: A. W. Sijthoff, 1954), p. 22.

United States that ultimately led to the Civil War produced a large volume of studies of the Constitution that were neither pure "law" nor pure "history" but rather analyses of the proper form and role of Constitutions and governments in human affairs. This development led an increasing number of writers and teachers to think of the study of politics and government as quite distinct from either the study of history or the study of law.

In 1856 a significant episode occurred. Francis Lieber, a German-born scholar who had made his career in the United States and had published in 1838 his *Manual of Political Ethics* (a work regarded by some scholars as the first systematic treatise in political science published in this country), was elected to the chair of history and political economy at Columbia College. Lieber asked the college's trustees to change the name of his chair to "history and political science," and they agreed to do so.[9] This change signaled the emergence of the study of politics and government separately from the study of history.

Lieber's innovation came to full flower after the Civil War, when political science finally emerged in the United States as a distinct academic discipline. By the early 1880s a number of American institutions were offering courses in "government," as distinct from history or political economy, and in the late 1880s and early 1890s many created separate "government" and "political science" departments. In 1886 the *Political Science Quarterly,* the first specialized political science journal, was established by Columbia. During the same period a number of political science treatises, in the modern sense of the term, were published, the most notable being Theodore Dwight Woolsey's *Political Science* (1878), Woodrow Wilson's *Congressional Government* (1885) and *The State* (1889), John W. Burgess' *Political Science and Comparative Constitutional Law* (1890), and James Bryce's *The American Commonwealth* (1888), the last by an Englishman.

Finally, in 1903 the American Political Science Association was founded, with Frank J. Goodnow (see Chap. 17) as its first president, and in 1906 it began publishing the *American Political Science Review.* Political science in the United States had become established as a distinct discipline and has remained so ever since.[10]

## Growth of Social Science

The "natural" or "physical" sciences of astronomy, chemistry, physics, and so on first emerged in their modern versions in the sixteenth century and from then on accumulated an impressive and growing body of empirically verified descriptive laws of the behavior of various facets of the physical universe. By the nineteenth century these disciplines had won great prestige in the eyes of many philosophers and laymen and had developed a well-understood "scientific method" for dealing with their subject matters. By the middle of that century a number of students of human affairs

---

[9] Haddow, *Political Science in American Colleges and Universities, 1636–1900,* pp. 138–140.

[10] The "formative years" from 1880 to 1903 are well described in Albert Somit and Joseph Tanenhaus, *The Development of American Political Science: From Burgess to Behavioralism* (Boston: Allyn and Bacon, Inc., 1967), chaps. 1–4. This book is the best short history of the American development of political science.

had come to accept the doctrine, most notably advanced by the French philosopher Auguste Comte in his *Cours de philosophie positive* (1830–1842), that human society in all its aspects can and should be studied in exactly the same spirit and by substantially the same methods as those used by natural scientists in their studies of physical phenomena. The idea of "social science," in the modern sense, was born and took a grip on the imaginations and aspirations of many students of human affairs that has since increased rather than diminished.[11]

It is not surprising, therefore, that many of the same nineteenth-century scholars who believed that politics and government should be studied apart from ethics, history, law, and political economy also came to accept Comte's "positivist" philosophy that these matters can and should be studied scientifically. Many who pressed for the independence of political and government studies took up the term "political science" to describe both the scope and the method of the discipline that they hoped to establish.

### Current Status of the Label

By no means every student of political and governmental affairs, then or now, has accepted both developments implicit in the label "political science." Some scholars, for example, have preferred to speak of the "political sciences," reflecting their conviction that *all* aspects of society related to government—law, economics, sociology, history, and so on—should be studied together and that politics and government alone constitute too narrow a focus for profitable study. This view, as we shall see, is predominant in most European universities.

Other scholars grant that politics and government are a proper subject for special study but deny that they can or should be studied "scientifically" in the Comtian or "positivist" sense of the term. They refuse to accept the term "political *science*" as a proper designation for the discipline, and in some American colleges and universities the appropriate departments are officially labeled "government," "politics," or "public affairs."

Later in this chapter we shall consider the major issues involved and the positions taken on the question whether or not the subject matter of "political science" can be studied "scientifically." For our present purposes, however, we should recognize that in the United States "political science" is by far the most common term for the kinds of studies that we shall deal with in this book. The name of the professional association is the American Political Science Association, and "political scientist" is the term most commonly used to describe teachers and scholars of these subjects.

Although "political science" may not be a precise designation for the scholarly enterprises we consider in this chapter, it is so widely accepted that everyone who engages in them knows what kinds of activity it refers to. Furthermore, any other label is likely to muddy the waters of identification and discussion more than "political science" does.

---

[11] The story is well told in Maurice Duverger, *An Introduction to the Social Sciences,* trans. by Malcolm Anderson (New York: Frederick A. Praeger, Inc., 1964), chap. 1.

## Western European Nations

Political science, as defined here, has had by far its greatest development in the United States. It is estimated that nearly 1,000 American degree-granting colleges and universities now offer courses under the title of "political science," "government," or "politics", they now award about 25,000 bachelor's degrees and more than 450 doctorates a year. A British observer estimated in 1954 that there were more political scientists in the United States than in all other nations combined,[12] and American predominance—at least in numbers—has certainly not diminished since then. In most of this chapter, accordingly, we deal with the current state of American political science, but the status of political science elsewhere in the world merits comment also.

The academic and professional status of political science varies considerably from nation to nation outside the United States. It is perhaps most firmly established in Sweden, where, following the early lead of Uppsala University, the other three universities have also established the study of politics and government as a separate academic field; it is also required in the government institutes that train civil servants. It is probably least firmly established in Asia, although it is a major independent area of study in most Indian and Japanese universities.

The other nations appear to fall between these extremes. In Great Britain, for example, some politics and government are taught in all universities and colleges, but only recently has modern empirical political science become well established at certain institutions. The most notable of the latter include some of the new universities, notably the Universities of Essex and Strathclyde; some of the older "red brick" universities, especially the University of Manchester; and the University of London, which operates the London School of Economics and Political Science. Political science has quite different statuses in the two ancient universities. At Oxford it plays a prominent role in the honors curriculum known, in arcane British fashion, as "modern greats," and research is conducted at a high level under the aegis of Nuffield College. At Cambridge, on the other hand, political science can be studied only as a minor option for an honors degree in history or economics, and the chair of political science, long held by the distinguished political historian Sir Denis Brogan, is now occupied by a political philosopher.

In France the plural term *les sciences politiques* remains almost as popular as it was in 1872, when the École Libre des Sciences Politiques was founded. This well-known institution, established on private initiative but later made part of the University of Paris, gives instruction in all matters considered relevant to the making of public policy: political ideologies, economic history and theory, political and social geography, and so on. It thus offers broader coverage than do political science departments in American universities. Similar institutions have been established at six of France's sixteen other universities, but for the most part politics and government are studied

[12] Robson, *The University Teaching of Social Sciences,* p. 15.

as part of the curriculum in law and are treated in a legalistic and formalistic manner. The other "political sciences" are scattered between the faculties of letters and of science. The main center for contemporary French political science research is the Fondation Nationale des Sciences Politiques (again, note the plural form), which also gives courses through the related Institut d'Études Politiques.

The other European nations generally follow the French pattern. A few have established special institutes similar to the École Libre (one outstanding example being the Deutsche Hochschule für Politik in Berlin), but they have no independent academic departments labeled "political science," and for the most part even the "political sciences" are dispersed among the various divisions of universities in these countries.

Political science in Western Europe received a major boost in 1970 from the establishment of the European Consortium for Political Research. This organization was modeled on the American Inter-University Consortium for Political Research, which was founded in the United States in 1962 mainly through the pioneering efforts of Warren E. Miller of the University of Michigan. (The reader will notice that much of the information about public opinion used in this book has been supplied by the ICPR.) By 1973 the ECPR had reached a membership of fifty-five institutions (including academic departments, research institutes, and the like) in thirteen countries. Through its executive offices at the University of Essex it provides a number of services, including data archiving and circulation, research training, and scholar exchanges. Almost from its beginning it has played a central role in advancing Western European political science.

### Eastern European Nations[13]

One of the more interesting recent scholarly developments has been the slow growth of modern social science in general, and of political science in particular, in some communist nations in Eastern Europe. The Yugoslavs began it in 1951, when they founded a national political science association. Joseph Stalin's death in 1953 made possible a general intellectual "thaw" that in turn made possible at least the beginnings of empirical research in place of exegeses of the sacred texts of Marxism-Leninism. The Poles took advantage of the new climate to establish their own association of political science in 1957, and the Soviets themselves founded one in 1960. At present Bulgaria, Czechoslovakia, Hungary, Poland, Romania, the Soviet Union, and Yugoslavia all have official political science associations affiliated with the International Political Science Association (IPSA).

Political science, however, really has no status as an independent discipline in the Soviet Union. The Soviet political science association is dominated by legal scholars, and no Soviet university offers work called "political science." Some inter-

---

[13] In this section I have drawn heavily from David E. Powell and Paul Shoup, "The Emergence of Political Science in Communist Countries," *American Political Science Review,* 64 (June 1970), 572–588.

esting empirical research is, to be sure, being conducted with modern methods, particularly in the fields of local government and public administration, but political science has a long way to go in the Soviet Union before it can win full recognition as a distinct and useful scholarly discipline. Much the same can be said for most of the other Eastern European nations, despite their official political science associations. In Poland and Yugoslavia, however, political science appears to be well established and on the rise. In the early 1960s some Polish universities incorporated political science courses in their curricula, and Poland established a national institute for political science research. Several major studies of the power structures of local communities and the behavior of Polish voters have been made. Some Polish political scientists have had Western training, use modern research methods with skill, and sometimes engage in cooperative research projects with Western scholars.[14] Much the same is true in Yugoslavia, where the University of Zagreb has had a faculty of political science since 1962 and publishes a journal, *Politicka Misao (Political Thought)*, devoted to research and discussion in political science. Most Yugoslavian work, however, is concentrated on elaborations of Titoist political philosophy rather than on empirical research. But political science, along with other disciplines of modern social science, now has its foot in the door in Eastern Europe, and the probabilities are that its role will grow in the years to come.

### The International Political Science Association

The growth of political science around the world is signaled by the growth of the International Political Science Association. IPSA was founded in 1948 at a conference in Paris sponsored by the U.N. Educational, Scientific and Cultural Organization. By 1970 it had as "collective members" the national political science associations of thirty-three nations[15] but only slightly more than 300 individual members. It has held world congresses for the exchange of scholarly ideas and findings every three years, most recently in Montreal in 1973. Every year it has sponsored one to three "round tables" at which specialists in various topics have met and discussed their work. In general, IPSA has done a great deal to facilitate international exchange among established political science enterprises and to promote the development of the discipline in many nations where it has been weak or nonexistent.

To be sure, many of IPSA's European and Asian members (considerably more than half its individual members are Americans) hold professorships of law, psychology, or sociology in their home institutions. But the very existence of such a body is encouraging the development abroad of political science, although it will be many years before it achieves in any other nation the size, academic independence, and prominence that it has in the United States.

---

[14] See, for example, the work of Professor Jerzy J. Wiatr of the University of Warsaw, discussed in Chap. 9.

[15] Fourteen of them were Western European (including the United States), seven Eastern European, four Asian, three from the British Commonwealth, three from the Middle East, and two from Latin America.

### How Disciplines Are Distinguished

Earlier we noted how the discipline of political science acquired its distinct identity in the United States. As the term is normally used, "discipline" means an organized division of scholarly inquiry generally recognized as distinct from other divisions, as reflected, for example, in the separate departments of a university or divisions of the National Science Foundation. A scholarly discipline is usually distinguished from others on one or more of the three main bases: its *concerns,* those aspects of the universe that command its particular attention; the *kind of knowledge* that it seeks about its special concerns; and its *special methods* of acquiring knowledge.

It is important to understand that political science differs from the other behavioral and social sciences[16] mainly in its *concerns* and little if at all in the kind of knowledge it seeks or the methods it uses. As we shall see, there are long-standing disputes among political scientists about what kind of knowledge we want, what methods we can and should use, and what social purposes we should serve. But there is much less controversy over which aspects of the universe constitute our core concerns—though conceptualization and articulation of these concerns have changed over the years and are still changing. This whole book, of course, is an effort to review some of the things political scientists have said about their main concerns, but it is useful at this point to state those concerns briefly, as a way of outlining what political science is "about."

### Special Concerns of Political Science[17]

Setting aside for the moment any question about what political scientists *should* study, we can catalogue what they *do* study under seven headings.

**Institutions**   Political scientists past and present have focused on the structure and operations of the world's "public governments" (as opposed to the "private governments" of such unofficial bodies as churches, trade unions, and so on) and upon the "politics" associated with those governments. The terms "governments" and "politics" have generally been given definitions similar to those in Chapters 2 and 3 of this book. At first political scientists were concerned exclusively with the institutions of "the state," and such institutions—constitutions, laws, legislatures, executives, ad-

---

[16] In addition to political science, they include, according to the Behavioral and Social Sciences Survey, anthropology, economics, geography, parts of history, linguistics, parts of psychiatry, psychology, and sociology.

[17] There are far too many discussions of what are and should be the concerns of political science to be cited here. The reader may find several particularly helpful: Eulau and March, *Political Science,* chap. 1, on which the discussion in this text draws heavily; Sorauf, *Political Science;* James C. Charlesworth (ed.), *Contemporary Political Analysis* (New York: The Free Press, 1967); Marian D. Irish (ed.), *Political Science: Advance of the Discipline* (Englewood Cliffs, N.J.: Prentice-Hall, Inc., 1968); and Charles S. Hyneman, *The Study of Politics: The Present State of American Political Science* (Urbana, Ill.: University of Illinois Press, 1959).

ministrators, courts, and the like—continue to be the prime concern of many scholars. But since the late nineteenth century most political scientists have also thought it important to study unofficial institutions—notably, but not exclusively, political parties and pressure groups—that directly and powerfully influence official institutions.

**Policy Processes**   Many political scientists have observed that how a political institution really works is often quite different from how its formal rules say that it works. Accordingly, they have sought to understand the *causes* of particular institutional decisions, and they regard institutional formalities as significant only to the extent that they help explain actual policy processes. For example, these scholars are less concerned about Congress' elaborate rules for receiving, referring, debating, and voting upon bills than about the personal, social, economic, and other interactions that explain why Congress passes some bills and lets others die in committee.

**Power**   Some scholars proceed from the assumption that the way to understand the real policy processes of any institution is to find out who holds its power, how they have come to hold it, and how they use it. Some, indeed, have argued that political scientists should abandon their traditional concentration on legal governments and consider power relations in all human organizations. Others, however, have come to believe that "power" itself is an ambiguous and slippery concept (see the discussion in Chap. 23), and will thus not do as the single focus of the whole discipline.

**Ideologies**   Some political scientists are mainly interested in political ideologies past and present. These ideologies are defined as "more or less coherent and consistent sets of beliefs, values, opinion, and aspirations [that] serve as sources of obedience or consent, or sources of revolt."[18] They include all kinds of doctrines—Platonism, liberalism, Marxism-Leninism, fascism, Maoism, existentialism, *negritude*, and so on. Those who study them examine both logical structure and impacts on people's political behavior and on institutional arrangements.

**Political Behavior**   It is important to understand the distinction implicit in modern political science literature between "political behavior" and "behavioralism." "Behavioralism" is a certain *approach* to the study of all political phenomena. "Political behavior," on the other hand, is a certain subset of those phenomena—the perceptions, attitudes, and activities of individual political actors. The actors studied range from the mass electorates examined in research on voting behavior (see Chaps. 5 and 8) to the various elites heading governmental and extragovernmental institutions (see Chaps. 9–10 and 14–18).

**Policy Impacts**   Most political scientists have concentrated on policy processes rather than on policy impacts. That is, they have sought to understand how government adopts some policies over others—*who* governs, rather than what effects the governors' decisions have. They have typically tried to identify the various interests at-

[18] Eulau and March, *Political Science,* p. 22.

tempting to influence a particular policy decision or range of decisions, to describe and evaluate the strategic position and tactics of each, and to explain why the winners win and the losers lose. The policy output—the law, executive decree, or judicial decision—is considered the final product; and, when the reasons for the choice of one output over all the others possible have been explained, analysis ends. Few people would argue that policy processes are trivial concerns or that society does not need to know how its decisions are made. In recent years, however, some political scientists have come to think that, without abandoning its traditional interest in policy processes, political science should pay a good deal more attention to policy *impacts*—to how particular policies actually affect the life situations and attitudes of persons. Until these impacts are studied with the same zeal and skill that policy processes have attracted political science may contribute little to the *evaluation* of existing policies or the consideration of possible future policies.[19]

**Functions**   One influential group of political scientists has recently concentrated on the extent to which and the manner in which political institutions perform certain functions in their societies. They posit certain functions that must be performed in any society if it is to survive and prosper—interest articulation, interest aggregation, rule making, rule adjudication, and so on. Their concern is less with the internal workings of various institutions than with their roles in society. They focus on a concern implicit in the whole enterprise of political science: *What difference does it make* whether a society has one kind of political system or another, or is dominated by this ideology or that?

From the point of view of society this question is the real crux of political science. Most political scientists would agree that, if the discipline really has nothing to say about it, then it does not deserve and cannot expect society's continued support of its research and teaching efforts. But they are by no means agreed about what concerns political scientists should focus on, what questions they should ask, what methods they can and should use to obtain answers, and even whether asking significant questions or finding correct answers is the higher obligation.

Every student should understand that political scientists are currently divided among themselves on a number of issues involving their professional obligations and activities. Let us conclude our backstage tour by reviewing some of these issues.

## SOME ISSUES IN POLITICAL SCIENCE

Since the mid-1960s protest movements have played increasingly important roles in American life and politics—inside our colleges and universities as well as outside—as

---

[19] For various views on the possibilities and problems inherent in impact studies, see Austin Ranney (ed.), *Political Science and Public Policy* (Chicago: Markham Publishing Company, 1968). Two of the more successful impact studies are James W. Davis, Jr., and Kenneth M. Dolbeare, *Little Groups of Neighbors: The Selective Service System* (Chicago: Markham Publishing Company, 1968); and Theodore L. Becker (ed.), *The Impact of Supreme Court Decisions* (New York: Oxford University Press, 1969). See also the various issues of the *Policy Studies Journal,* published quarterly since 1972 by the Policy Studies Organization. The rapid growth of this organization is evidence of the rapid growth of interest among political scientists in developing studies of policy contents as well as processes.

they have in many other nations. Although these movements overlap and cut across one another to some degree, the more important strains in American protest include black militancy and nationalism; protest against American foreign policy, particularly the war in Vietnam; women's demands for social rights and opportunities equal to those of men; and a general, rather diffuse protest by youth against the morals, life styles, and politics of "middle America." In American academic institutions these forces have often converged in demands for increased student power over whom the colleges and universities should admit, what they should teach and how, and what functions—if any—they should perform for government (especially the military) and industry. It is a rare campus that has not experienced some form of "academic civil war": student strikes, boycotts, occupation of buildings, sit-ins—and suspensions, expulsions, and criminal prosecutions.

Everyone who reads a newspaper or watches television is well aware of these events. But it may be news to some that comparable protest movements have arisen within most of the learned disciplines and their professional associations. In the APSA and among political scientists in general the most prominent protest group has been the Caucus for a New Political Science, organized in 1967 to change the direction of the APSA and, through it, of the whole discipline. Although the caucus still has only a few hundred members, its manifestos and platforms—together with the replies that they have evoked from the political science "establishment"—have focused more sharply many of the discipline's most vexing intellectual disputes.[20] While I, like most political scientists, have been a participant in many of these disputes (on the side of the "establishment," reader be warned), let me try to summarize the views set forth on a few of the principal issues.

## POLITICAL PROTEST OR POLITICAL RESEARCH?

The 1969 Caucus platform begins with a statement of its basic charge: "The political science profession has invested its energies primarily in celebrating and supporting the economic, social, and political status quo, both here and abroad." Its principal objective is also stated: "The resources of the APSA must be used to redirect some of the energies and expertise of the discipline to encourage the development of a *new* political science—devoted to radical social criticism and fundamental social change."

The political science "establishment" replies that political scientists have, as have other professionals, a basic moral obligation to distinguish what they do as citizens from what they do as scholars and teachers. As citizens they have the same political obligation as students, workers, and any other citizens: to work for whatever governmental forms and policies they think best by whatever means they think permissible and effective. But they are morally entitled to claim special attention for their views *as political scientists* only to the extent that those views are grounded in and consistent with a valid and reliable body of special professional knowledge. When that knowledge clearly supports or opposes a certain policy, they have a professional

---

[20] The Caucus' origins and leadership are described in communications to *P.S.*, 1 (Winter 1968), 38–40; and *P.S.*, 2 (Winter 1969), 47–49. The fullest statements of Caucus views are to be found in its quarterly newsletters.

obligation to say so. When it does not, they have an equal obligation *not* to advance policy preferences as if they were inevitable conclusions from their professional knowledge.

The study of political science does not guarantee good political behavior.
Source: © 1961 United Feature Syndicate, Inc.

Above all, according to the "establishment," the first task of political scientists is not to take the lead in changing society but to make certain that its special body of knowledge is valid and reliable, in order to help people to understand the conditions and consequences of past social change and the probable consequences of future change. The validity of everything political scientists do in their professional capacities rests, in the end, on the quality of their professional knowledge. If the generalizations of political science are vague, inconsistent, or unverified, then the profession's first obligation is to sharpen, reconcile, test, and verify them. In this connection a high-school teacher once told a bumptious pupil, "Your trouble isn't that you don't know anything; your trouble is that so much of what you know isn't so!" To the extent that the problem in political science is that so much of what it "knows" isn't so—or is only partly so or is so only under some circumstances—political scientists have an obligation both to learn more than they know now and never to claim that they know more than they do.

## BEHAVIORALISM, ANTIBEHAVIORALISM, OR POSTBEHAVIORALISM?

### *The Meaning of "Behavioralism"*

Much of the controversy over the proper concerns and methods of political science since 1945 has centered on what is variously called "political behavior," "behavioralism," or "behaviorism." Most political scientists regard themselves as generally "probehavioral" or "antibehavioral,"[21] but there has been no clear agreement on just what the conflict is about. At first the term "political behavior" was often used to designate the activities that in this book are called "voting behavior" (see Chap. 8). In the 1970s, however, this usage has been generally dropped, and most of the disputants agree with Robert Dahl that what is at issue is a particular *approach* to the study of all political and governmental phenomena.[22] The preferred usage now is

---

[21] In 1963 Somit and Tanenhaus analyzed the views on various professional issues of a random sample of 431 political scientists. They found that the dispute over behavioralism separated the profession substantially more sharply than did any other issue; Somit and Tanenhaus, *American Political Science: A Profile of a Discipline* (New York: Atherton Press, 1964), pp. 21–24.

[22] The conflict is accurately described and calmly analyzed from a probehavioral position in

therefore "the behavioral study of politics," and its advocates are most often called "behavioralists."

But what is the behavioral approach? Some have confused it with the "behavioristic" doctrines of such psychologists as J.B. Watson. Others have defined it as the substitution of the individual human being for the political institution as the basic unit of political analysis. Still others consider it a protest against the formalism and weak evidential base of prewar political science.[23]

Despite this confusion, however, the controversy over behavioralism has centered on the general issue of the proper meaning and role of science in political science, and the following two questions in particular.

### What Science Is

The word "science," like the word "democracy," has acquired such favorable emotional connotations for so many people in our time that it is used for all sorts of disparate things. We often hear people speak, for example, not only of the "sciences" of chemistry and physics, but also of the "sciences" of wrestling and cooking, of "scientific" bidding in bridge, and of Christian Science as a form of religion.

Most political scientists, however, use the term "science" to denote a particular method of inquiry—distinguished from other methods of inquiry by its insistence upon certain objectives, techniques, and standards.[24]

**Objectives**  The main objective of science is to discover, declare, and verify the fundamental "laws" that govern the universe. A scientific law, of course, differs from a governmental law in that the former is *descriptive* (states the regular and recurring patterns of behavior observed in this or that body of natural phenomena and thus how things *do* behave), whereas the latter is *prescriptive* (states a rule of behavior that human beings *should* obey but may not obey).

Scientists, of course, would not try to discover scientific laws if they thought that no such laws existed and that there were no discoverable uniformities and regularities in nature. They operate on the basic assumption, as one philosopher has

Robert Dahl's "The Behavioral Approach to Political Science: Epitaph for a Monument to a Successful Protest," *American Political Science Review,* 55 (December 1961), 763–772. See also Evron M. Kirkpatrick's comprehensive survey of the relevant literature, "The Impact of the Behavioral Approach on Traditional Political Science," in Ranney (ed.), *Essays on the Behavioral Study of Politics* (Urbana, Ill.: University of Illinois Press, 1962), pp. 1–29.

[23] The various meanings are analyzed in David Easton, "The Current Meaning of 'Behavioralism' in Political Science," in Charlesworth (ed.), *The Limits of Behavioralism in Political Science* (Philadelphia: The American Academy of Political and Social Science, 1962), pp. 1–25.

[24] The following discussion is based largely upon the conception of science presented in Morris R. Cohen, *Reason and Nature* (New York: Harcourt Brace Jovanovich, Inc., 1931), pp. 83–114. The problems of applying scientific method to the study of social and political problems are well considered in Abraham Kaplan, *The Conduct of Inquiry: Methodology for Behavioral Science* (San Francisco: Chandler Publishing Company, 1964). The problems of application to political science are thoughtfully explored in Martin Landau, *Political Theory and Political Science* (New York: Crowell-Collier and Macmillan, Inc., 1972).

put it, that "the universe is a cosmos, not a chaos. The scientist has faith that . . . events in the world can be comprehended if he can learn some law or set of laws that govern them, and he believes that his methods can lead to the discovery of these laws."[25]

**Scientific Method**[26]    Modern science has developed a well-defined and generally accepted method for discovering descriptive general laws. The principal operations in that method can be enumerated here, although they are by no means always performed in this order.

First is the selection of problems. Scientific inquiry begins when scientists become dissatisfied with the existing level of knowledge on a particular matter. They may be dissatisfied with the way in which some aspect of the universe—like bad weather or disease or pollution—affects human life and may conclude that the ill cannot be cured until we know more reliably what causes it. They may be dissatisfied with the adequacy of some accepted explanation of a particular phenomenon—perhaps the phlogiston theory of combustion or the supply-and-demand theory of pricing—and may resolve to seek a better one. In any case, scientific inquiry begins because scientists are bothered by some problem and wish to solve it.

Second, the scientists formulate working hypotheses—that is, tentative statements about the forces governing the particular phenomena that their problems lead them to study.

Third, they gather data and test the hypotheses. On the basis of their hypotheses they make certain predictions about the future course of events: They reason that, if their guess about the forces governing the phenomenon under study is correct, then under conditions A and B events X and Y must occur. They then gather data about what events actually have occurred under conditions A and B. On the basis of these data they then decide whether their hypotheses provide a valid, invalid, or partially valid explanation of the forces at work.

Fourth is the use to which the results are put. Students of scientific method often distinguish between "pure" and "applied" science (sometimes called "engineering"). "Pure scientists" are concerned only with knowledge and understanding, and use the results of their studies only to support, refute, or modify existing scientific theories. Applied scientists or engineers, on the other hand, are interested in using scientific laws to manipulate natural or social forces to achieve "practical" results beyond mere understanding. They use the results of scientific inquiry to construct or modify physical devices or social institutions for the betterment of human life. They build a nuclear power plant, create a new form of municipal government, develop a new vaccine or antitoxin, and so on.

---

[25] Lewis White Beck, *Philosophic Inquiry* (Englewood Cliffs, N.J.: Prentice-Hall, Inc., 1952), p. 118.

[26] In recent years several useful manuals have been produced introducing undergraduate students to research methods in political science. Among them are William Buchanan, *Understanding Political Variables* (New York: Charles Scribner's Sons, 1969); M. Margaret Conway and Frank B. Feigert, *Political Analysis: An Introduction* (Boston: Allyn and Bacon, Inc., 1972); and James L. Payne, *Foundations of Empirical Political Analysis* (Chicago: Markham Publishing Company, 1973).

**Standards of Science** Scientists evaluate their own research and the research of others according to three main standards. The first is *accuracy and measurement*. Investigators seek to describe the aspect of the universe they are investigating as accurately as possible. Accuracy is a standard not only of the physical sciences but also of all forms of human investigation. Physical scientists believe that the most accurate form of description is measurement reducing all phenomena to units of similar nature that can be expressed and compared in numerical terms. For example, they prefer to describe the temperature of a liquid as "83°C." rather than as "hot," the weight of a man as "230 pounds, 10 ounces" rather than as "heavy," and the height of a mountain as "15,352 feet, 7 inches above sea level" rather than as "high."

The second standard is *universality*. Scientists seek generalizations that apply, as do the laws of gravitation and conservation of energy, to particular phenomena wherever they may be found, not merely to some instances.

The third standard is *system*. The ultimate goal of science is systematic theory—that is, a body of logically consistent and connected statements explaining all aspects of the universe.

### How Scientific Should Political Scientists Try to Be?

The preceding description of science is, of course, a model—an ideal that may be pursued and against which actual research may be measured and evaluated. It is, furthermore, a rigorous and demanding model, to which the actual work of chemists, physicists, biologists, and botanists—to say nothing of political scientists—by no means always measures up.

Political scientists take many different positions on the questions of how closely political science can approach this model and whether or not it should even try to do so. Most behavioralists argue that political science can become much more scientific than it is now and that it should settle for nothing less than becoming as scientific as possible. Most antibehavioralists argue that there are no regularities in human behavior comparable to the presumed uniformities in nature. They insist that the existence of free will in human beings differentiates them fundamentally from stars, atoms, and other animals. Human behavior, accordingly, is always determined by whim, caprice, and reasoned judgment, rather than by compulsions beyond individual control. It is even insulting and immoral, some of them argue, to view human beings as subject only to such compulsions.

Others argue that, if such regularities do exist in human behavior, they are not significant for understanding important relations among people or that they cannot be understood by means of "scientific" techniques. "What counts can't be counted," some are fond of saying. These critics argue that behavioral political scientists ask only questions that can be answered by their very limited and narrow "scientific" methods and that their questions are therefore always about trivial or peripheral matters, never about the perennial great problems of political philosophy or the burning political issues of our own time.[27]

---

[27] See Charles McCoy and John Playford (eds.), *Apolitical Politics: A Critique of Behavioralism* (New York: Thomas Y. Crowell Company, 1967).

Critics of behavioralism are by no means agreed on what approach should replace it. Some insist that political science should abandon *all* attempts to find laws of human behavior, for "scientism" and "gnosticism" make the sacrilegious assumption that *no* knowledge is beyond man and that *no* questions are too sacred for men to ask. Man puts himself in the place of God, these critics say, and turns his eyes from the pursuit of the eternal principles of right and wrong to open the door for the triumph of evil in human affairs.[28] Others argue that the goal should be political and moral wisdom, rather than scientific descriptive knowledge, and that the best way to gain such wisdom is to examine and ponder the great classics of political and moral philosophy.[29] Some Caucus leaders argue that the desperate need for a radical political science can be met only by turning from behavioralism to "existentialist phenomenology" as an intellectual base.[30]

This conflict over the places of "behavioralism" and "science" is closely related to a third major issue.

## THE PROBLEM OF VALUES

### Value-Free Political Science?

Some time ago a number of political scientists (together with many of their colleagues in the other social sciences) were debating the desirability of erecting a value-free political science—describing only what *is* and totally excluding views about what *should be*.[31]

This debate has now largely faded away, mainly because most political scientists, behavioralist or otherwise, recognize that a value-free political science simply is not possible. Every political scientist is a human being and every human being, as we shall see in Chapter 2, has a set of values, a body of beliefs about what is "good, true, and beautiful"—whether sharply aware of all of them or not. No political scientist can completely divorce all professional investigations and teaching activities from all values, as begins to become apparent when we ask, Why does anyone bother to undertake any kind of research? Different researchers no doubt have different reasons. Some may feel that research is "good for its own sake"—that is, it will interest, absorb, and otherwise entertain them. Others may believe that they will make money and acquire prestige. Others may wish to benefit mankind. Still others may wish to keep their parents from upbraiding them for laziness. And many may work from a combination of these and other reasons. The point is that any researcher —including one who attempts value-free research—undertakes such work because it seems to be a valuable thing to do. If we did not think so, we would not undertake

---

[28] See Eric Voegelin, *The New Science of Politics* (Chicago: University of Chicago Press, 1952).

[29] See Herbert J. Storing (ed.), *Essays on the Scientific Study of Politics* (New York: Holt, Rinehart and Winston, Inc., 1962).

[30] Marvin Surkin, "Sense and Nonsense in Politics," *P.S.*, 2 (Fall 1969), 573–581.

[31] See the debate between William F. Whyte, "A Challenge to Political Scientists," *American Political Science Review*, 37 (August 1943), 692–697; and John H. Hallowell, "Politics and Ethics," *American Political Science Review*, 38 (August 1944), 639–655.

it, and we cannot determine what is and what is not a valuable thing except according to our own values.[32]

### How Values Should Be Treated

Granted that there is no way of totally excluding values from the study of politics and government (or anything else), even if it were desirable to do so, the question remains how values should be treated in political science. Charles Hyneman has detected in the current professional literature three main treatments of values. First, there is identification of peoples' values and the description of the value systems of particular societies. Second, there is "value analysis": the determination of compatibilities and incompatibilities among the values held by men, women, and societies and of what values reinforce or challenge one another. Third, there is the statement of the author's or the teacher's personal value preferences, with appeals to others to join in supporting them.[33]

Some political scientists insist that all three are proper ways to treat values and that the best works are those that move forward on all three lines. Others, particularly those most committed to the "scientific" study of politics, believe that only the first is proper for political scientists. A few argue that the third is not only proper but also the main justification for the very existence of political science and the primary task of all political scientists who take seriously their responsibilities to God or their communities.

### Distinguishing Value Preferences and Descriptive Statements

Most political scientists believe that at least some kinds of value questions are proper for professional consideration. Many (though by no means all) add, however, that political science will be served best if its practitioners strive always to keep their value preferences and their descriptive statements as distinct as they possibly can. The reasons for this conviction can be briefly summarized.

Whatever may be the views of particular political scientists about the relative professional importance of describing a particular political-governmental system or of urging fellow citizens to preserve or alter it, we can work toward our end most effectively when we can accurately describe and thoroughly understand the system as it is.

The validity of any descriptive statement about these matters depends upon its correspondence to the reality of the system, not upon its correspondence to the political scientist's preferences.[34] For example, to say that political parties are uncohesive, irresponsible, and do not play the role they should is very different from saying that they have no role whatever; to say that World War III will destroy the

---

[32] For a perceptive discussion of how political scientists' values affect the kinds of questions we ask and how we go about finding answers, see Easton, *The Political System: An Inquiry into the State of Political Science* (New York: Alfred A. Knopf, 1953), chap. 9.

[33] Hyneman, *The Study of Politics*, pp. 181–189.

[34] This position is well stated by Kaplan, *The Conduct of Inquiry*, chap. 10.

world and should be prevented is very different from predicting that it will be prevented.

The more political scientists permit their "should" feelings to occupy the center of their attention, the more likely they are to distort their perceptions of how things actually are. To illustrate this point we may note that in the heyday of the Progressive era in the United States, from about 1890 to about 1920, American political scientists wrote a great deal about political bosses and machines. Most of these writers were deeply repelled by both institutions, and their dislikes apparently dominated their thinking. Most of their writings emphasized how bad bosses are and contained lengthy exhortations to their readers to throw the rascals out and thus to forward the cause of good government. So convinced were they that nothing good can be said about bosses that they could explain the continuing survival of the latter in the face of many contemporary reform movements only in terms of apathy, laziness, and lack of public spirit among the voters. Indeed, they talked about politics as if it were simply a contest between good men (reformers) and bad men (bosses)—a contest that the latter won with disheartening frequency.

This body of literature did not, however, provide an adequate explanation of *why* the "bad" men usually won or, for that matter, why the "good" men occasionally won. Its authors took little account, for example, of the hypothesis that no one is entirely "good" or "bad" but rather a mixture of both, the proportions of which change from time to time. Their preoccupation with the "badness" of the bosses, in other words, stopped them from exploring even so elementary a question as whether or not bosses performed services that the majority of voters regarded as necessary and that no other social or political institutions were providing—that is, whether or not some hypothesis other than the low moral character of voters might more adequately explain the phenomenon of bossism.[35]

The moral of this story, many political scientists believe, is that, while recognizing that we cannot entirely divorce our research and teaching from our values, we must nevertheless try our best not to confuse our notions of how things should be with our perceptions of how things actually are. Our ability to avoid this kind of confusion is likely to be important in our efforts to understand how politics and government operate. Such an understanding in turn is vital to the effective performance of whatever we may conceive as the proper functions and the achievement of the ultimate goals of political science.[36]

*Postbehavioralism?*

One leading political scientist has bravely tried to pitch an intellectual tent that will accommodate all the conflicting points of view and factions within the discipline. In

---

[35] For different perspectives on these questions, see Richard Hofstadter, *The Age of Reform* (New York: Vintage Books, 1955); and James C. Scott, *Comparative Political Corruption* (Englewood Cliffs, N.J.: Prentice-Hall, Inc., 1971).

[36] For a recent thoughtful statement of this view, see Eulau, "Values and Behavioral Science: Neutrality Revisited," in *Micro-Macro Political Analysis* (Chicago: Aldine Publishing Co., 1969), pp. 364–369.

his presidential address to the APSA's 1969 annual convention, David Easton announced that the "behavioral revolution" has now been completed (and is presumably victorious) and that those who now challenge, as do members of the Caucus, "establishment" values and activities are not engaged in an antibehavioral counter-revolution but in a new "postbehavioral revolution." Their insistence upon emphasizing substance over method, upon "relevance," and upon "politicization" of the profession in order to press for radical social change is, Easton declared, an effort, not to *replace* behavioralist concerns with theoretical rigor and empirical verification, but to *add* others. The "new revolution" is thus postbehavioral, not antibehavioral. He urged behavioralists to welcome it and all political scientists to spend more scholarly time and resources on "applied, action-oriented research." He concluded by proposing that political scientists

> take the initiative by calling for the establishment of a Federation of Social Scientists.... The tasks of such a Federation would be to identify the major issues of the day, clarify objectives, evaluate action taken by others, study and propose alternative solutions, *and press these vigorously in the political sphere.*[37]

There is still no sign that political science will take the lead in establishing such a federation. There is also no sign that either the Caucus or the behavioralists have accepted Easton's view that they are really complementary rather than antagonistic. And the political scientists who oppose all "scientism" and "gnosticism"—to say nothing of "radical social change"—seem to think that the behavioral revolution itself can still be turned back.

It therefore seems likely that the cross-cutting intellectual and factional disputes outlined in this chapter, which now divide the profession of political science, will continue to do so for some time to come.

## POLITICAL SCIENCE AND THE GOVERNING OF MEN

Every political scientist should walk humbly with his profession, and most do. Ambitious as are the objectives of the physical sciences, the ultimate goals of political science are even more so, for they are nothing less than to acquire an understanding of government and politics that will enable us to use the instruments to realize our vision of the good life. If our reach should indeed exceed our grasp, then, however else we may criticize political science, we cannot condemn it for pursuing petty and insignificant goals.

When political scientists measure the knowledge they have against the knowledge they want—or compare their achievements with those of the natural sciences or even of some of the other social sciences—they should feel very humble indeed, and most do. Yet even at its present stage of development political science is far from a complete failure, for surely human society is far better off for having the kind of

---

[37] Easton, "The New Revolution in Political Science," *American Political Science Review*, 63 (December 1969), 1060; italics added. See also George J. Graham, Jr., and George W. Carey, *The Post-Behavioral Era* (New York: David McKay Company, Inc., 1972).

information and understanding—developed mainly by political scientists—that will be summarized in this book than it would be without it.[38]

Political science may well never become as exact or useful a discipline as is chemistry, physics, or even medicine or meteorology. But surely its efforts to become *more* exact and *more* useful hold high promise of benefiting mankind. As the great American historian and political scientist Charles A. Beard stirringly declared:

> No one can deny that the idea is fascinating—the idea of subduing the phenomena of politics to the laws of causation, of penetrating to the mystery of its transformations, of symbolizing the trajectory of its future; in a word, of grasping destiny by the forelock and bringing it prostrate to earth. The very idea is worthy of the immortal gods. . . . If nothing ever comes of it, its very existence will fertilize thought and enrich imagination.[39]

---

[38] For a judicious estimate of the failures and successes of political science and a convincing conclusion that it has scored a number of impressive scholarly successes and has made valuable contributions to human welfare, see Dwight Waldo, *Perspectives on Administration* (University, Ala.: University of Alabama Press, 1956), chap. 1.

[39] Charles A. Beard, quoted in Easton, *The Political System,* p. vii.

# II

# POLITICAL SYSTEMS AND THEIR ENVIRONMENTS

# 2

# POLITICS IN HUMAN LIFE

"Ye shall know the truth, and the truth shall make ye free" (John 8:32).

"While you live, tell truth and shame the devil!" (Shakespeare, *Henry IV, Part I,* Act III, scene 1).

"Tell it like it is."

The idiom has changed, but the message has not. From the mists of prehistory to our own time most human beings have believed that knowledge is our greatest power. Understanding the physical and social world in which we live need not commit us to accepting it as the best or the only possible order of things. But understanding is surely our greatest tool for creating a better order.

It is not surprising, therefore, that many of us are deeply concerned about the political and governmental environment in which the great questions of our time are being decided. Who among us never asked such questions as, Why is it so hard to get a satisfying job? What right has the government to take so much of my income in taxes? What makes nations go to war? Who really runs this country?

But before we can *tell* it like it is we have to *know* it like it is. Unfortunately, most of us are better at asking the questions than at answering them. For one thing, finding valid answers is more difficult and more painful: Not only does it take more time, energy, and training, but also the person who offers answers exposes himself to criticism and even ridicule that seldom disturb the person who only asks questions. Then, too, most of us have to go to school and then earn a living, and we simply cannot devote much time or energy to finding better explanations of how and why political systems operate as they do. So, although the demands of our daily lives do not and should not keep us from asking questions and insisting that our teachers and leaders tell it like it is, they prevent most of us from finding answers in any but the most casual and sporadic manner.

Be that as it may, a few people, called "political scientists," *do* make full-time jobs of investigating and teaching about the nature of politics and government. The purpose of this book is to describe something of what they have learned. The purpose of this chapter is to explain what politics is "about"—that is, what kinds of human behavior are political and therefore relevant to the book's concerns.

## WHAT POLITICS IS

### IN EVERYDAY CONVERSATION

We all know *something* about "politics." The word and its derivatives pop up again and again in everyday thinking, conversation, and reading. When a football player tell us that "X was elected captain because of politics, not merit," a university president charges that "politicians are interfering with higher education," or a newspaper columnist writes that "farm subsidies are economically senseless, but it is politically impossible for Congress to abolish them," most of us think that we know what such statements mean. Indeed, we are likely to nod sagely and perhaps add a sigh for the imperfections of human nature.

These and similar commonly heard statements give some clues to what politics means to most of us. For one thing, it has something to do with allocating values—with deciding who gets the lion's share and who the mouse's share. For another, it operates not only in "the government" but in private groups as well—for example, in a football team as well as in Congress. And, finally, it often connotes selfish squabbling for private gain, rather than statesmanlike cooperation for the common good.

Most political scientists[1] incorporate the first two aspects in their conceptions of politics but reject the third. They observe that even people who dislike "politicians" and admire "statesmen" can never agree on which public figures should be given which label. To some, for example, Franklin D. Roosevelt was a great "statesman," but to others he was a "politician of the cheapest sort." Similar disagreements have existed about almost every other prominent leader from Thomas Jefferson and Abraham Lincoln to Winston Churchill, Charles de Gaulle, Richard Nixon, and Moshe Dayan.

Basically such disagreements arise from the fact that for many people "statesman" is a laudatory term and "politician" is quite the opposite. Consider, for example, the finding of a 1973 Gallup Poll that only 23 percent of the American people

---

[1] In the pages to come readers will often encounter variations on the phrase "most political scientists believe." This usage is intended to alert them to the fact that the beliefs described are not shared by every political scientist in the world. As we have seen in Chap. 1, there is probably no single professional statement that *all* political scientists would support, and there are a number of important moral and epistemological issues on which they are sharply divided. Accordingly, when a particular view predominates in the relevant scholarly literature, it will be presented in this text as the position of "most political scientists." When there are several competing views, none of which predominates, each will be summarized, and whatever preference I may have and why will be indicated.

said they would like to see their children go into "politics" as a life's work.[2] But consider also the findings of many other polls that among the persons most admired by most people are high elected officials, like the President, governors, and congressmen. What are we to make of this? Does it mean that people think it is good to be a high elected official—but bad to do what must be done to get elected? That seems both inconsistent and unfair, but there it is.

Some observers suspect that for most people a "statesman" is simply a government figure they like and a "politician" is one they dislike. This suspicion has led some commentators to say that "a statesman is a dead politician," and others that "a statesman is a politician held upright by pressures from *all* sides." It has also inclined most political scientists to use the terms "politics" and "politicians" in the more neutral senses that we shall use in this book.

## POLITICS AS POLICY MAKING

In its broadest sense politics includes the decision-making and -enforcing processes in any group that makes and enforces rules for its members.[3] Several political scientists have studied these processes in such groups as labor unions, business corporations, medical associations, and the like. But most political scientists have concentrated on the processes of governments rather than on those of private organizations,[4] and it seems desirable to adopt the same focus in an introduction to the discipline.

As the word will be used in this book, accordingly, politics is *the process of making government policies.* Let us see just what is implied by this definition.

When government officials are called upon to take some course of action (or inaction) in a particular field, they are always faced with a number of alternatives which *might* be pursued—that is, are technically possible. They cannot, however, undertake all these courses simultaneously if for no other reason than that some would cancel out others. In such a situation public officials always select from the available alternatives the few that they intend actually to put into effect. The courses of action thus chosen are, for the moment, government policies; and the process by which policy makers choose which alternatives they will and will not use is, according to our definition, politics.

A good illustration of this point can be taken from the response of the Nixon administration to the energy crisis of 1973–1974. For decades prior to the crisis the demands of American industry and consumers for more energy to run automobiles, heat homes, operate factories, and the like had increasingly outstripped the nation's production of fuels. Consequently, we bought an increasing proportion of our fuels, especially petroleum, from other nations, including the oil-rich Arab nations of the

---

[2] Reported in the Milwaukee *Journal*, July 13, 1973, p. 5.

[3] See Harold D. Lasswell and Abraham Kaplan, *Power and Society* (New Haven, Conn.: Yale University Press, 1950); and Robert A. Dahl, *Modern Political Analysis* (Englewood Cliffs, N.J.: Prentice-Hall, Inc., 1963).

[4] We shall consider the distinctions between governments and private organizations in Chap. 3.

Middle East. In 1973 war broke out between these nations and Israel, and our support of the Israelis led the Arabs to shut off all oil shipments to us. Some said there was no real crisis—that the sudden shortage of oil was really being manufactured by our own oil companies to force prices up. But in the administration's view the crisis was quite real, and it meant that we suddenly had less fuel than we needed to run our affairs.

In meeting this crisis, the administration had a wide range of alternatives. At one extreme, it could accede to all the Arab demands, get the oil coming again—and perhaps pay the price of allowing Israel to be conquered. At the other extreme, it could invade the Arab nations, seize the wells—and perhaps pay the price of thermonuclear war with the Soviet Union. Or it could avoid both extremes by instituting a strict program of rationing; or by trying to persuade both sides to end the war; or by accepting the analysis that there was no real crisis and forcing domestic oil companies to release their hoarded supplies; and so on. But the administration obviously could not do *all* of these things simultaneously, for some (for example, seizing the Arab wells) would cancel out others (for example, giving in to the Arab demands). In fact the administration rejected both extremes and chose to combine a program of limited restrictions on domestic fuel consumption with efforts to end the war and a crash program to develop new domestic sources of energy. Taken together, then, these few courses of action chosen from among the many that might have been followed constituted, in the terminology of this book, the Nixon administration's *policy* toward the energy crisis. Like any other government policy, it was and remains subject to continual revision.

## POLITICAL SYSTEMS AND SYSTEMS ANALYSIS

Ever since the time of Plato and Aristotle, as we saw in Chapter 1, some scholars of politics have sought to discover universally valid descriptive "laws"—that is, statements which accurately describe and explain political institutions and processes in all nations and at all times. Many scholars have argued that the quest requires a general conceptual framework within which the countless variations in detail from one society or time to another can be described and compared, and essential similarities and differences can be understood. A number of such frameworks have been proposed over the years, and a few have even been tested as guides for empirical research. In our own time, however, many political scientists have found "systems analysis," explicated in a political context principally by David Easton, to be a useful scheme.[5]

---

[5] See Easton, *A Systems Analysis of Political Life* (New York: John Wiley & Sons, Inc., 1965); and Easton, *A Framework for Political Analysis* (Englewood Cliffs, N.J.: Prentice-Hall, Inc., 1965). See also Gabriel A. Almond and G. Bingham Powell, Jr., *Comparative Politics: A Developmental Approach* (Boston: Little, Brown & Company, 1966), especially chap. 2; and the articles on general systems theory, social systems, political systems, and international systems in David L. Sills (ed.), *International Encyclopedia of the Social Sciences,* Vol. 15 (New York: The Macmillan Company and The Free Press, 1968), pp. 452–486. For an alternative framework, generally called "exchange theory," see Sidney R. Waldman, *Foundations of Political Action: An Exchange Theory of Politics* (Boston: Little, Brown & Company, 1972).

As in any general conceptual scheme, the concepts and interrelations of political systems analysis are necessarily highly abstract and often may seem far removed from the grubby concreteness of the political life that each of us personally experiences. But they can help guide us to an understanding of many things we do not directly experience and thus broaden and sharpen our political vision. And, as we shall use the ideas and terminology of systems analysis frequently in the chapters to come, a simple illustration of the essential features of any political system is presented in Figure 1, and definitions of the basic terms of systems analysis follow:

**FIGURE 1**
**Essentials of a political system.** Source: adapted from David Easton, *A Systems Analysis of Political Life* (New York: John Wiley & Sons, 1965), diagram 2, p. 32; reprinted from Austin Ranney (ed.), *Political Science and Public Policy* (Chicago: Markham Publishing Company, 1968), p. 9.

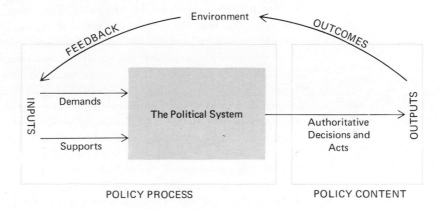

*Political system* Those institutions, processes, and interactions through which values are authoritatively allocated in a society.

*Environment* Those social, biological, sociological, and personality forces both inside and outside a particular society that affect and are affected by the political system but are analytically distinct from it.

*Inputs* Those events in the environment that act upon the political system and evoke some kind of response from it. According to Easton, there are two kinds of input: *demands,* which are expressions of desire that values be allocated in particular ways, and *supports,* which are expressions of willingness to accept particular value allocations or the processes by which the allocations are made.

*Conversion processes* Those institutions, processes, and interactions by which the political system converts demands and supports into outputs.

*Outputs* Those actions by the political system that affect the system's environment in some manner, consisting mainly of *authoritative decisions and acts*—that is, laws, executive orders, judicial decisions, and the like promulgated by the *authorities* (people generally recognized as having the legitimate power and duty to allocate values).

*Outcomes* Those changes in the environment brought about by the political system's outputs.

*Feedback* Those changes in the nature, intensity, and volume of demands and supports brought about by the outcomes.

Let me illustrate this way of looking at things political by rephrasing the earlier energy-policy illustration in systems-analytic terms. In 1973 diplomatic and military events in the American international political environment combined with certain long-standing economic, social, and psychological trends in our domestic environment to stimulate various new demands. Some were for changing our Middle East policies, others for increasing the supply of domestic as well as foreign oil, others for increasing the prices and profits of domestic fuel producers and retailers, others for equitable distribution of the fuel shortage's burdens, others for strict government regulation or public ownership of the domestic oil industry, and so on. Obviously many of these demands were in sharp conflict with others, but even so most persons and groups pressing them agreed, explicitly or implicitly, that the disputes should be dealt with by the nation's established political processes, and not by assassination or civil war. The demands entered the political system and triggered various input processes: pressure groups organized, propagandized, lobbied, and demonstrated. The authorities—the President, his "energy chief," lesser bureaucrats, congressmen, state governors, and so on—heard the various arguments and made some of their own. From such conversion processes as argument and counterargument, negotiation, bargaining, deals, and trials of political strength emerged several policy outputs. These included administration efforts to settle the Middle East war, a law lowering highway speed limits, a "jawbone" program exhorting (but not requiring) people to lower thermostat settings in their homes and places of work, and funding research on new domestic energy sources. These and other outputs soon produced several outcomes, including a modest decline in overall fuel consumption, sharp increases in the prices of fuels and the profits of fuel producers and merchants, and even a decline in traffic fatalities. These outcomes, in turn, produced a feedback of increased complaints from fuel consumers. This feedback further altered the environment and produced new and renewed demands for restricting fuel-industry profits, gasoline and fuel oil rationing, abandoning our pro-Israel policies, and others too numerous to list here.

Thus in this as in all other public issues the political process continues to travel through its continuous "loop": demands and supports ——> conversion processes ——> outputs ——> outcomes ——> feedbacks ——> new demands ——> and so on, world without end. And in such terms we shall in chapters to come consider many political and governmental processes as they resemble and differ from one another in various modern nations.


## POLICY PROCESS AND POLICY CONTENT

Figure 1 shows a distinction between policy process and policy content that underlies much of the discussion in this book. It offers a political version of the familiar distinction between means and ends: Most of us think of ends as particular desired states of affairs and of means as actions that can be taken in an effort to achieve those ends. Similarly, in a political system the policy process includes all the interactions like demand structure, expression of demands, and political conversion processes that produce outputs. Policy content is roughly synonymous with the political system's outputs.

In the years since World War II most political scientists—especially those of the "behavioral" persuasion—have focused mainly on policy processes. Typically policy content has been the dependent variable;[6] that is, most scholars have sought to explain *why* political systems produce particular policies or patterns of policies. Only a few have studied the impacts of various policies on the way people live, and only a few have given *scholarly* attention to deciding and proclaiming that this or that policy is good or bad. (Many, of course, have been active in politics as ordinary citizens.)

To a large number of today's students this emphasis on process over content may well make political science seem irrelevant in grappling with war, racism, poverty, and other urgent social problems of our time. Yet, in our understandable eagerness to find solutions and to apply them without delay, we may overlook, to our great loss, two of humanity's most hard-learned lessons: No single person or profession can tackle all problems at once and hope to produce solutions or useful knowledge. In most circumstances, *how* decisions are made is even more important for social and political health than what the decisions are.

This dilemma is, of course, related to the age-old problem of choosing appropriate means for achieving desired ends. We all face this problem many times in our personal lives: Shall we tell friends "little white lies" to avoid hurting their feelings? Shall we shout opponents down to keep them from expressing racist or prowar opinions? Shall we help to blow up a university building to protest the administration's failure to hire black faculty members and offer courses in black history?

Making any such choice certainly involves the question of efficacy: Will this means in fact achieve or help to achieve our goal more quickly and fully than others that we might use? Will it damage other values that we also cherish? But it also involves a tough moral question: Are we justified in using this means? Is it morally *right* to use it to pursue this (or any) end?

So it is in politics. Every person or group pressing political demands and every public official responding to them constantly makes judgments of both efficacy and morality. For example, to achieve their goal of eliminating Jewish influence in the Third Reich the Nazi leaders decided that the "final solution"—extermination of all Jews—would be both effective and morally justified. To most of us their decision remains morally hideous beyond expression, but this should not obscure the fact that Adolf Hitler, Heinrich Himmler, and their henchmen were quite aware of the moral questions involved and quite satisfied with their answers. Nor are Americans immune to this kind of reasoning. One of the most striking—some would say horrifying—facts to emerge from the "Watergate" revelations of 1974 was proof that a number of leaders of the Committee to Reelect the President believed that reelecting Richard Nixon was so important a goal that it justified using burglary, forgery, sabotage, and the concealment of illegal campaign funds. In my own university a student named Karleton Armstrong felt that the lofty goal of ending American involvement in Vietnam was so compelling that it justified blowing up a university building, in the

---

[6] "Variable" is a technical term often used in the literature of the social sciences, and it will appear frequently in this book. Throughout the book, it means any characteristic of a social situation or institution that may appear in different degrees or forms in different situations and institutions. A "dependent variable" is one whose characteristics are considered as being affected by other variables; it is roughly equivalent to an "effect." An "independent variable" is one considered as affecting the characteristics of other variables; it is roughly equivalent to a "cause."

process of which another student was killed. These various political actors sought very different goals; but in choosing their modes of political action they made, as we all must make, both practical and moral judgments.

In this book we shall generally consider policy processes more than policy contents, for they have been the focus of most political science research in recent years and we simply know more about them.[7] We should be clear, however, that this decision is a matter of emphasis only. Obviously we can study policy processes only through observing the determination of policy contents. And we should also be clear

---

[7] At present, however, a growing number of political scientists believe that their profession can and should substantially increase its concern with policy content without changing its professional stance from analytical and scientific to hortatory and "political." For various points of view on the problems and possibilities of this shift in emphasis, see Austin Ranney (ed.), *Political Science and Public Policy* (Chicago: Markham Publishing Company, 1968). See also the articles in three new policy-centered scholarly journals: *Public Policy, The Public Interest,* and the *Policy Studies Journal.*

that policy processes are not isolated; they are affected by policy contents and outcomes in many ways, some of which we shall consider.

We should also never forget, however, that how a decision is made is in some respects more important than what the decision is. For one thing, it may determine the content of the decision: Elections in which large numbers of blacks are denied the right to vote are likely to produce officeholders with views on racial discrimination quite different from those of officeholders chosen through elections in which blacks vote in large numbers. For another, it may produce side effects that nullify or over-shadow the decision itself: Student strikes and occupation of buildings may force a public university's administration to institute new programs, but they may also so antagonize the citizens and legislature of the state that funds for all new programs and some old ones as well are shut off. And for yet another, it may strengthen or destroy the whole political system: When people pressing a particular demand believe that their views have had a full and fair hearing, even though the decision goes against them, they are likely to accept it as fair though incorrect; they are likely to channel their efforts to reverse it through established procedures. But, when the "losers" believe that the policy process has been hopelessly rigged to deny them even a chance of winning, they may well conclude that overthrowing the entire system is the necessary first step toward achieving their policy goals. Once they set their feet on that path, everyone is in great danger, for who can say with certainty that a new political system will not produce even worse policy contents and outcomes than did the old? Revolutions are undoubtedly sometimes necessary, desirable, inevitable, or all three, but the political systems they produce can rarely be predicted with accuracy. They are not always as satisfactory—even to the original revolutionaries—as were the systems overthrown.

In any event the "let's win and never mind how" point of view is prevalent enough in our world so that, though political scientists could hardly justify the total neglect of policy contents, they may perhaps be forgiven their emphasis on policy processes.

## SOME CHARACTERISTICS OF POLITICS IN ALL SYSTEMS

Most of this book is devoted to description of the principal political systems in the modern world. Throughout we shall repeatedly encounter two basic facts about governing. First, certain general themes are in varying degrees characteristic of politics and government in all modern societies; that is, they are essentially alike wherever we look. Second, there are significant variations in these phenomena from one society to another—variations that help to produce important differences in the lives and fortunes of the peoples concerned. An understanding of both the general themes and the principal variations is necessary for the student of political science. In this chapter and the next we shall consider the general themes; later, in Chapters 12 and 13, we shall take up the variations.

### POLITICS AS CONFLICT

Politics, as the term is used in this book, is the process of making government policy. But what is the process like? What are its main characteristics? The first we will note is that politics in all systems involves conflict—that is, some form of struggle among

WE BRING THE TROOPS HOME— WHICH RAISES UNEMPLOYMENT— SO WE CREATE NEW JOBS— WHICH RUIN THE ENVIRONMENT— SO WE LIMIT INDUSTRIAL EXPANSION—

**Politics is choices and consequences.**
Source: ©1971 Jules Feiffer. Courtesy Publishers-Hall Syndicate.

human beings trying to achieve different goals and to satisfy opposing interests. A basic, though perhaps painful, first step toward understanding the governing process is thus to face the fact that political conflict is not an unfortunate and temporary aberration from the norm of perfect cooperation and harmony. It arises from the very nature of human life itself.

## Conflict in Human Life

One universal and basic trait of human life is that people live together, not in isolation from one another. When we reflect upon our lives and try to understand what has happened to us and why, we realize that our stories must be told largely in terms of our relations with other people—parents, teachers, sweethearts, friends, enemies, bosses, subordinates, and so on. To be human is to interact with—to affect and to be affected by—other human beings every day of our lives. And to interact with our fellows is, to some extent at least, to be in conflict with them. Let us see why.

Although all human beings are alike in certain respects, no human being is exactly like any other in every respect. One of the most significant respects in which people differ from one another is in the total set of values that each holds. A value, as the term is used here, is an object of desire—what someone wants, whether it be passing grades, a Jaguar, social prestige, peace of mind, or a brave new world. Social scientists agree that not only do different people want different things but also every person in some way *acts* to realize certain of his or her values. Wherever human beings come into contact with one another, then, their values are in some conflict. In a world of limited resources, to the extent that some values are satisfied other values must necessarily go unsatisfied. For example, if taxes are increased to support higher welfare payments, taxpayers will be unhappy; if the Republicans win the presidency, Democrats will be unhappy; if farm prices are high and industrial prices low, farmers will be happy and industrialists and workers unhappy; and so on.

Accordingly, we all find that to some extent we are in competition with our fellows. As we live our daily lives and try to enter the college of our choice; study what interests us; and then find a job that is absorbing, socially useful, and still remunerative enough to let us live as we wish, we discover that other people also want comparable satisfactions and that not everyone can or does have equal success in attaining them. We all want a better, more just world—but we do not all agree on what is the best way to achieve it. We all strive in all sorts of ways—working and resting, studying and practicing, speaking and demonstrating, voting and abstaining, telling the truth and lying, obeying the rules and breaking them—to achieve particu-

Political Systems and Their Environments

WHICH CRIPPLES THE ECONOMY— SO WE GO TO WAR— TO SALVAGE THE ECONOMY— AND AT FOUR YEAR INTERVALS WE ELECT A NEW PRESIDENT— TO GET OUR MIND OFF OUR PROBLEMS.

©1971 JULES FEIFFER 6-6    Dist. Publishers-Hall Syndicate

lar goals in competition with our fellows, who pursue different goals or the same goals in different ways. Conflict, then, is an essential and inescapable consequence of our living together rather than in isolation from one another.

### Political Conflict in Society

Wherever human beings live together in a society, most feel that certain values can be fully satisfied only by rules effectively binding everyone in the society. For example, most Americans who believe that racial segregation in public schools must be ended would not be satisfied with the tokenism of entering a few blacks in unsegregated schools while all others were forced to continue to study under Jim Crow laws. They demand that any black child whose parents wish him to attend an unsegregated school be allowed to do so, and they will settle for nothing less, even if it means busing. For another example, most people who favor a complete "quarantine" of Cuba would not be satisfied if each businessman could decide for himself whether or not he would do business with Havana. They are likely to demand that all businessmen be prevented, forcibly if necessary, from dealing with the Castro regime.

In many non-Western and traditional societies, as we shall see in Chapter 3, the political aspect of life is not as clearly differentiated from the social and personal aspects as it is in Western and advanced societies, nor are political authorities as clearly differentiated from religious and family authorities. Even so, the desire for authoritative rules binding on everyone is a potent force in such societies, and it seems appropriate to call the making of such rules "politics" in non-Western as well as Western societies.

In Western and advanced societies, most people regard government action as the most promising way to obtain authoritative and binding rules. Conflict over what the rules shall be is thus, according to our definition, political conflict. To be sure, not all conflicts among individuals and groups in any society are fought out in the political arena. Many occur largely or entirely outside a clearly differentiated political sphere. The point is that no society—Western or non-Western, traditional or modern, democratically or dictatorially ruled—is entirely without political conflict; and, as we shall observe repeatedly throughout this book, in modern societies most value conflicts about which people feel strongly sooner or later become, for good or ill, mainly political in nature.

Just as interpersonal conflict is an inescapable part of human life, then, political conflict is an inescapable part of human society.

## POLITICAL CONFLICT AS GROUP CONFLICT

Many political scientists emphasize a second general characteristic of politics: that most people engage in political conflict not as isolated individuals acting without reference to or support from others, but in association with others, in political groups. Most political conflict is thus seen as conflict among groups, rather than among individuals. For example, the contest between George McGovern and Richard Nixon for the American presidency in 1972 was far from a contest between those two men alone. Each was supported, opposed, and influenced by various political parties, labor unions, ethnic groups, business associations—and also by majorities of such unorganized but potent groups as blacks, whites, the middle class, workers, youth, women, the middle-aged, and so on. To describe the election campaign and outcome solely in terms of what McGovern and Nixon said and did would be to present only a partial and very misleading picture. For another example, the bitter fights in several American metropolitan areas in the 1970s over whether suburban white children should be bussed to predominantly black central-city schools and black city children to predominantly white suburban schools to achieve racial balance in both involved not only the children, parents, and school officials directly concerned but also many national pressure groups, both national political parties, and ultimately the President, Congress, and Supreme Court of the United States.

The defendant in a murder trial may appear at first glance to be an individual with no group support or interest behind him. Certainly the standard title of such a trial— *The People of the State of New York* v. *John Doe*—seems to suggest that the contest is taking place between Mr. Doe on one hand and everybody else in New York on the other. If so, it seems a highly unequal contest, and we wonder how Mr. Doe can have the slightest chance of winning. The fact is, however, that he has considerable support from others. For example, many people in the community believe that every person accused of a crime should be given a fair trial, and they have written into the state constitution such protections as the guarantee of counsel paid for by the state if he cannot afford to hire one himself, the power to subpoena witnesses on his own behalf, and the right to prevent the seating of jurors prejudiced against him. Neither Mr. Doe nor any other individual engaged in political or governmental conflict is alone.

Politics, then, is usually best viewed as the conflict among groups over the formulation of government policy. Let us now consider the different kinds of groups and determine which are the most prominent in politics.

### Varieties of Human Groups

**Categoric Groups**   A categoric group, or "social stratum," is any aggregate of individuals sharing one or more common characteristics: for example, people under twenty-one years of age, people earning more than $5000 a year, residents of Illinois, tool-and-die makers, blonds, tight ends, and so on. The individuals in any particular categoric group may or may not be conscious of their common characteristic, regard it as important, and direct their behavior accordingly. Few brown-eyed people, for example, feel strong bonds with other brown-eyed people or are acutely aware of a wide gulf between their interests and the interests of blue-eyed people; they are not likely, therefore, to unite with other brown-eyed people to advance the cause of brown-eyedness against the blue-eyed peril. Most blacks, on the other hand, can hardly help being aware of their differences from whites, and they form organizations like the National Association for the Advancement of Colored People or the Black Panther party to improve their social status. Any particular categoric group thus may or may not be socially or politically significant.

**Organized and Unorganized Interest Groups** The American political scientist David B. Truman defines an interest group as "any group that, on the basis of one or more shared attitudes, makes certain claims upon other groups in the society for the establishment, maintenance, or enhancement of forms of behavior that are implied by the shared attitudes."[8] In this sense, an interest group is a categoric group whose members are to some extent conscious of their common characteristics, regard themselves as having a common value or "interest" arising from these characteristics, and to some extent direct their behavior to advance this common interest. Doctors of medicine, for example, share the common characteristic of having received a certain kind of training and the MD degree from a medical school. They are also conscious that their training and skills differ from those of chiropractors, herbalists, and faith healers. Most medical doctors, therefore, join a professional association (the American Medical Association), which, among other functions, works to withhold legally from people who do not have the MD degree such privileges as calling themselves "MDs," "physicians," or "surgeons"; performing operations; and prescribing certain drugs. These attitudes and behaviors make doctors, in our terms, an interest group.

Some interest groups pursue their goals with little or no conscious, planned cooperation but make their weight felt mainly through spontaneous parallel action. When the price of meat rises above a certain level, many housewives may individually and without mutual consultation decide to boycott the butchers and feed their families macaroni and cheese until meat prices come down—as they did in early 1973. Although they thus became a full-fledged interest group and their parallel activity had a powerful impact on the price of meat, they constitute, in our terms, an unorganized interest group.

On the other hand, members of certain other interest groups regularly try to achieve their common goals through direct association, conscious planning, and organization. Medical doctors, for example, do not try to uphold their preferred position over chiropractors through individual and uncoordinated protests and letters to the editor. They *organize*—that is, they meet together; form a professional association with bylaws, dues, and officers; decide what to do; and assign various tasks to members of the association. If they do these organizing jobs well, their members and officers act together cooperatively much as the organs of the body act together—hence the origin of the term "organized" to describe such a group.

**Political Interest Groups** Any interest group, organized or unorganized, that pursues at least some of its goals through political action—that is, by seeking to obtain government policies that will further its goals or hinder opposing groups from achiev-

---

[8] David B. Truman, *The Governing Process* (2d ed.; Alfred A. Knopf, 1971), p. 33.

ing theirs—is a political interest group. Some political commentators use the term "pressure group" to denote such associations, but the term has doubtful utility because of its bad moral connotations and because the word "pressure" usually refers to certain kinds of tactics employed by some, but not all, politically oriented groups. In this book, therefore, the neutral descriptive term "political interest group" will be used, except in the discussion of groups using pressure tactics in Chapter 10.

### Characteristics of Group Conflict in Politics

Group conflict in politics in every human society displays to some degree certain main characteristics.

**Multiplicity**  Every distinction among human beings—whether based on race, religion, age, occupation, educational level, or the like—generates categoric groups, some of which become political interest groups. The more complex the society, the more distinctions there are among its members, and the more likely it is to contain large numbers of political interest groups. A highly complex society like that of the United States probably contains more categoric groups than can ever be counted. The surest proof of this statement is the incredible variety of bases on which organized interest groups are formed in this country. The following list is a small sample of the national associations listed in the *World Almanac,* but it illustrates how many diversified interests Americans find worth organizing to advance.[9]

> Alcoholics Anonymous
> American Civil Liberties Union
> American Feline Society
> American Institute of Architects
> American League to Abolish Capital Punishment
> American Society for the Advancement of Atheism
> Anti-Defamation League of B'nai B'rith
> Association for the Promotion of the Study of Latin
> Association of Professional Ball Players of America
> Big Brothers of America
> Blizzard Men and Ladies of 1888
> Chinese Women's Association
> Circus Fans Association of America
> Ducks Unlimited
> Federation of the Handicapped
> Future Farmers of America
> Hay Fever Prevention Society
> International City Managers' Association
> International Concatenated Order of Hoo Hoo
> International Log Rolling Association
> Izaak Walton League of America
> The John Birch Society

[9] *World Almanac, 1974* (New York: Newspaper Enterprise Association, Inc., 1974), pp. 269–283 *passim.*

Magicians Guild of America
National Collegiate Athletic Association
National Horseshoe Pitchers Association of America
National Speleological Society
Planned Parenthood Federation of America
Rodeo Cowboys Association
Save-the-Redwoods League
Soaring Society of America

Another way of illustrating the multiplicity of interest groups in the United States is to list the number of units (in 1970 figures) measurable on a few of the more obvious bases of group formation.

Number of families (households): 163,450,000
Religious denominations: 254
Local congregations: 329,672
Business firms: 12,001,000
Farms: 2,954,000
National and international unions: 185
Local unions: 49,000
Units of government:
    Nation: 1
    States: 50
    Counties: 3,044
    Municipalities: 18,517
    Townships and towns: 16,991
    School districts: 15,781
    Special districts (park, sanitary, and drainage districts, and so on): 23,885

Politics is largely a contest among political interest groups, and the United States—like any complex modern nation—has an almost infinite number of active and potential contestants.

**Opposition**  Every political interest group has opposition—that is, some group or combination of groups seeking conflicting goals. No proposal for governmental policy therefore ever enlists *all* members of the society in its support. The closest a nation comes to unanimity is usually on a win-the-war policy during times of armed conflict. Even then an opposition of pacifists, who oppose all war measures, and of traitors, who actively work for enemy victory, still exists. Every political interest group, accordingly, encounters some opposition in its efforts to induce the government to adopt policies favorable to it.

There are many variations in the kind of opposition that particular groups encounter in particular situations. Opposing groups may be organized or unorganized, large or small, powerful or weak, and so on. The degree of hostility between opposing groups ranges all the way from the mild disagreement between groups favoring and opposing free barber service for congressmen to bitter and uncompromising civil war. As we have already noted, not all group conflict is fought out by political means, but many of the most serious and divisive types of competition in modern societies are conducted in the political arena. Such political competition may include competition among cities, states, and regions for industry, teachers, labor, population, fuel, and water; competition between labor and management over wages, hours, working conditions, and union status; competition among ethnic groups for status, power, and prestige; competition among religious groups for membership and status; competition among various income groups over allocation of taxes and government expenditures and various kinds of special privilege; and competition among businessmen, farmers, and workers for favored positions in the economy. Other examples will no doubt suggest themselves to the reader.

**Overlapping Membership**   The more complex a society is, the less likely are its political interest groups to have mutually exclusive memberships—that is, to include people each of whom is a member of one particular group and no other (see Fig. 2). Political interest groups in complex societies relate to one another as shown in Figure 2b, sharing some of their members with other groups; seldom do two groups claim identical membership, however.

**FIGURE 2**
**Membership of political groups.**

a.  Mutually Exclusive
     Membership

b.  Overlapping  Membership

The phenomenon of overlapping membership arises in a society that has many distinctions among its members and therefore many bases for group formation; each individual belongs to a great many different groups simultaneously, and few individuals belong to exactly the same groups. (See Fig. 2.) Readers can check the validity of this generalization by comparing their group memberships with those of their close friends and associates. They are likely to find, for example, that friend X is a college student, Protestant, of Scottish descent, a fraternity man, and a member of Young Americans for Freedom (YAF); friend Y is a college student, Protestant, of German descent, an independent, and a member of Students for a Democratic Society (SDS); and friend Z is a college student, Unitarian, of English descent, an independent, and a member of Students for Violent Non-Action (a student inactivist group founded at The University of Chicago).

**Imperfect Mobilization**   Because membership in political interest groups overlaps, no group can mobilize the total support of all its members. The degree of support it can muster is likely to vary considerably from issue to issue in at least two respects. First, the number of members who support a group to any degree fluctuates. Recent studies of voting behavior, for example, have shown that all the major voting groups studied—older and younger people, Protestants and Roman Catholics, rich and poor, whites and blacks, and so on—are divided among themselves in their voting preferences and activities. Table 1 illustrates this point by showing how some American

**TABLE 1**

Divisions within Certain Population Groups
in the 1972 Presidential Election

| | Percentages | | | | |
| --- | --- | --- | --- | --- | --- |
| Voting Group | Voted for Nixon | Voted for McGovern | Other Vote | Did Not Vote | Total Percentage[a] |
| Men | 49% | 23% | 2% | 25% | 99% |
| Women | 41 | 26 | 2 | 32 | 101 |
| | | | | | |
| Age 18-24 | 30 | 30 | 1 | 40 | 101 |
| Age 25-29 | 39 | 31 | 1 | 29 | 100 |
| Age 30-59 | 49 | 24 | 2 | 24 | 99 |
| Age 60 and over | 47 | 19 | 1 | 32 | 99 |
| | | | | | |
| White | 49 | 22 | 2 | 28 | 101 |
| Black | 8 | 54 | 2 | 36 | 100 |
| | | | | | |
| Protestant | 46 | 21 | 1 | 31 | 99 |
| Roman Catholic | 45 | 30 | 2 | 23 | 100 |
| Jewish | 26 | 60 | 2 | 12 | 100 |
| | | | | | |
| Grade-school education | 33 | 22 | 2 | 44 | 101 |
| High-school education | 44 | 22 | 2 | 32 | 100 |
| College education | 53 | 31 | 2 | 15 | 101 |
| | | | | | |
| Annual income under $4000 | 32 | 25 | 1 | 43 | 101 |
| Annual income $4000-14,999 | 44 | 25 | 1 | 30 | 100 |
| Annual income $15,000 or more | 59 | 26 | 2 | 13 | 100 |
| | | | | | |
| Working class | 40 | 24 | 2 | 34 | 100 |
| Middle class | 50 | 26 | 2 | 22 | 100 |
| | | | | | |
| Urban | 36 | 35 | 1 | 27 | 99 |
| Suburban | 51 | 22 | 2 | 26 | 101 |
| Rural | 44 | 20 | 2 | 34 | 100 |

[a]Some rows do not sum to 100 because of rounding adjustments.

*Source:* These figures come from a national sample survey conducted by the Survey Research Center, University of Michigan, and were furnished to the author through the Inter-University Consortium for Political Research.

population groups were split in the 1972 presidential election. It also illustrates the second respect in which support within particular groups varies: the intensity with which their members support them. In the 1972 election some members (ranging from 12 to 44 percent) in every group did not provide even so limited a form of support as voting.

Labor, farmers, businessmen, youth, Roman Catholics, and other such groups are by no means disciplined political armies ready to spring into action whenever their leaders give the command. Nor are they constant factors in political conflict. Like every political interest group, each contains members who also belong to other groups. On a given issue some—but not all—of its members will approve of the group's political activities; and of those who do approve, some will participate active-ly and enthusiastically, and others will not lift a finger.

In certain societies under certain conditions a few political interest groups may appear to approach 100 percent mobilization. In the modern Republic of South Africa, for example, nearly all the Afrikaners (white residents of Dutch descent) have appar-ently given enthusiastic support to the drive for apartheid (total segregation of whites from blacks and complete white supremacy). Such a situation usually means that the nation is dangerously near to civil war; but even in South Africa some Afrikaners are not unqualified advocates of apartheid.

## POLITICS AS AGGREGATION AND INTEGRATION

Up to this point we have focused upon the universality and inevitability of political conflict in human society. But this focus should not mislead us into viewing politics as solely a kind of permanent jungle warfare, red in tooth and claw, in which every person's hand is implacably turned against every other's. To depict politics as unrelieved conflict is no less a distortion than depicting it as an unfortunate aberration from the norm of peace and harmony.

The crucial point was forcibly put by the eighteenth-century philosopher Jean Jacques Rousseau:

> What made the establishment of societies necessary was, if you like, the fact that the interests of individuals clashed. But what made their establishment possible was the fact that these same interests *also* coincided. *In other words:* It is the overlap among different interests that creates the social bond, so that no society can possibly exist save as there is some point at which all the interests concerned are in harmony.[10]

In the terminology of present-day social science, political systems encompass not only competing demands and interests but also aggregating and integrating forces as well. "Government" is the collective label political scientists usually apply to the institutions and processes in a society that work to combine demands, convert them into authoritative policy outputs, and thus to moderate conflict and to integrate and preserve the society. Competition *within* an accepted framework is the essence of a political system. In Chapter 3 we shall consider some features of the governing process that are common to all political systems.

[10] Jean Jacques Rousseau, *The Social Contract,* trans. by Willmoore Kendall (Chicago: Henry Regnery Company, 1954), bk. 2, chap. 1; italics in the original.

# 3

---

# THE GOVERNING
# OF NATIONS

In some respects the process of learning what it means to be a human being is not pure joy. From birth we become involved in increasing numbers of social organizations, and, as we become aware of our involvement, we learn that each claims the right to make and enforce rules governing our behavior. We are born into a family, and our parents tell us that we must drink our milk, brush our teeth, keep our rooms neat, and not draw on the walls or swear. We go to school, and our teachers tell us that we must attend class, pass examinations, and not break windows. We join a church, and our ministers tell us that we must attend services, say our prayers, and live according to certain ethical standards. We find a job, and our bosses tell us that we must do our work, obey orders, and refrain from giving away company secrets to competitors. And so it goes all the days of our lives.

Furthermore, each organization backs up its rules with sanctions—penalties that can be imposed upon those who violate the rules. Parents can spank us and "ground" us on weekends; teachers can keep us after school and send us to the principal; college professors can fail us, and deans and presidents can throw us out of school; churches can expel us from membership; bosses can fire us.

The older we grow, the more conscious we become of the rules and sanctions of another organization that claims authority over us: "the government." It orders us to stay in school until we are sixteen, requires us to pay certain proportions of our incomes in taxes, tells us where we can and cannot park our cars, and in general surrounds us with more rules than we can count. And, if "the government" catches us violating its rules, it fines or imprisons us or even puts us to death.

Government is thus a very special kind of social organization—so special in fact, that the discipline of political science concentrates mainly on its operations and roles in various societies. In this chapter we shall consider the nature of government, how it differs from other social organizations, and why political systems (especially the variety called "nations") have governments.

## THE NATURE OF GOVERNMENT

### THE RULES PEOPLE LIVE BY

No human being acts in purely random fashion without rhyme, reason, or pattern. Although behavior patterns may be difficult to figure out and may change as we grow older, move, acquire new friends, enter new occupations, and so on, there still is, at each point in our lives, a pattern of some kind.

Every society, moreover, recognizes certain "normal" behavior patterns—that is, certain ways in which most members behave. Most Americans, for example, wear *some* clothes, even on hot summer days when they might be more comfortable without them. Most wear "modern" clothes, not togas, loincloths, or sarongs. Most eat with knives and forks rather than chopsticks or fingers, pay money for what they buy, drive on the right-hand side of the road, and refrain from eating human flesh or killing disobedient children. Some of what they do is governed by habit: It never occurs to them to do otherwise. Much, however, is governed by rules; that is, most Americans consciously believe that they ought to act in certain ways, or they know that if they act differently their associates will disapprove or they will be punished. Some of the rules people live by are closely associated with government; others are not. Let us briefly examine each type.

### Moral Precepts

Every human being directs his behavior to some extent according to a moral code, a series of principles according to which certain kinds of behavior are right and good and others are wrong and bad. We may consciously bear in mind and try to obey such Christian commandments as "Thou shalt not kill," "Honor thy father and thy mother," and "Do unto others as you would have them do unto you." Or we may adhere to such non-Christian commandments as "Never give a sucker an even break" and "Look out for number one first and everyone else second."

Part or all of a person's moral code may come from religious sources. The commandments may emanate from a church and have behind them some sort of supernatural sanction, like a priest's warning that nonobservance will displease God and thus condemn the violator to the eternal fires of hell. Part or all of a person's moral code may also come from nonreligious sources. The commandments may emanate from the individual's philosophy of the good life and have behind them such non-supernatural sanctions as fear that violating them will bring highly undesirable personal and social results and inner conviction that "virtue is its own reward."

Whatever their source, moral precepts differ from other kinds of social rules in that those who obey them do so not because they fear concrete retribution from other people but rather because they believe that it is good to do so, regardless of what others may think.

## Customs

We all also direct our behavior to some extent according to what we think others expect of us. For example, neither a man's church nor his private moral philosophy requires him to wear a business suit instead of a toga or a monk's habit to the office, to leave a tip for the waitress at a restaurant, or to begin his letters "Dear _____" and close them "Sincerely yours." Yet he regularly follows all these rules because he knows that if he does not most of his associates will regard him as peculiar—and few people wish to be singled out as peculiar.

Customs, or, as some sociologists call them, "folkways" and "mores," are powerful regulators of human activity in all societies. According to anthropologists, in most primitive societies customs are the most powerful regulators of all, and even in the literate and more "civilized" modern nations they play an important role.

That different groups have different customs should not blind us to the fact that customs in general are powerful determinants of human behavior. For example, many college students grow their hair long, wear blue jeans, and regard themselves as rebels against conformity. Many insurance executives have short haircuts, wear gray-flannel suits, and regard themselves as upholding the sartorial decencies. But how many insurance executives have long hair and wear blue jeans, regardless of what their friends and associates think, because to do so expresses their individuality? For that matter, how many college students have short haircuts and wear gray-flannel suits, regardless of what *their* friends and associates think, because to do so expresses *their* individuality? Is it possible that all of us, however much we may feel that we are doing our own thing, are conformists to *some* group's customs? Insurance executives, students, and professors alike may find that asking such questions about themselves and their peers produces some illuminating insights into how people live in a society and its subgroups.

## Law

The kind of behavior-limiting rules with which we are mainly concerned are those which collectively go under the label "the law." In Chapter 18 we shall examine in detail the nature, sources, and types of law, but for our present purposes we need to understand just what law in general is and how it differs from moral precepts and customs.

The literature of political science, jurisprudence, and sociology offers many definitions of law.[1] As the term is used in this book, however, law is *the body of rules emanating from governmental agencies and applied by the courts.* Law, as distinct from customs, emanates from a specific source and, as distinct from moral precepts, is regularly enforced by the courts. It consists of *governmental* rules, and in the kinds of political systems we shall consider government differs from all other rule-making organizations in several significant respects.

---

[1] For a convenient summary of various definitions, see Kenneth Redden, *An Introductory Survey of the Place of Law in Our Civilization* (Charlottesville, Va.: The Michie Company, 1946), chap. 1.

## POLITICAL SYSTEMS, DIFFERENTIATED AND UNDIFFERENTIATED

In Chapter 2 a political system was defined as "those institutions, processes, and interactions through which values are authoritatively allocated in a society." We should begin our study of government by recognizing that the world's political systems encompass an enormous variety of institutions, processes, and interactions. In some primitive societies, for example, the political system is not clearly differentiated from the systems of social, familial, or religious relations; all are mingled in ways that may seem exotic to us. Consider, for example, Gabriel A. Almond and G. Bingham Powell's description of the Eskimos:

> The political system of the Eskimo is among the simplest known to man. The Eskimos are scattered from the Bering Straits to Greenland in small communities, each numbering around one hundred inhabitants, most of the members of each community related by blood or marriage. There are only two specialized roles that are politically significant, those of the headman and the shaman, and these are both mixed roles. The shaman is the religious leader, but he also may punish those who violate taboos. In the extreme case he may order an offender exiled, which in the Arctic may mean death. The headman is a task leader, making decisions about hunting or the selection of places for settlement. In matters related to political order he is an influential leader rather than a leader with power to coerce.
>
> Violations of order are handled mostly through such means as fist fights and "song duels," or in extreme cases through family feuds. An individual who threatens the community by repeated acts of violence, murder, or theft may be dealt with by an executioner, who is given the task by the community or assumes the responsibility for the execution with the approval of the community.[2]

Institutions in a system like that of the United States provide a striking contrast: For example, the United States Supreme Court has even prohibited compulsory recitation of prayers and Bible reading in public schools because they violate our Constitution's command that church and state be kept separate.

Political scientists have focused mainly on the "differentiated" political systems, in which the institutions and processes by which values are authoritatively allocated are understood to be distinct from religious, artistic, scientific, and other social institutions and processes. We shall keep this focus in the chapters to come, but it is well to remember that by no means every person in the world lives in a system in which government can be clearly distinguished from all other social organizations.

## A DEFINITION OF GOVERNMENT

The term "government" is commonly used in two related but distinct senses: It sometimes refers to a particular aggregate of people, each with individual idiosyncra-

---

[2] Gabriel A. Almond and G. Bingham Powell, Jr., *Comparative Politics: A Developmental Approach* (Boston: Little, Brown & Company, 1966), pp. 42–43. For illustrations of African "stateless societies" see John Middleton and David Tait (eds.), *Tribes without Rulers: Studies in African Segmentary Systems* (London: Routledge & Kegan Paul Ltd., 1958).

sies, faults, and virtues and performing certain functions in a particular society; and it sometimes refers to a particular set of institutions, a series of accepted and regular procedures for performing the functions mentioned. I shall incorporate both senses, defining government as a *body of people and institutions that make and enforce laws for a particular society.* In the terminology of systems analysis, it includes both the authorities and their regularized patterns of behavior.

Defined thus, government is undoubtedly one of mankind's oldest and most nearly universal institutions. Some political philosophers, to be sure, have speculated about what life would be like in a state of anarchy, that is, in a society without any government, differentiated or undifferentiated. Yet there is no recorded instance of an actual society, past or present, that has operated for long with no government whatever. Evidently people at all times and in all societies have felt—for reasons we shall consider shortly—that some sort of government is vital to life as they wish to live it.

Humanity's universal desire for government has not, however, led all people at all times and in all societies to establish the same kind of government. Indeed, one of the most striking facts about actual governments, past and present, is that no two have been exactly alike. They have varied in complexity all the way from simple chieftainships, as among the primitive Baganda tribes in Africa, to the highly complex systems of the United States and the Soviet Union. They have varied in the treatment of their peoples all the way from the mass executions and brutality of Nazi Germany to the permissive "welfare state" of Sweden. Evidently different societies require different kinds of government to fulfill their particular needs.

In Chapters 12 and 13 we shall examine some of the principal respects in which modern governments differ from one another. Our present concern is with how government differs from all other types of social organizations in a modern, differentiated society.

## HOW GOVERNMENT DIFFERS
## FROM OTHER SOCIAL ORGANIZATIONS

### *Comprehensive Authority over Involuntary Membership*

Rules made by any particular social organization other than government apply, and are intended to apply, only to members of that organization. When the University of Illinois rules that all freshmen must take a course in personal hygiene, no one expects this rule also to apply to freshmen at Yale or Oxford or Slippery Rock. If General Motors should decide to split its stock four for one, no one considers that Ford, U.S. Steel, or American Telephone and Telegraph must do the same thing. The rules of American government, on the other hand, apply, and are intended to apply, to *all* members of American society. When Congress rules that every American with an annual income above a certain level must pay a portion of that income in taxes, no one imagines that this rule is not *intended* to apply to people who think that income taxes stifle initiative, who cannot afford to pay the taxes *and* buy new cars, or who let payment slip their minds. When Congress says *every* American, everyone understands that it means precisely that.

Membership in most social organizations other than government is, moreover, voluntary—that is, people become members of such organizations and subject themselves to their rules only by deliberate choice and conscious act. One does not automatically become a Presbyterian at birth because one's parents are Presbyterian or because one is born in a Presbyterian hospital. One can officially join the church only by going through such formal procedures as baptism and confirmation. Membership in a nation, however, is largely involuntary—that is, most people *initially* become citizens of a nation and subject to its rules without any deliberate choice or conscious act. All nations officially regard as citizens either all persons born in their territories, all children born of their citizens, or some combination of both. Most nations also provide for the official voluntary acquisition and abandonment of membership by adults, but initial membership in a national society is involuntary.

## Authoritative Rules

Rules made by various nongovernmental organizations are often in conflict with one another. A labor union may order its members to overturn cars and use clubs and fists to keep strikebreakers from crossing picket lines, yet the church to which some of the union members belong may teach that physical violence should never be used. In most societies there is no clearly defined and generally accepted hierarchy among organizations and therefore no automatic way to determine which organizations' rules shall prevail and which shall be ignored in situations of conflict. There is no universal agreement that a church is more important than a labor union or vice versa, so that each union member who is also a church member must decide for himself whether to obey the church or the union.

The rules of government, however, are quite another matter, for in every nation these rules are generally recognized as *authoritative*—that is, they are generally considered to be more binding upon all members of the society, church and union members alike, than are the rules of any nongovernmental organization. In conflict between the laws of government and the rules of any other organization, there is general agreement that the former should prevail. If a particular religious group prescribes human sacrifice as part of its ritual and the government forbids the taking of human life by any organization other than itself, most members of the society will regard the governmental prohibition as more binding than the religious prescription. If the local building code requires that brick walls must be at least twelve inches thick and local engineers consider eight inches to be a far more reasonable safety standard, most of the town's citizens—including most of its engineers—will obey the twelve-inch requirement, however misguided they believe it to be.

## Legitimate Monopoly of Life-and-Death Sanctions

Of course, all government rules are not always obeyed by all members of society. Every social organization has to deal with individuals who disobey its rules, and government is certainly no exception. All organizations deal with rule breakers by imposing sanctions, but government differs from other organizations in the kind of sanctions it is authorized to impose. Nongovernmental organizations are authorized to withhold certain privileges, impose fines, and require certain penances. Their ultimate legitimate weapon, however, is expulsion. If a church or labor-union member refuses to pay the fines or do the required penances, the most extreme penalty the organization can impose is expulsion. Government can do all these things to people who disobey its rules, and it can also impose two additional sanctions that are forbidden to other organizations: It can imprison or execute lawbreakers.

It is important to understand that governments are not the only organizations that do in fact impose life-and-death sanctions, for that is clearly not so. Gangsters of the Mafia sometimes kill people who violate their codes, and Ku Klux Klansmen sometimes kill civil-rights workers. The point is that government alone has the *legitimate* power to execute rule breakers. By "legitimate" I mean that most people in the society believe that if any agency may rightfully use the ultimate sanction, government is the only one. Any nongovernmental organization or private person using it is committing murder, perhaps the worst of all crimes.

### Overwhelming Force

All social organizations can muster some physical force to enforce their rules. At the very least they can enlist the fists of their members; many also collect rocks, bricks, clubs, razors, knives, and perhaps even firebombs, pistols, rifles, and submachine guns. No American needs to be told that some organizations sometimes actually use force to promote their causes. No nation, sad to say, conducts its internal political conflict entirely without violence.

Government differs from other social organizations not in the occasional use of force to enforce its rules but in the sheer amount of force it can muster. The difference is so great that we can almost think of government as monopolizing all force. And we are not far from the truth, for the rocks and pistols that nongovernmental organizations can round up are feeble indeed in comparison to the armed police, military forces, intercontinental missiles, and hydrogen bombs that governments can turn to.

### The Highest Stakes

These special characteristics of government combine to make political stakes the highest that people play for. Controversies among Roman Catholics about the permissibility of "the pill" and the authority of the Pope are of great importance to Roman Catholic clergy and laity, but much less so to Protestants, Jews, and Muslims. The struggles over student power at Columbia and Berkeley may dominate the lives of all who study and teach on those campuses, but they are, at most, of merely spectator interest to the United Mine Workers or the American Medical Association. But the confrontation between the United States and the Soviet Union over the Arab-Israeli conflict in the Middle East could quite conceivably escalate into thermonuclear World War III, and the conflict within each of the two nations over the Middle East policy that it should follow involves no less a stake than the survival of mankind.

As any poker player knows, when the stakes rise, the nature of the game changes. Despite some instructive similarities with their counterparts in other social organizations, the processes of politics and government operate in an atmosphere and for stakes that make them quite different from their nongovernmental analogues. It

**The ultimate sanction —
or cruel and unusual
punishment?** Source:
UPI Photograph.

Political Systems and
Their Environments

is well to remember this point whenever we are tempted to simplify decision making
in the National Security Council or the Kremlin or the White House as just another
version of what goes on in our family or dormitory.

## WHY SOCIETIES HAVE GOVERNMENTS

In Chapter 2 we observed that political conflict exists wherever human beings live together in society. No society therefore has a choice of whether or not it will have political conflict; it has a choice only of how such conflict will be conducted. It decides only what methods contestants may employ to promote their causes, what channels of communication and points of contact will be available to them and—perhaps most important of all—what methods will be used to resolve the various conflicts, that is, by what processes society will determine which competitors "win" and "lose" and how "losers" will be induced to accept the verdict.

Logically any society could choose anarchy. That is, it could establish no authoritative and binding procedures whatever for settling such questions, and let groups conduct political conflict in any manner they saw fit; and it could leave to the contestants themselves the determination of the "winners." A society could thus solve the basic problem of government by having no government at all. At first glance,

The Governing of Nations

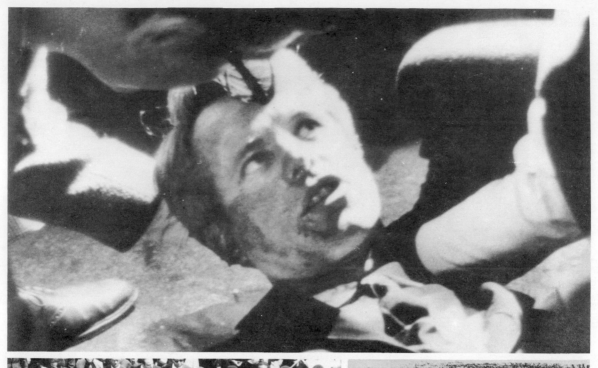

Political Systems and
Their Environments

such a solution seems very tempting indeed, for who among us has not sometimes dreamed of living in a society without tax collectors, cops, and truant officers?

Yet no society has long embraced anarchy as its permanent method for conducting political conflict. Why not? There appear to be two main explanations.

### Desire for Authoritative Rules

In Chapter 2 we noted that most groups in modern nations have some values that can be satisfied only by rules applying to and binding upon *all* persons in the nation—that is, by governmental rules. Let us illustrate this point further from perhaps the bitterest group conflict in current American politics. The National Association for the Advancement of Colored People (NAACP) and those for whom it speaks have their hearts set on achieving rights and opportunities for blacks fully equal to those enjoyed by whites. They work for the day when all decisions on whether or not a particular black will be hired for a particular job, be paid a particular wage, vote, hold public office, and so on, will be made strictly according to his personal abilities and qualifications, with no weight whatever given to the color of his skin. They seek a society in which blacks will be judged, as they believe only whites are now, as individuals and not as stereotyped members of an allegedly inferior ethnic group.

They do not, of course, speak for all blacks. Some blacks, as we shall see in Chapter 22, are so alienated from white culture and government that they are pressing for a new kind of segregation: some form of autonomous all-black society within the United States but not controlled by it. Many blacks, however, still support the NAACP's goal of equal rights in a genuinely integrated society. This goal can never be achieved, they believe, merely by attempting to persuade every individual white American, business firm, and election official, one by one, to forswear discrimination voluntarily; such a process would take forever, and they are not willing to wait that long. Nor are they willing to settle permanently for some version of the present situation, in which some employers and election officials discriminate against blacks and others do not; such a solution would mean that some blacks would always be second-class citizens.

The NAACP and its supporters believe that they will achieve their goal of equality only when American society enforces some kind of antidiscrimination rule applicable to *all* Americans, including those who prefer discrimination and white supremacy. They regard anything short of such a rule as only a second-best solution. For the time being they may have to settle for it, but they will never be permanently and fully satisfied by it. They also believe that such a rule must be genuinely binding —that is, it must be obeyed by all Americans and not merely by those who approve of it. If it is not, then the group's goal of ending all discrimination everywhere in America cannot be achieved. Accordingly, they are unwilling to let each American decide for himself whether or not he will obey the rule. They demand that nondiscrimination be embodied in the *law,* society's most solemn and authoritative rule of conduct. They also demand that society punish people who violate the law. That is why they fought so hard for the passage of the Civil Rights Act of 1964 and now fight for its full enforcement.

Most Americans who feel strongly that racial discrimination should be abolished in the United States believe that they can achieve their goal only through an antidiscrimination rule that applies to the whole society and is genuinely binding upon every American. Only government can adopt and enforce such a rule. By the same token, those Americans who believe that white supremacy must be maintained can achieve their goal only by preventing the adoption and enforcement of such a rule. That is why they fought so hard against the 1964 Civil Rights Act. And so it is with the conflicting groups on many other issues in the United States and in other societies past and present. Every society contains groups with goals that only government action can fulfill; as long as it does, no society will long be willing or able to settle for anarchy.

### Desire to Preserve Society

The desire for general and binding rules does not always and automatically lead to rejection of anarchy and establishment of government. After all, many of the world's nations also believe that certain rules of conduct should be enforced upon all of mankind. Some communists, for example, would like to impose their politicoeconomic system on all the earth's peoples, whereas some anticommunists would like not only to prevent the spread of communism but also to stamp it out entirely wherever it now exists. Yet neither the communist nor the noncommunist nations clamor for the establishment of a world government with power to settle this issue authoritatively. Both sides prefer to contest this and other international political issues in the context of the present state system, which closely approaches international anarchy (see Chap. 23).

There is no a priori reason why interest groups within a particular nation should not attempt to achieve their goals by the same means that the world's nations now use. The NAACP, for example, might proclaim a nondiscrimination rule and attempt through destruction, torture, and assassination to force all Americans to obey it; white supremacists might resist with machine guns, poison gas, and hydrogen bombs.

The NAACP and its opponents *might* do these things, yet for the most part they do not. Like most groups in most societies most of the time, they apparently prefer to pursue their objectives in the context of government, not anarchy. Why? The answer lies in the characteristics of political conflict we observed in Chapter 2. Each member of both the antidiscrimination group and the white-supremacy group is also a member of many other groups. It is very unlikely, therefore, that either group could mobilize the full support of all its members for the "total war" that the suggested tactics would bring on. Both groups, furthermore, have important interests and objectives in common. Both are part of American society and receive many benefits from it—for example, more personal freedom, a higher standard of living, and more voice in government decisions than they could have in many other nations. Each group therefore has a considerable stake in preserving the United States. Each group knows that the nation could not survive if its political issues were regularly settled by civil war; in this imperfect world a nation that can no longer govern itself is not likely to pass into a state of blissful anarchy. It is far more likely to be conquered and governed by some other nation that *can* keep internal conflict under control.

In deciding what tactics to pursue, the NAACP and its opponents—and, indeed, all interest groups in all societies—must make these decisions; they must calculate their chances for success in a possible civil war and must decide whether or not what they stand to gain from such a war is more valuable than what they stand to lose from the destruction of their society.

Sometimes groups in certain societies choose anarchy and civil war in extreme situations. Violence, rebellion, and large-scale violations of law are by no means unheard of in human affairs, and in later chapters we will consider these phenomena at greater length. But only in international "society" do anarchy and war appear to be generally accepted as the regular and preferable principles of organization. In almost any society most people act most of the time as if they believe that its preservation is necessary to the kind of lives they wish to lead and that some form of government, rather than anarchy, is the only method of settling political conflict that can preserve it. Viewing government in this light makes it easier to put up with tax collectors, cops, and truant officers.

## THE NATURE OF NATIONS

### THE MODERN STATE SYSTEM

Every human being lives in some kind of political society, and most live in more than one simultaneously. Most Eskimos, for example, live in isolated communities of about 100 inhabitants each. They are ruled mainly by decisions made within these communities but also by the laws of larger political units (for example, Canada and the United States) that exercise authority over their territories. The Tallensi peoples of Western Africa also live in small communities through which they make many of the rules controlling their lives, but their villages lie in the territory of the Republic of Ghana, and they are subject to its laws as well.

This multiplicity of governments goes much farther in larger and more complex societies. In the United States most of us live in cities governed by mayors and councils; counties governed by boards of supervisors; states governed by governors and legislatures; and the United States, governed by the President and Congress.

In a complex society like ours such subsystems and their governments are formally interrelated in a hierarchy of authority: State governments can override certain decisions by city and county governments, and the national government can override certain decisions by state governments. At the peak of this hierarchy stands the national government. No government has the legal and generally recognized authority to override decisions of the national government of the United States, and the national governments of all other countries are legally supreme, or "sovereign," in their own territories.

Political scientists use the term "state system" for this division of the world's population into "nations" or "nation-states" (see below), each of which has complete governing authority within its particular territory and none of which acknowledges a government superior to its own. Political scientists have studied and written about national political systems more than about any others, and for that reason we shall focus on them in this book. Let us now see what traits distinguish nations from other kinds of political societies.

### FEATURES OF THE MODERN NATION AND NATION-STATE

Like many other terms in political science, the term "nation" is widely used, useful—and somewhat ambiguous. Sometimes it is used to mean a particular legal entity, such as the United States of America or the Dominion of Canada; sometimes it is used to mean a group of people with common political loyalties or cultural bonds, such as "the Apache nation" or "the Jewish people." Some political scientists reserve the term "nation" for the group of people and the term "nation-state" for the legal entity, but most use the two terms interchangeably.[3] I shall follow this common usage, but whenever the distinction is especially important I shall specify which meaning is being used.

One result of this ambiguity is that there is always some question about just which political systems should be called either "nations" or "nation-states" and how many there are. Systems like the United States, the Soviet Union, and India are universally acknowledged to be nations, and systems like New York, Derbyshire, and the Auvergne are recognized as cities, counties, and regions respectively. But there is dispute over the proper labels for marginal systems like the Vatican City and Tibet. Accordingly, political scientists agree that at present the world state system includes *about* 151 nations, but "about" seems unlikely ever to be replaced by "exactly."[4]

The characteristics most often stipulated for the nation are a definite territory, a definite population, a government, formal independence, and a sense of national identity.

### Definite Territory

Each of the world's nations is located on a particular area of the earth's surface and has definite, generally recognized boundaries that do not overlap the area of any other nation. To be sure, the exact locations of mutual boundaries are sometimes disputed by adjoining nations, like China and India in the 1960s, but the *principle* of definite boundaries is accepted by all nations.

### Definite Population

Each nation regards only certain people as citizens or subjects and all others as aliens.

### Government

Each nation has an officially designated set of persons and institutions authorized to make and enforce laws for all people within its territory.

### Formal Independence

Each nation's government is sovereign—that is, it is formally recognized by other nations as having the exclusive right to make policy for that nation's territory and

---

[3] A useful discussion by an Israeli political scientist is Benjamin Akzin, *State and Nation* (London: Hutchinson, 1964). Two leading works on the characteristics of modern nations that particularly emphasize the psychological phenomenon of nationalism are Hans Kohn, *Nationalism: Its Meaning and History* (New York: Crowell-Collier and Macmillan, Inc., 1955); and Karl W. Deutsch, *Nationalism and Social Communication: An Inquiry into the Foundations of Nationality* (New York: John Wiley & Sons, Inc., 1953).

[4] For a recent discussion of the classification problem and a list of nations, see Bruce M. Russett, J. David Singer, and Melvin Small, "National Political Units in the Twentieth Century: A Standardized List," *American Political Science Review,* 62 (September 1968), 932–951; and some criticisms in *American Political Science Review,* 62 (September 1968), 952–955. For new nations added since 1968, see *The World Almanac & Book of Facts, 1974* (New York: Newspaper Enterprise Association, Inc., 1974), pp. 542–619.

*"My country right or wrong or in any of the gray areas that lie between."*

inhabitants. Each nation thus has supreme legal authority over its own affairs and in this respect is fully equal to any other nation. This *legal* principle is known in international law as "the principle of the sovereign equality of nations." In actual behavior, some nations may be more subject to influence by foreign nations than others. If the United States strongly suggests that Guatemala adopt a certain policy, Guatemala is more likely to accept the suggestion than the United States would be to act on a similar suggestion put to it by Guatemala. *Legally* speaking, however, Guatemala has as much power to make decisions for Guatemala as the United States has for the United States.

### Nationalism and the Sense of National Identity

The psychological basis of the state system is the prevalence of senses of different nationality—citizens' love for and loyalty to their particular nations. For many of the world's inhabitants, especially those in the long-established nations,

The Governing of Nations

59

nationalism is the highest allegiance, more compelling than loyalty to church, social class, race, even family. The most striking evidence of the power of nationalism over human thought and behavior is that nowadays wars, the supreme test of people's loyalties, are fought mainly among nations, rather than among races or churches or social classes. When the United States has fought with Germany, American workers, capitalists, Roman Catholics, and Lutherans have killed and been killed by German workers, capitalists, Roman Catholics, and Lutherans.

In the world's newly independent nations (see pp. 61–65), however, nationalism is often much weaker, and strengthening the citizens' identification with the nation rather than with tribes, religious sects, or linguistic groups is one of the greatest problems that national leaders face. The bitter civil wars in the 1960s between Nigerian nationalists and Biafran separatists and between Congolese nationalists and Katangan separatists are among the best-known recent manifestations of the failure of political loyalties to coincide with legal boundaries inherited from colonial days. Leaders of the new nations have dealt with the problem of developing national identity and loyalty in varying ways and with varying success, but only a few have solved it completely.[5]

The problem is by no means unknown in older nations; for example, there is separatism in Quebec, conflict between Catholics and Protestants in Northern Ireland, and conflict between Flemings and Walloons in Belgium. Yet in most long-established nations nationalism is the basic political loyalty for most citizens. Why the difference? What makes one aggregate of people think of themselves as a nation, whereas others do not? Social scientists are still unable to answer these questions to their full satisfaction. Most agree, however, that nationalism is found among peoples who display most, though not necessarily all, of the following traits.

**Identification with National Territory**   Not only does each nation occupy and rule over a particular territory, but most of its citizens also to some degree psychologically "identify" with it. They have affection for its physical features—its rivers and lakes, mountains and plains, deserts and prairies—and this affection is powerfully evoked by phrases like "the white cliffs of Dover," "the rock-bound coasts of Maine to the sunny shores of California," and "how quiet flows the Don."

**Common History**   Most citizens of each nation are to some degree conscious of being part of a continuous historical entity, and this historical consciousness furnishes them with strong reminders of their common roots and a powerful source of resolution to carry on in such a way that what their forefathers created "shall not perish from the earth." It apparently makes little difference whether the nation's history is, as in the United States and Great Britain, largely one of success and domination or, as in Poland and the Republic of Ireland, largely one of defeat and oppression. Accordingly, most nations instruct their children in national history and

---

[5] For stimulating discussions of many aspects of this problem, see Karl W. Deutsch and William J. Foltz (eds.), *Nation-Building* (New York: Atherton Press, 1966); Lucian W. Pye, *Communication and Political Development* (Princeton, N.J.: Princeton University Press, 1963); and David E. Apter, *The Politics of Modernization* (Chicago: University of Chicago Press, 1965).

erect monuments and statues commemorating the great episodes and figures of the past.

**Common Language and Literature**   Most of us feel a certain kinship with those who speak the same language we do with the same accent and idiom. When we meet someone who speaks substantially the same language but with a different accent and idiom, we tend to think of him as foreign, as when an American converses with an Englishman; when we meet someone who speaks a tongue entirely different from our own, we think of him as very foreign, as when an American deals with a Frenchman, a Swede, or an Indonesian. Those who share a common language—and a common literature that transmits not only the nation's language but also its history, traditions, and customs—are likely to feel both a certain kinship with one another and a certain separateness from people who do not share it. There are, to be sure, some bilingual and trilingual nations like Canada and Switzerland, but they are exceptional, and most nations have one official language that is spoken by the great majority of their citizens.

**Common Culture**   The citizens of each modern nation also share a particular culture. Most of them conduct their lives—courtship, marriage, child rearing, work, and recreation—in ways generally accepted and approved in their own nations. Each culture differs in at least a few respects from that of any other nation. Each citizen thus feels a certain kinship with his fellow citizens, whose way of life is similar to his own; at the same time he entertains a certain feeling of strangeness and difference from citizens of other nations, who live somewhat differently.

**Desire for Political Independence**   The traits described so far do not constitute full-fledged nationalism unless the people who share them also believe that their collective aspirations can be satisfied only by full political independence. Californians, Texans, and New Yorkers apparently feel that they are somewhat different from less fortunate folk, but their feelings do not result in genuine nationalism, for they are content to remain under the United States government and do not agitate seriously for complete political independence. But the aspirations and demands of the people of India, Indonesia, and Ghana in the first half of the twentieth century could not have been satisfied merely by improved standards of living or a stronger voice in the councils of the European nations that controlled them. They could be satisfied only by complete political independence, by recognition of their status as fully independent and sovereign nations and of their consequent right to make all their own political decisions without guidance or interference from any other nation. Only when the shared traits of a particular people result in a demand for political independence can we accurately describe their collective feelings and aspirations as nationalism.

## DEVELOPING NATIONS

The worldwide rebellion against Western colonialism since World War II has produced the greatest proliferation of new nations in history. Of the 151 modern nations mentioned earlier, no fewer than 82 (54 percent) have achieved formal independence since 1945. Africa outdistances all other areas with thirty-eight new nations, followed by Asia with twenty, the Middle East with twelve, the Caribbean with seven, and Latin America with five. Nationalism and the state system, far from dying out, are thus stronger than ever in global politics.

Political scientists generally call the new nations (and most of the older nations in Latin America, the Middle East, and Asia as well) "developing nations," as opposed to the "developed nations" of Western Europe, the former British Commonwealth, and the United States. Many people in the African and Asian nations object to this term, arguing that it implies a single standard of perfection aimed at by all nations but achieved only by those in the West.[6] There is some validity in this criticism, but the term "developing nation" is now so widely used that it would be pointless to coin another here. We need only note that the principal indexes of "development" include such economic and social statistics as per capita gross national product; ratios of population to number of medical doctors, number of vehicles, number of telephones, and number of radios; and percentage of the population that is literate. The main political measures include the degree of competition for public office permitted, the freedom and extent of political communications, and success in articulating and aggregating the demands of interest groups.[7]

Social scientists have studied the developing nations intensively in recent years, and their findings are far too copious and complex to summarize in detail here.[8] But we shall discuss some leading themes.

The developing nations encompass the whole range of forms of government (see Chap. 12), including multiparty democracy as in Israel and Lebanon; near-democracy dominated by one party, as in Mexico and Malaysia; one-party dictatorships, as in Algeria and Guinea; and nonparty traditional dictatorships, as in Saudi Arabia. Many developing nations face in varying degrees the difficulty of converting anticolonial fervor into effective national unity; they must, as in Uganda and Nigeria, pacify divisive factions ranging from irredentist objectors to armed secessionists. All are struggling with problems of economic growth, industrial and agricultural modern-

---

[6] Fred R. von der Mehden, *Politics of the Developing Nations* (Englewood Cliffs, N.J.: Prentice-Hall, Inc., 1964), pp. 4–6.

[7] Early and influential discussions are "Introduction" and "Conclusion" in Almond and James S. Coleman, *The Politics of Developing Areas* (Princeton, N.J.: Princeton University Press, 1960).

[8] Probably the most influential works, after Almond and Coleman, *The Politics of Developing Areas,* have been the six volumes of the series "Studies in Political Development" sponsored by the Committee on Comparative Politics of the Social Science Research Council and published by Princeton University Press; they have examined the impact on political development of such institutions and processes as communications, bureaucracy, education, political culture, and political parties. Other leading general works include Apter, *The Politics of Modernization;* Deutsch and Foltz, *Nation-Building;* Rupert Emerson, *From Empire to Nation* (Cambridge, Mass.: Harvard University Press, 1960); and John H. Kautsky, *Political Change in Underdeveloped Countries* (New York: John Wiley & Sons, Inc., 1962). Particularly interesting for theoretical statements are Lucian W. Pye, *Aspects of Political Development* (Boston: Little, Brown & Company, 1966); and the dissenting view by Samuel P. Huntington, *Political Order in Changing Societies* (New Haven, Conn.: Yale University Press, 1968). In addition, there are studies of single nations, too numerous to be mentioned here.

Political Systems and Their Environments

ization, and increasing literacy while mediating the differences—and hostility—between the relatively advanced cities and the more primitive rural areas.

In fact, the new nations have found that, when the last colonial overlord departed for London, Paris, and Amsterdam, their problems did not magically leave with him; indeed, they multiplied. These nations are learning what others have learned before them: that preserving a nation is every bit as arduous as establishing one.

## GOVERNMENT AND THE LIFE AND DEATH OF NATIONS

In David Easton's words, "the question that gives coherence and purpose to a rigorous analysis of political life as a system of behavior is . . . how do any and all political systems manage to persist in a world of both stability and change?"[9] For not all national political systems *do* manage to persist. Some, like Estonia, Latvia, Lithuania, and Tibet, have been conquered and subjugated by more powerful nations. Others, like the West Indies Federation and Malaysia, have peacefully split into several even smaller nations. Still others, like Newfoundland and Zanzibar, have voluntarily become parts of other nations.

Such national "deaths" are relatively rare, but every nation, no matter how powerful, constantly faces external challenges to its security and independence. And every nation, no matter how long-lived, constantly faces internal threats to its cohesion and stability. It is the latter dangers that concern us here.

The main internal threats to a nation's survival arise from the nature and volume of demands on its political system and the manner in which they are pressed. Each of these factors, be it noted, is a *variable,* a matter of more or less, rather than of either-or. For example, some groups in a nation may press unyieldingly for demands totally unacceptable to others, or no group may press any demand that it really regards as nonnegotiable. Several groups may press for economic benefits whose total cost would exceed the nation's resources, or they may all be willing to give up half a loaf to be sure of enjoying the other half. Some groups may turn to assassination or mass rebellion when they fail to achieve their goals, or all groups may press their demands only by nonviolent methods.

There can be many variations between the extremes of each variable. But, as we saw in Chapter 2, demands aplenty there will surely be—far more demands than the political system can possibly satisfy. The inevitable incompatibility of some demands guarantees that no policy output can ever equally satisfy everyone concerned.

### FACTORS HOLDING A NATION TOGETHER

Happily for the survival of nations, major inputs in any political system include supports as well as demands. In Easton's scheme there are two main kinds of support: *specific* supports for particular authorities, which result from particular outputs pleasing to the supporters, and *diffuse* supports, which are general supports for the system's

---

[9] David Easton, *A Systems Analysis of Political Life* (New York: John Wiley & Sons, Inc., 1965), p. 17.

authorities and conversion processes, arising not from supporters' gratitude for particular outputs but from their general belief that the authorities and processes are legitimate, the proper people and ways to make decisions.[10]

The degree of diffuse support for the system among any particular segment of the population depends mainly upon the extent to which the latter believes that the authorities give its demands full and fair hearings; that belief in turn depends largely on whether or not the system's outputs have in fact satisfied the group's demands enough to warrant the hope that it will continue to be reasonably content under the existing system and need not incur the great costs and risks of trying to overthrow it.

If American workers cared only for higher wages, businessmen only for higher profits, blacks only for an immediate end to all forms of racial segregation, and southern whites only for eternal preservation of complete racial segregation, the four groups could hardly continue to live together as Americans. The fact is, however, that most workers, businessmen, blacks, and southern whites have—and act as if they have—a real interest in maintaining the particular modes of conducting political conflict that the American system provides. Each group stands to lose a great deal by destroying these modes through civil war or decrees from a foreign army of occupation. Each group shares at least one interest in common with most of the nation's other groups: preserving the society in which they all live.

When most members of any major group no longer feel this way, then some form of civil war is likely—and the nation may or may not survive it. No American should forget that it happened to us in precisely this way in 1861, and the result was history's bloodiest civil war. There is no divine guarantee that it will never happen again.

## STABILITY AND CHANGE

Political scientists talk so much about "system stability" and "system maintenance" that they are sometimes accused of harboring a conservative, "establishment" preference for the status quo. The fact is that some do indeed have such a preference, but others of equal professional eminence have quite the opposite preference. The reason for the concern with stability and maintenance is not political but scholarly: Change can be conceptualized and measured only with reference to some model of stability. To determine that change A but not change B tends to take place under condition X, whereas change B is more likely under condition Y, does not in itself reflect a preference for A or B over the status quo. It reflects knowledge about what encourages and retards particular kinds of change—knowledge equally available and useful to both advocates and opponents of any particular change or of change in general.

At any rate, it is clear that nations do not face choices between change and no change, for some kind of change is inevitable. A nation's population changes—in birthrate, size, density, age distribution, life expectancy, and a host of other ways; its environments change too—through new technology, depletion or enrichment of resources, increasing or decreasing conflict with other nations, and so on. These

[10] Easton, *A Systems Analysis of Political Life,* especially p. 249.

changes inevitably produce changes in the nature, volume, and expression of demands. However satisfactory the system's responses may have been in the past, it cannot and predictably will not meet the new configuration of demands in exactly the same way as before.

The question that every nation faces every day is therefore not whether or not there will be change but what kinds of change there should be and will be. Who will be favored at the expense of whom? How will priorities be implemented? What consequences will they have for the people involved and for the system itself?

## THE BASIC TASK AND TOOLS OF GOVERNMENT

As most rulers of nations see it, the basic task of any government, whether democratic or dictatorial, is to keep the nation alive—to guard its independence against external enemies and to preserve its cohesion in the face of internal conflict. To accomplish this task it must satisfy the social needs that have called it into being: It must receive political demands, convert them into authoritative rules, and enforce those rules in such a way that no major group of citizens feels compelled to tear the nation apart. National survival is thus the ultimate test of any government.

There is no universal or infallible method for accomplishing this task, no surefire way to prevent civil wars or to win foreign wars. In Chapter 20 we shall review the wide range of policy outputs modern governments produce. But we may note here that all governments rely upon combinations, varying in emphasis from time to time and from government to government, of a few basic "tools," which can only be partially illustrated here.

### Interest Articulation[11]

If a nation's government is unaware of a particular set of demands, it can hardly deal with them. If it is dimly aware of the demands but unaware of their incidence or intensity, it is not likely to deal with them effectively. And if it does not consider urgent and widely supported demands with at least some effectiveness, it risks anger, alienation, perhaps even rebellion from the slighted groups.

Consequently governments need effective channels for articulation of interests —ways in which political groups can formulate, express, and transmit their demands. In later chapters we shall consider some of the leading methods and channels now used to articulate interests—for example, pressure groups, propaganda and protest, mass and face-to-face communications, public opinion polls, and campaigns and elections. Here we note only that any political system needs effective ways to make its authorities aware of important political demands within the society.

### Interest Aggregation

In Chapter 2 we noted that some political demands inevitably conflict with others; there is thus no way that a government can fully satisfy every demand. To be dealt

---

[11] For a more detailed discussion of articulation and aggregation of interests see Almond and Powell, *Comparative Politics,* chaps. 4, 5.

with at all satisfactorily, demands must be aggregated, adjusted so that they do not automatically cancel one another out, and combined into more general programs that government can accept, modify, or reject as alternatives for public policies. As we shall see, many aggregating processes commonly occur outside formal government in discussions among individuals and in negotiations and deals within and among pressure groups and political parties. Some also occur inside the legislative, executive, and administrative agencies of government. But however interest aggregation is achieved, it is a necessity for any political system and a vital tool of any government.

### Coercion and Compromise

Every government, democratic or dictatorial, perpetually faces the key question of how to ensure acceptance of its policies and obedience to its laws. One obvious and important answer, of course, is coercion, the threat or imposition of sanctions. Governments can apply many kinds of sanctions to lawbreakers—physical, economic, psychological, violent, nonviolent. They can deny a license to engage in a particular business or profession, take away the right to vote and hold public office, withdraw financial aid or expel from school, or even exile. And, of course, they can fine, imprison, "brainwash," torture—and kill. As mentioned earlier, government's legitimate monopoly of the use of such sanctions is a prime difference between it and all other social organizations.

Governments generally use coercion to achieve one or both of two main objects: to "make examples" which, it is hoped, will convince potential lawbreakers that the consequences of breaking the law will be worse than any likely gains and to take out of circulation any person who, undeterred by these threats, breaks the law anyway. No doubt there is often an element of revenge as well, but the principal justification for government coercion is deterrence.

Yet no government can rely on coercion alone. It is impossible to execute or imprison all citizens or even a large proportion of them; really massive resistance to a law or policy simply cannot therefore be overcome by coercion alone. Nor is open defiance the only form of resistance that government has to worry about. A policy that commands only sullen, foot-dragging, minimal compliance is not likely to accomplish its objectives. Voluntary compliance by most persons affected is the minimum condition for an effective policy, and enthusiastic popular support can make up for a good many technical deficiencies and miscalculations. Any government, however brutal and ruthless it may sometimes be, seeks this kind of voluntary compliance for all its policies.

How do governments obtain it? There are myriad ways, but to some degree they are all variations on the basic theme of compromise. Given the inevitability of conflicting interests and incompatible demands, for every "winner" in political conflict there is bound to be a "loser." No government can escape this hard fact of life, but it can strive to structure the content and impact of each policy so that the "losers" will feel that continuing to live under the existing regime, though perhaps far from ideal, is at least bearable. A government can best encourage diffuse support by giving each contestant *something* of what he wants, so that none experiences total "defeat." But then it must deny total victory to "winners," compromising the maximum demands of opposing interests.

The resulting policy is likely to contain some logically inconsistent provisions and may even appear downright ridiculous when judged by the canons of logic. But a government is likely to be more concerned with preserving its society than with perfect logic, and if the policy helps to do the job no one will care much about its lack of logical symmetry.

The current conflict over the education of black children in the nation's public schools provides a classic example of the uses and limits of compromise. Consider, for a moment, what is happening in this explosive and highly dangerous struggle. One set of demands comes from extreme white supremacists who demand that racial segregation be permanently restored in the schools and that whites decide what both the all-black and all-white schools teach. Another set comes from extreme black nationalists, who also insist upon racial segregation but demand that only blacks decide what black schools shall teach. A third set comes from integrationists of both races, who press for the education of black and white children together in the same schools under policies developed by black and white teachers and parents working together. Each group feels deeply that its position is right. Completely satisfying the demands of any one would mean total defeat for the other two, a defeat that none is likely to accept peacefully. The civil-war potential in this conflict is high. It has already boiled over into violence many times, most recently in the wrecking of school buses by enemies of forced integration.

How has the nation's political system dealt with this conflict? In 1954 the U.S. Supreme Court ruled that school segregation is unconstitutional, a major but not a total victory for the integrationists. The Court ordered that local school boards show "good faith" in ending segregation in their districts. It also recognized that desegregation must come more slowly in some areas than in others by ordering the various Federal district courts to proceed "with deliberate speed" to see that the local school boards complied with the order. Only in 1969, fifteen years after the original decision, did the Court declare that "with deliberate speed" means "now." Since 1955 legal segregation has been almost completely abolished in some states (like Missouri and Maryland), abolished only in parts of others (like Texas), and relatively little changed in still others (like South Carolina and Mississippi). "De facto" school segregation, reflecting segregation in housing, has been attacked in some northern cities through busing of children from their home school districts to integrated schools in other districts, but in other cities it continues much as before. A number of school districts have instituted classes in African and Afro-American history and culture and even in Swahili. Others have turned over control of teachers and curricula in black districts to local citizens; as in New York in 1968–1969, this policy has sometimes stirred not only teacher-board and teacher-parent clashes but also hostility between blacks and whites and between Jews and Gentiles.

Each of the three groups has thus received some but not all of what it wants. The white supremacists have experienced a mortal wound to the old ways, but have at least prevented "outsiders" from imposing immediate and total change in their way of life. The integrationists have probably won the most, but their goal of full integration is still unachieved. The black nationalists have not achieved all-black schools run by blacks for blacks, but they have won a much bigger say in what the schools teach, and their prospects for a progressively larger say in the future are excellent. None of the three groups is, of course, entirely happy with the present situation, but the publicity given occasional strikes, demonstrations, and even bombings should not blind us to the fact that most people in all three groups apparently find the present situation and future prospects sufficiently bearable to refrain from civil war.

Our present policy toward the races in the schools can hardly satisfy anyone's vision of perfect logic or justice, but it has so far enabled the nation to deal with this bitter issue by means other than all-out civil war or iron-handed repression of dissidents. From the point of view of government, that is all the justification it needs. One who understands why already understands a good deal about governing.

# 4

# POLITICAL CULTURE AND SOCIALIZATION

Two of the best-known purveyors of advice to Americans traveling abroad offer these tips on how to deal with customs officials:

> Some officials are straight; some are as crooked as an anteater's nose. Don't try to pull anything with the Americans, British, Dutch, Scandinavians, Swiss or Greeks. You'd have an easier time smuggling rubber underwear to a friend on his way to the chair.
>
> A hoary trick for getting fast clearance is this: Offer the man a cigarette before he opens your bag. If he takes it, hand him the rest of the package—or put it next to him in plain sight on the counter. When he accepts it, you're in. The inspection will be quick and easy.[1]

A British scholar suggests comparable distinctions for people contemplating political careers in Great Britain, Nigeria, or Ghana:

> In Britain, the distinction between the official and private capacities of high office is widely understood and accepted. As a private person, a Minister of the Crown is not expected to be particularly hospitable or lavish in his hospitality. In West Africa, if a man holds high office, he is often expected to entertain his relations, tribesmen, and political supporters, for such generosity may be a condition of continued political eminence.[2]

---

Political Culture and Socialization

[1] Nancy and Temple Fielding, *Fielding's Super-Economy Europe, 1969–70* (New York: Dell Publishing Co., Inc., 1969), p. 55.

[2] M. McMullan, "A Theory of Corruption," *Sociological Review,* 9 (July 1961), 195–196.

These quotations offer minor examples of differences among the "political cultures" of the nations mentioned. They illustrate the point, discussed more generally in Chapter 12, that any political system both shapes and is shaped by its environment. One of the most significant aspects of that environment is the particular political culture within which political issues are shaped, expressed, and resolved or unresolved.

In this chapter, accordingly, we shall examine the main components of political culture and outline how they are born, perpetuated, and changed.

## PEOPLE AND THEIR POLITICS

Although political scientists deal mainly with aggregates of human beings (legislatures, courts, protest movements, political parties, and the like), it is well to remember that the individual person is the basic unit of all social behavior, and that the "political actor"—the individual person who engages in some form of politically relevant activity[3] —is the basic unit of political behavior. Students of politics can thus learn a great deal about the nature of political mankind from biology, psychology, psychiatry,and other disciplines focused on the individual. Let us briefly summarize some of the findings of these disciplines that are most useful in understanding political cultures and political systems.

### BIOLOGICAL NATURE AND NEEDS

We may begin by borrowing James C. Davies' formula for how people acquire their opinions and determine their behavior: $B = f (SO)$ "Behavior is a function of the interaction of the situation and the organism."[4] To look at the organism first, it is clear that one of the most powerful drives affecting human behavior is people's desire to maintain their biological existence (although it is by no means their only desire). To satisfy this desire at even the minimum level of bare existence they must eat, sleep, clothe and shelter themselves; defend themselves against attacks by animals and other people; and protect themselves from the onslaughts of nature in the form of floods, fire, hurricanes, and so on. Most people also wish to engage in sexual relations, to reproduce themselves, and to protect their mates and offspring. Furthermore, most people want to achieve these goals at levels beyond that of bare existence: They wish to live in comfort and enjoy pleasure. They are thus likely to favor policies that they believe will help them to achieve good things for themselves and their families and oppose policies they believe will prevent or make difficult their achievement.

### PSYCHOLOGICAL PROCESSES

Our formula for human behavior emphasizes the *interaction* of the situation and the organism. Accordingly, one critical factor in behavior is the person's neurological-mental-psychic apparatus for receiving, ordering, and interpreting the stimuli he or

---

[3] To keep matters straight, it should be clear that the term "political actor" includes, but is not restricted to, such famous Californians as Ronald Reagan, George Murphy, and Shirley Temple Black.

[4] James C. Davies, *Human Nature in Politics* (New York: John Wiley & Sons, Inc., 1963), pp. 2-3.

*"All that political paranoia you helped me get rid of, Doctor—what do I do now that it turns out I was right?"*

she receives from the external situation and translating them into action. One useful way to picture this apparatus is as a "cognitive map" of the physical and social world in which each person lives. This "map" has three main elements. First, it includes many *perceptions*— "signals" of sight, sound, touch, taste, and smell from the outside world that provide the raw material for the person's picture of the world. Second, it includes *conceptualization*— the mental categories into which he or she sorts the perceptions and relates them to one another to give them meaning. And, third, it includes *affect*— the emotional coloration of good or bad with which the person endows the patterns of meaning thus created.

### Perception and Cognitive Dissonance

Students of political psychology have found many variations in people's cognitive maps. In the matter of perceptions, for example, they have found that people do not invariably receive and record political signals as photographic film receives and records light waves; rather, their perceptions are powerfully affected by the nature and degree of "cognitive dissonance" that the signals arouse.[5] For example, if person A hears person B, whom he admires, advocate position X, which A already agrees with, well and good; but if B advocates position Z, which A opposes, there is painful "dissonance" between A's admiration of B and his opposition to Z. He may resolve the dissonance and ease the psychological pain simply by blocking out the signal that B advocates Z. A striking illustration of just such blocking has been provided by a

---

[5] The leading exposition of this approach is Leon Festinger, *A Theory of Cognitive Dissonance* (New York: Harper & Row, Publishers, 1957).

famous study of voters in Elmira, New York, during the 1948 presidential election. A leading issue in that election was the Taft-Hartley Act, which restricted certain labor-union practices. Many people held strong views on the act, and the two leading candidates repeatedly took strong opposing stands on it: Republican Thomas E. Dewey favored the act, and Democrat Harry S. Truman opposed it. The investigators asked their Elmira respondents' own views on the act, their voting intentions, and their perceptions of how the candidates stood on the act. By sorting their responses into various groups, the investigators discovered some interesting facts, as summarized in Table 2; almost all the voters whose views of the act were in fact shared by the candidate whom they preferred correctly perceived his stand (96 percent and 95 percent); but large proportions of those whose views were opposed by their favored candidate simply blocked out the dissonant signals and saw their man as holding a position that he did not in fact hold (54 percent and 40 percent). Many people's cognitive maps are thus not photographically exact reproductions of the external world; they are perceptually "touched up" to make them easier to live with.

TABLE 2

**Impact of Cognitive Dissonance on Elmira Voters, 1948**

|  | Dewey Voters' Perceptions of Candidate's Views | | Truman Voters' Perceptions of Candidate's Views | |
| Candidate | For the Act | Against the Act | For the Act | Against the Act |
| --- | --- | --- | --- | --- |
| Dewey | 96% | 54% | 85% | 95% |
| Truman | 27 | 43 | 40 | 10 |

Source: Adapted from Bernard R. Berelson, Paul F. Lazarsfeld, and William N. McPhee, *Voting*, by permission of The University of Chicago Press. Copyright 1954 by The University of Chicago Press. Chart CII, p. 221.

## Levels of Conceptualization

The day after the 1964 American presidential election, the San Diego *Union* editorialized, "The vote for Senator Barry Goldwater indicated that four out of ten Americans are sincerely and devotedly conservative." By the same reasoning, the vote for Lyndon B. Johnson showed that six out of ten Americans are sincerely and devotedly liberal, but the *Union* neglected to add this conclusion. Both propositions rest upon the assumption that Americans are highly ideological—that they see politics as a conflict between liberalism and conservatism and base their opinions and votes on the ideology to which they adhere.

This assumption has been sharply questioned by social science research. In 1956, for example, the Survey Research Center of the University of Michigan asked its respondents a series of open-ended questions on what they liked and disliked about the parties and presidential candidates. It found that only 12 percent of the sample replied in terms that could be called "ideological" in even the broadest sense of the term. The most common type of conceptualization, characteristic of 42 percent of the sample, was what the SRC labeled "group benefits" (for example, "The Democrats are for the workingman," and "The Republicans are for big business"). Another 24 percent gave answers based on the "nature of the times" (for example, "Times are good so why change parties?" and "Republicans cause depressions"). The remaining 22 percent had no issue content in their conceptualizations (for example, "I Like Ike" and "I'm a Democrat").[6]

But *issue* voting is quite different from ideological voting, and it has increased markedly in American presidential elections in the 1960s and 1970s: The SRC found that most voters in 1972 felt strongly about certain issues, particularly ending the Vietnam war, amnesty for draft evaders, government health insurance, unrestricted abortions, and legalization of marijuana. Moreover, most voters perceived McGovern and Nixon as holding sharply different positions on those issues, and most voted for the candidate whose positions they preferred. There is still some dispute among political scientists about how extensive and permanent issue voting has become in America,[7] but most would agree with the SRC's conclusion that "apparently it took twelve years of national leadership focused on national problems and policy alternatives to transform the American electorate and to overlay the traditional politics of the 1950's, rooted in the Great Depression and the social cleavages made deep by economic distress, with a new issue politics."[8]

## PHYSICAL ENVIRONMENT

One major external influence on human beings' political opinions is the physical conditions in which they live. If, for example, climate, soil, and resources make biological survival difficult, people are likely to view proposals for government policy through a perspective different from that held by people living in physical environments that make biological survival easy. If a particular nation's physical geography renders it vulnerable to invasion, its people are likely to view issues of foreign policy and national defense differently from the way people living in a relatively inaccessible nation view them.

One school of political analysis, known as "geopolitics," holds that any nation's basic foreign policy is determined entirely by the necessities of its geographical position and that its citizens have no real choices in making such policy.[9] Most political scientists, however, believe that this point of view greatly oversimplifies the policy-making process. They argue that, though a nation's physical environment undoubtedly exerts considerable influence over the policies it adopts, it is only one of many influential factors.

---

[6] Angus Campbell, Philip E. Converse, Warren E. Miller, and Donald E. Stokes, *The American Voter* (New York; John Wiley & Sons, Inc., 1960), chap. 10.

[7] See the discussions by Gerald M. Pomper, Richard W. Boyd, John H. Kessel, and Richard A. Brody and Benjamin I. Page in the *American Political Science Review*, 66 (June 1972), 415–470.

[8] Arthur H. Miller, Warren E. Miller, Alden S. Raine, and Thad A. Brown, "A Majority Party in Disarray: Policy Polarization in the 1972 Election," a paper presented at the annual meeting of the American Political Science Association, 1973, New Orleans, La. The point is underscored by Jeane J. Kirkpatrick, "The Revolt of the Masses," *Commentary*, February 1973, pp. 55–75. The growing importance of issue voting was first marked by V. O. Key, Jr., *The Responsible Electorate: Rationality in Presidential Voting, 1936–1960* (Cambridge, Mass.: Belknap Press of Harvard University Press, 1966).

[9] A leading exposition of this point of view is Halford J. Mackinder, *Democratic Ideas and Reality* (reissue of the 1919 edition; New York: Holt, Rinehart and Winston, Inc., 1942).

## The Nature of the Process

Another general category of external pressures on the political opinions of individuals includes those exerted by various social groups. Some of these groups—notably pressure groups and political parties—make conscious efforts to influence the political opinions of their own members and of nonmembers as well. In Chapters 8–10 we shall inspect the nature and opinion-influencing operations of these groups.

Here, however, we are concerned with the influence of social groups of which the individual is himself a member. In Chapter 2 we noted that every person in modern society belongs to many categoric groups—that is, aggregates of people who share at least one such characteristic as sex, age, race, occupation, and religion. We further noted that some categoric groups are also interest groups—that is, groups whose members are conscious of their shared characteristics, regard themselves as having certain common goals arising from those characteristics, and to some extent direct their behavior accordingly. Finally, some interest groups are political in the sense that they pursue their goals at least partly by seeking to influence governmental action.

Several social psychologists have investigated this aspect of the opinion-forming process. Some have focused mainly upon the influence of "primary groups"—that is, of groups whose members have regular face-to-face contact. Others have studied the broader and more impersonal "categoric" groups already mentioned. These investigators have concluded that primary groups generally have a more direct and powerful influence on the opinions of their members than do larger and more impersonal groups but that the latter do have considerable influence on the opinions of most people.

Perhaps it would be valuable to descend from the dizzying heights of theory and polysyllabic words for a moment to check these generalizations with our own experience. If we think of those with whom we have most daily contact—parents, schoolmates, sweethearts, friends, and so on—we can ask ourselves, "Are our opinions about most things, including politics, pretty much like their opinions—or do our opinions sharply differ from theirs on many matters?" All who ask and honestly answer this question about themselves will learn that the social psychologists are talking not only about "other people" but also about *us!*

Just how does all this agreement come about? By what processes do we form pretty much the same opinions as the other members of the primary groups to which we belong? Investigations and experiments conducted by social psychologists reveal how the process works.[10]

---

[10] The leading studies include George C. Homans, *The Human Group* (New York: Harcourt Brace Jovanovich, Inc., 1950); Sidney Verba, *Small Groups and Political Behavior* (Princeton, N.J.: Princeton University Press, 1961); and Robert T. Golombiewski, *The Small Group* (Chicago: University of Chicago Press, 1963).

In every social group, and particularly in every primary group, certain pressures are working for uniformity of opinion among the members, pressures which operate on each individual member and powerfully affect his or her opinions, political and otherwise. This pressure arises from several sources. First, membership in particular groups limits to some extent the stimuli the members receive and therefore affects their ideas of what the world is really like. A Ku Klux Klansman in Mississippi, for example, is likely to be confronted with somewhat different facts about racial segregation and prevailing interpretations of those facts than is a Unitarian minister in Vermont. The Klansman and the minister are thus likely to have different opinions about such matters as the intelligence of blacks and the degree to which blacks in Mississippi are unhappy about segregation. Second, people want the acceptance and approval of their associates and to be regarded as "with it" and "okay," rather than as "out of it" or "weird"—*at least in the eyes of those people and groups that matter to them* (see pp. 75–79). Many social psychologists believe that this desire, far more than "patriotism" or "national ideals," accounts for the great physical courage shown under fire by so many soldiers. Third, if a person values highly his membership in a particular group, like his family, fraternity, church, or local chapter of Students for a Democratic Society, and derives much personal satisfaction from it, he may well feel that if he holds an opinion sharply different from that held by most of the other members, the group might expel him or disintegrate altogether, thus depriving him of the satisfaction it brings.

Sometimes these group pressures are applied through the communications by certain members of the group who serve a kind of "sergeant at arms" function. Sometimes they are applied through informal communications among members of the group holding no official position. (In Chap. 6 we shall inspect some processes of social and political communication.) The strength of the pressures applied to any particular individual depends upon several factors, including the importance of group membership to the individual's own personal satisfactions and the number and strength of the counterpressures exerted by other groups with conflicting goals of which he or she is also a member.

### Types of Influential Group Memberships

Social scientists generally agree that primary groups have more influence upon the political opinions of their respective members than the more impersonal categoric groups. Most primary groups, however, are segments of particular categoric groups. One useful way to describe the more influential types of group membership is thus to consider pairs of related primary and categoric groups.

**Families and Ethnic Groups** The first group of which most of us become conscious is our family. We learn many of our values, reality perceptions, thinking and acting habits, and so on, from parents, brothers, and sisters. Indeed, we often hear that most people "inherit" their party affiliations and political attitudes from their parents. We shall see later how much truth there is in this allegation.

Most families are based largely or exclusively on blood relationships and are therefore parts of particular ethnic groups. Social scientists define an ethnic group as an aggregate of people who share a common ancestry and certain special customs and

Political Culture and
Socialization

behavior patterns. The most often-discussed ethnic groups are the "races" (Caucasian, Negroid, Mongoloid, and so on), but the term also includes groups from particular areas and nations (Irish-Americans, Spanish-Americans, Polish-Americans, Italian-Americans, and so on). Social scientists believe that the political opinions of most people are influenced to some extent by membership in particular ethnic groups but that such influence is less strong than is that of families. Ethnic-group influence appears to be greatest among members of minority groups (for example, blacks, Chicanos, and Jews in the United States and Afrikaners in South Africa) that feel threatened by larger groups.[11]

**Friends and Age Groups**   The second group of which most of us become conscious is our circle of friends and playmates. Most of us want the approval of our friends and are strongly influenced by their opinions not only in childhood and adolescence but in adult life as well.

Who are our friends? The old maxim "Birds of a feather flock together" applies to most of mankind. Most of our friends are people very much like ourselves: They live in the same general kind of neighborhoods, attend the same general kinds of schools and churches, come from similar economic levels and social classes, and often work at the same general kinds of jobs. Most of our friends are also close to us in age. A perennial complaint of older people is that they "cannot understand the younger generation," and yet another complaint among older people is that young people's passion for the singing of Rudy Vallee, Frank Sinatra, the Beatles or the Rolling Stones (depending on which generation is "young" at the moment) reflects lack of taste and even morality. Much of our literature is focused upon the conflict between the old and the young, and most social scientists agree that membership in particular age groups has some influence upon most people's opinions.

**Congregations and Religious Groups**   Many of us begin to attend Sunday school at an early age and later join church youth organizations and become members of congregations. Most religions are deeply concerned with both values and conceptions of the universe, and most churches try to indoctrinate their communicants. There is no doubt that many people's attitudes on many matters are powerfully influenced by their membership in particular congregations and religious groups.

Many churches, moreover, make official pronouncements on certain political issues and have some direct influence on the political opinions and behavior of their communicants. Nations that encourage particular religions or restrict others (for example, Spain and certain Latin American nations) allow the favored religions particularly influential roles in the formation of political opinions and public policy. But even in nations that, like the United States, have no officially "established" or favored religion, the churches have considerable influence upon the political opinions of a great many people.

---

[11] See Raymond E. Wolfinger, "The Development and Persistence of Ethnic Voting," *American Political Science Review,* 59 (December 1965), 896–908; and Mark R. Levy and Michael S. Kramer, *The Ethnic Factor: How America's Minorities Decide Elections* (New York: Simon and Schuster, Inc., 1973).

**Schoolmates and Educational Groups** Modern nations vary greatly in the amounts of formal education their citizens receive, but in most both the proportion of those attending school and the average time spent in school are increasing year by year. The U.S. Census estimated that in 1972 23 percent of the population of the United States had had at least some college education, 75 percent had had some high-school education, and 99 percent had had some grammar-school education. All three figures were higher than those in the 1960 Census reports, and those in the 1980 reports will doubtless be higher still. The opinions of most Americans, therefore, are exposed to the influence of both schoolmates and school authorities.

The purposes of education in all nations, democratic and dictatorial alike, include instructing the young in some of the skills and techniques that they need to perform useful roles in society (for example, reading, writing, counting, and perhaps driving automobiles and running machine lathes) and also indoctrinating them in the political values and beliefs about reality favored by most of the nation's citizens. In the United States the schools are committed to educating their pupils in the principles of democracy and "the American way," just as in the Soviet Union the schools are committed to educating Soviet youth in the principles and attitudes of communism. In all nations the schools are generally considered such important shapers of opinion that they are perennial subjects of controversy. We are all familiar with the periodic clashes in this or that part of the country over whether or not the schools are indoctrinating the young in the *proper* values and beliefs. We often hear charges from the Right that the schools are teaching "sexual immorality," "socialism," and "atheism"; we also hear charges from the Left that the schools are "apologists for capitalist exploitation" or "inculcating racist attitudes." As most schools in most modern nations, democratic and dictatorial alike, are governmentally rather than privately owned and operated, what they do and how they do it are always political issues, and they are subject to constant powerful pressures, from public officials, parents, students, teachers, churches, economic pressure groups, protest groups, and so on.

**Work Associates and Occupational Groups** Most adults spend half or more of their waking hours at work. In terms of sheer frequency of face-to-face contact their immediate work associates constitute one of their most important primary groups, and social scientists have discovered a high degree of uniformity in the opinions, political and otherwise, of such groups.

All groups of work associates are also segments of larger and more impersonal occupational groups: college professors, retail merchants, carpenters, unskilled laborers, farm operators, business executives, and white-collar workers. As we shall see in Chapter 5, however, the evidence suggests that membership in this kind of categoric group has less influence on political opinions than does membership in many of the others that we have discussed.

**Neighbors, Income Groups, and Social Classes** The remaining kind of primary group of which most of us are conscious is our neighbors—the people who make their homes in our immediate residential areas. Social scientists have long observed that most neighborhoods are composed of people who are similar in several respects. Most of those living in particular neighborhoods are likely to be of the same or similar ethnic groups, religious groups, educational levels, and income levels.

They are also likely to be members of the same social classes—a concept that requires some definition and explanation. According to Karl Marx and his communist disciples, a class is strictly and solely a group of people holding particular positions in the production process and only two such classes exist: the *bourgeoisie,* who own the instruments of production and exploit the people who operate them, and the *proletariat,* who operate but do not own the instruments of production and are exploited by the bourgeoisie. The Marxist conception of classes proclaims a sharp distinction and irreconcilable hostility between the two classes and views all politics as a struggle between them for total domination.

Non-Marxist social scientists, however, use the concept of class in quite a different sense. They see society as divided into many more than two classes and conceive of each class as based upon a number of distinctions, including ethnic affiliation, length of family residence in the nation and in the local community, educational level, income, occupational prestige, and so on. As most of these factors are difficult to measure and express mathematically, the class boundaries are indistinct, and the classification of particular individuals is often difficult. The one generally used criterion of class membership that is relatively definite and measurable is wealth and income level, but few, if any, non-Marxist social scientists consider it the sole factor determining social class.[12] Whatever their particular definitions of class, however, most social scientists agree that class membership has a powerful influence upon the political opinions of most people.[13]

### The Variable Impact of Group Membership

It is important to remember that no social group has the same political impact on every one of its members, as is clear from the data in Chapter 2 about the internal division of every social group in political preferences, involvement, and behavior. As Table 1 showed (p. 43), in the 1972 election most black Americans preferred George McGovern but a few favored Richard Nixon, and over a third did not vote at all. Most whites in the Deep South preferred Nixon, but a substantial number did not vote.

Most social scientists believe that the impact of membership in a particular social group upon a particular person's political views and behavior depends upon several factors.[14]

**Group Salience for the Individual**  Some people regard their status as women, blacks, Roman Catholics, or union members as the most important thing in their lives, and the particular reference group has a powerful effect upon their attitudes and

---

[12] For a brief but lucid explanation of non-Marxist social scientists' conception of class, see John W. Bennett and Melvin M. Tumin, *Social Life, Structure and Function* (New York: Alfred A. Knopf, 1948), chap. 25.

[13] See Richard Centers, *The Psychology of Social Classes* (Princeton, N.J.: Princeton University Press, 1949); Seymour Martin Lipset, *Political Man* (New York: Doubleday & Company, Inc., 1960), chaps. 7–9; and Robert R. Alford, *Party and Society* (Skokie, Ill.: Rand McNally & Company, 1963).

[14] This discussion is based upon the analysis in Campbell, Converse, Miller, and Stokes, *The American Voter,* chap. 12.

behavior. Other women, blacks, Roman Catholics, and union members identify less strongly with these groups and also base their behavior on cues from other sources. The evidence from many studies of political psychology supports the proposition that the stronger the members' identifications with their groups the more likely they are to think and behave in ways that distinguish members of their groups from nonmembers. There is also much evidence that, other things being equal, the intensity of identification with a particular group is closely related to length of conscious membership in it. Persons who have been raised in Democratic families and have always thought of themselves as Democrats are more likely to be strong partisans than are those who were raised Republicans and have only recently become Democrats.

**Perceived Political Relevance of the Group**   Strong identification with a particular group is not enough in itself to shape a person's politics. Some union members, for example, may identify strongly with their union but exclusively as an instrument for obtaining better wages, hours, and working conditions, rather than as an organization taking partisan political stands or supporting political candidates. Their political attitudes and behavior are less likely to be influenced by the union's stands than those of unionists who identify strongly and think it proper for the union to take stands.

**Transmission of Group Political Standards**   The leaders of some social groups—including organizations as varied as the American Medical Association, the American Federation of Labor–Congress of Industrial Organizations, Students for a Democratic Society, and the John Birch Society—make regular efforts to "sell" their members on organization views and candidates. Leaders of other groups, on the other hand, make weak efforts or none at all, and the evidence suggests that the organization's salience and political relevance increase as such "transmissions" from the leadership increase. This result is one aspect of the general phenomenon of political communication, which we shall consider in detail in Chapter 6.

But, whatever their biological or social sources may be, the political attitudes of the mass membership of any political system are among the most powerful forces shaping its inputs, conversion processes, and outputs. Taken together, these attitudes constitute what political scientists call "political culture." We turn now to a closer look at the components and consequences of this concept.

## POLITICAL CULTURE: THEME AND VARIATIONS

### THE CONCEPT OF POLITICAL CULTURE

We shall use Gabriel A. Almond and G. Bingham Powell's definition of political culture: "Political culture is the pattern of individual attitudes and orientations toward politics among the members of a political system. It is the subjective realm which underlies and gives meaning to political actions."[15]

---

[15] Gabriel A. Almond and G. Bingham Powell, Jr., *Comparative Politics: A Developmental Approach* (Boston: Little, Brown & Company, 1966), p. 50.

The political scientists who have worked most with the concept of political culture[16] have not approached all aspects of any nation's total culture. They have focused on those most relevant to understanding how and why a nation's political system operates as it does. They have asked questions about popular attitudes toward the following political objects:

*The National Political System as a Whole*   Do most people identify mainly with the national system or with some territorial, ethnic, religious, or tribal subsystem? Are they proud of the national system? Do they believe that it has a major impact on their lives?

*Particular Political Roles or Structures*   Do people expect fair treatment from public officials? Do they think that the officials are corrupt? Do they believe that they themselves should be active in public affairs? Do they believe that they can influence what public officials do?

*Individual or Group Role Incumbents*   Do people approve of the ways in which current officeholders are performing their duties? Do they feel that the incumbents should be removed so that others can do the jobs better?

*Specific Public Policies and Issues*   Do Americans approve of their government's program for dealing with the energy crisis? Do Englishmen want labor-union leaders fined for failing to prevent wildcat strikes? Do West Germans want reunification with East Germany even at the cost of losing American friendship?

## COMPONENTS OF POLITICAL CULTURES

Political culture is generally viewed as having three main components.

### Empirical Beliefs

Empirical beliefs are what people *understand* about how things *are* in the political world. For example, all but one-tenth of a sample of Americans interviewed in 1961 believed that their national government had an impact on their daily lives, whereas two-thirds of a comparable Mexican sample believed that the Mexican national government had no such impact. For another example, 89 percent of a British sample expected fair and equal treatment from police, whereas 57 percent of the Mexican sample expected *un*equal police treatment.[17] Both sets of attitudes have obvious consequences for the interrelationships of ruler and ruled.

---

[16] The two leading works in this area are Almond and Verba, *The Civic Culture* (Princeton, N.J.: Princeton University Press, 1963; abridged paperback ed., Boston: Little, Brown & Company, 1965), a comparative study of political attitudes in the United States, Great Britain, West Germany, Italy, and Mexico; and Lucian W. Pye and Verba (eds.), *Political Culture and Political Development* (Princeton, N.J.: Princeton University Press, 1965), a volume of essays analyzing the political cultures of Japan, England, West Germany, Turkey, India, Ethiopia, Italy, Mexico, Egypt, and the Soviet Union.

[17] Almond and Verba, *The Civic Culture*, p. 80, Table 1, p. 108, Table 2.

## Value Preferences

Value preferences are beliefs about public goals that *should be* sought and personal virtues that *should be* maximized by governmental action. For example, some Americans may say, with Stephen Decatur, "My Country: may she ever be right; but right or wrong, my country!" But others may say, with Henry David Thoreau, "The only obligation [to government] which I have a right to assume is to do at any time what I think right." Some people place the highest values on "law and order," stability of the system, "domestic tranquillity," and the like; others prefer "social justice," "keeping up with the times," and "dialogue" or "confrontation" between opposing visions of the good life.

## Affective Responses

Affective responses are favorable or unfavorable emotions toward perceived political objects. For example, 85 percent of an American sample interviewed in 1961 expressed pride in American government and political institutions, whereas only 7 percent of a German sample and 3 percent of an Italian sample expressed such pride in their own comparable institutions.[18] Sizable majorities of a sample of Wisconsin adults interviewed in 1964 agreed (64 and 82 percent, respectively) with statements that "the political parties more often than not create conflicts where none really exists" and that "the best rule in voting is to pick the man regardless of his party label." But 67 percent *dis*agreed with the proposition that "it would be better if, in all elections, we put no party labels on the ballot," and 68 percent agreed that "democracy works best where competition between parties is strong."[19] It seems that most Wisconsinites (and Americans?) do not think very highly of their political parties but nevertheless have no urge to abolish them.

It is important to note that all the prevailing empirical beliefs, value preferences, and affective responses that together constitute a nation's political culture do not have to be logically consistent with one another; indeed the evidence suggests that most political cultures, particularly those in the "advanced" nations, fall far short of logical consistency and symmetry. In the United States, for example, most of us endorse such Christian sentiments as "Love thy neighbor as thyself" and "Help those less fortunate than yourself"—but also such distinctly un-Christian sentiments as "a corporation's first obligation is to its stockholders" and "the Lord helps those who help themselves." Most of us believe in "efficient" and "businesslike" government—but also in separation of powers and checks and balances, which inevitably cause a great deal of inefficiency by making it difficult for any one leader or party to take real charge.

Do these anomalies in political cultures prove us fools, knaves, or simply human beings behaving as human beings? Without choosing any of these labels, we

---

[18] Almond and Verba, *The Civic Culture*, p. 102, Table 1.

[19] See Jack Dennis, "Support for the Party System by the Mass Public," *American Political Science Review,* 60 (September 1966), 600–615.

can observe that every nation's political culture contains some anomalies—and that, however inconsistent and illogical, every nation's political culture constitutes one of the most powerful influences shaping its political system.

## POLITICAL CULTURES AND SUBCULTURES

No nation's political culture is evenly diffused among all its social strata and political groups. Its components are found in varying strengths in different segments of the population, and some segments may hold views shared little or not at all by others. When the views of a particular segment vary significantly in content or intensity from those of the nation as a whole, the segment is said to have its own distinctive political subculture.

There are, for example, the "elite" and "mass" subcultures. In almost no human organization do all members participate all the time with equal energy, commitment, and influence. In any organization, and particularly those of such enormous scale as modern national political systems, only a small fraction of the members are especially committed to and informed about the organization's affairs, work especially hard on its business, initiate suggestions for action that later become policy, and thus have special influence. These active members are often called the organization's "elite." The remaining great majority, the masses, know and care much less about organization affairs, spend little if any effort on its business, and at most react to the suggestions made by the elite.[20] This point should be well understood. Many college students assume that the way they and their friends look at politics is pretty much the way most people, or at least most young people, look at politics. But this assumption is incorrect and very misleading, for in many important respects college students are an elite quite unrepresentative of most of the population. They attend college, which less than 30 percent of persons under the age of twenty-five do and even fewer older people have done. By no means all college students take political science or other social science courses. Politically, students who do are a great deal more involved, aware, and "ideological" than are most people of any age who have not gone to college. As a result, the way that these college students feel about politics is not likely to be a useful guide to the way that most people off campus—and many on it—feel. Compared with those who have not attended college, the college-educated are much more likely to conceptualize politics in ideological terms, to know and care more about issues, to have a high sense of political efficacy (as we

---

[20] We have no precise measurements of the relative sizes of elites and masses in modern nations, but several estimates have been made. Lester W. Milbrath, for example, has estimated that in the United States 5–7 percent of the population consists of "gladiators" (roughly synonymous with our term "elite"), another 60 percent of "spectators" (who vote fairly regularly, at least in presidential elections, and read and talk some about politics), and 33–35 percent of "apathetics" (who almost never vote and are little aware of the political world around them); see Milbrath, *Political Participation* (Skokie, Ill.: Rand McNally & Company, 1965), pp. 21–22. The data in Almond and Verba, *The Civic Culture,* pp. 89–99, suggest even higher proportions of apathetics in Italy and Mexico.

shall discuss), to take conservative positions on social-welfare questions, and to adopt internationalist positions on foreign-policy questions.[21]

One recent and dramatic illustration of this point is the difference between student and nonstudent reactions to the behavior of the Chicago police in suppressing the street demonstrations during the 1968 Democratic national convention—behavior watched on television by millions. If one were to gauge public opinion only from talking to college students and reading editorials in college newspapers, one would conclude that the entire nation was outraged by the "police brutality" and Mayor Richard Daley's encouragement of it. No doubt many students believed that that was how everyone *did* feel. But they were wrong. All the public-opinion polls taken after the convention showed that most people *approved* the actions of the Chicago police.[22] The point is not the justice or injustice of either the students' or the nonstudents' views; it is that politically active college students are an elite and it is very wrong to assume that their views predominate among the nonstudent masses.

Equally illuminating is the finding that current American politics is far from what student leaders often claim it is: a clash between youth and age. The evidence suggests, on the contrary, that differences in political attitudes and behavior are a good deal sharper between college youth and noncollege youth than they are between college youth and college-educated older people. The authors of the most authoritative sample survey of voting behavior in the 1968 election summarized the situation:

> Although privileged young college students angry at Vietnam and the shabby treatment of the Negro saw themselves as sallying forth to do battle against a corrupted and cynical older generation, a more head-on confrontation at the polls, if a less apparent one, was with their own age mates who had gone from high school off to the factory instead of college, and who were appalled by the collapse of patriotism and respect for the law that they saw about them. . . .
>
> In the degree that the feelings and opinion reflexes of the common man, *including age peers of lower circumstances,* were comprehended at all by campus activists, they tended to be a subject for derision or disdain. Strange to say, such hostile postures communicate with great speed even across social gulfs, and are reciprocated with uncommon reliability.[23]

It seems, then, that introspection and discussions with friends are not reliable techniques for helping college students to understand mass public opinion. The same

---

[21] Campbell, Converse, Miller, and Stokes, *The American Voter,* pp. 175, 200, 250, 491. For some more recent evidence supporting this point, see Jack Dennis and Austin Ranney, "Working within the System: Academic Recess and College Student Participation in the 1970 Elections," *American Politics Quarterly,* 1 (January 1973), 93–124.

[22] A Gallup poll released September 16, 1968, showed that 56 percent of a national sample approved the police action, 31 percent disapproved, and 13 percent had no opinion; see *Congressional Quarterly,* September 20, 1968, p. 2502.

[23] Converse, Miller, Jerrold G. Rusk, and Arthur C. Wolfe, "Continuity and Change in American Politics: Parties and Issues in the 1968 Election," *American Political Science Review,* 62 (December 1969), 1104–1105; italics added. The same was true in 1972: see Miller, Miller, Raine, and Brown, "A Majority Party in Disarray."

can be said for college professors,[24] business executives, and Presidents of the United States.

Many other political subcultures are also significant. In the United States the black subculture unquestionably and understandably differs in many ways from the white one. There are comparable differences between Flemings and Walloons in Belgium, among many of the language groups in India, among tribal groups in most new African nations, and so on. In many nations Jews and gentiles, Roman Catholics and Protestants, or Muslims and Hindus have distinct political subcultures. The sharpness of the cultural differences between the North and the South in the United States is matched by that of north-south differences in Italy. Physical and biological scientists in the Soviet Union have a status and subculture quite different from those of writers and manual workers. And in almost every nation, as we shall see, the political subcultures of the poor and the uneducated differ markedly from those of the well-educated.

Every nation, then, has a number of political subcultures that must be identified and understood for full comprehension of the psychological bases of its politics. Yet in most nations many beliefs are sufficiently widespread among most members of most educational, ethnic, religious, and other groups that we are justified in speaking of a nation's "political culture" and comparing one national culture with another. In what significant respects, then, do national political cultures differ from one another?

## SOME VARIABLES OF POLITICAL CULTURE

### Relevant General Attitudes

Students of political cultures have identified a number of popular attitudes that underlie and help explain both political and other kinds of behavior. One of the most studied of these variables is the trait of trusting or distrusting other people. A five-nation study of the United States, the United Kingdom, Germany, Italy, and Mexico showed, for example, that most Italians feel that only members of their own immediate families merit trust and devotion and that everyone else is a potential enemy, to be watched and guarded against—and never to be trusted.[25] Laurence Wylie has furnished another example in his classic study of life in a French village; he was struck by how often each villager warned him against the others:

> "Of course, you can trust me and my family and a few other people I'll point out to you, *mais les autres, ils . . . .*" *Les autres, ils . . .* was the inevitable opening of a diatribe against the other villagers. *"The others,* they criticize you, insult you, meddle in your business, try to tell you how to bring up your children and your

---

[24] An absorbing study of how unrepresentative of the mass public professors are is Everett Carll Ladd, Jr., and Seymour Martin Lipset, *Academics, Politics, and the 1972 Election* (Washington, D.C.: American Enterprise Institute for Public Policy Research, 1973).

[25] Conductors of the study asked respondents to agree or disagree with the statement, "Most people can be trusted." Only 7 percent of the Italians agreed, compared with 55 percent of the Americans, 49 percent of the British, 30 percent of the Mexicans, and 19 percent of the Germans; see Almond and Verba, *The Civic Culture,* p. 267, Table 4.

dog and how to treat your grandmother. *They* try to turn other people against you by casting doubts on your honesty and morality. *They* talk behind your back and then when you catch them at it they try to lie their way out of it. *They* don't respect your rights and your property. *They* are unreasonable and dishonest."[26]

Another significant general variable is efficacy-powerlessness; to what extent do ordinary people feel that they personally can have some direct influence upon national and local public officials? The five-nation study revealed significant differences, reported in Table 3, in the proportions of people who felt that they could do something about an unjust local regulation or national law.

TABLE 3

**Levels of Subjective Civic Competence, by National**

| Percentage Reporting | U.S. | U.K. | Germany | Italy | Mexico |
|---|---|---|---|---|---|
| National and local competence | 67% | 57% | 33% | 25% | 33% |
| National competence only | 8 | 5 | 4 | 2 | 5 |
| Local competence only | 10 | 21 | 29 | 26 | 19 |
| Neither national nor local competence | 15 | 17 | 34 | 47 | 43 |
| | 100% | 100% | 100% | 100% | 100% |
| N | 970 | 963 | 955 | 955 | 1007 |

*Source:* Gabriel A. Almond and Sidney Verba, *The Civic Culture* (Princeton, N.J.: Princeton University Press, 1963), p. 186, Table 2. Reprinted by permission of Princeton University Press.

Other politically relevant general variables include the dimensions ideology-pragmatism, interpersonal civility-hostility, faith-cynicism, optimism-pessimism, and identification-alienation. All help to explain the structure and operation of particular political systems, but certain other variables are more obviously related to politics.

## Political Attitudes

**Identification with the Nation**    Political scientists agree that one of the most powerful determinants of a nation's political stability and governmental effectiveness is the extent to which its citizens give their primary political loyalties to it rather than to one of its regions or tribes or religions. Many new African and Asian nations have thus faced "crises of identity" shortly after achieving independence. Some, like Ghana, Burma, and the Philippines, have weathered them very well, though not without scars, whereas others, like India, Nigeria, and Malaysia, have had much rougher going.[27] There are also significant variations among the developed nations. National identity is very strong, for example, in Japan, Norway, and Sweden. It is strong in the United States, though challenged by black separatism (see Chap. 22) and echoes of the Confederate loyalties of a century ago. It is strong in Great Britain, though challenged by Welsh and Scottish nationalism. But it is greatly diluted in Italy

---

[26] Laurence Wylie, *Village in the Vaucluse* (New York: Harper & Row, Publishers, 1964), p. 194; italics in the original.

[27] The leading study in this area is Pye, *Politics, Personality, and Nation Building* (New Haven, Conn.: Yale University Press, 1962).

by *campanalismo* (loyalty to the home town or the region rather than to the nation);[28] and most West Germans still identify with prepartition Germany, long for reunification, and have developed only limited identification with the present Federal Republic.[29] But, pure or diluted, strong or weak, the degree of citizens' identifications with their nation powerfully affects the stability and effectiveness of its political system.

**Legitimacy of the Authorities**  No government can rely entirely on physical force to guarantee compliance with its rules. Realistically speaking, it can shoot or torture or imprison only a small fraction of its citizens, and when a resolute resistance group larger than that fraction refuses to obey, the authorities are authoritative no longer. The first prerequisite for necessary voluntary compliance is the prevalence of popular confidence that the authorities have won their posts rightfully, that they make and enforce their decisions through proper procedures, and that their decisions are within the generally accepted boundaries of legitimate governmental concerns and do not encroach on what is rightfully private and personal. Where such confidence is widespread, as, for example, in Norway, Switzerland, and New Zealand, governments need only minimum force to deal with lawbreaking. Where the authorities' legitimacy is widely challenged, however, lawbreaking is a major problem and revolution an ever-present possibility.

That is why so many America-watchers have become deeply concerned over the evidence from a number of public opinion polls showing a sharp increase since the early 1960s in ordinary Americans' alienation from their government institutions and perhaps from the whole society.[30] Some of this evidence is arrayed in Table 4. The data in Table 4 show all too clearly that the Watergate revelations of 1973 and the impeachment crisis of 1974 only accelerated the increase in alienation originating in the mid-1960s. Years before the burglaries by the "plumbers" and the lying and cheating by the Committee to Reelect the President were exposed, President John Kennedy, Senator Robert Kennedy, and Dr. Martin Luther King, Jr., were assassinated; major riots broke out in the black ghettos of most major cities; the Vietnam war got worse and worse while three administrations said it was getting better and better; the forced busing of schoolchildren escalated racial conflict in the North as well as the South; universities became arenas for political conflict rather than agencies for studying it; and so Watergate was one more blow, albeit a grievous one, to an already-dwindling confidence in American institutions and society. The alarming growth in political alienation, in short, has been in large measure a response to events; and events may yet reverse the trend. We shall see.

**Citizens' Obligation to Participate**  Most governments, democratic and otherwise,

---

[28] Joseph LaPalombara, *Interest Groups in Italian Politics* (Princeton, N.J.: Princeton University Press, 1964), pp. 56–57.

[29] Lewis J. Edinger, *Politics in Germany* (Boston: Little, Brown & Company, 1968), pp. 85–89.

[30] The much-abused term "alienation" is sometimes used to mean feelings of powerlessness, sometimes meaninglessness of events, sometimes the absence of clear standards of right and wrong, and so on: see Ada W. Finifter, "Dimensions of Political Alienation," in Finifter (ed.), *Alienation and the Social System* (New York: John Wiley & Sons, Inc., 1972), pp. 189–212.

**TABLE 4**

**The Growth of Political Alienation in America, 1956-1972.**

| | Percentage of Respondents Agreeing | | | |
|---|---|---|---|---|
| Statement | 1956 | 1964 | 1968 | 1972 |
| "You can trust the government in Washington to do what is right just about always or most of the time." | 72% | 77% | 61% | 53% |
| "The government is run for the benefit of all the people." | 76 | 68 | 51 | 38 |

| | Percentage of Respondents Expressing "a Great Deal of Confidence" in Institution | | |
|---|---|---|---|
| Institution | 1966 | 1971 | 1973 |
| Executive branch of the Federal government | 41% | 23% | 19% |
| Congress | 42 | 19 | 30 |
| The Supreme Court | 51 | 23 | 33 |

| "Do you feel we always have one crisis or another in America, or do you feel there is something deeply wrong in America?" | Percentage of Respondents | | | |
|---|---|---|---|---|
| | March 1968 | June 1968 | Aug. 1973 | Sept. 1973 |
| Always one crisis or another | 55% | 26% | 46% | 37% |
| Something deeply wrong | 39 | 66 | 48 | 53 |
| Not sure | 6 | 8 | 6 | 10 |
| | 100% | 100% | 100% | 100% |

*Source:* For item 1: Arthur H. Miller, Thad A. Brown, and Alden S. Raine, "Social Conflict and Political Estrangement, 1958-1972," paper delivered at the Midwest Political Science Association Annual Meeting, May 1973, p. 6. For items 2 and 3: Louis Harris polls, reported in *Congressional Quarterly Weekly Report,* December 8, 1973, pp. 3214-3215.

want their citizens to participate in at least some political activities. In the Soviet Union, for example, the model citizen is what some Western scholars call an "eager robot":[31] That is, he is supposed to accept unquestioningly the policies laid down by top party officials and enthusiastically do his best to carry them out in his factory, collective farm, or wherever. He is permitted, sometimes even encouraged, to criticize lack of zeal and excessive inefficiency among middle- and lower-level bureaucrats and managers (though never among party leaders). We can only estimate what proportion of the Russian masses approximate this ideal, but we know that it is higher than many Westerners believe and perhaps lower than Russian leaders would prefer.[32]

Quite aside from how much and in what ways citizens of Western democratic systems *do* participate, it is clear that in some nations few feel any moral obligation to do so. In the five-nation study already cited, for example, respondents were asked, "What part do you think the ordinary person ought to play in the local affairs of his town or district?" Fifty-one percent of Americans replied that he should be active (attend meetings, join organizations involved in community affairs, and the like), and another 27 percent said that he should be "interested" (at least keep informed and

[31] The phrase is used in Ralph T. Fisher, Jr., "The Soviet Model of the Ideal Youth," in Cyril E. Black (ed.), *The Transformation of Russian Society* (Cambridge, Mass.: Harvard University Press, 1961).

[32] Frederick C. Barghoorn, *Politics in the USSR* (Boston: Little, Brown & Company, 1966), pp. 33–34.

Political Culture and Socialization

vote). But the corresponding figures for Italians were 10 and 22 percent, for West Germans 22 and 38 percent, and for Mexicans 26 and 33 percent.[33]

**Perceived Political Efficacy**   Closely related to a citizen's sense of obligation to participate in politics are his feelings about his ability to do so and the likelihood that his participation will have some impact. Does he know enough to deserve a hearing? Will the "powers that be" give him one? Can he have some influence on what they do? To see how feelings of efficacy are distributed among and within their five nations, Almond and Verba asked each respondent what, if anything, he might do to try to change an unjust or harmful local regulation or national law and how likely it was that he would succeed if he did try. Some of the replies are summarized in Table 5 (see also Table 3).

TABLE 5

Levels of Subjective Civic Competence,
by Nation and Education

| Nation | Total | Percentage of Respondents Who Say That They Can Do Something about an Unfair Local Regulation | | |
|---|---|---|---|---|
| | | Primary Education or Less | Some Secondary Education | Some College Education |
| United States | 77% | 60% | 82% | 95% |
| Great Britain | 77 | 74 | 83 | 88 |
| Germany | 62 | 58 | 83 | 85 |
| Italy | 53 | 45 | 62 | 76 |
| Mexico | 53 | 49 | 67 | 76 |

*Source:* Taken from data in Gabriel A. Almond and Sidney Verba, *The Civic Culture* (Princeton, N.J.: Princeton University Press, 1963), p. 186, Table 2; and p. 206, Figure 1. Copyright © 1963 by Princeton University Press. Reprinted by permission of Princeton University Press.

The most striking message of the data in Table 5 is not that Great Britain and the United States have higher levels of perceived political efficacy than do West Germany, Italy, and Mexico; it is that the differences among the educational groups *within* each nation are, with one exception, greater than the overall differences *among* the nations. The overall difference between Britain and the United States at one end of the range and Italy and Mexico at the other is 24 percentage points; but the differences between the most and least educated groups are 27 percent for Germany and Mexico, 31 percent for Italy, and 35 percent for the United States; only in Great Britain is the difference among educational groups as low as 14 percentage points. Furthermore, the differences among the five nations grow smaller in each higher educational group: among those with primary education or less there is an internation spread of 29 percentage points; among those with secondary education it declines to 21 percentage points; and among those with college education it declines to 19 percentage points.

Comparable findings in many other studies have led most political scientists to suspect that many significant differences among the political cultures of modern nations reflect not so much variations in unchanging and unchangeable "national characters" as variations in certain processes common to all political systems. Perhaps the most important and certainly the most studied of these processes is political

[33] Almond and Verba, *The Civic Culture,* p. 169, Table 1.

socialization. We shall therefore conclude this chapter by reviewing what is known about the conduct and consequences of political socialization in modern nations.

## POLITICAL SOCIALIZATION

### THE CONCEPT

A leading study of political socialization begins with the following report of a conversation between one of the authors and his three-and-a-half-year-old son held while the father was trying to find a parking place.

> Child: "There's somewhere."
> Father: "I can't park there."
> Child: "Why?"
> Father: "It's not allowed."
> Child: "Who say so?"
> Father: "I'll get a ticket."
> Child: "Uh."
> Father: "A policeman will stop me."
> Child: "Oh."

> When a three-and-a-half-year-old child, safely seated in the backseat of his father's car, helpfully sought to point out a parking space and entered into this laconic conversation, he learned if not his first political lesson at least the beginning of an important one. He was being introduced to the notion that his father is not omnipotent, that there is a power external to the family to which even his father has to submit, and that somehow the policeman represents the power.[34]

We do not yet know if the child will grow up to be a policeman, a penologist, or a protester hurling rocks at the "pigs." But we do know that most of his adult political attitudes will be *learned:* such attitudes are not instinctive. Political scientists call this learning process "political socialization" and define it as *"those developmental processes through which persons acquire political orientations and patterns of behavior."*[35]

In later chapters we shall consider the socialization of various political elites: the processes by which legislators, administrators, judges, party officials, and other political leaders acquire the attitudes and skills appropriate to their specialized roles. But "political socialization" generally means socialization of the *masses,* the processes by which ordinary people develop their attitudes toward their political systems. That kind of socialization is our subject here.

### PROFILE OF THE DEVELOPING POLITICAL SELF[36]

For most people political socialization begins early in life (evidently at least by three and a half!) and continues until very old age or death. There are, of course, many

---

[34] David Easton and Jack Dennis, *Children in the Political System* (New York: McGraw-Hill, Inc., 1969), pp. 3–4.

[35] Easton and Dennis, *Children in the Political System,* p. 7; italics in the original.

[36] For more detailed accounts, see Easton and Dennis, *Children in the Political System,* chaps. 4–14; Herbert H. Hyman, *Political Socialization* (New York: The Free Press, 1959), chap. 3; and Richard

variations in the content and pace of socialization from one person to another and one culture or subculture to another. But there are enough similarities among people in the United States and other developed nations[37] that we can outline the developmental cycle in general terms.

### Beginnings[38]

Political socialization begins as early as the fourth or even third year of life, when the child first perceives some basic political objects—for example, the President, the policeman, "the government"—as somehow different from his family or the people next door. About the same time he also learns that he is part of some collectivities larger and more remote than his family—that he is an American, a black, a Jew, a southerner, and so on. By the age of seven many children even have party preferences and say unhesitatingly, "I am a Democrat" or "I am a Republican."[39] In these beginning stages the child's identifications have more affective than cognitive content—that is, he is quite sure that he is a Democrat but not so sure about how Democrats differ from Republicans or why he is one rather than the other. But many of the cognitive gaps are filled in quite soon.

### Childhood

From age six to age eighteen our typical child lives at home and attends public schools through twelfth grade (legally he *must* attend until he is sixteen). From his parents, teachers, and other socializing agents (see later discussion) he not only acquires such basic skills as reading and arithmetic but also learns a good deal about the political world. He moves from a highly personalized conception of "the government" as synonymous with "the policeman" and "the President" to more abstract and general notions of its group character and norms. He perceives with increasing clarity the different identities and activities of the President, the policeman, the mayor, the governor, and eventually the legislature and the courts. This development process is well illustrated by the summary of proportions of children of various ages in New Haven, Connecticut, who gave "reasonably accurate" answers to questions about selected political objects. Table 6 shows that almost all the younger children could *name* the President of the United States and the mayor of New Haven. But, though

---

E. Dawson and Kenneth Prewitt, *Political Socialization* (Boston: Little, Brown & Company, 1969), chap. 4.

[37] Until the late 1960s most of the published research on political socialization was by Americans about Americans, and only a few shaky cross-national generalizations were made. Happily, however, the volume of research on socialization in Western European countries and some developing countries is growing, and the 1970s should produce a much firmer empirical base for general propositions about the process.

[38] See especially Fred I. Greenstein, *Children and Politics* (New Haven, Conn.: Yale University Press, 1965); and Robert Hess and Judith Torney, *The Development of Political Attitudes in Children* (Chicago: Aldine Publishing Company, 1967).

[39] Easton and Hess, "The Child's Political World," *Midwest Journal of Political Science,* 6 (August 1962), 229–246.

**TABLE 6**

**"Reasonably Accurate" Responses to Selected
Political-Information Items, by School Year**

| Information Asked | School Grade | | | | |
| --- | --- | --- | --- | --- | --- |
| | 4th | 5th | 6th | 7th | 8th |
| President's name | 96% | 97% | 90% | 99% | 100% |
| Mayor's name | 90 | 97 | 89 | 99 | 97 |
| President's duties | 23 | 33 | 44 | 65 | 66 |
| Mayor's duties | 35 | 42 | 50 | 66 | 67 |
| Governor's duties | 8 | 12 | 23 | 36 | 43 |
| Role of state legislature | 5 | 5 | 9 | 24 | 37 |
| N | 111 | 118 | 115 | 135 | 180 |

*Source:* Fred I. Greenstein, "The Benevolent Leader: Children's Images of Political Authority," *American Political Science Review,* 54 (December 1960), p. 937, Table 2.

considerably fewer than half the fourth-graders (average age nine) could say anything "reasonably accurate" about the more abstract and general matter of these and other public officials' *duties,* much higher proportions of eighth-graders (average age thirteen) could. This difference illustrates the proposition that political cognition in children generally develops from the individualized and personalized to the more general and abstract. The process continues, and by age fourteen children's political perceptions are nearly as sharp and as clear as they ever will be, and their affective responses to many political objects (for example, their party preferences) are well established.

*Adolescence*

Adolescence, according to the dictionary, is "the period of life from puberty to maturity terminating legally at the age of majority": that is, from age thirteen or fourteen (younger for girls) to age eighteen. Many secondary-school teachers say that the period starts "horribly" (eighth and ninth grades, consisting mainly of thirteen- and fourteen-year-olds, are said to be the most difficult of all to teach) but ends better. Parents say that no one knows what problems are until one has tried to live with an adolescent.

However that may be, students of political socialization do not entirely agree on how much and what sort of politically relevant attitudinal and behavioral change takes place in these years of general *Sturm und Drang.* One prominent view is that there is substantially less change in the political self between ages fifteen and eighteen than between ages eleven and fifteen.[40] Most psychologists believe that adolescence is the most painful and difficult period in general personality development: Sexuality emerges, the "silver cord" binding child to parents is severed, the first independent decisions are made, and so on. The psychic maladjustments often produced by these personal crises sometimes find political outlets, particularly in strong commitments to utopian proposals, both leftist *and* rightist, for sweeping away the corrupt

[40] Joseph Adelson and Robert P. O'Neil, "Growth of Political Ideals in Adolescence. The Sense of Community," *Journal of Personality and Social Psychology,* 4 (1966), 305–306.

**Generation gaps.** Source:
© 1970 Jules Feiffer.
Courtesy Publishers-Hall
Syndicate.

I THOUGHT I WAS LEFT.

UNTIL THE COLLEGE KIDS CAME ALONG.

I THOUGHT I WAS LEFT.

UNTIL THE HIGH SCHOOL KIDS CAME ALONG.

I THOUGHT I WAS LEFT.

UNTIL THE ELEMENTARY SCHOOL KIDS CAME ALONG.

I'M LEFT.

Political Systems and
Their Environments

92

institutions and hypocritical attitudes of the adult establishment and replacing them with a new society cleansed of war, greed, exploitation, racism, and all the other evils that adults perpetrate.

Yet studies of adolescent psychology suggest that only a small minority express their rebellion in active political ways—by becoming members of the Students for a Democratic Society or the Young Americans for Freedom, for example—though the politicized adolescent minority has been highly visible in recent years in Berkeley, New York, Ithaca, Madison, Paris, Rome, Tokyo, and a host of other university cities around the world.

## Adulthood

After reaching his majority the typical person acquires an ever-greater stake in his society and therefore in what government does or fails to do. He completes his formal education; takes a job or opens a business; marries; acquires a house, an automobile, a television set, and a lot of debts. As a result of these and other changes in his life, he becomes more politicized: He feels more concerned about political affairs; he knows more about them; his preferences grow more intense; his group affiliations (his party identification and ethnic or religious identification) become stronger and more salient; and he is more likely to vote and to participate in politics in other ways.[41]

For most people politicization in the adult years means intensification and activation of attitudes and preferences already acquired in childhood and adolescence. Typical adults do not, for example, switch their early party preferences; rather they move from being "independents" or "weak identifiers" toward the "strong identifier" end of the partisanship scale.[42]

Yet a small proportion of adults *do* switch their party preferences, ideological stances, even national loyalties. Such switches may result from changes in personal circumstances, as when a Democratic woman marries a Republican man and becomes a Republican to keep peace in the house (or to save her forensic ammunition for more important matters). Or switches may result from the shattering of earlier loyalties by cataclysmic political events, as when some German Jews and other Germans renounced their German citizenship after Adolf Hitler came to power. Such "switchers" seldom constitute more than a small fraction of the population, often cancel one another out with no net gain for any party or ideology, and usually have little political impact. But when they do constitute a relatively large fraction and move mainly in one direction, as when large numbers of Republicans became Democrats in the early 1930s, they can produce basic changes in the parties' electoral strengths and the nation's public policies.[43] After all, if only 5 percent of the 78 million American voters, a very small fraction of the electorate, were to abandon their traditional party loyalties, their 3.9 million votes (if all or most had changed from Democratic to Republican) could decide many presidential and congressional elections. Political

---

[41] Campbell, Converse, Miller, and Stokes, *The American Voter*, pp. 146–149, 324–327.

[42] Campbell, Converse, Miller, and Stokes, *The American Voter*, pp. 161–165.

[43] Campbell, Converse, Miller, and Stokes, *The American Voter*, pp. 149–160.

changes in adulthood have been important in the United States and elsewhere, and they can be again.

## Old Age

When does political old age begin? If the difference between frequent voting and frequent nonvoting is a meaningful boundary between some degree of active political life and none, then it appears that in the United States political old age begins in the early sixties. Voting studies show a steady increase in voter turnout at each higher age-level from twenty-one to about sixty-two and a decline thereafter.[44] This decline no doubt results partly from increasing physical infirmities, but it also suggests that the decline in general social and economic involvement (especially after retirement) produces some "depoliticization" that is the reciprocal of the increasing politicization of the young. Seventy-year-olds still vote substantially more than do twenty-five-year-olds but not as much as do people between thirty and sixty. And, though political socialization may still be taking place among "senior citizens," it is at a considerably reduced rate.

Thus end the Five Ages of (Political) Man.

## AGENTS OF SOCIALIZATION

We noted earlier that a person's political orientations and behavior patterns are not congenital or instinctive. They are learned. Political socialization, like all learning, is a process of interaction between the learner and certain elements of his human environment generally called "socializing agents." Among those to which political scientists have paid most heed are the family, school, peer groups, and the mass media.

## The Family

The nuclear family—particularly parents but also to some degree brothers and sisters —is for most people the most powerful single socializing agent. It is the first human group of which they become aware; during the psychologically crucial formative years from birth to age five or six they are in far closer contact with it than with any other group or social influence;[45] and the psychic pressures toward conformity in primary groups generally, which we discussed earlier in this chapter, are strongest of all in the family.

Thus it is not surprising that there is a widespread tendency for children's political attitudes, preferences, and levels of interest and activity to resemble those of their parents. The strength of parental political influence varies according to several

---

[44] Campbell, Converse, Miller, and Stokes, *The American Voter*, p. 494, Figure 17–1.

[45] One fascinating exception are the kibbutzim (collective settlements) of Israel, in most of which children are raised in special communal centers rather than in their parents' homes. Apparently the main political effects are that kibbutz children are more "ideological" and more like one another in their attitudes than are children raised in their parents' homes in the rest of Israel; see Leonard J. Fein, *Politics in Israel* (Boston: Little, Brown & Company, 1967), pp. 116–118, and the works cited there.

## TABLE 7
### Intergenerational Resemblance in Partisan Orientation, Politically Active and Inactive Homes, 1958

| Party Identification of Offspring | One or Both Parents Politically Active | | | Neither Parent Politically Active | | |
|---|---|---|---|---|---|---|
| | Both Parents Democrats | Both Parents Republicans | No Consistent Parental Partisanship | Both Parents Democrats | Both Parents Republicans | No Consistent Parental Partisanship |
| Strong Democrat | 50% | 5% | 21% | 40% | 6% | 20% |
| Weak Democrat | 29 | 9 | 26 | 36 | 11 | 15 |
| Independent | 12 | 13 | 26 | 19 | 16 | 26 |
| Weak Republican | 6 | 34 | 16 | 3 | 42 | 20 |
| Strong Republican | 2 | 37 | 10 | 1 | 24 | 12 |
| Apolitical | 1 | 2 | 1 | 1 | 1 | 7 |
| | 100% | 100% | 100% | 100% | 100% | 100% |
| N | 333 | 194 | 135 | 308 | 187 | 199 |

Source: Angus Campbell, Phillip E. Converse, Warren E. Miller, and Donald E. Stokes, *The American voter* (New York: John Wiley & Sons, Inc., 1960), p. 147, Table 7-1.

factors, as indicated by the data in Table 7. The table shows that parental influence is stronger in children from families in which both parents have the same party identification and weaker in those from politically divided families. It is stronger (see the boxed figures) when one or both parents have been openly interested in politics and have often discussed political questions with or at least in front of their children and weaker when the parents have shown no political interest or activity. When parental partisanship and interest are strong and visible, children are more likely to develop strong party identifications, more likely to have the same preferences as their parents, more likely to be interested in politics, and more likely to vote and participate in other ways.[46]

The strength of these factors, in turn, depends partly upon the society's and the parents' ideas about what kind of conversations (if any) parents should have with or in the presence of their children. For example, a well-known comparative study of French and American political attitudes has revealed, surprisingly, that Frenchmen are generally somewhat less emotionally involved in politics than are Americans. The authors believe that the explanation for this difference is suggested by the fact that, whereas 86 percent of the Americans could describe their fathers' party preferences and general political leanings, only 26 percent of the French respondents could say anything at all about their fathers' political *tendances*. Why this strikingly low figure? The French respondents explained it well with their frequent comments: "Il ne disait rien à ses enfants"; "il n'en parlait jamais."[47] If papa does not discuss politics with or in front of his children and if they do not know how he feels about politics, then

---

[46] It is interesting in this connection that studies of white radical college students in SDS and similar organizations show that the rebels' parents tend to have strong liberal ideologies and to be very politically interested and active. The children seem to be "going their parents one better," rather than rebelling against them. See Kenneth Keniston, *The Young Radicals* (New York: Harcourt Brace Jovanovich, Inc., 1968).

[47] Converse and Georges Dupeux, "Politicization of the Electorate in France and the United States," in Campbell, Converse, Miller, and Stokes, *Elections and the Political Order* (New York: John Wiley & Sons, Inc., 1966), pp. 279–281.

Political Culture and Socialization

the socialization process will be much more indirect and the family less influential in it. But even in France the family is still temporally the first and one of the more powerful of the socializing agents.

### School

All governments try to instill at least some political attitudes and behavior patterns in their citizens. All, for example, try to maximize national patriotism and obedience to law. Some (like the democratic systems of the West) try to encourage voter turnout and other forms of popular political participation. Others (like Francisco Franco's Spain) try to encourage the belief that political affairs are best left to those few who are especially qualified to rule.[48] Still others (like the Soviet Union and the People's Republic of China) try to encourage popular support of the leaders' policies by training every citizen as an "eager robot."

Whatever their objectives, governments rely heavily upon the public schools to implant the desired attitudes. For one thing, it is difficult to monitor and control what parents tell children.[49] For another, the public schools are organized, financed, staffed, and programmed by the government; children are required to attend school from ages five or six usually until middle adolescence. The schools thus provide the government's most effective direct channel for shaping their citizens' political attitudes and behavior while they are young and pliable.

Formal education is certainly powerful in developing children's political selves. Perhaps the best evidence is the nearly universal tendency, already noted, for the most educated people to have the strongest sense of political efficacy, to be the most politically interested and informed, and to take the most active roles in political affairs. Many people are indeed prone to regard education as the last and best hope for curing social ills; war, they say, will never disappear until people have been educated to understand its futility and horror, white racism will never disappear until white people are educated to recognize blacks as full equals, and so on. But formal education is certainly not an absolute, irresistible weapon for forming children's—or adults'—attitudes. When children hear one thing in school and quite another at home or from their playmates, there is no reason to think that they will believe teachers and textbooks rather than parents and peers. Wylie tells how the civics textbooks used in the school of his French village discoursed eloquently and at length on the democratic ideal of trust in others, the high mission of government, the important contributions of political parties, and so on. But, he writes, *outside* school the children

> constantly hear adults referring to Government as a source of evil and to the men who run it as instruments of evil. There is nothing personal in this belief. It does not concern one particular Government composed of one particular group

---

[48] Juan J. Linz, "An Authoritarian Regime: Spain," in Erik Allardt and Yrjo Littunen (eds), *Cleavages, Ideologies and Party Systems* (Turku: Westermarck Society, 1964), pp. 304–311.

[49] In the Soviet Union, indeed, "the family does act as an impediment to full and enthusiastic acceptance of the official system of beliefs, especially of those which stress militancy, total conformity, and instant adaptation to shifting official demands"; see Barghoorn, *Politics in the USSR,* p. 109.

of men. It concerns Government everywhere and at all times—French Governments, American Governments, Russian Governments, all Governments. Some are less bad than others, but all are essentially bad.[50]

In France as elsewhere schools and families working together would be a good deal more effective than is either working at cross-purposes with the other.

### Peer Groups

In addition to parents, siblings, and teachers, most people spend a great deal of their lives in the company of "peer groups"—of people outside their families who are approximately the same age and share similar statuses, problems, and concerns. Schoolmates are one obvious peer group, work associates another, friendship "cliques" yet another. What do we know about the role of such groups in political socialization?

We know at least that in developed societies like the United States and Sweden the socializing influence of parents and teachers begins to wane in early adolescence and that from then on peer groups become increasingly important influences on political attitudes and behavior.[51] As people grow older, some peer groups that were highly influential in their adolescence (for example, schoolmates, fraternity brothers, and perhaps radical student organizations) are superseded by others made salient by their new life circumstances: work associates, neighbors, and, above all, a husband or wife. One proof is the political homogeneity of various primary groups. Several studies of American voting behavior have revealed that the most politically homogeneous of all American groups, primary or secondary, are husband-wife pairs, followed fairly closely by friendship groups and then by groups of work associates.[52]

In primitive and traditional societies, on the other hand, most people have many fewer contacts and much less involvement with people outside their families, and such peer groups as they do have are relatively much less powerful socializing agents at any age than in the developed nations. It seems likely, however, that one significant effect—and cause—of "political modernization" in these societies will be

---

[50] Wylie, *Village in the Vaucluse,* p. 208. For a report of the relative ineffectiveness of American high-school civics courses in developing political interest and efficacy, see Kenneth P. Langton and M. Kent Jennings, "Political Socialization and the High School Civics Curriculum in the United States," *American Political Science Review,* 62 (September 1968), 852–867.

[51] James S. Coleman, *The Adolescent Society* (New York: The Free Press, 1961); Georg Karlsson, "Political Attitudes among Male Swedish Youths," *Acta Sociologica,* 3 (1958), 220–241; and Verba, *Small Groups and Political Behavior* (Princeton, N.J.: Princeton University Press, 1961), pp. 90–109.

[52] In 1952 the SRC asked their respondents the voting intentions of their spouses, their five best friends, and the people that they worked with. They found 90 percent of the husband-wife pairs in agreement, compared with 84 percent of the friendship groups and 77 percent of the groups of work associates; see Campbell, Gerald Gurin, and Miller, *The Voter Decides* (New York: Harper & Row, Publishers, 1954), p. 201, Table C.1. A study of voters in the 1948 election found comparable degrees of homogeneity among friendship and work-associate groups; see Bernard R. Berelson, Paul F. Lazarsfeld, and William N. McPhee, *Voting* (Chicago: University of Chicago Press, 1954), pp. 94–98.

a sharp decrease in the family's traditional near-monopoly of socialization and a concomitant increase in the influence of the schools, peer groups, and the mass media.

## Mass Media

In Chapter 6 we shall consider at some length how mass communications media (television, radio, newspapers, and so on) shape public opinion and its expression. Here we need note only that in all nations with technologically advanced mass communications the media play a direct role and a much greater indirect role (through "opinion leaders"; see Chap. 5) in shaping the basic orientations, as well as the specific opinions, of most people. They may play—or have the potential of playing—an even greater role in the developing nations, for there the media provide the best tool—better than the schools—for regimes that seek to change their citizens' traditional orientations and behavior. After all, schools affect mainly the young, but it may be deemed necessary to change adult orientations immediately without waiting for the new generation to take over. The mass media can reach the largest number of people—adults *and* children—in the shortest time. Leading illiterate masses out of their ancient ways into new ones is, at best, a tricky business, and the communicators must be careful not to attempt too sharp a break too quickly. But socialization through the mass media is the best short-run technique available, and many scholars —and leaders of developing nations—believe that it is crucial to political modernization.[53]

## POLITICAL SOCIALIZATION AND POLITICAL SYSTEMS

Every political system operates as it does largely because of the kind of people, elites and masses both, who make the demands, provide the supports, and constitute the targets for its outputs. Their basic beliefs about the way things are, their convictions about the way things should be, and their accustomed modes of political behavior all fix very real limits on whether or not and how government can achieve its goals— whether the goals are racial equality or apartheid, peace or world conquest, cutting taxes or putting men on the moon. People's beliefs and convictions are not congenital or instinctive; they are *learned* through the process that we call "political socialization." Some socializing agents, particularly the schools and the mass media, are directly controlled to some degree by governments in order to spread "desirable" attitudes and behavior patterns among their citizens. Other agents, particularly families and peer groups, are much freer from direct government control. Many families and peer groups thus preserve and pass on values and cognitions that differ significantly from those that governments want their people to absorb.

Political socialization is by no means a conservative, change-resistant, system-maintaining force in every political system in all circumstances. Some Western nations are like Norway and New Zealand in that almost all their citizens are strongly identified with them, approve of their political institutions, regard their authorities

[53] See Pye (ed.), *Communications and Political Development* (Princeton, N.J.: Princeton University Press, 1963).

and rules as entirely legitimate, and have no significant subculture to dispute the basic consensus. In such nations the governments' efforts at political socialization through the schools and mass media are reinforced by families and peer groups, which contribute significantly to the regimes' stability and resistance to change.[54]

Other Western nations resemble the United States and Great Britain: Most people identify with the nation and approve its institutions, but one or more significant subcultures (black separatists in the United States, Welsh and Scottish nationalists in Great Britain) sharply challenge majority attitudes and values. In these nations the families and peer groups of the alienated subcultures may operate their own socialization processes resisting those of the official schools and dominant media; if they are successful, their children will be more alienated and militant than the parents, and the stability and even survival of the system may be seriously jeopardized.

In some developing nations the elites that have led the drive against colonialism and now rule are determined to instill new national loyalties and new modes of political and economic behavior as soon as possible. Parents, village elders, tribal chiefs, and others may, however, resist the new ways. The young hear one thing at school and on the radio and quite another thing at home and from their peer groups. This conflict often produces great psychic tension and results in political unrest, regional and tribal separatism, perhaps even civil war.

However that may be, it is clear that "public opinion"—popular attitudes toward specific political issues, which we shall consider in Chapter 5—does not arise and take shape spontaneously. It is, in an important sense, *derived.* It consists of various people's reactions to political events and personalities. It is shaped and limited by the nation's political culture. And that culture consists in good part of the basic values and perceptions of reality acquired by its people during their lifelong political socialization.

[54] See Harry Eckstein, *A Theory of Stable Democracy* (Princeton, N.J.: Center of International Studies, 1961).

# III

# POLITICAL INPUTS

# 5

# PUBLIC
# OPINION

Most people in the Western world are accustomed to think that public opinion plays a significant role only in democracies. Yet this view is far too parochial. As one of the greatest political scientists of our time put it:

> Governments must concern themselves with the opinions of their citizens, if only to provide a basis for repression of disaffection. The persistent curiosity, and anxiety, of rulers about what their subjects say of them and their actions are chronicled in the histories of secret police. Measures to satisfy each curiosity by soundings of public opinion are often only an aspect of political persecution; they may also guide policies of persuasion calculated to convert discontent into cheerful acquiescence. And even in the least democratic regime opinion may influence the direction or tempo of substantive policy. Although a government may be erected on tyranny, to endure it needs the ungrudging support of substantial numbers of its people.[1]

For these reasons, in both democratic and dictatorial systems the cultivation of public opinion is a major preoccupation of most powerful political groups. In the democracies political parties, candidates, and pressure groups spend millions of dollars bombarding ordinary citizens with television "spots," billboard displays, newspaper advertisements, bumper-sticker slogans, and the like, all intended to nudge public opinion in the desired direction. A "public-relations counsel" sits at the elbow of many public figures, advising them how to cultivate "a good public image."

---

[1] V. O. Key, Jr., *Public Opinion and American Democracy* (New York: Alfred A. Knopf, 1961), p. 3.

Commercial polling organizations are hired by newspapers to issue frequent reports on how the public views the parties, candidates, and issues of the moment.

But dictatorial regimes are also vitally concerned with public opinion. Their ministries of propaganda (or "public education" or "public information") spend millions of dollars to whip up enthusiasm for the rulers' policies. And most use a variety of devices—including even public opinion polls—to learn how the masses feel about current policies and how they are likely to react to contemplated future policies. For the success of dictatorial rulers' policies depends very much upon whether the masses enthusiastically support and implement them, sullenly accept the necessity of going through the motions, or flatly refuse to carry them out except at gun point.

All government and most political actors thus treat public opinion as a mighty force. But exactly what *is* it? What forces shape it? How can we be sure what public opinion demands, permits, or prohibits on this or that matter of public policy? These questions have long fascinated students of politics, and in this chapter we shall review some of their findings.

## PUBLIC OPINION IN DEMOCRATIC SYSTEMS

As an introduction, let us sketch the opinion processes in an imaginary democracy and then call attention to some of their main characteristics. Let us imagine a New England town with a total citizenry of fifteen people. Members A, B, and C have farms on the town's north road and propose that the town pave it; A and B feel very strongly about it, but C is less worked up. D, E, and F, who own farms on the south road, feel discriminated against and oppose any such move, although F is less angry about it than the other two. G, H, and I are merchants who believe that paving the road will mean higher taxes, and they plan to oppose it—unless opposition means the loss of A, B, and C's business. J and K are widows living on income from real estate, and they too oppose the proposal because of the higher taxes it will bring, but they consider it unladylike to be too openly political. L and M, the town's odd-job men, own no farms, pay no real-estate taxes, dislike people who do, and could not care less about the whole matter. N and O, the town's ministers, have parishioners on both sides, find that no moral or religious issue is involved, and decide that it would be prudent to stay out of the fight.

At the town meeting A moves that the north road be paved. A, B, and C vote yes; D, E, F, G, H, I, J, and K vote no; L and M have not even bothered to attend the meeting; and N and O, though present, do not vote. A's motion is defeated, eight votes to three. Then A has an inspiration: He moves that *both* the north and south roads be paved and that one of them be officially named after the late husband of J. On this second proposal, A, B, and C again vote yes and are joined not only by D, E, and F but also by J and by N (the late Mr. J was one of N's favorite parishioners). Only G, H, I, and K vote against it, and the proposal carries by a vote of eight to four.

What can we say about "public opinion" in this imaginary democracy? For one thing, on neither issue did *all* the town's members express opinions. For another, not all the members of any side felt equally strongly about the matter. For yet another, when the first issue was replaced by the second, there was a reshuffling of the individuals composing the "pro" and "con" groups. Although both issues may be said to have been decided in accordance with "public opinion," it is inaccurate to picture the latter as a body of attitudes on all issues held by all fifteen members of the community constituting an entity known as *the* public. How, then, should we picture "public opinion" in this or any real-life situation?

## A DEFINITION

The nineteenth-century British politician Sir Robert Peel doubtless spoke for many of his confreres then and since when he referred to "that great compound of folly, weakness, prejudice, wrong feeling, right feeling, obstinacy, and newspaper paragraphs, which is called public opinion."[2] Most present-day political scientists would reject Sir Robert's rather pejorative definition, but they by no means agree on how public opinion should be defined.[3]

In this book we shall use V. O. Key's definition: "Public opinion consists of those opinions held by private persons which governments find it prudent to heed."[4] To elucidate a bit: A political *attitude* is a relatively general "set," or predisposition, toward a politically relevant class of objects, events, or behavior—for example, A's notion that "blacks are lazy and shiftless" or B's idea that "Whitey never gives the black man a decent chance to show what he can do." A political *opinion*, on the other hand, is a more specific view of what government should or should not do: for example, X's view that "the government should stop this immoral business of women getting abortions whenever they wish" or Y's view that "the government should provide free abortions for any woman who wants one." *Public Opinion* is the sum of all private opinions of which government officials in some measure are aware and which they take into account in determining their official actions.

According to this definition, then, public opinion is the cutting edge of a nation's political culture (see Chap. 4). It is, moreover, specific to particular political situations and issues; it is not a body of ideas on *all* issues held by *all* the members of the community known as *the* public. Each issue produces its particular constellation of opinion groups, always including one that expresses no opinion whatever (every "public opinion poll" on a political issue always discovers that some responses must be classified as "don't know" or "don't care"). From issue to issue there is always some reshuffling among the individuals composing the various opinion groups: some of the "pros" and "cons" on one issue reverse sides or become "don't cares" on the next, and some of the previous "don't cares" take sides.

## DIMENSIONS OF PUBLIC OPINION

Political scientists find it useful to think of public opinions as having two dimensions: *preference* and *intensity*. The preference dimension measures the property of being for

---

[2] Quoted in Bernard C. Hennessy, "Public Opinion and Opinion Change," in James A. Robinson (ed.), *Political Science Annual,* Vol. 1 (Indianapolis, Ind.: The Bobbs-Merrill Company, Inc., 1966), p. 245.

[3] For a survey of the most prominent current definitions, see Harwood L. Childs, *Public Opinion* (Princeton, N.J.: D. Van Nostrand Company, Inc., 1965), pp. 12–26.

[4] Key, *Public Opinion and American Democracy,* p. 14.

or against some party, candidate, or policy; the intensity dimension measures how strongly people feel about their preferences.[5] In terms of actual political conflict, each dimension is as important as the other: If 60 percent of the voters prefer George McGovern, 40 percent prefer Richard Nixon, and all feel strongly enough to vote, McGovern wins by a margin of three to two; but if only half the "McGovernites" and all the "Nixonites" care enough to vote, Nixon wins by a margin of four to three. History, indeed, records many victories of small but intensely motivated groups over larger but more apathetic oppositions.[6]

Political candidates and public officials thus need to know not only what people prefer but how strongly they prefer it. Academic opinion analysts try to measure these preferences by arraying them on scales, rather than lumping them into "pro" and "con" catchalls. For example, in 1972 the Survey Research Center of the University of Michigan asked a national sample of adult Americans this question: "Do you think the government in Washington should see to it that white and black children go to the same schools or stay out of this area as it is not its business?" Of 2420 respondents, only 43 failed to express an opinion. The opinions of the others were distributed as follows: 995 (41.9 percent) said the government should see to it that white and black children go to the same schools; 182 (7.6 percent) gave equivocal answers; 1200 (50.5 percent) said the government should stay out of this area as it is not its business.[7] Presented graphically, as in Figure 3, this range of opinion constitutes a classic example of what opinion analysts call a "U-shaped curve," which reveals a state of intense conflict. Most people have opinions, most of those who have opinions hold them strongly, and those who feel strongly are more or less evenly divided between the two extreme positions. Proposals for forced racial integration of the schools by the Federal government will thus be strongly pressed and hotly opposed, and the capacity of the political system to resolve the dispute peacefully will be taxed far more than if most persons were clustered in the middle categories of intensity and preference.

## SOME CHARACTERISTICS OF PUBLIC OPINION

Public opinion in a number of democratic systems has been studied intensively, and some of the principal findings are summarized here.

### Consensus and Conflict

Suppose that the 29,168,110 Americans who voted for McGovern in 1972 were all deeply convinced (as some no doubt were) that Nixon would ruin the nation. Surely

---

[5] See Robert E. Lane and David O. Sears, *Public Opinion* (Englewood Cliffs, N.J.: Prentice-Hall, Inc., 1964), pp. 6–9.

[6] The many difficulties that the intensity factor poses for such conceptions of majority rule as that presented in Chapter 13 of this book are discussed by, among others, Robert A. Dahl, *A Preface to Democratic Theory* (Chicago: University of Chicago Press, 1956); and Willmoore Kendall and George W. Carey, "The 'Intensity' Problem and Democratic Theory," *American Political Science Review*, 62 (March 1968), 5–24.

[7] These data have been furnished by the Inter-University Consortium for Political Research, which is based at the University of Michigan.

"Public opinion" is often pictured as the position held by a single, continuing body of people, "the public," on every issue.
Source: Herbert Block, *The Herblock Gallery* (New York: Simon and Schuster, Inc., 1968), p. 196.

"I'd hate to have him aiming at a small one"

"You go first, sonny, then point me toward him"

Public Opinion

FIGURE 3
A U-shaped curve of
opinion distribution on a
Federal imposition of
racial integration of the
schools, 1972 (percentage
base excludes those with
no opinion). Source:
Survey Research Center,
University of Michigan.

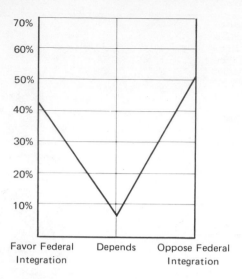

they would not quietly have permitted the disaster to happen? They would have launched a rebellion to save the United States by putting McGovern in Nixon's place. These suppositions are not entirely idle fancies. Armed rebellion against election winners is common in many nations: Venezuela, for example, became an independent republic in 1821, but the first freely elected president to serve his full term in office and to be succeeded by a freely elected successor was Romulo Betancourt (1959–1964) —138 years after the nation's birth. The 1973 overthrow of Chile's President Salvador Allende by a military coup ended a long history of peaceful acceptance of election results. Nor need Americans feel superior to the hot-blooded *latinos:* In 1860–1861 eleven southern states refused to accept the election of Abraham Lincoln, and the result was the bloodiest civil war in history.

Democracy requires that minorities peacefully accept the decisions of majorities, but such minority acquiescence depends partly upon majority forbearance: Majorities must not try to impose policies that minorities find so unbearable that they would rather fight, however hopelessly, than submit. For they may agree with the Mexican revolutionary leader Emiliano Zapata that "it is better to die on your feet than live on your knees." Thus democracy requires a substantial degree of *consensus* to limit conflicts and temper passions.[8]

If most political issues were to divide public opinion as reflected in the U-shaped curve shown in Figure 3, it is difficult to see how consensus could be maintained and democracy survive. But public opinion studies show that in fact a great many issues produce J-shaped curves of the sort shown in Figure 4, which makes clear that among Americans there is predominant opposition to the busing of school children for purposes of racial integration of schools.

Studies of public opinion in the United States and other democratic regimes have shown that the J curve reflects the consensus that exists on many political issues,

---

[8] For an extended exposition of this view, see Ranney and Kendall, *Democracy and the American Party System* (New York: Harcourt Brace Jovanovich, Inc., 1956), chap. 3.

**FIGURE 4**
A J-shaped curve of
opinion distribution on
the question "Where
would you place yourself
on this scale concerning
the question of whether
racial integration of
schools justifies busing
children to schools out
of their own neighbor-
hoods or whether letting
children go to their
neighborhood schools is
so important that busing
should be opposed?"
(Percentage base excludes
those with no opinion.)
Source: Survey Research
Center, University of
Michigan, 1972.

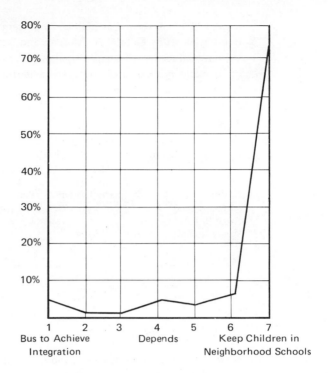

whereas the U curve reflects serious conflicts that are relatively rare. There is good reason to believe that democracy requires neither perfect consensus nor sharp conflict but rather conflict *within* consensus. Conflict without consensus means civil war, but consensus without conflict means no choices to be made, no public interest or partici- pation in politics, and social and political stagnation. As social theorist Talcott Par- sons has summed it up, in a healthy democracy, "divisive tendencies are controlled by being placed in the context of the hierarchy of solidarities . . . so that the cleavages that develop tend to be toned down and muted on their own level and referred to higher orders of integration for resolution."[9]

## Information

Studies of public opinion in the democratic nations have consistently shown that most citizens have little information on which to base their opinions. For example, in 1956 the SRC asked respondents' opinions on a variety of issues and then asked them to describe what the government was actually doing on each matter. The "no opinion" groups ranged from 10 to 30 percent of the sample; the groups holding opinions but unfamiliar with what the government was doing ranged from 10 to as high as 39 percent; and those who both held opinions and knew what actual govern-

---

[9] Talcott Parsons, " 'Voting' and the Equilibrium of the American Political System," in Eugene Burdick and Arthur J. Brodbeck (eds.), *American Voting Behavior* (New York: The Free Press, 1959), p. 100.

ment policy was ranged as high as 78 percent but fell as low as 45 percent.[10] In their five-nation study Gabriel A. Almond and Sidney Verba asked respondents to name the national leaders of the principal parties in each country and to identify the heads of as many ministries or executive departments as they could. The responses are tabulated by country in Table 8.

TABLE 8

Ability to Name Own Party's Leaders
and Governmental Ministers, by Nation[a]

| Nation | Named 4 or More Party Leaders | Named No Party Leader | Named 4 or More Ministers | Named No Minister |
|---|---|---|---|---|
| United States | 65% | 16% | 34% | 28% |
| Great Britain | 42 | 20 | 34 | 23 |
| West Germany | 69 | 12 | 40 | 20 |
| Italy | 36 | 40 | 23 | 53 |
| Mexico | 5 | 53 | 21 | 47 |

[a]Percentages are of total sample from each nation.

*Source:* Reprinted from Gabriel A. Almond and Sidney Verba, *The Civic Culture,* by permission of Princeton University Press. Table II, p. 96.

### Involvement and Sense of Efficacy

Many college students, teachers, and graduates are likely to cluck their tongues at the generally low level of information shown in Table 8. After all, they assume, politics is terribly important these days; even the most ordinary citizen in a democracy has the power to influence policy, and people must be pretty lazy or stupid or both to know as little as they do. But these assumptions are not necessarily justified. To a great many people politics is far less important than finding jobs, marrying, raising families, and other basic personal concerns. In any democratic system only a fraction of the citizens are highly involved in politics; most are only somewhat involved, and a fair proportion are involved little or not at all. For example, the 1960 American presidential election was the closest in this century. Yet when the SRC asked its respondents how interested they were in the outcome, only 38 percent replied "very much," and 25 percent replied "not much"; only 63 percent of the persons of voting age actually voted.

College people who study political science are especially apt to overlook this lack of interest. For them politics *is* interesting, and they acquire a lot of information, but not everyone is as interested and informed as they are. Public opinion studies have generally shown that the most educated people are the most involved politically mainly because they tend to have a stronger sense of political efficacy than do the less educated. That is, more of them believe that their opinions and votes are the determinants of public policy and that elections in particular and politics in general do matter a lot.[11]

---

[10] Angus Campbell, Philip E. Converse, Warren E. Miller, and Donald E. Stokes, *The American Voter* (New York: John Wiley & Sons, Inc., 1960), p. 174, Table 8–1.

[11] For evidence of this pattern in the United States, see Campbell, Converse, Miller, and Stokes, *The American Voter,* p. 479; for its operation in other nations, see Gabriel A. Almond and

## Stability and Change

One of the more puzzling traits of public opinion is that opinions on some questions seem to zig and zag almost overnight (for example, the metamorphosis of the Russians from our "gallant allies" in 1945 to our "godless enemies" in 1946), whereas on others it changes at a glacial pace, if at all (for example, note the high stability of party preferences discussed in Chap. 8).

Why the difference? Public opinion analysts find this question highly complex, and they are far from having a complete and definitive answer. Part of it, however, is the degree to which opinion is "structured." If the topic is one on which most people have held opinions for a long time, few are likely to change their views; other things being equal, the longer a person holds a view the more intensely he adheres to it.[12] On the other hand, if it is a new question, on which most people have no strong views, opinions will be more amenable to change. In the United States opinion on such long-standing and emotion-laden issues as legalizing abortion or Federal intervention to secure the rights of blacks will, in Key's metaphor, have "high viscosity" and flow into new channels turgidly if at all, whereas opinion on such new or generally unexciting issues as private ownership of communications satellites or fair-trade laws is likely to move and change more freely.[13]

## Latency

Political leaders regularly have to decide whether or not a contemplated action is politically safe. Often they can discern no clear public opinion on the question at the moment, and they are thus forced to estimate how the public will respond after action is taken. They must act, in political scientist Carl Friedrich's phrase, according to "the law of anticipated reactions." But estimating the nature and possible consequences of latent public opinion is exceedingly difficult. How many people now silent and unconcerned will become aroused if action is taken? Will most of them approve or disapprove? Will their concern flare up and then die away in a few weeks, or will it persist and grow stronger? Will they translate their feelings into votes for or against a particular party or leader, or will they give them no partisan interpretation? Even the best public opinion polls are poor instruments for estimating the potential degree and direction of latent opinions. But, though the opinion analyst can and should explore this difficult question slowly with ever more scientifically rigorous methods, the politician has to deal with it every day with whatever tools he has at hand. For latent public opinion may become active, and active public opinion is bound to provide some guidelines for, and set some limits on, what political leaders can do with political safety and effectiveness.[14]

---

Sidney Verba, *The Civic Culture* (Princeton, N.J.: Princeton University Press, 1963); chap. 6; and Seymour Martin Lipset, *Political Man* (New York: Doubleday & Company, Inc., 1960), chap. 6.

[12] For the operation of this principle in the intensification of party identifications, see Campbell, Converse, Miller, and Stokes, *The American Voter*, pp. 161–164.

[13] Key, *Public Opinion and American Democracy*, pp. 235–242.

[14] Key, *Public Opinion and American Democracy*, pp. 282–287.

# PUBLIC OPINION POLLS AND OPINION MEASUREMENT

## THE PROBLEM OF MEASURING PUBLIC OPINION

Many people in many lands have long been interested in discovering what public opinion on various issues is. Even in the Soviet Union (as we shall see later), the Communist party must be aware of mass opinion at any given moment in order to determine how far ahead of that opinion its policies may go. Its "agitprop" apparatus thus has the job of measuring, as well as of molding, public opinion.

The problem of measuring public opinion has been of much greater concern in the more democratic regimes. Ideal democracy, after all, means government acting in accordance with the desires of popular majorities. If genuine democracy is to be approximated, there must be some way of learning how popular majorities feel about political issues; if the government does not and cannot know those feelings, it can hardly act in accordance with them.

Some democratic philosophers, most notably Jean Jacques Rousseau, have dreamed of a "plebiscitary" democracy, in which the majority will on each and every issue is always clear and determines through some kind of continuous machinery whatever action the government takes. No actual democratic system, including the famed New England town meetings and the Swiss cantonal Landsgemeinden, has ever been organized along these lines. The principal official devices for sounding public opinion in modern democracies have been either indirect and periodic, like representation and elections, or direct and intermittent, like the initiative and referendum (all these devices are described in Chaps. 7 and 14).

Modern social science has developed a device that some theorists believe capable of both direct and continual measurement of public opinion—the "sample survey" or "public opinion poll." No government has yet adopted such polls as part of its official policy-making apparatus (although many government agencies conduct polls to learn "how the land lies"), but polls have come to occupy a central position in the analysis and measurement of public opinion. I shall therefore conclude this description of the opinion process in the democracies by describing the nature, techniques, problems, and role of public opinion polls.

## THE NATURE OF PUBLIC OPINION POLLS

### What Is a Public Opinion Poll?

In the broadest sense of the term, a public opinion poll is any effort to ascertain public opinion on a question by directly asking some members of the public what they think and taking the views of this "sample" to represent what the whole public ("population" is the accepted technical term) thinks. In this broad sense it includes everything from conducting elections and referenda to asking friends or passersby on the street.

The term is, however, most generally used for a particular kind of procedure: determining the views of a scientifically-selected cross section and taking them to represent the views of the whole public. Polls in this sense are conducted by commercial pollsters all over the world, including such famous firms as the American Institute of Public Opinion (headed by George Gallup), Louis Harris and Associates, Roper Research Associates, and Sindlinger and Company.[15] Many European and Asian nations have similar firms, and some of the most distinguished work is done by academic survey organizations like the Survey Research Center of The University of Michigan (SRC) and the National Opinion Research Center of The University of Chicago (NORC).

### Straw Votes: The Polls' Predecessors[16]

As early as 1824 a Pennsylvania newspaper sent some of its reporters to ask voters how they intended to vote in that year's presidential election. Ever since then newspapers and magazines have tried to sound opinion, especially on elections, by sending out reporters or mailing questionnaires to their subscribers or the general public. In most of these "straw votes" no particular effort has been made to question a representative cross section of the public, and those who have conducted straw votes have relied mainly upon obtaining as large a number of respondents as possible to ensure accuracy. Most of these surveys register opinion only within a particular area, and few are extended to the entire nation.

Perhaps the best known of all the straw votes, however, was national in scope. From 1916 through 1936 *Literary Digest* magazine investigated public opinion not only on the outcome of presidential elections but also on a number of other political issues. It mailed ballots to its subscribers, to people listed in telephone directories, and to automobile owners. By the 1930s the magazine was mailing more than 20 million ballots in election years and receiving more than 5 million answers—a truly enormous "sample." By means of this procedure it was able to predict correctly the outcome of all the presidential elections between 1916 and 1932, and its success was one of the major reasons for its wide circulation. In 1936, however, the magazine predicted, on the basis of its poll, that Governor Alfred M. Landon of Kansas, the Republican candidate, would win with 59 percent of the popular vote and 370 electoral votes; in the actual election he lost by a landslide, receiving only 37 percent of the popular vote and a mere 8 electoral votes. The failure of the *Digest* by so wide a margin made the magazine a national laughingstock, and in less than a year it went out of business altogether.

### Development of Representative-Sample Surveys

The method of sounding public opinion by interviewing small but carefully selected representative samples of the public has been used in consumer research and marketing since the early 1920s. It was first applied to the measurement of political opinions on a national scale by Gallup in 1934; in 1935 he founded the American Institute of Public Opinion. At about the same time two other pollsters, Elmo B. Roper, Jr., and

---

[15] A useful, though somewhat outdated, description of the chief American polling firms that work in politics (forty-two in all) is presented in *Congressional Quarterly*, May 3, 1968, pp. 992–1000.

[16] See Claude E. Robinson, *Straw Votes. A Study in Political Prediction* (New York: Columbia University Press, 1932).

Archibald Crossley, launched similar operations. The 1936 election that witnessed the collapse of the *Literary Digest* poll also saw the emergence and first popular success of the new-style pollsters. The latter not only correctly predicted the outcome of that election; they also explained publicly, in advance, that the *Digest* would fail because its sample was heavily overloaded with upper-income people attached to the Republican party, whereas their own samples, though much smaller than that of the *Digest,* represented each voting group in its proper proportion. The combination of their success in predicting the election outcome and the plausibility of their basic approach launched the new polls, and, with a few setbacks here and there (notably in the 1948 presidential election), they have flourished ever since.

At present more than twenty democratic nations have private organizations that conduct public opinion polls with the Gallup techniques. Most are actually affiliated with the American Institute of Public Opinion and are often called the "British Gallup Poll," the "Norwegian Gallup poll," and so on. Most are also members of the World Association for Public Opinion Research.

Polls have developed farthest in the United States, where they have become big business. The commercial polling organizations together now gross more than $100 million a year. Most of their research is concentrated on consumer and marketing problems, on contract for manufacturers, and the results are not published. Part of their revenue, however, comes from polling opinion on political questions and selling the results to newspapers, and it is this aspect of the polls that most of us know. Private polling has also become an important campaigning device for political parties and candidates at the national and state levels and in many local communities as well. Both the Democratic and Republican national committees use public opinion experts to analyze published polls and to conduct private ones; the polls and analyses of Louis Harris played a key role in the strategy and success of John F. Kennedy's drive for the Democratic nomination and the presidency in 1960.[17]

In addition to the commercial polls, others are operated by universities for the purpose of studying the process of opinion formation. Some government agencies also conduct polls to sound public opinion on policies and operations. The most extensive of them has been made by the Department of Agriculture, which has a Division of Special Surveys in its Bureau of Agricultural Economics; the division is charged with investigating public opinion on farm problems, farm programs, and related issues. Polling was also used extensively by the Office of War Information in World War II to check on the success of its propaganda program.[18]

## HOW THE POLLS WORK[19]

There is some variation in detail in the procedures used by the various polling

---

[17] See Lewis A. Dexter, "The Use of Public Opinion Polls by Political Party Organizations," *Public Opinion Quarterly,* 18 (Spring 1954), 53–61; and Theodore H. White, *The Making of the President, 1960* (New York: Pocket Books, Inc., 1961), *passim.*

[18] H. H. Remmers, *Introduction to Opinion and Attitude Measurement* (New York: Harper & Row, Publishers, 1954), chap. 9.

[19] A useful short introductory manual is Charles H. Backstrom and Gerald D. Hursh, *Survey Research* (Evanston, Ill.: Northwestern University Press, 1963).

organizations, but they all follow the same four basic procedures and the same basic principles.

### Drawing the Sample

The polls operate on the basic premise that the opinions of a properly drawn sample may be regarded, within certain well-established margins of "sampling error," as close to the opinions of the entire population. The utility of a sample is determined not by its size but by its *representativeness:* a relatively small sample that is truly representative of the population is far more useful than a much larger one that, like the one selected by the *Literary Digest,* is not representative. The first step in conducting a poll, therefore, is to draw a representative sample of relatively few individuals. The Gallup and Harris polls, for example, use national samples of only 1500–5000 people out of a national voting-age population of 140 million.[20]

The particular members of the sample are usually selected by one or a combination of the following two procedures.

**Stratified Quota Sampling**    The pollsters select certain characteristics of the population—like sex, age, size of community of residence, income, and so on—and construct their samples so that each characteristic appears in the sample proportionally as often as it does in the population. The difficulty with this method is that it assumes that the particular characteristics selected play significant roles in shaping opinions when they may not at all. More and more pollsters are therefore using the second procedure.

**Probability Sampling**    The objective in drawing a probability sample is to ensure that every member of the population has as good a chance of being selected as has every other member; there will then be no "systematic bias" in any particular direction or directions. This procedure involves a number of operations too technical to be described here, but it is fair to say that they are all aimed at making the selection of sample members as truly random as possible.

### Phrasing the Questions

The next step is to phrase the questions that respondents will be asked. The main object is to avoid "leading questions," for they are bound to influence the answers and thus distort whatever picture of public opinion emerges. The problem of designing the right kind of questions has received a great deal of attention from pollsters, and although it has not yet been perfectly solved most pollsters agree that considerable progress has been made.

---

[20] The final Gallup poll in the 1972 presidential election was based on an initial sample of nearly 5000 respondents weeded by the Gallup organization to a total of 3500 "likely voters": *The Gallup Opinion Index*, December 1972, p. 9.

### Obtaining the Answers

The next step is to obtain answers from the respondents. Sometimes pollsters use mailed questionnaires, by far the cheapest method. The most effective method, however, is personal interviews, preferably face to face but sometimes by telephone. The Gallup organization, for example, normally employs 250–300 interviewers in a national poll, a ratio of one interviewer to each 15–20 respondents. Interviewing of this sort requires certain special skills, for it is necessary to avoid all "interviewer bias"— distortion of answers because of the effect of the interviewer's personality on the respondent, the latter's desire to impress the interviewer, and so on. Considerable study of proper interviewing techniques has been made, and most interviewers are trained in these techniques before they are sent out.

### Coding and Interpreting Answers

Ideally all answers should be tabulated so that each person's opinion on a particular issue can be treated as a mathematical unit equivalent to every other person's opinion on that issue, for only such units can be analyzed and manipulated statistically. Answers to yes-or-no questions or to questions about preferences among political parties and candidates are thus the easiest with which to deal. Answers to questions about issues are usually ranged along scales, allowing for variations between the two extreme answers on each question. The actual coding, sorting, and interpreting process has been greatly expedited by the use of card-punch machines and electronic computers, which are now generally used at this stage of the operation.

## SOME QUESTIONS ABOUT POLLS

For many years the polls have been the subject of a great deal of discussion, not only by social scientists but by the general public as well. Although they have won acceptance and approval in most quarters, they are still somewhat controversial and have both critics and defenders. The debate appears to center on three main questions.

### How Accurate Are They?

Perhaps the most frequent question about polls is whether or not they accurately report public opinion on the questions with which they deal. So far no entirely satisfactory method has been developed to check the accuracy of their reports of public opinion on "issues"—questions of whether the government should follow this or that policy. Preelection polls, however, have the great advantage of being checkable by actual election returns; and, although such unpredictable factors as the weather on election day may influence the actual voting figures, most people believe that the best method yet developed for checking the accuracy of polls in general is to examine their record in predicting the popular vote in elections.

By this standard, then, how accurate are the polls? Their record in predicting the outcomes of American presidential elections is shown in Table 9. The major polls have correctly forecast the outcomes of nine of the ten presidential elections since they were established, and all failed to predict President Harry S. Truman's reelection

**TABLE 9**

**The Record of the Presidential Polls**

| Year | Actual Democratic Vote | Gallup Poll | Harris Poll | Yankelovich Poll | Roper Poll | Crossley Poll |
|------|------------------------|-------------|-------------|------------------|------------|---------------|
| 1936 | 60.2% | 53.8% | — | — | 61.7% | 53.8% |
| 1940 | 54.7 | 55.0 | — | — | 55.2 | — |
| 1944 | 53.8 | 53.3 | — | — | 53.6 | 52.0 |
| 1948 | 49.4 | 44.5 | — | — | 37.1 | 44.8 |
| 1952 | 45.0 | 46.0 | — | — | 43.0 | 47.0 |
| 1956 | 42.0 | 40.5 | — | — | 40.0 | — |
| 1960 | 49.4 | 49.0 | — | — | 47.0 | — |
| 1964 | 61.3 | 61.0 | — | — | — | — |
| 1968 | 42.7 | 40.0 | 43.0 | — | — | — |
| 1972 | 37.5 | 38.0 | 39.0 | 40.0 | — | — |

*Source:* The figures for 1936–1960 are reprinted by permission from James MacGregor Burns and Jack Walter Peltason, *Government by the People:* The Dynamics of American national, state, and local government © 1963. Reprinted by permission of Prentice-Hall, Inc., Englewood Cliffs, New Jersey. Figures for 1964, are added by the author.

**The failure of the polls in 1948 lowered their prestige only temporarily.**
Source: *The Herblock Book* (Boston: The Beacon Press, 1952).

*"Now, about predictions for next year——"*

in 1948—a failure that has received about as much publicity as all their correct predictions together.

Most observers agree that on this and other evidence the record of the polls in predicting election results has been very good indeed and far better than that of straw votes or of the hunches of politicians and political commentators. Some of the polls' critics, however, argue that success in predicting election results is no sign that polls are equally capable of revealing public opinion on issues. They charge that in dealing

Public Opinion

with issues polls are subject to two great limitations. First, they have no entirely satisfactory way to measure the *intensity* of respondents' opinions. This deficiency is crucial, the critics believe, for intensity is a very important factor in determining the outcome of conflict among groups holding different opinions. The pollsters are aware of this problem and have improved their methods for dealing with it (see pp. 112–116). The second limitation, according to the critics, is the *irresponsibility* of respondents' opinions. People may give one answer to a question when they know that the only likely result is the addition of one more unit to a polling organization's punch cards and quite another when they know that their answers will have a direct and immediate impact upon policy formation and political events. The interview situation is thus artificial, and opinions expressed may or may not correspond closely with respondents' real opinions. Pollsters also recognize this difficulty, which they believe is even more difficult to overcome than that of measuring intensity; but they agree that it is not insoluble.

### How Much Influence Do They Have?

Ever since modern pollsters began to achieve their present prominence and prestige people have asked just how much influence the polls actually exert on the policy-making process. There are two main aspects of this problem. First, do public officials read poll results and make policy accordingly? There is every reason to believe that most public officials do read the results, but there is little direct evidence on whether or not what they read influences what they do. Such evidence as there is suggests that poll results are for many public officials one, but by no means the only, factor influencing their decisions (see Chap. 15).[21] Second, do poll results exert a "bandwagon" effect on the voters? Do many undecided or weakly committed voters read preelection polls and decide that they might as well be on the winning side? Again there is little direct evidence, but what there is suggests that any such effect operates on a negligible proportion of the voting public.[22]

### How Much Influence Should They Have?

Next to the question of the polls' accuracy the question most often raised asks how much influence they *should* have on the formation of public policy. Some pollsters

---

[21] They are probably used most in planning electoral strategy. For example, the British prime minister, as we shall see in Chapter 7, has the power to order a general election at any time within five years from the date of the previous election. After the Labour party's victory in the 1966 election Prime Minister Harold Wilson reportedly watched the polls continuously to check on his government's popularity. They showed a steady deterioration until late in 1969, when Labour's popularity began to rise. By late May 1970, the polls showed Labour again in the lead, and Wilson ordered the election held in June. But the polls were wrong and he had miscalculated, for his Conservative opponents won the election. These events touched off a British debate about the accuracy and proper uses of the polls strikingly similar to that stimulated in the United States by the polls' failure to predict correctly the outcome of the 1948 presidential election.

[22] During the 1968 election there were charges that the Gallup, Harris, and other published polls were being deliberately manipulated to influence public opinion and election outcomes. For a refutation of these charges, see Archibald M. Crossley and Helen M. Crossley, "Polling in 1968," *Public Opinion Quarterly*, 33 (Spring 1969), 1–16.

argue that they should have great influence. Indeed, Gallup has argued that polls have made possible a sort of continuous national "town meeting" and that public officials should be guided by what they reveal about public opinion on the issues before government.[23] Some critics, notably political scientist Lindsay Rogers, have argued that such a national town meeting is neither possible nor desirable. Not only are the polls inaccurate and misleading, Rogers insisted, but also the whole idea of direct democracy is nonsense in a modern nation because of the great complexity of the problems its government faces and because of the ignorance of its rank and file.[24]

Most political scientists consider both views too extreme. They believe that polls are here to stay, not as the key element of democratic government machinery but as a valuable aid in grappling with one of government's most vexing perennial problems: finding out what the public wants its government to do so that government can respond. The problem is so difficult, in fact, that public officials in the democratic systems must sometimes envy the policy makers in the more dictatorial regimes like the USSR. After all, harried democratic leaders must sometimes sigh, *those* fellows don't have to worry about public opinion; they can just go ahead and do whatever has to be done with never a thought to its popularity. But can they? We shall spend the remainder of this chapter finding out.

## PUBLIC OPINION IN THE USSR

### PUBLIC OPINION IN COMMUNIST IDEOLOGY

#### Relations between the Party and the Masses

According to communist ideology, democracy is government *for* the people (the proletarian masses): policies are made by the Communist party for the benefit of the masses, and approval of those policies by the masses is a desirable but secondary consideration (see Chap. 13). The elite character of the party is openly and proudly proclaimed by Communist leaders, and they confine party membership to the small segment of the population they consider most "class-conscious," intelligent, and skilled in the principles of Marxism-Leninism. The present membership of the Communist Party of the Soviet Union (CPSU) includes about 9 percent of the total adult population.[25]

According to communism's great prophet, N. Lenin, the party must avoid two equally grave mistakes: adopting only those policies that accord exactly with existing mass opinion and pursuing policies that go so far beyond what the masses can understand and accept that they become unenforceable. The proper object for the party, said Lenin, is to make policies far enough ahead of mass feelings to induce progress yet not so far ahead that they cannot be enforced.

[23] George Gallup, *Public Opinion in a Democracy* (Princeton, N.J.: Princeton University, 1938), p. 15.

[24] Lindsay Rogers, *The Pollsters* (New York: Alfred A. Knopf, 1949).

[25] John A. Armstrong, *Ideology, Politics, and Government in the Soviet Union* (3d ed.; New York: Frederick A. Praeger, Inc., 1974), p. 56.

The task of the CPSU and its agents is therefore twofold: to gauge mass sentiment in order to learn what policies are possible at any given moment and to mold public opinion so that ever more "advanced" policies become possible. We shall examine in a moment the agencies that have been developed to accomplish these tasks.

### Samokritika and Party Policy

People in the West sometimes mistakenly think of the Soviet Union as a place in which no public critical or adverse comment on government policies or officials is ever made. Not only is this picture misleading; it also overlooks the peculiar communist institution of *samokritika* ("self-criticism"), defined by the Soviet *Political Dictionary* as "exposing the deficiencies and errors in the work of particular persons, organizations, and institutions on the basis of a free, businesslike discussion by the toilers of all the problems of economic-political life . . . [and] developing the ability to see, to uncover, to acknowledge one's mistakes and to learn from them."[26]

All communist leaders, from Lenin to Kosygin and Brezhnev, have stressed the desirability of *samokritika*. As it actually operates, this institution permits—indeed, encourages—*certain kinds* of public criticism. No one, for example, is permitted to attack the basic structure of the communist regime itself, to oppose any basic party policy, or to criticize top party leaders, for criticisms of this sort presumably give aid and comfort to the "enemies of the people" and are therefore treasonable. Accordingly, no criticism of the Presidium of the Central Committee of the CPSU or any attack upon the essentials—as distinct from the details—of any major policy has ever been published or broadcast in any official medium.[27]

The permissible targets for open public criticism consist mainly of the errors of minor and intermediate public officials and the details of policy and administration. For example, ordinary workers at a collective farm would not be permitted to argue publicly that the whole idea of collective farms is bad, but they are encouraged to publicize a view that their farm's manager is inefficient, that the farm is not fulfilling its quotas, or that some of their fellow workers are not working hard enough.[28] The main channels for such permissible criticisms are letters to the editor and editorials in newspapers, articles in journals, and satirical cartoons.

Party leaders often take note of these criticisms and sometimes change policy

---

[26] Quoted in Alex Inkeles, *Public Opinion in Soviet Russia* (Cambridge, Mass.: Harvard University Press, 1950), p. 197. Although outdated in some respects, this work is still the leading analysis of public opinion processes in the Soviet Union.

[27] John N. Hazard, *The Soviet System of Government* (4th ed.; Chicago: University of Chicago Press, 1968), p. 59. There is, however, a small but courageous group of Soviet notables who have openly criticized the regime through unofficial media. The most notable examples are the distinguished physicist Andrei Sakharov and the Nobel prize-winning novelist Alexander Solzhenitsyn, who in early 1974 was exiled and stripped of his Soviet citizenship for his persistent and outspoken criticisms.

[28] For a typical list of criticisms recently published in *Izvestia,* see L. G. Churchward, *Contemporary Soviet Government* (London: Routledge & Kegan Paul, Ltd., 1968), p. 113.

*"About three more men and we would have large-scale production."*

*"Comrade Chairman, the tractors are ready to work."*

*"Fine, the spare parts are over there in the stall."*

details or administrative practices and personnel as a result. On a few occasions the party has even permitted public discussion of policy essentials. Two notable examples are the public debates in the 1940s on the merits of the laws relating to marriage, divorce, and abortion and of the staggered five-day week.[29] For the most part, however, the objects of *samokritika* are limited to lesser officials and to the details and execution of party policies.

## THE AGITATION-PROPAGANDA OPERATION

### Communist Conceptions

For reasons already mentioned, Communist leaders place great emphasis on indoctrinating the masses with "correct" political attitudes in order to generate enthusiastic support for party policies. In organizing its indoctrination activities, the CPSU distinguishes sharply between "agitation" and "propaganda" (a fact that escapes most noncommunist political analysts). "Propaganda," as Communists use the term, means indoctrination of party members and nonparty intellectuals in the principles of Marxism-Leninism. It involves lengthy discussions and considerable reading and is aimed only at those whom the party considers eligible to join the proletarian elite. "Agitation," on the other hand, means presenting a few simple ideas to the masses as dramatically as possible in order to inspire them to behave as the party wishes. The ideas are kept few and simple because of the Communist conviction that the masses cannot comprehend and respond to very many or complex ideas.

### Techniques of Mass Indoctrination

The entire enormous program of political indoctrination is operated, not by the regular state schools, but by a party agency: the Propaganda-and-Agitation Section

---

[29] J. A. Brown, Jr., "Public Opinion in the Soviet Union," *Russian Review,* 9 (January 1950), 37–44. See also Merle Fainsod, *How Russia Is Ruled* (rev. ed.; Cambridge, Mass.: Harvard University Press, 1963), pp. 211–212.

of the central Secretariat operating under the Central Committee of the CPSU. The Section has a subsection, or "sector," responsible for propaganda, another for agitation, another for "mass work" among youth groups and trade unions, and so on. It also administers the various communications media and supervises the execution of their agitation missions.[30]

**Bolshevik Agitators**   The communists believe that face-to-face communication is more effective than are the mass media in bringing about desired attitudes in the masses. Consequently the Communists have relied more heavily upon their agitation apparatus than upon the mass media. There are now well more than 3 million "Bolshevik agitators," a ratio of about one agitator to every sixty-five adults. These agitators are picked by the party from its rank and file, the most promising members of the Komsomol (the Communist youth organization), and nonparty intellectuals. Agitation is considered one of the most valuable services that one can render to the party; to be chosen as an agitator is thus a high honor. The party tries to place at least one agitator in every government agency, factory, collective farm, military unit, and so on. He is charged with explaining party policies to the nonparty masses in his particular agency, whipping up enthusiasm for these policies, and reporting to his superiors on the kind of reception that policies receive and the general attitudes of the masses with whom he has contact. The main technique of the agitator is to lead "discussions" with his fellow workers, but he is also expected to convince them by his own example, as well as by words. For instance, if the party decides that all tractor factories must increase output 10 percent, the agitators in those factories are expected to increase their own personal output and thus to provide a good example for their coworkers. If some workers in the discussions organized by the agitators grumble, "Increasing our output is all well and good, but how can we do it as long as we have to bother with the red tape our manager insists on?" the agitators are expected to report this complaint to their superiors. Bolshevik agitators are thus both "educators" of the masses and reporters of mass opinion.

**Newspapers**   Although the communists rely most heavily upon agitation, they also use the media of mass communications, especially newspapers. The number of newspapers and their total circulation have increased enormously in Soviet Russia since czarist days; they now cover just about every part of the Soviet Union. The two greatest national papers, from which all regional and local newspapers take not only their general direction but also much of the specific material they print, are *Pravda* (the official organ of the Central Committee of the party) and *Izvestia* (the official organ of the Supreme Soviet, the formal national governing body).

The task of the Soviet press, of course, is not to "present the news" in any Western sense of the term but rather to explain and arouse enthusiasm for party policies and to serve as a channel for *samokritika*. The latter function is accomplished mainly through letters-to-the-editor columns, which occupy considerable space in every Soviet newspaper. Agitation is performed through exhortations to the masses and, above all, through reporting news and events inside and outside the Soviet Union

[30] Armstrong, *Ideology, Politics, and Government in the Soviet Union,* pp. 77–79.

in such a way as to construct the picture of the world that the party leaders wish the masses to have. A director of the TASS news agency put the matter very succinctly: "News is agitation by means of facts."[31]

**Radio** Most people on this side of the iron curtain think of a radio as a receiving apparatus with no direct or exclusive connection to any particular broadcasting station and capable of receiving signals from a number of different broadcasting stations. The owner of the set therefore has some option about which programs he listens to. "Radio" does not mean that to most Russians. More than 80 percent of the radio receivers in the Soviet Union are wired directly to particular broadcasting transmitters and can receive signals only from those transmitters. Most people with receivers therefore have access to only one set of programs. The receivers are located not only in homes but also in such public gathering places as communal dwellings and dormitories, factories, barracks, offices, public squares, and the like. The content of the programs, closely controlled by the party, consists of such "cultural" material as symphonic music and such "educational" material as "news" and political comment, instruction in technical matters and political ideology, sports, and literary and dramatic programs, all of which are used to promote communist political ideas.

**Motion Pictures** The other prominent medium of mass communication—motion pictures—is used largely for political, technical, and cultural instruction and not for "entertainment" in the Western sense.

## CONTRASTS BETWEEN DEMOCRATIC AND COMMUNIST SYSTEMS

Public opinion of a sort does exist in the USSR, as it does in any dictatorial system. The essential differences between such opinion and the processes by which it is formed and their counterparts in the democratic systems consist in the different roles of government in the two regimes.

In the democratic nations, as we shall see, governments (people who hold public office) are simultaneously both participants in the policy-making process with preferences of their own and the agencies that determine and register the outcomes of contests over public policy among all competing groups. Government is therefore only one of the political groups that have access to the media of communication, and its policy preferences are by no means the only ones in circulation. Its desires are not the only factor that directly and powerfully influences public policy.

In the communist regimes, on the other hand, the government has a legal monopoly over all the media of mass communications and also a great many advantages in controlling face-to-face contact. The only issues that are genuinely controversial, therefore, are those on which the government allows controversy. Only on these issues can public opinion in anything like the democratic sense be said to exist.

Despite their monopoly of mass communcations media, however, leaders in the Soviet Union and other communist nations have not been able to mold the masses'

---

[31] N. G. Palgunov, quoted in Frederick C. Barghoorn, *Politics in the USSR* (Boston: Little, Brown & Company, 1966), p. 115.

*"I think I may say, without fear of contradiction . . ."*

views exactly to their own liking. Even Joseph Stalin had to yield to the Russian peasants' stubborn anticollectivism to the extent of allowing them to cultivate some privately owned plots. The considerable resistance to the Red Guards' Mao-inspired savaging of "bourgeois revisionist" citizens and ideas in the People's Republic of China in the late 1960s showed that in twenty years of communist rule Chairman Mao's thoughts, as published in the *Little Red Book,* still had not captured the Chinese mass mind as he had intended. Popular resistance to Moscow-dominated regimes in Hungary in 1956 and in Czechoslovakia in 1968–1969 demonstrated that public opinion in both nations was in opposition to what party leaders had tried to impose.

In the communist nations as in the democracies, then, it is clear that the mass communications media are not the only channels by which ideas can be transmitted effectively enough to take root and influence politics significantly. In the next chapter we shall review the main channels of modern political communication and assess their strengths, limitations, and relative impacts on the formation of public opinion.

# 6

---

# COMMUNICATION
# AND
# POLITICS

To some Americans the most frightening book published in 1969 was *The Selling of the President 1968*.[1] Its author, newspaperman Joe McGinniss, relates in chatty detail how some advertising agencies and television sales experts "packaged" and "sold" Richard Nixon to the American people in the 1968 presidential election.[2] As McGinniss describes these experts' assessment, the main problem was Nixon's pre-1968 "image" as a cold, square, slightly shifty politician on the make. They sought to change this image into a new one of a serious, friendly, experienced, firm but not fanatical statesman who could be relied on to cool the nation's passions, restore law and order to its streets, and extricate us from the mess in Vietnam. In the words of former Republican National Chairman Leonard Hall, "You sell your candidates and your programs the way a business sells its products."[3]

Of course, many people would argue that the Democrats tried to do the same thing for Hubert Humphrey but failed. Few potential contributors of funds thought that Humphrey could win, and many were still angry about the Democratic national convention. The Humphrey campaign was run on a shoestring and could not begin to match the slick professionalism of the Nixon campaign.

Judging from the reactions to McGinniss' book, some Americans are politically frightened and morally repelled by the implicit political message that advertising,

---

[1] Joe McGinniss, *The Selling of the President 1968* (New York: Trident Press, 1969).

[2] The agencies were Fuller & Smith & Ross, Inc., and Feeley & Wheeler, and the "advertising creative director" was Henry Treleaven, then on leave from his post as chief media director of the J. Walter Thompson advertising agency.

[3] Quoted in McGinniss, *The Selling of the President 1968*, p. 27.

especially on television, is an absolute weapon for controlling people's minds and can be used to sell a presidential candidate just as irresistibly as it can sell a toothpaste or a deodorant. Were we officers or stockholders in an advertising agency, any of us might be willing to have everyone else believe that we sold such absolute weapons. But as students of political science we are obliged to ask, *is it true?*

The answer, based on many scholarly studies of the impact of advertising, mass communications, political campaigns, and related topics is neither yes nor no but *it depends.* After all, Nixon's well-financed campaign in the two-way race of 1960 yielded 34,108,157 votes, or 49.5 percent of the total, for a narrow loss; in the three-way race of 1968 the campaign McGinniss describes yielded 31,785,480 votes, or 43.4 percent of the total, for a narrow win. And Nixon's campaign of 1972, which used television and other communications gimmicks less than either of its two predecessors, yielded 47,165,234 votes, or 60.7 percent of the total, for a landslide victory. What are we to make of this? It is hard to believe that any truly "absolute" weapon will produce a near-miss one time, a glancing hit the next, and a shot right to the bull's-eye the next when it is used at less than full power. The fact is that political advertising on television is one element, but only one element, in a much broader communications network, and its effectiveness, like that of any political communication, depends not only upon how well "spots" and "talk shows" are produced but also upon what candidate is being "sold" against what opposition to what electorate under what circumstances.

Even more repellent to democratic values were the "dirty tricks" of forgery and sabotage used by the Committee to Reelect the President to discredit the presidential campaigns of Edmund Muskie and George McGovern in 1972. But even they are regarded by most observers as having had relatively little effect upon the November results.[4]

In the pages to follow we shall examine what social scientists have learned about the nature and interrelations of the principal elements of political communication; and it may be that when we have finished, McGinniss' message and CREP's "dirty tricks" will seem, if not less repulsive, at least less frightening.

## THE NATURE OF POLITICAL COMMUNICATION

### COMMUNICATION, SOCIETY, AND POLITICS

Communication is the transmission of meaning through the use of symbols. It is the process by which a person or group tries to make another person or group aware of its feelings about a particular matter. In this broad sense communication occurs in many different ways—through pictures, music, mathematical symbols, gestures, facial expressions, even physical blows. The most common form of communication in

---

[4] Theodore H. White, for example, estimates that, had the full facts of the scandal been known prior to election day, they would have swung at most 3 or 4 million voters from Nixon to McGovern, and Nixon would have won handily even so: *The Making of the President, 1972* (New York: Bantam Books, Inc., 1973), pp. 399–400. At the time he wrote, of course, White, like most Americans, did not know the full facts of President Nixon's participation in the "coverup."

human society, however, is the system of oral and written verbal symbols that we call "language."

Communication is the basic social process. A "society," after all, is an aggregation of human beings who in some fashion live together and act collectively to promote their common interests. If they cannot or do not communicate with each other in any way, they can neither become aware of their common interests nor act to promote them. So the equation is simple: no communication, no society.

Certainly communication plays a significant role in politics and in the process of forming political opinion, for it is the basic medium through which political groups are formed and seek to influence public policy.[5] That some people are rich and others poor, for example, has no political significance in itself. By talking and reading, however, poor people learn that some of their fellows are also poor but others are not; they learn that they are members of a particular economic group different from and, to some extent, opposed to another economic group. After talking and reading some members of each group decide that they want the government to follow policies favorable to their interests. And through talking and reading—and perhaps also through cartoons, billboards, protest marches, and other nonverbal means—they try to induce public officials to adopt those policies.

Communication, in short, is the main catalytic agent by which the social and psychological characteristics of men are applied to the dynamic processes of political conflict.

## ELEMENTS OF POLITICAL COMMUNICATION

The nature and role of political communication are most easily understood through separate consideration of its constituent elements.

### The Communicator

All groups that consciously try to influence government policy—and some that have no such conscious purpose—are political communicators. The main types of such communicators in the modern democracies are political parties and pressure groups, whose organization and activities are described in Chapters 9 and 10. Many government agencies in many democracies, however, also try to influence the opinions of those outside the formal structure of government. Several national agencies in the United States government, for example, maintain "public relations" or "public information" bureaus which print and distribute pamphlets, send out speakers, and otherwise try to create public support for their programs. In the USSR (see Chap. 5) such programs are a major activity of government, which has a monopoly of all the media of mass communication and tries to achieve control of all face-to-face communications as well.

---

[5] Political scientist Karl W. Deutsch has developed a stimulating "cybernetic" model of political systems as communications structures in *The Nerves of Government* (New York: The Free Press, 1963). This model is a special political application of a general social theory advanced by mathematician Norbert Wiener, *Cybernetics* (2d ed.: New York: John Wiley & Sons, Inc., 1961).

## The Message: Propaganda versus Education

Every political communicator has a message—a series of communications intended to induce others to adopt opinions favorable to his goals. Much of the social science literature on communications has concentrated upon this particular aspect, and the distinction between propaganda and education has been heavily emphasized.

The term "propaganda" was first used in the seventeenth century to describe a new effort by the Roman Catholic Church to "propagate" its faith; in 1622 Pope Gregory XV created the College of Propaganda, a committee of cardinals. The term retained its largely religious connotations until World War I, when it not only took on a mainly political meaning but also acquired, in the minds of a great many Americans, odious moral connotations because of the efforts of each side, particularly the Allies, to influence the American attitude toward the war. Since that time many people have thought of propaganda as a certain *way* of influencing opinions—a way marked by such reprehensible practices as selecting and distorting facts, using emotional rather than rational and logical appeals, and discouraging critical examination of the content of the message. People who use the term in this fashion generally contrast it with education, which they regard as the presentation of the whole truth solely for the general benefit of the whole society rather than for the selfish benefit of the "educator."

Many present-day students of political communication, however, have largely abandoned this distinction. They believe that "propaganda" has become merely an epithet and "education" a "God-word," that "propaganda" has come to mean communications by a group of whose objectives one does not approve and "education" communications by a group that one likes. Such students speak only of "communications" and not of "propaganda" or "education."

## Transmitters, Receivers, and Responses

The message must be transmitted to receivers if it is to have any political significance, and in a later section of this chapter we shall deal with the nature, organization, and relative effectiveness of the most prominent communications media in the democracies.

The receivers of any particular message by any particular communicator through a particular medium do not involve all members of the community. Who the receivers are significantly influences the political effects of any communication. Receivers' responses reflect these effects upon attitudes and actions, effects that, as we shall see, vary greatly from situation to situation.

## THE MEDIA OF POLITICAL COMMUNICATION

The media of political communication are usually divided into two categories: mass media, in which each message is aimed at large numbers of receivers and involves no face-to-face contact between communicator and receivers, and "face-to-face" media, which carry messages to only a few receivers at a time, with direct contact between communicators and receivers. Let us review the status of each type in modern nations.

## Newspapers

In dictatorial systems like the Soviet Union all mass media, including newspapers, are government-owned and -operated monopolies used to persuade the masses to support government policies with enthusiasm. In democracies a few newspapers, like *L'Humanité* of Paris, are owned and operated by political parties, mainly as agencies for drumming up electoral support. Most newspapers, however, are privately owned and operated and are run mainly for the same purpose that every other kind of private business is run: to make profits for their owners.

In the United States newspapers obtain their revenue partly from subscriptions but mainly from advertising, which accounts for 65–90 percent of their total income. Increased circulation is therefore a prime goal of all American papers, for it not only brings in more direct revenue but also attracts more advertisers. This necessity inclines editors to print material they think will interest readers and not unduly offend present and potential advertisers. No newspaper that is not a rich man's plaything or the "house organ" of a political party can afford to print only what its editors think readers ought to read; it must print what they think readers want to read, and this necessity plays a great part in determining what is regarded as news.[6] In addition to news, most papers print substantial numbers of "features"—comics, recipes, fashion notes, bridge columns, and so on.

Most newspapers also print material avowedly intended to influence the political opinions of their readers, mainly in the form of unsigned editorials and signed political "columns." The evidence suggests that such material is considerably less than irresistible to readers. In both the United States and Great Britain, for example, almost every voter regularly reads a newspaper, and the great majority of American and British newspapers editorially favor the Republican and Conservative parties, respectively; yet the Democratic and Labour parties, despite their usual lack of editorial support (the 1964 American presidential election was a major exception), continue to win their share of the elections.

We should not, however, leap to the conclusion that newspapers have *no* significant influence on public opinion. Many observers believe that most people obtain their notions of what is going on in politics mainly from what they read in the news columns of their newspapers and that these notions fix the basic direction of their opinions. Although readers may not be impressed or convinced by editorials arguing that an incumbent governor is a great man and should be reelected, they may well be impressed by news stories describing corruption and inefficiency in the administration and draw conclusions quite different from those that the editors intend. The effect of newspapers on public opinion is no less powerful when it comes indirectly through news stories rather than directly through editorials.

Newspapers have a larger audience than any of the other mass media. In the

---

[6] For several illuminating empirical studies of how newspapers decide what is and is not news, see Lewis Anthony Dexter and David Manning White (eds.), *People, Society, and Mass Communications* (New York: The Free Press, 1964), pp. 141–199.

United States, for example, approximately 90 percent of all adults regularly read at least some part of a daily newspaper. For basic economic reasons the largest number of newspapers and the largest audiences are found in nations with the highest rates of per capita wealth, industrial development, and literacy.[7] More than 80 percent of the total newspaper circulation in the entire world is in Europe and North America.

Since World War I there has been a marked trend toward increased concentration of newspaper ownership and control in all the democracies and particularly in the United States. Although in the United States total circulation has greatly increased in this period, the total number of newspapers has significantly decreased from more than 2600 daily publications in 1909 to 1792 in 1973. In 1909 nearly 700 American cities had two or more competing dailies each, but by 1960 the number had fallen to 61 cities. By the mid-1960s, more than 40 percent of all readers of daily newspapers had no locally published competitive paper as an alternative, and more than 95 percent of all American newspapers faced no local competition.[8] Some newspapers have gone out of business, others have merged, and "chain" newspapers (newspapers in different cities owned and operated by one national firm like the Scripps-Howard, Hearst, and Freedom chains) have spread. Some observers fear that a continuing decline in newspaper competition will make it impossible for proponents of all competing points of view to have access to this important communications medium and will thus seriously cripple the free circulation of ideas that democracy requires. Most people, however, think that this concentration of ownership and control has not yet gone far enough to create a "clear and present danger."[9]

### Television and Radio

The United States is the only nation in which most radio and television broadcasting is privately owned and operated. Not that broadcasters in the United States have a completely free hand: The Federal Communications Commission (FCC) closely regulates both kinds of broadcasting, using its licensing power as its main instrument. Every broadcasting station must obtain an FCC license before it can operate, and each license comes up for renewal approximately every three years. In order to qualify for a new or renewed license the broadcaster is supposed to comply with a number of FCC standards and rules. Perhaps the most famous political rule is the section of the Communications Act of 1934 that requires any station which grants free time to one political party to give equal free time to all opposing parties. A station may, however, *sell* to any party whatever time the party can afford without furnishing the opposition with free equal time. The FCC also controls such matters as the operating frequency and power of broadcasting stations, their legal and financial relations with the net-

---

[7] Richard R. Fagen, *Politics and Communication* (Boston: Little, Brown & Company, 1966), p. 58, Table IV.1, reports the following positive correlations between nations' gross national product per capita and levels of mass-media development: radio receivers per 1000 population .85, daily newspaper circulation per 1000 population .80, television sets per 1000 population .75, per capita attendance at movies .65.

[8] Theodore Peterson, Jay W. Jensen, and William L. Rivers, *The Mass Media and Modern Society* (New York: Holt, Rinehart and Winston, Inc., 1965), pp. 66–67.

[9] See Peterson, Jensen, and Rivers, *The Mass Media and Modern Society,* pp. 67–68.

works, the proportions of "live" and "recorded" material presented, and the like. It has exercised little if any direct political censorship, but it has had some (though not enough, according to its critics) effect upon the content of programs and upon the financial and legal structure of the broadcasting industry.[10]

In the other democracies some or all of the radio and television stations are owned and operated by the government. In Denmark, for example, all broadcasting is conducted by a government-owned and -operated monopoly. In Sweden broadcasting is also controlled by a monopoly but one in which both the government and private interests participate. The systems of greatest interest to most Americans, however, are probably those in France, Great Britain, and Canada.

In France, as in Denmark, all radio and television broadcasting is a government monopoly. Since the early 1960s it has been administered by the Office de Radiodiffusion-Télévision Française. The ORTF is supervised by the Ministry of Information, and its director general and his principal assistants are directly appointed—and removable—by the government. Almost every French household now has a radio, and television now reaches about 90 percent of the population. Opponents of President Charles de Gaulle (1958–1969) frequently charged that during referendum and election campaigns he took unfair advantage of his official position to give himself and his supporters the lion's share of broadcasting time. In the 1967 parliamentary election, for example, ORTF allocated 50 percent of available broadcast time to the candidates of the Gaullist majority and 50 percent to those of "the opposition"— meaning that the various parties opposing de Gaulle for a variety of reasons had to divide their half several ways and that no one opposition candidate had nearly as much time as did his government opponent. How much this allocation helped Gaullist causes and candidates is a matter for speculation, but under the regime of Georges Pompidou, after de Gaulle's resignation in 1969, political broadcasting time was allocated somewhat more evenly.[11]

Great Britain has a mixture of publicly and privately owned broadcasting. The British Broadcasting Corporation (BBC) was chartered as a "public corporation" by the government in 1927 but is not itself directly owned or controlled by the government as are its Danish and French counterparts. Its board of governors is appointed by the Queen on the advice of the Prime Minister, but its members are not "political" in the partisan sense, and they make policy without direct supervision by any regular government agency. Every owner of a radio or television set must purchase a license from the post office, and the revenue is returned to the BBC. The rest of BBC revenue comes from the sale of its weekly publication, *Radio Times.* Most BBC programs are planned and broadcast centrally and relayed over a series of local and regional stations, although some local and regional variations in programming are permitted. In general the programs of the BBC are designed with relatively less concern for what viewers and listeners want and more concern for what broadcasters think they should have than in the United States.

---

[10] Murray Edelman, *The Licensing of Radio Services in the United States, 1927 to 1947* (Urbana, Ill.: University of Illinois Press, 1950).

[11] See the succinct and informative discussion in Henry W. Ehrmann, *Politics in France* (Boston: Little, Brown & Company, 1968), pp. 161–168.

In 1954 Parliament authorized private television (but not radio) broadcasting for commercial profit. It established a body somewhat comparable to the American FCC, the Independent Television Authority. The ITA owns and operates the transmitting stations, but the programs are produced by private companies under contract to the ITA. There are now fifteen such companies, most of them organized on regional bases. Some are controlled by motion-picture interests, others by newspapers, and others by general investors. Advertisers do not directly sponsor programs as in the United States but purchase time between programs when series of advertisements are broadcast—singing commercials and all.[12]

In the 1959 general election the BBC and ITA jointly proposed to the three leading parties that the time available for party-controlled telecasts be divided four parts for Conservatives, four for Labour, and one for Liberals (presumably reflecting the parties' respective strengths); the parties accepted. In the 1964, 1966, and 1970 general elections the ratio was changed to 5:5:3, reflecting increased Liberal strength. In all four campaigns each party prepared its own broadcasts for its allotted times. The BBC and ITA also put on their own forums, interviews, and other political broadcasts and tried—not entirely to the satisfaction of party leaders—to divide the attention they gave to candidates and programs according to the same formula. There were some complaints about inequities in 1959, considerably more in 1964, but relatively few in 1966, 1970, and 1974. This British variation on the familiar "equal time" rule now appears to be well established and likely to continue for some time to come.[13]

The Canadian system is an interesting hybrid of American, British, and European practices.[14] The Canadian Broadcasting Corporation (CBC) was created and is periodically renewed by direct acts of Parliament, the most recent being the Broadcasting Act of 1968. Consequently, the Canadian Parliament directly controls the CBC's finances, whereas the British Parliament has no such control over the BBC's finances. The CBC used to be supported by receiver license fees on the British model, but since the 1950s it has been financed by a combination of commercial revenue and annual parliamentary grants and loans. Privately owned broadcasting stations also exist and are licensed and regulated by an entirely separate agency, the Canadian Radio-Television Commission (CRTC), which is analogous to the American FCC. These arrangements result in three parallel and separate broadcasting groups: the CBC's national network, the privately-owned CTV national network, and a number of independent private stations. Some of the latter are affiliates of the CBC, use some CBC programs at no cost, and the CBC shares in any commercial revenues raised by

---

[12] A concise description of the British system of broadcasting is given in *Britain, An Official Handbook, 1964* (London: Central Office of Information, 1964), pp. 480–488.

[13] For details, see the chapters on television and radio in David E. Butler and Richard Rose, *The British General Election of 1959* (New York: St. Martin's Press, Inc., 1960), chap. 7; Butler and Anthony King, *The British General Election of 1964* (New York: St. Martin's Press, Inc., 1965), chap. 10; Butler and King, *The British General Election of 1966* (New York: St. Martin's Press, Inc., 1966) chap. 7; and Butler and Michael Pinto-Duschinsky, *The British General Election of 1970* (New York: St. Martin's Press, Inc., 1971), chap. 9.

[14] I am grateful to Mr. T. J. Allard, Executive Vice-President of the Canadian Association of Broadcasters, for providing the information in this paragraph.

the stations in connection with CBC programs. The net result is that, although the Canadian system was originally fashioned on the British model, it now more nearly resembles the American: the CBC somewhat resembles our Public Broadcasting System, and the CRTC more closely resembles our FCC.

As are newspapers, radio and television are most concentrated in the wealthier and more literate nations. Since the early 1920s there has been a tremendous increase in the area reached by radio and in the size of its audience. For instance, in the United States, only 300,000 households had radio sets in 1922; over 60 million households had sets in 1970. In 1922 there were only 286 broadcasting stations; in 1972 there were 4422 commercial AM stations and 2468 commercial FM stations.[15] The other Western democracies have not quite achieved these figures, but they too have enjoyed greatly increased radio coverage since the early 1920s. And in recent years there has also been an enormous increase in radio coverage in the developing nations of Africa, Asia, and Latin America.

Even more striking has been the phenomenal growth in television coverage since the early 1950s, greater in the United States than elsewhere but also great in Western European nations. At the end of World War II television was still mainly a laboratory plaything. By 1972 almost every American family lived in an area in which television signals could be received, and 96 percent of all households had television sets.[16] In 1950 there were 107 TV broadcasting stations, but in 1972 the number had risen to 774 commercial stations and 227 educational stations.[17] The growth of television, however, has not driven radio out of business. In the other democratic nations television has not yet expanded as much as it has in the United States, and in those nations radio is still an important medium. Even in the United States, daytime radio has continued to be popular and only evening radio has lost most of its audience and therefore most of its commercially sponsored programs.

The proportion of time given to the presentation of news and political commentary is somewhat smaller in the United States than in other democratic countries, but nowhere is it more than about 10 percent of total broadcasting time. Radio and television nevertheless play significant roles in the formation of political opinion. Several studies have shown that whereas more people read parts of daily newspapers than listen regularly to radio or watch television, the latter media receive considerably more total hours of attention per day than do the newspapers. These studies also reveal that most people trust the accuracy and impartiality of news presentation on radio and television more than they trust what they read in their newspapers. The two electronic communications media, accordingly, are important sources of popular ideas about world affairs and as such have a powerful impact upon the formation of public opinion.

---

[15] *The American Almanac, 1974* (The Statistical Abstract of the United States, prepared by the Bureau of the Census; New York: Grosset & Dunlap, Inc., 1974), p. 497, Table 809.

[16] *The American Almanac, 1974,* p. 499, Table 814.

[17] *The American Almanac, 1974,* p. 497, Table 809.

In all the democracies motion pictures are produced mainly by private firms, although government agencies occasionally issue "documentary" films. Only in the dictatorial regimes is all film production monopolized by the governments. In the democracies, however, the movie business not only is regulated in its financial and organizational aspects but also is subject to greater censorship than are newspapers and broadcasting. Some of this censorship is self-imposed (in the United States in the form of the industry's famous rating system)[18] and some is imposed by various national and local government agencies. Both types of censorship are intended mainly to prevent the showing of "obscene" and "salacious" material; there is little direct political censorship.

The movie industry in the United States is by far the largest in the world. It has a capital investment of more than $3 billion and employs more than 185,000 people. American films are widely shown outside the United States: about half the feature films shown in Europe, Central and South America, and Africa are made in the United States, although the American share of these film markets is declining.

In the United States and other nations where television has expanded rapidly the movies have been hit almost as hard as radio. Surveys by the United Nations Economic, Social and Cultural Organization in the 1960s revealed that in such nations movie audiences had declined slowly but steadily and fewer feature films were being made. Furthermore, as audiences declined, they also became younger; it is now estimated that considerably more than half are teen-agers and more than 70 percent under the age of thirty.[19] In most developing nations, on the other hand, the movies have held and even expanded their audiences, which continue to be larger than those for any other medium except newspapers and radio.

Even more than radio and television programs the movies produced in the democracies are intended to entertain audiences and to make money for their producers, rather than to sell particular political points of view. Direct and obvious political propaganda in movies is therefore relatively rare, although it is more common and more overt in the growing number of "adult films." Not that movies have no effect whatever upon the political opinions of those who watch them: Most observers agree that the reality perceptions of many moviegoers are strongly affected by what they see, and that these perceptions in turn powerfully influence political attitudes. Perhaps the most striking illustration of this point is the impact of American movies upon attitudes toward the United States in the foreign nations where they are shown. The picture of American life and society presented in Hollywood's products is, indeed, almost the only direct source of information about the United States that citizens of many nations have. This thought may make American readers shudder, especially as most of the exported films are "situation comedies," but there seems little doubt of its truth. Some people complain that the rather optimistic picture of

---

[18] Since 1968 the Motion Picture Association of America has classified each film as "G" (recommended for general audiences), "PG" (recommended for people over the age of sixteen), "R" (people under sixteen admitted only when accompanied by an adult), and "X" (people under sixteen not admitted at all).

[19] Peterson, Jensen, and Rivers, *The Mass Media and Modern Society*, pp. 127–128, 131.

American life usually painted by such movies is infantile and politically misleading, and they sometimes argue that "the movies should be more like life." Others reply: "Nonsense. Life should be more like the movies!"

## The Minor Media

The other mass communications media are minor in the sense that they make regular contact with far smaller proportions of the population than do newspapers, broadcasting, and motion pictures. Magazines have the largest audience of any of these media, followed by books (which are read by about 30 percent of the adult population of the United States), pamphlets, billboards, posters in buses and trains, the "legitimate" theater, and so on. The influence of the minor media on politics, however, is probably greater than the size of their audience suggests. Books and magazines, for example, are most heavily "consumed" by those whom the social psychologists call "opinion leaders" (see below). Nevertheless, none of these media has either the audience or the general impact of the three major mass media.

## FACE-TO-FACE MEDIA

### General Nature

We have noted that every person belongs to a number of primary groups composed of people with whom he regularly has direct contact: his family, his work associates, his schoolmates, his lodge brothers, members of his congregation, and the like. Over a generation ago social psychologists Kurt Lewin and Muzafer Sherif launched a study of the effects of membership in such groups upon formation of opinions, and a considerable body of generalizations based on empirical studies of specific groups has subsequently been developed. For our purpose the most significant of these generalizations can be summarized here.[20]

Every member of a primary group is subject to various pressures to conform his opinions to those of his associates. For one thing, he is likely to read the same newspaper, watch the same television programs, and see the same movies as do his fellows, and his reality perceptions thus tend to be the same as theirs. For another, he may dread being regarded as "bullheaded" or "weird" by his associates. Whenever he expresses an opinion contrary to those of his associates, some of them may try to "set him straight," and he may learn that the price of clinging to his views is the cessation of friendly relations with other members of his group—a price most people are unwilling to pay. Face-to-face communications thus exert a powerful influence upon the political reality notions, values, and preferences of most of us.

---

[20] See the discussion of primary-group influences on opinion in Chapter 4. See also Kurt Lewin, *A Dynamic Theory of Personality* (New York: McGraw-Hill, Inc., 1935); and Muzafer Sherif, "An Experimental Approach to the Study of Attitudes," *Sociometry,* 1 (1937), 90–98.

## Opinion Leaders and the Two-Step Flow of Communication

In their pioneer sample survey study of social influences on voting behavior in the 1940 American presidential election, Paul F. Lazarsfeld, Bernard Berelson, and Hazel Gaudet found that most people described personal conversations with family and friends rather than what they had read or heard in the mass media. This finding led the investigators to formulate the theory, now widely accepted by social scientists, that the mass media have their main impact on public opinion and political behavior *indirectly* through the mediation of "opinion leaders" in a "two-step flow" of communication. In the investigators' words:

> In every social group there are some individuals who are particularly active and articulate. They are more sensitive than others to the interests of their group, and more anxious to express themselves on important issues. . . . We found that one of the functions of opinion leaders is to mediate between the mass media and other people in their groups. It is commonly assumed that individuals obtain their information directly from newspapers, radio, and other media. Our findings, however, did not bear this out. The majority of people acquired much of their information and many of their ideas through personal contacts with the opinion leaders in their groups. These latter individuals, in turn, exposed themselves relatively more than others to the mass media. The two-step flow of information is of obvious practical importance for any study of propaganda.[21]

Many subsequent studies have elaborated and refined this theory. It has been found, for example, that in most primary groups particular opinion leaders are influential on particular topics but not on every topic of interest to the groups. For example, one group member may be influential on matters of fashion and dress, another on sports, another on television programs, another on politics, and so on. The political "influential" reads, listens, and talks more about politics than do the others, but on nonpolitical matters he is likely to be one of those influenced rather than influential.

What traits distinguish political opinion leaders from other group members? In most respects they are "superrepresentatives" of their groups; that is, they are typical of the group members in socioeconomic status, education, and attitudes. They differ from the others mainly in that they are more involved politically; they therefore "consume" more of the mass media's political content, have more facts and figures at their fingertips, and are more eager to initiate political discussions. Their special influence, like that of opinion leaders on other topics, results mainly from their greater initiative and knowledge, but it operates within a context of their commitment to the group's basic values and goals. In many respects, then, they are unofficial, self-selected democratic analogues to the Bolshevik agitators described in Chapter 5.[22]

The process of political communication is a two-step flow. First, the mass media

---

[21] Paul F. Lazarsfeld, Bernard Berelson, and Hazel Gaudet, *The People's Choice* (2d ed.; New York: Columbia University Press, 1948), pp. xxii–xxiii.

[22] For summaries of early research on opinion leaders, see Elihu Katz, "The Two-Step Flow of Communication: An Up-to-Date Report on an Hypothesis," *Public Opinion Quarterly,* 21 (1957), 61–78; and Katz and Lazarsfeld, *Personal Influence* (New York: The Free Press, 1955).

broadcast their political messages to a largely unreceptive audience far more interested in relaxation and entertainment than in politics, but the signals come through loud
and clear to a small, attentive public of political opinion leaders. Second, the political
opinion leaders pass on the messages—or revised versions of them—by means of
personal conversation around the dinner table, at the shop, or across the back fence.
The influence of any mass communications medium on public opinion therefore
cannot be measured merely by determining the size of its audience. It is equally
important to know who is in the audience.

## THE EFFECTS OF COMMUNICATION[23]

Most students of communications systems and the sociopolitical environments in
which they operate have concluded that their interrelations are best viewed as a
"two-way street": Communication affects environment, and environment conditions
communication. Although we are mainly interested here in the effects of communication upon societies and their governments, we should bear in mind that societies and
governments also shape the nature and effects of mass and face-to-face
communication.[24]

### EFFECTS OF THE ENVIRONMENT ON COMMUNICATION

#### Communicators' Bosses

No newspaper editor, television producer, or director of any other mass communications medium is entirely his own boss, consulting only his conscience about what
messages he should beam, to whom, and how. Most work for other people and must
perforce use their technical skills to achieve their bosses' goals above their own.

In trying to understand the communications system of any nation it is thus
important to know who pays the piper, for they will surely call the tunes. The United
States and the Soviet Union offer instructive examples. Theodore Peterson, Jay W.
Jensen, .and William L. Rivers correctly point out:

> The mass media in America are business, whether big or little; they are, as
> George Gerbner has said, "the cultural arm of American industry." That is the
> primary fact about the mass media in the United States, oriented as they are to
> marketing. One must understand that fact to grasp the essential meaning of the
> media and their relationship to the American social order. A similar understand-
> ing is necessary for analysis of the Soviet communication system. To grasp the
> essential meaning of the Soviet mass media and their relationship to Communist

---

[23] In this section I have drawn heavily on Joseph T. Klapper's excellent summary of many
empirical studies, *The Effects of Mass Communication* (New York: The Free Press, 1960).

[24] This point of view is emphasized by, among others, Klapper, *The Effects of Mass Communication;*
Berelson, "Communications and Public Opinion," in Wilbur Schramm (ed.), *The Process and Effects
of Mass Communication* (Urbana, Ill.: University of Illinois Press, 1954), pp. 342–356; and V. O. Key,
Jr., *Public Opinion and American Democracy* (New York: Alfred A. Knopf, 1961), chap. 15.

society, one must first recognize that the Soviet communication system is an arm of the political order, as it is in any authoritarian society.[25]

Despite their many differences, then, both the American and Soviet communications systems operate to preserve their respective political and social orders. To sell the largest possible amount of goods, business-directed American media operators generally tiptoe around controversial subjects that might offend potential customers and make them tune out. The American media heavily emphasize entertainment within generally accepted ideas of what "turns people on"; they aim to give customers what they want, rather than what media directors think they ought to have. The Soviet party-directed media operators select subjects and treatments that seem best calculated to "sell" the party's policies and to foster "correct socialist attitudes"; they aim to give the masses what the party thinks is good for them, rather than what the masses, in their ideological backwardness, might want. In both nations, then, the managers of the mass media are neither great villains nor shining heroes; they are simply employees.

### Audiences

No communicator addresses his audience in a social vacuum, nor are audiences formless lumps of social clay that he can mold into any shape he wishes. They already have certain attitudes and values, some of which they hold strongly. If he simply bores them, his messages will not reach them at all. If he catches their attention but offends, repels, or angers them, not only will he win no converts but he may even make converts for his competitors. To some extent, therefore, every communicator must tell his audience what it wants to hear lest he lose it altogether. The rule is simple: no audience, no communication; no communication, no results; no results, no job. These rules express the hard facts about the environment to which all communicators in every political system must accommodate if they wish to stay in business.

### EFFECTS OF COMMUNICATION ON POLITICAL OPINION AND BEHAVIOR

We noted at the beginning of this chapter that some people regard advertising and propaganda, especially with their modern computerized technologies, as "absolute weapons." They view people as bundles of psychological "knee-jerk" reflexes that they cannot themselves control; they believe that, if a skilled propagandist taps the correct reflex in the correct way, he can make people do anything he wishes, from buying a particular brand of soap to voting for a particular candidate.

Let us admit that the great success of the advertising industry and the ability of dictators like Adolf Hitler and Mao Tse-tung to mobilize the masses fanatically behind them lend a certain credibility to this view. But social science research has shown it to be largely spurious. Berelson sums up what we have learned about the effects of communication on opinion and behavior: "Some kinds of *communication* on

---

[25] Peterson, Jensen, and Rivers, *The Mass Media and Modern Society*, p. 25.

some kinds of *issues,* brought to the attention of some kinds of *people* under some kinds of *conditions,* have some kinds of *effects.*"[26] Each of the italicized words in this sentence signals a significant variable in the process, each of which may appear quite different in different circumstances.

### Kind of Communication

A communication may have "reportorial" or "editorial" content or both. Although most attention has been directed to the latter, the evidence suggests that reportorial content is more effective in influencing opinions. If we tell a man, "The Arab terrorists want to overthrow our government," he may or may not be impressed; but if we tell him, "The Arab terrorists have just murdered the mayor and blown up the city hall," we are likely to stir a more active response.

Another aspect of communication that has long interested social scientists is the relative effectiveness of various media. Their research indicates that, the more direct and personal the medium of communication, the more effective it is likely to be.[27] The superiority of the face-to-face media in this respect results, according to one study, from the following characteristics.[28]

1. They are nonpurposive. Face-to-face political discussion occurs casually in the course of ordinary everyday conversation, and the receiver cannot "turn it off" as he can a television set. Most people, furthermore, tend to "screen" propaganda from the mass media for opinions with which they already agree and to ignore opinions counter to their own. They cannot so easily control the content of personal conversations.
2. Communicators can be flexible when encountering resistance. They can shape and alter their arguments in quick response to the observed reactions of the listeners. The mass media, on the other hand, alter their messages much more slowly even when they know exactly how their audiences are reacting, which they rarely do.
3. They provide immediate personal rewards for compliance and punishment for noncompliance: They take advantage of the general human desire to be liked by one's associates. The propagandist on radio or television and the political columnist or editorialist in the newspaper are remote and impersonal figures to most of their audiences, which therefore have no particular desire to be liked by them. They do not offer the personal reason to respond favorably that an associate would.
4. Pressures may be exerted by a trusted and intimate source whom the receiver knows, rather than by some remote and impersonal—and therefore less trustworthy—"pressure group."

As a result of these factors not only are the face-to-face media generally more effective than are the mass media, but also the more direct mass media—radio, television, and the movies—appear to be more effective than are newspapers and

---

[26] Berelson, "Communications and Public Opinion," p. 345. Italics in the original.

[27] See Klapper, "The Comparative Effects of the Various Media," in Wilbur Schramm (ed.), *The Process and Effects of Mass Communication* (Urbana, Ill.: University of Illinois Press, 1954), pp. 91–105.

[28] Lazarsfeld, Berelson, and Gaudet, *The People's Choice,* chap. 15.

books, which depend mainly upon the printed word. Most political parties and pressure groups are fully aware of the advantages of face-to-face communication and try to organize their campaigns accordingly.

### Kind of Issue

Communication is most effective when it deals with new and unstructured issues—those on which no strong opinions already exist. Most of us are more likely to accept strong judgments, favorable or unfavorable, of people and groups about which we know little or nothing than of those that we know well. For example, if we tell a railroad president, "All politicians are crooks!" he may well agree, but if we tell him that "X railroad is the most inefficient in the world," he will probably reply that the situation involves too many complex factors to justify such an extreme statement. On the other hand, if we make both statements to a politician, he will probably enter qualifications and reservations about the first and heartily agree with the second.

Communication is likely to be more effective on issues that the receivers regard as relatively unimportant than on those they believe to be crucial. They may have views on both kinds of issues, but their opinions on what they regard as the important ones are likely to be far stronger (and therefore less changeable) than their opinions on issues that seem relatively unimportant.

### Kind of People

Obviously, communicators can affect the opinions only of those who receive their message. People who consume relatively few mass communications are thus less likely to be affected than are those who spend much time reading, listening to the radio, or watching television. Conversely, people who do a lot of reading, listening, and viewing are likely to be better informed and less easily influenced than are those who devote less time to communications media. Strongly predisposed people are less likely to be influenced by communications than are weakly predisposed people.

### Conditions

A communicator who has a monopoly over the media of communications is obviously in a better position to influence opinion than is one who must worry about large-scale counterpropaganda, which, of course, explains why ruling groups in the Soviet Union and other dictatorial regimes are careful to control the media of communication as much as they possibly can. It also explains why the model of democracy outlined in Chapter 13 requires free access to communications media, and it accounts for the concern that some observers have expressed over tendencies toward increasing concentration of ownership and control of the mass media in modern democratic systems. Most observers agree, however, that this tendency has not yet gone so far as to approach monopoly; at any rate, the effectiveness of mass communications is limited by the other factors we are considering here.

Berelson has argued that the long-range effects of communication are more significant than the short-range effects. Among the former he includes providing meanings for key political terms, furnishing basic pictures of what the world is like, emphasizing and perpetuating certain social values, and so on.

Of the short-range effects of communications, as observed in political campaigns, for example, the least frequent is *conversion:* inducing people to switch preferences from one candidate or position to another. A more common effect is *initiation:* initiating attitudes on issues that have previously had little or no visibility for the mass public and on which most people have no prior opinions. Still more frequent is *reinforcement:* bolstering the preferences that audiences already have and providing them with arguments with which to counter both their own doubts and unsettling propaganda from the other side. The most frequent effect is *activation:* making supporters feel that their preference is so right and the issue so important that they will act to advance it, by voting, attending meetings, contributing money, and so on.[29]

Most political-campaign directors in the developed nations are well aware of these probabilities. As a result, most campaigns are designed not to convert people supporting the opposition but to keep adherents faithful to the cause and to ensure that they go to the polls when it counts.

## COMMUNICATION IN DEVELOPING NATIONS[30]

We observed earlier in this chapter that in any political system communication is the essential process by which people's attitudes and interests are translated into political action. Up to this point we have concentrated on communication in developed nations East and West. It is time now to point out that communication plays a critical role in the effort of every developing nation in Africa, Asia, and elsewhere to preserve and strengthen its national identity and to meet the economic and social needs of its people.

Communication, as Richard R. Fagen has pointed out, played a key role in the new nations' struggles for independence. Typically the colonial power, for reasons of administrative efficiency, expanded and modernized transport and other communications facilities, encouraged change in the static structure of the traditional society, promoted greater physical and social mobility, and increased literacy and homogeneity of language. Those changes had the unanticipated effects of greatly expanding the subject people's social and political horizons and forging many rival local and tribal loyalties into more nearly national loyalty. The new loyalty, in turn, produced increasingly militant demands for political independence, spawned an organized effort

---

[29] See Lazarsfeld, Berelson, and Gaudet, *The People's Choice,* chaps. 8–10; and Klapper, *The Effects of Mass Communication,* chaps. 2–4.

[30] The most comprehensive discussion is Lucian W. Pye (ed.), *Communications and Political Development* (Princeton, N.J.: Princeton University Press, 1963). See also Fagen, *Politics and Communication.*

to press those demands—by armed rebellion if necessary—and led to ultimate withdrawal of the colonial power.[31]

After achieving independence, however, each new nation has faced many difficult problems of political development: strengthening citizens' identification with the nation, mobilizing popular understanding of and support for economic-development efforts, and developing in the population both new technological skills and a desire for achievement to replace the passivity typical of traditional societies. Only thus can a new nation operate a productive economy and meet its people's needs.[32]

Many scholars believe that these goals can be achieved only through replacing the communications system of the preindependence society with a modern system comparable to those of the developed nations. The traditional communication process, Lucian W. Pye tells us, typically lacks professional communicators. Information flows along the established traditional hierarchy and never reaches much of the population; it is therefore simply incapable of meeting the demands of political and economic development. The job can be done only with a modern communications system, including both a structure of professionally organized mass media and a cadre of opinion leaders who exert influence because of their involvement and knowledge, rather than because of their inherited statuses in a traditional social order.[33] Establishing such a system of mass media is costly, and complementing it with a network of opinion leaders takes time, but, as studies of such diverse "transitional" nations as India, Turkey, Thailand, and the People's Republic of China show, it can be done. Clearly it *must* be done if new nations are to "modernize" in the full sense of the term.

In developed and developing nations alike, then, communication is not an absolute weapon sure to achieve all by itself any political objective. But no such objective can be achieved *without* communication, and, the more effectively the tool is used, the greater is the impact of the other forces making for political success, however defined.

---

[31] Fagen, *Politics and Communication,* pp. 108–109.

[32] See David C. McClelland, *The Achieving Society* (Princeton, N.J.: D. Van Nostrand Company, Inc., 1961).

[33] Pye, *Communications and Political Development,* pp. 24–26.

# 7

---

# THE ELECTORAL PROCESS

Abraham Lincoln's northern political opponents, and they were many, called him a "dictator." In clear defiance of the Constitution he had suspended the writ of habeas corpus, clapped his political adversaries in jail, raised an army, withdrawn money from the Treasury, and started a war, all without even asking Congress for prior authorization.

Lincoln's supporters replied that he had certainly used the emergency powers of the presidency to their fullest but that he was no dictator. Why? Because in the elections of 1862 and 1864 the voters had had a chance to throw first his supporters and then Lincoln himself out of office. Any public official who can be turned out of office in a free election, they declared, is no dictator, for as long as such elections are held the people, and not the President or any other public official, hold the ultimate ruling power, as democracy requires.

Most democrats then and now believe that this distinction between a strong democratic executive and a dictator is both fundamental and valid. They agree that the basic institution of democratic government, the ultimate weapon for establishing and preserving popular control of their leaders, is the institution of free elections. As Gerald Pomper correctly points out, secure popular control

has not been provided by depending on the good will of rulers, on the presumed identity of interests between governed or governors, or on institutional controls, such as a federal structure, or supervision by a monopolistic political party. To the ancient question "Who will guard the guardians?" there is only one answer: those who choose the guardians.[1]

---

[1] Gerald M. Pomper, *Elections in America* (New York: Dodd, Mead & Company, Inc., 1968), p.

## A MODEL OF A FREE ELECTION

No model of a free election, viewed as a basic institution of democratic control, is fully realized in the actual electoral system of any modern democracy. But such a model (see Chap. 13) can provide a useful set of bench marks for analyzing, understanding, comparing, and evaluating existing electoral systems. Most students of electoral systems would agree that a genuinely free election must satisfy at least six requirements and perhaps others as well.[2]

### MEANINGFUL CHOICES

In order to exercise effective control over their public officials, voters must have a choice between at least two candidates for each office to be filled. Clearly this requirement rules out the single-candidate elections organized by the Soviet Union, which we shall discuss later. Some observers say that it also rules out the "Tweedledum versus Tweedledee" contests supposedly characteristic of American elections, elections that provide no real choices on such important issues as capitalism versus socialism, militarism versus pacifism, black power versus white racism, and so on. Others reply that, though a choice between George McGovern and Richard Nixon, for example, does not provide alternatives at the absolute *extremes* of these ideological spectrums, it does provide a significant choice between two quite different points along each spectrum. But all agree that a truly free election must furnish the voters meaningful choices, however defined.

### FREEDOM TO KNOW AND DISCUSS THE CHOICES

If two candidates for an office are allowed to run but only one is permitted to present his views publicly and to have his name printed on the ballot, then he is effectively the only candidate. There must be full freedom for all candidates and their supporters to publicize their names and policy positions so that the voters can hear what they have to say. Some observers would add that, if this requirement is to mean anything, every candidate must be guaranteed at least some financial support so that all candidates, rich and poor alike, have at least minimum opportunities to publicize their views and appeal for popular support.

### A MANAGEABLE NUMBER OF CLEAR CHOICES

Because of a political deadlock over reapportioning the state's legislature, the Illinois Supreme Court ordered that all assembly districts be abolished for the 1964 election

---

263. This same view underlies W. J. M. Mackenzie, *Free Elections* (New York: Holt, Rinehart and Winston, Inc., 1958).

[2] See Pomper, *Elections in America,* pp. 263–266; and MacKenzie, *Free Elections,* chap. 20.

Elections as choices
between two foils.
Source: "Nixon Rated
Cartoons" by Ranan
Lurie, published by
Quadrangle, the New
York Times Book Co.

LURIE'S OPINION

© 1972 by United Feature Syndicate, Inc.

and that all candidates for the 177 seats in the state's General Assembly be elected "at large." The ballot contained 236 names, and the voter was to vote for any 177! For anyone but a full-time specialist in Illinois politics this task would have been impossible. But, happily, the names of the 236 candidates were printed in two columns of 118 names each, labeled "Republican" and "Democratic"; by marking the party "circle" at the top of either column voters could (and most did) vote their party's "straight ticket." As 1964 was a very good year for Democrats, all 118 of their candidates and only 59 Republicans were elected (each party had agreed to run only 118 candidates instead of the full 177). The point is that the two political parties *organized* the election and thus gave Illinois voters a manageable number of meaningful choices. "Structuring the vote" in this way is accomplished mainly by political parties in Western democratic systems,[3] but *some* agency must do the job in any system that approximates our model of democracy.

## EQUAL WEIGHTING OF VOTES

The essence of democratic government is the location of ultimate ruling power in *all* people, rather than in a select few or an all-powerful one. All adults must have an equal opportunity to register their choices by voting. We shall mention later some of the practical problems that have arisen under this requirement: setting a proper minimum voting age, deciding whether or not to deprive convicted criminals of their votes, and so on. But the *principle* of universal adult suffrage is generally accepted as a necessary (but not sufficient) condition for free elections.

If some people's votes are weighted more heavily than other people's, this basic democratic principle of political equality is violated, and the favored voters constitute a kind of oligarchy. "One man, one vote" is the only principle for apportioning legislative districts and counting votes which satisfies the requirements of our model of a free election. We shall examine this principle in more detail in Chapters 13 and 14.

## FREE REGISTRATION OF CHOICES

Students of free elections agree that voters must be able to go to the polls without any obstruction or fear of subsequent reprisal. It also means that they must be able to vote without coercion or fear of reprisal, which, in turn, requires that they be allowed to cast their votes *secretly.*

## ACCURATE REGISTRATION, COUNTING, AND REPORTING

The voting procedures—whether marking a paper ballot, pulling levers on a voting machine, or punching holes in an IBM card—must permit voters to register their choices accurately and unambiguously. The counting procedures must provide accurate totals of the preferences registered for each alternative. And reporting procedures must guarantee that the totals, which control who wins the contested offices, are honestly published. If any of these principles is ignored, the others are rendered meaningless.

From the six basic requirements of our model of a free election we turn to a survey of some problems that democratic nations have encountered in trying to satisfy these requirements and of various solutions they have chosen.

---

[3] This point is well made in Leon D. Epstein, *Political Parties in Western Democracies* (New York: Frederick A. Praeger, Inc., 1967), chap. 4.

# SUFFRAGE IN DEMOCRATIC SYSTEMS

## SUFFRAGE AND DEMOCRATIC THEORY

### The Principle of Universal Suffrage

One of our requirements for a free election is that all adults have an equal opportunity to register their choices by voting. This principle of "universal suffrage" has, however, never been interpreted to mean that *everyone* in the community must have the right to vote. No democratic nation, for example, has ever permitted ten-year-old children to vote, and no democratic theorist has ever called this omission "undemocratic." Most democratic systems also exclude aliens, lunatics, and criminals in prison, and few democrats think that such exclusions violate the principle of universal suffrage.

As a democratic ideal, in other words, the principle of universal suffrage requires that every member of the community, rather than every person who happens to be present in the community on election day, have the right to vote. Generally, only those who have demonstrated their inability (for example, by confinement in a mental institution) or their unwillingness (for example, by conviction for a felony) to assume the obligations of loyalty to the nation and obedience to its laws are considered not to be full-fledged members of the community and therefore are not entitled to vote in its elections.

### Democratization of the Suffrage

The history of suffrage has been essentially the same in all modern democratic countries. In each, one kind of restriction after another has been abandoned, and consequently ever-greater proportions of the population have been included in the electorate. In all the nations considered here this trend has reflected increasing commitment among people who already had the franchise not only to the principle that all members of the community should have the vote but also to an expanding conception of who should be considered full-fledged members.

In the first American election under the new Constitution in 1789, for example, only about one in every thirty adults was eligible to vote! Women were the largest single ineligible group, but most states also excluded slaves and males owning no property or paying no taxes; a few states even excluded adherents of certain religions. Through the succeeding decades, however, these restrictions were gradually removed one by one. All religious qualifications had been removed by the early nineteenth century, and by the end of the Civil War, in 1865, most states had removed all property-owning and taxpaying requirements. The Fifteenth Amendment to the national Constitution (1870) prohibited denial of the right to vote "on account of race, color, or previous condition of servitude"—although for a century some southern states continued to use illegal and indirect means to bar blacks from the polls simply because they were black. But, as we shall see in Chapter 22, this shameful evasion of the Fifteenth Amendment had almost completely ended by the early 1970s. The most recent major legal steps in the United States came in 1920, with the adoption of the Nineteenth Amendment, which prohibited denial of the right to vote "on

The latest change in suffrage requirements: Eighteen-year-old high school students line up to register to vote. Source: UPI Photograph.

account of sex" and thus admitted women to full voting equality with men, and in 1971, with the adoption of the Twenty-Sixth Amendment, which lowered the minimum voting age to eighteen.

In the other democracies the story has been substantially the same: the gradual elimination of religious, property-owning, and taxpaying requirements in the nineteenth century and the adoption of woman suffrage in the twentieth.

## CURRENT SUFFRAGE REQUIREMENTS

The main qualifications for voters in modern democratic systems are summarized here.

### Citizenship

Most democratic nations permit only their own citizens to vote but make no distinction between native-born and naturalized citizens. This requirement rests upon the conviction that only people loyal to the nation, who prefer it to all others, should be permitted to vote in its elections. Citizenship is generally regarded as the best formal indication of such loyalty.

Political Inputs

148

### Age

Just about every society requires each of its members to attain a certain minimum age before being admitted to full participation in community affairs, on the ground that infants and children are incapable of such participation. Most primitive societies, for example, have special rites and ceremonies for the induction of young people into adulthood and full membership. Every modern democracy requires that its citizens reach a certain minimum age before they can vote.

Every such age limit is, of course, arbitrary in the sense that it does not reflect different ages of maturity among different individuals. In all democratic nations, however, the difficulty of conducting individual "maturity examinations" is generally regarded as greater than the possible injustices resulting from applying one minimum-age requirement to all. The most common limit is twenty-one years. The lowest limit is eighteen years (in Great Britain, Israel, Uruguay, and the United States); the highest is twenty-five (in Denmark). In most nations the rule is uniform for all voters, but Italy permits only citizens over twenty-five to vote for senators and all citizens over twenty-one (and married men over eighteen) to vote for deputies.

### Residence

Most democratic systems also require voters to have lived in the nation and their particular voting districts for certain periods of time. For example, in Illinois a voter must have lived in the state for 30 days before the election in which he wishes to vote.

### Registration

In order to prevent such election frauds as "voting the graveyard" and "repeating" (which we shall discuss later), most democratic systems supply officials in each election district with a full roster (usually called a "register") of all eligible voters, against which the names of those asking for ballots can be checked. Some registration systems are permanent, in that once the roster is compiled it is kept up to date by elimination of ineligible individuals and addition of eligible ones. Others are periodic, in that at regular intervals the entire register is scrapped and a new one drawn up.

The most significant distinction among registration systems is the assignment of responsibility for compiling the register. At one end of the scale stand Great Britain and most European democracies, which require the registering officer to make periodic door-to-door canvasses of his district and to enroll any eligible person who is not already on the register. The United States stands at the other end: Most states require each would-be voter to take the initiative by coming to the registration office and applying formally; only a few permit or encourage door-to-door canvassing and registration in the home or in the neighborhood. In the United States most voters must take the initiative on two occasions: during the registration period and again on election day. In Great Britain and most other democracies the voters must take the initiative only on election day. Most analysts believe that this difference is one of the main causes for lower voting turnouts in the United States.[4]

## Other Requirements

Beside these four universal requirements, some democratic systems have others. Chile and Great Britain, for example, exclude certain public officials and members of the nobility. The Philippines and some American states exclude people who cannot read and write. South Africa excludes by law (and some American states formerly excluded by illegal practices) members of certain races. Switzerland excluded women until 1971. Most democracies exclude lunatics and convicted felons.

Of all these special requirements, however, only those barring members of certain races disqualify substantial portions of the adult population; the suffrage rules of most modern democracies, accordingly, come very close to approximating the democratic ideal of universal suffrage.

## NONVOTING AND COMPULSORY VOTING

John Locke, Jean Jacques Rousseau, Thomas Jefferson, and other early advocates of democracy apparently assumed that once members of a community were given the legal right to vote, they would exercise it as a matter of course at every opportunity. The evidence indicates, however, that actual voting participation in the modern democracies does not measure up to this expectation. Table 10, for example, shows the percentage of legally eligible voters actually voting in recent general elections in a number of democratic nations. It reveals that only India had as low a turnout rate among eligible voters as did the United States. But a fair comparison of the American rate with others must allow for the facts that in the United States a substantial number of voters are temporarily disfranchised because of moving just before the election and that others fall afoul of our demanding registration laws. William G. Andrews has estimated that the turnout rate of those not excluded or discouraged from voting is closer to 80–85 percent—a figure that exceeds those in most British Commonwealth nations.[5]

Many of democracy's well-wishers regard failure to vote as both a disgrace and a threat to democratic survival. Many political scientists have therefore sought the causes of nonvoting (which we shall examine in Chap. 8) and have recommended such remedies as easing registration, reducing the frequency of elections and the number of elective offices, vote drives by civic organizations and advertising councils, and—that analgesic for all social ills—more education.

---

[4] See Mackenzie, *Free Elections,* pp. 117–118; his judgment was confirmed by the *Report of the President's Commission on Registration and Voting Participation* (Washington, D.C.: U.S. Government Printing Office, 1963), pp. 11–14.

[5] He reached this conclusion after a detailed analysis of probable exclusions and voting turnout in the 1960 presidential election; see William G. Andrews, "American Voting Participation," *The Western Political Quarterly,* 19 (December 1966), 639–652.

**TABLE 10**

**Voting Turnouts in Recent General Elections**

| Nation | Year | Percentage of Persons of Voting Age Voting |
|---|---|---|
| Argentina | 1973 | 86 |
| Austria | 1971 | 92 |
| Canada | 1972 | 75 |
| Chile | 1970 | 84 |
| Costa Rica | 1970 | 80 |
| Finland | 1972 | 81 |
| France | 1973 | 81 |
| India | 1971 | 55 |
| Ireland | 1973 | 75 |
| Japan | 1972 | 72 |
| Mexico | 1970 | 68 |
| Netherlands | 1972 | 83 |
| Norway | 1969 | 83 |
| United Kingdom | 1974 | 79 |
| United States | 1972 | 56 |
| Venezuela | 1973 | 92 |
| West Germany | 1972 | 91 |

*Source: Keesing's Contemporary Archives,* published by Keesing's Publications, Longman Group Limited, Bath, England.

The most drastic remedy, however, is compulsory voting, pioneered by Belgium (1893), the Netherlands (1917), and Australia (1924). The Australian law specifies that every person eligible to vote must, within twenty-one days of becoming eligible, enroll with the registrar in his district. After each election the registrar sends to each person on the roster who did not vote a form on which the nonvoter must explain why. If he offers a legally valid excuse (for example, illness or religious scruples) and if it is verified, no penalty is imposed. Otherwise he is fined.

Some nations, like Uruguay, have adopted compulsory-voting laws but have not enforced them. Others have enforced such laws and have experienced marked increases in average election turnouts (from 70 to 95 percent in Belgium, from 64 to 94 percent in Australia). There is, however, no general agreement among political scientists—or, for that matter, among Belgians and Australians—on whether or not the total effect of compulsory voting has been beneficial. Some commentators argue that compulsion has greatly increased the number of irresponsible votes and enlarged the "automatic anti" vote. Others believe that, by lessening nonparticipation, it has also lessened indifference and thus strengthened democracy.[6]

The most we can conclude is that in the few democratic systems that have adopted compulsory voting there is no powerful sentiment to abolish it and that most modern democracies depend upon other agencies, notably political parties (see Chap. 9), to attract voters to the polls.

---

[6] For a general survey, see Henry J. Abraham, *Compulsory Voting* (Washington, D.C.: Public Affairs Press, 1955).

# NOMINATIONS AND CANDIDATE SELECTION

## RECRUITMENT OF CANDIDATES

### The Process

Most free elections involve choices among competing candidates—persons legally eligible for the offices contested whose names are printed on official ballots (or, less often, written in by voters). The first step in the conduct of free elections is thus the process by which a few of the many citizens eligible for office actually come to be named on the ballot—a process that we shall call "candidate recruitment." It has two major parts. The first is *nomination,* which includes the legal procedures by which eligible individuals are formally designated as candidates and have their names accepted by public authorities for printing on the election ballots. As we shall see, these procedures vary substantially from one democracy to another, but they are all alike in one significant respect. In elections for all but the most minor offices they are preceded and dominated by extralegal activities of political parties, which I shall call *candidate selection* and which constitute the second aspect of recruitment.

**Everyone has a stake in who wins nominations.** Source: "Nixon Rated Cartoons" by Ranan Lurie, published by Quadrangle, the New York Times Book Co.

Some kind of recruiting process precedes elections in just about every organization in which they are held. When football teams elect their captains, for example, it is customary for various team members to talk over the possibilities informally and to settle upon the particular players whom they will support. When a local Rotary Club or Sierra Club is about to elect a new president, the outgoing president appoints a nominating committee, which selects someone for the honor and presents his name to the association's members, who then elect him.

Both procedures are similar to that by which the Democratic national convention in 1972 decided that the party's presidential candidate would be George McGovern rather than Hubert Humphrey or George Wallace. McGovern's nomination did, of course, involve a decision by a highly organized party, whereas the other examples involved decisions by smaller factions and committees. In all three instances part of the electorate met before an election and decided which of the several individuals legally eligible for the elective post they would support—which would be the candidate of their particular faction, committee, or party.

### Significance

In a democracy every voter has the legal right to vote for any person eligible for any office. In practice, however, he does not have such complete freedom and could not use it if he had. In the United States, for example, about 85 million people presently fulfill all the legal qualifications for the presidency. But, if every voter had been required to choose among all these people in 1972, to be fair to all he would have had to learn the personal qualifications and positions of everyone! This kind of familiarity is obviously impossible. No human being can even perceive the nature of each of 85 million alternatives, let alone choose intelligently among them. But no such impossible task actually confronted the voters in 1972. The various political parties, through their nominations, had reduced the practical alternatives from 85 million to about 10. As Americans have a two-party system, most voters were faced with choosing between only McGovern and Nixon. The major parties' nominating processes thus reduced the alternatives from 85 million to 2.

Most of us can learn the personal qualifications and political opinions of two candidates and can make a meaningful choice between them. The reduction process therefore made meaningful choice possible for the voters. Surely it was as significant a part of the total selection process as was the general election in November, in which the voters reduced the alternatives from 2 to 1.

For these reasons the nominating process not only plays a crucial role in the selection of elected officials but is also an indispensable mechanism enabling the voters in a democratic system to participate meaningfully in selecting those who govern.

### FORMAL NOMINATING PROCEDURES

It is clear from the foregoing discussion that candidate selection by the parties is the most important part of candidate recruitment. Yet the parties' activities are restricted and influenced by the legal nominating machinery within which they must operate.

Before we consider party activities (in Chap. 9), we shall briefly review the principal formal nominating procedures in modern democracies.

### The United States

The laws regulating nominations in the United States differ sharply in several respects from comparable laws in other modern democratic systems. For one thing, American laws are far more elaborate and detailed. Most of them are enacted and enforced by the states rather than by the national government, and their details vary considerably from one state to another. Every state, however, regulates most nomination procedures rather closely.

**The Direct Primary**   Perhaps the sharpest contrast between American formal nominating procedures and those in other democratic systems is provided by the unique use of the "direct primary." It is a procedure by which nominations are made *directly* by the voters in government-supervised elections rather than indirectly by party leaders or convention delegates. Its stated purpose, indeed, is to remove the control of nominations from party "bosses" and to place it in the hands of "rank-and-file party members." Every one of the fifty states uses it for some nominations, and most states require it for all. But no other nation in the world uses it at all.

In general, the direct primary is designed to ensure that nominations are made as nearly as possible in the same way in which regular elections are conducted. Any qualified person who wishes to receive a particular party's nomination for a particular public office may file with election officials a petition containing his or her name, address, the nomination desired, and the signatures of a legally designated number of party members. When the filing period has elapsed, the election authorities print ballots for each party including the name of everyone who has petitioned for each office. On primary day the members of each party go to the polls and, under the same conditions of secrecy that prevail at regular elections, mark their preferences for each office. The person who receives the largest number of votes for each office on each party's ballot is certified as that party's official nominee, and the nominee's name and party designation are then printed on the ballot for the ensuing general election.

The only major differences among the direct-primary systems of the various states relate to the eligibility of voters in particular party primaries. Some states use the *closed primary,* in which the voter publicly states a party affiliation and, if challenged, must pass some test of party membership (usually by taking an oath that he or she is a party member). Other states use the *open primary,* in which the voters make no public statement of their party affiliations and may vote in the primary of any party that they choose.

Most observers agree that the general use of the direct primary has had a profound effect upon politics and political parties in the United States, although there is no general agreement upon just what that effect has been and whether it has been good or bad. Some observers believe that the direct primary has accomplished its main purpose of "democratizing" the nominating process by giving ordinary voters the power to overrule party leaders. Others argue that, because the leaders usually control the primaries, there has been no real change. Some commentators even believe that the direct primary has lessened the amount of conflict between the parties and has thus increased the number of one-party areas in the United States, and others insist that it is one of the main causes for the decentralization, lack of cohesion, and absence of discipline characteristic of American political parties.[7]

One point is clear: There is little disposition within the United States to abandon the direct primary—and not much more disposition in the other democracies to adopt it.

**The Caucus**   A "caucus" is a small face-to-face gathering of people, held in secret, for the purpose of agreeing on the nominees and policies they will support. The oldest and most informal of all nominating procedures, it is presently used in America for only a few minor offices.

**The Convention**   A nominating convention is an assembly of delegates picked in some fashion by the members of a party to represent them in the selection of the party's nominees. This procedure was dominant in the nineteenth-century United States and still is used in some states (for example, Delaware and Indiana) to select nominees to various state and local offices. The best-known nominating conventions, of course, are the national conventions of the major parties, which meet every four years to pick the parties' presidential and vice-presidential nominees and to write their national platforms.[8]

**The Petition**   In some states aspirants to certain public offices can have their names printed on the election ballots merely by filing petitions signed by legally designated numbers of voters. This procedure is used mainly for nominations to such local offices as school-board membership, for which nonpartisan elections (elections in which no party designations appear on the ballot) are held, but sometimes it also enables new parties and small parties to get their candidates on the ballots.

*Other Democratic Nations*

The formal nominating procedures of the other democratic nations are far simpler than those used in the United States. Two principal methods are currently in use.

**Petitions**   The formal procedure for becoming a candidate for the British House of Commons is simplicity itself. Any British subject or Commonwealth citizen over twenty-one years of age is eligible. Those declared ineligible include peers, High

---

[7] See the discussion of these questions in V. O. Key, Jr., *American State Politics: An Introduction* (New York: Alfred A. Knopf, 1956) chaps. 4–6; Frank J. Sorauf, *Party Politics in America* (Boston: Little, Brown & Company, 1968), chap. 9; Austin Ranney and Leon D. Epstein, "The Two Electorates: Voters and Non-Voters in a Wisconsin Primary," *Journal of Politics*, 28 (August 1966), 598–616; and Ranney, "The Representativeness of Primary Electorates," *Midwest Journal of Political Science*, 12 (May 1968), 224–238.

[8] The most thorough historical and analytical study of presidential nominating conventions is Paul T. David, Ralph M. Goldman, and Richard C. Bain, *The Politics of National Party Conventions* (Washington, D.C.: The Brookings Institution, 1960). There have been a number of major changes in both parties' conventions since 1968. For descriptions and analyses, see Judith H. Parris, *The Convention Problem* (Washington, D.C.: The Brookings Institution, 1972); and Austin Ranney, *Curing the Mischiefs of Faction: Party Reform in America* (Berkeley, Calif.: University of California Press, 1974).

Court judges, members of the permanent civil service, clergymen of the Church of England, the Church of Scotland, or the Roman Catholic Church, and convicted felons. He secures from election officials an official nomination paper, on which he states his name, address, occupation, and the constituency in which he wishes to "stand." The form must also be signed by two voters from that constituency acting as proposer and seconder and by eight other such voters acting as assenters. The completed form must be filed with the "returning officer," along with a deposit of £150. This deposit will be forfeited to the Treasury if the candidate fails to poll more than one-eighth of the votes cast in his constituency in the ensuing election. The purpose of this requirement is to discourage frivolous and "nuisance" candidacies, and it appears to have accomplished its purpose rather well. When these minimal requirements have been met, the candidate's name is placed on the ballot (only since 1969 has Britain allowed the candidates' party labels to be printed on the ballot) for the forthcoming election.[9]

Approximately the same procedure is followed in such other democratic countries as Canada, France, Japan, and New Zealand.

**Party-List Designations**  In most nations using some form of the party-list system of proportional representation the authorized agent of each recognized political party (usually an executive officer or committee) draws up a list of candidates for each constituency and presents it to the election authorities. When the latter have verified the eligibility of the names on each list, they are placed on the ballot without further ado. In some nations (for example, Israel) this procedure is the only one by which a candidate can be placed on the ballot. In other nations (like Chile, Denmark, and Finland) 50–100 independent voters can also nominate a single candidate or list of candidates by petition. In general, however, the initiative rests mainly or exclusively with party officials and agencies.

## ELECTIONS

### ADMINISTERING ELECTIONS

*Timing and Frequency*

In the United States, the terms of the President and members of Congress are fixed by constitutional provisions, and elections for these offices are held at regular intervals fixed by law. The term of the President is fixed at four years, the terms of senators at six years, and the terms of representatives at two years. A presidential election must be held every four years, a general election for representatives every two years, and an election for one-third of the members of the Senate every two years. Special elections to fill the places of legislators who have died or resigned may be held at other times, but the timing of all general elections is fixed by law.

The situation is more fluid in the parliamentary democracies. The British constitution, for example, requires that a general election for all members of the House

---

[9] A. N. Schofield, *Parliamentary Elections* (2d ed.; London: Shaw & Sons, Ltd., 1955), pp. 124–142.

Examples of election posters used in Swaziland to help tribesmen vote. Each candidate is known by a symbol, like a clock; only symbols appear on ballots for illiterate voters. Source: Wide World Photos.

of Commons (and in effect for all members of the ministry and cabinet) must be held at least every five years. But the British can hold a general election at any time before the five-year period has expired; the prime minister simply asks the monarch to dissolve Parliament and hold new elections. In conditions of national emergency, furthermore, a majority of the House of Commons can extend the life of a particular parliament beyond the normal five-year period. To understand how this system works, we need only recall that a general election was held in Britain in 1935; when the next one came due in 1940 the nation was fighting a desperate war, and the sitting parliament was therefore continued annually for the next five years. After the defeat of Germany in 1945 a general election was held, and the new parliament lived out its full statutory life. The general election of 1950 returned a Labour majority too small to govern effectively, and therefore in 1951 Prime Minister Clement Attlee asked the King to dissolve Parliament. The new election returned a Conservative majority, which governed until 1955, when Conservative leaders called a new election, which returned their party to power. General elections have since been held in 1959, 1964, 1966, 1970, and 1974. The same kind of formal flexibility obtains in the other parliamentary democracies.

Some political scientists believe that much of what is objectionable in American elections results from their rigid timing according to the calendar, rather than according to changing public opinion and party conflict. They argue that, if public opinion is up in arms about some mistake that public officials have made (for example, in early

1974 when the polls showed the Watergate affair and the energy crisis had reduced President Nixon's popular approval to only about 25 percent), there is no effective way for the people directly to "turn the SOBs out" if no election is scheduled at the time. In 1974 this system of fixed elections produced an unanticipated and unwelcome side-effect: the forced resignations first of Vice President Agnew and then of President Nixon meant that, for the first time since the early years of the Republic, neither of their successors as President and Vice President held office because they had won a popular election. If, on the other hand, an election happens to fall in a period of political quiet and public apathy—which has not infrequently happened in the United States—then party leaders are tempted to campaign with all sorts of extravagant charges ("The Democrats coddle Communists!" "The Republicans are the tools of Big Business!") in order to rouse the voters from their torpor. Either way, these writers argue, it is sheer coincidence if election day in a presidential democracy happens to arrive when the people really want an election.[10]

This argument may well be valid, but we should also recognize that the power of dissolution is used sparingly in most parliamentary democracies and that it gives the party in power a substantial advantage over the opposition. Two recent British examples demonstrate this point clearly. In 1956 the Conservative government joined with France in a surprise attack upon the Egyptians to regain control of the Suez Canal; the British and French were forced to withdraw, and in early 1957 Conservative Prime Minister Anthony Eden suddenly retired because of "ill health." Had an election been scheduled then, the Conservatives might well have lost. As it was, they were able to defer calling an election until their standing had improved; they actually increased their majority in the autumn of 1959. In the general election of 1964 the Labour party returned to power by the narrowest of margins, winning 317 seats out of 630 in Parliament. This narrow majority made it exceedingly difficult for Labour to govern, but Prime Minister Harold Wilson bided his time. When, in early spring 1966, the polls and other indicators showed that Labour's popularity was rising sharply, he called a new general election, which Labour won handsomely, with 363 seats. Many observers believe he miscalculated in calling a June election in 1970, but none doubts that Wilson's power to call the election at the most favorable time for his party was a significant advantage. Apparently, then, flexible elections cause problems too.

### The Secret Ballot

In the eighteenth and nineteenth centuries many democratic theorists believed that voters should register their preferences publicly rather than privately. Even so eminent a democrat as John Stuart Mill argued that in most circumstances secret voting is undesirable, on the grounds that "the duty of voting, like any other public duty, should be performed under the eye and criticism of the public; every one of whom has not only an interest in its performance, but a good title to consider himself

---

[10] See Pendleton Herring, *The Politics of Democracy* (New York: Holt, Rinehart and Winston, Inc., 1940), p. 290.

wronged if it is performed otherwise than honestly and carefully."[11] Before the mid-nineteenth century no democratic nation tried to guarantee the secrecy of the vote. According to one common procedure each voter simply came before the election officials and announced, in the presence of anyone who cared to listen, which candidates he preferred. A growing number of reformers condemned this procedure on the ground that it exposed voters to intimidation and bribery and made genuinely free voting impossible. They won their first success in 1856, when the British colony of South Australia adopted a system of voting that came to be known as the "Australian ballot." One of its basic features was the requirement that votes be cast and counted in such a way that no one could tell how a particular person had voted. At the present time every democratic nation has adopted this requirement, and guaranteeing the secrecy of the ballot is a main objective of election laws and administration in all of them.

## SOME PROBLEMS IN DEMOCRATIC ELECTIONS

### Fraud

One prime objective of a free election is to register clearly and accurately the voters' choices among various candidates. Any flaws in election laws and administration that prevent the full achievement of this objective are therefore a matter of great concern to democracy's well-wishers.

One of the most publicized kinds of deviation from this standard is fraud—the illegal manipulation of voting, ballots, and the counting process by individuals or groups for the purpose of winning more votes than they otherwise could. The history of every modern democracy includes many instances of election fraud, and some commentators regard it as one of the gravest threats to the health of democracy. Election riggers have over the years developed a bag of tricks far too varied to be described in detail here, but among the more widespread methods are "padding the register" (putting fictitious names on the roster of eligible voters), intimidation and bribery of voters, "stuffing the ballot box" (including large numbers of fraudulent ballots in the count), altering and spoiling (and thus invalidating) ballots during the counting process, and falsely reporting the count. Most democratic nations have enacted laws to prevent such practices, but their efficacy depends not only upon how diligently they are administered by election officials but also upon how much the general public insists that they be enforced.

No one can say precisely how much fraud exists in the elections of any particular democratic nation, let alone in all of them. Most students of the subject have concluded, however, that the incidence of fraud has greatly declined in the past century and that a very small proportion of the elections in any modern democracy is marred by large-scale fraud.[12]

---

[11] John Stuart Mill, *Utilitarianism, Liberty, and Representative Government* (Everyman's Library ed; London: J. M. Dent & Sons, Ltd., 1910), p. 300.

[12] Unfortunately, the most recent systematic estimate of the incidence of fraud in American elections is Joseph P. Harris, *Election Administration in the United States* (Washington, D.C.: The

**It's difficult to run against an incumbent.**
Source: Reprinted with permission Toronto Star.

*Representativeness*

Even if all fraud were removed from election administration, the problem of establishing the kind of electoral system best calculated to register the voters' preferences clearly and accurately would remain. Few problems of modern democracy have been debated so thoroughly as that of how to achieve the best representation. Modern democratic nations have adopted a wide variety of electoral systems; each system has its advocates and its critics, and I shall now describe how each of the principal systems operates and estimate its actual political effects.

## PRINCIPAL DEMOCRATIC ELECTORAL SYSTEMS[13]

The following discussion outlines the essential features of the two main types of

Brookings Institution, 1934), pp. 37–75, 316–320, 377–382. For a more recent but briefer estimate, see Key, *Politics, Parties and Pressure Groups* (5th ed.; New York: Thomas Y. Crowell Company, 1964), pp. 636–638.

[13] The main comprehensive surveys are Mackenzie, *Free Elections;* Enid Lakeman and James D. Lambert, *Voting in Democracies* (London: Faber & Faber, Ltd., 1955); George van den Bergh, *Unity in Diversity: A Systematic Critical Analysis of All Electoral Systems* (London: B. T. Batsford, 1956); and Douglas W. Rae, *The Political Consequences of Electoral Laws* (rev. ed.; New Haven, Conn.: Yale University Press, 1971).

electoral systems in modern democratic polities: majority and proportional systems.

## MAJORITY SYSTEMS

Most readers are probably familiar with the two types of majority systems, those requiring only pluralities and those requiring absolute majorities, for both are used in English-speaking countries.

### *Those Requiring Pluralities*

**Single-Member Constituencies**   The most common version of the majority system requires a plurality in each single-member constituency. It is used for elections to such bodies as the American House of Representatives, the British House of Commons, the lower houses of the Canadian, Indian, and some other parliaments, and many state, provincial, and local legislative bodies in the United States and the British Commonwealth. Each constituency elects only one member of the legislative assembly at each election. The voter votes directly for one candidate, usually by marking an $\times$ in the box beside the candidate's name. When the votes are counted, the candidate receiving the largest number of votes (a plurality) in each constituency is declared elected. Some commentators call this the "first-past-the-post system."

**Multimember Constituencies**   In each election to the Turkish National Assembly and to certain state and local legislatures in the United States, Canada, and Great Britain, each constituency chooses two or more representatives. Each voter is permitted to vote for as many candidates as there are posts to be filled from his constituency. The candidates receiving the highest pluralities are declared elected. This system is also called "block voting."

### *Those Requiring Absolute Majorities*

Some democrats are disturbed that the plurality systems just described make possible the election of a public official by less than an absolute majority of the votes (when three or more candidates are running); the officials therefore have more of their constituents "against" them than "for" them. To guarantee that every elected representative will have the approval of more than half those voting, several alternatives have been adopted by some democratic governments.

**The Preferential Ballot**   The preferential ballot is now used in elections to the Australian House of Representatives and to four Australian state parliaments. It instructs the voter to mark the candidates in the order of his preference by placing numbers rather than $\times$s beside their names. If no candidate receives a majority of first-place preferences on the first count, the candidate with the fewest first-place preferences is "dropped," and his ballots are redistributed according to the second-place preferences on each. Such redistribution is continued until one candidate's ballots constitute an absolute majority of all those cast. That candidate is then declared elected.

**The Second Ballot** In French presidential elections and in the direct primaries of the dominant Democratic party in ten southern American states, each voter casts his ballot for one candidate by marking an $\times$ beside the candidate's name. If no candidate receives an absolute majority (50 percent plus one) of the votes cast in the first election, a second, or "runoff," election is held two weeks to a month later between the candidates who finished first and second in the first election. As only two candidates run in the second election, one must receive an absolute majority.

In the 1969 French presidential election, for example, none of the seven candidates won a majority in the first election, held on June 1. This result necessitated a second election, on June 15, between the two leading candidates, Georges Pompidou (44.5 percent of the votes in the first election) and Alain Poher (23.3 percent). In the second election Pompidou received 57.8 percent of the votes; Poher 42.2 percent. It is interesting to note that nearly 4 million *fewer* votes were cast in the second election than in the first, mainly because Communist leader Jacques Duclos, the third-ranking candidate in the first election with 21.3 percent of the vote, appealed to his supporters to boycott the second election.[14]

## PROPORTIONAL SYSTEMS

### The Rationale

Since the mid-nineteenth century some democratic theorists have argued that the majority systems make genuinely democratic representation impossible and have proposed that all such systems be replaced with some kind of proportional representation ("PR" for short). Their arguments can be briefly summarized here.[15]

A truly democratic representative assembly should be to the political divisions in the nation as a map is to the territory it represents or a mirror to whatever is placed before it (these metaphors recur frequently in the pro-PR literature). It should ensure that every point of view held by members of the community has spokesmen in the assembly in proportion to its adherents in the community.

The majority system cannot provide such an assembly. Wherever it is in force the majority party has more assembly seats than its share of the total popular vote warrants, and all other parties have fewer seats than their shares of the vote entitle them to. Furthermore, the majority system forces a two-party system upon the population, for third and fourth parties have little or no chance of electing members of the assembly. The legislatures that result from this kind of party system can express the many shades of public opinion no more accurately than a black-and-

---

[14] *New York Times,* June 3, 1969, p. 3; and *New York Times,* June 16, 1969, p. 1.

[15] For a thorough summary and analysis of the case for PR, see Hanna Fenichel Pitkin, *The Concept of Representation* (Berkeley, Calif.: University of California Press, 1966), chap. 5. Perhaps the leading defense of PR is Clarence G. Hoag and George H. Hallett, *Proportional Representation* (New York: Crowell-Collier and Macmillan, Inc., 1926).

Ballots for four major electoral systems: a. the majority system (U.S. Senate); b. the cumulative-vote system (Illinois House of Representatives); c. the party-list system (Belgian Chamber of Representatives); d. the preferential ballot (British Borough Council).

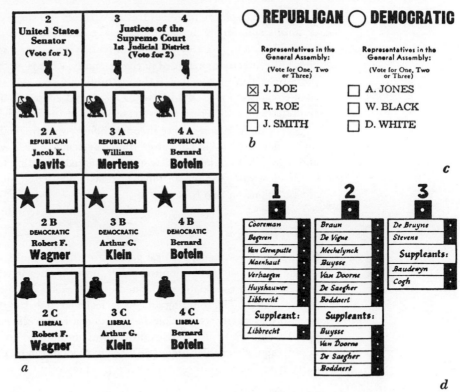

| 2 | 3 | 4 |
|---|---|---|
| **United States Senator** (Vote for 1) | **Justices of the Supreme Court** 1st Judicial District (Vote for 2) | |
| **2 A** REPUBLICAN Jacob K. **Javits** | **3 A** REPUBLICAN William **Mertens** | **4 A** REPUBLICAN Bernard **Botein** |
| **2 B** DEMOCRATIC Robert F. **Wagner** | **3 B** DEMOCRATIC Arthur G. **Klein** | **4 B** DEMOCRATIC Bernard **Botein** |
| **2 C** LIBERAL Robert F. **Wagner** | **3 C** LIBERAL Arthur G. **Klein** | **4 C** LIBERAL Bernard **Botein** |

*a*

○ **REPUBLICAN** ○ **DEMOCRATIC**

Representatives in the General Assembly:
(Vote for One, Two or Three)

☒ J. DOE
☒ R. ROE
☐ J. SMITH

Representatives in the General Assembly:
(Vote for One, Two or Three)

☐ A. JONES
☐ W. BLACK
☐ D. WHITE

*b*

*c*

**1**
Cooreman
Begeren
Van Clemputte
Maenhaut
Verhaegen
Huyshauwer
Libbrecht
Suppleant:
Libbrecht

**2**
Braun
De Vigne
Mechelynck
Buysse
Van Doorne
De Saegher
Boddaert
Suppleants:
Buysse
Van Doorne
De Saegher
Boddaert

**3**
De Bruyne
Stevens
Suppleants:
Baudewyn
Cogh

*d*

| Mark order of preference | Names of Candidates |
|---|---|
| | **BROWN** (John Brown, of 52, George St., Bristol, Merchant). |
| | **JONES, JOHN** (John Jones, of 5, Mary St., Bristol, Retired Teacher). |
| | **JONES, WILLIAM DAVID** (William David Jones, of 10, Charles St., Bristol, Merchant). |
| | **ROBERTSON** (Henry Robertson, of 8, John St., Bristol, Builder). |

### INSTRUCTIONS TO VOTERS

VOTE BY PLACING:

the figure 1 in the space provided opposite the name of the candidate who is your first choice; *and further (if you so desire)*

the figure 2 opposite the name of the candidate who is your second choice; *and further (if you so desire)*

the figure 3 opposite the name of the candidate who is your third choice; *and so on as far as you may choose.*

The Electoral Process

white photograph can represent the many colors and shades of reality. Their pictures of public opinion are bound to be grossly distorted.

Then, too, in a truly representative system every member of the community should be directly represented in the assembly. That is, each voter should be able to point to at least one member of the assembly and say, "My vote helped put her there, so she represents me." But under the majority systems all those who vote for losing candidates lack such direct representation, and their votes have been wasted.

For these reasons, these theorists believe that the majority systems should be replaced with some kind of "proportional system"—one in which no votes are wasted and in which all points of view are represented according to their relative strengths in the electorate. The proportional systems now used in modern democratic nations are variations on two basic types.

## Party-List Systems

In all party-list systems political parties are the basic units for which representation is sought. They all involve multimember constituencies, in which voters are confronted with lists of candidates nominated by the leaders or executive committees of the various parties. The counting process is designed to distribute seats in the legislative assembly as nearly as possible in accordance with each party's share of the total popular vote. Party-list systems differ from one another only in the degree to which voters can register their preferences for individual candidates, as well as for whole party lists. There are three main subtypes presently in use.

**No Choice Among Candidates**   In the elections for the Israeli Knesset (parliament) the entire nation is one constituency electing all 120 members. Any party that can muster the signatures of 750 eligible voters can submit a list of up to 120 candidates, arranging them in whatever order it wishes. Each party has a separate ballot paper, and the voter selects the paper of his party and deposits it in the ballot box. There is no way that he can indicate preference either for particular candidates on his party's list or for candidates on the lists of other parties. Whatever number of seats each party is entitled to according to its percentage of the total popular vote is filled by the candidates heading its list.[16]

Israel is the only democratic nation currently using this particular type of party-list system, but it was also used for elections to the German Reichstag from 1919 to 1933, the Czechoslovakian parliament from 1919 to 1938 and 1945 to 1948, and the French National Assembly in 1945 and 1946.

**Limited Choice Among Candidates**   In the second type of party-list system the voter may vote either for one party's list in its entirety or for a limited number of individual candidates (from one to four, depending on the nation) on a particular list. If he chooses the latter course, he indicates his desire to move his preferred candidates to the top of his favored party's list; if a majority of the voters for a particular list indicate a preferred order of candidates other than that specified by the party, the seats to which it is entitled are filled by the candidates in the order indicated by the

---

[16] Leonard J. Fein, *Politics in Israel* (Boston: Little, Brown & Company, 1967), pp. 97–98.

☛ **Gilt als Wahlzettel** — *Vaut comme bulletin de vote* ☚

**Kanton Bern — *Canton de Berne***

**Nationalratswahlen — 1951 — *Elections au Conseil national***

Ausseramtlicher Wahlzettel — *Bulletin non officiel*

**Sozialdemokratische Partei des Kantons Bern**

*Parti socialiste du canton de Berne*

### LISTE Nr. 8

1. **Aebersold Ernst,** Schulinspektor, Biel (bisher)
2. **Bratschi Robert,** Generalsekretär des Schweiz. Eisenbahnerverbandes, Bern, Präsident des Schweizerischen Gewerkschaftsbundes (bisher)
3. **Fawer Albert,** Gemeinderat, Biel (bisher)
4. **Freimüller Eduard,** Dr., Gemeinderat, Bern (bisher)
5. **Geissbühler Karl,** Zentralseckretär SAS, Köniz (bisher)
6. **Grimm Robert,** Direktor BLS, Bern (bisher)
7. **Grütter Fritz,** Präsident der Sozialdemokratischen Partei des Kantons Bern, Bern (bisher)
8. **Meyer Fritz,** Gemeindepräsident, Roggwil (bisher)
9. **Roth Hans,** Sekundarlehrer, Interlaken (bisher)
10. **Schmidlin Fritz,** Gemeinderat, Bern (bisher)
11. **Steiner Arthur,** Vizepräsident des Schweizerischen Metall- und Uhrenarbeiterverbandes, Bern (bisher)
12. **Stünzi Walter,** städtischer Fürsorgeverwalter, Thun (bisher)
13. **Weber Max,** Dr. Prof., Präsident des Verbandes Schweizerischer Konsumvereine, Wabern (bisher)
14. **Aeschbacher Karl,** Maschinensetzer, Zentralpräsident des Schweizerischen Typographenbundes, Bern (neu)
15. **Bircher Ernst,** Zentralpräsident des Verbandes der Bekleidungs-, Leder- und Ausrüstungearbeiter der Schweiz, Bern (neu)
16. **Felser Max,** Sekretär des Schweizerischen Bau- und Holzarbeiterverbandes, Nidau (neu)
17. **Geyer Jakob,** kaufmännischer Angestellter, Burgdorf (neu)
18. **Häusler Gottfried,** Lehrer, Büetigen (neu)
19. **Michel Oskar,** Gemeindepräsident, Bönigen (neu)
20. **Müller Fritz,** Spengler-Installateur, Belp (neu)
21. **Müller Hans,** Lehrer, Herzogenbuchsee (neu)
22. **Müller Richard,** Dr., Sekretär der PTT-Union, Bern (neu)
23. **Rubi Christian,** Geschäftsführer des Schweizerischen Skischulverbandes, Wengen (neu)
24. **Sägesser Fritz,** Stationsvorstand, Heustrich-Emdtal (neu)
25. **Schneider Erwin,** Sekretär der Sozialdemokratischen Partei des Kantons Bern, Bern (neu)
26. **Stähli Walter,** Mechaniker, Stettlen (neu)
27. **Staub Werner,** Zentralsekretär des Schweizerischen Textil- und Fabrikarbeiterverbandes, Gemeindepräsident, Duggingen (neu)
28. **Steinmann Fritz,** Kupferschmied und Gemeinderatspräsident, Langnau i.E. (neu)
29. **Zingg Karl,** Sekretär des Gewerkschaftskartells des Kantons Bern, Bern (neu)
30. **Bratschi Robert,** Generalsekretär des Schweiz. Eisenbahnerverbandes, Bern, Präsident des Schweizerischen Gewerkschaftsbundes (bisher)
31. **Grimm Robert,** Direktor BLS, Bern (bisher)
32. **Grütter Fritz,** Präsident der Sozialdemokratischen Partei des Kantons Bern, Bern (bisher)
33. **Steiner Arthur,** Vizepräsident des Schweizerischen Metall- und Uhrenarbeiterverbandes, Bern (bisher)

**Unmittelbar vor Einwurf in die Urne vom Wahlausschuss auf der Rückseite abstempeln lassen**
*Faire timbrer au des par le bureau electoral immediatement avant la mise dans l'urne*

voters rather than in that chosen by the party leaders. In elections for the Belgian Chambre des Représentants, the Danish Folketing, and the Tweede Kamer of the Dutch Staten-Generaal, the voters are permitted to indicate preference for only one candidate. In elections for the Norwegian Storting, both houses of the Swedish parliament, and the Eerste Kamer of the Dutch parliament, the voters are permitted to indicate preferences for from two to four candidates.

**Full Freedom of Choice Among Candidates** Under the third type of party-list system each voter has as many votes as there are seats to be filled from his particular constituency, and he may distribute those votes as he wishes. He may register several votes for a particular candidate or one vote each for several different candidates. He may also vote for particular candidates on several party lists. The votes are totaled for all candidates on each list, and seats are allotted to each party in accordance with its proportion of the total vote for all lists. Each party's quota of seats in each

The Electoral Process

constituency is then filled by the party's candidates receiving the largest numbers of votes. This system, also called "panachage," is now used in elections to the Swiss National Council and to a number of cantonal councils, as well as in elections to the Eduskunta (parliament) of Finland.[17]

### The Single-Transferable-Vote System

All party-list systems, as we have seen, operate on the assumption that the voter is most interested in supporting a particular political party. All single-transferable-vote systems operate on the contrary assumption that voters are more interested in individual candidates than in parties and should be given maximum freedom to indicate their preferences for individuals.

Each constituency elects several members to the legislative assembly, and any individual can obtain a place on the ballot by petition, with or without a party designation. The voter indicates his order of preference among the various candidates as in the preferential-ballot systems described, marking numbers in the boxes beside their names. The ballots are first sorted according to the first-place choices for each candidate. Then an "electoral quota" is figured according to one of several possible formulas.[18] If no candidate receives enough first-place choices to satisfy the quota, the candidate with the fewest first-place choices is dropped, and his ballots are redistributed according to the second-place choices on each. The process of dropping the low candidates and redistributing their ballots is continued until a sufficient number of candidates have satisfied the quotas and are declared elected.

This system is now used for the election of members of the Irish Dáil, the Senate of Northern Ireland, the Australian Senate, the South African Senate, particular houses of the parliaments of the Australian states of Tasmania and New South Wales, and some city councils in the United States.[19]

## POLITICAL EFFECTS OF ELECTORAL SYSTEMS

Both the majority and proportional systems have strong partisans among present-day democratic theorists.[20] We have already summarized the main arguments for PR, and we should note here that its critics declare that, wherever it has been tried, it has

---

[17] The best way to understand the panachage system is to observe its use in an actual election. Such an illustration would take far too much space here, but the reader is referred to a description of the election of the Swiss National Council from the Canton of Lucerne in 1959; Christopher Hughes, *The Parliament of Switzerland* (London: Cassell & Co., Ltd., 1962), pp. 175–178.

[18] The formula favored by most advocates of this system is

$$\frac{\text{total votes}}{\text{total seats} + 1} + 1 = \text{quota}$$

[19] See the description of the system's operation in the 1957 election for the Irish Dáil by Basil Chubb, in "Ireland," in D. E. Butler (ed.), *Elections Abroad* (New York: St. Martin's Press, Inc., 1959), chap. 3.

[20] The leading advocates of PR are listed in note 15. The leading critics include F. A. Hermens, *Democracy or Anarchy?* (Notre Dame, Ind.: The Review of Politics, 1941); Herman Finer, *Theory and Practice of Modern Government* (New York: Holt, Rinehart and Winston, Inc., 1949), pp. 556–558; and Ernest Barker, *Reflections on Government* (New York: Oxford University Press, 1942), pp. 78–81.

encouraged multiple parties, deepened ideological fissures, and lowered consensus. It has also, they say, transformed every government that uses it into a weak coalition of quarreling and mutually suspicious parties, and it has failed to elicit popular mandates on immediate and practical political issues.

In a book of this sort I cannot present the full argument for each side, let alone decide which is the more convincing. But political science research has provided a great deal of empirical material and analysis that should provide the basis—if not the conclusions—for this debate. In his systematic study of the consequences of various electoral systems for the distribution of popular votes and public offices among political parties, Douglas W. Rae came to certain conclusions that may be summarized here.[21]

First, every electoral system tends to award to parties with large shares of the vote more than their proportional shares of parliamentary seats; the reverse is true of parties with small shares of the vote. The party with the largest single share of the vote profits most from this tendency, which generally operates to deny small parties any seats at all. This pattern is more pronounced in majority than in proportional systems, but it operates to some extent in all. Second, majority systems tend to produce two-party competition except when minority parties are very strong in particular areas.[22] Third, proportional systems discriminate against small parties without strong local bases less than do majority systems; they thus encourage greater "fractionalization" of party systems.[23] Fourth, in order to achieve a legislative majority capable of ruling, more parties willing to join coalitions are necessary in proportional than in majority systems. Finally, the most important single factor affecting the degree of proportionality[24] in an electoral system is the size of its electoral districts: The more members elected from each district, the more proportional are seats to shares of the vote. Israel, which elects all its national legislators "at large" from one all-nation district, has the highest proportionality of any electoral system. It also has the largest number of parties represented in parliament of any present-day democracy and one of the most fractionalized party systems.[25]

Those are some of the most notable facts. It may also be mentioned that most of the democratic electoral systems adopted since World War II—in Japan, Italy, and Israel, for example—employ some form of PR. On the other hand, few if any of the English-speaking nations now using majority systems are seriously considering adopting PR. Whatever the respective merits of the two systems may be, it is clear

---

[21] Douglas W. Rae, *The Political Consequences of Electoral Laws.*

[22] This is an important qualification of some observers' claims that majority systems always produce two-party competition.

[23] That is, a more even division of votes and parliamentary seats among a larger number of parties; see Chap. 9.

[24] That is, how closely each party's share of the vote approximates its share of the parliamentary seats.

[25] The number varies somewhat from one election to the next, but the modal number of parties represented in the Knesset is sixteen; Fein, *Politics in Israel,* pp. 226–227, Table VI.1. For the judgment that Israel's party system is among the world's most fractionalized, see Rae, *The Political Consequences of Electoral Laws,* p. 141.

that in the foreseeable future neither is likely to become *the* democratic method for electing public officials.

## NOMINATIONS AND ELECTIONS IN THE SOVIET UNION

### FORMAL PROCEDURES

At first glance the formal nominating and electing procedures in the Soviet Union appear to justify Joseph Stalin's famous boast that the Russian Constitution is "the most democratic in the world." Article 135, for example, guarantees the suffrage to "all citizens of the USSR who have reached the age of eighteen, irrespective of race or nationality, sex, religion, education, domicile, social origin, property status or past activities . . . with the exception of persons who have been legally certified insane."[26] Moreover, just about every eligible Soviet voter votes, and voting turnouts are far higher than the best that the Western democratic systems can claim: In elections to the Supreme Soviet from 1962 to 1974 the average turnout was a staggering 99.9 percent! Even the most optimistic get-out-the-vote organizations in the Western democracies must despair of ever matching this figure.

When the Western observer looks a bit more closely at the formal procedures and actual conduct of Soviet nominations and elections, however, he can only conclude that they correspond little if at all to the standards of free elections outlined earlier in this chapter.

#### Nominations

The Supreme Soviet is a bicameral body, and the members of each house are elected by pluralities from single-member constituencies. The election laws state that nominations of candidates for these posts may be made by Communist Party branches, trade unions, cooperative societies, youth organizations, cultural societies, and such work units as factories and collective farms. When one of these groups has met and agreed upon a candidate, it must submit his name and the minutes of the nominating meeting to the local election commission, which prints the candidates' names on the ballot fifteen days after the end of the submission period. How could nominating rules be simpler or more democratic?

Yet these superdemocratic procedures have never produced more than one candidate for each office to be filled. The reason is that the Communist Party, the only legal party in the Soviet Union, has members in every trade union, cooperative society, cultural organization, collective farm, and factory. It requires very little imagination to understand what happens in these "nominating" organizations when a party member proposes a candidate or opposes candidates suggested by nonparty members. Most nominations, as a matter of fact, are made in mass meetings in factories and on collective farms, rather than in private meetings of the various

---

[26] Quoted in Randolph L. Braham, *Soviet Politics and Government* (New York: Alfred A. Knopf, 1965), p. 578.

associations, and, once the attending party members have made known their views—as they always do—the matter is settled. If the machinery should happen to slip up somewhere and present an election commission with two nominations, the commission, which also includes party members, can eliminate the competition in the fifteen-day period before the ballots are printed.

The evidence strongly suggests that the party does exercise close control over nominations. For example, its membership is only about 9 percent of the whole population, but more than 80 percent of the nominees for membership in the Supreme Soviet are party members. Even nonparty deputies are carefully selected to represent such major elements as workers, farmers, the old, the young, women, the intelligentsia, and so on. And no nonparty candidate, we may be sure, is *anti*party![27]

Soviet leaders are neither furtive nor apologetic about their single-candidate system. As a recent Soviet writer, P. Tumanov, put it:

> During the nomination of candidates for Deputy many meetings name several candidates. Why does only one candidate's name remain on the ballot? Back in 1936, M. I. Kalinin, speaking at the pre-election rally in Leningrad, said: "If in our country in a number of places candidates withdraw their names in favor of a single candidate, this is the consequence of their social kinship and the community of their political goals. After thorough discussion, tens and thousands of voters have agreed on a single candidate. This is also a hallmark of socialism, a sign that there is no, and cannot be any, discord among our laboring masses, the kind of inner discord that exists within bourgeois society."[28]

### Elections

After a campaign period of about two months the election is held. The voters go to the polls and receive ballots from the local election official. The law gives them two choices: If they approve the candidate printed on the ballot, they need only fold it, unmarked, in front of everyone in the room and drop it in the ballot box; if they wish they can retire to a screened voting booth, cross out the official candidate's name, fold the ballot, and drop it in the ballot box—with everyone knowing exactly what they have done. They cannot write in the name of another candidate but are restricted to voting against the official candidate. It is not surprising that only a minute fraction of the voters take their ballots into the screened booth.

When 99.9 percent of the voters have performed this ritual, the polls are closed, the ballots are counted, and *Pravda* and *Izvestia* announce the outcome:

> The dazzling victory of the Party and non-Party bloc in Soviet elections is a clear expression of the monolithic cohesion of the Soviet people, of its faith, love and devotion to the Communist Party and to the Soviet Government, to its

---

[27] See the description of the nominating process in Derek J. R. Scott, *Russian Political Institutions* (New York: Frederick A. Praeger, Inc., 1966), pp. 95–96.

[28] Quoted in John A. Armstrong, *Ideology, Politics, and Government in the Soviet Union* (rev. ed.; New York: Frederick A. Praeger, Inc., 1967), p. 111.

wholehearted readiness to march behind the Party along the road to communism.[29]

## WHY THEY BOTHER

Even though the election results are a foregone conclusion, once the official candidates are named campaigning is quite as noisy and energetic as in the most hard-fought contests in the Western democracies. For a full two months the voters are flooded with radio speeches, newspaper stores and editorials, pamphlets and broadsides, and door-to-door campaigning by Bolshevik agitators (see Chap. 5).[30] Mass meetings and parades are held several times a week, and in general a tremendous effort is made to arouse 100 percent of the voters to vote.

**In communist elections reality differs from formality.** Source: *The Herblock Book* (Boston: The Beacon Press, 1952).

*"We now bring you more late election returns"*

To those of us accustomed to Western democratic procedures the whole elaborate Soviet system of nominating, campaigning, and electing seems pointless and ridiculous. That is because we think of nominations and elections as methods by

---

[29] Quoted in L. G. Churchward, *Contemporary Soviet Government* (London: Routledge & Kegan Paul Ltd., 1968), pp. 108–109.

[30] Frederick C. Barghoorn estimates that the "huge army of more than 2,000,000 agitators is swollen during election campaigns to more than 3,000,000"; Barghoorn, *Politics in the USSR* (Boston: Little, Brown & Company, 1966), p. 167.

which a truly sovereign electorate chooses among many rivals for public office and political power; it is difficult for us to understand why the communists bother to go through the motions of democracy when they know that they have—and *want* to have—rule by the party elite rather than by the masses.

When we view the matter from the communist point of view, however, it makes a kind of sense. Elections are above all a device for mobilizing the masses' approval and even enthusiasm for party policies while giving them the feeling—however spurious it may seem to democratic eyes—that they are participating in the nation's governing processes. They also provide the regime with a facade of democratic legality that may be useful in its dealings with other nations—for example, Algeria and Guinea—that wish to cloak the hard realities of a dictatorial regime in the garments of democracy.[31] And even the tiny variations in the numbers of abstentions and negative votes may provide a useful barometer for detecting changes in public opinion.[32]

The purpose of democratic candidate recruitment and elections is to establish popular *control* over public officials. The purpose of communist nominations and elections is to create popular *support* for policies and leaders already determined by the party oligarchs. In few other institutional comparisons is the contrast and distance between the Western and communist conceptions of democracy so apparent.

[31] See Merle Fainsod, *How Russia Is Ruled* (rev. ed.; Cambridge, Mass.: Harvard University Press, 1963), pp. 381–383; Armstrong, *Ideology, Politics, and Government in the Soviet Union,* pp. 111–112; and Barghoorn, *Politics in the USSR,* pp. 167–168.

[32] Vernon V. Aspaturian, in Roy C. Macridis and Robert E. Ward (eds.), *Modern Political Systems: Europe* (Englewood Cliffs, N.J.: Prentice-Hall, Inc., 1963), p. 511. For an interesting analysis of Polish one-party elections as barometers in this sense, see Jerzy J. Wiatr, "Elections and Voting Behavior in Poland," in Ranney (ed.), *Essays on the Behavioral Study of Politics* (Urbana, Ill.: University of Illinois Press, 1962), pp. 244–251.

# 8

## VOTING BEHAVIOR

Most of us sometimes become upset, frightened, or angry about what our government is doing or not doing. Some of us are concerned about unemployment and demand government-guaranteed jobs. Some of us are concerned about the rising crime rate and our inability to walk safely after dark on the streets of our big cities, and we demand the restoration of law and order. And some of us are concerned about the rapid deterioration of our physical environment and demand drastic antipollution measures before it is too late.

There comes a time for most of us when we feel that mere talk is no longer enough, that it is time for action—now! But what kind of action? "I'm only one person," we often hear people say. "What can *I* do?"

In a democratic system there are many answers to that question. We can join existing political parties or form new ones and try to elect new public officials. We can join pressure groups to "put the heat on" incumbent officials to make them do something or stop doing something. We can file court suits against the officials. We can demonstrate, boycott, and strike. The physical means are readily at hand even to assassinate the President or start a revolution. We *can* do any of these things, but most of us evidently find most forms of political action too demanding, too costly, too dangerous, or too destructive of other values. Like most citizens of the world's other democratic nations, we confine ourselves to voting for or against particular parties and candidates in periodic elections.

Voting may or may not be the most effective way for ordinary citizens to make

Political Inputs

government do as they wish.[1] But in every modern democratic regime votes are the basic units of political power. When all is said and done, the groups that mobilize the largest numbers of voters in support of the policies and public officials they favor receive the largest shares of what they want out of politics. If a man has every quality necessary to be a great President except the ability to make people vote for him, his other qualities will not make him *any* kind of President. A political party may have the most intelligent and foresighted program possible, but if it cannot convince the voters its program will never become public policy. A pressure group may lobby so skillfully that it lines up everyone in the legislature on its side, but should the voters throw those legislators out of office at the next election its lobbying efforts may well have been for naught. Even the power of money, sometimes mistakenly regarded as an irresistible force in politics, ultimately depends upon its ability to produce votes.

Most party politicians and pressure group leaders know these political facts of life. For them the whole question of what makes voters vote as they do is a matter of the most vital concern. No doubt few political leaders think of themselves as having anything as fancy as a "working theory of voting behavior." All, however, have just that in the form of practical rules of thumb that guide their campaigning operations: Voters become more stirred up against people and issues than for them; people vote mainly to advance their own economic self-interest; if a district has a lot of Polish and Italian voters, some Polish and Italian candidates ought to appear on the ticket; and so on.[2]

Despite the obvious importance of voting behavior in the decision-making processes of democratic systems, few social scientists made any but the most casual efforts to study it before World War I. In 1924, however, the American political scientists Charles E. Merriam and Harold F. Gosnell published a pioneer study of the causes of nonvoting.[3] Since then a considerable body of literature on nonvoting and many other aspects of voting behavior has been published. As a result voting behavior (or "political behavior" as it is sometimes misnamed: see Chap. 1) has become not only a full-fledged "field" of political science but also, by general agreement, one of the most advanced. And, although the bulk of such research has been devoted to American voters, there are also excellent studies of British, Finnish, French, German, Italian, Norwegian, and Swedish voters.

In this chapter we shall review their principal findings.

---

[1] In Chap. 10 we shall say more about various forms of political action, with particular attention to their effectiveness, costs, and consequences.

[2] There are many studies of political campaigning focusing on candidates' and campaign directors' notions about why voters vote as they do and the kinds of campaigns that attract the most voters. See, for example, Karl A. Lamb and Paul A. Smith, *Campaign Decision-Making: The Presidential Election of 1964* (Belmont, Calif.: Wadsworth Publishing Company, Inc., 1968), on presidential campaigning; Murray B. Levin, *Kennedy Campaigning* (Boston: The Beacon Press, 1966), on senatorial campaigning; David A. Leuthold, *Electioneering in a Democracy* (New York: John Wiley & Sons, Inc., 1968), on campaigning for the United States House of Representatives; John W. Kingdon, *Candidates for Office: Beliefs and Strategies* (New York: Random House, Inc., 1968), on campaigning for a state legislature; and Richard Rose, *Influencing Voters: A Study of Campaign Rationality* (New York: St. Martin's Press, Inc., 1967), on national campaigning in Great Britain.

[3] Charles E. Merriam and Harold F. Gosnell, *Non-Voting* (Chicago: University of Chicago Press, 1924).

## DIMENSIONS[4]

Political scientists picture voting behavior as having two principal dimensions, as shown graphically in Figure 5. The horizontal axis represents the voters' *preference,* that is, the degree of their approval or disapproval of particular political parties, candidates, laws, policy proposals, or whatever. The seven categories shown are those used by the Survey Research Center of The University of Michigan for measuring American voters' attitudes toward the major parties in our two-party system. Similar scales can, however, be constructed (with many more categories) for measuring voters' preferences in multiple-party systems by arranging the parties on some kind of left-right continuum (see Chap. 9).

**FIGURE 5**
**The dimensions of voting behavior.**

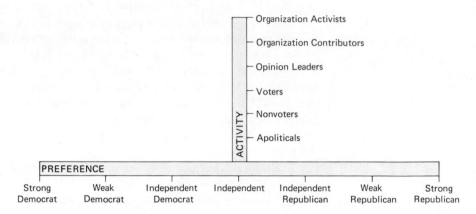

The vertical axis represents the voters' *activity*—what, if anything, they do about their preferences. Its six categories are usually defined as follows. *Organization activists* are people who regularly devote substantial time and energy to working in political parties or pressure groups: party leaders and precinct captains, pressure group leaders and lobbyists. It is estimated that no more than 1 percent of the adult population in most democracies belongs in this category.[5] *Organization contributors* occasionally donate money, do volunteer campaign work, or otherwise actively lend a hand. Perhaps 5 percent of adults may be classified here. *Opinion leaders,* as we saw in Chapter 6, are people who regularly "talk politics" with their families, friends, and work associates and thus have a noticeable impact on the formation of political opinion; about 25 percent of adults fit this description. *Voters* are people who cast ballots in most elections but do nothing more to support their preferences, about 44 percent of

---

[4] This discussion closely follows that in Hugh A. Bone and Austin Ranney, *Politics and Voters* (3d ed.; New York: McGraw-Hill, Inc., 1971), pp. 4–6.

[5] Lester W. Milbrath, *Political Participation* (Skokie, Ill.: Rand McNally & Company, 1965), pp. 16–19, estimates the proportions of American adults generally found at each level of activity. Similar estimates are given by Robert E. Lane, *Political Life* (New York: The Free Press, 1959), pp. 52–56. Jean Blondel estimates that in Great Britain about 1 percent of adults are organization activists and 4 percent organization contributors—figures remarkably similar to the American estimates; see Blondel, *Voters, Parties, and Leaders* (Baltimore, Md.: Penguin Books, Inc., 1963), pp. 94–95.

Political Inputs

adults.[6] *Nonvoters* seldom or never vote but still have some trace of interest in political affairs; they constitute about 24 percent of the adult population. *Apoliticals* have no discernible knowledge of or interest in politics; they constitute perhaps 1 percent of adults.

**Levels of political involvement and activity—an endless treadmill for modern man?** Source: Drawing by Lee Lorenz, © 1969 The New Yorker Magazine, Inc.

## INTERVENING VARIABLES

In any democratic system the aspect of voting behavior that first concerns both practicing politicians and political scientists is the *result*—how many people vote and which way—because it is at that point that voters have their most direct and powerful impact on the governing process. Voting studies thus take voters' preferences and activities as their main dependent variables—the varying effects whose causes they wish to understand and explain.

---

[6]The proportions in the last three categories obviously vary widely from one democracy to another. The figures in the text are crude estimates of the "average" proportions in most democracies.

Voting Behavior

Voting behavior is a species of the genus public opinion. As we saw in Chapters 4 and 5, a great many independent variables affect most political attitudes and behavior—biological natures and needs; psychological constitutions, including perceptions and conceptualizations; memberships in primary and secondary groups; communications received; and so on. Should we, then, simply assume that these factors also explain voting behavior and let it go at that?

The authors of the most distinguished study of American voting behavior say no.[7] They point out that, when we ask people why they voted as they did in a particular election, few are likely to reply, "Because I have a high socioeconomic status," "Because I live in a suburb," or "Because daddy told me to." They will probably say, "Because I am a Democrat," "Because I want to restore law and order in this country," or "Because I think Nixon is a crook." Most people regard their own votes as reflecting their opinions on parties, issues, and candidates rather than as "knee-jerk" responses to their own social statuses. Psychological factors *intervene* between the voters' life situations and their votes or failures to vote in any particular election.

We therefore have to understand not only the ultimate independent variables of people's psychobiological cores and social states but also the intervening variables: party identifications, issue orientations, and candidate orientations.

## PARTY IDENTIFICATION

### Meaning

Party identification is "the sense of general attachment or belonging which an individual feels toward a given party."[8] It is thus an inner psychological attitude, rather than an overt organizational attachment like party membership (see Chap. 9). Political scientists usually seek to measure party identification by asking questions comparable to the SRC's standard "Generally speaking, do you usually think of yourself as a Republican, a Democrat, an independent, or what?" Of those replying "independent," they ask a follow-up question "Do you think of yourself as closer to the Republican or Democratic party?" Their responses can be classified in the seven categories illustrated on the preference dimension in Figure 5.

### Development

From the evidence so far compiled, it appears that party identification is the first attitude that most people acquire in their political socialization: As we saw in Chapter 4, by age seven or eight most Americans will tell an interviewer, "We [that is, the respondent's family] are Republicans (or Democrats)." Evidently we acquire our initial party identifications, like our religious preferences, mainly from our parents,

---

[7] Angus Campbell, Philip E. Converse, Warren E. Miller, and Donald E. Stokes, *The American Voter* (New York: John Wiley & Sons, Inc., 1960), chap. 2.

[8] Campbell and Henry Valen, "Party Identification in Norway and the United States," *Public Opinion Quarterly,* 25 (Winter 1961), 505.

as aspects of our identifications with our families. The more united the parents are in their party preferences and the more vocal they are about them, the more likely their children are to have the same preferences for the rest of their lives.[9] In most people these early preferences are likely to grow stronger through life as a result of the general principle, noted in Chapter 4, that, the longer one maintains identification with any group, the more intense the identification becomes. On the other hand, where, as in France, the usual family relationship does not allow for political discussion by parents with or in front of children, fewer people have stable long-run party identifications.[10]

### Fluctuation

Another reason for the lower incidence of stable party identifications in France is that the parties themselves have been less stable than in many other democracies. The parties of the Third Republic (1870–1940) disappeared under the Vichy regime (1940–1944), reappeared in somewhat altered form and with some new names under the Fourth Republic (1946–1958), and have undergone more reshuffling in the Fifth Republic (1958–). Furthermore, under the Fourth Republic some parties (the Rassemblement du Peuple Français, Social Republicans, and Poujadists) were purely "flash" parties: They emerged, fought one or two elections, and disbanded. In recent years France has offered fewer durable parties with which Frenchmen could form lasting identifications than most other democracies have provided for their citizens.

In the United States, however, the present party alignment has lasted since 1854, in Great Britain and Norway since 1900, in Switzerland since 1919, in Canada since 1918, and so on. In these countries party identifications tend to be noticeably stronger and more stable than in France, but some fluctuations occur nevertheless. According to the SRC some Americans switch parties for personal reasons: A woman marries a man with an opposing party loyalty and shifts hers to keep peace at home; a man achieves a socioeconomic status higher than that of his father or moves to a new neighborhood and switches to the predominant party in his new environment; and so on. Politically, however, the significant fluctuations are those in which massive numbers of voters switch from one party to another and thus change the balance of electoral power. Such a shift certainly occurred in the United States between 1930 and 1936 when many Republicans became Democrats;[11] in Great Britain in 1918–1924, when many Liberals switched to Labour or the Conservatives; and in France after 1958, when many supporters of the left, center, and moderate rightist parties became supporters of the new Gaullist party, the Union pour la Nouvelle République.

---

[9] For American evidence, see Campbell, Converse, Miller, and Stokes, *The American Voter*, pp. 146–149. For British evidence, see David Butler and Stokes, *Political Change in Britain* (New York: St. Martin's Press, Inc., 1969), pp. 45–55.

[10] Converse and Georges Dupeux found that whereas 91 percent of American respondents had some idea of their fathers' parties, only 29 percent of their French respondents did; "Il ne disait rien à ses enfants" was a reply often heard in France. Converse and Dupeux, "Politicization of the Electorate in France and the United States," *Public Opinion Quarterly*, 26 (Spring 1962), 11–13.

[11] See Campbell, Converse, Miller, and Stokes, *The American Voter*, pp. 149–160.

**TABLE 11**

**The Distribution of Party Identifications in the United States and Norway**

UNITED STATES, 1968–1972

| Year | Democrats (52–55%) | | | Independents (11–13%) | Republicans (33%) | | |
|------|--------|------|-------------|---------------|-------------|------|--------|
| | Strong | Weak | Independent | | Independent | Weak | Strong |
| 1968 | 20% | 25% | 10% | 11% | 9% | 14% | 10% |
| 1970 | 20 | 23 | 10 | 13 | 8 | 15 | 10 |
| 1972 | 15 | 26 | 11 | 13 | 10 | 13 | 10 |

NORWAY, 1957

| Labor (45%) | | Liberal (17%) | | Christian (10%) | | Agrarian (15%) | | Conservative (13%) | |
|--------|------|--------|------|--------|------|--------|------|--------|------|
| Strong | Weak | Strong | Weak | Strong | Weak | Strong | Weak | Strong | Weak |
| 21% | 24% | 4% | 13% | 6% | 4% | 6% | 9% | 5% | 8% |

*Source:* The American figures were compiled by the Survey Research Center, University of Michigan, and furnished through the Inter-University Consortium for Political Research. The Norwegian figures come from Angus Campell and Henry Valen, "Party Identification in Norway and the United States," *Public Opinion Quarterly*, 25 (Winter 1961), p. 517, Table 2.

## Distribution

Party leaders and candidates are naturally most interested in the distribution of party identifications, for it is one of the prime (though not the only) factors controlling their chances of winning elections. Table 11 shows recent distributions in a two-party and a multiparty nation. It reveals several things of political importance. First, in the United States the Democrats were clearly the majority party in 1972: 52 percent of the respondents expressed some degree of preference for them, to only 33 percent for the Republicans. The Democrats thus enter any national election with a long head start, and it takes powerful short-range countervailing forces, like Dwight D. Eisenhower's great personal popularity in the 1950s or their own internal division in 1972, to overcome their lead. In Norway, the Labor party had almost a majority of the population in 1957 (45 percent to a combined total of 55 percent for all the others). The only way to prevent a Labor government was thus for all the other parties to combine behind one government that excluded Labor. The difficulty is demonstrated by the fact that from 1945 to 1965 Labor was in power all the time except for twenty-eight days in 1963; it lost again in 1965 and 1969, but returned to power in 1971.

Table 11 also shows that Norwegians had somewhat stronger party attachments than did Americans: 42 percent expressed strong identifications, compared with 30 percent of the Americans.[12] I shall describe some consequences of this difference in a moment.

---

[12] In France in 1958, by contrast, 10 percent of respondents refused to tell interviewers their party preferences. Of the remainder only 60 percent identified themselves with parties or even general *tendances* like "left" and "right"; see Converse and Dupeux, "Politicization of the Electorate in France and the United States," p. 9.

As we have noted previously, in most modern democracies the most visible political contestants today are the same political parties (or at least parties bearing the same labels) that have been prominent for periods ranging from sixty years to more than a century.[13] In such nations the parties constitute "virtually the only interesting political objects that are surely perceived by the quasi-totality of the population."[14] Party identification thus serves people as the principal device for making sense of the political events, personalities, issues, charges, and countercharges flooding them from the communications media. That is, the one political fact that most of us are sure of is that we are Democrats or Republicans; when in doubt—as we often are—about this issue or that candidate, we can still choose, by simply going along with our parties' positions or candidates.

It is not surprising therefore that political scientists have consistently found powerful associations between intensity of party identification and most other aspects of voting behavior. For example, the most partisan among us are also the most interested in and best informed about political affairs, the most likely to vote, and the most likely to try to influence others to vote.

The least partisan are quite different. We are all familiar with the inspiring picture of "independents" as ideal citizens—people who are deeply concerned with civic affairs, acquaint themselves with the facts about the issues and candidates, and make their decision on each according to its merits, their thinking uncontaminated by loyalty to party labels. Without commenting on whether or not good citizens *should* be this way, we must recognize that the voting studies have found only a tiny fraction of self-styled "independents" who do fit this ideal. Quite the contrary: typical "independents" are far less interested in politics than strong partisans, know much less about issues and candidates, care little about how elections come out, and are much less likely to vote. Their independence, in short, results from plain apathy, rather than from high-minded rejection of partisanship.[15]

Remember, though, that the previous paragraph applies only to the "independent independents"—that is, people who express no preference of *any* kind for one party over the other. There are also the "independent leaners"—those who do not regard themselves as *members* of either party but still feel that one party is better than

---

[13] The principal exceptions are the new democracies like Sri Lanka, India, and Israel and nations that have recently replaced dictatorial regimes with democratic ones: France, West Germany, Italy, and Japan.

[14] Converse, "Information Flow and the Stability of Partisan Attitudes," *Public Opinion Quarterly,* 26 (Winter 1962), 582.

[15] See Campbell, Converse, Miller, and Stokes, *The American Voter,* chap. 6. This phenomenon is evidently not uniquely American. For example, Blondel says of British "floating voters" (those who have no party preferences and switch back and forth between the parties from one election to another), "They seem to be less committed, not because of a genuine independence of mind, but more out of apathy." Blondel, *Voters, Parties, and Leaders,* p. 72. Bo Särlvik says of Swedish voters, "The stronger the voter's ... intensity of partisan preference the greater will be his propensity to vote": Särlvik, "Political Stability and Change in the Swedish Electorate," *Scandinavian Political Studies,* 1 (1966), 206.

the other. They are quite different from the "independent independents": there are more of them (21 percent to 13 percent in 1972); they are much more interested in politics; they know much more about the issues and candidates; they care much more about how elections come out; and they are far more likely to vote. Indeed, they generally score higher on all these counts than do the weak party identifiers. In terms of political involvement, knowledge, and activity, the strong party identifiers are first, the independent leaners are second, the weak identifiers are third, and the independent independents are a distant last.

Party identification, then, has a powerful impact on voting. Yet it is obviously not the sole determinant of voting behavior; if it were the Republicans would never win a presidential election, when in fact they have done splendidly in every election since World War II except that of 1964. To some degree this record can be explained by the countervailing effects of the two other intervening variables.

## ISSUE ORIENTATION

A political issue is a question about what government should or should not do over which people disagree. Much of what we hear about politics in our newspapers and on television—especially during election campaigns—describes interparty (and often intraparty) disputes over issues: Senator A says that the United States should impose strict price controls to stop inflation, while Senator B says that prices should be left free from government meddling to find their true economic level. Some people—probably most readers of this book—who pay considerable attention to discussions of politics in the mass media assume, quite erroneously as we saw in Chapter 5, that everyone else is as interested as they are and knows as much about issues as they do. Consequently, many students of political science, like many political commentators, tend to exaggerate the influence of issues and ideology on the mass electorate.

Why "exaggerate"? The authors of *The American Voter* correctly point out that in order to have a measurable impact upon voting behavior, an issue must fulfill three conditions. First, it must be cognized in some form—that is, the voters must be aware of its existence and have some kind of opinion about it. Second, it must arouse enough intensity of feeling to make them weigh it in deciding how to vote. And, third, they must perceive that the position of a particular party or candidate on the issue is nearer to their own than is that of the opposition. Only when an issue fulfills all three of these conditions for large numbers of voters can it exert significant influence on the outcome of an election.[16]

Voting-behavior studies have generally revealed that those for whom issues are most likely to fulfill all three conditions are those with the strongest party identifications. They, in turn, are likely to derive their issue positions from the stands that their parties take; if, as we saw in Chapter 4, their parties and candidates take issue positions contrary to their own, many of them will simply ignore the fact and continue to act as if the parties they favor support the positions they favor.

The main consequence of this pattern is the general rule that the more ideological the parties and the larger the proportion of the voters strongly identified with

[16] Campbell, Converse, Miller, and Stokes, *The American Voter*, pp. 169–171.

*"How does he stand on reciprocal trade agreements?
That's what I want to know."*

them, the more likely are people's stands on issues to be predictable from their party identifications. This association is weaker in the United States, where the major parties espouse less clear and consistent ideologies, to say the least, than do those in many other nations. It is stronger in Great Britain, where the parties are more ideological than in the United States, though less so than in many European democracies.[17] And it is even stronger in nations like Norway, where a number of durable parties have for many years expounded quite different social philosophies and taken widely divergent stands on public issues. To illustrate, Angus Campbell and Henry Valen asked both Norwegian and American respondents whether or not they thought that there were important differences in what the respective sets of major parties stood for. Forty percent of the Americans thought that the Democratic and Republican parties were about the same, but only 11 percent of the Norwegians saw no important ideological differences among their five major parties. The intranational comparisons were also suggestive: Among the Americans, only about one-third of the strong party identifiers saw no major differences between the parties, compared with almost half the weak identifiers. Among the Norwegians, only 2–6 percent of the strong identifiers saw no differences, compared with 12–17 percent of the weak identifiers.[18]

But things may be changing. In Chapter 4 we noted the considerable rise of issue voting in America in the 1960s and 1970s, and observed that in 1972 most voters

[17] See Butler and Stokes, *Political Change in Britain,* chap. 9. See also Blondel, *Voters, Parties, and Leaders,* pp. 75–87.

[18] Campbell and Valen, "Party Identification in Norway and the United States," p. 517, Table 2.

perceived McGovern and Nixon as holding sharply different positions on many of the most salient issues. However, there is still a question as to whether the voters also saw sharp issue differences between the two *parties*—differences that presumably would persist when McGovern and Nixon no longer headed their respective tickets. To get at this, the Survey Research Center asked its 1972 respondents to rate each party's stand on a number of leading issues. Their responses are summarized in Table 12.

TABLE 12

Americans' Perceptions of Parties' Issue Stands, 1972

| Issue Positions | Percentage Perceiving Party as Holding Position | |
|---|---|---|
| | Democrats | Republicans |
| Vietnam war | | |
| Immediate withdrawal | 50% | 12% |
| Middle of-the-road | 44 | 62 |
| Complete military victory | 6 | 26 |
| | 100% | 100% |
| | | |
| Busing for racial integration of schools | | |
| Bus to achieve integration | 25% | 11% |
| Middle-of-the-road | 56 | 47 |
| Keep children in neighborhood schools | 19 | 42 |
| | 100% | 100% |
| | | |
| Progressive or regressive taxation | | |
| Increase tax rate for high incomes | 37% | 16% |
| Middle-of-the-road | 47 | 51 |
| Have same rate for everyone | 16 | 33 |
| | 100% | 100% |
| | | |
| Legalization of marijuana | | |
| Make use of marijuana legal | 16% | 5% |
| Middle-of-the-road | 55 | 48 |
| Set penalties higher than they are now | 29 | 47 |
| | 100% | 100% |
| | | |
| Equal social roles for women | | |
| Men and women should have equal social roles | 36% | 27% |
| Middle-of-the-road | 58 | 62 |
| Women's place is in the home | 6 | 11 |
| | 100% | 100% |

*Note:* Respondents were asked to place each party's position on a 7-point scale, and I have combined scale positions 1 and 2 for one extreme, 6 and 7 for the other extreme, and 3, 4, and 5 for the middle-of-the-road position.

*Source:* Survey Research Center, University of Michigan, data furnished by the Inter-University Consortium for Political Research.

The responses in Table 12 show that small majorities of the respondents perceived *both* parties as taking middle-of-the-road positions on most of these issues. But substantial minorities believed that the parties were taking sharply opposed positions on every one of the issues except that of equal social roles for women. It therefore appears that Americans nowadays see greater "issue distances" between the parties than they saw in the 1950s. Yet, in presidential elections at least, many voters continue to make their choices not so much on party or issue grounds but on the basis of what they consider to be the two candidates' personal qualities.

VOTE FOR ✔
PENDELTON

*"Well, my first wish is for charisma, my second one is for clout, and my third wish is for deep humility."*

## CANDIDATE ORIENTATION

"Candidate orientation" means voters' opinions on the candidates' personal qualities considered apart from their own party affiliations or stands on issues. For example, when one votes for Richard Nixon mainly because he is the Republican candidate, party identification is the prime factor; when one votes for Nixon mainly from a conviction that he will prevent busing children to force racial integration in the schools, issue orientation is most prominent; and when one votes for Nixon because he is thought to be a mature, experienced, and prudent leader (perhaps in contrast with an unstable and radical McGovern), candidate orientation is the prime factor.

Contrary to what we sometimes read or hear (as in Joe McGinniss' book emphasizing the "selling" of Nixon's "image" in 1968, discussed at the beginning of Chap. 6), candidate orientation is never the only consideration in voting and often not even the most important one. Its power varies with several circumstances—the visibility of the office, the type of election, whether things are going well or badly, and so on. It is strongest when the voters vote directly for the occupant of the office, when they choose between well-publicized candidates, and when the incumbent is often in the news so that the office is prominent in most voters' "cognitive maps." It is thus probably at its strongest in elections for the chief executives of presidential democrat-

Voting Behavior

**FIGURE 6**
Democratic shares of
party identification, and
votes, 1952–1972.

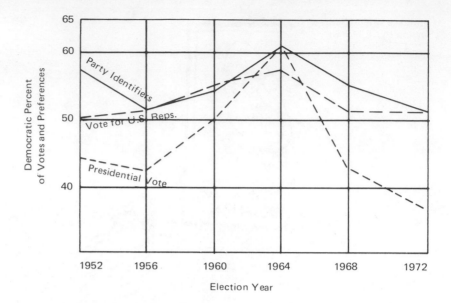

ic systems. This is clearly shown in the case of the United States by the comparison in Figure 6 of three different measures of the Democratic party's electoral strength in the period 1952–1972. In those 20 years the Democrats' share of voters' party identifications varied between a low of 51 percent in 1956 and a high of 61 percent in 1964 (a difference of 10 points). Their share of the total national vote for U.S. representatives varied even less, from a low of 50 percent in 1952 to a high of 57.5 percent in 1964 (a difference of 7.5 points). But in presidential voting their share fell as low as 37.5 percent for George McGovern in 1972 and soared as high as 61 percent for Lyndon B. Johnson in 1964—a difference of 23.5 percentage points![19]

In its study of the 1972 presidential election the SRC asked its respondents to order twelve political figures on a "feeling thermometer," running from 0° (cold) to 100° (warm), with 50° representing the "indifference point." Table 13 shows the mean scores for each figure among the whole sample and also among the major racial and ideological subgroups. The scores in Table 13 show that the figures with the most ideological images were Kennedy, McGovern, Wallace, and Agnew, for they evoked the greatest disagreements between the left-leaning and the right-leaning respondents. The scores also show, perhaps surprisingly, that blacks thought more highly of three white male figures than they did of Shirley Chisholm, the first black female presidential aspirant in history.

---

[19] Survey data confirm the importance and variability of candidate orientation in presidential elections. Donald E. Stokes reports that the SRC's studies of the 1952, 1956, 1960, and 1964 elections show relatively small variations in the distribution of party identifications and issue orientations but great variations in reactions to the candidates' personal qualities; the Republicans had both the most popular candidate (Eisenhower) and the most unpopular candidate (Barry Goldwater): Stokes, "Some Dynamic Elements of Contests for the Presidency," *American Political Science Review,* 60 (March 1966), 19–28.

**TABLE 13**

Average Ratings of Major Political Figures, 1972

| | Total Sample | By Race | | By Policy Orientation | | |
|---|---|---|---|---|---|---|
| | | Whites | Blacks | Left | Center | Right |
| Richard Nixon | 65.5% | 67.3% | 49.2% | 54.4% | 67.8% | 72.8% |
| Edward "Ted" Kennedy | 55.3 | 51.9 | 86.4 | 67.1 | 54.3 | 44.6 |
| Spiro Agnew | 54.3 | 56.1 | 36.6 | 41.6 | 56.0 | 62.9 |
| Thomas Eagleton | 53.9 | 53.6 | 57.6 | 57.2 | 54.8 | 51.5 |
| Hubert Humphrey | 53.1 | 50.9 | 73.4 | 58.5 | 54.0 | 48.0 |
| R. Sargent Shriver | 50.0 | 48.0 | 69.8 | 59.1 | 49.9 | 42.5 |
| Edmund Muskie | 49.9 | 49.2 | 58.1 | 55.6 | 49.9 | 45.5 |
| George Wallace | 49.4 | 52.7 | 19.8 | 33.4 | 49.7 | 60.7 |
| George McGovern | 48.9 | 45.9 | 76.4 | 61.9 | 46.7 | 39.4 |
| Henry "Scoop" Jackson | 48.5 | 48.6 | 48.2 | 46.6 | 50.7 | 48.1 |
| John Lindsay | 47.9 | 46.9 | 58.7 | 54.9 | 46.9 | 43.1 |
| Shirley Chisholm | 45.6 | 42.2 | 73.2 | 57.8 | 43.0 | 37.2 |
| (Range of Ns) | (1306– 2633) | (1205– 2376) | (101– 257) | (332– 706) | (389– 735) | (456– 912) |

*Source:* Arthur H. Miller, Warren E. Miller, Alden S. Raine, and Thad A. Brown, "A Majority Party in Disarray: Policy Polarization in the 1972 Election," *American Political Science Review,* 68 (September 1974), Table 5.

Elsewhere in the western hemisphere the personalities of such top candidates as Eduardo Frei (Chile), Rómulo Betancourt (Venezuela), Juan Perón (Argentina), and José Figueres (Costa Rica) have had comparable effects upon election outcomes. And, although Charles de Gaulle was directly elected to only one of his two terms as President of France (in 1965), his personality certainly played a critical role in French elections—to say nothing of world politics—until he resigned in 1969.

Candidate orientation has been said to be less significant in the parliamentary democracies, where the prime ministers are not directly elected but achieve office as a result of their parties' performances at the polls (see Chap. 16). In some of these nations, however, the personalities of party leaders appear to be growing more and more prominent in election campaigns—the "Americanization of politics" some call it. For example, the most acute analysts of recent British general elections conclude that the Conservatives' cause was damaged in 1964 by many voters' negative reactions to Tory leader Sir Alec Douglas-Home. Labour, on the other hand, prominently featured Harold Wilson in campaign posters and broadcasts, and the voters' approval of him made a significant contribution to his party's victory.[20] The Conservatives then chose a new leader, Edward Heath, partly, it is said, because his public "image" would compare more favorably with that projected by Wilson. In the 1966 campaign both parties focused more than ever on their leaders.[21] Other indirectly elected prime ministers whose personalities have notably attracted voters to (and repelled them from) their parties have included Gough Whitlam in Australia, Pierre Elliott Trudeau in Canada, David Ben-Gurion in Israel, Willy Brandt in West Germany, and, perhaps greatest of all, Jawaharlal Nehru in India. Although candidate orientation probably

[20] Butler and Stokes, *Political Change in Britain,* chap. 17; and Butler and Anthony King. *The British General Election of 1964* (New York: St. Martin's Press, Inc., 1965), pp. 146–150, 370–371.

[21] Butler and King, *The British General Election of 1966* (New York: St. Martin's Press, Inc., 1966), pp. 29–30, 104, 134–139.

remains more powerful in the presidential than in the parliamentary democracies, it does appear to be growing steadily more important in many of the latter.

But direct election does not in itself guarantee high candidate orientation, for the less visible the office, the less important are the candidates' personal qualities in affecting the outcome. In many American states, for example, the voters first choose—usually with some confidence—their candidates for President, Congress, governors, and state legislatures. But then the long ballots frequently confront them with choices for state secretary of state, treasurer, comptroller of public accounts, attorney general, and superintendent of public instruction; then may come choices for county supervisor, clerk, treasurer, sheriff, auditor, clerk of the circuit court, coroner, superintendent of schools, justices of the peace, sanitary commissioners, park commissioners, and recorder of deeds. By the time voters get down to the contest for recorder of deeds, even the most conscientious are likely to say to themselves, "I don't know either of these candidates, I don't know what the recorder of deeds does, I can't imagine it makes any difference which candidate wins the office, and I'm tired!" They either leave that part of the ballot unmarked or vote for the candidate of their party, knowing absolutely nothing else about the candidates. Direct elections for such offices, we may say with confidence, seldom elicit high candidate orientation! As elsewhere, party identification remains the most powerful psychological variable intervening between the voters' behavior at elections and the wider context of politically relevant events, institutions, and communications in which they live.

## VOTING PATTERNS

Psychologists study voting behavior because it helps them understand human attitudes and behavior in general. Sociologists study it to learn more about the general effects of status and group affiliations on social structure and change. Both disciplines have made invaluable contributions to our understanding of how and why people vote. But political scientists study the behavior of individual voters in order to understand the behavior of electorates, for their object is to comprehend the forces affecting the outcome of elections, which, as we shall see, are the principal democratic devices for holding government responsible to the people.

Voting studies in various democracies have unearthed a number of patterns in the behavior of electorates that reveal much about the operation of democracy in the modern world. I shall conclude this chapter by outlining some of these principal patterns.

### SOME CORRELATES OF PREFERENCE

#### Social Status

The factor most generally associated with voters' preferences in all democracies is social status, which includes income, occupation, and education—their unequal shares in their societies' good things. In all modern democratic systems upper-status citizens tend to prefer the parties of the right; lower-status citizens prefer parties of the left.[22] But in no democracy does either group give *all* its votes to a single party; everywhere some upper-status voters support left-wing parties, and some lower-status voters support right-wing parties.

In the United States a majority of the more "advantaged" vote Republican and the less "advantaged" Democratic. In Great Britain the same is true of Conservatives and Labour, respectively. In Japan the middle and upper classes favor the Liberals, whereas the lower classes support the Socialists.[23] In Finland support for the Agrarians and Conservatives, on one hand, and the Communists and Social Democrats, on the other, follows similar patterns.[24] And the Continental European parties have comparable class bases.

### Region

In no modern democratic country are all the classes, occupations, and religious affiliations in the population evenly distributed over the whole territory. Rather, each nation has several geographical regions, each of which is populated more heavily by some types of people than by others. As a result, the parties' electoral support is never evenly distributed throughout the nation; each party has its political oases and its political deserts. In the United States, for example, the Democrats dominate most of the nation's big cities, whereas the Republicans draw much of their support from small and medium-sized towns and big-city suburbs. The rural areas are the most evenly divided.[25] In Great Britain Labour's support is concentrated in the big cities, mining areas, and depressed rural areas of Scotland, Wales, and the north of England; the Conservatives draw heavily from big-city suburbs and the prosperous middle-sized towns and rural areas of the south and west of England. In West Germany the Christian Democrats' strength is drawn mainly from Westphalia, the Rhineland, and Bavaria, whereas the Social Democrats depend mainly upon West Berlin, Hamburg, Bremen, and Hesse.[26]

In most modern democracies national party competition thus results less from even competition in all regions than from the competition of each party's one-party regions with the others. Mapping a nation's electoral geography is usually indispensable to understanding its politics.

---

[22] In Chap. 9 I shall say more about the meaning of the "left-right" scale as applied to political parties. The most complete documentation of this general point is Seymour Martin Lipset, *Political Man* (New York: Doubleday & Company, Inc., 1960), chap. 7. See also Robert R. Alford, *Party and Society* (Skokie, Ill.: Rand McNally & Company, 1963).

[23] Chitoshi Yanaga, *Japanese People and Politics* (New York: John Wiley & Sons, Inc., 1964), p. 275.

[24] Erik Allardt and Yrjö Littunen (eds.), *Cleavages, Ideologies, and Party Systems* (Turku: Westermarck Society, 1964), p. 102, Table 2. For descriptions of the class bases of political parties in New Zealand, France, Italy, West Germany, and Norway, see the relevant articles in Seymour M. Lipset and Stein Rokkan (eds.), *Party Systems and Voter Alignments: Cross-National Perspectives* (New York: The Free Press, 1967).

[25] William H. Flanigan, *Political Behavior of the American Electorate* (Boston: Allyn and Bacon, Inc., 1968), pp. 45–46.

[26] Lewis J. Edinger, *Politics in Germany* (Boston: Little Brown & Company, 1968), pp. 244–248.

## Religion

Some democratic countries have parties more or less directly tied to particular religious faiths: The Christian Democrats in West Germany and Italy (Roman Catholic), and the Netherlands' Catholic People's party (Roman Catholic), Anti-Revolutionary party (Calvinist), and Christian Historical Union (Protestant) are examples. They receive most of their support from their coreligionists, although not all their coreligionists support them.

Other democratic nations, like the United States and Great Britain, have no such religious parties, yet the adherents of particular faiths tend to support particular parties. In the United States since the early 1930s substantial majorities of Roman Catholics and Jews have usually supported the Democrats, whereas smaller but distinct majorities of Protestants have supported the Republicans (see Table 1, Chap. 2). And John Kennedy's Roman Catholicism played a major role in the 1960 presidential election. In Great Britain the members of the Church of England have generally supported the Conservatives, whereas Labour has drawn heavily from Nonconformists (Protestants other than Anglicans), Jews, and nonbelievers.[27]

## Ticket Splitting

Strictly speaking, a split ticket is any ballot on which a voter has not voted for all the candidates nominated by one party. Thus a "ticket splitter" and a "floating voter" are not the same thing: the former is a voter who votes for candidates from different parties for different offices in a given election year, while the latter is a person who votes for most or all of one party's candidates in one year and switches to the other party's candidates in a later year.

The structure of the American governmental and electoral system has always invited ticket splitting: Federalism and separation of powers provide the voters at most elections with a number of different executive and legislative offices to be filled and lists of party candidates to choose from at the national, state, and local levels. This method, of course, is in sharp contrast with that in the parliamentary democracies, particularly those with plurality election systems, which usually require the voters to vote for only one office (for example, a member of a legislative body) at any given election. The 1972 elections provided some dramatic illustrations of this uniquely American phenomenon: In Utah only 26 percent of the voters voted for Democrat George McGovern for President, but a whopping 70 percent voted for Democrat Calvin Rampton for Governor—two concurrent landslides moving in opposite directions! In Vermont McGovern got only 36 percent, but Democrat Thomas Salmon won the governorship with 55 percent; and in Maine McGovern received 38 percent, but his party's senatorial candidate won with 53 percent. Over the entire nation, indeed, while McGovern won only 37.5 percent of the presidential votes, his

---

[27] A useful analysis of the relative role of religious differences and other factors in Western European party cleavages is Rose and Derek Urwin, "Social Cohesion, Political Parties and Strains in Regimes," *Comparative Political Studies,* 2 (April 1969), 7–67.

fellow Democrats running for the House of Representatives won 51.7 percent of all the votes and elected a majority of the members (239 out of 435, or 55 percent).

This kind of ticket splitting has long been a special feature of American electoral politics, and there is some reason to believe it has been increasing in recent years. For example, the fifteen national elections from 1946 through 1974 produced split results (a President of one party and a Congress controlled by the other party) eight times. These facts make split-ticket voting appear to be the norm, not the aberration, in national elections; and much the same was true of the state elections: in states holding gubernatorial and U.S. senatorial elections concurrently between 1960 and 1972, over half yielded split results.[28]

What kinds of people split their tickets? In what other ways do they differ from people who vote straight tickets? In terms of socioeconomic characteristics, they seem to be somewhat more highly educated, more in the professional and white-collar occupations, better paid, and younger.[29] An SRC study made in the 1950s also found a number of interesting motivational correlations. The least split-ticket voting was found among people for whom all three intervening variables pointed in the same partisan direction. Of the three, strong party identification was more highly correlated with straight-ticket voting than were strong issue partisanship and strong candidate partisanship. The SRC concluded that ticket splitters are of two basic types: "indifferents," who care little about how the election comes out but who have some interest in local candidates or wish to please friends; and "motivateds," who have strong but conflicting feelings about parties, issues, and candidates. Very few, however, are civics-book "independents," with strong feelings about the issues and candidates but no preferences between parties.[30]

## SOME SOCIAL CORRELATES OF VOTING AND NONVOTING[31]

Table 14 summarizes authoritative estimates by the U.S. Bureau of the Census of what proportions of various social groupings in the United States actually voted in the presidential elections of 1968 and 1972. The table shows in detail the much-remarked decline in the voting turnout in 1972, and suggests that it cannot all be blamed on apathetic or alienated eighteen-year-olds or black Americans. The more interesting comparisons are those among the various social groupings in each election, for they tell us a great deal about some of the principal social correlates of voting and nonvoting.

---

[28] Walter DeVries and V. Lance Tarrance, *The Ticket-Splitter: A New Force in American Politics* (Grand Rapids, Mich.: William B. Eerdmans Publishing Company, 1972), chap. 1; in the 1972 elections (not covered by the DeVries-Tarrance book), six states gave both offices to the same party and six split them between the parties.

[29] See the Gallup Poll quoted in DeVries and Tarrance, *The Ticket-Splitter,* pp. 59–60.

[30] Campbell and Miller, "The Motivational Basis of Straight and Split Ticket Voting," *American Political Science Review,* 51 (June 1957), 293–312.

[31] Lipset, *Political Man,* chap. 6, is the most comprehensive cross-national survey. He reports that the correlates shown for the United States in Table 14 of this book generally apply to all Western democratic systems.

**TABLE 14**

Voting Turnout of American Social Groups, 1968–1972

| Social Group | Percentage Voting | |
| --- | --- | --- |
| | 1968 | 1972 |
| National | 61% | 56% |
| **Sex** | | |
| Women | 66 | 62 |
| Men | 70 | 64 |
| **Education** | | |
| Elementary | 55 | 47 |
| High School | 69 | 61 |
| College | 81 | 79 |
| **Age** | | |
| 18–20 | 33 | 48 |
| 21–24 | 51 | 51 |
| 25–34 | 63 | 60 |
| 35–44 | 71 | 66 |
| 45–64 | 75 | 71 |
| 65 and over | 66 | 63 |
| **Race** | | |
| White | 69 | 65 |
| Black | 58 | 52 |
| **Residence** | | |
| Metropolitan | 68 | 64 |
| Nonmetropolitan | 67 | 59 |
| South | 60 | 55 |
| Nonsouth | 71 | 66 |
| **Employment** | | |
| Employed | 81 | 66 |
| Unemployed | 52 | 50 |
| Not in labor force | 63 | 59 |

*Source: The American Almanac, 1974,* (The Statistical Abstract of the United States, prepared by the Bureau of the Census; New York: Grosset & Dunlap, Inc., 1974), p. 379, Table 612.

*Note:* Many of the social groupings, such as women and men, show higher voting turnout figures than the "national" figures because they are derived from a sampling of the voters, while the "national figures" are compilations of actual totals. Sample surveys almost always show higher reports of voting over non-voting than the voting returns show.

## Social Status

Perhaps the most universal pattern of voting behavior is the greater participation among high-status people than among low-status people. This is apparent in the voting figures themselves. Many studies of many different democratic nations have shown the same patterns as those in Table 14: Substantially higher proportions of nonvoters among low-income groups than among high-income groups, among grammar-school-educated people than among high-school-educated people, among high-school-educated people than among college-educated people, among blue-collar workers than among white-collar workers, and—most striking in the United States—among blacks (including those whose right to vote is well protected) than among whites. The Census Bureau estimates that in the 1968 election 58 percent of blacks voted, compared with 69 percent of whites, and that in the 1972 election the percentages were 52 percent for blacks and 65 percent for whites.

At first glance these disparities seem strange. After all, government is as useful to the "disadvantaged" in changing the status quo as to the "advantaged" in preserving it. Many formerly disadvantaged groups—like the Irish and Italians in the nineteenth-century United States—have found politics an excellent weapon for improving their statuses. Yet the disadvantaged generally use politics far less than do the advantaged. Why?

S. M. Lipset suggests that a major reason is that low-status groups have poorer access to information than do high-status groups and are thus less likely to know how useful government can be. Furthermore, low-status occupations are less likely than high-status occupations to produce people with the organizing skills and the free time necessary for political leadership. Finally, low-status people are less likely than high-status people to join voluntary associations that might increase political awareness and stimulate planned political action.[32]

The SRC, however, has suggested that nonvoting and low levels of political activity in general basically arise from low levels of political involvement and feelings of political ineffectiveness. The middle-aged black laborer on Chicago's South Side who reached only the fifth grade and has never voted and never expects to vote simply does not care how elections come out. He thinks that it makes no difference whether a Democrat or a Republican occupies the White House or the governor's mansion and that "little" people like him have no influence on what government does or does not do. Whatever "they," the big boys, decide, he and his will have to live with. On the other hand, the middle-aged white executive in Evanston who went to college and votes regularly views politics quite differently: He believes that his vote does have some effect on what government does and that voting is a way to make the world a little more like he wants it to be.[33]

*Sex*

Table 14 shows that American women vote proportionately less than do American men, though the difference is narrowing; this pattern is duplicated in every other democratic nation for which we have data. These sexual differences are most pronounced among the least-educated groups and almost disappear among the college-educated, but in most social groups in most democracies distinctly fewer women than men vote. The difference seems to result partly from the demands of home and children, which restrict women from going out to vote. More important is the persistent and widespread idea among both men and women (and imposed on women by men, according to the Women's Liberation Movement) that politics is a rough, dirty men's affair and that involvement in it is somehow unfeminine. One woman respondent told an interviewer, "Woman is a flower for men to look after"; another said: "I have never voted, I never will. . . . A woman's place is in the home"; and a third declared, "Voting is for the men."[34] Such notions tend to disappear among women who have been to college, but they have long maintained a strong hold among the less educated of both sexes in most nations.

---

[32] Lipset, *Political Man,* pp. 190–203. For a useful summary of knowledge about voting and nonvoting, see Lester W. Milbrath, *Political Participation* (Skokie, Ill.: Rand McNally & Company, 1965).

[33] Campbell, Converse, Miller, and Stokes, *The American Voter,* chap. 17.

[34] Quoted in Lane, *Political Life,* pp. 210–211.

Voting Behavior

FIGURE 7
The age-voting curve.

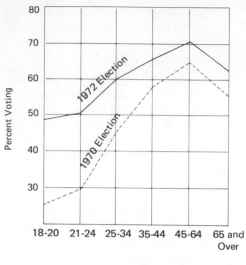

Age Groups

## Age

The frequency of student political demonstrations, marches, rallies, protests, and riots all over the world suggests that young people are far more excited about politics than their elders. Yet the data in Table 14 (shown graphically in Figure 7), as well as other voting studies, show the contrary. Generally speaking, the proportion of voters to nonvoters is lowest among those who have just attained voting age. It increases in each successively older group through the thirties, forties, and fifties and reaches a peak among people in their late fifties and early sixties. Then it declines, apparently because of ailing health and lower physical mobility.

The SRC explains this pattern by the general rule, which we noted earlier, that the longer people hold particular preferences, the more strongly they feel about them. People in their forties and fifties have simply had more time than those in their twenties to develop strong attachments to parties and other political groups. This extra time appears to bring the world into sharper perceptual and emotional focus for them than for their younger compatriots. Moreover, as people grow older, find jobs, marry, raise children, accumulate property, and thus acquire stakes in society, government action becomes more immediately important in their personal lives than it has been in their earlier years.[35] The radical campus activist, though sometimes undoubtedly a potent political force, is nevertheless atypical of his generation.

## CONSISTENT PRESSURES AND CROSS-PRESSURES

Each person's voting decision has two components: should one vote at all? If so, for what party or candidate? One's answers to these questions may be viewed as the end products of various pressures—that is, of various social and psychological forces

---

[35] Campbell, Converse, Miller, and Stokes, *The American Voter*, pp. 493–498.

impelling one in different directions. For example, affluence and a college education, as we have seen, incline one to vote, and to vote Republican, whereas poverty and a grade-school education lead to a Democratic preference, diluted by a tendency not to vote at all. Similarly, strong identification with the Democratic party, agreement with the Democrats' perceived positions on the most important issues, and great admiration for the Democratic candidate's perceived personal qualities impel one to vote and vote Democratic, whereas the opposite attitudes incline one to vote but vote Republican. The pressures are quite similar in all Western democracies.[36]

For many people these social and psychological pressures are most often consistent and mutually reinforcing. But some voters are sometimes "cross-pressured": Some of their affiliations and attitudes point toward a Democratic vote but others toward a Republican vote. What do *they* do? The answer is shown in Table 15.

TABLE 15
**Effects of Consistent Pressures and Cross-Pressures on Voting Behavior**

| Consistent Pressures | Cross-Pressures |
| --- | --- |
| Straight-ticket voting | Split-ticket voting |
| Early decisions on voting | Late decisions on voting |
| High interest in politics | Low interest in politics |
| High levels of political information | Low levels of political information |
| Consistent attitudes | Conflicting attitudes |

*Source:* William H. Flanigan, *Political Behavior of the American Electorate* (Boston: Allyn and Bacon, Inc., 1968), p. 65.

One striking illustration of the patterns shown in Table 15 is Lipset's finding that

> In European countries like France and Austria, where most working-class men back anticlerical leftist parties, their often religious wives are faced with a conflict between voting with their church or with their class and their husbands. This vivid and not uncommon conflict undoubtedly contributes greatly to the low voting rates of working-class women.[37]

A classic illustration of cross-pressures at work in recent American politics is provided by the dilemma of Roman Catholic Republicans in the 1960 presidential election. As Republicans they were inclined to vote for Nixon; as Roman Catholics, however, they were inclined to vote for Kennedy, who was only the second of their coreligionists ever nominated for the nation's highest office. Protestant Democrats, of course, faced the opposite dilemma. For many on both sides it was an agonizing choice, as is clear from this excerpt from an interview with a Roman Catholic Republican committeewoman in a border state:

I'm so confused this election year. *How is that?* I'm a Republican and a

---

[36] For a general summary of the social characteristics associated, in Western democracies, with high or low turnout and left or right preferences see Lipset, *Political Man,* chaps. 6–7.

[37] Lipset, *Political Man,* p. 208.

Catholic, and religion and politics are important to me. I'll have to make a decision, looks like I'll have to go against my church.... *Is there anything about Kennedy that might make you want to vote for him?* No, there is not. The only thing he is a Democrat. I could not vote for him for that reason. I *couldn't*. On the other hand he is a Catholic—oh, dear! Why does it have to be that way?[38]

**The nervous (cross-pressured?) voter in 1968: a cartoonist's view.**
Source: Drawing by Robert Osborn. Robert Osborn © 1967, 68, 69 by The New York Times Company. Reprinted by permission.

We are not told what this lady did about her cross-pressures, but we do know that many other Roman Catholic Republicans—and Protestant Democrats—wrestled with comparable dilemmas. We know that the majority of Protestant Democrats stayed with Kennedy and the majority of Roman Catholic Republicans with Nixon. But we also know that proportionally more Protestant than Roman Catholic Republicans voted for Nixon and that proportionally more Roman Catholic than Protestant Democrats voted for Kennedy. We also know that the more religious the "cross-

[38] Quoted in Converse, "Religion and Politics: The 1960 Election," in Campbell, Converse, Miller, and Stokes, *Elections and the Political Order* (New York: John Wiley & Sons, Inc., 1966), p. 96.

pressured" person was, the more likely he was to "vote his religion" rather than his party identification.[39] The chances are, then, that our Roman Catholic Republican committeewoman voted for Nixon but felt very badly about it and was relieved that the presidential choices in later elections did not present her with the same dilemma. She doubtless had plenty of company.

A more recent American illustration is the plight of northern unionized white manual workers in the 1968 presidential election. Ever since the New Deal in the early 1930s they had been solidly Democratic, helping to keep the Democrats the majority party. But from the early 1960s on there was increasing "white backlash" among them: growing opposition to the civil-rights laws pushed by Democrats (see Chap. 22) to help blacks move into white neighborhoods, join white unions, compete with whites for jobs, and generally threaten white workers' accustomed way of life. Democratic candidate Humphrey was a long-time leader in achieving integrationist civil-rights legislation, and the candidate more likely to resist such efforts appeared to be either Nixon or third-party candidate Wallace. On election day a plurality (32 percent) of northern white manual workers, many of them under the prodding of their union leaders, stayed with the traditional Democratic affiliation, but 9 percent voted for Wallace and 26 percent for Nixon; the latter percentage was considerably larger than the one they had given the popular President Eisenhower in 1956. And 31 percent did not vote at all—a markedly higher figure than usual among northern workers.[40]

In our capacity as voters, we are all subject to many social and psychological influences, some of which we understand and some of which we do not. When all these influences impel us in a particular direction, we are likely to move and move in that direction, but when they work against one another we may only wander about in circles. The art of political navigation for party and pressure-group leaders thus still depends upon the undependable rule of thumb, "dead reckoning," that it has always depended upon in a free society.

---

[39] Converse, "Religion and Politics."

[40] These SRC data have been furnished by the Inter-University Consortium for Political Research. See also Converse, Miller, Rusk, and Wolfe, "Continuity and Change in American Politics: Parties and Issues in the 1968 Election," *American Political Science Review,* 63 (December 1969), 1083–1105, especially 1102.

# 9

# POLITICAL PARTIES AND PARTY SYSTEMS

One of the more influential books in recent political science begins with the following declaration:

> It should be stated flatly at the outset that this volume is devoted to the thesis that the political parties created democracy and that modern democracy is unthinkable save in terms of the parties. As a matter of fact, the condition of the parties is the best possible evidence of the nature of any regime. The most important distinction in modern political philosophy, the distinction between democracy and dictatorship, can be made best in terms of party politics. The parties are not therefore merely appendages of modern government; they are in the center of it and play a determinative and creative role in it.[1]

Strong as such statements may seem, for over a generation many political scientists have held them to be no more than the simple truth. Indeed, a number of distinguished studies have been conducted from the premise that we can gain more insight into the essential nature of any nation's political and governing processes by examining the nature and role of its party system than by concentrating mainly on its formal governing apparatus.[2]

---

[1] E. E. Schattschneider, *Party Government* (New York: Holt, Rinehart and Winston, Inc., 1942), p. 1.

[2] For example, Maurice Duverger, *Political Parties: Their Organization and Activity in the Modern State,* trans. by Barbara and Robert North (New York: John Wiley & Sons, Inc., 1954); Sigmund Neumann (ed.), *Modern Political Parties* (Chicago: University of Chicago Press, 1956); Joseph LaPalombara and Myron Weiner (eds.), *Political Parties and Political Development* (Princeton, N.J.:

Still, there have always been a few professorial skeptics. Anthony King has voiced serious doubts about whether political parties in Western democracies in fact play leading parts in all the activities they are said to monopolize or dominate—for example, structuring the vote, stimulating participation, formulating programs, and articulating and aggregating interests.[3] Leon D. Epstein, William J. Keefe, and Frank J. Sorauf share King's doubts and add the further caveat that parties in most political systems are much more the products than the shapers of their systems' special characteristics.[4]

American college students, as noted earlier, have always been more inclined than almost any other element of the population to declare themselves "true independents" with no preference whatever for either of the nation's "Tweedledee and Tweedledum" major parties. And recent public opinion polls have shown a marked decline in strong party identification and a corresponding rise in independence among Americans in general since the mid-1960s (see Table 11 in Chapter 8). There is reason to believe that comparable trends are taking place in many other Western democracies besides the United States.

For all of these reasons, it is hard to escape the conclusion that Western political parties are, as institutions, under more severe attack today than they have been in a long time. If their traditional role is truly in the process of being abolished or radically altered, the consequences are likely to be very great for the whole nature of Western-style democratic politics. But before we decide whether or not this is indeed the case, let us consider what their traditional role and structures have been. That is the task of the present chapter.

## POLITICAL PARTIES IN DEMOCRATIC SYSTEMS

### WHAT IS A POLITICAL PARTY?

Politics, as viewed in this book, is essentially a contest among people and groups for influence over the policies of government. Several different types of groups engage in this contest, including such "unorganized interest groups" as consumers and women and such "organized interest groups" and "pressure groups" as the American Medical Association (AMA) and the Students for a Democratic Society. Each type of group pursues its objectives by means that differ somewhat from those used by other types. Accordingly, each plays a somewhat different role in democratic political systems.

---

Princeton University Press, 1966); and James S. Coleman and Carl G. Rosberg (eds.), *Political Parties and National Integration in Tropical Africa* (Berkeley, Calif.: University of California Press, 1964).

[3] Anthony King, "Political Parties in Western Democracies: Some Sceptical Reflections," *Polity*, 1 (Winter 1969), 111–141.

[4] Leon D. Epstein, *Political Parties in Western Democracies* (New York: Frederick A. Praeger, Inc., 1967), chaps. 1 and 9; William J. Keefe, *Parties, Politics, and Public Policy in America* (New York: Holt, Rinehart and Winston, Inc., 1972), pp. 1–6; and Frank J. Sorauf, *Political Parties in the American System* (Boston: Little, Brown & Company, 1964), p. 57.

Political parties are a particular kind of political group. How can we distinguish them from the other kinds? There is surprising disagreement among political scientists about precisely how political parties should be defined and differentiated from other forms of political organization.[5] Most would agree, however, that in any democratic or dictatorial system a political party has at least the following characteristics:

1. It is an aggregation of people to whom a *label*—Republicans, Communists, Social Democrats, or whatever—is generally applied by both themselves and others.
2. Some of these people are *organized;* they deliberately act in concert to achieve whatever goals their party has.
3. The larger society recognizes as *legitimate* their right to organize and promote their party's cause.
4. Some of the party's goal-promoting activities work through the mechanisms of representative government.
5. A party's key activity is thus *selecting candidates* and *nominating* for public office.

By these criteria, then, a political party differs from a group like thirty-year-olds in that it is organized. It differs from a group like the AMA mainly in that it nominates candidates directly; its selections usually go on the ballots under its name. Pressure groups, as we shall see in the next chapter, resemble parties in many respects: They often contest elections by endorsing candidates, raising money, issuing campaign propaganda, even ringing doorbells. But most of them are concerned mainly with what government *does,* whereas parties are equally or more concerned with who holds office. The "who" and "what" of government are not completely separate, of course, but are analytically separable aspects of the same thing. Our distinction is based on the parties' generally greater emphasis on the "who" aspect, clearly manifested in formal nominations under their own labels. Pressure groups do not provide this kind of sponsorship.

## PARTY IDENTIFICATION AND MEMBERSHIP

### Identifiers, Supporters, and Members

In Chapter 8 we noted that all but a small fraction of the citizens of most modern democratic systems have some party identification; that is, they feel "some sense of general attachment or belonging . . . toward a given party." We also noted that most people acquire such attachments early in life, that the identifications grow stronger as they grow older, that they exert a major influence on voting behavior, and that they are one of the most stable and powerful factors affecting the outcomes of free elections.

---

[5] See, for example, Epstein, *Political Parties in Western Democracies,* pp. 9–14; Neil A. McDonald, *The Study of Political Parties* (New York: Random House, Inc., 1955), chap. 1; and V. O. Key, Jr., *Politics, Parties, and Pressure Groups* (5th ed.; New York: Thomas Y. Crowell Company, 1964), pp. 163–165. The discussion in the text is drawn mainly from Austin Ranney, "The Concept of 'Party,'" in Oliver Garceau (ed.), *Political Research and Political Theory* (Cambridge, Mass.: Harvard University Press, 1968), pp. 143–162.

But being a member of an organization usually means something different from being an identifier or even a supporter. The loyal Green Bay Packers fan who attends all the games, cheers his side, jeers the opposition, and offers free (though unheeded) advice to the coach and players is a team identifier and supporter, but no one would call him a member. Membership implies both the assumption of obligations to the organization and guaranteed direct access to its decision-making processes. Accordingly, the survey respondent who tells an interviewer "I am a Democrat" but never contributes money, rings doorbells, addresses envelopes, attends rallies, or makes any contribution to the party other than occasionally voting for its candidates is, like our Packers fan, an identifier and occasional supporter but never a member.

### Party Membership Rules

In most democracies other than the United States political parties are considered purely private organizations, like bowling leagues or learned societies. There are few if any laws regulating their internal organization and decision-making processes. All such matters—including qualifications for membership and admission procedures— are controlled by each party, which makes and enforces rules for itself.

Under the rules adopted by most non-American parties, people become party members, usually of a ward or branch organization near where they live, by formally applying and being approved by a local party council or leader. They assume some obligation to the party, mainly to pay annual dues.[6] The main privilege that they receive is participation in party activities, notably selection of candidates for public office.

But not in the United States. In each of the fifty states the qualifications for party membership are defined by law, in order to control who can vote in a particular party's direct primary elections (see Chap. 7). To qualify as Republicans in a closed-primary state, qualified voters must publicly state their party preferences to a registration official; they then receive the Republican primary ballot. The laws usually permit a party representative to challenge the voters' good faith, but the latter need only swear affidavits of their sincerity, and there the matter ends. Such challenges are thus rare and the voters' self-designations are really the sole determinants of their memberships. In open-primary states they can vote in the primary of any party that they choose without even having to state their choices publicly. Accordingly, the American Democratic and Republican parties are unique among the world's parties in that neither has effective control of its own legal membership and there is no formal distinction between member and supporter.

Many political scientists believe this lack of control to be one major cause of the American parties' decentralization, low cohesion, and lack of clear and consistent

---

[6] The dues are not necessarily burdensome. In Great Britain, for example, the minimum annual "subscription" for members of the Labour party is approximately $1.38; members of the Conservative party it is about 58 cents; R. L. Leonard, *Elections in Britain* (Princeton, N.J.: D. Van Nostrand Company, Inc., 1968), p. 54. The dues are somewhat higher in most Continental European parties.

programs. Whatever may be the truth of this charge, it is significant that in at least three states (California, New York, and Wisconsin) some adherents of both parties have tried to overcome the debilitating effects of loose legal membership and organization by aping parties in other democracies. They have established dues-paying party "clubs," which operate outside the legal machinery; they support particular candidates in primaries and assume the main burden of raising funds and campaigning.[7] But in most states party members continue to be legally and in fact those who so designate themselves.

## Members and Militants

Although party membership involves more than simple self-designation in most democratic systems, by no means all members of any party are equally involved, active, or influential in party affairs. As in any human organization, some members—whom we shall call the party's "militants," or "activists"—feel particularly strongly about the party's goals, devote much time and energy to its operations, and consequently have the most to say about what it does. This universal trait of parties is part—but only part—of what the Swiss political sociologist Robert Michels meant by his famous "iron law of oligarchy," and no political scientist would deny that it fits the facts. But Michels also went on to argue that the "oligarchies" of militants always operate effectively unchecked by their rank and file and to advance their own selfish interests, rather than the general interest of the party and all its members.[8] But the latter propositions do not flow inexorably from the first; indeed, most political scientists agree that they do not fit the facts.[9]

To give just one illustration, membership in the British Conservative party is open to anyone "who declares his or her support of the party's objects" and pays dues equivalent to 60 cents a year to his local Conservative constituency association. The average membership of these associations is around 5000, but only a fraction—estimated at 1–3 percent—is continually active in association affairs. Most of the time these few dominate the associations' only important business: selecting the parliamentary candidates for their constituencies. But on a number of occasions the quiescent rank and file have rebelled against the militants' choices and replaced them with others.[10] What is operating, then, is no iron law of oligarchy but rather what might

---

[7] See James Q. Wilson, *The Amateur Democrats* (Chicago: University of Chicago Press, 1962); Epstein, *Politics in Wisconsin* (Madison, Wis.: University of Wisconsin Press, 1958), chap. 5; and Ralph A. Straetz and Frank J. Munger, *New York Politics* (New York: New York University Press, 1960), pp. 21–23.

[8] Robert Michels, *Political Parties: A Sociological Study of the Oligarchical Tendencies of Modern Democracy,* trans. by Eden and Cedar Paul (New York: The Free Press, 1915; reprinted 1949).

[9] Certainly they do not fit the facts of American parties. The most thorough study of the distribution of power in American parties at the local level describes them not as oligarchies but as "stratarchies"—agglomerations of different party groups operating more or less independently at different levels: Samuel J. Eldersveld, *Political Parties: A Behavioral Analysis* (Skokie, Ill.: Rand McNally & Company, 1964), pp. 9, 98–117.

[10] See Ranney, *Pathways to Parliament* (Madison, Wis.: University of Wisconsin Press, 1965), chap. 3.

be called a "tendency toward the uneven distribution of influence"—which is quite a different matter.

### Direct and Indirect Members

Most democratic parties are like the British Conservatives, in that membership is direct; each member joins the party directly and not through some intermediary body. But membership in some parties can be indirect; the parties are partly federations of organized interest groups, and any member of an affiliated group is automatically a member of the party. For example, the British Labour party has many thousands of individual members who directly join local Labour associations (called "constituency Labour parties") and pay annual dues just as do their Conservative counterparts. But also most of Britain's trade unions are directly affiliated with the Labour party at the national level, and many local union branches are also affiliated at the constituency level. Part of every union member's dues goes directly into the Labour party's coffers unless he specifically requests that it be withheld. This process is known as "contracting out," and relatively few union members bother to do it even when they support the Conservatives! In the party's annual conferences each union has a vote proportional to the number of its members who do not contract out. Many union members are thus indirect members of the Labour party because of their union membership.[11]

Similar relations characterize some other socialist parties (like the Belgian Socialist party), and some Roman Catholic parties (like the Austrian People's party and the Belgian Social Christian party) that are federations of Roman Catholic workers' unions, peasants' associations, industrialists' organizations, and so on. But direct affiliation by individuals remains by far the most common form of democratic party membership.[12]

## PARTY ORGANIZATION

### Extragovernmental Structures

In all democratic nations most officials elected with a common party label form some sort of organization for mutual consultation on policy and strategy. A few of the smaller European parties have only this kind of organization and are little more than tiny collections of legislators who insist on retaining their ideological purity and reject all compromise and alliance with larger parties. Only by courtesy can they be called "parties" at all.

As making nominations and contesting elections are highly important to democratic parties, most maintain organizations outside government for purposes of nominating and campaigning for candidates. Many parties shape their extragovernmental organizations to fit the electoral structures in which they must operate and maintain

---

[11] The most authoritative account is Martin Harrison, *Trade Unions and the Labour Party since 1945* (London: George Allen & Unwin Ltd., 1960).

[12] See Duverger, *Political Parties,* pp. 5–17.

some kind of organization for each district that elects one or more major public officials. In the United States, for example, we elect the President and Congress for the nation; a governor, legislature, and other executive officers for each state; a board of supervisors for each county; and a council for each city. To maximize its chances of winning elections at each of these levels, each major party holds a quadrennial national convention, maintains a national committee, congressional and senatorial campaign committees, state central committees, county committees, and city committees. There are also many committees for congressional and judicial districts and so on.

Most democratic parties are similarly organized. The British Conservative, Labour, and Liberal parties maintain organizations in the parliamentary constituencies, combine them in regional federations, hold annual conferences, and maintain executive committees to administer national party affairs between conferences. The major Canadian parties are amalgams of the British and American types; to a basically British system they add organizations at the provincial level and formally select their national party leaders at national conventions organized along American lines. The major French parties (except the Communists) have local "sections" in the towns and villages, which are combined into federations at the department level (see Chap. 19), and have national congresses and executive councils comparable to those of the British parties. The same is true of the leading West German, Italian, and other European parties.

European Communist parties are organized somewhat differently. Carrying on the old Bolshevik tradition of soviets, they continue to use the "cell" as their basic unit. The cell was originally supposed to have an occupational rather than a geographic base, each cell to include all party members who worked in a particular factory, office, government bureau, ship, or whatever. But the Communists have found it increasingly necessary to add area cells to the old work cells, to accommodate party members who are not concentrated in particular work units—doctors, lawyers, small merchants, and the like. Today more than three-quarters of all Communist party members are organized in area cells rather than in work cells. It seems that, willy-nilly, the Communists have had to copy their bourgeois rivals to function effectively.

### Conflict between Intragovernmental and Extragovernmental Organizations

In most democratic parties some degree of conflict between intragovernmental and extragovernmental organizations is endemic and occasionally sharp. One of the bitterest such clashes in recent years took place in the British Labour party. The party's 1960 annual conference adopted a resolution in favor of unilateral abandonment of nuclear weapons and withdrawal from alliances using them—for example, the North Atlantic Treaty Organization. But party leader Hugh Gaitskell and most members of the parliamentary wing of the party refused to accept this policy directive. They continued to support NATO and British possession of nuclear weapons and worked hard within the unions and constituency organizations to persuade the extraparliamentary party to reverse itself. Their efforts were rewarded when at the 1961 annual conference the unilateral nuclear-disarmament policy was dropped and Gaitskell's position adopted.[13]

Some French parties provide examples of even sharper disjunctions between intragovernmental and extragovernmental organizations. In France a clear distinction is made between the *groupes* (collections of deputies meeting together in single caucuses, or *bureaux*) and the *partis* (nominating and campaigning organizations operating outside the National Assembly). As one scholar has remarked, "After national elections, the elected representatives of a party often form small groups and thereafter act independently of the party under whose label they ran."[14] Some *groupes*, like the Communists, Socialists, and the Mouvement Républicain Populaire (MRP) correspond in both name and policy to their *partis*, or organizations of *militants*, outside the National Assembly. Others, like the Entente Démocratique and, notably, the Union des Démocrates pour la V^e République (UDR), formerly led by Charles de Gaulle and Georges Pompidou, are primarily *groupes* with little or no extragovernmental organization. The UDR reflects *le grande Charles's* distaste for party politics: Its deputies campaign for election on the simple platform of loyalty to the Fifth Republic's constitutional structure (which in 1968 was enough to elect 296 deputies out of 482, one of the few single-party majorities in French history).[15]

Even in the United States clashes between intragovernmental and extragovernmental party organizations are not unknown. For example, after the 1956 election the Democratic National Committee established an advisory council to make official party pronouncements on policy. But the party's leaders in Congress—House Speaker Sam Rayburn and Senate Majority Leader Lyndon Johnson—refused to join the council or to consider its declarations in any way binding upon the Democratic majorities in Congress.[16] Similar efforts by Republicans outside Congress between 1964 and 1968 met with similar coolness from Republican congressional leaders.

It seems, then, that some tension between the intragovernmental and extragovernmental organizations is inevitable in democratic parties.


## PARTIES' PRINCIPAL ACTIVITIES

### Selecting Candidates

From the democratic point of view, selecting candidates is the most important of all party activities. The nominating process, as noted in Chapter 7, plays a crucial role in the selection of public officials, and parties' near-monopoly over formal nomina-

---

[13] The story is well told and the general problem of conflict between the parliamentary parties and their mass supporters outside brilliantly analyzed in Robert T. McKenzie, *British Political Parties* (2d ed.; New York: Frederick A. Praeger, Inc., 1964), chap. 10.

[14] Roy C. Macridis, "France," in Macridis and Robert E. Ward (eds.), *Modern Political Systems: Europe* (Englewood Cliffs, N.J.: Prentice-Hall, Inc., 1963), p. 171.

[15] Henry W. Ehrmann, *Politics in France* (2d ed.; Boston: Little, Brown & Company, 1971), p. 335, Table VII.

[16] Cornelius P. Cotter and Bernard C. Hennessy, *Politics without Power: The National Party Committees* (New York: Atherton Press, 1964), chap. 11.

tions in all the democracies gives them great power to shape governments and policies. As E. E. Schattschneider has pointed out, "The parties frame the question and define the issue [who will occupy public office]. In doing this they go a long way toward determining what the answer will be."[17] They also accomplish a task that must be accomplished if the voters are to have manageable and meaningful choices: What Leon D. Epstein calls "structuring the vote," which he defines as

> the imposition of an order or pattern enabling voters to choose candidates according to their labels (whether or not the labels appear on the ballot). The structure may be little more than that provided by the label itself and the voters' acquaintance with it, or it may involve a vast educational and campaigning apparatus mobilizing voters for a party cause. In one way or another, parties provide a basis—although not the only one—for electoral choice.[18]

The process of candidate selection is no less crucial for the success and internal control of the parties themselves. For one thing, the ability to make *binding* nominations—nominations that are regularly accepted and supported by most of the party's workers and members—is one of the prime requisites for electoral success. For another, control of the party's nominations is the principal stake of power fought for by the various factions and leaders of any party that has a good chance of winning elections. One who controls the party's candidate selection controls who speaks for the party officially before the electorate; the choice and phrasing of the official party policies; the distribution of whatever patronage and power may come to the party as the result of winning elections; and what kind of party it is going to be. Most party leaders and workers, accordingly, believe that winning intraparty struggles with opposing factions over nominations is at least as necessary for their purposes as winning interparty contests for public office.

Given the central importance of candidate selection for democratic nations and their political parties, it is surprising that political scientists have only recently begun to study selection procedures and processes. On the basis of the studies now available we can say that selection processes vary substantially from one nation to another on several dimensions.[19]

**Centralization**    At one extreme of the centralization dimension all power over selection of party candidates for all elective offices is concentrated in a national party agency; at the other extreme it is entirely dispersed among regional and local party organizations. Probably the most centralized selection processes at present are those of the Israeli parties. In Israel the entire nation constitutes a single parliamentary constituency, and each party submits one national list of up to 120 candidates for the Knesset. Each list is prepared by the party's national executive committee or comparable inner circle, and, although the "selectors" generally try to achieve a reasonable

---

[17] Schattschneider, *Party Government,* p. 51.

[18] Epstein, *Political Parties in Western Democracies,* p. 77.

[19] The most comprehensive general summary is Epstein, *Political Parties in Western Democracies,* chap. 8.

geographical spread in their list, the choice of particular names *and* of their order on the list is entirely theirs. They can place any candidate in a desirable position on the list and can veto any aspirants whom they disapprove by keeping them off the list entirely or by putting them so far down on it that they have little chance of election.[20]

At the opposite extreme stand the national parties of the United States. To be sure, each party's presidential candidate is selected at a quadrennial national convention—but one made up of delegates from largely autonomous state parties. Furthermore, each of the party's 100 senatorial and 435 congressional candidates is selected in a *local* (state or district) direct primary or (occasionally) convention, and neither the national committee, the national chairman, nor any other national party agency has any formal or informal power to place or veto any local candidate.

Somewhere between the Israeli and American systems stand those of other nations. In Great Britain, for example, national agencies of both the Conservative and Labour parties have the power to veto any locally chosen parliamentary candidate and some opportunity to place people in "winnable" constituencies. But both parties have used their veto powers only rarely, and more often than not their efforts at placement have been stymied by local constituency organizations' refusals to submit to national guidance.[21] In Norway, on the other hand, each party's list in each of the twenty parliamentary constituencies is chosen by a provincial nominating convention made up of delegates from the party organizations in the constituency's cities, towns, and rural communes. Henry Valen has observed, "The decisions made by the nominating provincial convention are final [and] the national party headquarters has neither access to the meeting nor any right to veto the list."[22]

**Closure**  Another significant dimension of candidate selection is closure—the degree to which the rank and file, however defined, are guaranteed the opportunity to participate in selecting the candidates. At one theoretical extreme the selection process is controlled by a small party elite operating behind closed doors with no opportunity for other party members to know why a particular candidate has been selected, let alone to influence the selection. At the other extreme the process is open to all party members, and the candidate is selected publicly by mustering a larger number of the members' votes than has any of the rivals.

No actual selection system perfectly exemplifies either extreme. The Israeli parties' processes are probably the most nearly closed, and those of the American parties the most nearly open. But even in the United States the formally wide-open selection processes stipulated by direct-primary laws in many states and localities are often in fact dominated by small groups of party "slatemakers," who choose candidates in secret and then push them in the primaries. For example, in Illinois very few aspirants selected and backed by Chicago Mayor Richard J. Daley's Cook County "machine" have ever lost a Democratic primary for statewide office. De facto closure

---

[20] Lester G. Seligman, *Leadership in a New Nation* (New York: Atherton Press, 1964), p. 67.

[21] See Ranney, *Pathways to Parliament,* chaps. 3–6; and Michael Rush, *The Selection of Parliamentary Candidates* (Camden, N.J.: Thomas Nelson & Sons, 1969), chaps. 2–3, 5, 8.

[22] Henry Valen, "The Recruitment of Parliamentary Nominees in Norway," in Pertti Pesonen (ed.), *Scandinavian Political Studies,* 1 (1966), 122.

frequently overrides de jure openness in states and localities, perhaps more than we know.[23]

But, whether centralized or decentralized, open or closed, the parties' various procedures and processes for selecting candidates for public office have profound effects upon all their other activities and upon the conduct of elections, choice of public officials, and formation of government policies.

### Contesting Elections

Having made their nominations, most democratic parties exert some effort to get their candidates elected. There is great variation in the financial and personnel resources that they can throw into election campaigns and also in the importance they place upon electoral victory as a goal. At one extreme of the scale, in presidential campaigns the major American parties together now spend more than $300 million on such vote-getting operations as door-to-door canvassing, television and radio speeches and spot announcements, mass rallies, pamphlets and comic books, billboards, lapel buttons, and the like. At the other extreme, some minor American parties and many European parties spend practically no money at all and confine their campaigning to street-corner speeches and telephone calls.[24]

Political scientists generally agree that in most democratic systems party campaigning is the principal organized activity that arouses popular interest in elections and stimulates the citizens to vote. We learned in Chapter 8 that the more partisan people are, the more likely they are to vote and to participate in politics in other ways and that the least partisan people are the least active. If maximum participation in the election of public officials is as desirable as most theorists of democracy think it is, then political parties deserve a large measure of praise—which they do not always receive—for encouraging such participation more effectively than does any other social organization.

### Organizing Government

Every modern democratic government requires a great deal of organization. If all of a government's tens of thousands of public officials acted entirely on their own without consultation or cooperation with the others, chaos would surely result. In Chapters 15–19 we shall consider some of the more prominent official intragovernmental organizations that provide modern democratic governments with order and direction, but we should recognize here that official agencies do not by any means do the job alone. In every modern democratic country the successful candidates of most

---

[23] See, for example, the description of practices in Pennsylvania in Sorauf, *Party and Representation* (New York: Atherton Press, 1963), chaps. 3–5.

[24] The most authoritative analyses of the costs and financing of American party campaigns are David Adamany, *Campaign Finance in America* (North Scituate, Mass.: Duxbury Press, 1972); Herbert Alexander, *Money in Politics* (Washington, D.C.: Public Affairs Press, 1972); and various publications of the Citizen's Research Foundation of Princeton, N.J., directed by Alexander. The most comprehensive cross-national study of party finance is Richard Rose and Arnold J. Heidenheimer (eds.), *Journal of Politics,* 25 (August 1963).

political parties form some kind of intragovernmental party organization. For example, the legislators belonging to a particular party usually join together in a "caucus" or "conference"; select "policy committees" and "floor leaders"; determine who will serve on which legislative committees; and consult on matters of legislative policy and strategy. The parties thus backstop the formal organization of the legislature with informal organizations based on similar political objectives and attitudes, thus lending some order and direction to legislative activities.

We shall note later the considerable variation in the cohesion, discipline, and direct impact on public policy of intragovernmental party organizations. The point here is that most groups of successful party candidates do set up such organizations and thus have some impact on government operations.

### Ancillary Activities

Many democratic parties conduct other activities in addition to the three basic operations just described. They hold social affairs—banquets, picnics, "socials," and so on—at which the rank and file can mingle with the leaders. They establish youth organizations to mobilize new voters and to recruit workers and leaders. Some parties sponsor boy-scout groups, summer camps, and adult-education classes in such non-political subjects as foreign languages. Some publish daily newspapers and other periodicals. Some even organize and finance the funerals of deceased party members. The lives of many Europeans, indeed, are touched by political parties at almost every major juncture: They are named after party heroes, attend both party and public schools, join party-sponsored children's and youth groups, receive wedding gifts from the party, do most of their socializing at party affairs, join party-sponsored trade unions, and are laid to rest at party-organized funerals. Such close contact is less common in the United States, but many Americans know their political parties as more than merely nominating and electioneering bodies.

## DIFFERENCES AMONG PARTIES IN DEMOCRATIC SYSTEMS

### SELECTIVITY OF MEMBERSHIP

Left to their own devices, most democratic parties do not try to enroll every Tom, Reginald, and François. They prefer to restrict their memberships to people whom they can count on to do party work, participate intelligently in party decisions, accept cheerfully decisions made even if they disagree, and—above all—keep silent about internal party affairs in public. They prefer devoted, knowledgeable, and responsible *cadres* to apathetic, ignorant, and irresponsible *masses*. Although they are always trying to increase the numbers of their supporters, they are far more interested in the quality than in the quantity of their members.

The socialist parties produced in Western Europe by the enfranchisement of manual workers in the late nineteenth and early twentieth centuries have taken a different tack, however. Their first object was to educate the workers to prepare them for taking control of the government and the economy, and they had no rich members or corporations to call upon for party funds. Consequently they held repeated membership drives and established highly democratic party constitutions both to attract and to involve as wide a membership as possible.[25]

Legally speaking, the American direct-primary laws force the Democratic and Republican parties to be the most nearly "mass" parties in the world. Yet in many parts of the nation their affairs are actually managed, not by the millions of legally registered party members, but by small cadres of party activists. Even European socialist party leaders grow yearly less interested in maximizing their memberships. For party funds they now count far more on contributions from labor unions than on those from individual members; to bring out the vote they rely increasingly on the mass media rather than on local enthusiasts; and they are not eager for the sort of elbow joggling characteristic of a mass membership (as in the British Labour party—see p. 202).

It appears, then, that the heyday of the mass party is over and that most democratic parties will become more and more cadre-directed in fact if not in form.[26]

## THE NATURE AND ROLE OF IDEOLOGY

Every democratic party appeals to the voters through some sort of platform or program—some set of statements about how its candidates will use government power if elected. Some platforms are more ideological than others. The term "political ideology" implies a basic and wide-ranging philosophy encompassing convictions on what ultimate values are most worth achieving, the fundamental nature of human life and politics, and the proper relations of means to ends. In this sense, the Communist Manifesto of 1848 is a highly ideological program, whereas the Republican national platform of 1972 (or any other year) is not.

Democratic parties vary greatly in both the nature of their ideologies and the role that their ideologies play in shaping party attitudes and operations. At one extreme stand both European and American parties of the "missionary" type. As an example, let us consider the Socialist Labor party of the United States. This party, founded in the second half of the nineteenth century, is committed to what may be called a "noncommunist Marxism." That is, its members believe that true Marxism (as opposed to what they believe to be its outrageous perversion by the Soviet leaders), particularly its explanation of history and society in terms of class conflict between the bourgeoisie and the proletariat and its goals of victory for the proletariat and a classless society, provides the key not only to understanding what society now is but also to setting objectives toward which it should strive. The Socialist Laborites are convinced that history and truth are on their side. In their electioneering activities they seek not votes but converts. Although their ideology runs counter to the beliefs of a majority of the electorate, they will not alter it to make it more popular—as some Christian churches will not abandon their doctrines of the Trinity and the Virgin Birth in order to cater to skeptics. If the party's ideology is unpopular with the voters, then it is the voters who must change, not the ideology. The ideology is believed to be *true*, and no part of it may be altered or soft-pedaled in any misguided effort to

---

[25] See Duverger, *Political Parties*, pp. 62–71.

[26] The point is convincingly made in Epstein, *Political Parties in Western Democracies*, chap. 5.

gain popularity. The party's strategy for winning power, if indeed it has such a goal, is gradually to convert the masses, over many decades or even centuries, if need be. In this sense, then, the Socialist Labor party is a missionary party, as are many European parties (whose ideologies I shall describe) and other American parties like the Socialist Workers party. Some European Social Democratic and Christian Democratic parties are not above trimming their ideological sails occasionally to make themselves more attractive to the voters, but even so they are much closer to the missionary type than are the major parties in the English-speaking nations.

**Neither American major party espouses a particular clear and consistent ideology.** Source: *The Herblock Book* (Boston: The Beacon Press, 1952).

*"I have the same trouble"*

At the other extreme of the scale stand the Democratic and Republican parties of the United States. If either of them has an ideology, as I have defined it, no one has ever been able to state it satisfactorily. The Republican party includes liberals and internationalists, sometimes known as "moderate Republicans," and conservatives and isolationists, sometimes known as "Reagan Republicans"; neither faction can establish claim to being the only "real Republicans." The Democratic party encompasses southern conservatives and white supremacists, as well as northern liberals and antisegregationists, but neither faction can set itself up as the only "true Democrats." Each party directs its appeals at and draws electoral support from every major interest group in the nation. Rather than attempting to convert a majority of the voters to a rigid and unchanging ideology, each party seeks to discover what each interest group wants and then tries to put together some kind of program that will attract maximum support among a maximum number of groups. A party's success is measured not by the ideological consistency of its program, leaders, and supporters but by the number of elections that it wins.

Political Parties And Party Systems

209

The major American parties are thus "brokers" among the conflicting demands of interest groups. A. Lawrence Lowell first applied this term to them in the early years of this century:

> The process of forming public opinion involves . . . bringing men together in masses on some middle ground where they can combine to carry out a common policy. In short, it requires a species of brokerage, and one of the functions of politicians is that of brokers. . . . If politicians are brokers, party is the chief instrument with which they work.[27]

The other democratic parties of the world can be ranged along a scale between these two extremes. The Liberal and Progressive-Conservative parties of Canada, for example, are almost as nonideological as the major American parties. The British, Australian, and New Zealand Conservative and Labour parties have somewhat more clearly defined ideologies, but they too are essentially broker parties. Such "centrist" parties of France as the Union pour la Nouvelle République (UNR), the MRP, and the Radicals fall somewhere near the middle of the scale. The left-wing and right-wing parties of most European democracies fall nearer the missionary extreme. Later in this chapter we shall note some highly "fractionalized" party systems and the main ideologies espoused by their leading parties.

## THE SOCIAL COMPOSITION OF LEADERSHIP AND SUPPORT

In the kinds of people who become their leaders and who provide their electoral support, the broker parties tend to be cross sections of their communities, and the missionary parties tend to be segments. In Chapter 8 we observed that in the United States and Great Britain each major party draws at least some electoral support from every major ethnic, occupational, religious, economic, and educational group in its community and the same is true of each major party in Canada, Australia, and New Zealand. In each nation, to be sure, each major party usually draws more heavily from some groups than others, but no broker party can accurately be described as a "rich man's party," or a "Roman Catholic party" or a "white man's party."

This cross-sectional character of broker parties is also reflected in the nature of their leadership. In the United States, for example, both the Republicans and the Democrats include among their local, state, and national committeemen and chairmen, as well as among their candidates, Jews and gentiles, Roman Catholics and Protestants, lawyers, businessmen, farmers, trade unionists, and so on. In Great Britain many leaders of the Conservative and Labour parties are graduates of the prestigious public schools (Eton, Harrow, Winchester, Marlborough, and so on) and of the universities of Oxford and Cambridge. The Conservative party, to be sure, draws

---

[27] A. Lawrence Lowell, *Public Opinion and Popular Government* (New York: David McKay Company, Inc., 1914), pp. 61–64. Compare this view with Gabriel A. Almond and James Coleman's conceptions of interest groups as the "articulators" of narrow interests and of political parties as the "aggregators" of those interests into general policies with which all groups can live; Almond, "Introduction" in Almond and Coleman (eds.), *The Politics of the Developing Areas* (Princeton, N.J.: Princeton University Press, 1960), pp. 33–45.

more leaders and electoral support from among businessmen than does the Labour party, and the latter draws more heavily from among trade unionists—but neither monopolizes the support or supply of leaders from either group.[28]

The missionary parties, on the other hand, tend to draw almost all their electoral support and leadership from particular segments of the community and hardly make a dent in other segments. The European Communist parties, for example, find their votes and their leaders almost entirely among the working class, poor farmers, and a few intellectuals; they draw hardly at all from middle-class groups. The Liberal parties draw almost exclusively from middle-class groups, and the Roman Catholic parties receive little or no support or leadership from Protestants.

Broker parties, then, tend to be cross-sectional in their leadership and electoral support, whereas missionary parties tend to be segmental. These tendencies have significant effects upon party conflict in different nations.

## CENTRALIZATION

We have noted that most parties have some kind of national organization and some intermediate and local organizations. Democratic parties differ sharply, however, in the distribution of intraparty power among the various organizational levels. These differences are most clearly revealed in the varying ways that nominations are controlled.

From this point of view the major American parties are the most decentralized in the world. Their main national organizations, the quadrennial national conventions, nominate only the candidates for President and Vice President—and even they are usually controlled by shifting and temporary coalitions of state and local organizations and leaders.[29] Each candidate for U.S. senator is nominated by a state direct primary or convention, and each candidate for representative by district primary or convention. If the national leaders of either party object to a particular congressional nominee because he is not a "true Democrat" or a "real Republican," they are helpless to block his nomination—if he has the support of his local organization or local primary voters. On several occasions, most notably when Franklin D. Roosevelt tried to "purge" anti–New Deal Democrats in the primaries of 1938, a popular national party leader has attempted to prevent unacceptable local candidates from receiving the party's nomination. Not only has every such effort failed because the national leader has been unable to enlist the help of local organizations, but the very attempt has been regarded by many voters and party leaders as a serious violation of basic American political morality.[30] In the Democratic and Republican parties alike, power over nominations, the highest stake in any democratic party's internal game, rests in

---

[28] See Jean Blondel, *Voters, Parties, and Leaders* (Baltimore, Md.: Penguin Books, Inc., 1963), pp. 56–59; and W. L. Guttsman, *The British Political Elite* (London: MacGibbon & Kee, 1963), chaps. 1, 4, 8–10.

[29] The most comprehensive description of American national party conventions is Paul T. David, Ralph M. Goldman, and Richard C. Bain, *The Politics of National Party Conventions* (Washington, D.C.: The Brookings Institution, 1960).

[30] For a fuller account of these "purge" efforts, see Ranney and Willmoore Kendall, *Democracy and the American Party System* (New York: Harcourt Brace Jovanovich, Inc., 1956), pp. 286–289.

a congeries of state, county, and district organizations and leaders. It is highly decentralized. Later we shall see to what extent other powers of American parties are also decentralized.

The United States is not the only democratic country with some decentralized major parties. The French Radicals have long been a loose federation of local associations, which, in Maurice Duverger's words, "resembles an incoherent agglomeration of associations linked by vague and variable bonds, resultant upon hidden intrigues, rivalries between cliques, struggles amongst factions and personalities."[31] Many European conservative parties are similarly decentralized. In Switzerland all the major parties, with the possible exception of the Socialists, are organized mainly in the cantons,[32] and the national parties are even looser alliances of local parties than is common in the United States. There are no outstanding national party leaders, but only leading cantonal figures, who are generally unknown to most people outside their own bailiwicks.[33] In the Scandinavian countries candidates for national legislatures are selected by district committees or conventions, and national party leaders can only advise on who should and should not be selected.[34]

Most democratic parties, however, are somewhat more centralized in their nominating procedures and other activities. In Great Britain, for example, the Conservative and Labour constituency associations select the parliamentary candidates, but both parties' national agencies have the power to veto unacceptable candidates. The Conservatives have used this power very sparingly, Labour somewhat more often; still, both are certainly more centralized than are most parties in Switzerland and Scandinavia.[35] Canadian parties, despite their federal organization, nominate candidates in much the same way.[36] And in most European nations using the party-list form of proportional representation (see Chap. 7) national party agencies select the candidates for their lists and determine the order in which they appear. Decentralization, though far from unknown in democratic parties, is still less common than is centralization.


## DISCIPLINE

In any human organization "discipline" includes the means available to group leaders to induce members to act according to rules laid down by the leaders. The whole

---

[31] Duverger, *Political Parties,* p. 42.

[32] Cantons are subnational governing units comparable to but more powerful than the American states; see Chap. 19.

[33] Roger Girod, "Switzerland," in Erik Allardt and Yrjö Littunen (eds.), *Cleavages, Ideologies, and Party Systems* (Turku: Westermarck Society, 1964), pp. 132–133.

[34] Dankwart A. Rustow, "Scandinavia: Working Multiparty Systems," in Sigmund Neumann (ed.), *Modern Political Parties* (Chicago: University of Chicago Press, 1956), p. 171.

[35] See Ranney, *Pathways to Parliament,* chap. 10.

[36] See John Meisel, *The Canadian General Election of 1957* (Toronto: University of Toronto Press, 1962), pp. 120–124.

concept of discipline, then, implies some kind of hierarchical relations, or chain of command, between the group's leaders and members.

The leaders of every democratic political party have at least some disciplinary weapons, but these vary widely in nature and effectiveness. The President of the United States, for example, can, if he wishes, distribute patronage appointments to faithful supporters in his party and withhold them from recalcitrant party members; he can make his public support of fellow partisans in their election bids dependent upon their support of his policies; he can even try to "purge" mavericks in the party primaries. None of his weapons is very effective, however: There is only so much patronage available; many congressmen of his party do not need his support to be elected—and know it; and he can rarely bring off a "purge." Presidential discipline in either American party is thus little more than persuasion, pleas, and cajolery, and every President, as even Franklin Roosevelt and Lyndon Johnson learned, must expect considerable opposition to his policies from members of his own party.

A British prime minister or opposition leader is in a stronger position. Every member of his party in Parliament knows that when "the whip is laid on" (when the party leader notifies the members that they are expected to vote in a particular way on a particular bill) he disobeys at his political peril. The prime minister (and, potentially, the leader of the opposition) controls the distribution of ministerial offices; and, as the ordinary MP cannot, as in the United States, rise to power and influence by seniority, the only path to political success must be paved with the leaders' good will (see Chap. 16). Also, as we have seen, the national party agencies, which the leader controls, can veto the renomination of a rebel MP and thus effectively deny him his parliamentary seat (though this veto is seldom used).[37] But the leader's greatest power depends upon the British parliamentary system's assignment of governmental authority to the majority-party "team." When that team can no longer muster a parliamentary majority, it must give way to the opposition team. Any MP's vote against his own party is, in effect, a vote to put or keep the other party in power. It is not surprising, then, that in Britain party discipline is widely (though not universally) regarded as a virtue.[38]

Most of the missionary parties of Europe and Scandinavia assign to their national leaders the power to expel from the party members of the national legislature who refuse to vote the "party line." Such expulsion is somewhat less likely than in Britain to deny the expelled legislator his legislative seat, but it does exclude him from participation in the party's decision-making processes. It is, therefore, a somewhat less powerful disciplinary weapon than that held by British party leaders—but far more powerful than any available to American party leaders.

---

[37] In 1948–1949 the Labour party's national executive committee expelled five rebel MPs from the party. All five stood for reelection in 1950 and were soundly defeated by regularly approved Labour candidates. No Conservative MP has been disciplined in this fashion since before World War II. Indeed, just since 1970 at least three Labour MPs (S.O. Davies, Dick Taverne, and Edward Milne) have been denied renomination by their constituency parties but have run as independents and defeated the official party candidates. It thus appears that the British party organizations' disciplinary powers over their MPs have grown weaker than in many years.

[38] This point is well made by Epstein; see, particularly, "Cohesion of British Parliamentary Parties," *American Political Science Review,* 50 (June 1956), 360–377.

## LEGISLATIVE COHESION

The differences in centralization and discipline are reflected in different degrees of cohesion within various democratic parties. As the term is normally used, a party's "cohesion" means the extent to which members in public office vote alike on major issues of public policy. A party whose legislative members vote alike on every issue is said to have perfect legislative cohesion, and a party whose legislative members split fifty-fifty on every issue is said to have no legislative cohesion whatever.

Many political scientists believe that the degree of legislative cohesion is one of the most significant of all indexes of a party's nature, for it reveals the extent to which the party *as a party* influences the formulation of public policy.[39]

Democratic parties vary widely in legislative cohesion. The major British parties are among the most cohesive, as demonstrated by their ability to count upon all their members in the House of Commons to vote as the party leaders desire. On the few occasions on which some members cannot go along with the leaders' policies (for example, in 1971, when many Conservative members of Parliament could not support their leaders' moves to bring Britain into the European Economic Community, and many Labour MPs defied their leaders' decision to oppose entry) the dissenters are more likely to abstain from voting than to vote against their leadership. At the other extreme, many small French parliamentary *groupes* split internally on almost every public issue and therefore have little or no legislative cohesion. The other democratic parties fall somewhere between these two extremes. The larger French, Scandinavian, and German parties, for example, are almost, but not quite, as cohesive as the British parties; the major American parties in Congress, though relatively uncohesive, are considerably more cohesive than are the smaller French *groupes.* In the various American state legislatures the parties cover almost the whole range of cohesion.[40]

I have described some of the major respects in which democratic political parties differ from one another. These differences are also expressed in the types of party systems prevailing in modern democratic nations, and I turn now to a brief description of the nature and political consequences of each type.

## FRACTIONALIZATION OF DEMOCRATIC PARTY SYSTEMS

In analyzing and comparing political parties in various modern democratic polities, political scientists often speak of "party systems." This term denotes certain general characteristics of party conflict in particular polities, which can be classified according to various criteria. On the basis of the factors described in the preceding section, for example, we can speak of ideological and broker party systems or of centralized and decentralized party systems. Most political scientists, however, emphasize interparty

---

[39] See Schattschneider's statement that the relatively low cohesion of American parties in Congress is *"the most important single fact concerning the American parties.* He who knows this fact, and knows nothing else, knows more about American parties than he who knows everything except this fact." Schattschneider, *Party Government,* pp. 131–132; italics in the original.

[40] For the data underlying these generalizations about American legislative parties, see Keefe and Morris S. Ogul, *The American Legislative Process: Congress and the States* (2d ed.; Englewood Cliffs, N.J.: Prentice-Hall, Inc., 1968), pp. 298–322, and the studies cited there.

competition—that is, competition among the number of parties that regularly attract substantial portions of the available votes and public offices—on the premise that this variable has the most direct and powerful impact upon the general character of the governing processes.

## THE INDEX OF FRACTIONALIZATION

Until recently political scientists generally classified all party systems, on the basis of their competitiveness, as either one-party, two-party, or multiparty systems. Their techniques for systematically measuring degrees of competition were, however, developed mainly for analysis and comparison of the party systems of the American states and were thus of little use in investigating the many variations among the European party systems usually lumped together as multiparty systems.[41] To fill this void, Douglas W. Rae recently devised an ingenious index of party fractionalization that expresses, for any party system, two dimensions of competitiveness: the *number of parties* receiving shares of the popular vote and seats in the national legislature and the *relative equality* of their shares. Rae's scale is anchored at one extreme by a model one-party system, in which one party receives all the votes and seats for an index score of 0.00. As we shall see, the party system of the Soviet Union fulfills all these requirements. As the number of parties and the relative equality of their shares of the votes and seats increase, the index score rises. In a theoretically perfect two-party system two parties would split all the votes and seats exactly evenly, for a score of 0.50. If ten parties split the votes and seats evenly, the system would have a score of 0.90.[42]

Rae applied his index to the party systems of twenty Western European democratic nations and obtained the scores and rankings shown in Table 16.

For each of the twenty nations ranked, the legislative fractionalization score was a bit lower than the electoral fractionalization score, bearing out Rae's conclusion that all electoral systems—even those using proportional representation—discriminate to some degree in favor of the larger parties. This ranking also enables us to go beyond the oversimplifications of the traditional one-party–two-party—multiple-party trichotomy and refer, in spectrum fashion, to some systems (for example, the United States, New Zealand, and Australia) as less fractionalized, some (for example, Ireland and Sweden), as moderately fractionalized, and some (for example, Finland, Switzerland, and Israel) as highly fractionalized.

Figure 8 makes the general picture more concrete by showing the vote shares

---

[41] The principal techniques are described and evaluated in David G. Pfeifer, "The Measurement of Inter-Party Competition and Systemic Stability," *American Political Science Review,* 61 (June 1967), 457–467.

[42] Douglas W. Rae, *The Political Consequences of Electoral Laws* (New Haven, Conn.: Yale University Press, 1967), pp. 53–58. Rae's formula for computing the index ($F_e$) is

$$F_e = 1 - (\sum_{i=1}^{n} T_i^2),$$

where $T_i$ = any party's share of the total votes for legislative seats, expressed as a decimal fraction.

**TABLE 16**

Mean Fractionalization Scores for 20 Western
Democratic Party Systems, 1945-1964

| Nations[a] | Mean Fractionalization (Shares of Popular Vote) | Mean Fractionalization (Shares of Legislative Seats) |
|---|---|---|
| United States | 0.50 | 0.48 |
| New Zealand | 0.54 | 0.49 |
| Australia | 0.56 | 0.49 |
| Great Britain | 0.58 | 0.52 |
| Austria | 0.61 | 0.56 |
| Canada | 0.66 | 0.52 |
| Belgium | 0.67 | 0.62 |
| Luxembourg | 0.70 | 0.66 |
| Ireland | 0.70 | 0.67 |
| Sweden | 0.70 | 0.68 |
| Norway | 0.73 | 0.67 |
| West Germany | 0.73 | 0.69 |
| Iceland | 0.73 | 0.71 |
| Italy | 0.74 | 0.71 |
| Denmark | 0.75 | 0.74 |
| The Netherlands | 0.78 | 0.77 |
| France | 0.81 | 0.77 |
| Finland | 0.81 | 0.78 |
| Switzerland | 0.81 | 0.79 |
| Israel | 0.81 | 0.80 |

[a] Ranked in order of increasing fractionalization.

*Source:* "A Note on the Fractionalization of Some European Party Systems," by Douglas W. Rae is reprinted from *Comparative Political Studies,* Vol. 1, No. 3 (October 1968) pp. 413-429 by permission of the Publisher, Sage Publications, Inc.

and fractionalization scores in recent elections for four party systems, covering the whole range of fractionalization (from an index of 0.50 for the American system to one of 0.82 for the Finnish system).

## CHARACTERISTICS OF MORE FRACTIONALIZED SYSTEMS

The party systems of the Western European democratic nations generally rank on the high side of the fractionalization scale. In each of these nations at least three, and often as many as five or six, parties regularly win enough votes and legislative seats to be called "major" parties. Hardly ever does a single party win a majority of the seats; the cabinets and ministries are thus composed of coalitions, rather than of representatives of single parties.

### Leading Party Ideologies[43]

Most of the major parties in the Western European democratic nations are closer to the missionary than to the broker type. The names, of course, vary somewhat from one nation to another, but seven main ideologies can be found in most of the multiparty systems.

---

[43] A recent examination of the ideological thrusts and socioeconomic group support of the leading parties in seventeen Western nations is Rose and Derek Urwin, "Social Cohesion, Political Parties, and Strains in Regimes," *Comparative Political Studies,* 2 (April 1969), 7–67.

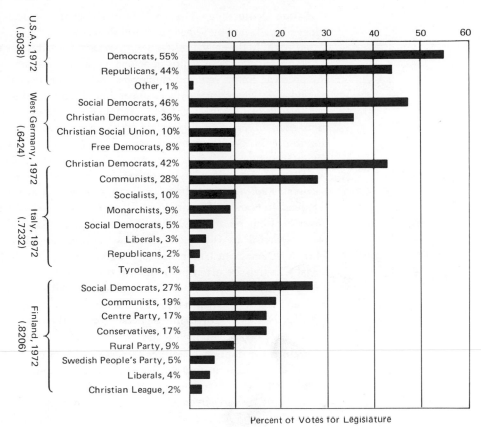

**FIGURE 8**
**Fractionalization in four Western party systems.**
Source: newspaper reports of election returns.

U.S.A., 1972 (.5038)
Democrats, 55%
Republicans, 44%
Other, 1%

West Germany, 1972 (.6424)
Social Democrats, 46%
Christian Democrats, 36%
Christian Social Union, 10%
Free Democrats, 8%

Italy, 1972 (.7232)
Christian Democrats, 42%
Communists, 28%
Socialists, 10%
Monarchists, 9%
Social Democrats, 5%
Liberals, 3%
Republicans, 2%
Tyroleans, 1%

Finland, 1972 (.8206)
Social Democrats, 27%
Communists, 19%
Centre Party, 17%
Conservatives, 17%
Rural Party, 9%
Swedish People's Party, 5%
Liberals, 4%
Christian League, 2%

Percent of Votes for Legislature

**Communism**    At the extreme left of the ideological scale[44] stand the Communist parties, whose ideology and structure I shall describe fully at the end of this chapter. In some nations (India is a leading example), there are two Communist parties, one .devoted to Moscow's line and the other to Peking's.

**Democratic Socialism**    One long step to the right of the communists stand the democratic socialist parties, which espouse some brand of noncommunist Marxist socialism somewhat similar to that of the American Socialist Labor party. Every European democracy has such a party, and among the more powerful are the Norwegian Labor party, the Swedish and Danish Social Democratic parties, the French and Belgian Socialist parties, the Finnish and West German Social Democratic parties, and the Austrian Socialists.

---

[44] Although they have no precise generally agreed-upon meanings, the terms "left" and "right" are so commonly used in descriptions of political ideologies and party conflict that they deserve a brief explanation. The ideological scale underlying them is constructed between extreme "socialism" and its total absence. "Socialism," too, has no very precise meaning, but as we are using it, it means government ownership and operation of economic enterprise (see Chap. 20). Those parties more sympathetic to socialism are thus more to the "left," and those more sympathetic to laissez-faire capitalism are more to the "right."

Political Parties And Party Systems

**Christian Democracy**   The ideology of Christian democracy is based on the doctrines promulgated by Pope Leo XIII in the encyclical *De rerum novarum* (1891) and by Pope Pius XI in the encyclical *Quadrigesimo anno* (1931). It holds that, though capitalism works many unjust hardships upon the workers, socialism is the wrong solution to the problem. Employers and employees should remember that they are all children of God and that spiritual redemption and purity, rather than material wealth, should be the goals of society. In order to promote those goals wealth should be distributed more equitably, and employers and employees should form partnerships for mutual distribution of profits. Economies should be reconstructed so that the excessive individualistic materialism of capitalism and the excessive collectivistic materialism of socialism will be replaced by a cooperative commonwealth in which the twin material barriers to spiritual well-being—excessive poverty and excessive wealth—will be removed. In France, Belgium, West Germany, Switzerland, and Italy, each of which has many Roman Catholics, Christian Democratic parties have been established. The most powerful are the Italian Christian Democratic party and the West German Christian Democratic Union, but such others as the French MRP and the Belgian Parti Social Chrétien are often prominent in the governing coalitions of their respective nations. These parties do not all interpret the papal encyclicals in exactly the same way, and can in fact themselves be scaled, with the French MRP standing toward the left and the Italian Christian Democrats toward the right.

**Liberalism**   In European politics "liberalism" was originally the doctrine of the individual's liberation from the domination of both church and state; its ideals were rooted in the Enlightenment and the French Revolution. The conflict between church and state, particularly over control of education, was a leading issue in nineteenth-century European politics, and the liberal parties were generally either first or second in strength.[45] Twentieth-century European politics, however, is focused mainly on economic issues, and the liberal parties have become "middle-of-the-roaders" between the socialists and the right-wing parties. Generally today they are no larger than fourth or fifth among the parties of any nation. Among the better-known liberal parties are the French Radicals, the Belgian Party of Liberty and Progress, the West German Free Democrats, the Swedish Liberals, and the Swiss Radical Democrats.

**Democratic Conservatism**   A number of right-wing European parties accept and defend the democratic form of government but argue that all the modern tendencies toward socialism, the welfare state, and other basic revisions of traditional socioeconomic systems should be halted or reversed. Leading examples of such parties are the French Independents and the Conservative and Agrarian parties in the Scandinavian nations.

**Antidemocratic Conservatism**   Some right-wing European parties not only wish to return to the socioeconomic systems of generations ago but also advocate more or less

---

[45] See Guido de Ruggiero, *The History of European Liberalism,* trans. by R. G. Collingwood (New York: Oxford University Press, 1927).

drastic revisions in their governmental system, in order to destroy majority democracy and to return to older forms of government. These changes, however, are sought only by peaceful and constitutional means. Examples of such parties are the Austrian Independents and the Italian Monarchists.

**Antidemocratic Radicalism**  At the extreme right of the European ideological spectrum stand the parties that advocate total destruction of democracy by any means necessary. They are the heirs of Benito Mussolini and Adolf Hitler, and, though they do not use the term themselves, most of them may accurately be described as "neofascist." They include such parties as the Italian Movimento Sociale Italiano and the French Union and French Fraternity party, which, under the leadership of Pierre Poujade, had an unsavory but brief career from 1954 to 1958.

*Political Consequences*

The more fractionalized party systems have both critics and defenders among political commentators. The critics charge them with producing unstable and ever-changing governments, splitting their communities into hostile and uncompromising ideological camps, failing to elicit clear popular mandates on issues, and thus weakening democracy's ability to survive. They often point to the party systems of Germany's Weimar Republic (1919–1933) and to the French Third and Fourth Republics (1871–1939 and 1945–1958 respectively) as examples of the damage that highly fractionalized and ideological party systems can cause. The defenders of such systems claim that the broad range of party ideologies accurately reflects the various shades of public opinion in their communities and thus more nearly realizes the ideals of representative democracy than do the oversimplified two-party systems of the English-speaking nations.

We cannot come to a final conclusion about this debate here, but it does seem clear that any resolution will have to take into account several considerations. First, political and governmental instability is not an inevitable result of higher party fractionalization. The systems of West Germany, the Scandinavian nations, and the Netherlands, for example, normally produce governments that are quite as stable as any in the less fractionalized nations. Even Israel, with one of the most fractionalized of all party systems, produces stable governments dominated by the Mapai party.[46] Second, it seems highly unlikely that the structure of fractionalized party systems is the sole or even the main cause of the deep ideological or ethnic divisions in nations like France and Belgium. Most students of French politics believe that the proliferation of parties has been the *result* of ideological and social fissures in the French nation far more basic and complex than the particular kind of party system.

---

[46] However, a recent study of party systems and government stability in nineteen parliamentary democracies in the period 1945–1969 shows that cabinets in the nations with more fractionalized party systems generally changed significantly more frequently than those in nations with less fractionalized party systems. Michael Taylor and V. M. Herman, "Party Systems and Government Stability," *American Political Science Review,* 65 (March 1971), pp. 28-37

I am not claiming that more fractionalized systems are "better" than less fractionalized ones; I merely suggest that a nation's party system is only one determinant—and in many instances not the most important one—of the nature of its basic political conflict.

## CHARACTERISTICS OF LESS FRACTIONALIZED SYSTEMS

The party systems of the English-speaking democracies, including the United States, Great Britain, New Zealand, Australia, and Canada, are generally less fractionalized than are those of the Western European nations; the American system comes closest to the model of a two-party system. The major parties of these nations differ in various ways, but they are also very much alike in certain important respects. Among their leading similarities five may be mentioned.

First, they tend to be of the broker, rather than of the missionary, type. Some (like the various labor and socialist parties) have somewhat more definite ideologies than do others (like both American parties and the various conservative parties), but all are more concerned with winning elections here and now than with eventually converting the whole population to pure and uncompromising ideologies.

Second, they tend to draw their leadership and electoral support from all elements of their communities, rather than from particular segments.

Third, they direct their appeals for votes at all major interest groups. The American Republicans and British Conservatives, for example, never say to organized labor: "We stand for business first, last, and always, and if we get into power we intend to destroy the unions! If you don't like it, take your votes elsewhere!" Rather they say: "We stand for the welfare of *both* business and labor, neither of which will benefit from a victory by our opponents. If you want fair and decent treatment for labor and management alike, vote for us instead of for them." Their programs and platforms are not as clear and internally consistent as are those of the missionary parties, for they are designed to appeal to many, often incompatible, interests, with a view to winning as many votes as possible.[47]

Fourth, they are moderate parties. They try to put forth programs that will not unduly antagonize any major element of the electorate, and they try to avoid or postpone taking a clear stand on any truly "hot" issue on which the community is sharply divided. Furthermore, any unreconstructed extremist in the ranks of either major party must either moderate his views as the price of retaining his position in the inner circles of the party (for example, Aneurin Bevin in the British Labour party) or maintain his extreme position and be isolated from most other party leaders (like George Wallace in the Democratic party and Representative "Pete" McCloskey in the Republican party).

---

[47] Economist Anthony Downs has developed an influential model of party and voter strategy based on the assumption that parties will shift ideologies to maximize votes; Downs, *An Economic Theory of Democracy* (New York: Harper & Row, Publishers, 1957).

Fifth, they tend to be a good deal alike in their basic views and specific programs. They agree generally on the basic form of government and the general direction of public policy. When one replaces the other in power, there is seldom a drastic shift in government policy. They are not, however, identical; the voters do have a real choice, for they usually disagree about the *pace* at which certain policies should be adopted and implemented and often on many details of such policies. Consequently, most voters believe that the parties are sufficiently different to warrant a preference for one over the other.

The major American parties, as we have seen, are considerably more decentralized than are their counterparts in the other English-speaking nations, but otherwise the major parties in all the less fractionalized systems are essentially similar.

## THE ONE-PARTY SYSTEMS OF THE DICTATORSHIPS[48]

Dictatorship is as old as government itself. But dictatorship conducted through the medium of a single all-powerful political party is an invention of the twentieth century. Indeed, one of the traits that have most clearly distinguished the governments of the Soviet Union, the People's Republic of China, Nazi Germany, and Fascist Italy from older authoritarian regimes is the central role played by such parties, each of which has had many of the trappings of parties in more democratic systems—but none of their competition.[49]

Yet there are different degrees of dictatorship, as there are of democracy. Hence it is not surprising that there are many significant differences among the less fractionalized and unfractionalized party systems of modern dictatorships and near-dictatorships. Western political scientists have paid some attention to these differences, especially in their studies of party systems in the new nations of Africa and Asia. But it was a Polish political scientist who recently suggested the usefulness of distinguishing among three different subtypes of one-party systems. In order of increasing fractionalization they are *monoparty* systems, in which only one party is legally permitted to exist; *hegemonic* systems, in which several parties are permitted to exist but do not contest elections because they have formed permanent coalitions within which one is accepted by all the others as the directing body; and *dominant* systems, in each of which several parties are permitted to exist and to contest elections but only one regularly wins all but a small fraction of the popular votes and public offices.[50]

Let us briefly examine each type.

---

[48] The best recent general discussion is Samuel P. Huntington and Clement H. Moore (eds.), *Authoritarian Politics in Modern Society: The Dynamics of Established One-Party Systems* (New York: Basic Books, Inc., Publishers, 1970).

[49] See Carl J. Friedrich and Zbigniew K. Brzezinski, *Totalitarian Dictatorship and Autocracy* (rev. ed.; Cambridge, Mass.: Harvard University Press, 1965), chap. 3.

[50] Jerzy J. Wiatr, "One-Party Systems: The Concept and Issue for Comparative Studies," in Allardt and Littunen, *Cleavages, Ideologies, and Party Systems,* pp. 281–290.

# MONOPARTY SYSTEMS

## Some Common Characteristics

All democratic parties, including even those of the missionary type, cherish democratic government at least as much as they cherish their particular social and economic aims. Accordingly, they tolerate the existence of opposing parties, use only peaceful and democratic methods to pursue their goals, and accept the verdicts of the voters in elections. Essential to all democratic party systems is the general acceptance of the idea of the *loyal opposition*—the conviction that, though opposing parties may be misguided, committed to incorrect ideologies and policies, they are nevertheless loyal to the nation and have a right to engage in its politics.

Communist and fascist parties, which monopolize the field in a dictatorship, bear no more than a superficial resemblance to democratic parties. Essentially they are like combat armies, and many of them, indeed, use military terms ("vanguard," "phalanx," "spearhead") to describe themselves and their operations. An even more apt analogy is that between a totalitarian party and a militant religious order. Every totalitarian party arises from and is committed to a kind of secular religion, each with its sacred texts *(Das Kapital, Mein Kampf)*, its prophets (Marx and Lenin, Hitler), its total explanation of the nature of society (dialectical materialism, the destiny of the Aryan race), and its ethical system (the end justifies the means). The party has its "priesthood" and its "evangelizers." Yet in one sense opposition is indispensable to a totalitarian party, for, to justify its military organization and the fanatical devotion that it demands of its members, a communist or fascist party needs a mortal enemy (the capitalists, the Jews) with whom it is locked in a struggle to the death.

Many of us in the democratic world are puzzled over why the rulers of communist and fascist regimes bother with the pseudodemocratic trappings of political parties at all. When we look a little closer at the totalitarian parties, however, we can see that they perform several roles of vital importance for their masters.

In the nations in which they are the sole legal parties, they provide tightly knit, well-organized, and fanatically devoted oligarchies that can operate the formal governing structures as directed by their leaders. Second, they provide useful psychological and organizational bridges between the nations' masses and their rulers—bridges that older, more aristocratic oligarchies lacked, with the result that they were more vulnerable to revolts by the masses.

In these and other respects, then, communist and fascist parties are essentially alike. In order to see how they differ, let us briefly examine the structure of each type of monoparty system.

## The Soviet Prototype

The monoparty system of the Soviet Union is the oldest and still the most powerful of all such systems, and it has served as the model not only for all other communist systems but also for many aspects of the fascist systems. Since 1918 the Communist party has been the only legal party in the Soviet Union. All attempts to form rival parties are officially regarded as treason, and the 1936 Constitution describes the party as "the vanguard of the working people" and "the leading core of all organizations of the working people, both public and State" (Article 126).

How do the Soviets justify permitting only one party to exist in what they claim is the most democratic government in the world? According to the doctrine enunciated by Stalin and his disciples, every political party represents a class. In nations where several classes exist, several political parties must also exist; but in Soviet Russia only the working class officially exists, and therefore only one party—the Communist party—is needed to represent it. Any other party could only oppose the interests and welfare of the proletariat, and that, of course, would be counterrevolutionary treason. "True democracy" (government in the interests of the workers) can permit only one party.

**Structure and Composition of the Party**  The Communist Party of the Soviet Union (CPSU) presently has about 14 million members, about 9 percent of the USSR's adult population. This small proportion does not mean, of course, that communism is "unpopular" in Russia; the party is *intended* to be an elite rather than a mass organization. A Soviet citizen can become a party member only after having been recommended by three party members of at least three years' standing and after having successfully passed many tests during a year's candidacy. Furthermore, in periodic purges the leadership expels all members whom it deems "inactive" or "politically incorrect" (about 50,000 members are expelled each year).[51] Lenin originally intended the party to be composed mainly of manual workers, but they now constitute only about one-fifth of its membership, and more than half the party's members come from the intelligentsia.[52]

The basic units of party organization, once called "cells," are set up in work places—factories, farms, military units, and so on. Above them are a series of district, provincial, and union republic committees and bureaus. Heading the whole party is the national party congress, which is supposed to meet every four years but has not always done so (no congress was held from 1939 to 1952, for example). The congress nominally chooses the central committee, composed in 1974 of 241 members and 155 alternates. The central committee is divided into several committees, of which by far the most powerful (the actual ruling oligarchy of the Soviet Union) is the Politburo, composed in 1974 of sixteen members and seven alternates.

Communist ideologues have made much of the principle of "democratic centralism," which calls for full and free discussion within the party before a decision is made but closed ranks and no criticism of a policy once it has been adopted. In practice, however, democratic centralism has meant that the party's rulers—Stalin himself before his death in 1953 and the Politburo since then—make the decisions and that their decisions are binding on all the lower party echelons, whose members may criticize only those few matters permitted by the ruling oligarchy.

Closely allied with the party structure are several auxiliary organizations characteristic of all one-party systems. They include the secret political police (now called the KGB), charged with detecting and disposing of all dissenters, deviationists, and

---

[51] John A. Armstrong, *Ideology, Politics, and Government in the Soviet Union* (3d ed.; New York: Frederick A. Praeger, Inc., 1974), p. 56.

[52] Merle Fainsod, *How Russia Is Ruled* (rev. ed.; Cambridge, Mass.: Harvard University Press, 1963), chap. 8.

other enemies of the regime. They also include the various youth organizations intended to indoctrinate the young in communism and to single out the more able for future party membership and leadership. The main youth organizations are the Little Octobrists (ages seven to ten), Young Pioneers (ages ten to fifteen), and the Komsomols (Young Communist League, ages fourteen to twenty-eight).

**Role of the Party**  Like all totalitarian parties in power, the CPSU is first of all a ruling oligarchy, "the government of the government," "a state within a state." Most major legislative, executive, administrative, and judicial agencies of the formal government have parallel party organizations, which control and operate particular formal agencies so that the whole government does what the party leaders want it to do.

Through its agitation-propaganda operations (see Chap. 5) the party also keeps a check on mass opinion in order to learn what policies are possible at the moment and to shape that opinion so that ever-more "advanced" policies can be successfully adopted with minimum physical coercion and terror.

The party is thus the brain and nervous system of the Soviet leviathan. One who knows the party structure and operations but not the formal structure knows far more about how the Soviet Union is governed than does one who knows the formal structure but not the party.

### Fascist Monoparty Systems

In its pre-1945 Italian and German versions, fascism, like communism, was a kind of secular religion at war with all other ideologies. It had its sacred texts and prophets, its total explanation of society, and its ethical system. It, too, regarded parties as priesthoods of true believers charged with spreading the doctrine and liquidating infidels.[53] That fascism deified the nation and the race, whereas communism glorifies the working class, should not obscure the essential similarities of the two movements.

The organizational similarities are even more striking. The Fascist party in Mussolini's Italy from 1922 to 1945 and the National Socialist German Workers' (Nazi) party in Hitler's Germany from 1933 to 1945 were the only legal parties in their respective nations. The structure of each paralleled the structure of the formal government and became the actual governing body. As in communist one-party systems, the fascist parties thus acted both as ruling mechanisms and as agencies for generating mass support of policies formulated by the leaders.

In the organization of fascist parties the *Führerprinzip* (leadership principle) was *formally* more prominent than it has been in communist organization, although in practice neither Hitler nor Mussolini dominated his party or nation more completely than Stalin dominated his. Both the Fascist and Nazi parties were organized like armies, with the Duce and the Führer as absolute overlords and the black-shirted

---

[53] See A. James Gregor, *The Ideology of Fascism* (New York: The Free Press, 1969); and S. J. Woolf (ed.), *The Nature of Fascism* (New York: Random House, 1969).

Fasci di Combattimento, brown-shirted "storm troopers," and black-uniformed "elite guard" as "shock troops" (the official titles of the various party organizations).

The main channel for entering each fascist party was its youth organizations; the Italian Balilla and Avenguardia for persons from the ages of six to twenty-one and the German Hitler Youth. Both parties conducted periodic purges (including the murderous Nazi "blood purge" of 1934) to eliminate all but the most fanatically devoted members, and like the communist parties, both were intended as elites rather than as mass organizations.

## HEGEMONIC PARTY SYSTEMS

Several Eastern European nations first liberated from the Germans and then occupied by the Red Army during and after World War II have established "people's democracies"—regimes modeled on, but not identical with, the Soviet order. One prominent feature of these "sovietoid" regimes is what Jerzy Wiatr calls their "hegemonic" party systems.[54] The main common features of such systems are exemplified by the parties and elections in his native Poland.[55]

First, more than one political party is legally permitted to exist, organize, and participate in presenting candidates for office. There are three legal political parties in Poland: the Polish United Workers (Communist) party (PUWP), the United Peasant party (UPP), and the Democratic party (DP).[56]

Second, the other legal parties are joined with the hegemonic party in a "people's front," which presents a single all-party list of candidates at each election and thus eliminates all *interparty* electoral competition. In Poland the PUWP, UPP, and DP have formed a "permanent National Front," which presents a joint list of candidates in each of the nation's parliamentary constituencies. Furthermore, the Polish electoral law stipulates that, once the national authorities of a party have agreed to present a joint list of candidates, any separate list proposed by any party's local authorities is automatically invalid. The law also allows the joint list of candidates in any constitu-

---

[54] The evolution of these systems from the first phase of postwar "liberation fronts" (coalitions of all parties resisting the Germans) through the phase of coalition governments among autonomous parties to the present phase of hegemonic "people's front" coalitions is described by Andrew Gyorgy, "Satellite Parties in Eastern Europe," in Sigmund Neumann (ed.), *Modern Political Parties* (Chicago: University of Chicago Press, 1956), pp. 284–301.

[55] For Wiatr's descriptions in English of the Polish system, see "Elections and Voting Behavior in Poland," in Austin Ranney (ed.), *Essays on the Behavioral Study of Politics* (Urbana, Ill.: University of Illinois Press, 1962), pp. 235–251; "The Hegemonic Party System in Poland," in Allardt and Stein Rokkan (eds.), *Studies in Political Sociology* (New York: The Free Press, 1969); and "Political Parties, Interest Representation, and Economic Development in Poland," *American Political Science Review,* 69 (December 1970), 1239–1245. See also Richard F. Staar, "Elections in Communist Poland," *Midwest Journal of Political Science,* 2 (May 1958), 200–218.

[56] In the German Democratic Republic (East Germany) the Socialist Unity (Communist) party runs the show but tolerates and is joined in a national-front coalition by the Christian Democratic Union, Liberal Democratic party, National Democratic party, and Democratic Farmer's party; see Jean Edward Smith, *Germany beyond the Wall* (Boston: Little, Brown & Company, 1969), chap. 9.

Political Parties And Party Systems

ency to include as many as two-thirds more names than there are posts to be filled. The National Front can thus permit some competition among individual candidates, though none is possible among the parties. The Front has actually allowed a modicum of such competition, and on a few occasions a candidate from the top part of the official list has not been elected. In all elections the PUWP wins a majority of the seats in the Sejm (parliament); the UPP usually wins about 25 percent and the DP about 8.5 percent.

Third, and most important, the "hegemonic" party (the PUWP) is clearly and without challenge *the* dominant element in the National Front. The other parties have separate identities and even some separate activities, but the UPP and the DP do not decide for themselves what they will and will not do. That decision is reserved for the PUWP, which, in Wiatr's words,

> represents and expresses the socialist ideology underlying the entire political system. It determines the fundamental aims and values which constitute the basis for the functioning of the political and socio-political institutions of the country. Through the activity of its members on the institutions of state and social organizations, the party harmonizes the functioning of these institutions with the basic goals of the system. The party determines the general directives of policy-making by the state institutions.[57]

To a Westerner the hegemonic party system of Poland appears different from the monoparty system of the Soviet Union—but not very much.

## DOMINANT PARTY SYSTEMS

### Western Nations

For almost a century no Republican has been elected to any state office in Mississippi. In most elections there no Republican has even bothered to run, and on those rare occasions when one has he has rarely received even 5 percent of the votes. The Democrats have done better in Vermont but not much: Since the Republican party was founded in 1854 the Democrats have won statewide offices only six times and have never held more than a small fraction of the seats in the legislature. The Welsh coal-mining constituency of Ebbw Vale has for decades given Labour candidates majorities of 75 percent or more. Many working-class districts in Paris, Lyons, and Lille regularly give comparable majorities to the Communists.

In short, every democratic nation has areas with what may be called "dominant party systems." But they differ from the monoparty and hegemonic systems of the dictatorial regimes in one vital respect: The dominant parties' existing and potential rival parties are not outlawed, nor are their ideologies and programs officially suppressed. They have substantially the same opportunities to win votes and offices as do the dominant parties, but they have little success for various reasons.

---

[57] Wiatr, "Political Parties, Interest Representation, and Economic Development in Poland," p. 1241.

## Developing Nations[58]

A few developing nations, notably Ethiopia and Saudi Arabia, make no pretense of governing by popular selection of public officials, and they therefore neither need nor have political parties. But most at least go through the motions of popular elections, and many honor their substance as well.[59]

About a quarter of the developing nations have monoparty systems fashioned more or less closely after communist or fascist models.[60] Only one party is legally permitted in each, and efforts to form opposition parties are considered treasonable. The official party is usually the postindependence version of the politico-military movement that originally won the nation's independence from colonialism or overthrew its previous regime, and it is usually dominated by one man: For example, the Algerian National Liberation Front and Houari Boumédienne, the United Party of the Socialist Revolution in Cuba and Fidel Castro, and the Parti Démocratique de Guinee and Sekou Touré. The dictator generally uses the party, as the fascists and communists do, for several purposes: to advance national unity by stamping out all opposition, to mobilize popular enthusiasm behind his program, to give the masses an invigorating though spurious sense of participation in government, and to keep informed on how far he can push his program before popular resistance makes it unworkable.

When outsiders criticize these systems, the dictators and their party lieutenants usually reply with the classical fascist and communist arguments. The official party, they say, represents the nation, and opposition to it is opposition to the nation—treason. Quarreling parties and contested elections would only divide the people and make the nation easy prey for its colonialist enemies. And, they conclude, even if party competition might conceivably be tolerable in times of peace, plenty, and security, that time is not yet.

In other developing nations party competition is legally tolerated;[61] parties other than the national liberation party organize, nominate some candidates, contest some elections, and win a few seats in the national legislature. But the national liberation party regularly wins most of the votes and offices and monopolizes government power. Most conflicts over public policy are thus fought out *within* the dominant party, rather than in contests between it and opposition parties.

The two leading examples of such party systems are those of India and Mexico. The Indian National Congress was founded in the 1920s under the leadership of

---

[58] Useful discussions include Gwendolen Carter (ed.), *African One-Party States* (Ithaca, N.Y.: Cornell University Press, 1962); LaPalombara and Weiner, *Political Parties and Political Development;* Aristide R. Zolberg, *Creating Political Order: The Party-States of West Africa* (Skokie, Ill.: Rand McNally & Company, 1966); and Fred R. von der Mehden, *Politics of the Developing Nations* (Englewood Cliffs, N.J.: Prentice-Hall, Inc., 1964), chap. 4.

[59] Von der Mehden estimates that twenty-nine of the eighty-three nations that he considers have democratic two-party or more fractionalized party systems and genuine popular elections; Von der Mehden, *Politics of the Developing Nations,* pp. 61–64.

[60] Von der Mehden identifies twenty-one such nations, including Algeria, Guinea, Liberia, and Tunisia; Von der Mehden, *Politics of the Developing Nations,* pp. 56–59.

[61] Von der Mehden puts twelve nations in this class; Von der Mehden, *Politics of the Developing Nations,* pp. 59–60.

Mohandas K. (Mahatma) Gandhi and Jawaharlal Nehru to bring together all Indians in a movement for independence from British rule. From the time that independence was achieved in 1947 until recently, its successor, the Congress party, has regularly won three-quarters of the seats in elections for the national House of the People, and its leaders have always formed the national government. It has been opposed by a variety of small parties espousing communism, socialism, communalism, capitalist enterprise, and so on; but, although these parties together have usually won more than half the popular votes, their fragmentation and inability to coalesce have perpetuated the Congress party's dominance.[62]

The Mexican revolution of 1910 was followed by two decades of political confusion and instability, which were finally ended in 1929 with the establishment of a national party uniting most of Mexico's major groups and interests. The party underwent several reorganizations and changes of name, but in 1946 it adopted its present name, the Party of Revolutionary Institutions (PRI), and organization. Since then it has been opposed by the Conservative (PAN), Marxist (PPS), and dissident PRI (PARM) parties but has won all presidential elections by overwhelming margins and held more than 80 percent of the seats in Congress[63]

The Indian and Mexican systems and their counterparts in Gabon, Malaysia, and elsewhere provide a highly significant alternative to both the full competition of the two-party and multiparty democracies, on one hand, and the suppression of all competition and dissent in dictatorial one-party systems, on the other. Whether or not this "third way" can serve as a permanent mode of conducting political conflict no one can yet say, but it certainly offers new and struggling nations a way out of what many see as an impossible choice between too much party competition and none at all. For this reason, if for no other, it deserves as much careful study as scholars have lavished upon other kinds of party systems.

## CONCLUSION

Whatever may be their difficulties today, political parties remain among the greatest organizing agencies of most modern political systems. As we have seen, democratic and dictatorial systems alike depend upon their parties to perform such crucial tasks as generating policies, selecting leaders, and arousing popular support, thus enabling government to operate in densely populated modern nations. The differences in the kinds of party systems performing these tasks account for many of the differences between democratic and dictatorial regimes. In the light of such considerations, the editor of a pioneering comparative study of political parties concluded his book with much the same judgment with which Schattschneider began his:

> Hesitation and doubt ... reflect widespread uncertainties as to the true

---

[62] The Indian national party system is well described in Weiner, *Party Politics in India* (Princeton, N.J.: Princeton University Press, 1957). Party politics in one of India's states is analyzed in Paul R. Brass, *Factional Politics in an Indian State: The Congress Party in Uttar Pradesh* (Berkeley, Calif.: University of California Press, 1965).

[63] The Mexican system is thoroughly described in Robert E. Scott, *Mexican Government in Transition* (Urbana, Ill.: University of Illinois Press, 1959).

nature and direction of the revolution in our time. Above all, however, this revolution challenges our ingenuity to articulate workable programs, to organize functioning movements, and to put them to constructive action—weighty responsibilities which rest primarily with the people's great intermediaries: the political parties.[64]

[64] Sigmund Neumann. "Toward a Comparative Study of Political Parties," in Neumann, *Modern Political Parties* (Chicago: University of Chicago Press, 1956), p. 421.

# 10

# PRESSURE GROUPS AND MODES OF POLITICAL ACTION

Let us imagine an American male in his twenties today. He reads with growing horror scientists' predictions that within twenty years the air in every American big city will be so foul that no city dweller will dare to go out on the streets without a gas mask. And he knows that even now ear-splitting noise, incessant traffic jams, and universal filth are making American big-city life all but unbearable. Nor, he discovers, will life in the small towns and the country be much better much longer: Scientists also predict that by the end of this century the waters in our streams and the vegetation in our countryside will be so polluted with industrial effluents, poisonous pesticides, and garbage that most wildlife will have died and America the Beautiful, urban and rural alike, will have become America the Foul.

Then it hits him: America the Foul is what *he* will be living in when he reaches his forties—not some remote future generation but *his own*. And what America is to be, he suddenly realizes, America is right now becoming. Whatever must be done to prevent the nightmare from coming true must be done now—if, indeed, it is not already too late. The checklist of necessary preventive measures—outlawing internal-combustion engines and stopping all discharge of industrial and domestic wastes into our streams, lakes, and oceans—is scientifically well established. The social and economic changes necessary to institute these measures are immense. And the task of mobilizing the political force required to put the preventive measures quickly into effect and to ensure that they are resolutely enforced is truly staggering. Yet, he feels, the only alternative is to resign himself to early death or to a life not worth living.

The need is urgent, and the time is short. What can he *do* about it? For a starter, he knows that he cannot do much as an isolated individual among 200 million apathetic Americans. But he also knows that some of his friends, as well as other people whom he does not know personally, feel the same way he does. He can get together with them and organize a group—perhaps even a "movement" (which is only a larger and more intensely concerned group)—to fight pollution. The question then becomes what strategy and tactics should his group use to achieve its goals? It can, for one thing, form a political party and try to elect its own candidates to Congress and the state legislatures. But this task is hopeless. The Democratic and Republican parties so monopolize elections and the loyalties of the mass public that no new "single-issue" party like his group's Save-Our-Environment party can hope to have much success ever and certainly not soon enough to do any good. Further-more, forming such a party would probably earn the group a reputation as "a bunch of kooks" and isolate it from the main channels of political power. Such a position might make its members feel very righteous, but it would not accomplish anything concrete. They might well decide instead to become a "pressure group" like the Sierra Club or the National Wildlife Federation.

The point is that "pressure politics" is one—but only one—mode of political action that a group may use in pursuing its objectives. People in every society belong to several different types of groups, some of which play significant roles in the governing process (see Chap. 2). The main types, let us recall, are categoric groups (aggregates of individuals, like consumers, sharing one or more common characteristics), interest groups (categoric groups whose members are conscious of their common characteristics and who, to some extent, direct their behavior to promote the values or interests arising from these shared characteristics, as do the blacks), and organized interest groups (interest groups whose members consciously organize and cooperate to promote their common interests). A political party is one kind of organized interest group, and a pressure group like the Sierra Club is another. A pressure group differs from a political party mainly in that its tactics do not include nominating candidates as its own official representatives.

Pressure groups, then, are only one of several types of political groups. When politics is defined, as in Chapter 2, as "a struggle for power among interest groups," there is a danger that the statement will be taken to mean that politics is exclusively a struggle for power among *pressure* groups. It is important to understand that no such proposition is being advanced here; for "unorganized interest groups" like consumers, "organized interest groups" like political parties, and sometimes even largely solo actors like Ralph Nader play significant roles in the process of government. Pressure politics should be regarded not as the whole of politics but as a particular kind of tactics by which some political interest groups in every modern democratic nation pursue their objectives—and as a particular strategy that many such groups have found more useful than forming political parties or depending solely upon the good will of other interest groups and public officials.

What are the main types of pressure groups in modern democratic systems? How are they organized? How do they try to induce governments to adopt policies they favor and to reject policies they oppose? What factors determine the success of various groups? What impact have pressure groups upon the formation of public policy? Are they beneficial or injurious to democratic government? Our task in the present chapter is to consider some answers to these questions.

Pressure Groups and
Modes of Political Action

# LEADING TYPES OF PRESSURE GROUPS

Although every modern democratic nation has a number of pressure groups, those in the United States have received the most attention from political scientists. Most of the discussion in this chapter will, accordingly, deal with American experience, although I shall introduce examples from other democracies whenever the literature makes it possible.[1] American politics involves a number of local pressure groups and national "single issue" or "ad hoc" pressure groups like the National Council against Conscription, but I shall confine my description to groups commonly found in national politics and organized on a relatively permanent basis. Merely to list, let alone to describe, all such groups in any one democracy would fill a much bulkier volume than this one, and I shall therefore limit the discussion to a brief description of the major types and to a few of the more prominent examples of each.

## BUSINESS

Most modern democracies have two main types of business pressure groups. The first includes those that purport to speak for the interests of business as a whole, rather than for particular industries. In general these groups work for such policies as keeping government expenditures and taxation as low as possible, limiting government regulation of business, restraining trade unions, and subsidizing business and protecting it from the rigors of unrestrained competition. An outstanding American example is the National Association of Manufacturers (NAM), which, in recent years, has spent hundreds of thousands of dollars annually in its fight for measures like the Taft-Hartley Act and against measures like price controls. Another leading American example is the Chamber of Commerce of the United States. The British counterparts of these groups are the Federation of British Industries, the National Union of Manufacturers, and the Association of British Chambers of Commerce. The French versions are the Confédération Nationale du Patronat Français and the Petites et Moyennes Entreprises.

---

[1] There is now a vast literature on pressure groups in many nations. The most general comparative studies dealing with the advanced nations are Henry W. Ehrmann (ed.), *Interest Groups on Four Continents* (Pittsburgh, Pa.: University of Pittsburgh Press, 1958); and Graham Wootton, *Interest-Groups* (Englewood Cliffs, N.J.: Prentice-Hall, Inc., 1970). Comparable descriptions of pressure groups in various developing nations are included in Gabriel A. Almond and James S. Coleman (eds.), *The Politics of the Developing Areas* (Princeton, N.J.: Princeton University Press, 1960). Two works on the United States are Robert H. Salisbury (ed.), *Interest Group Politics in America* (New York: Harper & Row, Publishers, 1970); and L. Harmon Zeigler and G. Wayne Peak, *Interest Groups in American Society* (2d ed.: Englewood Cliffs, N.J.: Prentice-Hall, Inc., 1972). Two works on Great Britain are Samuel E. Finer, *Anonymous Empire* (2d ed., London: Pall Mall Press, 1966); and Allen Potter, *Organized Groups in British National Politics* (London: Faber & Faber, Ltd., 1961). A comparable work on France is Jean Meynaud, *Les Groups de Pression en France* (Paris: Armand Colin, 1959); and another on Italy is Joseph LaPalombara, *Interest Groups in Italian Politics* (Princeton, N.J.: Princeton University Press, 1964).

The second general type of business pressure group includes those that represent particular industries and are sometimes in conflict with one another, as well as with labor and consumers. American examples of such groups are the American Petroleum Institute, which has so successfully defended the oil producers' "depletion allowance" tax bonanza, and the Edison Electric Institute, which has battled hard against proposals for increased Federal controls over water pollution by electric-power plants. British examples include the British Iron and Steel Federation, the Newspaper Proprietors' Association, and the Road Haulage Association. One of the most powerful such groups anywhere is the French Confédération Générale des Viniculteurs, the wine-and-alcohol distillers' group whose successful fight against former Premier Pierre Mendès-France's efforts to limit the consumption of alcohol was considered to be one of the main causes of his fall from power in 1955.

Even in nations far more "socialistic" than the United States business pressure groups are large and powerful.

LABOR

Conflict between employers and employees over such matters as wages, hours, working conditions, and control of industrial policy has been prominent in every nation with a capitalist economy and a democratic government. Only in the more authoritarian regimes has there been "labor peace." The basic form of labor organization in this conflict is, of course, the trade union. Every modern democracy has one or more national federations of trade unions: the American Federation of Labor–Congress of Industrial Organizations (AFL-CIO) in the United States, the Trades Union Congress (TUC) in Britain, and the Confédération Générale du Travail (CGT), the Confédération Française des Travailleurs Chrétiens (CFTC), and the Force Ouvrière in France.

The American labor movement, much to the despair and disgust of many socialist ideologists, has emphasized pressure politics over party activity far more than have its counterparts in most other democracies. Toward the end of the nineteenth century the Knights of Labor, the first American national union, participated in the formation of the People's party (the Populists). The demise of this party after the election of 1896, however, inclined most labor leaders to follow the advice of Samuel Gompers, the first president of the AFL, to avoid identification of workers with any political party and to "reward your friends and punish your enemies" in both major parties. The present-day AFL-CIO, though it contributes much money and many votes to the Democratic party, has remained quite separate from it and completely rejects any notion of founding a labor party on British or European models.

The European tradition has been quite different. In most nations the labor and socialist movements have been closely intertwined from the start, and most European trade unions are committed to the idea that participation in a socialist labor party of some variety is the best way to advance the common cause. The unions also to some degree act as independent pressure groups, but they have chosen to place their main emphasis on party activity. As we saw in Chapter 9, the British TUC is closely associated with the Labour party, and most major unions are directly affiliated with the party at the national and local levels. The bulk of the party's funds, workers, and votes are contributed by the unions, and a good many union-sponsored MPs man the parliamentary party.[2]

French labor organizations are even more closely associated with political parties. The CGT, for example, is completely dominated by the Communist party and is often called the party's "industrial wing." The CFTC is almost as closely associated with the Mouvement Républicain Populaire and the Force Ouvrière with the Socialist party.

"Bread-and-butter unionism" (a policy of seeking only such immediate and practical goals as higher wages, shorter hours, and union security) thus continues to be the basic policy of the American labor movement, whereas European workers pursue the more ambitious goals of socialism and labor control of the economy. The differing emphases of American and European unions on pressure politics and labor-party activity are, in turn, direct consequences of their differing objectives.

## AGRICULTURE

In many modern democracies farmers, like businessmen, have established two main types of pressure groups. One type claims to speak for agriculture as a whole and presses for such policies as government-guaranteed floors under farm prices, protection of domestic farm products against competition from foreign crops, and government subsidization of services like rural electrification, farm credit, and soil conservation. The leading American pressure group of this type and one of the most powerful of all our national pressure groups is the American Farm Bureau Federation (AFBF). Its smaller but far from impotent rival is the National Farmers' Union. The leading British farmers' group is also called the National Farmers' Union, and the French version is the Confédération Générale de l'Agriculture.

In the United States there are also a number of special "commodity" pressure groups. The National Cooperative Milk Producers' Federation and the American Soy Bean Association are particularly well known because of their struggle over the passage and repeal of the special Federal tax on oleomargarine, in which the protax "big butter-and-egg men" finally lost out to the antitax "oleo interests." Also prominent is the National Wool Growers' Association, which recently won a unique and highly advantageous form of government protection for the incomes of wool producers, in the form of a guaranteed annual income.

Overrepresentation of rural areas, which is to some extent characteristic of the legislature in every democratic country, contributes heavily to the power of farmers' pressure groups. In all democratic nations they are more successful than one would expect from the ratio of farmers to the total population or from their proportional contribution to the national income.

## PROFESSIONS

In every modern democracy such leading professionals as doctors, lawyers, architects, and teachers have organized pressure groups to defend and promote their economic

---

[2] The authoritative account is Martin Harrison, *Trade Unions and the Labour Party since 1945* (London: George Allen & Unwin, Ltd., 1960).

and other interests. The American Medical Association, for example, has secured the passage of laws regulating medical education and use of the title "doctor of medicine," as well as restricting to persons who possess this title the power to prescribe certain drugs and perform surgery. In recent years it has doggedly, though unsuccessfully, fought efforts to establish "socialized medicine" (national compulsory hospitalization and medical insurance). The British Medical Association was unsuccessful in its campaign to block the Labour government's program of socialized medicine (in the strict sense of medical care directly subsidized and administered by the government) but has had a great deal of influence on the program's administration. The American Institute of Architects has obtained laws in most states restricting the label "architect" to people who have passed examinations whose content and grading are considerably influenced by the AIA. The American Bar Association and its affiliated state bar associations exert similar influence over the examinations by which the states admit people to the practice of law, and in some states the bar associations also have much to say about the selection of judges. The American Federation of Teachers (affiliated with the AFL-CIO) and the American Association of University Professors press for better pay for teachers and oppose government interference with academic freedom. Even the American Political Science Association, through its executive director in Washington, D.C., conducted an arduous and ultimately successful campaign to have political science included as one of the social sciences eligible for government research and fellowship support through the National Science Foundation.

## VETERANS

In the United States, as V. O. Key has dryly observed, "every war has been followed by the establishment of a society of veterans to bring pressure for the creation of conduits from the Federal Treasury to the pockets of the veterans."[3] One of the earliest of all American pressure groups was the Society of the Cincinnati, an organization of former officers of George Washington's army founded in 1783 to make sure that Revolutionary veterans received their due from the newly independent government. For many decades after the Civil War the Grand Army of the Republic, an organization of Union veterans, had great success in inducing the national government to grant generous pensions to old soldiers and was one of the most powerful pressure groups of its time. The most successful veterans' group of our own time is the American Legion, founded after World War I. The Legion, with more than 3 million members, not only has pressed, with considerable success, for pensions and bonuses for veterans of both world wars but has also secured the adoption of the "veterans' preference" rule by which veterans are given special consideration in obtaining Federal civil-service jobs. Smaller and less powerful than the Legion but nevertheless influential are organizations like Veterans of Foreign Wars (VFW), American Veterans of World War II (Amvets), and the American Veterans Committee. Veterans' pressure politics in Great Britain are carried on by the British Legion and in Australia by the Returned Soldiers' League.

[3] V. O. Key, Jr., *Politics, Parties, and Pressure Groups* (5th ed.; New York: Thomas Y. Crowell Company, 1964), p. 106.

## RELIGIOUS DENOMINATIONS

Many religious denominations are deeply concerned with such political issues as religious instruction in public schools, regulation of child labor, dissemination of information about birth control, and censorship of books, newspapers, magazines, and motion pictures. In order to press their positions more effectively such religious groups in the United States have been organized into the Legion of Decency, the National Catholic Welfare Conference, the Council for Social Action of the Congregational Churches, National Council of the Churches of Christ in the USA, the American Bible Society, the Woman's National Sabbath Alliance, and others.

## ETHNIC GROUPS

A number of minority ethnic groups, particularly in the United States, have established pressure groups to push government policies protecting them against hostile attacks and establishing full economic, social, and political equality with all other ethnic groups. Outstanding examples include the National Association for the Advancement of Colored People, the Congress of Racial Equality, and the Southern Christian Leadership Conference, whose objectives and policies will be described in Chapter 22. The white citizens' councils and the Society for the Preservation of the White Race are examples on the opposite side of the fight. Nonracial groups include the Jewish Defense League, the Anti-Defamation League of B'nai B'rith, and the Polish-American Society.

## REFORM

A number of groups, each organized by people of different economic, occupational, religious, and ethnic affiliations, urge the adoption of various governmental reforms. The prototype of such groups, and one of the most successful pressure groups in American history, was the Anti-Saloon League. Founded in 1893, this organization was far more influential than the parallel Prohibition party in securing adoption of the Eighteenth Amendment and the Volstead Act outlawing the manufacture and sale of intoxicating beverages; for three decades it exerted great power over many national congressmen and state legislators.[4] Present-day examples of such groups in the United States are the American Civil Liberties Union, which seeks to publicize and prevent all encroachments upon the constitutional freedoms of individuals and groups; the League of Women Voters, which has urged many governmental reforms in the interests of efficiency and democracy; and the National Municipal League, which has advocated such reforms as the short ballot, proportional representation, and the city-manager form of municipal government. In Great Britain the Fabian Society has enlisted many prominent intellectuals in drives not only for socialism but also for more specific reforms like reapportionment of the House of Commons and reduction of the power of the House of Lords. Also influential in British politics have

---

[4] An early and classic study of pressure politics in the United States is Peter Odegard, *Pressure Politics: The Story of the Anti-Saloon League* (New York: Columbia University Press, 1928).

**Protest from the Left: protesters and police at Republican National Headquarters, Miami Beach, July 1972.** Source: UPI Photograph.

been the Society for the Prevention of Cruelty to Animals and the Society for the Prevention of Cruelty to Children.

## PROTEST GROUPS[5]

In the broadest sense all the organizations mentioned are "protest groups"; that is, they all protest (publicly object to and urge the ending of) certain government actions or inactions that they consider inimical to their interests. In common usage, however, the term "protest groups" generally means organizations distinguished by two traits: claiming to speak for especially "disadvantaged" and powerless segments of society and placing heavy reliance on tactics like sit-ins, marches, demonstrations, civil disobedience, and even bombings and riots—all intended to dramatize their

---

[5] Analyses of protest politics in modern American life include a report submitted to the National Commission on the Causes and Prevention of Violence, Jerome H. Skolnick, *The Politics of Protest* (New York: Simon and Schuster, Inc., 1969); Michael Lipsky, "Protest as a Political Resource," *American Political Science Review, 62* (December 1968), 1144–1158; and James Q. Wilson, "The Strategy of Protest: Problems of Negro Civic Action," *Journal of Conflict Resolution, 3* (September 1961), 291–303.

Pressure Groups and
Modes of Political Action

constituents' plight and to force concessions and win support from "the establish-ment." We shall consider these tactics at greater length later, but we may note here some leading examples of protest groups in current American politics: women's rights organizations like NOW (the National Organization for Women); student organiza-tions like Students for a Democratic Society and the (Berkeley) Free Speech Move-ment; anti-Vietnam war groups like the National Mobilization Committee to End the War in Vietnam and the Committee for Draft Resistance; and black-nationalist movements like the Black Panther party and the Black Liberators. It is well, however, to remember that not all protest groups are oriented toward the left: Members of the Ku Klux Klan and the Mississippi White Knights have murdered black and white civil-rights workers, and paramilitary organizations like the Minutemen cache weap-ons and train for guerrilla warfare against the communist government that they expect to take over the nation in the near future.

The United States has no monopoly on protest groups. The All Japan Federation of Student Self-Governing Organizations (Zengakuren) has developed its skills in demonstrations and street fighting to the point at which it was able to block the visit to Japan of President Dwight D. Eisenhower in 1958 and to force many of Japan's major universities to remain closed during a substantial portion of the 1960s. In May 1968 university students in France went on strike, were joined by millions of factory workers, and nearly brought down the government. At the other end of the French spectrum repeated demonstrations by farmers and small shopkeepers against high taxes, inflation, and government regulations have fueled the *incivisme* (hostility of conservative rural and small-town workers to the political order and encouragement of efforts to evade its rules) that constitutes one of France's long-standing political problems. And for years in Great Britain the Campaign for Nuclear Disarmament used marches, blocking of streets, and attacks on the American embassy to protest Britain's possession of nuclear weapons and participation in the North Atlantic Treaty Organization.

## ADMINISTRATIVE AGENCIES

No democratic government's administrative agencies are entirely passive, politically neuter robots that respond only to commands by political executives, legislators, and pressure groups outside the government. They are staffed by human beings with values, preferences, concerns, and political knowledge and skills. Accordingly, they often push particular policies and oppose others (see Chap. 17).

The official stance of government workers as political neutrals largely denies them access to some of the ta..ics that other pressure groups use—public propaganda, influencing nominations, and contesting elections. But they are quite free to do most of the other things that extragovernmental pressure groups do, and their position inside the government gives them certain advantages that outside groups usually lack. For example, our present system of medicare was largely designed by civil servants in the Department of Health, Education and Welfare, and they planned and fought much of the battle to get it adopted by Congress. And few readers of our daily newspapers have to be told of the influence of the Federal Bureau of Investigation's longtime Director J. Edgar Hoover in shaping Federal crime-control legislation or of

**Protest from the Right: a Loyalty Day demonstrator.** Source: Benedict J. Fernandez, *In Opposition* (New York: Da Capo Press, 1968).

the importance of General Lewis B. Hershey, former Director of Selective Service, in determining the nature of our military-manpower procurement system from World War II to the 1960s.

In Chapter 17 we shall consider in more detail the operations and impact of administrators on policy making in the United States and elsewhere. But we should note here that in all modern democratic systems there are important pressure groups inside, as well as outside, government administrative agencies.

Pressure Groups and
Modes of Political Action

# MODES OF POLITICAL ACTION

## ORGANIZATION

"Let's get organized!" This cry is often heard in any group of people who have decided to pursue some common goal collectively. Most of us realize that a basic weapon in any such group's armory is organization—deciding what tasks are to be done, assigning them to particular members, selecting leaders, allocating decision-making power, and so on. An organized group has one great advantage over an unorganized group: It has a far better chance of mobilizing all its resources and placing its whole weight behind the drive for its objectives and thus of minimizing the wasted and contradictory efforts that often handicap unorganized groups.

Pressure groups are organized in several different ways. The NAM and the AIA, for example, are "unitary," in that their decision-making power is both formally and actually centralized in their national officers and boards of directors; one becomes a member directly of the national body. The AFL-CIO and the AFBF, on the other hand, are federal in that their powers and functions are formally divided between their state and local constituent groups and their national officers and directors; membership in the national body is mediated through membership in a constituent group. The federal organizations are often less cohesive than are the unitary ones, and both the AFL-CIO and the AFBF sometimes encounter rebellions from constituent bodies.

Most pressure groups are formally organized along democratic lines, with annual national conventions of representatives from the constituent groups empowered to set policy by majority vote. In practice, however, many such groups are run by small national bureaucracies. The AMA, for example, assigns formal decision-making power to a house of delegates, most of whose members are elected for two-year terms by the state medical associations. The house of delegates appoints a board of trustees to govern between its annual sessions, and in practice this board controls most of the AMA's decisions and sets most of its policies.[6] The pattern in other formally democratic pressure groups is similar.

## LOBBYING[7]

Many legislative chambers have adjoining lobbies in which legislators and their guests can meet and talk informally. From this practice has emerged the term "lobbying," which refers to direct efforts by representatives of pressure groups to persuade public officials to act as the groups wish. Legislators are still the main targets of lobbying, but executives, administrators, and even judges are also frequently and regularly approached.

As David B. Truman has pointed out, the first prerequisite for successful lobby-

---

[6] See Oliver Garceau, *The Political Life of the American Medical Association* (Cambridge, Mass.: Harvard University Press, 1941).

[7] The most comprehensive analysis of lobbying at the national level is Lester W. Milbrath, *The Washington Lobbyists* (Skokie, Ill.: Rand McNally & Company, 1963).

ing is access—the ability to be heard at one or more of the government's key decision-making points. Any group which consistently fails to obtain a serious hearing at any such point can hardly expect much success. The access of any particular group depends upon several factors: its general prestige and social position, the reputation and skill of its lobbyists, and so on. For example, a Roman Catholic cardinal or archbishop is more likely to have access to committees of the Massachusetts legislature than is a representative of the Jehovah's Witnesses, and a lobbyist whom the legislators have long known as a reasonable, practical, well-informed, and friendly person is more likely to obtain a serious hearing than is one with a reputation of being cantankerous, ignorant, or merely a "do-gooder."[8]

Having gained access to one or more decision-making points, the lobbyist can employ various techniques of persuasion. He can make a formal presentation of his group's position, marshaling facts, figures, and arguments to show it in the most favorable light. He can threaten the legislator or executive with dire consequences at the next election, and he can reinforce his threat by stimulating a flood of telegrams, postcards, and letters from the official's constituents. He can offer to trade his group's support of some pet project of the legislator or executive for the latter's support of his own group's proposal. This practice is a variety of "logrolling," which is conducted among lobbyists themselves, as well as between lobbyists and public officials. The lobbyist can even offer a bribe, either directly in the form of cash, mink coats, or deep freezers or indirectly in the form of the promise of a well-paid private job for the public official after he leaves office. The bribe method, however, has become so generally disapproved and therefore so dangerous that it is used far less frequently today than it was a century ago. Far more common, as the Watergate revelations made clear, is the large campaign contribution.

Lobbying is still the main weapon of most pressure groups, but the changing nature of society and government in modern democratic countries has forced many such groups to place increasing emphasis on other weapons as well.

## WORKING INSIDE POLITICAL PARTIES

Lobbying, needless to say, is likely to be far more successful with favorably predisposed public officials than with those who are indifferent or hostile. As political parties nominate most candidates for public office and thereby largely determine what kinds of people holding what views shall hold formal government power, no major pressure group can afford to ignore the internal operations of the parties. In Great Britain and the European democracies, as we have seen, most pressure groups are closely associated with particular parties and make relatively little effort to influence the policies and candidates of opposing parties. In the United States, however, the relatively amorphous and protean character of the major parties tends to keep the major pressure groups from openly and completely identifying themselves with either one. Rather, they try to secure the nomination of sympathetic candidates and the adoption of favorable planks in the platforms of both parties. Any particular

[8] David B. Truman, *The Governmental Process* (2d ed.; New York: Alfred A. Knopf, 1971), pp. 264–270.

group may work harder in one party than the other (for example, the NAM in the Republican party and the AFL-CIO in the Democratic party), but no group is as completely identified with either party as most British trade unions are with the Labour party.

The AFL-CIO, to offer just one example, sends spokesmen before the platform committees of both parties' national conventions. It encourages its rank and file not only to vote for prolabor candidates in the primaries of both parties but also to become precinct committeemen, delegates to party conventions, and even candidates for public office. Its representatives are particularly influential in platform writing and candidate selection at the Democratic national conventions. Neither party, indeed, is likely to nominate a presidential candidate regarded as totally unacceptable by the AFL-CIO or, for that matter, by the AFBF, the NAACP, or any other pressure group generally believed to have the power to swing large blocs of voters from one party to the other.

## ELECTIONEERING

Most American pressure groups pay homage to the idea of "keeping out of politics," but that only means avoiding any open and complete identification with a particular political party and eschewing third-party activity. It certainly does not mean having nothing to do with electioneering. Some pressure groups work hard to secure the election of sympathetic candidates and the defeat of hostile ones. They make endorsements, contribute both money and workers to the favored candidates' campaigns, propagandize their own members and the general public, help bring out the voters on election day, and generally perform all the election tasks of political parties. An outstanding example of such activity is the AFL-CIO's Committee on Political Education (COPE), which in recent years has been one of the largest and most effective campaigning organizations in the nation.

No pressure group can "deliver" anything like the entire vote of its membership to any particular candidate or party. One of the main reasons is that wherever the group has a large number of members both parties are careful not to nominate candidates clearly and violently hostile to its interests. In the 1952 and 1956 elections, for example, COPE and its predecessors "delivered" only slightly more than half the labor vote to the Democratic presidential candidate; and the Gallup Poll revealed that COPE's neutrality in the 1972 election resulted in an actual majority for Nixon over McGovern among members of labor union families. But in 1964, when COPE campaigned against Republican Barry Goldwater, who was widely believed to favor a national "right-to-work" law and "open shop" requirements in all labor contracts, more than three-quarters of the labor vote went to the Democrats. COPE's most recent triumph came in the 1968 presidential election: During the early weeks of the campaign the polls all showed that substantial proportions of northern white manual workers intended to defect from their normal Democratic preference in favor of the "backlash" candidacy of George Wallace. COPE and many union leaders went to work to convince their members that Wallace was antiunion and that they had better stick to the Democrats for the traditional bread-and-butter reasons. Postelection polls showed their success: Of the voters from households with one or more union mem-

bers each, 47 percent voted for Humphrey, 37 percent for Nixon, and only 13 percent
—slightly less than the overall national percentage—for Wallace.[9]

Such successes are occasionally necessary if there is to be any credibility to a
group's electoral promises or threats to public officials and party leaders.


## MASS PROPAGANDA

Lobbying and working inside political parties, reinforced by electioneering that
makes promises and threats credible, are political tactics aimed mainly at persuading
political "insiders"—elected officials, bureaucrats, party leaders, and the like. In the
nineteenth century most pressure groups in most democratic countries concentrated
on such methods and paid little or no attention to mass opinion. Commodore Cornelius Vanderbilt's famous dictum "The public be damned!"—whether or not he actually
said it—expressed the view common in his time that because the public's attitude
toward the objectives of pressure groups did not seriously affect their chances of
success, it was a matter of little importance. But in our own time the opinions of the
general public—whether they be "pro," "con," or "don't care"—have a direct and
powerful influence upon the success of any political group.

Most modern pressure groups are well aware of this influence. Accordingly,
they cultivate mass public opinion through a wide variety of "public relations"
operations and spend hundreds of thousands of dollars each year to create "favorable
climates of public opinion" for their objectives. We are all familiar, for example, with
so-called "institutional advertising" in the news media of groups like the American
Petroleum Institute, whose full-page newspaper and magazine ads are intended to sell
us not gasoline and heating oil (we need no urging to buy those products!) but the
idea that the oil industry is not making unfair profits and that the energy crisis is a
genuine crisis and not an artificial one created to boost the oil refiners' profits. Anyone
who has visited a doctor's office since the late 1940s has noticed that the piles of
magazines on the reception-room tables have been joined by stacks of pamphlets and
cartoons opposing "socialized medicine." Frequently both unions and employer
groups use full-page newspaper advertisements to plead their respective causes during strikes.

The old-fashioned lobbyist and "wire puller" has been joined, and in some
pressure groups superseded, by the modern public-relations counsel.


## DEMONSTRATIONS

For many years protest groups have relied heavily upon various methods of political
action collectively labeled "demonstrations." They include such diverse ploys as
picketing, mass marches, chanting slogans, heckling opponents, even standing mo-
tionless in silent vigil against whatever is being opposed. In our time these methods

---

[9] Three percent voted for other candidates. These figures are from the study of the 1968
electorate by the Survey Research Center of the University of Michigan, and have been furnished through the courtesy of the Inter-University Consortium for Political Research.

have been widely adopted by student protesters (marches to the college presidents' homes, mass walkouts on graduation ceremonies), civil-rights groups (freedom rides and freedom marches), antiwar groups (the 1969-1970 Moratorium marches)—and also white-supremacy groups ("white power" marches) and prowar groups (Loyalty Day marches).

Despite these differences in form and in the political objectives of the groups mounting them, demonstrations share certain common traits as a method of political action. First, they are a form of direct participation by group members, compared to indirect participation like paying dues so that leaders can purchase newspaper ads. There is reason to believe that such direct participation often intensifies participants' devotion to group goals. The members have an emotionally satisfying experience, and the leaders gain a more cohesive and effective group. Demonstrations thus have major advantages for any political group but particularly for a protest group. Second, demonstrations sometimes provoke reaction—and overreaction—from opposing groups and the police, which may arouse sympathy for the group from many outsiders who care little about its political goals but dislike anything that smacks of repression or brutality. And, third, though most demonstrations are intended to arouse sympathy and support among the general public, all are planned to attract attention, and many succeed. A television network charges far more than most protest groups can afford for time to present their views, but the same network often finds in a good rousing demonstration just the exciting visual material that fascinates its viewers ("fender-bender footage" it is called in the trade) and will give the group prime-time coverage on its news shows without charging a penny.

Because of their low cost and their power to solidify groups, arouse sympathy, and attract free publicity, demonstrations are likely to continue to be widely used, especially by protest groups.

## STRIKES AND BOYCOTTS

The term "strike" usually means a collective work stoppage by a group of industrial workers, but, as we shall see, it can also refer to work stoppages by other elements of the community for political purposes. In the United States most labor strikes are conducted for nonpolitical reasons: They are intended to make employers grant such nonpolitical demands as labor contracts providing higher wages, shorter hours, better working conditions, union security, and so on. In many European democracies, on the other hand, labor strikes are sometimes used for political purposes—to force the government to adopt or reject certain policies or even to overthrow the existing form of government. In France, for example, the Communist-dominated CGT has called a number of strikes since 1945 for the avowed purpose of preventing the French government from participating in such anticommunist organizations as the Marshall Plan, the European Defense Community, and NATO. The "syndicalist" theorist Georges Sorel advocated the general strike (a complete work stoppage by all workers) as the best means for overthrowing capitalism and establishing his brand of socialism, and in some European and Latin American nations general strikes have been used to drive certain public officials and sometimes whole governments out of power.

A less familiar but equally important form of strike is the type in which French and Italian farmers have destroyed their produce in efforts to compel their governments to treat them more favorably. Perhaps the most amusing instance of an unusual strike was that conducted by the French customs inspectors in 1947. In an effort to make the government raise their wages, these employees put on a two-hour "zeal strike": They enforced to the letter *every* customs law and regulation and thus unleashed a storm of protests by tourists that did much to induce the ministry to grant the wage demands. Apparently work "speedups" can sometimes be as effective as work stoppages![10]

A boycott is a concerted refusal by a group of people to deal with some other private group or public agency. Economic boycotts are concerted refusals to buy the goods or services of particular industries or firms and are sometimes used for mainly political purposes. A classic example in American politics began in 1955 in Montgomery, Alabama, when Mrs. Rosa Parks, in protest against local Jim Crow ordinances requiring segregated seating on public transportation, refused to give up her seat on a bus to a white man and move to the back. This refusal touched off a general boycott of the Montgomery bus system by blacks, organized and led by the Reverend Martin Luther King, Jr. The bus system found that it could not long survive without its black patrons and eventually the city rescinded its segregated-seating ordinance. This tri-

[10] *New York Times,* May 9, 1947, p. 10.

umph first brought King to the national prominence that he enjoyed until his assassination in 1968. A more recent example is the nationwide boycott of table grapes and lettuce organized by Cesar Chavez, the *chicano* president of the Amalgamated Farm Workers of America, to support his union's strike against grape and lettuce growers. The objectives of this boycott have been more economic and less political than were those of the Montgomery boycott, but it too has had political objectives and impact.

## NONVIOLENT CIVIL DISOBEDIENCE

In his leadership of the movement for Indian independence from British rule, Mohandas K. Gandhi developed a technique for political action that has had a major impact on the Western world. He called it "satyagraha," and its Western version is generally called "nonviolent civil disobedience."[11] Its leading American theorist and practitioner has been King, and during the early 1960s it provided the dominant philosophy and the principal tactics for much of the American civil-rights movement.

As Gandhi and King both practiced and preached it, civil disobedience requires that protest groups first explore all the possibilities for negotiation and arbitration with their opponents and the government. Only when these means have failed should they issue an ultimatum explaining exactly what they are going to do and why. Then they employ various tactics to make things inconvenient for their opponents (without using violence or doing them bodily harm) and to commit their own members to the cause more deeply through sacrifices for it. These tactics include economic boycotts and noncooperation with government authorities (refusal to pay taxes or to send children to school and peaceful disobedience of whatever laws—for example, traffic regulations or prohibitions against parades and picketing—that they think appropriate). A tactic which has become familiar to newsreel viewers in several nations is what Gandhi called *dharna*—sitting down in streets, corridors of public buildings, airport runways, and other channels of movement. When public authorities enforce the laws with the usual methods of arrest and imprisonment, the members of the group must offer no resistance but must, in King's words, "testify with their bodies" to the justice of their cause. The ultimate objective is not only to win support from neutral outsiders but eventually also to convert the opponents themselves.

The tactics of civil disobedience have scored many impressive victories. They contributed much to the winning of Indian independence. And there is no doubt that the contrast between the blacks' peaceful demonstrations for their rights and the often brutal measures of suppression taken by southern white sheriffs and troopers—Birmingham and Selma, Alabama, are but two examples—touched the hearts of a great many previously apathetic northern whites and won their wholehearted support for the blacks' cause.

---

[11] The theory and practice of satyagraha are described in Joan V. Bondurant, *Conquest of Violence: The Gandhian Philosophy of Conflict* (Princeton, N.J.: Princeton University Press, 1958). A famous early American individualist version of the same doctrine is Henry David Thoreau's *Of Civil Disobedience* in Henry S. Canby (ed.), *The Works of Thoreau* (Boston: Houghton Mifflin Company, 1937), pp. 789–808, in which he explained why he refused to pay taxes to support the Federal government, which was fighting the Mexican war, which he regarded as an outrage to justice.

## VIOLENCE

In early April 1968, Martin Luther King, Jr., Nobel Peace Prize laureate and apostle of nonviolent civil disobedience in the struggle for equal rights for American blacks, went to Memphis, Tennessee, to organize protest demonstrations on behalf of striking Memphis sanitation workers. On the evening of April 4 he stepped out onto the balcony of his motel for a breath of air. From a window in a nearby rooming house James Earl Ray, a white man, shot and killed him. The shock of the assassination touched off a wave of rioting and looting in more than 125 cities in 29 states across the nation. Within a week at least 46 people had been killed, more than 2600 injured, more than 21,000 arrested; property damage resulting from more than 3000 deliberately set fires was more than $45 million.[12]

Two months and one day later Senator Robert F. Kennedy was leaving a Los Angeles hotel after celebrating his victory over Senator Eugene McCarthy in the California presidential primary. In the crush on the way out was Sirhan Bisra Sirhan, a young Jordanian living in Los Angeles; he emptied a .22-caliber pistol at Senator Kennedy, killing him and wounding five other people.

That evening President Lyndon Johnson spoke to the nation "not only as your President, but as a fellow American who is . . . deeply disturbed, as I know you are, by the lawlessness and violence in our country, of which this tragedy is the latest spectacular example." He appointed the National Commission on the Causes and Prevention of Violence. The reports that it commissioned constitute the most thorough study yet made of the role of violence in American political life.[13]

This recent research on violence, both political and nonpolitical, stresses two main points that we would do well to heed. First, violence—the use of physical force to eliminate opposition or to bend it to one's will—is not a new phenomenon in American life, nor is it caused by some national sickness peculiar to our own time. It is, as black militant H. Rap Brown has correctly remarked, "as American as cherry pie." Nonpolitical violence—murders, rapes, muggings, assaults, family blood feuds, "wars" between strikers and strikebreakers, tavern brawls, and so on—has been widespread from our nation's beginnings.

Furthermore, violence for mainly political ends has been equally common in our history. The nation was born in a violent revolution against Great Britain. Although we have had only one full-scale civil war, it was the bloodiest in any nation's history. Much of our continental territory was violently taken from its Indian inhabitants. Four of our Presidents (Abraham Lincoln, James Garfield, William McKinley, and John F. Kennedy) have been assassinated, and unsuccessful attempts have been made on the lives of as many more. Vigilante movements, in which private citizens take law enforcement and the punishment or elimination of suspected criminals into their own hands, first arose in the 1760s and have recurred many times since. And in our own time the white-supremacy violence of the Ku Klux Klan and the Mississippi

---

[12] *The 1969 World Almanac and Book of Facts,* (New York: Newspaper Enterprise Association, Inc., 1969), p. 74.

[13] Skolnick, *The Politics of Protest;* and Hugh Davis Graham and Ted Robert Gurr (eds.), *Violence in America: Historical and Comparative Perspectives* (New York: Bantam Books, 1969). See also H. L. Nieburg, *Political Violence: The Behavioral Process* (New York: St. Martin's Press, Inc., 1969).

Pressure Groups and
Modes of Political Action

DID YOU VOTE? YES. DID HE WIN? YES. HOW WILL YOU FEEL ABOUT HIM A YEAR FROM NOW? BETRAYED. THEN WHY DID YOU VOTE? TO BE EFFECTIVE. DID YOU VOTE?

**The calculus of violence.** Source: © 1970 Jules Feiffer. Courtesy Publishers-Hall Syndicate.

White Knights is countered by the violence of black urban rioters. And to all this free-enterprise political violence we must add the violence, ranging from night sticks to atomic weapons, used by our police and armed forces in implementing our domestic and foreign policies.[14]

It is quite a record. Yet the second point stressed by recent research is that the United States has no monopoly on either political or nonpolitical violence. As sociologist Charles Tilly has put it, "As comforting as it is for civilized people to think of barbarians as violent and of violence as barbarian, Western civilization and various forms of collective violence have always been close partners."[15] Riots, rebellions, coups d'état, violent strikes and strikebreaking, sabotage, assassinations, Luddite machine smashing, and other forms of collective political violence have been used frequently by European political groups to try to bring about, or to prevent, various kinds of social and political change.[16]

We should add a third point: Whether we like it or not, violence—private *or* governmental—is a form of political action. It can be used for good purposes or bad, however we may define them. For example, many people believe that the assassination of President Kennedy in 1963 removed one of the Western hemisphere's most promising democratic leaders, whereas the assassination of President Rafael Trujillo of the Dominican Republic two years earlier had removed one of its bloodiest tyrants. In the Greek revolution of 1968 and the Chilean revolution of 1973 democratic regimes were overturned by military juntas, whereas in the Venezuelan revolution of 1945 a military dictatorship was overthrown in favor of a progressive democratic regime. Closer to home police in Selma, Alabama, forcibly broke up demonstrations for black voting rights, but U.S. marshals forcibly broke up efforts by whites to prevent James Meredith from becoming the first black to enroll at the University of Mississippi.

Any group's decision whether or not to use violence to gain its ends involves several subsidiary questions. Is it right to use violence in *any* circumstances? Pacifists say no, but most political groups say yes. What political price must be paid for using

[14] See the summary by Richard Maxwell Brown, "Historical Patterns of Violence in America," in Graham and Gurr, *Violence in America,* chap. 2.

[15] Charles Tilly, "Collective Violence in European Perspective," in Graham and Gurr, *Violence in America,* p. 4.

[16] See Tilly in Graham and Gurr, *Violence in America,* chap. 1.

Political Inputs

NO. | WHAT DID YOU DO? | BLOW UP A UNIVERSITY. | WHY DID YOU BLOW UP A UNIVERSITY? | TO BE EFFECTIVE. | HOW WILL YOU FEEL ABOUT IT A YEAR FROM NOW? | INEFFECTIVE. | I CAN GET THE SAME RESULTS A LOT EASIER.

violence? There are many possibilities: little or no price; losing present or potential allies in other groups; alienating the less militant members of one's own group; triggering counterviolence by opposing groups; touching off repressive measures by the government; injury and death to one's associates; and so on. Would violence satisfy the members' emotional needs as no nonviolent tactic can? Would they regard anything less as a "copout"? And, of course, is violence a better bet than the nonviolent alternatives to obtain significantly more of what the group wants?

To the extent that a political group's main purpose is to influence government policy—as distinguished from providing its members with emotional fulfillment—this last question seems the most important in deciding whether or not to use violence. For in any political system some groups obtain substantially more of what they want than others do. What main factors, then, affect "who gets what, when, and how"?

**Police violence is used to protect demonstrations as well as prohibit them: Milwaukee police remove a man charged with trying to interfere with one of Father Groppi's marches for an open-housing law, September 1968.** Source: Wide World Photos.

Pressure Groups and
Modes of Political Action

# FACTORS AFFECTING THE SUCCESS OF PRESSURE GROUPS

## SIZE

A pressure group's size is obviously one factor affecting its ability to obtain what it wants. Other things being equal (which, as we shall see, they never are), groups with many members are likely to be more successful than groups with few members, simply because the former represent many votes and the latter few votes. From this point of view, therefore, the AFL-CIO is more likely than is the American Association of University Professors to force the wages of its members upward, the American Legion is more likely than is the American Veterans Committee to have its particular veterans' program adopted, and the AFBF's campaign for flexible farm-price supports is more likely to succeed than is the National Farmers' Union's drive for fixed price supports.

Political success by no means invariably comes to the larger groups, however. In politics as in boxing, basketball, and football it is the *good* big man, not any big man, who always wins over the good little man. Thus, the remaining factors in our list all affect what makes a pressure group "good."

## SOCIAL STATUS

One of the major contests in post-1945 American politics has been over compulsory national health insurance. The fight against such legislation has been conducted mainly by the American Medical Association and that for it mainly by the AFL-CIO. At first glance this contest would seem to be highly unequal: The AMA has only about 180,000 members and the AFL-CIO more than 15 million. Yet, as so often happens in democratic politics, David defeated Goliath many times. How can this be?

Part of the explanation surely lies in the great social prestige of the medical profession and its AMA spokesmen. Most Americans think that doctors are not only persons of great learning, skill, and respectability but also selflessly dedicated to alleviation of human suffering. Many Americans, by contrast, regard trade unionists as rather uncouth, lazy, and ordinary people dedicated only to making as much money as possible for as little work as possible. Whether or not either attitude is justified by the facts is irrelevant; the point is that for many Americans who are themselves neither doctors nor union members the social prestige of doctors and the AMA is notably higher than that of unionists and the AFL-CIO. The doctors' access is thus at least as good as that of the unions; furthermore, man for man they command far more deference from society in general than do union members and thus find it easier than the latter do to acquire political allies and support. The same factor does much to explain the success of such other relatively small pressure groups as the American Institute of Architects, the Daughters of the American Revolution, the American Humane Society, and the Izaak Walton League of America.

## COHESION

One of the most frequent events in democratic politics is the defeat of a large but internally divided or apathetic pressure group by a small but cohesive and energetic

A.M.A. hates Regimentation

group. In politics as in war ten who work closely together are more powerful than a hundred who cooperate loosely or not at all. Recognizing the value of group cohesion, however, is far easier than achieving it. The membership of every pressure group, as we noted in Chapter 2, overlaps with those of other groups. Each of its members belongs to other groups, and some of the latter have objectives and make demands that are in conflict with those of the group in question. Accordingly, one factor that powerfully affects the group's cohesion is the "heterogeneity" of its members—that is, the number and variety of the other groups to which they belong.

Pressure Groups and Modes of Political Action

Another is the extent to which these other groups make demands that conflict with those of the group in question. Still another is the relative importance that each person attaches to his membership in this group or that. And yet another is how much danger each group's members consider it to be in at the moment.

Take, for example, the AFL–CIO in the 1956 presidential election. The union leadership strongly urged the election of Adlai Stevenson as the more liberal and prounion of the two candidates, and its political arm, COPE, spent a great deal of money and effort toward that end. Yet many AFL–CIO members thought of themselves as Republicans; others believed Eisenhower would be better able than Stevenson to prevent the Middle Eastern and Hungarian crises from involving the nation in World War III; still others regarded the Republicans as more likely than the Democrats to lower taxes. Each of these unionists had to decide whether an Eisenhower victory would place the union movement in so great a danger as to outweigh its advantages in maintaining peace and lowering taxes. Judging by the election results, a great many decided these questions in favor of Eisenhower rather than as AFL–CIO leaders had recommended. If the unions had achieved perfect or nearly perfect cohesion among their 15 million members, they might well have elected Stevenson, but, as so often happens among pressure groups, the conflicting loyalties and attitudes of many members greatly reduced the AFL–CIO's effectiveness in this situation.

LEADERSHIP

A pressure group's effectiveness, like that of an army, also depends to some extent upon the quality of its leadership. A large and well-equipped army led by a John Pope or an Ambrose Burnside may well be routed by a smaller and poorly equipped army led by a Robert E. Lee, but when a U. S. Grant takes command of the larger army, ultimate victory becomes merely a question of time. The same is true in politics.

The leaders of any political group must perform both internal and external functions for their group. They must make suggestions about such internal matters as who will perform which tasks and who will make which decisions; they must appeal to the membership to support group policies and maintain cohesion; they must oversee the punishment or expulsion of rebellious individuals or factions; and they must encourage the emergence and preside over the training of lower-echelon leaders and their own successors. They must also initiate the group's strategy and tactics in its struggle with the opposition, and represent the group in its dealings with other groups and the general pulbic, not only as its spokesmen but also as a symbol to outsiders of the group's human qualities. If they are widely regarded as loudmouthed, ignorant, and untrustworthy, their group will suffer accordingly. But, if most outsiders believe them to be reasonable, well-informed, and honest, their group will acquire allies and friends much more readily.

What kind of person makes a good political leader? Political scientists and psychologists have long pondered this question. For many years the "personality trait" explanation was popular; according to it the successful leader is a person who possesses certain personal qualities (an attractive appearance, intelligence, vigor,

*"He was beloved as a person but rather indecisive as a Leader."*

dedication, and so on) that would make him or her a leader in any kind of group.[17] Recent social science, however, favors a more "situational" explanation, according to which leadership is not a thing possessed by certain favored individuals but a *relationship* among leaders and followers that depends upon the nature of the group, its objectives, and the sociopolitical environment within which it operates. Men who successfully lead baseball teams or trade unions may well be unable to lead religious orders or scientific associations.[18] Modern social science, accordingly, cannot provide a full explanation of what makes a good leader that applies to all groups in all situations. There is no doubt, however, that leadership skill is a prime factor in the success of any pressure group.

## THE POLITICAL AND GOVERNMENTAL ENVIRONMENT

As the preceding discussion implies, the organization, tactics, and chances for success of any pressure group are powerfully affected by the political and governmental

[17] For a summary of this view of leadership, see Ralph M. Stodgill, "Personal Factors Associated with Leadership: A Survey of the Literature," *Journal of Social Psychology,* 25 (1948), 35–71.

[18] For a fuller explanation of this point of view, see Alvin W. Gouldner (ed.), *Studies in Leadership* (New York: Harper & Row, Publishers, 1950); and Lester G. Seligman, "The Study of Political Leadership," *American Political Science Review,* 44 (December 1950), 904–915.

Pressure Groups and
Modes of Political Action

253

system in which it operates; the variations in these systems among the democracies do much to account for the differences in the structure and impact of their pressure politics.

The political and governmental system of the United States, for example, is more decentralized than are those of most of the other modern democratic countries. Not only are our political parties decentralized and relatively uncohesive (see Chap. 9), but the formal government is decentralized as well: Power is divided between national and state governments, and power within the national government is widely dispersed among the President, his Cabinet members, administrative officials, committees and leaders in each house of Congress, the various Federal courts, and so on. The American system thus provides a great many points of access, and different groups make their most effective bids at different points in the system. Labor groups, for instance, have generally had more success in winning support from the President than from Congress. Veterans' groups, on the other hand, have done better in Congress than with the President. Before 1964 filibusters and threats of filibusters in the Senate (see Chap. 15) blocked all attempts to push antisegregation laws through Congress, but the antisegregation forces (see Chap. 22) won a number of signal victories in the form of Supreme Court decisions outlawing racial discrimination in voting, housing, and education. The very multiplicity of points of access created by our decentralized political and governmental system has thus done much to determine the special nature of American pressure politics.[19]

For many years political commentators talked as if pressure groups were a unique and somewhat reprehensible feature of the American system and averred that no such things existed, for example, in Great Britain. Recent scholarship has made it clear, however, that "even if compared with American examples, pressure groups in Britain are numerous, massive, well-organized, and highly effective" and that it may well be that "at the present time pressure groups are more powerful in Britain than in the United States."[20] The main differences between American and British pressure politics result from the greater centralization of British parties and governmental structure. The parties are highly centralized, disciplined, and cohesive, and a pressure group has far less chance than in the United States to win the support of some legislative members over the objections of party leaders. British pressure groups, as we have noted, thus work more closely with party leaders and are more closely associated with particular parties than are their American counterparts. The British governmental structure concentrates most decision-making power in the national government rather than in county or borough governments; within the national government power is concentrated mainly in the Cabinet and a few key ministries and administrative bodies. There are, accordingly, fewer points of access in Britain than in the United States, and, once a pressure group in Britain has succeeded at one of these points, it is far less likely than in the United States to lose out at some other point. Samuel H. Beer has put the point this way:

---

[19] See Truman, *The Governmental Process*, pp. 322–327, 507–508.

[20] Samuel H. Beer, "Pressure Groups and Parties in Britain," *American Political Science Review*, 50 (March 1956), 1, 3. See also Beer, *British Politics in the Collectivist Age* (New York: Alfred A. Knopf, 1965).

Not only do interest groups enjoy a greater degree of concentration, but the government with which they deal also is more highly centralized than ours: greater power to exert pressure is linked up with greater power to act. Whether that power to act will be used or not will depend on various factors. . . . Usually—this is the point to press—if you can bring over the Minister and the Chancellor of the Exchequer you have not much else to worry about. Compare the position of the American pressure group which, if it wants positive action, must win its battle at many different points—committees in both houses, the presidency, the secretary, the bureau chief. It is no wonder that our pressure politics is so much noisier and less tidy than Britain's.[21]

The studies of pressure groups in other democracies suggest that in general they follow British rather than American practices, but the main point that they demonstrate is that pressure groups play significant roles in the politics and government of all modern democratic systems.

## THE ROLE OF PRESSURE GROUPS IN DEMOCRATIC GOVERNMENT

### LEGAL POSITION

Freedom of organization and political action is generally considered an essential principle of democratic government. The constitutions of most modern democracies guarantee the rights of their citizens to organize associations for the purpose of advancing by peaceful means whatever ideals and interests their members hold dear. The Constitution of the United States guarantees "the right of the people peaceably to assemble, and to petition the Government for a redress of grievances" (First Amendment); the Constitution of the West German Republic declares that "all Germans have the right to form associations and societies" except those "the objects or activities of which conflict with the criminal laws or which are directed against the constitutional order or the concept of international understanding" (Article 9); and the French Constitution of 1946 declared that "everyone may defend his rights and interests by trade-union action and may join the union of his choice" (Preamble). Most democracies, indeed, have provided some form of direct "functional" representation of pressure groups in the formal government structure through such devices as economic councils, interest-group membership of administrative advisory boards and public corporations, and so on (see Chap. 14).

Not, of course, that in every democratic system any pressure group is legally free to pursue any objective by any means it sees fit. Most democracies prohibit such tactics as bribery, violence, libel, slander, and intimidation and prosecute in criminal actions any pressure group representative who employs such tactics. Most democratic nations, as we shall see in Chapter 17, also deny associations of public employees the right to strike.

The United States has gone farther than have most democracies in its efforts

---

[21] Beer, "Pressure Groups and Parties in Britain," p. 9.

to regulate the lobbying activities of pressure groups. The Federal Regulation of Lobbying Act (1946), for instance, requires every individual, association, and corporation seeking to influence legislation to register and file quarterly reports with designated officials of the House of Representatives and the Senate. These reports must contain such information as the specific bills in which the lobbyist is interested, the amount of financial receipts and names of those contributing more than $500, and the amounts and names of recipients of expenditures of more than $10. Several states have adopted similar legislation. These regulations have produced a considerable body of information about the nature and dimensions of lobbying, but whatever expectations their authors may have had that forcing lobbying into the open would shame it out of existence have been sadly disappointed.[22]

## IMPACT ON POLICY FORMATION

### What Is It?

There is little doubt that pressure groups have powerful impacts upon the policy-forming processes of every modern democratic polity. They are not, of course, the only political groups that have such impacts. In every democracy political parties have some influence on the shape of public policy, and in many democracies they have more direct and obvious influence than the pressure groups have. In Chapters 15–19 we shall see that the many formal agencies of government are more than mere collections of robots whose activities are entirely controlled by such extragovernmental forces as pressure groups and parties. The point to remember, however, is that pressure groups have a significant impact upon public policy in every modern democratic system.

### What Should It Be?

Some commentators have argued that the present power of pressure groups is very dangerous to democracy. They say that "special interests are one of the perils of our times," that "there is no escape from the pressure of organized power," and that only political parties, not pressure groups, can act as "the principal rallying point for the great public interests of the nation."[23] Pressure politics undoubtedly has acquired a bad name in some quarters because of the widespread belief that pressure groups represent only "narrow, special, and selfish interests" and that the more powerful they are the less consideration will be given to the "public interest."

Other commentators reply that as there is no objective scientific test by which a democratic polity can determine the true content of the "public interest" and the precise policies that will promote it, both the concept and the policies are best determined through a pluralistic process of peaceful discussion, negotiation, and

---

[22] See Milbrath, *The Washington Lobbyists,* chap. 16; and *Legislators and the Lobbyists* (2d ed.; Washington, D.C.: Congressional Quarterly Service, 1968).

[23] The first two comments are quoted in Truman, *The Governmental Process,* p. 501. The third is from E. E. Schattschneider, *Party Government* (New York: Holt, Rinehart and Winston, Inc., 1942), p. 206.

**Pressure groups influence foreign as well as domestic policy.** Source: *The Herblock Book* (Boston: The Beacon Press, 1952).

compromise among political parties, legislators, executives, administrators, judges—and pressure groups. So long as the political climate is such that no pressure group or party becomes a fanatical political army determined to exterminate all its competitors and so long as all these groups have overlapping rather than mutually exclusive memberships, "democracy under pressure" will remain healthy and able to adapt its policies to the ever-changing demands of ever-changing social, economic, and political conditions. Pendleton Herring has put it this way:

> Democracy provides us with an ideal under which experimentation with institutions and negotiation among interests is tolerated and justified. We are not forced to believe in unity; we may glory in diversity. It is enough if we achieve

Pressure Groups and
Modes of Political Action

a working union of interests, ideas, institutions, and individuals. If we would formulate and execute constructive national long-range policies under our democratic ideology, we must face a period of change, of experimentation and of danger. Yet face it we must.[24]

One point is clear: The rights of citizens to organize and advance their ideals and interests by peaceful methods of discussion and negotiation is an essential principle of democracy. It is the basic justification not only for permitting the existence of pressure groups but for tolerating political parties as well. In any nation in which this right is guaranteed, pressure groups, like political parties, will continue to be organized and to play a significant role in the policy-making processes of democracy.

---

[24] Pendleton Herring, *The Politics of Democracy* (New York: Holt, Rinehart and Winston, Inc., 1940), pp. 420–421. For more recent expositions of this "pluralist" view, see Robert A. Dahl, *Pluralist Democracy in the United States* (Skokie, Ill.: Rand McNally & Company, 1967); and Nelson W. Polsby, *Community Power and Political Theory* (New Haven, Conn.: Yale University Press, 1963). For some attacks on the "pluralist" position, see C. Wright Mills, *The Power Elite* (New York: Oxford University Press, 1956); and Henry S. Kariel, *The Decline of American Pluralism* (Stanford, Calif.: Stanford University Press, 1961).

Political Inputs

# IV

## GOVERNMENTAL STRUCTURES

# 11

# THE ANATOMY
# AND PHYSIOLOGY
# OF CONSTITUTIONS

Few Americans have to be told that a nation's constitution is a significant element of its governing system. Most of us (including some who are a little vague about what it contains) are very proud of our own Constitution. When a foreigner like the nineteenth-century British statesman William Gladstone declares that "the American Constitution is the most wonderful work ever struck off at a given time by the brain and purpose of man," we are likely to feel that he has spoken only the simple truth. When a foreigner like the nineteenth-century French scholar Alexis de Tocqueville writes that he has "never been more struck by the good sense and the practical judgment of the Americans than in the manner in which they elude the numberless difficulties resulting from their Federal Constitution," we are likely to inquire indignantly how a *Frenchman* of all people presumes to comment on the "numberless difficulties" resulting from *our* Constitution.

By no means all the world's peoples, as we shall see, revere their constitutions as Americans do their own. Yet most political scientists believe that scrutinizing a nation's constitution is one useful way to begin the study of its governing system. In the present chapter, we shall begin our survey of the ways in which modern nations govern themselves by explaining what a constitution is, the different statuses that constitutions enjoy in different nations, where constitutional rules may be found and what matters they deal with, and how constitutions grow and develop.

# WHAT IS A CONSTITUTION?

## DESCRIPTION OR IDEAL?

Despite the long-standing respectful attention that they have paid to constitutions, students of government have long disagreed about the proper definition of the term itself. Perhaps the oldest dispute centers on the question of whether or not it should be used purely descriptively. Some writers have taken the position that a community's constitution is simply the body of fundamental rules according to which it is governed—in systems terminology, the accepted conversion processes by which its authorities turn demands and supports into policy outputs. Any community that makes and enforces government policies in conformity with certain generally understood and accepted procedures, they believe, has a constitution of some sort. The fact that we may disapprove of a particular community's procedures, they insist, does not entitle us to dismiss that community as having no constitution whatever.

Other writers, however, have agreed with the eighteenth-century political philosopher Thomas Paine that only certain kinds of governmental rules and procedures deserve to be called "constitutions." In *The Rights of Man* (1791–1792) Paine argued that no community can properly be said to have a constitution unless it passes these tests: Its people must consciously and deliberately establish its basic rules and (presumably) promulgate them in the form of a written document; this document must be generally regarded as antecedent to and therefore binding upon the community's government; it must define and thus limit government authority; and government action exceeding those defined limits must be generally regarded as an exercise of "power without right." Paine avowed that any government that does not, as the government of Great Britain does not, measure up to these standards has nothing that deserves to be called a "constitution."[1]

## WRITTEN OR UNWRITTEN?

Paine's argument that the British have no constitution at all raises the question of whether constitutions must be written or may also be unwritten. Paine's position won many supporters in his own time, especially in the United States; even today we occasionally encounter in newspaper editorials and elsewhere the argument that, because Great Britain, unlike the United States and most other nations, has no single written document officially designated as its Constitution, the British are in the unhappy state—akin to that of a man in an automobile with a high-powered engine but no brakes—of having no constitution whatever.

Most students of government in Paine's time and since have, however, agreed with his contemporary Edmund Burke that, as the basic rules of British government are at least as well understood and generally obeyed as those promulgated in most written Constitutions, these rules are as entitled to the label "constitution" as are

---

[1] One of Paine's British contemporaries, Arthur Young, quipped that Paine talked "as if a constitution was a pudding to be made by a recipe"; quoted in Charles H. McIlwain, *Constitutionalism Ancient and Modern* (Ithaca, N.Y.: Cornell University Press, 1940), p. 4.

those of any nation with a written document. In the nineteenth and early twentieth centuries many writers discussed learnedly and at great length the differences between written and unwritten constitutions (with the British constitution always providing the sole example of the latter type) and concluded, among other things, that the latter are more flexible but less stable than are the former.

Most contemporary political scientists, however, pay little heed to this distinction. They agree with the argument first advanced by the British scholar-statesman James Bryce that this dichotomy is a distinction without a difference; for, as Bryce pointed out, all written Constitutions are partly unwritten, and parts of the "unwritten" British constitution are promulgated in official documents.[2]

## CONSTITUTIONS AND CONSTITUTIONALISM

As the term is used in this book, a constitution is *the whole body of fundamental rules, written and unwritten, legal and extralegal, according to which a particular government operates.*[3] The reader will note that this definition, unlike Thomas Paine's, is purely descriptive. It implies that every political system that authoritatively allocates values for a society in some way (see Chap. 2) has a constitution.[4] One constitution may establish a dictatorial regime, another a democratic one; one constitution may operate in a developed nation with a formal Constitution, another in a developing nation without one; one constitution may consist of a complex set of basic rules, another of a simple set. But these variations are all related to the *kinds* of constitutions that various systems have, not to whether or not they have them at all.

There are advantages in a descriptive conception of a constitution, but there are problems too. The main problem is the confusion that often arises over the distinction between the empirical question of what kind of constitution a particular nation has and the normative question of whether or not its constitution satisfies the standards of constitutional *ism*. Let us try to get this important distinction clear and firmly fixed in our minds.

A constitution, according to this book's definition, is a nation's basic rules for governing itself; every nation has such rules, and therefore every nation has a constitution. This usage joins with most present-day political scientists in denying both the validity and utility of Paine's dictum that a nation with a bad constitution has no constitution at all. We may not admire the constitutional rules of, say, Haiti, Cuba, or Saudi Arabia, but we cannot legitimately say that these nations have no constitutional rules at all.

Constitutionalism, on the other hand, is a particular set of ideals, competing with other ideals for people's loyalties, about the kinds of constitutional rules a nation *should* have. Constitutionalism is the doctrine that the power of government

---

[2] James Bryce, *Studies in History and Jurisprudence,* Vol. 1 (New York: Oxford University Press, 1901), chap. 3.

[3] This definition is a somewhat modified version of one given in Francis D. Wormuth, *The Origins of Modern Constitutionalism* (New York: Harper & Row, Publishers, 1949), p. 3.

[4] To distinguish between constitutions in this broad descriptive sense and written documents officially designated as Constitutions, I capitalize the term in the latter sense but not the former throughout the book.

should be limited so that human rights—free speech, free press, due process of law, security of person, and the like—are formally and in fact protected from abridgment by either public officials or private individuals. The antithesis of constitutionalism is totalitarianism. Canada and Sweden may thus accurately be said to have constitutional governments, whereas Haiti and Cuba may not—despite the fact that all four have constitutions of some kind.

In Chapters 21 and 22 I shall have a great deal more to say about the proponents, opponents, and survival prospects of constitutionalism in the modern world. First, however, we need to know more about the status and "natural history" of constitutions in modern nations, totalitarian as well as constitutional.

## CONSTITUTIONS IN DEMOCRATIC SYSTEMS

### THE STATUS OF CONSTITUTIONAL RULES

#### Superiority to Ordinary Law

Every nation's constitution, as the definition given above suggests, consists of rules, requiring certain kinds of behavior, permitting others, and prohibiting still others. By no means all governmental rules, however, have constitutional status. As that definition also suggests, a nation's constitution is made up of *fundamental* rules—rules that have special importance, fulfill special needs in the nation's total governing system, and are generally regarded as superior to the rules of ordinary law. Some languages, indeed, actually have different terms for constitutional and ordinary law. In German, for example, ordinary law is called *Gesetz* and constitutional law *Grundgesetz* or *Verfassung*. In French the two types are called respectively *loi* and *constitution* and in Italian *statuto* and *legge*.[5] Constitutional rules are generally considered different from the rules of ordinary law in several main respects.

**More Fundamental**   Constitutional rules establish and regulate the basic framework of government, prescribing the matters with which the government may (or may not) deal, the specific agencies that are to deal with them, the procedures that those agencies must follow, and the processes by which members of the various agencies are selected. Constitutional rules apply to more general and significant matters than does ordinary law and also fix the limits of ordinary law.

In some modern Constitutions, to be sure, we can find rules applying to matters that do not really seem fundamental. The Constitution of Afghanistan, for example, provided that "in Friday sermons the name of the King will be mentioned" (Article 7). The Constitution of Peru requires that "there shall be at least one school in every place where the school-going population amounts to thirty pupils" (Article 73), and the Swiss Constitution provides that "the bleeding of slaughter animals which have not been previously stunned is expressly forbidden" (Article 25A). The point is,

---

[5] Herman Finer, *Theory and Practice of Modern Government* (rev. ed.; New York: Holt, Rinehart and Winston, Inc., 1949), p. 117.

however, that although these rules may seem to outsiders petty and undeserving of constitutional status, the Constitution-makers of the nations involved apparently do not agree. It is they, and not their critics in other nations, who decide for their communities what is fundamental and what is not.

**Less Easily Changed**   Most written Constitutions, as we shall see, can be formally amended only through procedures more difficult and time-consuming than those by which ordinary laws are adopted. This additional difficulty is intended to accomplish several purposes, one of which is to ensure that the rate of constitutional change is slower than that of changes in ordinary law. The same objective is accomplished even in nations like Great Britain and New Zealand, in which constitutional rules may be changed by the legislature through the same formal procedures it uses to alter ordinary laws. The legislatures of these nations know what is at stake when they consider bills that involve constitutional change, and the historical record shows that they have not wrought such changes more rapidly or more frequently than have other nations. New Zealand, for example, has passed only about thirteen parliamentary acts tantamount to constitutional amendments since 1908, whereas Switzerland, which has a far more elaborate formal amending procedure, has adopted more than fifty constitutional amendments since 1848.

**More Binding**   In most nations it is generally understood that any rule of ordinary law that contravenes a constitutional rule has no legal standing and may not legitimately be enforced. The reasoning behind this prohibition is that, because constitutions are fundamental and ordinary laws derivative, the latter may not violate the former. The only legitimate way to adopt such a law is to change the constitution to eliminate the contradiction.

### Maintaining Constitutional Supremacy

If constitutional rules are generally regarded as more binding than conflicting rules of ordinary law, the question remains, Who decides whether particular ordinary laws do or do not contravene the constitution? What agencies maintain constitutional supremacy? The world's nations answer these questions with either, but not both, of two institutional arrangements.

**Judicial Review**   Judicial review, as the term is used in this book, is *the power of a court to render a legislative or executive act null and void on grounds of unconstitutionality.* Although some English judges in the seventeenth century claimed this power, it first became generally established and accepted in some of the American states during the late eighteenth century and was made part of the national constitutional system by Chief Justice John Marshall's decision in *Marbury* v. *Madison* (1803). During the nineteenth and twentieth centuries the institution of judicial review gradually spread to other nations; the period after World War I was the time of its widest adoption.[6] At present

---

[6] David Deener, "Judicial Review in Modern Constitutional Systems," *American Political Science Review,* 46 (December 1952), 1079–1099.

the Constitutions of about thirty nations expressly assign this power to the courts, and in two other nations the Constitutions have been construed—as in the United States—as establishing judicial review.[7] In several nations (for example, Nicaragua, Portugal, and Syria) judicial review exists only on paper, for both the courts and the legislatures do whatever the ruling dictators or elites order, and the judges do not exercise their formal powers. In other nations (for example, Canada, the United States, and West Germany), however, the courts can—and on occasion do—declare legislative and executive acts null and void on grounds of unconstitutionality, and their decisions are accepted as authoritative by the respective legislative and executive bodies. In Chapter 18 we shall examine further the functioning and consequences of judicial review in such nations.

**Review by Other Agencies** The Constitutions of fewer than ten nations now expressly assign power to review the constitutionality of legislative and executive acts to various popularly elected bodies like legislatures, cabinets, and combinations of both. The remaining nations have neither constitutional provisions nor judicial declarations on the subject. This lack does not mean that these nations do not distinguish between constitutional rules and ordinary law or that their constitutions are not regarded as supreme. It means only that the duty of maintaining constitutional supremacy and the power to decide whether or not legislative and executive acts contravene the constitution rest in bodies other than courts—popularly elected legislatures and cabinets in the democracies and dictators or ruling oligarchies in the dictatorial regimes.

## WHERE CONSTITUTIONAL RULES ARE FOUND

The fundamental rules that compose a nation's constitution may be found in some combination of the following four locations.

### A Written Constitution

Every nation, with the few exceptions already noted, has a written document formally and officially designated as its Constitution. Despite their formal centrality, however, the rules set forth in such a document may or may not be important in the total constitution of any given nation. We can discern at least three general patterns. The rules stated in the written Constitutions of the United States, the nations of the British Commonwealth and West Europe, and some Latin American countries have high status and constitute the nucleus around which the total constitutions are built. In such nations as the Soviet Union, Hungary, Albania, and Czechoslovakia, on the other hand, lip service may be paid to the written Constitutions, but everyone understands that they may be set aside with no fuss or sense of wrongdoing whenever certain public officials decide that reasons of state require it—that is, whenever these

---

[7] The most recent comprehensive world collection of national Constitutions is Albert P. Blaustein and Gisbert Flaz (eds.), *Constitutions of the Countries of the World* (12 vols.; Dobbs Ferry, N.Y.: Oceana Publications, 1971————).

officials believe that observing the rules will make it inconvenient for them to do something that they want to do. In nations like Paraguay, Nicaragua, Haiti, and Saudi Arabia the written Constitutions are frequently ignored; their rules are violated, and they receive relatively little attention or respect.[8]

### Organic Laws

Few written Constitutions establish and outline the organization of every major agency of government. The gaps are usually filled in the legislature with rules that, though adopted by ordinary legislative procedures, are nevertheless regarded as almost as important as the rules in the Constitution itself. These special legislative rules are usually called "organic laws." They differ from other laws in their relation to the basic organization and procedures of government rather than to specific government policies.

The Constitution of the United States, for example, provides that "the judicial Power of the United States, shall be vested in one supreme Court, and in such inferior Courts as the Congress may from time to time ordain and establish" (Article III, Section 1). Most elements of our national court system—the district courts, courts of appeal, tax courts, patent court, and so on—have been established by acts of Congress, beginning with the Judiciary Act of 1789. The Constitution also refers to "the executive Departments" but does not prescribe what departments there shall be or how they shall be organized; all the existing departments, from the Department of State (established in 1789) to the Department of Transportation (established in 1967), have been created by acts of Congress. Despite their legislative rather than constitutional origins, these courts and executive departments are certainly parts of the American constitutional system, and it is scarcely easier to alter the legislation creating them than it is to amend the Constitution itself. The organic laws of most other nations enjoy this same special status.

### Judicial Decisions

Every written Constitution and organic law, as we shall see, is necessarily couched to some extent in ambiguous language—that is, in terms whose application to specific situations is not agreed upon by all reasonable persons. Many of the written parts of any constitution must therefore be interpreted. Every government agency in every nation interprets the constitution every time it acts, for presumably it will act only when it believes it has the constitutional authority to do so. Many such interpretations are so obvious and uncontroversial that they go unchallenged. A few, however, become controversial, and in constitutional governments many controversies over constitutional interpretation are fought out in cases at law. Although the courts in such nations have no monopoly on interpreting the Constitutions and organic laws, they do deal with many of the controversies over such interpretations, and their

---

[8] J. Roland Pennock and David G. Smith suggest distinguishing between formal and effective constitutions in such instances: *Political Science: An Introduction* (New York: Crowell-Collier and Macmillan, Inc., 1965), pp. 241–242.

decisions are generally regarded as authoritative. In each of these nations the decisions of most courts are written, collected, and published, and these collections furnish another important source of constitutional rules.

Perhaps the outstanding example of a major constitutional institution established by judicial decision rather than by a constitutional provision or an organic law is the American institution of judicial review itself. The Constitution of the United States nowhere expressly authorizes the courts to exercise this power, nor did any act of Congress do so before 1803. In that year, however, the Supreme Court, in *Marbury* v. *Madison,* interpreted the Constitution in such a way as to give the courts the review power; this interpretation was subsequently accepted by the other agencies of government and by the people, and judicial review thus became an established part of our constitutional system. Even today, however, to the question, "Where is the national courts' power of judicial review authorized?" the answer is, "In the Supreme Court's decision in *Marbury* v. *Madison.*"

### Constitutional Customs

The first three varieties of constitutional rules are all expressed in written form and for that reason are relatively easy to find and deal with. The fourth is different. The category of customary constitutional rules includes all those regularized, clearly understood, and generally accepted and obeyed fundamental rules of government that are not expressed in the formal and official manner of written Constitutions, organic laws, and judicial decisions. The only written form in which these customs may be found is in nonofficial documents like commentaries by scholars of jurisprudence, constitutional law, and political science. But customary rules are no less binding or authoritative than the other kinds of rules. Some people find this statement difficult to believe, for they assume that "the law" is the only really powerful regulator of government activity and believe that any procedure not prescribed by a written law is observed only at the whims of the citizens. A few examples of constitutional customs, however, should make clear their authoritative and binding nature.

The Constitution of the United States expressly provides that the President be elected by the Electoral College, the members of which are to be selected by the states in whatever manner the latter choose. The authors of the Constitution clearly intended the electors to choose the President according to their own individual judgments entirely free from popular pressure. Yet for more than 100 years all the electors have been pledged to vote for particular presidential candidates, and from 1789 to 1972 in only 10 of a possible 15,500 instances did electors vote for men other than the candidates to whom they were pledged.[9] As all electors are now popularly elected,

---

[9] Estes Kefauver, "The Electoral College," *Law and Contemporary Problems,* 27 (Spring 1962), 188–212, especially 208–209. Five such instances have occurred since World War II: In 1948 Preston Parks was a candidate for elector in Tennessee on both the regular Democratic ticket pledged to Harry S. Truman and the Dixiecrat ticket pledged to Strom Thurmond (he voted for Thurmond); in 1956 segregationist W. F. Turner, an Alabama elector pledged to Adlai Stevenson, voted for segregationist Alabama Judge W. B. Jones; in 1960 Henry D. Irwin, an Oklahoma elector pledged to Richard Nixon, voted instead for Senator Harry F. Byrd of Virginia; and in 1968 Lloyd W. Bailey, a North Carolina elector pledged to Nixon, voted for George Wallace (but

the Electoral College has become, in effect, a machine for rubber-stamping the choice of the American people.

In arithmetical terms, the machine has thus worked 99.91 percent of the time—which, to say the least, matches the record of compliance with our written laws and the Constitution. Yet students often ask, "But what happens if an elector *does* violate his pledge?" The answer, based on the ten instances mentioned, is that he is not subject to any national legal penalty, for neither the Constitution nor any act of Congress expressly requires him to honor his pledge. In only nineteen states would any present defector violate state law. Yet legal penalties, as we observed in Chapter 3, are by no means the only sanctions against deviant political behavior; there are also such penalties as social ostracism, smashed political careers, and so on.

**Sometimes constitutional customs are more advanced than are written procedures.**
Source: *Straight Herblock* (New York: Simon and Schuster, Inc., 1964).

*"We're almost ready to take off again"*

In short, we know that only .09 percent of the time electors have violated their pledges. We know that even in the very special circumstances of the 1960 election—the closest election in the twentieth century, in which many embittered southern

not for Wallace's running mate, General Curtis LeMay). In 1972 Roger L. MacBride, a Virginia elector pledged to Nixon, voted instead for Libertarian Party presidential candidate John Hospers.

electors pledged to John F. Kennedy might have bolted and thrown the election into the House of Representatives—the system worked almost perfectly, with only 1 defector out of 537 electors.[10] It therefore seems likely that the custom will hold firm almost all the time in the future as in the past. It also seems likely that, if it should break down and result in the election of a President whom a majority of the people oppose, it will swiftly become law (a possibility that in itself undoubtedly inhibits some potential defectors). So custom though it be, it is as rigid and unyielding as any rule embodied in our Constitution, organic laws, and judicial decisions.[11]

The Constitution of Canada expressly authorizes the Governor-General, who is the Queen's official representative, to appoint the ministers (the heads of the executive departments) and places no limitations on his choice. By custom, however, he—like the Queen and all "constitutional monarchs"—appoints only those whom the Prime Minister recommends, and he would never do otherwise. Nor does the Prime Minister have an absolutely free hand in making his recommendations: He knows, for instance, that he is expected to recommend both French- and English-speaking ministers, to provide for approximately equal representation from the provinces of Quebec and Ontario, and to make sure that the western provinces have some representation. These expectations are so firmly established and taken for granted that no prime minister would dare to disappoint them.

The Constitutions of the United States and Canada authorize the lower houses of the respective national legislatures to elect their own "speakers" (presiding officers) but say very little about the powers and duties of such officers. The speaker of the American House of Representatives, as we shall see in Chapter 15, is customarily the principal leader of the majority party in the House, whereas the speakers of the Canadian and British Houses of Commons are customarily removed from just about all connections with political parties and are almost completely nonpartisan officials. No speaker of either of these bodies would step out of the role that constitutional custom assigns to him.

As these illustrations make clear, these customary rules are every bit as firmly established as part of the general body of constitutional rules as are those written down in the Constitution, organic law, and judicial decisions.


## WHAT CONSTITUTIONAL RULES COVER

Although the rules of written Constitutions are, as we have seen, by no means the only rules in any nation's constitutional system, they provide an obvious and often

---

[10] The eight Mississippi electors who voted for Harry Byrd in 1960 ran as "unpledged" electors and thus violated no pledge; the six Alabama electors who joined them had announced in advance that they would not support Kennedy and so, strictly speaking, they too violated no pledge.

[11] Nevertheless, many Americans apparently do not wish to rely on "mere customs" in so important a matter. After considerable discussion and pressure, the House of Representatives in 1969 approved a formal constitutional amendment abolishing the Electoral College altogether and establishing direct popular election of the President and Vice-President. In 1970, however, the amendment failed to win Senate approval, and the direct-election reform seemed far from realization.

useful point of departure for studying any particular system. In some nations the written Constitution has high status and forms the nucleus around which the whole constitutional system is built. Even nations that largely ignore their Constitutions do not junk them altogether. Apparently, even they believe that such documents accomplish some purposes, even though those purposes do not include regulating the actual conduct of the governing process.

Although there are almost endless variations in the detailed provisions of the world's Constitutions, most of their contents fall into some combination of five main categories.

### Statements of Ideals

The bulk of most Constitutions is made up of legal rules intended as direct and fairly specific guides for and limitations on the behavior of public officials. Many Constitutions, however, also contain statements of general ideals and objectives, intended to set the tone and spirit of the whole document. To this extent, such Constitutions are more than collections of legal rules; they are also political manifestos or testaments.

Statements of ideals are more often than not located at the beginning of the Constitutions, and they usually state by what authority the Constitutions are established and for what purposes. The Preamble to the Constitution of the United States, for example, proclaims,

> We, the People of the United States, in Order to form a more perfect Union, establish Justice, insure domestic Tranquility, provide for the common defense, promote the general Welfare, and secure the Blessings of Liberty to ourselves and our posterity, do ordain and establish this Constitution for the United States of America.

Similar statements appear in the Constitutions of Brazil, Cuba, Finland, Korea, Liberia, the Philippines, and many American states.

Many of the Constitutions of the communist nations also describe their origins. The Russian Constitution of 1936 proclaims,

> The political foundation of the USSR is the Soviets of the Working People's Deputies, which grew and became strong as a result of the overthrow of the power of the landlords and capitalists and the attainment of the dictatorship of the proletariat.[12]

The Bulgarian Constitution of 1947 begins,

> Bulgaria is a People's Republic with a representative government established and consolidated as a result of the heroic struggle of the Bulgarian people against the monarcho-fascist dictatorship, and of the victorious national uprising of September 9, 1944.[13]

---

[12] Chapter I, Article 2, in Amos J. Peaslee (ed.), *Constitutions of Nations* (2d ed.: 3 vols.; The Hague: Martinus Nijhoff, 1956), Vol. 3, p. 485.

[13] Chapter I, Article 1, Peaslee, *Constitutions of Nations,* Vol. 1, p. 262. The Constitutions of Albania, Czechoslovakia, Hungary, Poland, and Romania begin with similar statements.

## Structure of Government

All Constitutions specify the major organs of the government, what kinds of people shall be eligible to occupy positions in these organs, and how they shall be selected and retired. Many also outline the organization of government agencies and describe in broad terms their proper interrelation.

## Distribution of Powers

Most Constitutions have rules specifying what the various main governing officials are authorized to do. These "powers of government" may be distributed in one or both of two ways. First, the Constitution can assign to each government organ—the legislature, the executive and administrative agencies, and the courts—power to act on certain matters. The Constitutions of the "presidential" democracies (see Chap. 15) follow the principle of "separation of powers": Each branch of government is assigned certain powers and, by implication at least, is largely forbidden to exercise powers assigned to the other branches. The Constitutions of the parliamentary democracies, on the other hand, not only authorize the legislative bodies to supervise, regulate, and select the heads of the executive agencies but also allow them to supervise the courts as well. The 1926 Constitution of Saudi Arabia locates full power in the King and permits (but does not require) him to appoint such advisers and administrators as he wishes.

Second, all federal Constitutions distribute powers between the national and local governments. The Constitution of the United States assigns certain specific delegated, or enumerated, powers to the national government and reserves the rest to the states. The Constitutions of Canada and India, on the other hand, have three lists of powers: those belonging exclusively to the national government, those belonging exclusively to the local governments, and those belonging to the two levels "concurrently." In most federal governments these lists can be formally altered only by joint action at both levels of government.

Some unitary Constitutions also list the powers of both levels of government, although these lists can be changed without the consent of the local governments. In most unitary governments, however, the powers of the local governments are stated in the organic laws rather than in the Constitutions.

## Rights of Individuals

Just about every Constitution declares that certain rights must be guaranteed to those within its jurisdiction. These rights are of two main varieties. First, there are limitations on government. The oldest and most familiar form of constitutionally guaranteed individual rights is expressed as things that government may not do to individuals. The Constitution of the United States, for example, declares that Congress may not abridge any individual's freedom of speech, press, or religion and that no state may deny to any person the "equal protection of the laws." Most other Constitutions list individual rights in much the same manner.

Second, there are obligations of government. Many of the more recent Constitutions include positive obligations of government to every individual. The most common are guarantees of the rights to work, to education, and to security in old age. Some Constitutions add rights that the framers of the American Constitution would hardly recognize as proper matters for constitutional guarantees. The Irish Constitution of 1937, for example, provides that "the State shall . . . endeavour to ensure that mothers shall not be obliged by economic necessity to engage in labour to the neglect of their duties in the home";[14] and the 1948 Constitution of Italy states that "the Republic favors through economic measures and other provisions the establishment of families and the fulfillment of their functions, with especial regard to large families."[15]

### Formal Amendment Procedures

Most Constitutions specify the procedures by which they may be formally amended. Very few modern Constitutions (that of New Zealand is an example) are flexible in the sense that they can be amended by the same procedures used to pass ordinary laws. Most Constitutions are "rigid"; they can be formally amended only by special procedures more difficult to accomplish than is the ordinary legislative process. In his survey of modern Constitutions, K. C. Wheare found that the special amendment procedures of the "rigid" Constitutions have one or more of four main objectives.[16]

First, they are designed to ensure that the Constitutions will be changed only "with deliberation, and not lightly or wantonly." Every special amending procedure is intended to accomplish at least this end.

Second, they are intended to give the people an opportunity to express their views before changes are made. Some Constitutions (for example, those of Ireland, Denmark, Australia, and Switzerland) require that all proposed amendments be approved by the voters in referenda before they take effect. Other Constitutions (like those of Belgium, the Netherlands, and Sweden) require that amendments must first be approved by the legislatures, which must then be dissolved; general elections must be held, and the amendments must then be passed in identical form by the new legislatures. The Swiss Constitution (and the Constitutions of some American states) permit voters to initiate as well as ratify constitutional amendments.

Third, they are intended to prevent alteration of the powers of national and local governments by either level acting alone. In the United States, for example, there are two amending procedures, but the only one used so far provides that amendments must be proposed by a two-thirds vote of both houses of Congress and ratified by the legislatures or conventions of three-fourths of the states. In Switzerland and Australia amendments proposed by the national legislatures must be ratified by majorities of all those voting in nationwide balloting and also by majorities of the voters in a majority of the cantons or states.

Fourth, they are designed to safeguard the rights of certain linguistic, religious, or cultural minorities. The Swiss Constitution, for example, specifies that German,

---

[14] Article 41, Section 2, Peaslee, *Constitutions of Nations,* Vol. 2, p. 459.

[15] Article 31, Peaslee, *Constitutions of Nations,* Vol. 2, p. 486.

[16] K. C. Wheare, *Modern Constitutions* (New York: Oxford University Press, 1951), chap. 6.

French, and Italian shall have equal status as official languages of the federation, and the Canadian Constitution makes similar provisions for French and English.

## CONSTITUTIONAL CHANGE

### Substituting Constitutions

No nation has been content to keep its constitution forever in exactly the same form in which it originated. Many have become so dissatisfied with their written Constitutions, for one reason or another, that they have replaced them with new ones, and some have changed Constitutions several times. Of the sixty-seven nations that had achieved independent national status before 1939, thirty-one now have Constitutions adopted since 1945; twenty-four others have Constitutions adopted between 1900 and 1945, and only twelve have Constitutions adopted before 1900. Although the United States is far from being the oldest nation in the world, its Constitution, written in 1787 and put into effect in 1789, is the world's oldest written Constitution still in effect.

Most, although not all, substituting of Constitutions has occurred in three historical periods: during the European liberal revolutions in the mid-nineteenth century; in the period 1918–1920, in response to changes in national status and forms of government wrought by World War I; and in the late 1940s as the result of changes in national status and forms of government brought about by World War II and communist conquests in Eastern Europe and Asia.

### Formal Amendment

Junking old Constitutions and replacing them with new ones is by no means the only—or even the most important—method of constitutional change. Another is formal amendment of the established Constitutions. In most nations this method had been the least significant of the various methods of constitutional change. Most groups seeking change have found other methods easier to use and equally productive of satisfactory results. Ascertaining how many times a particular Constitution has been amended, therefore, tells us very little about the full dimensions of constitutional change in the nation. For example, there have been twenty-six formal amendments to the Constitution of the United States, fifty-one to the Constitution of Switzerland, and only four to the Constitution of Australia. Yet no one concludes from these data that the constitutional system of Switzerland has changed far more than have the systems of Australia or the United States. To understand how much constitutional change has taken place in these or other nations, we must look not only at the number of formal constitutional amendments but also at other indexes.

### Statutory Revision

Because a nation's organic law is, as we have noted, part of its constitutional system, any major change in such law is a constitutional change. For example, in 1789 the American Congress established the Department of War and in 1798 added the Department of the Navy. For the next century and a half these two agencies constituted the nation's military establishment. In the late 1940s, however, Congress demoted the two departments from Cabinet rank, created a separate Air Force, and placed all military forces under the authority of a brand-new executive department, the Department of Defense. Congress has also since 1789 created other executive departments, increased the size of the Supreme Court and altered its appellate jurisdiction, established regulatory bodies like the Interstate Commerce Commission (1887) and the Federal Communications Commission (1934), and so on. All these actions represented changes in our constitutional system at least as significant as, say, the Third, Eleventh, and Twelfth Amendments to the Constitution. Similar observations apply to changes in the organic law of other nations.

## Judicial Revision

The power of the courts to interpret the Constitution necessarily involves the power to revise the constitution. To illustrate with the most famous example of recent years, the Fourteenth Amendment to the Constitution of the United States specifies that "no State shall . . . deny to any person within its jurisdiction the equal protection of the laws." In the case of *Plessy* v. *Ferguson* (1896) the Supreme Court held that the laws in southern states requiring racial segregation in transportation (and, by implication, in all other facilities as well) did not violate this clause if the facilities provided for each race were substantially equal to those provided for the other races. In *Brown* v. *Board of Education of Topeka* (1954), however, the Court reversed this ruling and held that racial segregation is in itself a violation of the "equal protection" clause and that all state laws requiring racial segregation in public schools are therefore unconstitutional. This decision, as many southern objectors quite correctly pointed out, changed the constitution almost as drastically as the Fourteenth Amendment had; but this occasion was by no means the first time the Court had altered the constitution, nor will it be the last.

Perhaps the most striking example of the power of courts to change constitutional systems is provided by the contrast between Canadian and American constitutional development. The Canadian Constitution gives the provinces (Quebec, Ontario, and the rest) a few specific, or delegated, powers and leaves all the rest to the national government. Yet the interpretation of the Constitution by the Judicial Committee of the British Privy Council (which held this power from 1867 to 1950) greatly whittled down national power and expanded the powers of the provinces. The Constitution of the United States, on the other hand, places the delegated powers in the hands of the national government and reserves the rest to the states. Yet the Supreme Court, through such devices as the doctrine of "implied powers,"[17] has so

---

[17] First promulgated in *McCulloch* v. *Maryland,* 4 Wheaton 316 (1819), this doctrine declares that the clause in Article I, Section 8, which empowers Congress to make all laws "which shall be necessary and proper" for carrying into execution its delegated powers, means that Congress may pass any law that is "helpful" in executing its delegated powers and is not expressly prohibited by the Constitution.

generously and broadly interpreted the national government's delegated powers that the whole balance of lawmaking power has shifted markedly away from the states. It may be said that judicial interpretation has made the Canadian constitution more and more like the original American constitution and vice versa. These judicial changes on both sides of the border are regarded by most political scientists as far more drastic revisions of the two constitutions than any wrought by formal amendments to either Constitution.

### Change in Practice

We have already noted that the authors of the American Constitution intended the Electoral College system to remove the election of the President from popular pressure and that the practice of popularly selecting electors pledged to candidates nominated by national political parties has, without changing a word in the Constitution, converted the Electoral College into a machine for registering the people's choice for the presidency. This change in our constitutional system is at least as drastic as any brought about by the formal amendments.

Changes in practice have altered the American constitutional system in several ways. Not only have they changed the operation of parts of the Constitution in the manner just noted, but new practices have succeeded old, and some have led to formal amendments. Before 1940, for example, it was generally understood that no President would serve more than two terms in office, and at least two presidential aspirants, U. S. Grant and Theodore Roosevelt, were rejected (by a political party and by the voters respectively) largely because it was felt that their reelection would violate constitutional custom. In 1940 and 1944, however, President Franklin D. Roosevelt was elected to a third and a fourth term; the defenders of the old tradition managed, in 1951, to secure the adoption of the Twenty-Second Amendment, which prohibits a President from serving more than two elective terms or a total of ten years in office. A revision of constitutional practice in 1940 was again altered by a formal amendment to the Constitution in 1951.

A more recent example is the growing practice of presidential "impoundment" of funds authorized by Congress. The Constitution (Article I, Section 8) explicitly gives the power to spend public funds to Congress, and also stipulates (in Article II, Section 3) that the President "shall take Care that the Laws be faithfully executed." Even so, Franklin D. Roosevelt in the 1930s launched the practice of occasionally ordering administrative agencies under his direction not to spend certain funds authorized by Congress. The practice was continued by his successors, and has so far been used most extensively by Richard Nixon in the early 1970s—for example, in his refusal to spend congressionally-authorized funds on programs to fight water pollution. Nixon argued that impoundment in this and other instances was necessary to fight inflation: if Congress would not hold down federal spending, he would. Many congressmen argued that this claim, if allowed to stand, would effectively give the President an absolute veto over all federal programs and that it constituted an unconstitutional takeover of Congress's power to make appropriations. Whatever the merits of the argument, it was by no means clear that either Congress or the courts would or could end or even limit presidential impoundment. If the practice survives, the

Constitution will have undergone yet another major change through changing practices rather than formal amendments.[18]

## CONSTITUTIONS IN DICTATORIAL SYSTEMS

We noted earlier that all nations, dictatorial as well as democratic, have constitutions of some kind, for every political system, however organized, operates according to *some* body of fundamental rules. The dictatorial systems' actual ways of dealing with public opinion, nominations and elections, political parties, and other forms of political organization—and their legislative, executive, administrative, and judicial procedures—constitute their "de facto," or effective, constitutions.

Surprising though some readers may find it, however, most dictatorial regimes also have written Constitutions. Some have simply permitted the previous Constitutions to continue nominally in force and have operated largely by new unwritten rules. Adolf Hitler, for example, never bothered to set aside the Weimar Constitution of 1919. He evaded its restraints by forcing the Reichstag to adopt an enabling act (authorized by the Constitution for emergencies) giving him the power to rule by decree. From then on he ruled as if no Constitution existed and the constitution was whatever the Führer willed. Most communist regimes, on the other hand, have adopted new written Constitutions after seizing power. The Soviet Union has had no fewer than three Constitutions, one promulgated in 1918, a second in 1924, and the most recent in 1936. Most of Russia's Eastern European satellite nations also adopted new Soviet-model Constitutions between 1947 and 1952; the People's Republic of China adopted a new Constitution in 1954.

Political scientists have studied the nature and role of written Constitutions in communist nations substantially more thoroughly than those in other dictatorial systems. We shall therefore confine our brief survey to the communist systems.

### THE COMMUNIST CONCEPTION OF A CONSTITUTION[19]

In several respects the written Constitutions of the communist systems closely resemble those of the more democratic regimes. Their formal contents, for instance, are quite similar—not surprisingly, for, as we have seen, any government, whatever its form, must deal with certain problems common to all governments. The 1936 Constitution of the Union of Soviet Socialist Republics contains a statement of general ideals and purposes (Chapter I), a specification of the relative rights and powers of the national and federal levels of government (Chapter II), delineation of the principal policy-making agencies at both the national and lower levels (Chapters III, IV),

---

[18] The most complete analysis of the issue is in Louis Fisher, *President and Congress* (New York: The Free Press, 1972).

[19] For the Russian conception, see especially Merle Fainsod, *How Russia Is Ruled* (rev. ed.; Cambridge, Mass.: Harvard University Press, 1963), chap 11; and Alfred G. Meyer, *The Soviet Political System: An Interpretation* (New York: Random House, Inc., 1965), pp. 97–104. For the Eastern European "people's democracies," see Zbigniew K. Brzezinski, *The Soviet Bloc: Unity and Conflict* (rev. ed.; Cambridge, Mass.: Harvard University Press, 1967), pp. 77–83.

stipulation of the principal administrative agencies at both levels (Chapters V–VII), an outline of the agencies of local government (Chapter VIII), an outline of the judicial system (Chapter IX), a list of "fundamental rights and duties of the citizen" (Chapter X), organization of the electoral system (Chapter XI), stipulation of "arms, flag, and capital" (Chapter XII), and specification of the amending procedure (Chapter XIII).[20]

These superficial similarities with the contents of the democratic regimes' written Constitutions are, however, far less significant than are the communists' strikingly different ideas about what constitutions—in both their written and unwritten aspects—are and should do. In the democratic nations, as we have seen, constitutions are generally regarded as guides for and limitations on present and future action. Communists, on the other hand, conceive of constitutions mainly as registrations of what has been accomplished—expressions of present reality. This conception is exemplified in a leading communist exegesis of the 1936 Soviet Constitution:

> The Soviet Constitution is the fundamental law of the socialist state. It gives *legislative embodiment* to the social and state system of the country, defines the principles underlying the organization and activity of the state organs, *records* the fundamental rights and duties of Soviet citizens and establishes the country's electoral system. It *reflects* the achievements scored in the building of the first socialist state in the world—the historic gains of the Soviet people in economic, political and cultural life.[21]

Given the communists' view of what politics and government are all about, this conception is the only one that makes sense. Communists believe that a communist government—like all governments—cannot be a neutral agency presiding over, moderating, and controlling conflict among the nation's interests; it can only be a partisan instrument by which the ruling class establishes and maintains its power over all other classes. The main difference between communist constitutions and those of the "plutodemocracies" of the West, in the communist view, is that in communist nations the working class is in the saddle, whereas elsewhere the capitalist class rules. The capitalists may adopt the tactic of masking their power monopoly with a facade of general popular control, but the government is still their tool.

## SOVIET CONSTITUTIONS, WRITTEN AND UNWRITTEN

One Western scholar has written of the 1936 Soviet Constitution:

> In fact, the entire Constitution is largely inoperative, not to say fraudulent; at best, it does not give an adequate picture of the actual political system. It is not even a useful guide to lawyers or administrators within the system who

---

[20] An English translation of the 1936 Soviet Constitution is included in Randolph L. Braham (ed.), *Soviet Politics and Government: A Reader* (New York: Alfred A. Knopf, 1965), pp. 555–579.

[21] A. Denisov and M. Kirichenko, *Soviet State Law* (1960), quoted in Braham, *Soviet Politics and Government,* p. 256; italics added. See also Brzezinski, *The Soviet Bloc,* p. 77.

might wish to orient themselves in it. More than in many other political systems, the real constitution of the USSR remains unwritten. . . .

The declaration that sovereignty resides in the "organs of state power" is specious. The exclusive right of the Supreme Soviet to make laws becomes meaningless when we realize that many binding decisions do not take the form of laws—edicts issued by the Presidium of the Supreme Soviet; decrees published by the Council of Ministers; resolutions of the Central Committee of the Communist Party; and a host of other regulations of which the Constitution makes no mention. Only a minute portion of authoritative decisions in the USSR take the form of laws. The majority rule which supposedly governs the deliberations of the Supreme Soviet is a fiction, since nothing has ever been decided by this body except unanimously.[22]

If this assessment is valid, Westerners may well ask, why do the Soviets bother to adopt a written Constitution at all, let alone to amend it and substitute new ones several times over? The Soviets themselves do not and probably cannot answer this question, mainly because they do not accept its premises. Western scholars, however, offer several answers. They point out that the 1936 Constitution was written and adopted during the period of the Great Purges at home and the policy of the popular front with noncommunist antifascists abroad. The Soviet dictator Joseph Stalin badly needed some kind of symbolic reassurance for the Russian people that, despite the purges and what appeared to be great internal disunity, the Revolution *had* established socialism and the regime *could* afford to allow its citizens—at least those loyal to it—more freedom. He also needed some way of assuring socialist and liberal antifascists in Western Europe that the Soviet regime was not a monolithic dictatorship but had simply developed an Eastern version of constitutional democracy with which noncommunists could comfortably make common cause.[23]

That was over a generation ago. The purges are over. Stalin and Hitler are dead, World War II has been fought, the popular front is an item in history books. But still the 1936 Constitution and its offspring in the Eastern European "people's democracies" persist. Why? Mainly because, in the opinion of most Western scholars, the Soviet regime has needed this kind of symbol of legitimacy, continuity, and popular participation to sustain itself through the shifts of power in the Kremlin from Stalin to Malenkov to Khrushchev to Brezhnev to whoever is next.

Specific Soviet constitutional prescriptions and realities are all variations upon the central theme just stated. Yet we should recognize that, in democratic regimes, as well as dictatorial, deeper and more significant questions underlie all the legalisms and formalisms of Constitutions. To what extent do modern constitutions really limit and restrain government officials in their dealings with the people under their jurisdiction? By what means? Under what conditions? At what costs? What values are served when the limitations are effective and injured when they are not?

Where, in short, *should* individuals stand in relation to their governments? Where *do* they actually stand in modern democratic and dictatorial regimes? We shall deal with these urgent questions in Chapters 21 and 22.

[22] Meyer, *The Soviet Political System,* pp. 103–104.

[23] See Fainsod, *How Russia Is Ruled,* pp. 372–373; and Meyer, *The Soviet Political System,* p. 104.

# 12

# FORMS
# OF
# GOVERNMENT

In his *Essay on Man,* the eighteenth-century English poet Alexander Pope dismissed the subject of the present chapter with this widely quoted couplet:

> For forms of government let fools contest;
> What'er is best administer'd is best.

In the long sweep of human history, however, few people have agreed with Pope. As long ago as the fifth century B.C. Greek scholars classified the governments they knew as either "monarchies," "aristocracies," or "democracies" and argued that these different "forms" represented significantly different ways of governing. A generation after Pope's death the English colonies in the New World fought a war for independence from the mother country, arguing in their Declaration of Independence that "whenever any Form of Government becomes destructive of" the ends of "Life, Liberty, and the Pursuit of Happiness," it is the "Right of the People to alter or to abolish it" and "to institute new Government, laying its foundation on such principles and organizing its powers in such form, as to them shall seem most likely to effect their Safety and Happiness." In our own time most of the world's peoples have been involved in wars, both "hot" and "cold," between something called "democracy" and something called "fascist dictatorship" or "communist dictatorship."

Evidently most people believe that significantly different ways of governing do exist. Evidently they also believe that their particular nation's "form of government" so powerfully affects such basic values as individual freedom, social justice, and national independence, that preserving it—or overthrowing it—is worth fighting and dying for. In our time as in times past both those who attack "the system" and those who defend it believe that there *is* a system and that it matters deeply what kind of system it is.

In this chapter, we shall continue our introductory survey of the general themes and principal variations in politics and governments by considering the classification of "forms" of governments. We shall consider some of the classifications that analysts have found useful and outline some of the social forces that incline different nations to adopt different forms.

## CLASSIFYING GOVERNMENTS

### PARTIAL DESCRIPTION OF AN EMPIRICAL WHOLE

We often hear the governments of the United States and Great Britain called "democracies" and those of the United Arab Republic (Egypt) and the People's Republic of China (PRC) "dictatorships." Let us consider for a moment what these labels mean. They do not mean that the governments of the United States and Great Britain are *completely* different from those of the UAR and the PRC, for we know that all four governments make authoritative rules, punish those who violate the rules, mantain armed forces, collect taxes, and so on. Nor do the labels mean that the governments of the United States and Great Britain are exactly alike, for we know that certain British public officials (for example, the Queen and some members of the House of Lords) inherit their posts, whereas all American public officials are either elected or appointed to their jobs.

We know that to some extent the governments of all nations are alike, yet no two governments are *exactly* alike. How, then, can we justify calling some "democracies," as if they were identical, and distinguishing them from "dictatorships," as if the latter were also identical and completely unlike "democracies"? The answer is that *in certain respects* the governments of the United States and Great Britain seem essentially alike and that *in those same respects* they seem significantly different from the governments of the UAR and the PRC. The label of a particular nation's government reflects a form that we discern among certain items *selected* from its unique aggregation of laws, customs, and institutions. When we have labeled the government "democracy" or "federation," we have described it only partially, and many other valid statements may also be made about it.

### PARTICULAR PRINCIPLE OF ORGANIZATION

Granted that we describe a particular government's form in terms of only certain aspects of its total character, how, then, do we decide *which* of its many different aspects reveal its form? The answer is that we concentrate on those features we consider most relevant to the particular principle of government organization at the basis of our classification.

For example, the basic principle of organization involved in labeling "democracies," according to a point of view to be outlined in Chapter 13, is the location of ultimate decision-making power in all adult members of the community equally. Those who take this view classify the governments of the United States and Great Britain as democratic because they believe that in both nations government decisions are ultimately made in accordance with the wishes of their respective popular majorities and not according to the wishes of power elites or dictators. That the formal head of American government is an elected President, whereas the formal head of British government is a hereditary monarch is crucial only when we classify the two governments according to another principle (how the formal head of state is selected, resulting in "monarchies" or "republics"); it does not in itself make either government more or less democratic than the other.

When considering classifications of governments, therefore, we should bear in mind that determination of a government's form according to any particular principle of organization reveals little or nothing about its form according to any other principle.

## WHY CLASSIFY GOVERNMENTS?

Many cogent objections can be made to the whole business of classifying governments. For one thing, as we have observed, labeling a particular government "democratic" or "dictatorial" may reveal something of its operation, but it also leaves out a great deal—and there is a danger that once we have determined its form to our satisfaction we shall imagine that we know all that is worth knowing about it. Categories and their criteria are so simple and reality is so complex that proper classification of borderline cases is next to impossible: For example, it is easy to classify the United States and Great Britain as democratic and the UAR and the PRC as dictatorial, but what about nations like Mexico and the Republic of South Africa? Then again, classifying governments may be scientifically worthless. If, for example, we classify according to formal constitutional arrangements, we find that the written Constitutions of Albania, Bulgaria, Czechoslovakia, Hungary, Poland, the Soviet Union, and Yugoslavia expressly state that each nation's sovereignty lies in the people, yet we know that the ultimate decision-making power in these nations is actually held by the leaders of their Communist parties. Shall we, then, ignore the realities and concentrate on the formalities or vice versa? If we take the former course, our classifications will hardly be worth the effort it takes to make them. If we take the latter course, we may plunge into a hopeless search for realities that can be encompassed in simple forms.

These objections have some merit and should not be forgotten. Yet most political scientists believe that the gains in analytical power likely to accrue from a theoretically relevant and empirically useful classification are so great that the enterprise should not be abandoned altogether. One of the necessary early stages in the development of any science is what may be called its "taxonomic," or "natural history," phase, in which "the facts . . . are immediately apprehended by observation, expressed in terms of concepts with carefully controlled denotative meanings by description, and systematized by classification."[1] Only when this job is well advanced can the science reach the stage of explanation and formation of general

---

[1] F. S. C. Northrop, *The Logic of the Sciences and the Humanities* (New York: Crowell-Collier and Macmillan, Inc., 1947), p. 35.

theory. However difficult it may be, therefore, classifying governments is useful for political science.

Beyond these scholarly concerns, however, lies the fact, noted earlier, that most people evidently believe that the kind of political system that governs them profoundly affects their "lives, fortunes, and sacred honor" (Declaration of Independence)—so profoundly, indeed, that defending it or overthrowing it is worth fighting and dying for. To what extent and in what ways they are right are this book's main concerns.

## SOME LEADING CLASSIFICATIONS OF GOVERNMENTS

As each variable in governmental organization provides a potential basis for a "typology," or set of categories, it is not surprising that scholars have classified governments on all sorts of bases: "legitimate" and "usurped"; "de jure" and "de facto"; "theocratic" and "secular"; and even "governments of laws" and "governments of men." I shall confine the discussion to four typologies very prominent in contemporary political science; for each I shall state the particular principle of organization on which it is based and describe and illustrate the resulting forms.

### DIFFERENTIATION OF GOVERNMENTAL INSTITUTIONS

We noted in Chapter 3 that in most of the approximately 151 modern nations governmental institutions and processes are quite distinct from their nongovernmental counterparts. That is, there are "formal, named, and recognized" political roles "that are played by specialists, not by any or every member of the society."[2] One consequence, as we shall see in Chapter 20, is the perennial controversy in these nations over which concerns properly belong to the "public sector" and which to the "private sector." The disputants take for granted that the distinction between "public" (governmental) and "private" (nongovernmental) is clear and important and that the proper assignment of responsibilities and powers to each is both important and controversial.

In some primitive subnational societies, however, there is little or no comparable differentiation among the members' activities, roles, and understandings; they are what anthropologists call "stateless societies." For example, each of the small roving bands of the Nambikuara Indians of Brazil's Mato Grosso is led by a chief, or headman, but he has no special political authority or sanctions at his disposal. He leads mainly because he is better than the others at finding and gathering food. As these activities are the band's main preoccupation, his skills incline his fellows also to accept his initiatives in social and religious matters as well, though these distinctions are all quite meaningless to the Nambikuara.[3]

---

[2] Aidan Southall, "Stateless Society," in David L. Sills (ed.), *International Encyclopedia of the Social Sciences*, Vol. 15 (New York: The Macmillan Company and The Free Press, 1968), p. 157.

[3] Claude Lévi-Strauss, "The Social and Psychological Aspects of Chieftainship in a Primitive Tribe: The Nambikuara of Northwestern Mato Grosso," *Transactions of the New York Academy of Sciences* (2d series), 7 (1948), 16–32.

Between these two poles lie many degrees of differentiation. Gabriel A. Almond and G. Bingham, Powell suggest that political systems can usefully be classified in three main categories along this dimension:[4] *primitive* systems, in which political institutions are differentiated little or not at all (for example, among the Nambikuara and the Eskimos); *traditional* systems, in which political institutions are relatively clearly differentiated from nonpolitical ones but in which there are few or no specialized political "infrastructures"[5] (for example the bureaucratic governments of ancient Egypt, the Inca empire before Francisco Pizarro's invasion, and the Tudor monarchy of fifteenth- and sixteenth-century England); and *modern* systems, in which there are both differentiated political institutions and specialized political infrastructures (as in all "developed" and many "developing" nations; see Chap. 3).

## FORMAL DISTRIBUTION OF POWER AMONG GOVERNMENT LEVELS

Every nation has a national government with authority over the entire nation and a series of local governments, each of which has authority over a particular subnational geographical area known variously as a "state" or "province"; a "county," "shire," or "department"; a "borough," "city," or "commune"; and so on.

The written Constitutions of twenty-one nations provide for federal governments, in which power is divided between the national government and certain local governments, each of which is legally supreme in its own sphere. In these nations the constitutions usually delineate the matters over which the national governments and the local governments have authority and prescribe that neither level be subordinate to the other. The United States, Switzerland, Australia, Canada, and West Germany are usually given as examples of nations in which the consitutional division of powers is paralleled by actual division of authority. Such nations as Argentina, Mexico, Russia, and Venezuela, on the other hand, are regarded as "paper federations" only, for the local governments are actually totally subordinate to the national governments. We shall consider the peculiar nature and problems of federalism in Chapter 19.

The Constitutions of all other nations provide for unitary governments, in which the national governments are legally supreme over the other levels. Each permits local governments to exist and to conduct certain activities, but the national government has the full legal right to overrule them, and they are formally subordinate to it. The governments of Great Britain and France are usually given as examples of this type.

A possible third category is confederate government, in which the central government is subordinate to local governments and exists and operates only through their sufferance. Most political scientists believe, however, that such arrangements

---

[4] Gabriel A. Almond and G. Bingham Powell, Jr., *Comparative Politics: A Developmental Approach* (Boston: Little, Brown & Company, 1966), pp. 218–254.

[5] "Infrastructure" is another of those unaesthetic but useful technical terms employed by social scientists. In this book it refers to a complex of subsystems, roles, and activities operating outside formal government but closely supporting it: for example, pressure groups, political parties, and communications media.

Governmental Structures

leave the central government so little power that it cannot accurately be called "government" at all and that they are better described (as in the case of the United Nations) as covenants, treaties, or organizations among sovereign governments rather than as a form of government.[6]

## SUBSYSTEM AUTONOMY

In addition to the governmental subsystems just discussed, every modern nation also encompasses a great many economic, social, religious, and other subsystems. They include business firms, labor unions, service clubs, fraternal societies, religious denominations, local congregations, and countless others. Many specialists in comparative politics have come to believe that one of the most important differences in the ways nations are governed is the extent to which these nongovernmental subsystems are *autonomous,* that is, the degree of their freedom to manage their own affairs without government interference.[7]

The *totalitarian* nations cluster at one pole of this dimension. They are nations whose governments strive (though none fully succeeds) to penetrate all aspects of every citizen's life and to shape them to the total service of government. According to two leading scholars of modern totalitarian dictatorship, one essential characteristic of such a regime is an official ideology covering all aspects of human existence, to which every member of the society must adhere not only in externals but by conviction.[8] Both Joseph Stalin's Russia and Adolf Hitler's Germany outlawed all political parties but the official ones and either established or took over universities, labor unions, trade associations, youth organizations, and even literary and scientific societies. The theory of the Soviet geneticist Trofim Lysenko that organisms' acquired characteristics are transmitted by heredity was praised and officially accepted by the Soviet government not because it is scientifically valid but because it accords with the regime's ideology that people's characteristics are entirely the product of the social systems in which they live. Crime in this view is entirely a product of capitalism and would disappear in generations reared under true socialism. In both Russia and Germany neighbors were encouraged to spy on neighbors and to report any "deviationist" or "subversive" talk; workers were urged to spy on managers, students on teachers, even children on parents. Every citizen was taught that true patriots have no private life or concerns of any kind; their every thought and deed should in some way serve the interests of the nation and the programs of the government. We know now that neither Stalin nor Hitler succeeded in stamping out

---

[6] See K. C. Wheare, *Modern Constitutions* (New York: Oxford University Press, 1951), pp. 26–33.

[7] One of the most influential expositions of this view and the resulting typology is Robert A. Dahl, *Modern Political Analysis* (Englewood Cliffs, N.J.: Prentice-Hall, Inc., 1963), pp. 35–37. Almond and Powell add the dimension of mutual independence of the subsystems (for example, whether religious denominations are organized only in churches, as in the United States or also in labor unions, political parties, mass-communications media, and so on, as in France and Italy). Almond and Powell, *Comparative Politics,* pp. 259–271.

[8] Carl J. Friedrich and Zbigniew Brzezinski, *Totalitarian Dictatorship and Autocracy* (2d ed.; Cambridge, Mass.: Harvard University Press, 1965), p. 9.

all privacy, but each came close enough to warrant classifying his regime near the totalitarian extreme on the dimension of subsystem autonomy.

The opposite pole is usually called "pluralism" or "constitutionalism" (although each term is also used to denote somewhat different aspects of political systems). Many nongovernmental organizations operate with little or no interference by the government, and a considerable area of each citizen's life is truly private in that it is lived with little or no reference to or regulation by government. In the United States, for example, labor unions and trade associations are established and run by workers and owners respectively, rather than by government, though government does set some limits on their activities. There are many private universities, but even in the public universities curricula, courses, student rules, hiring and firing policies, and so on are largely determined by the faculties and administrations (and increasingly also by students), subject to some government control, to be sure, but with a high degree of autonomy. National religious denominations and local congregations operate with even greater autonomy and are subject to only the most general and minimal government restraints. Accordingly, the United States approximates—though it does not completely realize—the ideal at the other end of the continuum.

Many political scientists regard subsystem autonomy as one of the most crucial of all criteria for classifying governments. We shall consider its constitutional-totalitarian dimension further in Chapters 13 and 21.

## LOCATION OF ULTIMATE RULING POWER

### The Classical Typology

From the very beginning of the serious study of government most analysts have believed that the most important fact to know about a government is who really runs it, what the real power structure is. Accordingly, the typologies that have always overshadowed all others are those based on estimates of the actual location of ultimate ruling power—"ultimate" because it represents the final say over what government will do and "actual" because it may not coincide with any written Constitution or organization chart.

The oldest and most persistent typology of governmental forms rests on this key variable of location of real power. In the fifth century B.C. the Greek historian Herodotus classified all governments as either *monarchies* (government by single persons), *aristocracies* (government by elites), or *democracies* (government by all). A century later Aristotle made his famous revision of this typology, distinguishing between three forms in each of which a different segment of the community rules in the interests of all (monarchy, aristocracy, and polity) and three in each of which a different segment of the community rules in its own selfish interests (tyranny, oligarchy, and democracy). The Aristotelian scheme is shown graphically in Figure 9.

### Modern Versions

Although Aristotle's typology has been little used, the older monarchy-aristocracy-democracy classification has persisted in one version or another to the present day.

FIGURE 9
Aristotle's typology of
governments.

| | Rule in the Interests of All | Rule in the Interests of Themselves |
|---|---|---|
| Control of Ultimate Power by One | Monarchy | Tyranny |
| Control of Ultimate Power by a Few | Aristocracy | Oligarchy |
| Control of Ultimate Power by Many | Polity | Democracy |

In the 1970s, however, there is much less clarity or agreement about the meanings of these terms than there was in Herodotus' day, and the confusion has been extended to such related terms as "autocracy," "dictatorship," "authoritarianism," and "totalitarianism." It arises largely because there is probably no definition of any of these terms that all political scientists and political philosophers, let alone laymen, agree on. It is tempting, indeed, to suggest that we simply drop them all—especially "democracy," the most confused of the lot—and invent terms upon whose meanings we can all agree. But the prospects seem so dim that we may as well do the best we can to specify what *we,* at least, mean by each label. We should then at least be able to cope with the confusion, although we cannot hope to eliminate disagreements entirely. The most widely used modern labels based on the control variable are democracy, oligarchy, dictatorship, pluralism, and elitism.

**Democracy, Oligarchy, and Dictatorship**   Many political scientists conceive of democracy as a form in which government decisions are ultimately controlled by all the adult members of the society rather than by some specially privileged subgroup or one all-powerful member. They refer to all governments in which the decisions are ultimately controlled by fewer than all the society's adult members as either dictatorships or oligarchies, depending upon whether rule is personal or collective. These terms and definitions undeniably raise as many problems as they solve; and, as the ideas underlying them are so prominent in the study of modern governments, we shall explore them in much greater depth in Chapter 13.

**Pluralism and Elitism**   "Pluralism," like "democracy," in one sense describes how some political systems *do* operate and in another serves as an ideal that some people believe political systems should strive toward. Here we are concerned mainly with its descriptive usage. According to a leading modern scholar, pluralism is a political system in which "instead of a single center of sovereign power there [are] multiple centers of power, none of which is or can be wholly sovereign."[9] In a pluralist system, then, government decisions do not emanate from the commands of any "sovereign"—not even "the people" or "the popular majority"; rather each is produced by negotiation and compromise among the social groups concerned, and each group has something closely approaching a veto over any proposed policy that it believes will damage its interests unbearably.

Both as an empirical description and as an ideal the concept of pluralism rests

---

[9] Dahl, *Pluralist Democracy in the United States* (Skokie, Ill.: Rand McNally & Company, 1967), p. 24.

on a conceptual base different from those underlying classical monarchy-aristocracy-democracy and the modern democracy-dictatorship typologies. Both of the latter typologies are monistic: They assume that, as a matter of both logical necessity and observable fact, every political system harbors a "sovereign power," a person or set of persons who hold the legitimate ultimate power to make and enforce authoritative rules binding on all participants in the system. Those who use these typologies see the key question as whether the sovereign power is actually held by one man, an elite, or all the people. "Pluralists," on the other hand, argue that, whatever the formal constitutional arrangements for sovereign power may be, some systems have no effective single locus of power.

Some scholars believe that pluralism is an accurate characterization of the American political system, and some also believe that it is a desirable state of affairs because it prevents direct and extreme confrontations among clashing interests, helps to aggregate demands, reduces levels of political hostility, and maximizes the stability and internal calm of the system.

Others, however, are convinced that pluralism furnishes neither an accurate empirical description of nor a desirable ideal for the American system. Perhaps the best-known of these critics is the late American sociologist C. Wright Mills, who argued that behind the facade of popular elections and representation public policy in the United States is made by—or at least only with the permission of—a small, identifiable "power elite" of top business and military leaders, supported but not partnered by the leaders of big labor unions, big universities, and the major political parties.[10] Mills and others have also argued that the nation's goal should be some kind of "participatory democracy," in which all interests and points of view are clearly expressed and decisions are made through active discussion of issues and registration of preferences by all citizens. Such a system, they insist, is both possible and desirable.[11]

These issues are obviously of the highest importance, and we shall return to them in Chapter 13.

## FACTORS SHAPING FORMS OF GOVERNMENT

### POLITICAL SYSTEMS AND THEIR ENVIRONMENTS

Every political system operates in an environment, and certain characteristics of its particular environment contribute materially toward determining both its form of government and its policy outputs. It operates, for example, in a particular portion of the earth's surface—with rich or barren soil, temperate or extreme climate, oceans and mountains providing natural defenses or broad plains easing the task of foreign invaders, and the like. Its people may be mostly literate or illiterate, imbued with

---

[10] C. Wright Mills, *The Power Elite* (New York: Oxford University Press, 1956).

[11] In addition to Mills, some leading exponents of this view are Peter Bachrach, *The Theory of Democratic Elitism* (Boston: Little, Brown & Company, 1967); Christian Bay, *The Structure of Freedom* (Stanford, Calif.: Stanford University Press, 1958); Lane Davis, "The Cost of Realism: Contemporary Restatements of Democracy," *Western Political Quarterly,* 17 (1964), 37–46; and Carole Pateman, *Participation and Democratic Theory* (New York: Cambridge University Press, 1970).

patriotism or devoted to subnational loyalties, well fed and active or badly fed and passive, and so on.

The interrelations between British government and the British psychological climate, or "political culture," furnish an illuminating illustration. The British system locates full governmental power in the House of Commons, which can dismiss any minister at any time for any reason, depose judges, abolish local governments, regulate succession to the throne, and do almost anything else that it wishes—up to and including altering or abolishing any part of the British constitution. No British court can overrule any act of Parliament as "unconstitutional." All decisions of the House of Commons are made by simple majorities: The will of as few as 50 percent plus one of the members present determines the action of the whole House. Under normal conditions, furthermore, most members belong to one or the other of two political parties, Conservative and Labour. If we knew only these facts about the British system, we might well conclude that Britain must be perpetually teetering on the brink of civil war and that sooner or later (and probably sooner) the majority party would, in the pride of its unlimited power, force through some measure so disastrous to the interests of the minority party that rebellion would follow.

Yet the British system, for all the formally unlimited power it gives to the majority party, is, in fact, highly stable and resistant to revolution—far more so than say the system of South Vietnam despite the fact that its written Constitution provides elaborate formal checks on majorities and safeguards for minorities. How can this be? The answer, according to most students of British government, is that in British society it simply never seriously occurs to the majority party to try to ram through anything that would be totally unacceptable to the minority. For one thing, each party's leaders have more in common with their political opponents than with their own party's rank and file: Unlike the majority of the general public, most have attended universities; most come from managerial, professional, or upper white-collar occupations; and all belong to the small and select group of political "insiders," to whom the the world often appears different from the way it appears to most "outsiders." They thus share a great many common attitudes and values, despite the differences in their party allegiances.[12] Second, the deep conviction that certain things "are simply not done" is shared by all strata of British society from top to bottom, and crushing a formally defenseless minority is certainly one of those things. Then, too, most Englishmen are very proud of their political system and would not dream of taking steps that might profoundly upset it—nor would they follow the example of what Shakespeare called the "less happier lands," those countries outside "this fortress buylt by nature for herself against infection," and do something so un-English as starting a revolution.

The eighteenth-century political philosopher Thomas Paine believed that every nation is entirely free to discard its form of government and replace it with another at any time. Most present-day political scientists believe that this is true in only the

---

[12] See W. L. Guttsman, *The British Political Elite* (London: MacGibbon & Kee, 1963); Richard Rose, *Politics in England* (Boston: Little, Brown & Company, 1964), especially chaps. 1–3; and Robert McKenzie and Alan Silver, *Angels in Marble: Working Class Conservatives in Urban England* (London: William Heinemann, Ltd., 1968).

most superficial sense, for the kinds of people who constitute a nation's population and the structure of the society in which they live fix firm and enduring limits upon the kind of government the nation can sustain. The same considerations lead political scientists to believe that a particular nation's form of government can be understood only against the background of the environment in which it operates.

**FIGURE 10**
**Components of the total environment of a political system.** Source: David Easton, *A Framework for Political Analysis,* © 1965, Table 1, p. 70. Reprinted by permission of Prentice-Hall, Inc., Englewood Cliffs, New Jersey.

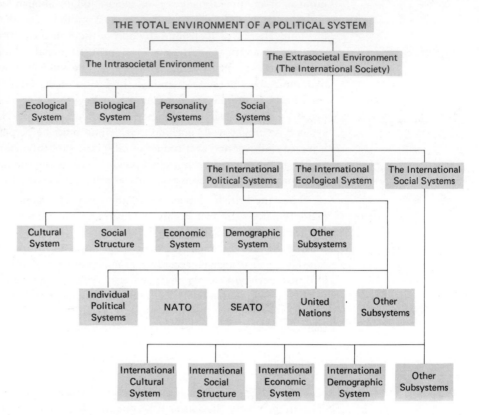

Much research remains to be done on the precise impacts of various environmental factors on national forms of government. Even so, most political scientists agree that democratic government is not likely to survive in a nation whose people are starving, illiterate, or bound to traditional and nondemocratic modes of thought and behavior.[13] A comprehensive formulation of the relations between a political system and its environment has been set forth by David Easton and is summarized in Figure 10.

The nature and impact of each environmental component listed in Figure 10 has been studied by geographers, biologists, ecologists, psychologists, economists,

---

[13] These points are made by, among others, S. M. Lipset, *Political Man* (New York: Doubleday & Company, Inc., 1960), chaps. 2, 3; Daniel Lerner, *The Passing of Traditional Society* (New York: The Free Press, 1958); and Phillips Cutright, "Political Structure, Economic Development and National Social Security Programs," *American Journal of Sociology,* 70 (1965), 537–548.

demographers, historians, and others. Political scientists, however, have concentrated mainly on certain social variables, which we shall consider in the remainder of this chapter.

## SOME LEADING SOCIAL VARIABLES

### Population

The populations of modern nations differ from one another in many ways, some of which condition and shape their forms of government. The size of a nation's population, for example, sets limits on the form and extent of direct popular participation in its government.[14] The number and intensity of the ethnic divisions within a population may affect the number and intensity of the nation's intergroup conflicts—and, indeed, the extent to which national identity and loyalty predominate over subgroup identities and loyalties. Age distribution, literacy, and educational levels may affect the kinds of roles that ordinary people can play in the governing process and also the kinds of social-welfare services provided by the government.

### Economy

Karl Marx, the nineteenth-century ideological founder of communism, argued that a nation's religions, social customs, arts, and form of government are simply reflections of its economic system—that is, reflections of the particular structure controlling the means of production, exchange, and distribution. Noncommunist social scientists long ago rejected Marx's central thesis as an enormous oversimplification of the complex environmental factors shaping society and government. But most also think that, though a nation's economy is by no means the only factor that affects its form of government, it is nevertheless one of the more significant. The level of technological advance and the division of labor, for instance, influence the number and variety of available occupations and thus the number and variety of interests among which political conflict may take place. The general level of wealth and disparity of incomes among different groups are bound to influence a nation's "civil-war potential," for, other things being equal, a perceived great disparity in income is likely to generate bitter dissatisfaction among the poor and greatly reduce the chances for a united community presided over by a stable government. If, on the other hand, the general level of wealth and physical comfort is high—if even the poorer groups consider themselves well off compared with their counterparts in other nations—then they are less likely to start a civil war to improve their lot.

### Social Structure

Broader still in its effect upon a nation's form of government is social structure, defined in this book as a residual category of all structures outside the strictly political

---

[14] The People's Republic of China has the largest population (estimated at 850 million in 1973) of any modern nation. The tiny central Pacific Republic of Nauru has the smallest (7,561). The United States, with over 200 million, ranks fourth behind the PRC, India, and the Soviet Union.

and economic spheres. For example, the degree of stratification of the nation's population into upper-, middle-, and lower-status, or "deference," classes and the degree of upward mobility among them may greatly affect national unity and therefore the kind of government the nation can sustain.[15] Then, too, the ways in which people conduct such basic activities as courtship and marriage, raising and educating children, worshiping, and communicating with one another all help to create a kind of gestalt within which the government must operate. They also set limits on the kind of government that the nation can operate successfully. We have already noted that the British form of government must to some extent be explained in the light of the British social structure; the same general considerations must be taken into account in the effort to understand any nation's form of government.[16]

### Social Tensions and Consensus

Every nation contains forces of national disintegration. They are usually described collectively as social tensions, the product of such variables as the kinds and number of group conflicts among the population, the degree to which group memberships intertwine and overlap, the degree of hostility among competing interests, and the general national atmosphere of security or insecurity within which social conflict takes place. Every nation also contains forces for unifying and preserving it, usually by maximizing consensus, by encouraging a general feeling among individual citizens and groups that preserving the nation is at least as important as achieving their own special interests. In Chapters 2 and 3 we dealt with some of these forces in our consideration of the factors that limit, diffuse, and moderate political conflict and those that maximize nationalism.

In every nation the interplay of these two clusters of forces affects not only the "civil-war potential" but also the kind of government that the nation can operate. Probably as much as any other social variable, the relative levels of social tensions and consensus determine whether or not a nation can maintain democratic government. The more dictatorial governments are relatively free to use propaganda and physical force without restraint in imposing their policies upon their peoples. But democracies, as we shall see in Chapter 13, must depend mainly upon free popular consent to public policies. Consequently, democratic governments can survive only in nations whose popular majorities refrain from trying to force unacceptable policies upon minorities and whose minorities accept and abide by majority decisions and try to change them only by peaceful and orderly methods. Only nations with relatively high degrees of consensus and low degrees of social tension are likely to have popular

---

[15] One of the most influential general expositions of this point is Barrington Moore, Jr., *Social Origins of Dictatorship and Democracy* (Boston: The Beacon Press, 1966).

[16] For excellent explanations of the American way of government in terms of the nation's underlying social structure, see perceptive discussions by the British "America watcher" Sir Denis Brogan, in *The American Character* (New York: Alfred A. Knopf, 1944) and *Politics in America* (rev. ed.; New York: Harper Torchbooks, 1969). See also a more recent analysis based mainly on polling data: Donald J. Devine, *The Political Culture of the United States* (Boston: Little, Brown & Company, 1972).

majorities and minorities that regularly show such forbearance, and only such nations can hope to have governments that are democratic to any notable degree.

## Political Culture

Ultimately all the social forces that we have been considering effectively shape forms of government mainly as they act upon peoples' minds and behavior. If, for example, a nation's population is in "objective fact" highly stratified in privileged and oppressed classes but the oppressed *think* that they are as well off as anyone else, then conflict between the classes is not likely to roil political waters.[17] And, however fairly a government may actually deal with a particular group's demands and activities, if most members of that group *believe* that they are being treated unfairly they are not likely to accept the government's decisions willingly or perhaps even peacefully.

In recent years a growing number of political scientists have come to think that one of the most powerful forces shaping a nation's form of government is its political culture. This concept, defined by one of its leading exponents as "the system of empirical beliefs, expressive symbols, and values which defines the situation in which political action takes place,"[18] has already been discussed in detail in Chapter 4 and so is only briefly mentioned here.

In Chapter 3 we noted that all governments—whether democratic or dictatorial, monarchical or republican, unitary or federal—are alike in many respects: they all have sovereignty over particular territories and the people in them; they all make rules regulating those people's behavior, and they all fine, imprison, or execute rule violators.

In this chapter we have briefly surveyed some of the different ways in which nations conduct these universal activities—some of the principal forms of government. And we have noted the conviction of most people that their nations' forms of government so profoundly affect such basic values as personal freedom, social justice, and national independence that preserving—or overthrowing—them is worth fighting and dying for.

Communist political analysts insist that only the distinction between capitalism and socialism matters, but most political scientists in the noncommunist nations believe that the choice between democracy and dictatorship is far more crucial. Accordingly, we shall continue our preliminary survey of general themes and principal variations in modern governments by examining each of the latter two forms in depth.

---

[17] For an instructive discussion of the differing political consequences of unperceived "objective" social stratification and conscious class identification, see Angus Campbell, Philip E. Converse, Warren E. Miller, and Donald E. Stokes, *The American Voter* (New York: John Wiley & Sons, Inc., 1960), chap. 13.

[18] Sidney Verba, "Comparative Political Culture," in Lucian W. Pye and Sidney Verba (eds.), *Political Culture and Political Development* (Princeton, N.J.: Princeton University Press, 1965), p. 513.

# 13

# MODELS OF DEMOCRACY AND DICTATORSHIP

In 1949 the United Nations Educational, Scientific and Cultural Organization (UNESCO) decided to find out how democracy stood in the postwar era. It sent questionnaires about the nature and desirability of democracy to 104 political and social philosophers in all parts of the world. A special committee of 6 scholars surveyed the replies and reported optimistically:

> For the first time in the history of the world, no doctrines are advanced as antidemocratic. The accusation of antidemocratic action or attitude is frequently directed against *others,* but practical politicians and political theorists agree in stressing the democratic element in the institutions *they* defend and the theories *they* advocate. This acceptance of democracy as the highest form of political or social organization is the sign of a basic agreement in the ultimate aims of modern social and political institutions. . . .[1]

Maybe so—and maybe not. After all, Benito Mussolini declared his fascist dictatorship to be "the realization of true democracy," and Joseph Goebbels hailed Hitler's Third Reich as "the most ennobled form of a modern democratic state."[2] Most Soviet-bloc nations describe themselves as "people's democracies," which, according to the theoretical journal of the Communist Party of the Soviet Union, are "new, higher forms of democracy as compared to the old, bourgeois-parliamentarian

---

[1] Richard McKeon (ed.), *Democracy in a World of Tensions: A Symposium Prepared by UNESCO* (Chicago: University of Chicago Press, 1951), pp. 522–523; italics added.

[2] Quoted in John D. Lewis, "The Elements of Democracy," *American Political Science Review,* 34 (June 1940), 467.

democracy."[3] Mao Tse-tung calls his Chinese regime a "people's democratic dictatorship."[4] Gamal Abdel Nasser spoke of his one-man rule over the United Arab Republic as "a peaceful, clean democracy."[5] Indeed, only a handful of old-fashioned absolute monarchs like King Faisal of Saudi Arabia and the Sultan of Oman scorn to call their rule "democratic."

Evidently, then, almost everyone in the world "believes in" democracy. But what does this statement really mean? Nothing more than that the word "democracy" arouses strongly favorable emotions in most people, who find it psychologically necessary to claim the label for whatever set of political institutions they prefer. Many, indeed, insist that only the particular set of institutions they favor constitute "true democracy," which they distinguish from the many false kinds by adding some adjective: "liberal democracy," "people's democracy," "guided democracy," "proletarian democracy," and so on—and on.

Some students of politics are not impressed by the near-universal popularity of "democracy"; rather, they are appalled by the fact that it is "a kind of conceptual Gladstone bag which, with a little manipulation, can be made to accommodate almost any collection of social facts we may wish to carry about in it."[6] They tend to agree with the French savant Bertrand de Jouvenel that "discussions about democracy, arguments for it and against it, are intellectually worthless because we do not know what we are talking about."[7]

Most political scientists, however, believe that, whether we like it or not, the word is here to stay and will continue to play an important role in political discourse. Therefore, perhaps the best we can do is to identify its principal meanings and specify which one we are using. In this book the term will be used in describing models of democracy and dictatorship that will help us compare and contrast actual governments. We begin, therefore, by considering the nature and uses of models in social science.

## THE NATURE AND USES OF MODELS IN SOCIAL SCIENCE

Modern social scientists use various kinds of models as tools to help them understand the complexities of empirical reality. Among these tools is what Abraham Kaplan calls a "semantical model, presenting a conceptual analogue to some subject-matter."[8] As the term is used here, each "semantical model" of democracy and

---

[3] Quoted in Zbigniew K. Brzezinski, *The Soviet Bloc* (rev. ed.; Cambridge, Mass.: Harvard University Press, 1967), p. 31.

[4] Quoted in John W. Lewis, *Leadership in Communist China* (Ithaca, N.Y.: Cornell University Press, 1966), p. 29.

[5] Quoted in Fred R. von der Mehden, *Politics of the Developing Nations* (Englewood Cliffs, N.J.: Prentice-Hall, Inc., 1964), p. 120.

[6] Carl L. Becker, *Modern Democracy* (New Haven, Conn.: Yale University Press, 1941), p. 4.

[7] Quoted in Giovanni Sartori, *Democratic Theory* (New York: Frederick A. Praeger, Inc., 1965), p. 9.

[8] Abraham Kaplan, *The Conduct of Inquiry* (San Francisco: Chandler Publishing Company, 1964), pp. 267–268, and, for a discussion of the various types and uses of models in social science, chap. 7.

dictatorship is an intellectual construct of a mode of political organization fully and perfectly in accord with a particular principle. Perhaps the best-known example of such a model is one widely used in economic analysis, that of the free market. The free market is a mental picture of an economic system in which all exchange takes place through free bargaining among sellers and buyers in the marketplace, the only motive influencing human behavior is the universal desire to "buy cheap and sell dear," and the price of any commodity or service is determined solely by the interplay of supply and demand.

Now everyone, including economists who use this model, knows that no actual economic system has ever operated in perfect accordance with these principles. People are, in fact, influenced by many motives other than their desire to buy cheap and sell dear—for example, their desire to be in fashion. Furthermore sellers often agree among themselves to "administer" prices regardless of supply and demand so that every seller can make a larger profit than he could under conditions of unrestricted, even cutthroat, competition; and every nation's government, as we shall see in Chapter 20, interferes in some way with the free interplay of supply and demand.

Why, then, do economists talk about this free market economy when no such system has ever existed? The answer is that they find it highly useful in isolating certain aspects of actual economies and studying them apart from all other aspects. Economists ask, "If an economy *were* organized in this fashion, what would be the effect on prices of variations in supply and demand?" They next observe what actually happens in a real economy when supply or demand changes. The difference between the effects predicted from the model and the effects actually observed gives them a rough measure of the nature and degree of influence of supply and demand relative to other factors.

Using models is thus one way in which social scientists can achieve something comparable to the results that physical scientists obtain through controlled experiments. The chemist in his laboratory, for example, can hold certain factors (like molecular structure, volume, weight, and density) constant, vary another (like temperature), and observe the outcome. Variations in the results, he assumes, are caused by variations in the one changing factor, for all the others have been held constant. Economists, however, cannot manipulate human economies in this fashion. But they can *imagine* what would happen in a free market economy when supply is increased, observe what happens in actual economies when supply is increased, and by comparing the two sets of results increase our understanding of the operation and influence of supply and demand relative to other factors.

Economists are noted for prefacing their comments on economic behavior with the phrase "other things being equal"—when they know full well that in fact other things never are equal. Nevertheless, they keep on thinking this way because they have learned, as have other social scientists, that models are highly useful in understanding the complexities of actual social institutions and situations.


## NORMATIVE VERSUS DESCRIPTIVE MODELS

In ordinary conversation we often use "model" to mean something worthy of imitation, an ideal to emulate: "He is a model boy" or "Her paper is a model of how to write an examination." Social scientists call this the "normative" use of the term, for it equates the model with good and its opposite with bad.

We should be clear, however, that here the term is used in a purely descriptive sense: It means simply an intellectual construct of a particular mode of political organization fully and perfectly in accord with a particular principle. Later in the chapter we shall consider a "model of dictatorship" as well as a "model of democracy." Our belief that governments *should* follow the democratic model should not cloud our observation that some governments *do* follow the model of dictatorship.

## MODELS OF GOVERNMENT

No actual government, as observed in Chapter 12, is organized according to a single principle. Every government is a "historic compound" of many different organizing principles. The government of the United States, for example, is organized in accordance with the principles of federalism, separation of powers, checks and balances, popular sovereignty, limited government, majority rule, minority rights, and many more. We cannot determine whether or not it is a democracy on the basis of *all* its myriad institutions, laws, and customs, for many of them are not relevant to the question at hand. So we must look *only* at those aspects of its total reality that are relevant. Our judgment of which aspects are relevant is inescapably determined by our conception of democracy, which is necessarily an abstraction from the total realities of American or any other actual government.

A model of democracy or dictatorship, then, has two major functions. First, it provides criteria of relevance by which to choose those aspects of an actual government that we must examine in order to determine whether it is more or less democratic or dictatorial. Second, it provides a set of standards against which we can measure actual governments for the purpose of classification.

## COMPARING REALITY WITH A MODEL

Let us see how a model can be used to understand and evaluate some aspect of reality. One essential principle of the model of democracy that I shall set forth is political equality, defined in the model as equal access to political power for every member of the community. Not only must each have the same right to vote as does everyone else, but each vote must also count for as much as every other vote. If some citizens have three or four votes apiece and others one or none, then clearly the favored citizens constitute a kind of ruling class, and their form of government is some kind of oligarchy.

So much for the model; now for the reality. In the American states before 1962 most legislatures were elected from districts of widely varying populations. In Vermont, for example, each town, regardless of its population, elected one state representative. The town of Stratton, with 24 inhabitants, elected one legislator, and so did the city of Burlington, with 35,531 inhabitants. Each Strattonite's share of the power to determine the legislature's membership was thus 1480 times greater than that of each Burlingtonian! In California the smallest state-senatorial district had a population of 14,294 and the largest 6,038,771—422 times as many people. Comparable disparities existed in most other states.

In a series of decisions from 1962 to the present, however, the U.S. Supreme

Models of Democracy and
Dictatorship

Court has examined the empirical question whether or not such disparities are consistent with the principle of political equality and has found that they are not. It has also considered the constitutional-normative question whether or not the disparities should be eliminated in obedience to the Fourteenth Amendment's injunction that "no State shall . . . deny to any person within its jurisdiction the equal protection of the laws" and has decided that they should.[9] The political-equality part of the model, then, has provided both a standard for measuring aspects of reality and a direction for political change.

Matters become more complicated, however, when we use whole models to classify whole governments.

## SPECTRUM CLASSIFICATION OF ACTUAL GOVERNMENTS

One more problem remains: If it is true that no actual government fully measures up to a particular model (see Fig. 11), how can we legitimately call any such government a "democracy"? The answer is simple. If we think in terms of two mutually exclusive categories, democracies (actual governments that fully and in every respect correspond to our model) and nondemocracies (governments that in some respects fall short of the model), then all the governments in the world undoubtedly must be placed in the latter category. But, if we think in terms of a spectrum, we can quite legitimately describe some actual governments as "more democratic" than others.

**FIGURE 11**
Spectrum classification of democracies.

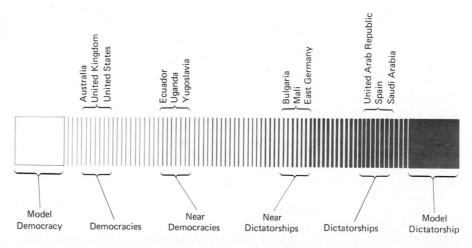

The familiar categories of rich and poor illustrate the principle of spectrum classification. We all use these categories every day, and nobody thinks that we are talking nonsense when we describe this person as poor and that one as rich. Yet consider for a moment the reasoning that underlies these classifications. We could

----

[9] For detailed accounts of the situation before and after the "reapportionment revolution" of the 1960s, see Gordon E. Baker, *The Reapportionment Revolution* (New York: Random House, Inc., 1966); and Congressional Quarterly, *Representation and Apportionment* (Washington, D.C.: Congressional Quarterly Service, 1966).

rank each person in the United States in increasing order of net worth. We could all agree that those at the top of the list were rich and those at the bottom poor. But where would we draw the line between the two categories? At exactly $10,000? If so, would we say that a person worth $9999.99 was poor and that acquiring one more penny would make that person rich? Clearly not. Yet the lack of a precise arithmetical dividing line between the categories does not prevent us—nor should it—from using the categories at all. They are, to be sure, gross categories, in the sense that they are not as precisely defined and delimited as are those in mathematics, but most of us find them useful all the same, particularly in describing people at the two extremes of the spectrum.

This same kind of reasoning, with all its advantages and limitations, underlies the classification and labeling of actual governments in this book. Graphically our spectrum may be shown as in Figure 11. But how do we construct such a spectrum and decide which nation belongs where? Essentially we begin by fixing one extreme of the scale with a particular model of democracy—a mental picture of what a government would be like if it were organized in complete and perfect accordance with what we regard as the essential principles of democracy. Some writers also fix the opposite extreme with a model of dictatorship—a mental picture of what a government would be like if one person had exclusive control of all government machinery and policies.

When the spectrum is thus anchored, we ascertain—either in a general and impressionistic way, by measuring quantifiable aspects, or by some combination of both—how each actual government measures up to the principles of our model of democracy or dictatorship.[10] From these data we can compile a "score" for each government and place it on the spectrum relative to those assigned to other governments.

Several social scientists have ranked the "democratic-ness" of actual governments by such procedures.[11] One of the most recent attempts has been made by Arthur K. Smith, Jr., who combined the scores of 110 nations on each of 19 variables measuring various aspects of his model of democracy[12] with their scores on an index of stability and change in democratic institutions during the period 1946–1965. The composite scores enabled him to rank nations from the most to the least democratic, as shown in Table 17. This table thus illustrates how a model of democracy can be used. Smith's rankings do not correspond exactly with those of other scholars,

---

[10] Many analysts rely mainly on such collections of information about the populations, societies, economies, and political institutions of most modern nations as those provided in Arthur S. Banks and Robert B. Textor, *A Cross-Polity Survey* (Cambridge, Mass.: M.I.T. Press, 1963); and Bruce M. Russett *et al., World Handbook of Political and Social Indicators* (New Haven, Conn.: Yale University Press, 1964).

[11] The procedures and rankings set forth by the leading scholars are well summarized and evaluated in John D. May, *Of the Conditions and Measures of Democracy* (Morristown, N.J.: General Learning Press, 1973).

[12] For example, each nation was scored on the variable "interest aggregation by political parties" as follows: "no political parties exist," 0; "interest aggregation by parties negligible," 1; "interest aggregation by parties limited," 2; "interest aggregation by parties moderate," 3; and "interest aggregation by parties significant," 4.

**TABLE 17**

**110 Nations Ranked according to Degree of Political Democracy, 1946-1965**

| Rank[a] | Country | Score | Rank | Country | Score |
|---|---|---|---|---|---|
| 1.5 | Australia | 137.7 | 56 | Cameroon | 96.5 |
| 1.5 | New Zealand | 137.7 | 57 | Cyprus | 96.4 |
| 3.5 | Denmark | 131.6 | 58 | USSR | 96.3 |
| 3.5 | Norway | 131.6 | 59.5 | Morocco | 96.2 |
| 3.5 | Sweden | 131.6 | 59.5 | Poland | 96.2 |
| 3.5 | United Kingdom | 131.6 | 61 | Czechoslovakia | 95.5 |
| 7.5 | Belgium | 127.9 | 62 | Indonesia | 95.0 |
| 7.5 | Luxembourg | 127.9 | 63 | Bulgaria | 94.1 |
| 7.5 | Netherlands | 127.9 | 64.5 | Paraguay | 94.0 |
| 7.5 | United States | 127.9 | 64.5 | Tanzania | 94.0 |
| 11.5 | Canada | 125.3 | 66 | Congo (Leopoldville) | 93.7 |
| 11.5 | Finland | 125.3 | 67 | Senegal | 93.5 |
| 11.5 | Ireland | 125.3 | 68 | Guinea | 93.4 |
| 14.5 | Iceland | 123.9 | 69 | Albania | 93.1 |
| 14.5 | Switzerland | 123.9 | 70 | Mongolia | 92.6 |
| 16 | Italy | 123.0 | 71.5 | Ivory Coast | 92.5 |
| 17 | Austria | 121.6 | 71.5 | Mali | 92.5 |
| 18 | Uruguay | 120.9 | 73 | Romania | 92.4 |
| 19 | Chile | 119.5 | 74 | East Germany | 92.0 |
| 20 | Philippines | 118.0 | 75.5 | Chad | 91.9 |
| 21 | West Germany | 117.4 | 75.5 | Gabon | 91.9 |
| 22 | Japan | 116.8 | 75.5 | Somalia | 91.9 |
| 23 | Israel | 116.5 | 78 | Syria | 91.7 |
| 24 | France | 115.5 | 79.5 | Dominican Republic | 91.6 |
| 25 | South Africa | 114.3 | 79.5 | Upper Volta | 91.6 |
| 26 | Costa Rica | 111.9 | 81 | Cuba | 91.4 |
| 27 | Greece | 111.8 | 82 | Ghana | 91.0 |
| 28 | Brazil | 111.7 | 83.5 | Congo (Brazaville) | 90.8 |
| 29 | Turkey | 110.7 | 83.5 | Niger | 90.8 |
| 30 | Venezuela | 109.8 | 85 | Central African Republic | 90.3 |
| 31 | Ecuador | 109.7 | 86 | Republic of Korea | 89.4 |
| 32 | Panama | 109.4 | 87 | Republic of Vietnam | 87.6 |
| 33 | Colombia | 108.6 | 88 | Dahomey | 87.2 |
| 34 | Ceylon | 108.0 | 89 | Kenya | 86.5 |
| 35 | Bolivia | 107.8 | 90 | United Arab Republic | 86.4 |
| 36 | India | 107.1 | 91 | Burma | 83.9 |
| 37 | Mexico | 106.4 | 92 | Malawi | 83.2 |
| 38 | Jamaica | 106.0 | 93 | Taiwan | 81.7 |
| 39 | Argentina | 105.9 | 94 | Iran | 80.8 |
| 40 | Honduras | 105.1 | 95.5 | Haiti | 79.1 |
| 41 | Trinidad-Tobago | 105.0 | 95.5 | Iraq | 79.1 |
| 42 | Guatemala | 104.1 | 97 | Algeria | 78.1 |
| 43 | Malaysia | 103.8 | 98 | Togo | 77.9 |
| 44 | Peru | 103.6 | 99 | Libya | 75.7 |
| 45 | Nicaragua | 103.2 | 100 | Cambodia | 73.0 |
| 46 | Sierra Leone | 102.9 | 101.5 | Jordan | 72.8 |
| 47 | Uganda | 102.0 | 101.5 | Pakistan | 72.8 |
| 48 | El Salvador | 101.7 | 103.5 | Portugal | 72.0 |
| 49 | Lebanon | 101.4 | 103.5 | Spain | 72.0 |
| 50 | Liberia | 101.0 | 105 | Thailand | 71.0 |
| 51 | Nigeria | 100.0 | 106 | Laos | 70.1 |
| 52 | Malagasy | 98.4 | 107 | Sudan | 69.4 |
| 53 | Hungary | 97.5 | 108 | Afghanistan | 63.8 |
| 54 | Tunisia | 97.3 | 109 | Ethiopia | 62.2 |
| 55 | Yugoslavia | 97.2 | 110 | Saudi Arabia | 55.8 |

[a]Ranks with fractions indicate identical scores.

*Source:* Arthur K. Smith, Jr., "Socio-Economic Development and Political Democracy: A Causal Analysis," *Midwest Journal of Political Science*, 13 (February 1969), 104-105. Note that since Smith made these rankings, the political systems of some nations—e.g., Chile, the Philippines, and Uganda—have become substantially less democratic by his criteria.

although the groups of nations at the top, center, and bottom of the scale are substantially similar in all rankings. The differences among them arise largely from differences in the models used.

Whether a particular government is called "democratic" or "dictatorial" thus depends largely upon the model against which it is being assessed. As much is said in other chapters of this book about democracies and dictatorships, I shall devote the remainder of this chapter to outlining the models used here and explaining why they have been chosen over other possible models.

## COMPETING MODELS OF DEMOCRACY

We began this chapter by noting that whatever reassurance we may gain from knowing that nearly everyone in the world "believes in" democracy is likely to evaporate when we recognize the endless confusion and disagreement about what democracy is. Despite this semantic mess, however, it seems unlikely that the word will disappear from political talk. Thus it may help if we at least try to understand what others mean by it—and make clear to others what we mean when we use it. Before outlining this book's particular model of democracy let us briefly review those that have been most influential in the modern world.

### COMMUNIST MODELS

#### *The Soviet Model* [13]

Disciples of Moscow's interpretation of the sacred doctrines of Marx and Lenin insist that only the Soviet Union and the "people's democracies," whose regimes are modeled on that of the Soviet Union, can legitimately be called "democratic." They are aware, of course, that most of us in the West regard the regimes of nations like Norway, Switzerland, and Sweden as "democratic," but they insist that all such noncommunist regimes are merely false fronts erected by capitalists to conceal the naked realities of their exploitation of the toiling masses.

The core of the Soviet conception is the conviction that true democracy is a regime in which government action always advances the *real* interests and welfare of the masses—that is, what is "objectively" good for the masses, not necessarily what the masses may want. Accordingly, democracy is essentially a matter of what government does, not of how government decides what to do. It is government *for* the people (the proletariat) but not necessarily government *by* the people. From this point of view, our spectrum between democracy and dictatorship seems trivial or meaningless.[14]

The Soviet communist model of democracy does have, however, a few proce-

---

[13] The most thorough analyses are N. S. Timasheff, "The Soviet Conception of Democracy," *Review of Politics,* 12 (October 1950), 506–518; and Ruth Amende Rosa, "The Soviet Theory of 'People's Democracy,'" *World Politics,* 1 (July 1949), 489–510.

[14] See Robert C. Tucker, *The Soviet Political Mind* (New York: Frederick A. Praeger, Inc., 1963), pp. 11–12.

dural elements worth noting. One is the notion of the Communist party as "the vanguard of the proletariat": During the present stage of historical development, it is held, the highly trained and deeply dedicated proletarian elite of the party knows far better than do the masses what is best for them and how to achieve it. To permit freedom of organization and expression for non- or anticommunist opponents of party policies would, by definition, be undemocratic: It would allow "capitalist exploiters," "social fascist reptiles," "deviationist adventurers," and other enemies of communism to retard and sabotage the party's programs, which means sabotaging the masses' welfare. The regime's toleration of only one party, suppression of most forms of dissent, and single-candidate elections are thus the only truly democratic modes of conducting government when the proletariat and their vanguard are in the saddle.

Closely related to this vanguard conception of the party's place in society is the doctrine of democratic centralism in the party's internal decision making. First expounded by Lenin and now written into the party's rules, democratic centralism proclaims full, free, and frank discussion of alternatives within the party before a decision is made but total and unwavering support of the policy by all after the party has made its choice. In practice, according to most Western students of the Soviet system, democratic centralism means that free discussion and dissent are confined strictly to certain matters selected by the party leaders. These matters are almost always limited to questions about the most effective way to carry out party policies; they never include direct criticism of the policies themselves or of the leaders who make them.[15]

Soviet Communist leaders are well aware, of course, that their policies can be truly effective only if they have the masses' enthusiastic support. Mere sullen foot-dragging acquiescence will cripple any policy, however enlightened. Accordingly, as we saw in Chapter 5, the Soviet leaders are concerned with a kind of public opinion, and the Soviet system includes devices for discovering the masses' reactions to party policies and for arousing mass approval and enthusiasm. But, in Soviet-style democracy, although the welfare of the toiling masses remains government's proclaimed paramount end, decisions about what measures will best achieve it remain strictly the monopoly of the party "vanguard."

### The Chinese Model [16]

The Chinese Communists' bitter attacks in recent years on their former Soviet comrades do not reflect any explicit Chinese departure from the principles of Marxism-Leninism. The main cause of their quarrel with the Soviets, they say, is the desertion by the latter of true communist principles for the heresy of "revisionism." Consequently, the Chinese communist model of democracy is very similar to the Soviet version.

---

[15] See Merle Fainsod, *How Russia is Ruled* (rev. ed.; Cambridge, Mass.: Harvard University Press, 1963), pp. 209–211; and Alfred G. Meyer, *The Soviet Political System: An Interpretation* (New York: Random House, Inc., 1965), pp. 152–155.

[16] This discussion is drawn mainly from J. W. Lewis, *Leadership in Communist China;* and H. Arthur Steiner, "Current 'Mass Line' Tactics in Communist China," *American Political Science Review,* 45 (June 1951), 422–436.

There are, however, a few differences in language and emphasis. The most noteworthy is the Chinese Communists' doctrine of the "mass line"—the integration of the party's leadership with the physical power of the masses in order to build true communism. The "mass line" is said to involve a two-way interaction: leadership by the party's cadres in farm, village, city, and factory to mobilize, inspire, and energize the masses to do what the party has decided must be done; and sensitivity of the party, through its cadres, to the masses' aspirations and feelings.

In its 1945 constitution, the Chinese Communist party clarified this concept by setting forth a number of deviations from the mass line that all cadres were adjured to avoid. The first, "tailism," was defined as "the erroneous practice of blindly following untutored popular demands"; clearly the party knows best in the Chinese model, as in the Soviet. The other proscribed deviations—"commandism," "isolationism," "bureaucratism," and "warlordism"—are all forms of behavior attributed to cadres and public officials who have become too far removed from and out of sympathy with the masses.

But in the People's Republic of China as in the Soviet Union, the question of who decides what is best for the masses is clearly answered:

> The party, as the vanguard of the working class, exercises leadership as its principal function in the mass line process.... The party controls by leading and the masses "control" by participating, and in this theory the "vanguard" cannot have interests different from those of the masses.... The masses, the Communists hold, are not as farseeing as the vanguard; the masses are more contaminated by reactionary ideologies and counter-revolutionary elements.... The ordinary Chinese, Mao implied, have neither the duty to create the mass line relationship nor the right to reject it. They cannot turn against the vanguard because they cannot reverse the tide of their own historical movement which creates the vanguard.[17]

## NONCOMMUNIST MODELS[18]

The noncommunist world has no single model of democracy to set against the Soviet communist model and its Chinese variant. There are, rather, several noncommunist models, no one of which has preempted, or is likely to preempt, the label "democracy" all for itself. These models share certain significant areas of agreement, but they are sufficiently different to warrant brief separate descriptions of the two most influential.

### The "Direct," or "Participatory," Model [19]

The word "democracy" was originally compounded from two Greek words: *demos,* meaning "the people," and *kratein,* meaning "ruling power"; its original meaning was

---

[17] J. W. Lewis, *Leadership in Communist China,* pp. 75, 83.

[18] For a useful survey employing a somewhat different typology from that used here, see M. Rejai, *Democracy: The Contemporary Theories* (New York: Atherton Press, 1967).

[19] One of many descriptions of the ancient Athenian origins of this model is A. H. M. Jones, *Athenian Democracy* (New York: Oxford University Press, 1957). Leading current expositions include Carole Pateman, *Participation and Democratic Theory* (New York: Cambridge University

"government in which the ruling power resides in the people." From the fifth century B.C. until the twentieth century most people using the word meant the government system of the city-state of Athens at the time of Pericles. Under the Periclean system all important decisions were made directly by the *ekklesia*, the general face-to-face assembly of all the citizens. Leading offices, like magistracies, were filled not by election but by lot, so that each citizen had as good a chance as any other to be selected; most public officials held their offices for one-year terms only and were not eligible for reselection. Even the Athenian equivalents of modern court trials were conducted directly either by the *ekklesia* or by "courts" of hundreds of citizens chosen by lot and acting as both judges and jurors. The two prime qualities of Athenian democracy, then, were popular *control* of public decisions and maximum popular *participation* in making the decisions and in holding public office.

Most present-day political theorists believe that this kind of widespread direct popular participation in day-to-day government is impossible in modern nation-states, almost all of which include millions of people, as opposed to perhaps 40,000 in Periclean Athens. Some theorists, however, argue that any ideal of democracy settling for less than maximum direct popular participation (for example, the "elitist" model to be presented next) cannot be a valid model of democracy. The moral goal of democracy, the basic purpose for which it exists, was and still is to develop the full human potential of each member of the community. The only logical way to direct government structure to this goal is to encourage maximum participation by all the people in the making of the decisions, public and private, that affect their lives.

But how? For one thing, they reply, a democracy should permit and encourage greater popular participation in smaller subgovernmental decision-making bodies like political parties, labor unions, corporations, schools, churches, and the like. In addition, it should delegate a larger share of public power to government units small enough to permit effective and meaningful mass participation in decision-making, particularly small municipalities and neighborhoods within big cities.[20]

Many other devices are also needed, these theorists say, but the first and most important step is to recognize that personal self-development is the moral goal of democracy and that maximum direct popular participation is the chief means of achieving it. When people generally understand and accept these basic principles, they can get on with the largely technical job of thinking up new and better means for increasing popular participation.

### The "Indirect," or "Elitist" Model[21]

Most, though not all, social scientists agree, as a matter of observation, that in almost no human organization do all members participate all the time with equal energy,

---

Press, 1970); and Peter Bachrach, *The Theory of Democratic Elitism* (Boston: Little, Brown & Company, 1967).

[20] See, for example, Robert A. Dahl, "The City in the Future of Democracy," *American Political Science Review,* 61 (December 1967), 953–970; and Milton Kotler, *Neighborhood Government* (Indianapolis, Ind.: The Bobbs-Merrill Company, Inc., 1969).

[21] The leading expositions of various versions of this basic model include Joseph A. Schumpeter, *Capitalism, Socialism, and Democracy* (2d ed.; New York: Harper & Row, Publishers, 1947);

commitment, and influence. In every organization a few members are more committed, more willing to work, more likely to take initiative and as a result to have more influence than the more passive majority. Social scientists usually call these more active and more influential members the organization's "elite."

Does the prevalence of influential elites in human groups mean that democracy is impossible? Not at all, say some political theorists. The essence of democracy lies not in absence of elites but in popular control of the elites. In this model control is exercised through the *competition* of elites for office and power, popular *selection* of the winners by the people in periodic elections, *limitations* on the power that any elite can exercise while in office, and *removal* of the incumbent elite whenever it fails to perform to the people's satisfaction—in sum, through the accountability of the elite in power at the moment to the people.

To such theorists a properly organized representative or indirect democracy is in principle every bit as democratic as the direct, or participatory, kind. Rather than wasting our energies in hopeless searches for ways to bring about universal popular participation in modern governments, they say, we should focus on the more significant quest for ways of establishing effective popular control of such governments. Town-meeting democracy may be a fine model for Athens, the rural cantons of Switzerland, or the small towns of New England, but the elitist model is equally democratic and a good deal more relevant to governing in the modern world.

### Some Agreements and Disagreements among Noncommunist Conceptions

Outside the communist world, then, the term "democracy" has many different meanings. All is not sheer chaos and hopeless confusion, however, for a survey and comparison of different meanings reveals that they share areas of agreement, as well as of disagreement.

**Areas of Agreement**    Almost all noncommunists believe, contrary to the heirs of Lenin, that democracy is *at least* a form of government—that is, a particular way of arriving at governmental decisions. They agree, furthermore, that a genuinely democratic government must have *at least* three characteristics.

> *Political Equality*    First, in a democracy each member of the community must have the same legal and actual opportunity to participate in the political decision-making processes enjoyed by every other member of the community. If, as in the communist regimes, certain people (for example, members of the only tolerated party) have more such opportunities than do others, the favored few are a "ruling class," and such regimes should be called "oligarchies" rather than "democracies."
>
> *Governmental Response to the Popular Will*    Second, a democratic government does whatever the people want it to do and refrains from doing whatever they do not

---

Robert A. Dahl, *A Preface to Democratic Theory* (Chicago: University of Chicago Press, 1956); Henry B. Mayo, *An Introduction to Democratic Theory* (New York: Oxford University Press, 1960); and Sartori, *Democratic Theory*.

Models of Democracy and
Dictatorship

want it to do. In a democracy the people—not an elite of party members or businessmen or college professors—are the final judges of what is in their best interests. Democracy is government *by* the people.

*Majority Rule Rather than Minority Rule*   Third, when the people disagree among themselves about what government should do and a decision must be made, the democratic way to decide is by majority rule. Each member of the community should register his wishes (in an election or referendum or by any of various methods described in previous chapters), the results should be totaled, and public officials should be mandated to act in accordance with the wishes of the greater proportion of the people (the majority) rather than with the wishes of the lesser proportion (the minority). Many noncommunists believe that popular majorities in a true democracy must not adopt certain kinds of policies, but none argues that minority rule is more democratic than majority rule in determining which of the permissible policies government will follow.

**Areas of Disagreement**   The main differences among noncommunists about the proper meaning of "democracy" center on two basic issues.

First, some noncommunists believe that popular majorities in a democracy must not do certain things, for example, abridge the rights of individuals, as outlined in Chapter 21. They argue that true democracy must have certain institutional machinery, like judicial review, to restrain majorities from ignoring or stepping outside their proper limits. Other noncommunists insist that any limitation upon popular majorities other than those imposed by the majorities themselves and removable by other majorities at any time means minority veto power and therefore minority rule. We shall return to this issue shortly.

Some noncommunists believe that democracy should be regarded solely as a form of government, a method of making public decisions not directly concerned with the content of those decisions or with the purposes to which government power may be directed. Others argue, however, that the concept of democracy, though it certainly includes certain ways of making political decisions, includes other considerations as well—a certain kind of economic system, certain kinds of relations among the races, a certain kind of religious philosophy, or the like. To such people democracy is more than simply a form of government. It is also a whole communal or personal way of life.

## A WORKING DEFINITION OF DEMOCRACY [22]

Let us recognize that neither science nor logic can prove that any particular conception of democracy is the only correct one—that is, one to which all people must adhere if they are not to be considered irrational or immoral. The proper meaning of "democ-

---

[22] The analysis of democracy to be given here is a somewhat revised version of that presented in greater detail in Austin Ranney and Willmoore Kendall, *Democracy and the American Party System* (New York: Harcourt Brace Jovanovich, Inc., 1956), chaps. 1–3. (I gratefully acknowledge the permission of Harcourt Brace Jovanovich, Inc., to borrow heavily from these chapters in the present analysis.)

racy," like that of any other word, ultimately depends upon convention: That is, its validity depends upon the degree to which it is generally understood and accepted. Let us further recognize that many people, communists and noncommunists alike, do not use "democracy" in exactly the same sense in which I am about to define the term.

Recognizing these differences does not, however, exempt us from the obligation of selecting a particular definition. The term "democracy" cannot be avoided in discussing certain aspects of governing. Throughout this book we are considering the political and governmental agencies and processes of "the democracies"—the nations that cluster toward the model-democracy end of the continuum shown in Figure 11. Our explanation of modern government is likely to be clearer and more useful if we understand from the outset what the model includes and why it has been chosen over others. But I certainly do not insist that this particular conception is the only one logically possible or morally permissible.

As the term is used in this book, democracy is a *form of government organized in accordance with the principles of popular sovereignty, political equality, popular consultation, and majority rule.* In order to understand this definition, let us briefly examine what is involved in each of its four principles.

### Popular Sovereignty

Briefly stated, the principle of popular sovereignty requires that basic governmental decision-making power be vested in *all* members of the community and not in any particular person or ruling class. This principle is the nucleus of the conception of democracy outlined here; the other three are logical elaborations of it. It has several major aspects.

**Sovereignty** Political scientists have long argued about the proper content and usefulness of the concept of sovereignty. For our purposes it is unnecessary to summarize or take sides in this debate. I merely reiterate a point first made in Chapter 3: One characteristic of any modern nation is its command of full and exclusive legal power to make and enforce laws for the people within its territory and under its jurisdiction. Such a nation is sovereign over its own affairs. And in every sovereign nation "sovereign power" is located somewhere in its political-governmental structure. In a democracy it must be vested in all members of the community.

**Vestment in the People** The principle of popular sovereignty does not logically require that all the people directly make all the daily decisions of government. Democracy does not demand that dog licenses and parking tickets be issued only when all members of the community specifically consent to them—any more than a dictatorship implies that the dictator must personally issue all licenses and tickets. The people in a democracy, like the dictator in a dictatorship, may lend, or "delegate," part of their decision-making power to legislators, executives, judges, or anyone else they wish. The people are sovereign as long as they, and not their delegates, have the power to decide such matters as what decision-making powers are to be delegated, to whom, under what conditions of accountability, and for what periods of time.

Models of Democracy and Dictatorship

**Members of the Community**   If democracy means government by the people, then we may reasonably ask, who *are* "the people"? Are they, for instance, all those physically present within the nation's borders at a given moment—including infants, aliens, lunatics, criminals in prison, and so on? I have implied an answer to this question by stating that in a democracy power rests in all *members of the community*, rather than in all persons who happen to be around.

The criterion for determining who may share in this power is thus membership in the community. The term "community" itself suggests something more than a mere aggregation of people: it implies some kind of bond, shared values, and some mutual interests, feelings, and behavior. The term "member" implies a special kind of relation between an individual and a group, involving both certain obligations to the group and certain privileges from it.

For example, a person's privilege to vote and hold office in a modern democratic nation is determined by the community's judgment of both the ability and the willingness of the person to fulfill the obligations of loyalty to the community and of obedience to its laws. Children and lunatics in such a nation are generally excluded from these privileges because they are judged incapable of understanding and fulfilling the obligations of loyalty and obedience. Aliens and criminals in prison are generally excluded because they are judged unwilling to accept these obligations. We may, of course, disagree with the application of these criteria to certain classes of citizens. Some people, for example, believe that it is undemocratic to deny the vote to persons under eighteen years of age or to persons who cannot read and write. The criteria of capability and willingness to assume certain obligations, however, are generally regarded in the democratic nations as proper standards for determining who should and should not be regarded as part of "the sovereign people."

**Sovereignty of All the People**   When ultimate power is vested in one person the government is a dictatorship, or an autocracy, as described in Chapter 12. When it is vested in only some members of the community, they constitute a ruling class, and the government is what I have described as an oligarchy or aristocracy. Only when it is vested in all the people is the government a democracy.

### Political Equality

The second principle of democratic government, political equality, requires that each member of the community have the same opportunity as every other to participate in the nation's political decision-making processes. This principle certainly means "one man, one vote," but it includes other matters as well. For instance, all citizens of the Soviet Union over the age of eighteen have the legally guaranteed right to vote, but they do not have political equality in our sense of the term. The fact that they can vote for only one Communist-sponsored and -approved candidate for each office deprives them of genuine choice. Their right to vote accordingly reflects no real power over political decisions. In the Soviet Union, as one observer puts it, "everyone is equal; but some are more equal than others!" Certainly the Communist party leaders who pick candidates are "more equal" than are the ordinary Soviet voters, who can only rubber-stamp the official slate or "scratch" their ballots.

Political equality requires such guarantees as the following: All members of the community must be able to vote and have their votes counted and given equal weight with all other votes cast; genuine alternatives must be put before the voters so that they may make real choices; all members of the community must have an equal chance to find out what the alternatives are and the arguments for and against each alternative; they must also have an equal opportunity to persuade others—and to be persuaded by them—of the desirability of particular alternatives.

The principle of political equality is, of course, a logical consequence of the principle of popular sovereignty. If some members of the community have greater opportunities than others—if, for example, their votes are given double or triple weight or only they are eligible for public office—then they become a kind of specially favored ruling class, which, according to the principle of popular sovereignty, is not permissible in a democracy.

The principle of political equality means equal *opportunities* for all members of the community, not actual equal participation. In no known or imaginable democracy does every person actually participate to exactly the same degree as does every other. As long as each member has a genuinely equal opportunity to participate to the degree that he or she wishes and can manage, the requirements of political equality are satisfied.

### Popular Consultation

The principle of popular consultation involves two requirements. First, a democratic nation must have some kind of institutional machinery through which public officials learn what public policies the people wish adopted and enforced. Second, having ascertained the policies preferred by the people, public officials must then put them into effect whether or not they believe them to be wise. This principle, like that of political equality, is a logical consequence of popular sovereignty. When officeholders do what they, rather than the people, wish, they and not the people are sovereign.

This principle is the most obvious point of difference between this conception of democracy and that of the communists. Communists, as we have seen, regard democracy as government *for* the people—government in which a special elite, the Communist party, decides what policies will best promote the "real" interests of the people. Popular approval of these policies is desirable but quite secondary to instituting the "right" policies.

Here, on the other hand, democracy is defined as essentially government *by* the people. The principle of popular consultation requires that the decision about which public policies best promote the people's interests must ultimately be made by the people themselves and not by any ruling class of party leaders, college professors, scientists, priests, or businessmen. According to this conception, the claim of a particular policy to the title "democratic" is determined by how it is made, rather than by its content. Policy content enters the picture only when it directly affects the nature of the decision-making processes themselves.

### Majority Rule

**The Principle** The final principle of democracy is probably the most controversial of the four, and I shall therefore take special pains to explain its meaning and why it seems to me essential to this conception of democracy.

When the people in a democracy unanimously agree that a particular policy should be adopted, the principle of popular sovereignty clearly requires that government follow that policy. Most political decisions in a democracy, however, eventually become choices among alternative views, each of which has its supporters among the sovereign people. In every such situation only one group can have its way, and the other group or groups must "lose." The problem is: How should a democratic government, resting as it does on the principle that basic decision-making power must be vested in *all* members of the community, determine *which* of the disagreeing groups will carry the day?

The principle of majority rule in a democracy requires that no government decision be made against the ultimate desires of popular majorities. When the people disagree on a particular issue, the government should act on that issue as the larger rather than the smaller number desire. This principle does not require that each and every government action be undertaken only after all the people have been consulted and a majority has specifically approved. It is up to popular majorities to decide how they want various kinds of decisions made. A majority may, for example, wish to reserve for itself and future majorities all government decisions, however minor— though no actual popular majority has ever done so. Or a majority may wish to leave all such decisions up to certain elected and appointed public officials and confine itself to deciding in periodic elections whether or not those officials should remain in office. Or it may leave some decisions to public officials and reserve others for direct popular decison by such means as initiative and referendum (see Chap. 14). As long as the procedures used to make governmental decisions are at all times approved by at least 50 percent plus one of the people and as long as the same proportion of the people can at any time revise those procedures, the principle of majority rule is satisfied.

**Limited Majority Rule**[23]     Some political commentators argue that "unlimited" majority rule is incompatible with true democracy, that in a true democracy certain kinds of action must not be taken by popular majorities. Such majorities, for example, must not destroy any principles of democracy by such actions as transferring sovereignty from the people to a dictator, giving certain people multiple voting power, prohibiting certain people from expressing their political views, or abolishing elections. Bare popular majorities must not destroy the kind of liberties and guarantees of due process of law described in Chapter 21. Any nation in which a bare popular majority does any of these things, these commentators insist, has no legitimate claim to be a democracy. For these reasons, they conclude, unlimited majority rule cannot be considered a principle of true democracy.

**Self-Limited Majority Rule**     People like the present writer who believe that unlimited majority rule must be a principle of democracy have no quarrel with the preced-

---

[23] For lengthier expositions of "limited majority rule," see Herbert McClosky, "The Fallacy of Absolute Majority Rule," *Journal of Politics* (November 1949), 637–654; and Thomas Landon Thorson, "Epilogue on Absolute Majority Rule," *Journal of Politics*, 23 (August 1961), 557–565. For a reply to the latter, see Ranney, "Postlude to an Epilogue on Absolute Majority Rule," *Journal of Politics*, 23 (August 1961), 566–569.

ing statements as far as they go. But the next—and crucial—question is: How are popular majorities to be prevented from destroying other democratic principles? Some opponents of unlimited majority rule do not answer this question directly but imply two answers: First, popular majorities in a true democracy must voluntarily restrain themselves from stepping over the line, and, second, when a popular majority in a particular nation fails to restrain itself and does destroy essential institutions and guarantees, that nation is no longer a democracy. Yet both propositions are entirely compatible with the conception of democracy presented here and its principle of unlimited majority rule, for they assume that majorities are *self*-limited only.

Other opponents of unlimited majority rule, however, insist that in a true democracy bare popular majorities must be limited by some agency independent of control by such majorities. They argue that there must be some restraining institution like judicial review or a requirement of "extraordinary" majorities (two-thirds or three-quarters, rather than 50 percent plus one) for certain kinds of action. Such an institution must permit a minority to veto any majority action that the former considers a threat to sacrosanct institutions and guarantees.

In this debate over the appropriateness for democracy of such minority veto devices, the issue between the opponents and advocates of self-limited majority rule is most clearly joined. Those like myself who favor self-limited majority rule argue that such devices are incompatible with the principles of popular sovereignty and political equality. To give minorities the power to veto, we believe, is to give them the power to rule. Why? Because in any decision-making situation there are always a number of possible alternatives that may be chosen, and one of them is almost always to continue the status quo. A minority with veto power can, to be sure, choose only the status quo, but if it is large enough (if it commands, for example, one-third plus one of the votes or a majority of the U.S. Supreme Court) it can force continuation of the status quo over any alternative policy desired by the majority.

Such minority veto power is incompatible with the principles of popular sovereignty and political equality. A person who votes No counts for two or three times as much as does a person who votes Yes, in violation of the principle of political equality. Under such a system each person who opposes change and prefers the status quo has more political power than does a person who desires change, and those who prefer the status quo thus become a sort of special ruling class. Minority veto power violates the principle of popular sovereignty.

For these reasons, then, the conception of democracy outlined here demands that the power of popular majorities to take any government action they choose be subject to no limitations other than those imposed—and removable—by such majorities. But what if a majority in a particular nation chooses to give all power to a dictator, abolish all freedom of speech and press, or deprive everyone but its own members of the right to vote? The answer is, of course, that the nation would immediately cease to be a democracy. Locating full *power* to take such actions in popular majorities is in itself, however, not inconsistent with democracy, for surely even the power to commit suicide as a democracy must be part of the all-inclusive sovereign power that democracy, as conceived here, locates in the people.

We may also ask, What if a particular majority chooses to set up judicial review or some other device to restrain future majorities? Under this conception such a decision is perfectly compatible with majority rule and the other principles of democracy provided that any future majority can at any time abolish judicial review or any other restraining device by the same simple-majority procedures by which the device was initially established.

The debate over the appropriateness of unlimited majority rule in democracy has to some extent been obscured by both sides' apparent assumption that there is such a thing as *the* majority—a single identifiable group that sticks together on issue after issue and continually beats down *the* minority. The opponents of unlimited majority rule, for instance, have sometimes argued that the majority is composed of the more ignorant, prejudiced, and selfish members of the community, who cannot be trusted to rule wisely in the interests of all. The defenders of unlimited majority rule have sometimes fallen into the same trap, arguing that the majority is composed of common men, like Henry Wadsworth Longfellow's village blacksmith, who may not read books or use fancy words but make their decisions on the much sounder grounds of "practical experience" and "common sense."

Both sides are, of course, talking about something that does not exist. As we observed in Chapter 5, every time one issue is succeeded by another in the center of the political stage there is always some reshuffling of the various "opinion groups." Neither the majority nor the minority on any given issue is made up of exactly the same people as the majority or the minority on any other issue. When, for example, the issue of who should be elected President of the United States in 1972 had been settled and was succeeded by the issue of whether Richard Nixon should be impeached and removed from office, some of the 1972 Nixon voters opposed impeachment but many supported it. The great majority of the McGovern voters favored impeachment, but even a few of them opposed it.

Actual majorities and minorities are (like "public opinion" in general) specific to particular issues, rather than permanent bodies whose members always side together on all issues. That is why I have specified that the only restraints on popular majorities (not "the majority") compatible with democracy are those imposed by majorities on themselves and removable at any time without any restraint by minorities.

## THE ADVANTAGES OF THE MAJORITARIAN CONCEPTION OF DEMOCRACY

I do not insist that the conception of democracy outlined here is the only one that is logically possible or morally acceptable. I do, however, suggest that it has at least two advantages.

### Accordance with the Historic Meaning of Democracy

The original meaning of "democracy," as we have seen, was "authority in the people," and it became one element of the ancient tripartite classification of governments as democracies, aristocracies (authority in a few of the people), and monarchies (authority in one person). From then until World War I, "democracy" continued to be given its original meaning by most people. Only since 1918 has it had the bewildering variety of meanings described at the beginning of this chapter. This book's conception of democracy, unlike many of its current rivals, thus closely accords with its generally accepted historical meaning.

The use of a word in a particular sense during most of its history does not, in itself, oblige us to continue it. If some new meaning makes the word more useful in political discussion and if the new meaning is generally accepted, we are well advised to abandon the old meaning in favor of the new. No other current conception of democracy can claim either of these advantages, however. None of the newer meanings commands general agreement. The fact that "democracy" now means different things to different people has actually *reduced* its usefulness in modern political discussion. The advantages lost in abandoning the old meaning of the word obviously have not been replaced by corresponding advantages in adopting new meanings.

### Accordance with Current Areas of Agreement among Noncommunists

The majoritarian conception of democracy also has the advantage of incorporating—without going beyond—the elements that most present-day noncommunists agree should be included in any proper conception of democracy. Noncommunists, as we have noted, agree that democracy is at least a form of government. They further agree that, as a form of government, it includes at least the principles of political equality, governmental response to the popular will, and majority rather than minority rule. They do not agree, however, on whether or not democracy is more than simply a form of government. Even those who maintain that it is also a "way of life" do not agree upon just what kind of social system, economic system, and personal attitudes and manners it requires.

It therefore seems reasonable to hope that the majoritarian conception will provoke less disagreement among people on this side of the iron curtain than another, more ambitious conception might. We may even hope that, though many people may believe the conception to be incomplete, few will think that it contains elements incompatible with *any* defensible meaning of the word.

At any rate, wherever it appears in this book, "democracy" means a form of government organized in accordance with the principles of popular sovereignty, political equality, popular consultation, and majority rule.

## DEMOCRACY AND CONSTITUTIONALISM

Democratic government, in this book's terminology, is not synonymous with "constitutional," "limited," or "free" government. The latter types, as explained in Chapters 21 and 22, are governments in which human rights are formally and actually protected from abridgment by either public officials or private groups. Such governments are called "constitutional" or "free" because of *what* they do or refrain from doing relative to those rights. A democratic government, according to the majoritarian conception, is defined by the *processes* by which it reaches decisions—not by the content of those decisions.

It would be theoretically possible for a benevolent despot to exercise his absolute decision-making power in such a way that all his subjects had full freedom of speech, press, and religion and were guaranteed all other individual "rights." He might even promulgate a constitution formalizing these particular limitations on his activities while reserving to himself the exclusive power to make all other political decisions. Such a government would certainly be "free" and even constitutional, but it would not, according to this book's definition, be democratic. A democratic government, on the other hand, might have no written constitution and no formal guarantees of civil rights whatever.

This distinction between democracy and constitutionalism, however, is more important logically than practically. Most of the nations that noncommunists generally call "democratic" would certainly also appear on any list of "constitutional" nations, and none of those generally called "dictatorial" would win a place on such a list. It therefore appears that most modern democracies have decided that one—though not the only—useful way to maintain their democratic decision-making processes is to accept and formalize in constitutions the personal freedoms and immunities that make possible genuine political equality and popular consultation. Democracy and constitutionalism are thus logically distinct, but in practice they are closely associated, and we rarely find a government that approximates one but not the other.

## THE ESSENTIALS OF DICTATORSHIP

### ORIGINS OF THE TERM

Explicating a model of dictatorship should take less time and argument than explicating a model of democracy. The reason is clear. As we have seen, the word "democracy" evidently kindles such a pleasant emotional glow in most people the world over that they feel impelled to insist that it applies best—perhaps exclusively—to whatever forms or outputs of government they favor. Any effort to claim it for other forms or outputs is thus always bound to encounter resistance and often resentment.

The word "dictatorship" has neither this popularity nor its attendant confusion. For most people it connotes something bad. The much rarer disputes over its usage therefore usually hinge not on what it means but on whether this or that actual government deserves the slur.

The word "dictator" originated in the ancient republic of Rome: When the city was threatened by foreign invasion or domestic rebellion and the Senate determined that regular governing procedures were inadequate to meet the danger, they appointed a *dictator* and gave him, for a limited period, absolute power to use all Rome's resources as he saw fit in order to save the city. When the danger had passed, the *dictator's* power reverted to the Senate and the people, and he returned, as did the great Lucius Quinctius Cincinnatus, to his former status of ordinary citizen. In the republic's late years, however, ambitious politicians seized the title and powers of *dictator* through armed rebellion or intimidation of the Senate, and for many centuries thereafter, a "dictator" was generally defined as one who seized and held absolute power illegitimately, in contrast to an "autocrat," who had equally absolute power but achieved it by such legitimate means as inheriting a throne.

# THE MEANING AND VARIETIES OF DICTATORSHIP TODAY

Political scientists have long since dropped these ancient distinctions and now use the term "dictatorship" to denote a form of government in which the ultimate ruling power is held and exercised by one person or a small elite. The dictator or dictatorial elite may acquire power by inheritance, as did Emperor Haile Selassie of Ethiopia; by overthrowing an established regime in a civil war, as did *El Caudillo* Francisco Franco in Spain and Chairman Mao Tse-tung in China; or by using the procedures of democracy to gain a foothold and then "liquidating" all opposition, as did Adolf Hitler in Germany. Dictatorship is the opposite of model democracy. Its essence is not the manner in which power is acquired but its distinguishing principles: sovereignty concentrated in one person or a small group, political inequality, no popular consultation, and minority rule.

Dictatorship thus conceived is a model in the same sense that democracy is a model: a full intellectual realization of a particular organizational principle, not a complete and precise description of any actual government. Just as there are degrees of democracy (degrees of approximation to the model), so there are degrees of dictatorship. In no actual government has one man actually controlled *all* decisions by himself. From Julius Caesar to Fidel Castro all dictators have had to rule through subordinates, who have had to intepret and carry out orders; as we shall see repeatedly in later chapters, any interpretation or implementation of an order necessarily creates an area of discretion effectively controlled by the subordinate, whatever the organization charts may indicate.

Actual dictatorships, like actual democracies, are thus matters of more or less, not of all or none. They come in many varieties: the monarchical regimes of Saudi Arabia and Oman, the military regimes of Burma and Taiwan, the corporate states of Spain and Portugal (see Chap. 14), and what might be called the "people's dictatorships" of Houari Boumediène in Algiers and Fidel Castro in Cuba.

## DICTATORSHIP AND TOTALITARIANISM[24]

### The Meanings of the Terms

We distinguish between dictatorship and totalitarianism as between democracy and constitutionalism. Democracy and dictatorship are particular ways of *allocating* ultimate power to make government policy. Constitutionalism and totalitarianism define limits or lack of them upon the permissible *exercise* of power.

A constitutional government, as we have seen, both formally and effectively protects human rights from abridgment by either public officials or private groups. The essential trait of a totalitarian regime is its claim to control every aspect of the citizen's life for the government's purposes as determined and interpreted by the

---

[24] The leading analyses of modern totalitarianism include Hannah Arendt, *The Origins of Totalitarianism* (New York: Meridian Books, Inc., 1958); Carl J. Friedrich (ed.), *Totalitarianism* (New York: University Library, 1964); and Friedrich and Brzezinski, *Totalitarian Dictatorship and Autocracy* (2d ed.; Cambridge, Mass.: Harvard University Press, 1965).

**The dictator: Idi Amin of Uganda.** Source: UPI Photograph.

rulers, with annihilation of personal privacy regularly used as a perfectly acceptable stratagem.

Most noncommunist political scientists believe that the closest approximations to complete totalitarian dictatorship in recent years have been Hitler's Germany, Joseph Stalin's Soviet Union, Mao's People's Republic of China, and François Duvalier's Haiti. The idea is carried to an imaginative extreme in George Orwell's frightening novel *1984.* Modern totalitarian dictatorship, observers believe, is a twentieth-century Western invention quite different in significant ways from the older forms of autocracy like the ancient despotism of Caligula, the oriental satrapy of Genghis Khan, the Renaissance tyranny of Cesare Borgia, and the absolute monarchy of Louis XIV. Each of those "dictators" had relatively limited political objec-

Governmental Structures

tives and made demands only on those parts of his subjects' lives and thoughts necessary to accomplish them. But modern totalitarian regimes set no limits on either their objectives or individual citizens' duty to sacrifice religion, family, and privacy to the leaders' demands.

### Essential Characteristics of Totalitarian Dictatorships

Two leading students of totalitarian dictatorships have listed six essential characteristics of this new kind of regime:[25]

1. An official ideology covering all aspects of man's existence to which every member of the society must adhere, not only by outer form but also by inner conviction
2. A single mass party, typically led by one man and consisting of a relatively small proportion of the total population, which acts as the official ideology's priesthood and the leader's apostles and "janissaries"
3. A system of terroristic police control based on modern technology
4. Nearly complete monopoly of control by the leader and party of all means of effective mass communication
5. Nearly complete monopoly of all means of effective armed combat
6. Central control of the entire economy through bureaucratic coordination of all previously private corporate entities

In strict logic, dictatorship and totalitarianism are as divisible as are democracy and constitutionalism. Theoretically speaking, there could be a totalitarian democracy —indeed, it seems to be what advocates of the "limited majority-rule" position, outlined above, seem to fear will develop if popular majorities are unchecked. In fact, however, there is no example in the modern world of a government that is both democratic and totalitarian. And, although all totalitarian governments have been dictatorships of the most ruthless sort, many dictatorships, like their ancient and medieval predecessors, are not very totalitarian as we use the term. Some, indeed, appear to be well described by the old characterization of Turkey's pre-1920s Ottoman Empire as "despotism tempered by anarchy." But no one would say that of Stalin's Russia or Hitler's Germany.

## CONCLUSION

Any classification of actual governments as approximations of democracy or dictatorship is likely to be tentative and imperfect at best. Given the present state of political science, described in Chapter 1, it could hardly be otherwise. Yet in a book like this one, which attempts to describe the main processes of politics and government the world over, I can hardly avoid talking about democracies and dictatorships, nor would I wish to do so.

We observed in Chapter 12 that anyone who talks of the form of an actual government has necessarily abstracted part of its total reality and that the particular

[25] Friedrich and Brzezinski, *Totalitarian Dictatorship and Autocracy,* pp. 9–10.

parts that one has chosen to investigate are determined by one's conception of a model, or perfect example of such a form. Anyone who uses the terms "democracy" and "dictatorship," therefore, bases them on conceptions of a complete democracy and a complete dictatorship, and anyone who describes an existing government as "democratic" or "dictatorial" is comparing that government's actual processes and institutions with preferred models.

My purpose in this chapter has been to make as clear as I can what "democracy" and "dictatorship" and the adjectives derived from them mean in this book, why I have chosen these particular conceptions over the alternatives, and by what reasoning I designate some actual governments as democratic and others as dictatorial.

# 14

# THEORY AND PRACTICE OF POLITICAL REPRESENTATION

Political representation is the key institution of every modern democratic political system—and disagreements about what "true" representation is and what institutions are best calculated to achieve it lie at the heart of most of the controversies about legislators, executives, administrators, and judges that we shall consider in Chapters 15 to 18.

It could hardly be otherwise. If "democracy" means anything, it means at least a government that does whatever a majority of the community's members want it to do and refrains from doing whatever the majority wants it not to do.[1] But democracy is only an impossible dream unless the government has some effective way of *finding out* what its citizens do and do not want and then translating those wishes into government action or inaction. The most obvious way to do so is simply to ask them: to listen to speeches and take votes at general meetings, to call them on the telephone, or to write letters to them. The ancient Athenians did something pretty much like this. Their basic ruling body, the *ekklesia*, consisted of all the citizens—which meant only all males aged twenty or more but no slaves, no resident foreigners, and no women. The general assembly met at least ten times a year and sometimes in additional special sessions. The members discussed policy, made laws, picked people

---

[1] This flat assertion, of course, bypasses those hotly disputed questions about accommodating majority rule to minority rights, determining who will be considered members of the community, responding to the different intensities of preference, deciding whether democracy requires social and economic as well as political equality, and so on, that we considered in the previous chapter.

to enforce the laws, and confirmed or voided specific applications of the laws made by those charged with carrying out the *ekklesia's* will between meetings.[2]

But Athens' citizens totaled only 30,000–40,000—a number that could easily be assembled in a public square. Even more important, because the economy of Athens was supported mainly by slaves and resident foreigners, most of the citizens had ample leisure time to attend *ekklesia* meetings and to think about the city-state's political problems in between. The polis (the political community) and its affairs were the most important thing in the lives of most Athenian citizens.

Modern industrial societies are vastly different on both counts. In the United States, for example, there were in 1972 an estimated 139,643,000 people of voting age (unlike the Athenians, of course, we include women). Furthermore, 19 percent of them lived in cities of 1 million or more population, 29 percent in cities of 100,000 or more, and 45 percent in cities of 25,000 or more.[3] It simply is not physically possible to run the government of the United States—or, for that matter, the governments of Switzerland, Illinois, New South Wales, and Los Angeles—as the government of ancient Athens was run.

Size, however, is by no means the only reason why Athenian-style democracy is not feasible in most modern polities. Americans—and the citizens of other modern democracies—do not have slaves as the Athenians did; most voters must spend the bulk of their time and energy making a living. Consequently, whether they live in New York City (population nearly 8 million) or Enosburg Falls, Vermont (population 1321), they do not and cannot make government their sole or even their main preoccupation. The best evidence is the disparity between the shining vision of participatory democracy in the ideal New England town meeting of American legend and the manner in which most New England towns are actually governed today. A recent study of town meetings in Maine reported:

> Town meetings are poorly attended, manipulated by minorities, unrepresentative of the community, and cumbersome to the point of rendering town government unresponsive. There are, of course, towns where the lie is given to this generalization, but they really are the exceptions that prove the rule. The farcical nature of the town meeting is accentuated in the larger towns: those with over 5000 population. A sampling of their town meeting attendance for the past five years revealed that only one attracted as many as 15 per cent of the potential voters. . . .[4]

Much the same can be said for the other storied example of participatory democracy, the Swiss Landsgemeinden, the ruling bodies of a handful of the most rural and thinly populated cantons (local governing units corresponding to the American states). The Landsgemeinde is an assembly of all the canton's citizens. It

[2] For details see Alfred E. Zimmern, *The Greek Commonwealth* (New York: Oxford University Press, 1931); and W. K. Prentice, *The Greek Political Experience* (Princeton, N.J.: Princeton University Press, 1941).

[3] *The American Almanac, 1974* (The Statistical Abstract of the United States, prepared by the Bureau of the Census; New York: Grosset & Dunlap, Inc., 1974), p. 23, Table 23.

[4] James Wilson and Robert W. Crowe, *Managers in Maine* (Bureau for Research in Municipal Government No. 24; Brunswick, Me.: Bowdoin College, n.d.), p. 10.

The nearest thing to ancient Athens? A Landsgemeinde meeting, Canton of Glarus, Switzerland. Source: Wide World Photos.

meets once a year, makes or alters the canton's laws, and selects the cantonal officials and representatives to the national Ständerat (upper house). Observers report that cantonal meetings are usually well attended and that the members exercise their legislative and supervisory authority conscientiously. Their main function, however, is to choose the persons who will administer the canton's affairs until the next annual meeting. Though the Landsgemeinden are perhaps nearer to the Athenian model than are most New England town meetings, they certainly are not models of continuous participatory democracy.[5]

Modern political systems, then, are not and cannot be governed by institutions like those of ancient Athens—though some advocates of "participatory democracy" would like to go as far as possible in this direction by maximizing the number of semiautonomous neighborhood governments, worker-controlled industries, and the

Theory and Practice of
Political Representation

[5] See the description in Georges Jean Sauser-Hall, *The Political Institutions of Switzerland* (Zurich: Swiss National Tourist Office, 1946).

like.[6] Most political scientists, however, believe that the best course is to retain the nation-state as the basic political unit and try to make its governing institutions more like those of the Athenian model even though they can never match it completely. They believe that the main device for this purpose is political representation, and that representative institutions, properly understood and properly organized, can provide most of the essentials of direct democracy.

In this chapter we shall explore the general nature of political representation, survey the leading theories about its proper organization, and review the organization and problems of existing representative systems in modern democratic nations.

## THE NATURE OF POLITICAL REPRESENTATION

### REPRESENTATION IN GENERAL

In its most general and commonly used sense, "representation" means "re-presentation," that is, "a making present of something absent—but not making it literally present. It must be made present indirectly, through an intermediary; it must be made present in some sense, while nevertheless remaining literally absent."[7]

It is difficult to imagine how we could live our lives without frequent use of some form of representation. We hand a television dealer a mere piece of paper known as a "check," and in return he gives us a twenty-four-inch electronic miracle of home entertainment. Schoolteachers across our land daily lead their pupils in a ceremony in which they pledge allegiance to a piece of cloth called a "flag." Some of us go to church and eat wafers of bread and sip glasses of wine, as our ministers tell us that we are consuming the body and blood of Jesus Christ. The very language that we use consists of "words"—configurations of scratchings on paper or vibrations in the air—to represent objects, persons, and ideas. Representation, in its many forms, is one of the most widely used instruments of human living.

### CONCEPTIONS OF POLITICAL REPRESENTATION[8]

Students of government are, of course, interested mainly in *political* representation— the processes by which members of a community can be "made present" in the

---

[6] See, for example, Carole Pateman, *Participation and Democratic Theory* (New York: Cambridge University Press, 1970); Peter Bachrach, *The Theory of Democratic Elitism* (Boston: Little, Brown & Company, 1967); and Milton Kotler, *Neighborhood Government* (Indianapolis, Ind.: The Bobbs-Merrill Company, Inc., 1969).

[7] Hanna Fenichel Pitkin, "The Concept of Representation," in Pitkin (ed.), *Representation* (New York: Atherton Press, 1969), p. 16.

[8] In this discussion I lean heavily on the analysis by Pitkin, "Introduction," in Pitkin, *Representation*, 1969, pp. 1–23. For other surveys, see Pitkin, *The Concept of Representation* (Berkeley, Calif.: University of California Press, 1966); J. Roland Pennock and John W. Chapman (eds.), *Representation* (New York: Atherton Press, 1968), especially chaps. 1–3; Robert G. Dixon, Jr., *Democratic Representation* (New York: Oxford University Press, 1968), chaps. 1–3; and Alfred de Grazia, *Public and Republic* (New York: Alfred A. Knopf, 1951).

decision-making processes of government without literally being there. For centuries many of the greatest Western minds have considered how political representation should be understood and what institutions and attitudes it requires. But agreement on these matters seems as far away today as it did in the seventeenth century. Perhaps the best we can do at this point is to review principal current conceptions of "true" representation. For they provide, whether explicitly or implicitly, the foundations for most of the past and present disputes about how public officials should be selected and should function.

### As Authorization

Thomas Hobbes (1588–1679) and his modern disciples have argued that a representative is one *authorized* by his constituents to act in their names. His action is considered the moral and legal equivalent of action by them, and they must bear the consequences exactly as if they themselves had acted. Accordingly, representativeness depends, not upon *what* the representative does, but upon whether or not he has been duly authorized to take action.

### As Responsibility

Some theorists insist that the crucial point is not how the representative gains his authority but whether or not and how it can be terminated by his constituents. To them a representative is one who is *responsible* to his constituents: his representativeness depends again not upon *what* he does but upon whether or not he can be effectively stripped of his power by his constituents if they do not like what he has done with it.

### As Correspondence

Other theorists argue that representation consists essentially of descriptive likeness between representatives and their constituents. According to this view, a legislature's representativeness depends, still not upon *what* it does, but upon the distribution of characteristics among representatives in the same proportions in which they are distributed among constituents. If, for example, 52 percent of the constituents are women, 11 percent black, and 32 percent Roman Catholic, then the legislature's members should be about 52 percent female, 11 percent black, and 32 percent Roman Catholic. (It is not clear whether or not a constituency of which 10 percent consists of morons must have representatives of whom 10 percent are also morons—although Senator Roman Hruska [Republican, Nebraska] did argue in 1970 that, because the United States has a lot of mediocre people among its citizens, they are entitled to representation by at least one mediocre judge on the United States Supreme Court.) This, of course, was the principle underlying the famous "quotas" imposed by the Democratic party in 1969–1972 requiring that the national convention's delegates should include women, young people, and members of minority groups "in reason-

Theory and Practice of
Political Representation

Representation as corre-
spondence: differences
between the 1968 and
1972 Illinois delegations
to the Democratic
National Convention:
(top) in 1968 Mayor
Richard Daley (upper
right), flanked by white
male delegates in suits
and ties, heckles Sen.
Abraham Ribicoff on
rostrum; (bottom) in
1972 there were more
blacks and youths,
including (front row)
Maureen Brenner, Rev.
Hosea Williams, and
Rev. Jesse Jackson, all
dressed informally.
Source: UPI Photograph.

Governmental Structures

able relationship to their presence in the population." The quotas were dropped in 1974.[9]

## As Symbolization

Some theorists believe that the representative should above all personify and symbolize his constituents' notions of what a public official should be. His representativeness depends, not on what he *does*, but on what he *is*. In this view, Dwight D. Eisenhower was a truly representative American president, not because Americans liked his Middle East policy or his opposition to farm price supports, but because they "liked Ike"—that is, they felt that he was a good man who looked and acted as the President should. By the same token, Charles de Gaulle was a truly representative French president, not because Frenchmen applauded his pulling France out of the North Atlantic Treaty Organization (NATO) or his insistence upon an independent nuclear *force de frappe*, but because he embodied for them the great France of Jeanne d'Arc and Henri IV, rather than the feeble, squabbling France of the Third and Fourth Republics.[10]

Whether or not symbolic representation is the essence of true representation, most students of dictatorship believe that it is an important element in the strength of successful dictators. To many Italians for many years, for example, the very person of Benito Mussolini personified their vision of themselves as stern, aggressive, martial Romans rather than as lazy, ineffectual, pasta-devouring *paisani*. To many Germans for many years Adolf Hitler personified the idea of the *Herrenvolk*—a German people destined to establish the dominance of "Aryan" civilization over all mankind. Much of Latin American politics is dominated by *personalismo*—the devotion of segments of the population to this or that *caudillo*, less because of his policies than because of the kind of man that he appears to be.

## As Action

Finally, some theorists hold, contrary to all the preceding conceptions, that the essence of representation lies in how the representative *acts*. Some argue that the true representative should act in the best interests of his constituents, whether or not his ideas of what is good for them agree with their own. Others insist that the true representative should act as his constituents want him to act—as, indeed, they would act themselves if they could be present. I shall have more to say about this dispute in a moment, but the point here is that both sides agree that representation is essentially a matter of what public officials *do*, rather than of how they are authorized,

---

[9] Cf. Austin Ranney, *Curing the Mischiefs of Faction: Party Reform in America* (Berkeley, Calif.: University of California Press, 1974). For an illuminating account of how the quota system made the 1972 Democratic national convention very representative in some ways and very *un*representative in others, see Jeane J. Kirkpatrick, "Representation in National Political Conventions: The Case of 1972," a paper presented at the 1974 annual meeting of the American Political Science Association.

[10] See Philip E. Converse and Georges Dupeux, "Eisenhower et de Gaulle: Les généraux devant l'opinion," *Revue française de science politique,* 12 (March 1962), 54–92.

held responsible, resemble their constituents, or personify their constituents' visions of great leaders.

These five conceptions are not mutually exclusive, and many people include two or more in various kinds of conceptual "mixes." As we noted earlier, the different mixes underlie and inform the various positions in past and present disputes over how representative systems should be organized. Let us see how.

## PROPER ORGANIZATION OF REPRESENTATIVE SYSTEMS

For many centuries most people in most societies have agreed that some kind of representation is a necessary and significant part of any satisfactory governmental structure. They have widely disagreed, however, over just what kind of representative system is best. The proper organization of representation has, indeed, been one of the most disputed issues in political literature since the early Middle Ages. The main issues in this persistent debate may be summarized here.

### WHAT SHOULD BE REPRESENTED

*Interests*

In most Western nations during most of the Middle Ages the dominant idea was that the great "estates" of the realm should be represented in the assemblies advising the king (the English Parliament, the French États-Généraux, and the Spanish Cortes, for example). In modern terminology, the estates were the great interests of the realm. They included the church, the feudal nobility, and the commons (the counties and towns); their spokesmen were, respectively, the "lords spiritual" (the top levels of the church hierarchy—cardinals, archbishops, and bishops), the "lords temporal" (the top levels of the nobility—dukes, earls, counts, barons, and so on), and the knights and burgesses of the counties and towns. Each estate was viewed not as a collection of individual human beings but, again in modern terminology, as an "interest."

All the lords spiritual and lords temporal were qualified to attend meetings of the assemblies, but the knights and burgesses of the House of Commons or the Third Estate were a different matter. Because the interests that they represented were those of certain *places*, the knights of the shires (counties) and the burgesses of the boroughs (towns) selected particular men from their areas to go to assembly and speak for them.[11]

There are several present-day versions of this medieval idea. Most familiar to Americans is the organization of the United States Senate and formerly the upper houses of many state legislatures to represent certain government units (states, counties, townships) equally, regardless of the differences in population. A similar principle operates in the organization of such other legislative bodies as the Australian

---

[11] See Maude V. Clarke, *Medieval Representation and Consent* (London: Longmans, Green & Co., Ltd., 1936).

Senate and the Swiss Ständerat; in a somewhat diluted form it also operates in the Canadian Senate and the West German Bundesrat.

Several recent social theorists have advocated another modernization of the medieval ideal, in a form generally called "functional representation." They argue that the significant units of the modern community are not its individual citizens but rather the basic interests, or "functions," of its citizens. The representative system should therefore be organized to represent them directly and efficiently rather than as at present. One version of the functional-representation doctrine was set forth in the early 1920s by the British political theorist G. D. H. Cole (who subsequently abandoned it). Briefly summarized, Cole's argument ran as follows: How can a legislator who is himself, say, a lawyer, a Roman Catholic, a veteran, and a white man possibly represent those of his constituents who are businessmen, workers, Protestants, Jews, nonveterans, blacks, and so on? Cole's answer, of course, was that he cannot and that such constituents simply go unrepresented. He concluded:

> The essentials of democratic representation . . . are, first, that the represented shall have free choice of, constant contacts with, and considerable control over, his representative. The second is that he should be called upon, not to choose someone to represent him as a man or as a citizen in all the aspects of citizenship, but only to choose someone to represent his point of view in relation to some particular purpose or group of purposes, in other words, some particular *function*. All true and democratic representation is therefore *functional* representation.[12]

Another version of this position was set forth in 1931 by Pope Pius XI in his encyclical *Quadrigesimo anno*. A basic object of representation, he declared, should be to "abolish conflict between classes with divergent interests, and thus foster and promote harmony between the various ranks of society." Instead of the present division between labor and capital, which cuts across industrial and functional lines, there should be a combination of workers and employers within each industry to promote the welfare of the whole industry and all persons engaged in it.[13] One version of the Pope's ideas later appeared in the "corporative" representative bodies of Italy and Portugal, which will be described later.

Several democratic nations have established certain advisory bodies directly representing various functional groups. Only one democratic nation, however, has incorporated this principle in the organization of its legislative assembly. The Constitution of Ireland provides that the upper house of the parliament, the Seanad, will represent certain interests, rather than individual persons. Of its sixty members, eleven are named by the prime minister and six by the nation's universities; the remainder are elected by the lower house from panels of candidates representing literature, art, and education; agriculture and fisheries; labor; industry and commerce; and public administration and social services. From 1922 to 1936 the Seanad possessed the power to delay bills passed by the lower house, but Prime Minister Eamon

---

[12] G. D. H. Cole, *Guild Socialism Re-stated* (Philadelphia: J. B. Lippincott Company, 1920), pp. 32–33. For a more recent statement of this position, see Fritz Nova, *Functional Representation* (Dubuque, Ia.: William C. Brown Company, Publishers, 1950).

[13] See John H. Hallowell, *Main Currents in Modern Political Thought* (New York: Holt, Rinehart and Winston, Inc., 1950), pp. 681–684.

de Valera and his supporters insisted that it is unreasonable to give to a body not directly responsible to the voters the power to upset the programs of a legislative body and executive that are responsible. In 1936, accordingly, the Constitution was amended to deprive the Seanad of all power to veto or delay bills passed by the lower house. Since then the Irish Seanad, though still nominally a legislative house, has become, in fact, no more than an advisory body.[14]

Two authoritarian nations have introduced the principle of functional representation in their legislative bodies and have thus established "corporate states." In 1926 the fascist regime of Mussolini established twenty-two "corporations," each representing a particular industry, like glass and ceramics, textiles, and water, gas, and electricity. Each corporation was composed of delegates from the official employers' and employees' organizations for its industry, delegates from the Fascist party, and a few technical experts. Each corporation was supposed to plan all production for its industry in order to promote the common interests of its owners, workers, and consumers. In 1930 the national council of corporations was created to supervise these activities. In 1939 Mussolini abolished the chamber of deputies, the lower house of parliament, which had been organized along traditional democratic lines, and replaced it with the chamber of fasces and corporations. The new legislative house was composed of delegates from the top echelons of the Fascist party and the national council of corporations; the reconstituted parliament thus had no members whatever directly elected by the citizenry.[15] From the democratic point of view, however, this change made little difference. The old chamber of deputies had been little more than a claque for the orations of the Duce, and the new chamber of fasces and corporations served the same purpose. The post-Mussolini regime abolished the corporate state (and, for that matter, the Duce himself) and restored the chamber of deputies in its traditional democratic form.

The other corporate state was Portugal from 1935 to 1974. The Constitution of 1935, written under the direction of that nation's long-time dictator, Antonio de Oliveira Salazar, established a parliament consisting of a national assembly, based on traditional democratic forms (if not realities—it was a one-party dictatorship), and a corporative chamber composed of representatives of such groups as local governing units and industrial, agricultural, commercial, financial, cultural, and religious organizations. Neither body could override any policy decision made by the dictator, but the corporative chamber was supposed to advise both the dictator and the national assembly on bills under consideration. Salazar formally proclaimed his "Decalogue of Principles for the New State," in the course of which he expounded the ideas underlying the Portuguese system of representation:

> The welfare of the collectivity transcends—and includes—the welfare of the individual. In the New State the individual exists socially, as member of a group, which may be natural, as the family; or professional, as the corporation; or

---

[14] The fullest account of the nature and problems of the Irish Senate is Donal O'Sullivan, *The Irish Free State and Its Senate* (London: Faber & Faber, Ltd., 1940).

[15] The best description of the organization of the Italian corporate state is G. Lowell Field, *The Syndical and Corporative Institutions of Italian Fascism* (New York: Columbia University Press, 1938).

territorial, as the municipal council—and it is in this social quality that all his necessary rights are recognized. . . . The nation is represented not by artificial groups or ephemeral parties but by real and permanent elements in national life.[16]

## People

In Chapters 10 and 15 we note that most modern democratic governments provide for at least indirect representation of interests, through either the formal establishment of advisory councils or the informal operations of pressure groups. But (with the exception of the upper houses in the federal legislatures already mentioned) official lawmaking representative bodies are based on a theory of representation going back at least to England's Civil War in the mid-seventeenth century. This theory, which some have called "liberal" and others "democratic," was succinctly stated by Chief Justice Earl Warren when the United States Supreme Court ordered that both houses of all state legislatures be apportioned according to the principle of "one man, one vote": "Legislators represent people, not trees or acres. Legislators are elected by voters, not farms or cities or economic interests."[17] The basic political units of the community are its individual citizens; each should be represented equally with every other, and the sine qua non of democratic government is its representatives' responsiveness to the wishes of the people. Representation must thus be organized according to the principles of popular sovereignty, political equality, popular consultation, and majority rule (see Chap. 13).

But how? That is the second great issue involved in organizing representation.

## HOW PEOPLE SHOULD BE REPRESENTED

### Fascist and Communist Theories

Representation, according to the fascist, and especially the Nazi, political theorists of the 1920s and 1930s, is no more than the process by which the leader whips the masses into line behind the policies that he knows are in the national interest. The democratic idea that representation requires consultation with the masses about their policy preferences is ridiculous. For, as Hitler himself pointed out, "the political understanding of the great masses is not sufficiently developed for them to arrive at certain general political opinions by themselves and to select suitable persons." One of his leading disciples, Alfred Rosenberg, added:

> [The masses are] the instrument on which the political leader must play. Insofar as he gets the right notes out of that instrument—that is, has the confi-

---

[16] Quoted in S. George West, *The New Corporative State of Portugal* (London: The New Temple Press, 1937), pp. 13–14. Portugal's corporate-state institutions were abolished by the liberal revolution of 1974.

[17] Reynolds v. Sims. 377 U.S. 533 (1964).

Theory and Practice of Political Representation

dence of the people in his leadership—he gets therewith the indispensable basis for the activity of his political leadership. *But a people can never lead itself.*[18]

The communist theory of representation is almost identical with the fascist theory. The communists regard the party as representative of the proletarian masses in the sense that it works only for the masses' welfare and knows far better than the masses themselves what policies are best for them. Representation therefore involves no procedures by which the masses can replace the members of the ruling elite or directly control it in any other way. Quite the contrary; according to communist theorists, if the masses were armed with such powers, they would probably use them to put in the saddle an elite that would exploit the proletariat. To communists, as well as to Nazis and other fascists, a representative system should consist of devices by which the masses are "educated" and their enthusiasm mobilized for policies made and enforced by the ruling elite. The "elections" and "plebiscites" held in such nations (see Chap. 7) bear only the most superficial resemblance to elections and referenda in the democratic nations of the West.

### Direct Representation

Most democrats hold that representation must be direct: That is, each citizen must have the power to elect one or more representatives, those representatives must hold office for only limited terms, and at the end of their terms the voters must be able to deny them reelection. In this way each representative's responsibility to his constituents will be direct, rather than "virtual," and the citizens will not depend upon the representative's sense of noblesse oblige to help keep the assembly responsive to the community's desires.

## HOW REPRESENTATIVES SHOULD BE SELECTED

Most democrats agree upon at least two basic principles of representation: The represented should be people, rather than areas or interests, and people should be represented directly, rather than through the superior wisdom of a ruling elite. But the theorists are divided on the other great issues. One of the most problematic is the selection of representatives. As we noted in Chapter 7, some democrats prefer some form of the "single-member district," or majority, system, whereas others argue that only some form of proportional representation can do the job. This disagreement arises partly from the fact that the former conceptualize representation mainly as a matter of what representatives do, whereas the latter think of it as mainly the correspondence of representatives to constituents—if not in social characteristics, then certainly in the proportions committed to the community's principal ideologies.

## HOW REPRESENTATIVES SHOULD BE APPORTIONED

We noted in Chapter 7 that every modern democratic nation except Israel is divided

---

[18] Both statements are quoted in René de Visme Williamson, "The Fascist Concept of Representation," *Journal of Politics,* 3 (February 1941), 29–41; italics in the original.

into a number of geographical subdivisions known as "districts" or "constituencies," each of which elects one or more members of the national legislative assembly. Apportionment is the process of drawing the constituencies' boundaries and thus allocating representatives and political power among the nation's regions and interest groups. The problem of achieving fair apportionment is most vexing in nations that use single-member districts, but it is present even in those that rely on proportional representation.

**Malapportionment of legislatures denies political equality.** Source: *Straight Herblock* (New York: Simon and Schuster, Inc., 1964).

*"You can't say we're denying your right to vote"*

Fair apportionment is difficult, especially among single-member districts, because a number of competing principles have legitimate claims and it is impossible to satisfy them all. The most obvious and in a sense the most basic is the principle of "one man, one vote," which, in apportionment terms, means the principle of *equal electorates.* It requires that each constituency have the same number of citizens as has every other. Any deviation from this standard means a violation of the basic democratic principle of political equality (see Chap. 13): if district A has a population of 500,000 and district B one of only 250,000, then each resident of B has twice as large a share of the nation's lawmaking power as has any resident of A. In the "reapportionment revolution" that it has wrought since 1962, the United States Supreme Court has held that the principle of equal electorates must be the primary rule

Theory and Practice of Political Representation

governing the apportionment of both houses of all state legislatures[19] and the United States House of Representatives.[20] Even minor deviations are constitutionally permissible only when "based on legitimate considerations incident to the effectuation of a rational state policy."[21]

What might qualify as "legitimate considerations"? The Court has yet to say, but in most modern democracies they include at least three. First, coincidence with local government boundaries is much cheaper and easier in terms of administration by local government authorities; it is therefore desirable to make the boundaries of national constituencies coincide with local ones wherever possible. Congressional districts and parliamentary constituencies are usually formed by combining counties or metropolitan wards, rather than by creating entirely new subdivisions without regard to existing local government boundaries. Second, because the new boundaries are drawn up by incumbent legislators, they are usually drawn to minimize the number of their fellows whose districts will be radically changed. Third, no matter how equal the districts' populations may be, it is always possible for the dominant political party to draw their boundaries in order to make the most effective use of its own votes and to waste those of the opposition. The basic technique is to concentrate large blocs of opposition voters in a few districts and distribute large blocs of favorable voters more broadly. Successful "gerrymandering" results in perhaps two opposition candidates regularly elected by margins of ten to one along with five of the dominant party's own candidates regularly elected by margins of three to two. The most faithful application of the other principles will not prevent gerrymandering; the main safeguards against it are the dominant party's sense that it had better show some restraint lest the opposition take revenge at some future date and, above all, the voters' insistence that apportionment not be used to give one party an unfair advantage over the other.[22]

The power to make and unmake apportionment rules and to draw constituency lines is therefore of considerable importance in any democratic government. In the United States the Constitution stipulates that each state, regardless of population, shall have two members of the Senate but leaves it up to Congress to allocate seats in the House of Representatives. Under the present law, after each national census (taken every decade beginning in 1790) Congress determines how many representatives each state will have but allows each state's legislature to draw the boundaries for its own congressional districts. Because the state legislatures also determine their own districts, collectively they play the key role in the nation's apportionment initiatives. But since *Baker* v. *Carr* (1962) the Federal and state courts have kept such a close watch on the legislatures' apportionment activities that the latter no longer enjoy the monopoly they held for so many years.

In Great Britain, Parliament has established four nonpartisan boundary commissions (one each for England, Scotland, Wales, and Northern Ireland) to review

---

[19] Baker v. Carr, 369 U.S. 186 (1962); and Reynolds v. Sims, 377 U.S. 533 (1964).

[20] Wesberry v. Sanders, 376 U.S. 1 (1964).

[21] Reynolds v. Sims, 377 U.S. 533 (1964).

[22] The most complete study of apportionment problems and rules in the United States is Dixon, *Democratic Representation.*

**Reapportionment and partisanship.** Source: Reprinted by permission of *The Milwaukee Journal.*

*"Well, I think mine is a reasonable redistricting plan for Wisconsin!"*

constituency boundaries every ten to fifteen years and to recommend revisions. The commissions' recommendations are accepted and sometimes revised by the ruling political party and enacted by Parliament.[23] The most recent "redistribution" increased the total number of constituencies from 630 to 635 and went into effect for the general election of February, 1974.

In France *découpage* (districting) usually results from an ad hoc agreement between the minister of the interior and the prefect of each *département*; partisan considerations—for example, minimizing the number of Communist deputies elected—have played an important role. In both Switzerland (1962) and West Germany (1963) national supreme courts have voided as unconstitutional apportionments that have strayed too far from the principle of equal electorates. And in all democratic nations

[23] The authoritative account is D. E. Butler, *The Electoral System in Britain since 1918* (2d ed.; New York: Oxford University Press, 1963).

apportionment controversies, though perhaps not as dramatic as that in the United States during the 1960s, are nevertheless endemic—and for good reasons.[24]

## THE PROPER RELATION BETWEEN REPRESENTATIVE AND CONSTITUENTS

The oldest and most debated issue among democrats involves the proper relation between representatives and their constituents. Two distinct positions on this issue were fully stated in the late eighteenth century, and most subsequent expositions have been restatements of these originals.

### The Mandate Theory

Some theorists, like John Lilburne and Jean Jacques Rousseau, have argued that the proper function of the representative assembly in a democracy is not to initiate policy but only to register the dominant policy preferences of its constituents. They start from the premise that the ideal method of popular consultation is face-to-face assembly of all community members. As this method is impossible in a large and thickly populated nation, the next best alternative is for members of the community to express their will through representatives. As long as the representative assembly confines itself to registering its constituents' views, representation involves no significant departure from democracy. But when the assembly begins to make policy on its own in either ignorance or defiance of its constituents' desires, it becomes a kind of oligarchy. As William Paterson put it during the American Constitutional Convention of 1787, "What is the principle of representation? It is an expedient by which an assembly of certain individuals chosen by the people is substituted in place of the inconvenient meetings of the people themselves."[25]

A logical corollary of Paterson's idea is the argument that the representative may rightfully act only on the basis of a *mandate* from his constituents to present their views in the representative assembly. If they wish him to support a proposal that he believes is wrong, he must either swallow his objections and vote as they wish or resign in favor of a representative who will. Under no circumstances should a representative vote contrary to his mandate, according to this view. If he does not know his constituents' desires on an issue, he should go home and find out before he votes.

### The Independence Theory

In 1714 a British member of Parliament, Antony Henry, received a communication from his constituents asking him to vote against the budget of that year. He is reputed to have replied:

---

[24] See Vivian Vale, "*Reynolds v. Sims* Abroad: A Briton Compares Apportionment Criteria," *Western Political Quarterly,* 22 (March 1969), 85–93.

[25] Quoted in Max Farrand, *Records of the Federal Convention of 1787*, Vol. 1 (New Haven, Conn.: Yale University Press, 1937), p. 561.

*Gentlemen:* I have received your letter about the excise, and I am surprised at your insolence in writing to me at all.

You know, and I know, that I bought this constituency. You know, and I know, that I am now determined to sell it, and you know what you think I don't know that you are now looking out for another buyer, and I know, what you certainly don't know, that I have now found another constituency to buy.

About what you said about the excise: may God's curse light upon you all, and may it make your homes as open and as free to the excise officers as your wives and daughters have always been to me while I have represented your rascally constituency.[26]

Certainly no one could accuse Mr. Henry of undue pandering to his constituents, but most advocates of the independence theory of representation have chosen somewhat softer words. They have argued that the kind of representative system advocated by Rousseau and Paterson is neither possible nor desirable in a modern nation. The problems of modern government are so complex and difficult that they can be understood and dealt with intelligently only by people who make them a full-time job. Constituents must necessarily spend most of their time and energy on earning a living and cannot possibly acquire the necessary information and understanding as effectively as can their representatives. The representative assembly must therefore initiate—and not merely register—policy if the nation is to avoid disaster. This approach need not convert democracy into a kind of legislative oligarchy, for the power to decide who will sit in the legislature is still the basic power to rule and that power is retained by the constituents.

A logical corollary of this position is the proposition that the representative should exercise his judgment on public affairs independently, without regard to what his constituents think. If at the end of his term they think that he has used his power badly, they can refuse to reelect him. But while he is in office his views, rather than theirs, should determine his votes.

The best-known exposition of the independence theory is that of Edmund Burke in 1774, the year that he was elected to the House of Commons from the city of Bristol; he immediately wrote and circulated a pamphlet in which he told his constituents what they should and should not expect from him as their representative. The essence of his position is presented in the following quotation.

[The constituents'] wishes ought to have great weight with [the representative]; their opinions high respect; their business unremitted attention. . . . But his unbiased opinion, his mature judgment, his enlightened conscience, he ought not to sacrifice to you, to any man, or to any set of men living. . . . If government were a matter of will upon any side, yours, without question, ought to be superior. But government and legislation are matters of reason and judgment, and not of inclination; and what sort of reason is that in which the determination precedes the discussion, in which one set of men deliberate and another decide, and where those who form the conclusions are perhaps three hundred miles distant from those who hear the arguments? . . . Parliament is not a *congress* of ambassadors

[26] Quoted in Peter G. Richards, *Honourable Members* (London: Faber & Faber, Ltd., 1959), p. 157.

from different and hostile interests, which interests each must maintain, as an agent and advocate, against other agents and advocates; but parliament is a *deliberative* assembly of *one* nation, with *one* interest, that of the whole—where, not local purposes, not local prejudices, ought to guide, but the general good, resulting from the general reason of the whole.[27]

As Hanna Pitkin has perceptively pointed out, the long-standing dispute between adherents of the mandate and independence theories arises from their quite different conceptions of true representation. The former say that government in which representatives can consistently do the opposite of what their constituents want is simply not representative. The independence proponents reply that representatives who never act on their own and serve merely as conduits for constituents' preferences are not representing. It it hard to disagree with Pitkin's comment:

> Confronted by two such arguments, one wants to say that both are somehow right. The man is not a representative if his actions bear no relationship to anything about his constituents, and he is not representative if he does not act at all. Of course, in either case he may still be formally the representative of a certain group, but the substance is missing.[28]

She concludes that we should not view representation as a single precise standard that, if rightly understood, will settle the controversy over mandate and independence once and for all. We should view it rather as a set of limits "beyond which we will no longer accept what is going on as an instance of representation." Complete independence, whatever its desirability may be on other grounds, certainly is inconsistent with our conception of democracy, which requires government *response* to citizens' desires. On the other hand, complete mandating is simply not possible, because on many issues that come before representatives their constituents have no clear or strong views at all and the representatives have no effective way of finding out such views. We should therefore be willing to accept as legitimate representation many degrees of independence from and deference to constituents within these outer limits.

This position appears to be the one that most representatives in modern democratic systems live by, regardless of what they say to their constituents and their colleagues. We shall examine the evidence for this statement in Chapter 15.

## DEMOCRATIC ORGANIZATION OF REPRESENTATION

As we have seen, by no means all democrats agree on what kind of representative system is best for democracy. It is not surprising, therefore, that no democratic system is organized in strict accordance with any of the principles just outlined. The representative systems of most democratic nations, indeed, are based upon combinations of several principles, some of which are logically inconsistent with one another.

---

[27] Edmund Burke "Address to the Electors of Bristol, November 3, 1774," in Burke, *Works*, Vol. 2 (Boston: Little, Brown & Company, 1871), pp. 95–96; italics in the original.

[28] Pitkin, "The Concept of Representation," p. 19.

## TABLE 18
## Selection of Representatives in Democratic Systems

| Nation | Legislators | | | | Chief of State | | | Head of Government | |
|---|---|---|---|---|---|---|---|---|---|
| | All Directly Elected | Some Indirectly Selected | Plurality System | PR[a] | Directly Elected | Elected by Legislature | Hereditary or Appointed | Directly Elected | Confidence of Legislature |
| Argentina | X | | | X | X | | | X | |
| Australia | X | | | X | | | X | | X |
| Austria | | X | | X | | X | | | X |
| Belgium | | X | | X | | | X | | X |
| Canada | | X | X | | | | X | | X |
| Colombia | X | | | X | X | | | X | |
| Costa Rica | X | | X | | X | | | X | |
| Denmark | | X | | X | | | X | | X |
| Finland | X | | | X | b | | | c | a |
| France | | X | X | | X | | | c | |
| Iceland | X | | | X | X | | | | X |
| India | | X | X | | d | | | | X |
| Ireland | | X | | X | X | | | | X |
| Israel | X | | | X | X | | | | X |
| Italy | | X | | X | X | | | | X |
| Jamaica | | X | X | | | | X | | X |
| Japan | X | | X | | | | X | | X |
| Lebanon | X | | | X | | X | | | X |
| Liechtenstein | X | | | X | | | X | | X |
| Luxembourg | X | | | X | | | X | | X |
| Malta | X | | X | | | | X | | X |
| Mexico | X | | X | | X | | | X | |
| Netherlands | | X | | X | | | X | | X |
| New Zealand | | X | X | | | | X | | X |
| Norway | X | | | X | | | X | | X |
| Panama | X | | | X | X | | | X | |
| San Marino | X | | | X | | X | | | X |
| Sri Lanka (Ceylon) | | X | X | | | | X | | X |
| Sweden | | X | | X | | | X | | X |
| Switzerland | | X | | X | f | | | | f |
| Trinidad and Tobago | | X | X | | | | X | | X |
| Turkey | | X | X | | X | | | X | |
| United Kingdom | | X | X | | | | X | | X |
| United States | X | | X | | X | | | g | |
| Uruguay | X | | | | X | | | X | |
| Venezuela | | X | | X | X | | | X | |
| West Germany | | X | X | X | | X | | | X |

a Proportional representation.

b In Finland the chief of state is the President of the Republic, who is indirectly elected by an electoral college. He has a number of independent powers and shares with the prime minister the job of heading the government.

c Under the Constitution of the Fifth Republic (1958) the French chief of state is the President of the Republic, who is directly elected by popular vote; for discussion of his unique position, see Chap. 16.

d The President of India, indirectly elected by an electoral college (members of the national legislature and the state legislatures), has no power as head of government.

e The Netherlands does not permit ministers to be members of the legislature; the prime minister is thus not in quite the same position as are his counterparts in the orthodox parliamentary democracies.

f In Switzerland the chief of state is the President of the Swiss confederation, a title automatically conferred upon the chairman of the federal council. This seven-person body is elected by the legislature for four-year terms, and the chairmanship rotates in order of seniority once each year. This body is also the "head of government," and Switzerland thus has a plural political executive.

g The President of the United States, who is both chief of state and head of government, is formally elected by an electoral college but actually elected by popular votes.

In Table 18 the methods used to select the main representative officials of the modern democratic societies are set forth.

## LEGISLATORS

### Selection

In every modern democratic system all members of at least one house of the national legislature are directly elected by popular vote. In some democratic countries, as Table 18 reveals, some legislators are selected by other means. All members of the Canadian Senate, for example, are appointed for life by the governor-general on the advice of the prime minister. Some members of the Indian council of states are appointed by the President, and the others are elected by the legislatures of the various states. All members of the Swedish upper house are selected by special electoral colleges. Most legislative bodies of this type (see Chap. 15) have little or no real power, and in all the democratic polities real lawmaking powers rest formally in bodies whose members are directly elected by the voters.

### Representation of Local Governing Units

In some democratic nations one national legislative house is intended to represent certain units of local government rather than the people directly. All the federal democratic systems, for example, constitute the upper houses of their national legislatures in this manner. The United States Senate has two members from each state, the Australian Senate ten from each state, and the Swiss council of states two from each canton and one from each half-canton. The Canadian Senate's structure somewhat reflects population differentials among the provinces (Quebec and Ontario have each twenty-four senators, and no other province has more than six). The West German Bundesrat is organized similarly, although the members of both bodies are nevertheless intended to represent the provinces and *Länder* as such, rather than individuals. Even some of the unitary democracies represent local governing units in one house each of their national legislatures. In Burma and the Netherlands, for example, the provinces derive all their formal power by grant from the national governments, yet the upper houses of the legislatures of both nations are composed of equal numbers of representatives from each province.

### Average Size of Constituencies

Most advocates of direct popular representation believe that the total number of constituents in each representative district should be kept as small as possible so that the representatives can maintain personal contacts with their constituents. This consideration seems of special importance in nations using single-member districts, for each constituency has only one representative to speak for it. This ideal is also common, however, among advocates of multiple-member districts and proportional representation.

Governmental Structures

**TABLE 19**

Size of Legislative Bodies and Populations
of Constituencies

| Nation | Size of Legislative Lower House | Average Population per Constituency |
|---|---|---|
| Argentina | 192 | 124,000 |
| Australia | 124 | 105,000 |
| Canada | 265 | 83,200 |
| Costa Rica | 57 | 32,300 |
| France | 487 | 106,600 |
| India | 522 | 1,079,500 |
| New Zealand | 80 | 37,000 |
| Turkey | 450 | 83,300 |
| United Kingdom | 635 | 87,800 |
| United States | 435 | 467,100 |
| West Germany | 248[a] | 248,700 |

[a]The assembly has a total of 499 members, 248 elected from single-member districts and the remainder by proportional representation.

Most modern democratic countries have discovered that the increased sizes of their populations during the past centuries have made the constant enlargement of the memberships of their legislative bodies the price of living up to the ideal of small constituencies. The first American House of Representatives in 1789, for example, had 65 members, 1 for every 30,000 people. The present House has 435 members, 1 for every 464,400 people—if the original ratio had been maintained, the House would now have no fewer than 6773 members! The United States, like most other democratic countries in recent years, has decided that ever-growing legislatures do even more damage to proper democratic representation than do ever-growing constituencies, and it has therefore put a ceiling on the total membership of the House, allowing the districts to continue to grow in size. Table 19 shows the populations of the average constituencies in various modern democratic polities using single-member districts. India and the United States have by far the largest constituencies of any of the modern democratic nations using single-member districts. As they also have by far the largest total populations of any of the nations listed, they can reduce the average size of their constituencies only by greatly enlarging the sizes of their legislatures. Apparently, both nations have decided that holding their constituencies to sizes comparable with those of other democratic countries is not worth the price of legislatures with thousands of members.

The figures in the right-hand column of Table 19 are, of course, only averages. In most of these nations there are considerable variations in constituency populations. In the United States before the post-1964 redistricting, for example, congressional districts ranged in population size all the way from 182,845 (the Second District of South Dakota) to 951,527 (the Fifth District of Texas). Redistricting, however, has recently narrowed these differences considerably: In 1972 the largest district had a population of 467,547 (the Fourth District of Michigan), and the smallest had a population of 410,949 (the Sixth District of South Carolina).[29]

[29] *Congressional Quarterly Weekly Report,* July 8, 1972, pp. 1661–1666.

The United States is by no means the only democratic polity in which wide district disparities have existed. In the 1964 general election constituencies for the British House of Commons ranged from 24,280 (Ross and Cromarty) to 90,996 (Epping).[30] And in Canada before the 1952 redistribution constituencies for the Canadian House of Commons ranged from 21,202 (Brant) to 95,942 (St. James).[31]

In the United States continuing pressure by the Supreme Court and in most other democratic nations the efforts of boundary commissions will minimize the variations in size among legislative constituencies. However, as long as standards other than the principle of equal electorates are also applied in drawing district boundaries, some disparities will be inevitable.

## EXECUTIVES

In most modern democratic nations, then, the directly elected legislative bodies are regarded as the basic elements of the legal representative systems. In addition to such bodies, however, each system also has certain other elements, including executive officials. Every democratic regime (see Chap. 16) has two top executive positions: a chief of state, who acts as the formal apex of the nation's governmental structure and may or may not exercise power over policy making, and a head of government, who directs the people and agencies in command of the actual decision-making apparatus. In each of the presidential democracies like Costa Rica, Venezuela, and the United States both positions are occupied by a president, who is elected, directly or indirectly, by a nationwide constituency. In all other democratic nations these positions are held by different officials selected in different ways. In such "constitutional monarchies" as Australia, Belgium, Sweden, and the United Kingdom the chiefs of state are either hereditary monarchs or officials appointed by such monarchs to act in their behalf. In the "parliamentary republics" like Austria, Ireland, and Italy the legislatures elect presidents who perform approximately the same functions as would constitutional monarchs. In all the democratic systems except the presidential ones, and also in Switzerland (which has a "plural executive"), the heads of government are prime ministers formally appointed by the chiefs of state but actually holding their posts because they have the "approval" of a majority of the directly elected legislators.

## JUDGES

In all the democratic nations except the United States and Switzerland judges are appointed rather than elected and therefore do not *directly* represent the people. In some states of the United States (but not in the national government) and in Swiss cantons judges are directly elected. Whether or not they are as representative as are directly elected legislators and executives is a matter that we shall consider in Chapter 18.

---

[30] R. L. Leonard, *Guide to the General Election* (London: Pan Books, Ltd., 1964), p. 35, Table 4.
[31] Robert M. Dawson, *The Government of Canada* (Toronto: University of Toronto Press, 1947), p. 369.

## APPOINTED ADMINISTRATIVE OFFICIALS

In every democratic polity the great majority of public officials are appointed administrators, who, by definition, do not *directly* represent the people. One of the recurring debates in modern democratic political theory (see Chap. 17) centers on the questions of how representative these administrators should be, in what sense they should be representative, and what institutional arrangements are best calculated to achieve the proper degree of representativeness.

## ADVISORY BODIES FORMALLY REPRESENTING INTEREST GROUPS

Many modern democratic nations have certain formal devices for directly representing interest groups in government policy making. In the United States, for example, the bar associations in some states are directly represented on the bodies that select judicial nominees, the medical associations are directly represented on the bodies that license physicians, and the architectural associations are directly represented on the bodies that license architects. Many administrative agencies maintain advisory boards made up of representatives named by the organized interest groups most directly affected by the particular agencies' activities.[32] In Great Britain representatives of labor, management, and "the public" usually sit on the governing boards of the various nationalized industries.

A few democracies have established more general advisory bodies representing their nations' main economic interests. The best-known example is the French economic and social council, established by the Constitution of 1946. The council is composed of representatives named by national organizations of workers, employers, farmers, civil servants, and various other interest groups. It is empowered to consider bills before the national assembly, either by request or upon its own initiative. It can only make recommendations, however, which the national assembly may or may not heed. The council has no power to veto, amend, or even delay a bill and is therefore purely advisory. It is used mainly as a source of information both on technical matters and on the opinions of the various interest groups; it appears to have negligible influence on policy making in France.[33]

In every modern democratic polity, however, the representation of interest groups is accomplished mainly through the informal and extralegal processes of lobbying, propaganda, demonstrations, and the like. The object of such groups, as we observed in Chapter 10, is to persuade or coerce the formal institutions of government to act, or to refrain from acting, as they wish. This activity may or may not be representation in any of the usual senses, but, as we have seen, it plays a major role in the policy making of every modern nation.

---

[32] The seminal study of direct interest representation in the United States is Avery Leiserson, *Administrative Regulation: A Study in Representation of Interests* (Chicago: University of Chicago Press, 1942).

[33] J. E. S. Hayward, *Private Interests and Public Policy: The Experience of the French Economic and Social Council* (New York: Barnes & Noble, Inc., 1966).

# DIRECT LEGISLATION

## RATIONALE

Some democratic theorists, as we have observed, have always regarded *any* system of representation as a more or less unsatisfactory method of popular consultation. Rousseau, for example, argued that representation in any form inevitably distorts public opinion to some degree, for, when one person's ideas are passed through the mind of a second person and expressed by the latter, they always come out in a form somewhat different from that which went in—an observation with which anyone who has ever read a set of examination papers will heartily agree. For this reason, Rousseau and his followers have argued, we cannot permit representation to be the sole method of finding out what the people want. At the very least we must supplement it with some device that expresses the popular will directly and without "interpretation" by any intervening agency.

Many people believe that the New England town meeting or the Swiss Landsgemeinde is the ideal device for this purpose, and some believe that public opinion polls can do the job. But town-meeting procedures are possible only in small communities, and too many people have too many doubts about polls' ability to measure public opinion accurately. Consequently, most people who have reservations about representation hold that some form of "direct legislation" is a necessary part of the machinery for democratic popular consultation. Few advocates of direct legislation have ever argued that it should replace representative assemblies entirely, but most have proposed it as a necessary supplement for such assemblies, always available to the people whenever the legislatures are not accurately expressing their desires.[34]

## ORGANIZATION

Two main devices are generally classed under the general heading "direct legislation."

### The Initiative

The initiative enables voters to initiate a law or constitutional amendment directly without any action in the legislature. Generally, a group of voters who desire a particular law or constitutional amendment that the legislature is unwilling to pass circulates a petition stating the proposition; when the required number of legitimate signatures (in some instances a flat number, in others a specific percentage of the votes cast at the most recent general election) have been secured, the proposition must be placed on the ballot at the next general election, and if it receives the necessary

---

[34] Most of the literature advocating direct legislation was written in the Progressive Era in the United States from the early 1890s to World War I. Two leading expositions of the position as outlined in this text are Nathan Cree, *Direct Legislation by the People* (Chicago: A. C. McClurg & Company, 1892); and William B. Munro (ed.), *The Initiative, Referendum, and Recall* (New York: Appleton-Century-Crofts, 1912).

majority (in some instances a simple majority, in others a two-thirds majority) it becomes law.

### The Referendum

The referendum permits the voters to approve or disapprove a law or constitutional amendment proposed by the legislature or a constitutional convention. The most common is the compulsory referendum: The proposal is automatically referred to the voters by the initiating body and does not become law until and unless it is approved by the required majority. A few governments also use the optional referendum: The legislature may refer a proposal to the voters if it wishes.

By far the most common form of direct legislation in modern democratic systems is the constitutional referendum. Roughly half the nations listed in Table 18, including Australia, Austria, Denmark, Ireland, and Japan, require popular approval of constitutional amendments proposed by their legislatures or constitutional conventions. A few more require a popular referendum if a proposed amendment is approved by less than a designated proportion (two-thirds or three-fifths) of the legislatures. The national government of the United States has no direct-legislation procedures of any sort, but they are widely used by the states: All but one have the compulsory constitutional referendum, thirteen have the constitutional initiative, twenty-two have the optional legislative referendum, and twenty have the legislative initiative.[35]

The oldest system of direct legislation among modern democracies is that of Switzerland, which used the constitutional referendum as early as 1802. Certain Swiss cantons adopted the constitutional and legislative initiative and referendum in the 1830s, and the national government incorporated the compulsory constitutional referendum in its Constitution in 1891. The Swiss system has long been regarded as the model by advocates of direct legislation, and it remains the most extensive system employed by the national government of any modern democracy.[36]

### RESULTS AND EVALUATION

A political scientist who has both participated in and studied referenda in California has told how they appear to him:

> Entering the polling booth on Tuesday, November 3, 1964, the typical California voter found himself confronted with an immense sheet of finely-printed green paper, a dirty black rubber stamp, a tiny ink pad, and thirty decisions to render. A few minutes later (the legal maximum is 10) he emerged and numbly surrendered to a clerk his ballot, now slightly embellished, like the fingers of his decision hand, with black ink stains.
>
> Most of his decisions were made on a lengthy array of propositions. In these,

---

[35] Clyde F. Snider and Samuel K. Gove, *American State and Local Government* (2d ed.; New York: Appleton-Century-Crofts, 1965), pp. 14, 169, 173.

[36] See Felix Bonjour, *Real Democracy in Operation* (Philadelphia: J. B. Lippincott Company, 1920), pp. 30–39.

questions on an assortment of issues were posed, each couched in language tedious and obscure—as only minds trained in the finest law schools could devise.[37]

This brave researcher has been joined by several others, who have studied the operation of direct legislation in Switzerland, in Germany's Weimar Republic (from 1919 to 1933), and in the American states.[38] They have all made substantially similar empirical observations. For example, initiative and referendum elections usually attract considerably fewer voters than do elections for public officials; occasionally, however, the turnout for a hotly contested election on a highly controversial measure will match that for office elections.[39] How does the minority that votes usually vote? Some people no doubt follow one voter's reported rule: "I always vote no, and I'm usually right!"[40] But most voters decide what consequences they think that the measure will have and how it will affect their own interests and vote accordingly. They thus generally vote down measures to increase taxes or limit public expenditures and generally approve measures authorizing public works and limiting the size of public debts. These preferences may seem logically inconsistent, but apparently to many voters they make good political sense.

Campaigns for and against most measures are conducted mainly by organized interest groups rather than by spontaneous citizens' opinion groups. The evidence suggests that, contrary to a belief cherished by editorial writers, newspaper endorsements have little effect upon the outcomes. Occasionally political parties take strong public stands on particular measures. When they are on the same side, the measure usually passes. When they are on opposite sides, the voters' party identifications usually exert strong but not all-powerful influences on their voting.[41] Similarly,

---

[37] John E. Mueller, "Voting on the Propositions: Ballot Patterns and Historical Trends in California," *American Political Science Review,* 63 (December 1969), 1197–1212.

[38] For the Swiss and Weimar experiences, see George Arthur Codding, Jr., *The Federal Government of Switzerland* (Boston: Houghton Mifflin Company, 1961), pp. 60–67; and Herman Finer, *Theory and Practice of Modern Government* (rev. ed.; New York: Holt, Rinehart and Winston, Inc., 1949), pp. 562–567. For recent studies of American experience, see Mueller, "Voting on the Propositions"; Raymond E. Wolfinger and Fred I. Greenstein, "The Repeal of Fair Housing in California: An Analysis of Referendum Voting," *American Political Science Review,* 62 (September 1968), 753–769; and Norman C. Thomas, "The Electorate and State Constitutional Revision: An Analysis of Four Michigan Referenda," *Midwest Journal of Political Science,* 12 (February 1968), 115–129.

[39] For example, the turnout in recent Swiss referenda has averaged about 50 percent—well below the average in legislative elections. It has ranged from 38 percent to 67 percent—the latter in the 1959 referendum on a proposal to grant voting rights to women (which lost); Codding, *The Federal Government of Switzerland,* p. 65. In the American states turnout in local referenda is often as low as 15 or 20 percent, but in the bitterly contested 1964 California referendum on Proposition 14 (to repeal the state's fair-housing law) 96 percent of those who voted for President also voted in the referendum; see Wolfinger and Greenstein, "The Repeal of Fair Housing in California," p. 753.

[40] Quoted in William Attwood, "Fluoridation: Why All the Controversy?" *Look,* June 24, 1958, p. 23.

[41] This influence was evidently not operating in California's 1964 referendum, in which the Democrats strongly supported the state's open-housing legislation and the Republicans strongly supported its repeal. Although Democrat Lyndon B. Johnson had won 59 percent of the state's

although measures initiated by government agencies by no means win all the time, they do considerably better than do measures proposed by citizens' groups.[42]

Political scientists do not agree on whether the net effect of direct legislation has been good or bad. Some argue that legislative decision making has two critical advantages over plebiscites. First, the legislative process encourages competing interest groups to retreat from their initial "nonnegotiable demands" and to work out compromises that will give all groups something of what they want and avoid total defeat for any. On the other hand, a referendum like that on Proposition 14 in California poses only two choices: the open-housing legislation that is on the books or no open-housing legislation at all. Referendum results thus often mean total victory for one group and total defeat for another. Closely related, these critics say, is a second advantage: Legislatures typically weigh the *intensity* of demands, as well as the numbers making them, whereas in a referendum every voter's preference is equal to that of every other, and there is no way of registering different intensities beyond the elementary dichotomy of voting and not voting. A white majority fairly strongly opposed to compulsory open housing can—as in California—defeat a black minority passionately convinced that open housing is the minimum justice to which they are entitled. Such results, the critics conclude, produce neither justice nor social peace nor governmental stability.[43]

The many defenders of direct legislation reply that all such considerations are less important than is the fact that the initiative and referendum enable the voters to express their policy preferences *directly* without distortion and dilution by legislative interpretation and deals.

Whatever may be the relative merits of representation and direct legislation, the former provides the main or sole legal framework for making government policy in all modern democratic systems. In recent years no democratic nation has added the initiative or referendum to its lawmaking institutions, and at least one (West Germany) that once had direct legislation has abandoned it. For better or worse, the periodic election of legislators, executives, and (in a few systems) judges is the principal formal device through which ordinary citizens can express their views about what government should and should not do.

In most of today's democratic polities the legislatures are the key official agencies for making public policy. In the following chapter, accordingly, we shall examine their organization, operation, problems, and changing role in modern government.

---

presidential vote and Republican Barry Goldwater only 41 percent, the Republican position on the referendum prevailed by a two-to-one margin; see Wolfinger and Greenstein, "The Repeal of Fair Housing in California," pp. 760–761.

[42] Codding reports that 67 percent of all proposals for legislative referenda generated by the Swiss Bundesversammlung (parliament) have been approved, compared with only 10 percent of proposals launched by popular initiative; Codding, *The Federal Government of Switzerland,* p. 66.

[43] See Wolfinger and Greenstein, "The Repeal of Fair Housing in California," pp. 768–769.

# V

---

# GOVERNMENTAL
# AUTHORITIES
# AND PROCESSES

# 15

---

# THE
# LEGISLATIVE
# PROCESS

In this and the next four chapters we shall consider the principal *official* policy-making agencies of modern governments. They are official because they are formally established by constitutions and laws and are generally regarded as parts of "the government"—in contrast to such unofficial, extragovernmental agencies as political parties, pressure groups, primary groups, social strata, and the like.

In the course of this survey we shall see that the organization of the legislatures, executives, and courts of the Western democratic systems, as well as their policy-making processes, are substantially alike in many ways. But we shall also discover that some democratic systems differ significantly from others in certain respects, particularly those relating to the official status and interrelations of legislative and executive agencies. These differences are important enough so that we shall begin our study of legislatures and executives by briefly examining and contrasting presidential and parliamentary democracies.

## PRESIDENTIAL AND PARLIAMENTARY DEMOCRACIES

### THE DOCTRINE OF SEPARATION OF POWERS

*Origins and Influence*

Suppose that the municipal council of a city passed an ordinance requiring the inoculation of all dogs against rabies. Suppose that the mayor and chief of police then announced, "We think this is a bad regulation, and we refuse to enforce it." Surely most of us, including many who objected to the ordinance, would think that the mayor and chief of police were acting wrongly. Why? Because we would believe that making the laws is the council's job and that it is up to the mayor and the police to enforce them, regardless of personal convictions.

Suppose, again, that a citizen were arrested for grand larceny. Suppose that the governor of the state then declared, "This poor man will not get a fair trial from the courts, so I will try him myself." Again, most of us would strongly object, on the ground that trying people accused of crime is the job of the courts, not of the governor.

Most of us, in fact, accept the idea that each agency of government has its own proper powers and that it should not try to exercise those of any other agency.

However fundamental and self-evident this premise may seem to us, it is relatively new in people's thinking about government. Until about the seventeenth century few political theorists tried to separate the governing process into legislative, executive, and judicial components. Government seemed one integral process, and the only significant variations from society to society were in who governed and how.

The prevalent institutions of government before the seventeenth century reflected this idea. The *ekklesia,* the council of five hundred, and the "courts" of Periclean Athens, for example, all made rules, apprehended suspected offenders, decided on guilt or innocence, and administered punishment; no one raised the question whether these bodies were legislatures or executives. The Roman Senate performed many judicial as well as legislative functions. The great medieval assemblies like the English Curia Regis and Parliament, the French *parlements,* and the Spanish Cortes, were also at one and the same time judicial and legislative agencies; indeed, the official title of the larger English assembly was the High Court of Parliament.

In the seventeenth and eighteenth centuries, however, a group of influential political theorists, including John Locke, the Baron de Montesquieu, Jean Jacques Rousseau, Thomas Jefferson, and the authors of *The Federalist,* developed a new conception of the governing process. This conception involved partly a description of how the governing process *does* work and partly a doctrine about how it *should* work. It remains the basis for the belief, widely held in the United States and some other modern democratic systems, that legislatures should legislate, executives execute, and judges adjudicate.

## Content [1]

The most thorough and influential exposition of this point of view—and one of the most influential books about government ever written—was *L'esprit des lois,* published in 1748 by Montesquieu. His argument can be briefly summarized.

The two significant elements of the governing process are the individual citizens and the official governmental agencies. In a properly run community the citizens establish a constitution that performs three functions. First, it stipulates what the

---

[1] For a more detailed description of the origins, influence, and content of this doctrine, see Herman Finer, *Theory and Practice of Modern Government* (rev. ed.; New York: Holt, Rinehart and Winston, Inc., 1949), chap. 6.

whole government may and may not do—what powers the government will have (for example, to collect taxes, declare war, protect private property). Second, it establishes certain government agencies and provides a procedure for selecting their members. And, third, it allocates certain powers to each agency.

The whole power of any government is, like Caesar's Gaul, divided into three parts, each substantially distinct from the others. There is the *legislative* power, the power to make the laws; the *executive* power, the power to enforce them; and the *judicial* power, the power to interpret them and apply them to individuals whom the executive has charged with violations. Whatever any public official does in his official capacity is thus either lawmaking, enforcement, interpretation, or application.

Like many of his contemporaries. Montesquieu believed that government is an eternal threat to people's liberties; yet anarchy and lawlessness also threaten them. How, then, can we establish a government that is strong enough to maintain law and order without becoming tyrannical? The answer, Montesquieu and his followers believed, is to give each of government's three basic powers to a separate and independent government agency. When all three agencies, or "branches," act in concert, government can do what it must do, but no single branch can ever control the whole power of government, and thus no executive, legislature, or court can ever use the whole power of government to work its way heedless of restraint. Any concentration of powers in a single agency is tyrannical, no matter whether that agency is an elected and responsible representative assembly or an irresponsible hereditary monarch. Only genuine separation of powers protects the liberties of people against the aggressions of government. James Madison spoke for all the Founding Fathers when he wrote in the forty-seventh *Federalist* paper:

> No political truth is certainly of greater intrinsic value, or is stamped with the authority of more enlightened patrons of liberty, than that . . . the accumulation of all powers, legislative, executive, and judiciary, in the same hands, whether of one, a few, or many, and whether hereditary, self-appointed, or elective, may justly be pronounced the very definition of tyranny.[2]

## PRESIDENTIAL DEMOCRACIES

"Presidential democracy" is the term that political scientists generally apply to any government organized according to the classical doctrine of separation of powers. The government of the United States is the oldest government organized in this way, but the category also includes such nations as Colombia, Costa Rica, Mexico, and Venezuela—all of whose governments are modeled more or less closely upon the North American prototype. In all presidential democracies there is some formal constitutional proclamation of separation of powers as the basic organizing principle. One form is a "distributing clause," like Article XXX of the Massachusetts Constitution of 1780:

---

[2] Max Beloff (ed.), *The Federalist* (New York: Crowell-Collier and Macmillan, Inc., 1948), pp. 245–246. For Montesquieu's similar argument, see *The Spirit of the Laws,* trans. by Thomas Nugent (New York: Hafner Publishing Company, 1949), bk. 11.

In the government of this Commonwealth, the legislative department shall never exercise the executive and judicial powers, or either of them: The executive shall never exercise the legislative and judicial powers, or either of them: The judicial shall never exercise the legislative and executive powers, or either of them: to the end it may be a government of laws and not of men.

The Constitution of the United States contains no such clause, but it specifies that "all legislative powers herein granted shall be vested in a Congress" (Article I), "the executive Power shall be vested in a President" (Article II), and the "judicial power . . . shall be vested in one supreme Court, and in such inferior Courts as the Congress may from time to time ordain and establish" (Article III).

In all presidential democracies the three types of power are kept formally separate by two main devices.

## Separation of Personnel

Under the Constitution of the United States no person may hold office in more than one of the three branches of government at a time: Article I, Section 6, declares that "no Person holding any Office under the United States, shall be a Member of either House during his Continuance in Office." If the Attorney General wishes to be a senator from New York, he must resign his executive position, as Robert Kennedy did. If a representative from Wisconsin wishes to be Secretary of Defense, he must resign his House seat, as Melvin Laird did. If the Assistant Attorney General wishes to become a justice of the Supreme Court, he must resign his executive post, as Byron White did. If a justice of the Supreme Court wishes to become U.S. Ambassador to the United Nations, he must resign his seat on the bench, as Arthur Goldberg did.

## Checks and Balances

In classical form the three branches of government are not splendidly isolated from one another; rather each is given a number of "checks" with which it can keep the others in proper "balance." Congress is empowered to check the President by refusing to pass bills that he requests, withholding appropriations for executive and administrative agencies, denying approval of the appointments of his top subordinates, and even impeaching him and expelling him from office. Congress is empowered to check the Supreme Court by limiting its appellate jurisdiction and withholding approval of the appointment of new members. The President is empowered to check Congress by vetoing its acts and to check the Supreme Court by his initial appointment of its new members. And the Supreme Court can check both Congress and the President through its power of judicial review (see Chap. 11).

## PARLIAMENTARY DEMOCRACIES

Most of the world's democratic nations neither accept the doctrine of separation of powers nor use checks and balances in the American pattern. They have, instead, what political scientists generally call "parliamentary systems." Great Britain, the British Commonwealth nations, the nations of Scandinavia and Western Europe, and such non-European democratic nations as India, Sri Lanka (Ceylon), and Japan fall into this category.

The essential characteristics of all parliamentary democratic systems is what some analysts have called "the fusion of powers"; that is, the constitution stipulates that the executive—the ministry, cabinet, and prime minister (see Chap. 16)—will hold office only as long as it "holds the confidence" of a majority of the legislature. In the United States, by contrast, if the Congress refuses to pass a bill that the President insists is important, both the President and Congress continue in office for the duration of their constitutionally fixed terms. In a parliamentary system no such impasse is possible. Once the prime minister and cabinet have proposed an important bill and insisted that the parliament pass it, if the parliament refuses, then government must stop until the impasse is resolved. Either the executive must resign and be replaced by another acceptable to the legislative majority, or a general election must be held to elect a new legislature—which then may reappoint the old executive or replace it with a new one.

The governments of the parliamentary democracies, as we shall see, vary in many important respects, but they all share this essential feature: Disagreement and deadlock between the legislature and executive on important measures cannot be tolerated and must be resolved by changing the membership and behavior of either or both agencies so that agreement—sometimes called "legislative confidence in the executive"—can be restored.

## THE THREE POWERS AS DESCRIPTIVE CATEGORIES

Most contemporary political scientists regard Montesquieu's classification of the powers of government as inadequate and misleading. They recognize that in all modern democratic systems no agency sticks exclusively to the job formally assigned to it. Legislative bodies often engage in executive activities (for example, their investigations of wrongdoing in government, schools, and trade unions). Courts often "make" law (as in their interpretations of Constitutions and statutes). Executive and administrative agencies often make and interpret laws as well as enforcing them (for example, making administrative regulations and holding hearings to determine whether licenses for radio and television broadcasting stations should be granted, renewed, or revoked).

A few political scientists have attempted to preserve the traditional conception, dubbing the judicial activities and powers of executive agencies "quasi judicial." Most, however, have concluded that the adjectives "legislative," "executive," and "judicial" should be used only as convenient tags for identifying particular government agencies; their utility depends strictly upon general agreement on which tags should be pinned to which agencies. They do not offer complete and accurate descriptions of what the agencies actually do.[3]

In this chapter, accordingly, we shall consider those agencies generally called "legislatures." In examining the legislative process we shall deal with the principal activities of these bodies, but we shall not be concerned with the question whether

---

[3] See Finer, *Theory and Practice of Modern Government,* chap. 7.

or not these activities are truly legislative in the orthodox sense of the term. For our purposes, *any* function performed by an agency called a "legislature" is a "legislative function"; we shall proceed from similar premises in subsequent chapters on the executive, administrative, and judicial processes.

## FUNCTIONS OF LEGISLATURES[4]

### STATUTE MAKING

Perhaps the most obvious and certainly one of the most important functions of legislatures in modern democratic systems is making statutes. The term "statute making," rather than the more commonly used "lawmaking," will be used because it more accurately describes what legislatures actually do. "Law" means any rule of behavior that officially emanates from a definite government source. The rules officially established by legislatures, which are generally known as "legislative acts" or "statutes," certainly constitute an important segment of any democratic system's total body of law, but the latter also includes such elements as "common law" and rules of equity determined by the courts, as well as the more significant executive and administrative decrees and regulations. Legislatures thus monopolize statute making but not lawmaking.

### CONSTITUENT

The legislatures in most democratic systems have certain powers over the establishment and amendment of their nations' constitutions. Many constitutions were originally drawn up by legislative bodies, and every legislature is authorized to play some role in formal amendment. In some democratic countries, like Great Britain and New Zealand, the national legislatures are the sole agencies authorized to amend the constitutions. In many others, like Australia, Switzerland, and France, the legislatures normally propose amendments, and the voters ratify or defeat them in referenda. In still others, like the United States, amendments are proposed by the national legislatures and ratified by state legislatures or conventions. Most democratic legislatures have considerably altered and added to their constitutions by statutory enactments; (in the United States, these alterations have included establishing the inferior Federal courts, the executive departments, and the regulatory commissions).

### ELECTORAL

Most democratic legislatures take a significant role in selecting certain public officials, who in turn play leading roles in the executive. The outstanding instances are the indirect "elections" of prime ministers by the legislatures of the parliamentary systems. These legislatures do not always, of course, directly cast ballots for various

---

[4] Two useful general comparative studies of many aspects of modern democratic legislatures are K. C. Wheare, *Legislatures* (New York: Oxford University Press, 1963); and Inter-Parliamentary Union, *Parliaments* (New York: Frederick A. Praeger, Inc., 1963).

candidates for this office, yet every time that one votes on a question of confidence (see Chap. 16) it is, in effect, reelecting or defeating the incumbent prime minister. Some commentators, indeed, believe that this kind of "election" has become the main function of the legislatures in these systems.

Even in the presidential democracies the legislatures have some electoral powers. The Constitution of the United States, for example, provides that, when no candidate for President or Vice-President receives a majority of electoral votes, the House of Representatives (each state casting one vote) will choose the President from among the top two or three candidates and that the Senate will choose the Vice-President in a somewhat different way. No President or Vice-President has been selected by these procedures since 1824, but Congress retains its electoral powers against the day when they may be used again.

## FINANCIAL

In every modern democratic system the legislature holds the basic official financial power: It determines the nature and amount of taxes, and all public moneys may be spent only as the result of legislative appropriations. As have so many other legislative functions, the main initiatives for and direction of governmental finance have passed from the legislatures to the executives in most democratic nations; most legislatures now merely revise budgets proposed by executive officials, rather than drawing up their own de novo. How much revision particular legislatures do depends upon the degree of control that the executives have achieved—a matter that we shall consider later in this chapter.

## EXECUTIVE

In addition to acting upon executive budgets, most democratic legislatures also pass upon certain other executive proposals. In most democratic countries, for example, international treaties are negotiated by the executives but must be approved by the legislatures before they become effective. In the United States the President appoints various kinds of officials (Federal judges, Cabinet members, heads of administrative agencies, and ambassadors) "by and with the Advice and Consent of the Senate" (Article II)—that is, the appointments are only provisional, or "interim," until approved by a majority of the Senate.

## JUDICIAL

Some democratic legislatures also perform judicial functions. The Constitution of the United States, for example, provides that the House of Representatives may impeach any civil officer of the national government (including the President, the Vice-President, Cabinet members, and judges) and that any person so impeached must be tried by the Senate; a two-thirds vote of the latter is necessary for conviction. The House has impeached a total of twelve officers since 1789: nine judges, one President (Andrew Johnson), one senator, and one Cabinet member. Only four, all judges, have been convicted and removed from office, but President Johnson escaped conviction in 1868 by the bare margin of one vote; and in 1974 President Nixon resigned when it became clear that the House was going to impeach him.

Similarly, the French national assembly can indict the President of the Republic and the ministers for treason and other crimes and misdemeanors, although indicted officers are tried by the high court rather than by a legislative body. The British House of Lords has lost most of its other powers but continues to be the nation's highest court of law. Most of the Lords' judicial work—and all its work as a court of appeals—is performed in the name of the whole House by a small group of ten to fifteen legal experts, including the lord chancellor, the nine lords of appeal in ordinary (the "law lords"), and other members of the House who have held high judicial office (for example, former lord chancellors).

## INVESTIGATIVE

The investigative function of democratic legislative bodies receives more publicity than do most of the others, especially in the United States; congressional "probes" like those by the Ervin Select Committee on Presidential Campaign Activities in 1973 and by the House Judiciary Committee on the impeachment of President Nixon in 1974 are the best-known recent examples. American legislatures, however, have no monopoly on this kind of activity. The British House of Commons establishes four or five "select" committees each year for the purpose of digging up information desired by the House on matters not covered by the "standing" committees. These select committees hold hearings, subpoena witnesses and records, and often submit reports that inspire changes in existing legislation, administrative practices, or both. Although the British, unlike the Americans, conduct much of their governmental investigations through royal commissions (bodies composed of both legislators and outsiders), the select committees nevertheless have a significant role in the shaping of legislative and administrative policy.

## INFORMATIVE

Some legislative investigations are conducted mainly to uncover information necessary for new legislation. A great deal of the activity, however, is intended mainly to inform other government agencies, extragovernmental bodies, and the general public about what is going on in the nation. For example, the Ervin committee investigations of the Watergate scandals in 1973 were intended only in part to provide the basis for new legislation regulating campaign finance and practices; in addition they were designed to determine whether or not the legislation already on the books had been violated by the President or members of his administration and campaign organization. For another example, the McClellan committee, in its investigation of Jimmy Hoffa's administration of the Teamsters' Union in the 1950s, intended mainly to acquaint the union's rank and file and the AFL–CIO national leadership with the nature and extent of the Teamsters' leaders' dishonesty, in the hope that the union might clean its own house.

Such investigations, then, are one aspect of the legislative function of informing the public, and legislative debate is another. In many legislatures party lines are so rigid that legislative debate hardly ever changes a member's vote. Yet debate

Congress investigates and informs: Former White House counsel John W. Dean, III, faces the Ervin committee investigating the Watergate affair. Source: UPI Photograph.

provides the main forum in which the "rights" and "wrongs" of issues are aired. It therefore serves much the same function of informing and activating public opinion that election campaigns are supposed to perform. Debates in the British House of Commons, although they almost never change legislative votes, sometimes change the opinions of those who elect the legislators, and some observers describe them as "a continuing election campaign." If an informed and enlightened citizenry is indeed a prime requisite for healthy democracy, informing the public is far from the least significant of the legislature's functions.

## STRUCTURE AND ORGANIZATION OF LEGISLATURES

### NUMBER OF HOUSES[5]

Approximately two-thirds of all modern democratic nations have bicameral (two-house) legislatures, and one-third have unicameral (one-house) legislatures. Although there are several variations in the structure of the bicameral legislatures, most are organized in substantially similar fashion. One of the two houses, generally called the "lower house," has the larger membership, has the shorter terms of office, and

The Legislative Process

[5] See Wheare, *Legislatures,* chap. 8.

is elected (under one of the electoral systems described in Chap. 7) by the widest franchise. Examples of such houses are the American House of Representatives, the British House of Commons, the French Assemblé National, and the Swiss National-rat. The other house, generally called the "upper house," has the smaller membership, has longer terms of office, and is selected in various ways. The members of the American Senate, for example, are elected by the voters in statewide constituencies for six-year terms; some members of the British House of Lords inherit their positions, and others are appointed for life by the monarch on the advice of the prime minister; the members of the Canadian Senate are appointed for life by the governor-general on the advice of the prime minister; and the members of the Austrian Bundes-rat are elected by the legislatures of the various *Länder* (provinces).[6]

Why should a nation establish two legislative houses rather than one? Historically there have been two main reasons. First, all the federal democracies have thought it necessary to give their subnational "sovereignties" equal representation in the national legislature: hence the establishment of the United States Senate with two members from each state, regardless of its population or wealth. Perhaps even more important, in both federal and unitary nations, has been the desire to provide an internal check on legislative action. The lower houses have been presumed to be closely in tune with popular appetites and passions and have therefore been regarded as dangerous to national stability and welfare. Many nations, accordingly, have at one time or another established higher property and age qualifications for those who elect members of the upper houses than for those who elect members of the lower houses, and a few nations still retain these special franchise requirements.

In recent years a number of democratic nations have formally or informally abandoned bicameralism, mainly on the ground that it is a barrier to the full realization of democracy in the sense that it does not locate full government power in the representatives of popular majorities. A few (for example, Denmark and New Zealand) have officially abolished their upper houses. Many more have reduced their powers so drastically that they are now little more than advisory bodies and the lower houses have become, for all practical purposes, unicameral legislatures. For example, until the nineteenth century the British House of Lords was in many respects more powerful than was the House of Commons. After the democratization of the Commons in 1832, however, the powers of the Lords began to slip away. The Parliament Act of 1911 stripped it of all but a few delaying powers, and an act of 1949 reduced these powers still more. Accordingly, the House of Lords is today merely an advisory and delaying body, with little or no formal legislative power. Most observers believe that it performs useful revising and suggesting functions, but Parliament has in practice become a unicameral legislature. The same thing has happened to a greater or lesser degree in most other unitary democracies, for example, France and Ireland. Only in some of the federal democracies (for example, the United States and Switzerland but not Canada and Australia) do the upper houses retain powers equal or superior to those of the lower houses.

---

[6] Norway's procedures are unique: The voters elect the 150-member Storting, which then proceeds to choose 38 of its members to serve in a second chamber, the Lagting; the remaining 112 are called the Odelsting.

### Selection

Every legislative body has officers, including such minor dignitaries as clerk, sergeant at arms, chaplain, and postmaster. The most significant and powerful officials are the presiding officers, only a few of whom acquire their positions by virtue of holding other public office. The Vice-President of the United States does preside over the Senate (possibly because the Founding Fathers wanted to give him something to occupy his time other than inquiring after the President's health every morning); but most presiding officers are selected by legislative bodies from among their own members (for example, the speaker of the American House of Representatives, the speaker of the British House of Commons, and the president of the French national assembly).

### Formal Powers and Functions

In their official capacities the presiding officers of all democratic legislatures have substantially the same powers and functions. They "recognize" legislators who wish to speak, put motions for assembly votes, rule on points of parliamentary order and procedure, supervise the referral of bills to committees, sometimes appoint members of the various committees, and generally direct the bodies' formal operations.

### Partisanship and Party Leadership

It seems reasonable to expect that, because the presiding officer of a legislative body has considerable control over who is heard and what is done, he will be fair to *all* the body's members, parties, and points of view and thus ensure to each group an equal chance to have its policies adopted. In order to ensure such fairness, the speaker of the British House of Commons is "purged" of all party connections. The leaders of the principal rival parties agree on a candidate, always a member who, though he has also been a party member, does not have a reputation for fervent partisanship; more often than not he is elected unanimously. After his election the speaker completely divests himself of all connections with political parties and clubs and never takes part in debate. In general elections he sometimes runs without opposition, and in every other conceivable way he is insulated from partisan politics so that he may be completely impartial in his dealings with all parties and all members.[7]

The speaker of the United States House of Representatives (and of most other American legislative bodies) provides a striking contrast. Not only is he openly and avowedly partisan (there is certainly no tradition that he run unopposed for reelection in his district), but he is, in fact, the principal leader of the majority party in the House and one of the main national leaders of his party. Some foreign observers find it difficult to believe that a speaker can at one and the same time successfully perform

---

[7] See W. Ivor Jennings, *Parliament* (3d ed.; New York: Cambridge University Press, 1957), pp. 54–65.

the two quite different jobs of neutral presiding officer and partisan leader. Yet most American speakers seem to do just that, for seldom does the minority party complain of the speaker's unfairness, and seldom does the majority party complain of his ineffective leadership.[8]

The presiding officers of other democratic legislatures fall somewhere between the British and American extremes of neutrality and partisanship, but most follow the British model more closely.[9]

## PROCEDURES[10]

### Rules

Legislatures in democratic systems conduct their business largely according to rules of their own making, limited only by a few constitutional requirements, like those requiring records of their proceedings and quorums to conduct business. There are, of course, many variations in detail among the rules followed by various legislative bodies, but most are modeled generally on the procedures of the "mother of parliaments," the British House of Commons. The familiar *Robert's Rules of Order,* according to which so many nongovernmental organizations operate (or are supposed to operate), are a kind of distillation of the procedures most generally followed by democratic legislative bodies the world over.

### Public and Private Bills

Legislatures in most democratic systems distinguish between public and private bills. A public bill is one that applies to the whole population and is intended to promote the general welfare: a tax law, a military draft act, a law against kidnapping, and so on. A private bill, on the other hand, is one that applies to and is intended to promote the welfare of a particular person or locality: an appropriation of money in compensation for property damage or personal injury, a bill admitting a particular alien to the nation outside the regular immigration laws, a bill appropriating money to improve the harbor at Porkville, Anystate, or the like.

Most democratic legislatures have established somewhat different procedures for handling public and private bills. In the British House of Commons, for example, private bills are filed with the examiner of petitions for private bills and with the government department most immediately concerned. Interested parties are invited to testify, and all bills that are opposed go to a private-bills committee, which holds

---

[8] See William J. Keefe and Morris S. Ogul, *The American Legislative Process* (2d ed.; Englewood Cliffs, N.J.: Prentice-Hall, Inc., 1968), pp. 42–43.

[9] See Wheare, *Legislatures,* pp. 22–29.

[10] The most complete recent study of rules and procedures in both houses of Congress, emphasizing their impact on the allocation of power and the outcomes of legislative struggles, is Lewis A. Froman, Jr., *The Congressional Process: Strategies, Rules, and Procedures* (Boston: Little, Brown & Company, 1967). Some comparable information for other legislatures is given in *Parliaments,* part 2, although little is said about the rules' effects on legislative outcomes.

hearings and makes recommendations that are almost always accepted by the whole House. The purpose of this procedure and similar ones in other legislatures is to keep private bills from clogging the regular legislative machinery and thus blocking consideration of more important questions.

### Main Steps in Handling Public Bills

Despite differences in procedural details, the legislatures of most democratic regimes put public bills through similar steps before they become law.

**Introduction** In most legislatures any member may introduce a public bill either by giving it a "first reading" on the floor and moving its adoption or, as in both houses of Congress, merely by dropping it in the "hopper" at the clerk's or secretary's desk. This formal equality in the right to introduce bills is, however, somewhat misleading. Many democratic legislatures, like the British House of Commons, make a formal distinction between government bills (those introduced by ministers on behalf of their ministries or "the government") and private members' bills (those introduced by ordinary members on their own initiative). Only the former are likely to be passed: The government introduces about 85 percent of all public bills in Great Britain, and about 95 percent of all public bills passed are government bills.[11] No such formal distinction is made in Congress, but a bill generally known to be an "administration bill" (one backed by the President and pushed by his spokesmen in Congress) has a better chance of passage than does one that lacks this kind of backing.

**Consideration by Committee** Later in this chapter we shall examine the structure, personnel, operations, and general role of committees in the legislative process. In the present context the important point is that in most democratic legislatures bills are referred to and considered by committees *before* they undergo general consideration and debate by the houses as wholes. Committees therefore have a great deal to say not only the contents of bills but also about what bills will even have the chance to become laws. In the British House of Commons, however, bills are referred to committee *after* general debate and *after* basic policies and most details have been established by the whole House (which means by the "government"). British committees, unlike those in most other democratic legislatures, are, in Herman Finer's words, "lowly handmaidens to help clean up amendments."[12] The nations of the British Commonwealth generally follow British practices in this regard, but the United States and most European democracies assign their legislative committees far more decisive roles, as we shall see.

**General Debate** The few bills that survive the screening process in committee are then "reported" back to the whole house in original or altered form and are given "second readings" (which usually means only that the presiding officer or the clerk

---

[11] Finer, *Governments of Greater European Powers* (New York: Holt, Rinehart and Winston, Inc., 1956), p. 383.

[12] Finer, *Governments of Greater European Powers*, p. 116.

announces the number and title of each bill about to be considered, not that anyone literally reads aloud its entire contents). At this point all legislators have a chance to express their views on the basic policy questions involved in the bill and also to offer amendments to it. If the bill survives this stage its chances of final passage are excellent.

**Final Passage**   After general debate has been held and all proposed amendments have been accepted, rejected, or revised, the bill is given its third and final "reading," and the question is put whether or not the whole bill, as amended, should be passed. An affirmative vote means that, as far as the particular house is concerned, the bill will be law.

**Consideration by Conference Committee**   In many supposedly two-house legislatures, as we have seen, the upper houses have the power only to suggest amendments and to delay bills passed by the lower houses. After a delaying period has elapsed and after a lower house has accepted or rejected an upper house's suggested amendments, the bill moves on to the next and final stage, regardless of further objections by the upper house. But in the United States (and some other nations) both houses have coordinate legislative power; each bill must pass both houses in identical form before it can move on to the final stage. When the two houses disagree on the final wording of a bill, whether on a minor detail or a major policy question, and neither is willing to accept the other's version, the differences must be ironed out and the bill worded in a manner acceptable to majorities in both houses. This problem arises in about one-third to one-half of all the bills that pass both houses of Congress, including just about every major public bill.

In all genuinely bicameral legislatures the necessary "ironing out" is accomplished by some version of the American conference committee, which operates as follows. The presiding officer of each house appoints from three to nine members to represent the house as conferees. The two sets of conferees constitute the conference committee, which meets in secret session to work out a version of the bill on which all or most of the conferees can agree. Usually this version is a compromise between those of the two houses, but on rare occasions the committee writes a substantially new bill. When they have reached agreement, the conferees report to their respective houses. The reports cannot be amended but must be accepted or rejected in their entirety; usually they are accepted, for the good reason that most members of both houses know that, if the conference committee's version is not accepted, there will probably be no bill at all.

Conference committees, accordingly, have a great deal of power over the final content of legislation—so much that some observers call them "the third house of Congress." Some such institution, however, is inevitable in any genuinely bicameral legislature.[13]

---

[13] The authoritative analysis of conference committees in the American Congress is Gilbert Y. Steiner, *The Congressional Conference Committee* (Urbana, Ill.: University of Illinois Press, 1951). For comparable practices in other nations, see *Parliaments,* pp. 185–189.

**Submission to the Executive**   After the legislature has officially enacted a bill, the latter is submitted to some executive agency for official promulgation and inclusion in the collection of statutes in force. In the parliamentary systems the executives—monarchs and presidents—have no choice but to accept the bills and to declare them law. In the presidential system, however, the presidents can veto bills; if the President of the United States vetoes a bill, it can become law only if repassed by both houses with a two-thirds majority in each. This procedure will be discussed further in Chapter 16.

## LEGISLATIVE COMMITTEES[14]

### Structure

Every democratic legislative body establishes committees of its members to perform various functions; they appear to be a universal response to two main needs. First, the sheer size of most legislatures prevents them from effectively handling questions of detail and wording. Most legislatures have several hundred members each, and, as participants in all governmental and other organizations have learned, hundreds simply cannot deal effectively with such matters but must confine themselves to considering broad questions of policy. Second, the sheer number of bills introduced necessitates some kind of process to weed out the few that deserve serious consideration. In an average session of Congress, for example, 10,000–12,000 bills are introduced—obviously far too many to receive serious consideration—and only about 500–1000 are passed.

In the United States and most European democracies most of this screening is accomplished by legislative committees. In the United States each house of Congress maintains a number of *standing committees* (those considered permanent) established according to subject matter: agriculture, appropriations, armed services, foreign affairs, and education and labor are examples. They range in size from nine to fifty members and include legislators of the majority and minority parties in approximately the same ratio that prevails in their respective houses. Nominally the members of each committee are elected by the whole house, but actually the leaders of each party (assembled in its "committee on committees") determine which of their legislators shall sit on which committees. In making these selections the leaders are bound by a series of informal but nonetheless powerful rules: All previous members of a committee must be reappointed if they so desire, every major area and interest must have a spokesman on a committee that deals with matters affecting it, and so on.

The *commissions* of the French national assembly are in some respects similar to

---

[14] A general survey of committee procedures and powers is included in *Parliaments,* pp. 141–151. A useful recent study of committee structure and operation in the American Congress is Richard F. Fenno, Jr., *Congressmen in Committees* (Boston: Little, Brown & Company, 1973). Also useful is a book intended mainly for new congressmen: Donald G. Tacheron and Morris K. Udall, *The Job of the Congressman* (Indianapolis, Ind.: The Bobbs-Merrill Company, Inc., 1966).

American legislative committees. The outstanding French variation is the institution of the *rapporteur* (reporter). As each bill is received by a particular *commission,* the latter appoints one member as *rapporteur* for that bill, in which capacity he takes the lead in studying it, in preparing the *commission's* report on it, and in defending the *commission's* position in the debate before the whole assembly.

The British House of Commons, in contrast to the American and French legislatures, maintains only five "alphabet" standing committees (so called because they are officially designated Committees A, B, C, D, and E, rather than "armed forces," "agriculture," and so on) and a sixth committee for dealing with Scottish bills. The British and French committees, as we shall see, are not specialized by subject matter and are far less powerful than their counterparts in most other legislatures.

Beside standing committees, democratic legislatures from time to time establish *select committees,* which make special inquiries into and recommendations on particular questions and dissolve when they have completed their tasks. Examples are the select committee of the United States Senate that in 1954 recommended the censure of Senator Joseph McCarthy for "conduct unbecoming a senator" and the select committee of the House of Representatives established in 1969 to investigate all aspects of crime in the United States. The genuinely bicameral legislatures sometimes establish *joint committees,* composed of equal representation from each house, to supervise certain matters (for example, the Joint Committee on Atomic Energy created to supervise the Atomic Energy Commission's administration of the American nuclear-fission program).

### Activities and Power

Most legislative committees have two main types of activities. The first is disposing of bills referred to them by their respective houses. A powerful committee has a wide range of choice in deciding how to dispose of a particular bill: It may figuratively deposit it in a special hollow cylindrical "file" and forget about it—the apparent fate of most bills—or it may immediately report the bill in its original form back to the whole house with a recommendation "that it do pass." It may also decide to work the bill over before making any recommendation. If the committee chooses the last course, it may hold hearings at which representatives of various interested groups are invited to testify. When the hearings are over the committee may go into "executive" (secret) session and rewrite the bill as little or as much as it sees fit, up to and including deleting everything but the title and substituting an entirely new bill!

Allowable committee activities include projects that the committee undertakes on its own initiative. It may decide to draw up and have a member introduce a brand-new bill of its own. It may decide to investigate possible wrongdoing in the executive, administrative, or judicial agencies or in schools, trade unions, athletics, and the like.

The power of legislative committees over the general legislative process varies considerably among modern democracies. At one extreme stand the committees of the American Congress and state legislatures, which are the most powerful in the world. Not only do they receive bills before general debate and before basic policy decisions have been made, but also they can and often do make major decisions on basic policy, as well as on matters of detail and wording. "Little legislatures," Woodrow Wilson called them, and the phrase is as apt today as it was when he wrote it in 1885.[15]

At the other extreme stand the committees of the British House of Commons. They do not receive bills until after the second readings—that is, after the basic policy decisions have been made, and they are authorized to make alterations and amendments only on minor matters. As they do not specialize in particular areas of legislation, they develop no particular expertise or vested interest in any policy area. Their members are subject to strong party discipline both inside the committees and out. The committees therefore play a relatively unimportant role in the British legislative process.

Under the Third and Fourth Republics the powers of the French *commissions* resembled American more closely than British practices. Charles de Gaulle's Constitution of the Fifth Republic, however, deliberately set out to reduce these powers and thus to reduce the fragmentation characteristic of the national assembly before 1958. The number of *commissions générales permanentes* (standing committees) was reduced from nineteen, each corresponding to a particular legislative area, to six unspecialized committees on the British model. They now can only suggest changes to the government, and it is the government's bills—not the committees' amendments and counterproposals, as under the Fourth Republic—that come before the whole assembly for debate and final action.[16]

The power of legislative committees in the other democracies falls between these extremes. On one hand, committee reports usually serve as the basis for debate and action in the whole legislature, and a committee has considerable power to redraft and amend the bills originally submitted to it. On the other, in most parliamentary democracies government control of legislative calendars and political parties' control of their members' votes are such that the committees can rarely impose on governments bills to which the latter object.[17]

In most democratic systems committees thus play a significant role in the legislative process, though nowhere are they quite as powerful as in the United States.

## DEBATE, FILIBUSTERS, AND CLOTURE

One view of the legislative process is that the stage of general debate is the one in which most of the crucial decisions are made. Debate is conceived as a series of speeches in which members of the legislature try by their eloquence to convince the others to vote as they recommend, with the most persuasive speakers carrying the day. Needless to say, this picture is not entirely accurate. It assumes not only that

---

[15] *Congressional Government* (Boston: Houghton Mifflin Company, 1885). A richly detailed and informative modern account of the internal decision making and external influence of the powerful House and Senate committees on appropriations is Fenno, *The Power of the Purse: Appropriations Politics in Congress* (Boston: Little, Brown & Company, 1966). A similar volume on another important committee is John F. Manley, *The Politics of Finance: The House Committee on Ways and Means* (Boston: Little, Brown & Company, 1970).

[16] Roy C. Macridis, "France," in Macridis and Robert E. Ward (eds.), *Modern Political Systems: Europe* (2d ed.; Englewood Cliffs, N.J.: Prentice-Hall, Inc., 1968), pp. 263–264.

[17] *Parliaments,* pp. 145–151.

most legislators are present during the debate and listen carefully to it but also that they are subject to no pressures or influences other than their own personal views; neither assumption, as we shall see, is justified by the facts in most modern democratic legislatures.

**Filibusters are a weapon of minorities.** Source: *Straight Herblock* (New York: Simon and Schuster, Inc., 1964).

*"Sure—I'm for equalizing things"*

In most legislatures some members—always holding minority views—have occasionally used debate not to convince others but to block action. In the "filibuster," some minority member (or members) holds the floor with a marathon speech, reading aloud from cookbooks, the Bible, the manual of arms, and other such sources. The purpose? To delay or entirely to prevent the vote on a bill that the filibusterer opposes yet knows will pass if a vote is taken; he knows that, if he can filibuster long enough, the pressure of other business will force the majority to give in and to shelve the controversial bill so that other work can be done.

During the nineteenth century, for example, the Irish Nationalist minority in the British House of Commons frequently delayed the business of the House with long harangues; they were trying to force the House to grant Irish independence just to be rid of the nuisance. In many European legislatures today communist minorities seize every opportunity to filibuster against all anticommunist proposals. In the United States Senate in 1964 the southern minority filibustered for seventy-five days against the Civil Rights bill before its supporters were able to force a vote.

Governmental Authorities
and Processes

The legislatures in most democratic systems have found it necessary to adopt some kind of cloture rule to enable a majority to end debate, take a vote, and get on with other business.[18] The basic form is simple cloture. At any point in the debate a member may move that "debate now end and the question be put." Such a motion is itself undebatable, and if it receives the required majority (usually a simple majority but in some legislatures and in *Robert's Rules of Order* a two-thirds majority) debate must cease and a vote be taken on the main motion immediately. Subsidiary forms of cloture are the "guillotine," an advance ruling that debate on particular sections of a bill may last only a specified length of time before a vote must be taken, and the "kangaroo," which permits the presiding officer to decide in advance which amendments to a bill may be debated at all. Both, however, are backed up by simple cloture, the basic weapon of any legislative majority against filibusters.

Perhaps the most famous filibusters have taken place in the United States Senate. Under Senate Rule XXII, adopted in 1917 and revised in 1949 and 1959, debate can be stopped only if two-thirds of the senators present and voting assent. The result is that any thirty-four senators—usually a smaller number is required—can block any bill.

The reader should understand, however, that legislative policy is influenced in the Senate far more by *threats* of filibusters than by actual filibusters, which rarely occur. The authors and sponsors of every bill have to consider the possibility of a filibuster when planning its content and their floor strategy. As Senator Clinton Anderson (Democrat, New Mexico) put it during the 1949 debate over changing Rule XXII:

> I am not suggesting that the filibuster is the regular order of the day on this floor. It does not have to be. However infrequently the hammer on the filibuster gun is drawn back and cocked, this veto power of the minority over the will of the majority is, as all of us well know, a factor never overlooked in legislative drafting, appropriations, strategy, and tactics in the Senate of the United States. It affects and conditions every piece of legislation from the time it is a twinkle in the eye of its parent through every stage of gestation and birth.[19]

## PARTY ORGANIZATION[20]

### Principal Agencies

Almost every member of every democratic legislature is elected as the nominee of a political party. In every legislature the members of each party form some kind of organization to consult on matters of policy and strategy, in order to advance their common cause most effectively. Although these legislative party organizations vary

---

[18] Finland and Sweden are among the few modern democracies that still have no formal procedure for limiting legislative debate; see *Parliaments,* p. 153.

[19] *Congressional Record,* 95, Part 2 (March 2, 1949), 1589.

[20] A useful guide, though somewhat outdated, to the extensive literature on American congressional party organization is Charles O. Jones and Randall B. Ripley, *The Role of Political Parties in Congress: A Bibliography and Research Guide* (Tucson, Ariz.: University of Arizona Press, 1966).

in detail from nation to nation and from party to party within a particular nation, most include some version of each of the following principal instruments.

**Caucus**   The most inclusive organization is some form of the caucus, an assembly of all the party's members in the particular house. The American versions are called "conferences" or "caucuses"; the British and dominion versions, "parliamentary parties"; the French versions *groupes;* and so on. Their main function is to select their parties' legislative leaders, although occasionally some also decide what stands their members should take on particular legislative issues.[21]

**Executive Committee**   The caucus usually selects a few of its members as a kind of executive committee, or board of directors, and authorizes them to determine the party's stand on legislative issues and to select the tactics by which the party will pursue its objectives. The American versions are called "steering committees" or "policy committees"; the British and dominion versions, "the leadership" or "the cabinet" and "the shadow cabinet" (see Chap. 16); the French versions the "party executive"; and so on.

**Floor Leaders**[22]   Each caucus also selects one of its members as its official floor leader and main spokesman. The American versions are called "the majority leader" and "the minority leader"; the British equivalents are called "the party leader" (the prime minister) and "the leader of Her Majesty's loyal opposition."

**Whips**   Finally, the caucus or leader selects a few members to act as assistant leaders, generally known as "whips."[23] Their functions are to inform the rank and file of the leadership's decisions about policy and strategy, to ensure that the members vote—and vote "correctly"—on key legislative issues, and to transmit to the leaders information about dissatisfactions and resentments that members may have.

### Power and Role

We noted in Chapter 9 that the legislative party organizations' discipline and cohesion vary widely among democratic parties. On any scale the British parliamentary parties would stand near the "high" end. The majority party picks the prime minister and accepts his appointments to the Cabinet and the ministry. These leaders, in turn, exercise nearly absolute control over the proceedings and decisions of the House of Commons and also constitute the British executive. Organized opposition is monopo-

---

[21] In many democracies with fractionalized party systems each group must have a minimum number of members (ranging from three in the Israeli Knesset to fourteen in the French national assembly) to enjoy the privileges of recognized party groups.

[22] A recent detailed study is Ripley, *Party Leaders in the House of Representatives* (Washington, D.C.: The Brookings Institution, 1967). An interesting comparison with British counterparts is Martin Redmayne and Norman Hunt, "The Power of the Whips," in Anthony King (ed.), *British Politics* (Boston: D. C. Heath and Company, 1966), pp. 142–147.

[23] This widely used term is of British origin and is derived from the "whippers-in" who keep the hounds from straying from the scent in fox hunting.

lized by the minority party's organization and the shadow cabinet, which not only keeps up a running fire of criticism and opposition to majority policies but also stands ever ready to form the government itself when the voters decide to give it a majority of the seats. As a result, British government is more completely *party* government than is any other in the democratic world, in the sense that party organizations and operations are the very core of its legislative and executive processes.

Nearest the "low" end of any scale would stand a few of the smaller center and right-wing parties of democratic polities with more fractionalized party systems. Their members ordinarily feel little obligation and no compulsion to vote or act together; they are thus little more than aggregations of independent legislators who happen to bear the same formal party labels.

The Democratic and Republican parties in the American Congress stand between these two extremes. On matters of personnel (electing the presiding officers and allocating committee positions, for example) they are quite as cohesive as are their counterparts in London. On most issues of public policy they are less cohesive than are the British parties but far more so than are the French Radical Socialists or Independents. To illustrate, since the late 1940s the AFL–CIO has kept score on how every senator and representative has voted on issues of particular concern to organized labor. Its summary for the period 1947–1972 shows that around 70 percent of the votes cast by Democrats in both houses supported labor and liberal positions, whereas only about 25 percent of those cast by Republicans did so. It also shows that some Democrats (for example, Senators James Eastland of Mississippi and Willis Robertson of Virginia) were as conservative as were the most conservative Republicans and that some Republicans (for example, Senators Jacob Javits of New York and Charles Percy of Illinois) were almost as liberal as were the most liberal Democrats. On most key issues in Congress, then, most Democrats oppose most Republicans, but each party has a few mavericks who vote mostly with the opposition.[24]

We also noted in Chapter 9 that in centralization, discipline, and cohesion the dominant parties in most democracies fall somewhere between the British and American parties on the scale. But in any democratic polity the parties' power over their legislative members' votes and actions determines the role of parties in the nation's legislative process. And it also sets the stage for the individual legislator's public life. Let us see how.

## LEGISLATIVE WAYS OF LIFE

For our present purposes legislators in modern democratic systems may usefully be divided into two general types. First is the "party man," exemplified by the ordinary "back bench" member of the British House of Commons—a legislator subject to such strong party discipline that, except under the most unusual circumstances, he feels compelled to vote as his party whips direct. Second is the "independent operator," exemplified by the ordinary member of the United States Senate or House of Representatives—a legislator whose subjection to party discipline is weak enough so that he can, if he wishes, feel safe in voting contrary to his whips' requests.

[24] Keefe and Ogul, *The American Legislative Process*, pp. 298–313.

## THE PARTY MAN[25]

### Life in the House

The basic features of legislative life for the ordinary British back-bencher are two: Practically speaking, his vote belongs to his party's leaders, and legislative success consists of appointment to ministerial office by those same leaders. If he is ambitious, whatever he does as a back-bencher must at least not convince his leaders that he is *not* of ministerial caliber. Even if he has no hope of reaching ministerial rank,[26] he has little freedom to use his *vote* to gain other goals.

What, then, can he do? For one thing, he can speak in parliamentary debates. If he is good at it, he may win the approval necessary for advancement to ministerial office; even if he does not, he may still enjoy the applause of his colleagues and favorable notices in the newspapers. For another, he can keep the ministers on their toes by asking sharp questions during question time (see Chap. 17). For still another, he can rise to eminence in his party's committees of back-benchers and through them can exert substantial influence on the leaders. He can introduce motions which may cause some public stir. He can introduce private bills, a few of which may even pass. And there is always the possibility, however remote, that by abstaining or threatening to abstain from voting in a major crisis he may help to bring down an unwanted government (as in the unseating of Neville Chamberlain's government in 1940) or reverse a disastrous government policy (as in the Suez crisis of 1956).

By American standards, the British back-bencher's position is not impressive. His vote is not his own, he has little independent power to put pressure on administrators, and he is paid very little (the equivalent of about $8000 a year); most MPs have to earn outside incomes too. But the back-bencher is by no means a complete cipher. He belongs to one of Great Britain's most exclusive clubs (about the only one in London that guarantees parking space for his car), he is an insider in the nation's most fascinating game, and his membership may be highly useful in his career as journalist, lawyer, or businessman. Relatively few MPs retire voluntarily, and many who are defeated in general elections try again and again to win their way back.

---

[25] The most complete recent description of the British back-bencher is Peter G. Richards, *Honourable Members* (London: Faber & Faber, Ltd., 1959). Another illuminating account, based on transcriptions of interviews with a number of MPs, is Anthony King and Anne Sloman, *Westminster and Beyond,* (London: Macmillan and Co., Ltd., 1973). See also Anthony Barker and Michael Rush, *The British Member of Parliament and His Information* (Toronto: University of Toronto Press, 1970). For comparable descriptions of the legislative life in other European democratic nations, see Frederic Debuyst, *La Fonction Parlementaire en Belgique: Mécanismes d'Accès et Images* (Brussels: Centre de Recherche et d'Information Socio-Politique, 1966); André Laurens, "Le Métier de Député," *Le Monde,* October 4–10, 1967; Gerhard Loewenberg, *Parliament in the German Political System* (Ithaca, N.Y.: Cornell University Press, 1967); and Christopher Hughes, *The Parliament of Switzerland* (London: Cassell & Co., Ltd., 1962).

[26] The odds are against him. Philip Buck's study of parliamentary careers from 1918 to 1959 showed that only 32 percent of Conservative and 24 percent of Labour MPs reached ministerial rank: *Amateurs and Professionals in British Politics, 1918–59* (Chicago: University of Chicago Press, 1963), p. 9.

Evidently, then, even the party man who never rises to ministerial rank finds sufficient satisfaction in being a back-bencher.

### Relations with Constituents

Because the ordinary back-bencher does not control his parliamentary vote, he has no individual voting record for his opponents to attack or his supporters to praise. But in his constituency he is much more than merely a name with a party label. He is expected to provide certain local services, and if he functions well he can have a significant voice in constituency affairs. Although the institution of ministerial responsibility (see Chap. 16) prevents him from exerting pressure on civil servants in the American sense, he can explain local problems and dramatize local needs through speeches in the House and private representations to ministers. Most MPs hold regular "surgeries" in their constituencies—that is, they have office hours during which they are available to all constituents who care to visit, express their views, or make requests. If the MP finds merit in a constituent's claim, he can call it to the relevant ministry's attention, although he can do no more. The conscientious MP graces local festivals, celebrations, and ceremonials with his presence. And at his constituents' request he procures for them tickets of admission to the Strangers' Gallery (from where they can watch the House in session) and frequently also invites them to tea on the handsome terrace overlooking the Thames. An MP who shirks his local duties is more likely to find himself in trouble with his constituency party organization than with the voters, but the point is that his local obligations are an important—and often wearying—part of his public life. In some respects, then, he has many of the independent operator's burdens with few of his powers.

## THE INDEPENDENT OPERATOR

### Life in the House [27]

The American congressman operates in quite a different milieu. He owes his nomination—and renomination—to local organizations and voters, and no national party agency can veto it. His chances of reelection may be marginally affected by the success and support of his national party leaders, but they depend mainly upon what the local voters think of him. Not only do his leaders have little effective power to punish him for deviant voting, but also a reputation for independence and "refusal to submit to party dictation" may well be worth thousands of votes in his district. Furthermore,

---

[27] Many major studies of American legislators have been conducted in recent years. Those on Congress include Donald R. Matthews, *U.S. Senators and Their World* (Chapel Hill, N.C.: The University of North Carolina Press, 1960); Charles L. Clapp, *The Congressman: His Work as He Sees It* (New York: Anchor Books, 1963); Ralph K. Huitt and Robert L. Peabody, *Congress: Two Decades of Analysis* (New York: Harper & Row, Publishers, 1969); and Lewis Anthony Dexter, *The Sociology and Politics of Congress* (Skokie, Ill.: Rand McNally & Company, 1969). Studies of state legislators include John C. Wahlke, Heinz Eulau, William Buchanan, and LeRoy C. Ferguson, *The Legislative System* (New York: John Wiley & Sons, Inc., 1962); James David Barber, *The Lawmakers* (New Haven, Conn.: Yale University Press, 1965); and Jeane J. Kirkpatrick, *Political Woman* (New York: Basic Books, 1974).

a vote against his party's "line" is in no sense a vote to put the other party in control of Congress or the presidency—fixed terms and separation of powers take care of that. His vote therefore belongs to him, and he can use it as he wishes, to promote whatever values he chooses. He may voluntarily decide to "go along" with his party on most issues—a majority of congressmen, as we have seen, do just that. But the fact that his party cannot effectively *order* him to vote this way or that makes his position very different from that of the British MP.

How do American legislators use this heady independence? Most political scientists have answered this question in terms of the different roles that different legislators choose (or are forced) to play. James D. Barber's study of Connecticut freshman legislators, for example, has distinguished among "spectators," "advertisers," "reluctants," and "lawmakers." The study by John C. Wahlke, Heinz Eulau, William Buchanan, and LeRoy C. Ferguson of legislators in California, New Jersey, Ohio, and Tennessee identifies several sets of roles: In their representational functions legislators are classified as "trustees," "politicos," and "delegates"; in their dealings with other legislators as "inventors," "brokers," and "tribunes"; and in their dealings with pressure groups as "facilitators," "neutrals," and "resisters." William S. White's and Ralph K. Huitt's studies of the Senate distinguish between "members of the inner club" and "outsiders."[28] The common theme of all these studies is that each legislator is impelled by his own psychological makeup, his perceptions of the legislative process in the capital and of the electoral process in his district, and his goals and ambitions to choose a certain role; the role that he chooses determines both his actions and his effectiveness.

Let me illustrate with an example, which I shall call "The Education of Senator X":

X, a brilliant and idealistic young liberal, is elected to the United States Senate from a midwestern state. Justly proud of his speaking ability and burning with zeal to push the liberal legislation for which he campaigned, he makes his "maiden" speech a few days after having been sworn in and in the ensuing weeks follows it up with a number of speeches on a wide variety of topics. All his speeches are eloquent and witty and receive favorable notice in the press, but somehow the other senators do not seem to be persuaded by them—not even the other liberals. Senator X therefore begins to accept outside speaking engagements, in the course of which he refers often to the stubbornness of the conservative senators, the lack of leadership among his fellow liberals, and the inertia and sloth of the Senate itself. His name appears in the headlines with increasing frequency, and his mail indicates that the folks back home think that he is wonderful. But it seems that the more popular he becomes outside the Senate, the less able he is to accomplish anything inside the Senate. He introduces many intelligently drafted and worthy major bills, but most of them never even leave committee.

Finally, in desperation, he goes to Senator Y, his party's floor leader, and asks: "Why can't I get anything done in this outfit? What am I doing wrong?" Senator Y

---

[28] William S. White, *Citadel: The Story of the U.S. Senate* (New York: Harper & Row, Publishers, 1956); and Ralph K. Huitt, "The Outsider in the Senate: An Alternative Role," *American Political Science Review,* 55 (September 1961), 566–575.

replies: "Look X, you are doing just about everything wrong. A couple of days after you had been sworn in you made a major speech. During your first six months you sounded off—at length—on every major issue that came up. Then you started shooting your mouth off outside the Senate and had the gall to say a lot of nasty things about some individual senators and the Senate itself. And now you keep introducing bills on every subject under the sun. Frankly, X, the boys think that you are a blowhard and a publicity hound. They think you don't know what you are talking about most of the time, and no matter how good the bills you introduce may be, the fact that you introduced them is, as far as most of the boys are concerned, reason enough to dump them. That's the way it is."

Senator X is, of course, stunned and angry. But, although he is as eager as the next man to be a hero to the folks back home, he also wishes to see his liberal legislation pass the Senate. He therefore decides to make a few changes in the light of Senator Y's comments. First, he picks four subjects—agriculture, civil rights, foreign affairs, and taxation—and speaks only on legislation in those areas. Second, he carefully prepares each speech, shows himself to be thoroughly conversant with all the facts and figures in each area, and confines himself to no more than one major speech on each major bill in each of his chosen areas. Third, he sharply reduces his outside speaking commitments and refrains from any direct criticism of the Senate or its individual members. Fourth, he makes a point of frequently seeking the advice of Senators A, B, and C, who are older and chairmen of key committees; he does several chores for each of them. Finally, he introduces only one or two major bills at each session.

After a while X notices that when he speaks in the Senate not only do the others listen but also some of them even quote him in their own speeches. His bills begin to receive serious and friendly consideration, and most are passed in some form or other. Other senators begin to come to him for advice. Finally, Senator Y stops him in the lobby one days and says: "X, you've straightened out just fine these past months, and all the boys on both sides of the aisle think you're okay. In fact, you are in line for the next vacancy on our policy committee, so keep it up!" As X walks away feeling very pleased, he thinks to himself that learning how the Senate really works involves a lot more than memorizing the Senate rules and the committee structure—and he only wishes that he had started his education a little sooner.

## Relations with Constituents [29]

Senator X, like every American congressman and most British MPs, cannot, however, concentrate solely on the game with his fellow legislators, for the voters back home are the final arbiters of his political success.[30] He must perform a number of services

---

[29] Two installments of a rigorous and imaginative study are: Warren E. Miller and Donald E. Stokes, "Constituency Influence in Congress," *American Political Science Review,* 57 (March 1963), 45–56; and Miller and Stokes, "Party Government and the Saliency of Congress," *Public Opinion Quarterly,* 26 (Winter 1962), 531–546.

[30] This fact is ignored in Allen Drury's best-selling novel *Advise and Consent* (New York: Pocket Books, Inc., 1962), which tells its story of senatorial decision making as if there were no voters and all the senators held office for life.

for them. Furthermore, local chores are even more important to him than to an MP: His personal electoral fortunes are less tied to those of his party, and, unlike the MP, he *can* exert direct pressure on executives and administrators. Failure to show results is thus more likely to count against him than against the MP at reelection time.

There is an even greater difference: Because the congressman controls his own vote, he has an individual voting record that may play a major role in his efforts to be reelected. In Chapter 14 we examined several theories about how a democratic legislator *should* determine his vote; now it is time to ask how American congressmen actually *do* make up their minds.

In their study of the United States House of Representatives Warren E. Miller and Donald E. Stokes consider three possible explanatory models: the Burkean independent legislator, the Rousseauistic constituency delegate, and the responsible party's team player. To discover which, if any, of these three best fits American congressmen, they interviewed a sample of 116 representatives and a sample of the voters in each of their districts. They found, as we would expect (see Chap. 5), that on most issues most constituents "are almost totally uninformed about legislative issues in Washington." Furthermore, few voters know anything more about their representatives than the party labels and for most the representatives' voting records are a total mystery.[31]

Miller and Stokes concluded that

> no single tradition of representation fully accords with the realities of American legislative politics. The American system is a mixture, to which the Burkean, instructed-delegate, and responsible-party models all can be said to have contributed elements. Moreover, variations in the representative relation are most likely to occur as we move from one policy domain to another.[32]

On civil-rights issues most representatives voted according to their constituents' *and* their own views, which usually coincided. On social-welfare issues their votes conformed more closely to their parties' stands than to their constituents' views. And on foreign-policy issues they voted more in line with their own views than with either their constituents' or their parties' views.

It appears, then, that the independent legislator is not so independent after all. If his constituents hold strong views on a salient issue, he had better not flout them if he wishes to keep his seat. He has fellow legislators whose cooperation he needs to accomplish anything. He has friends and supporters in organized pressure groups

---

[31] Significantly, however, this finding did not appear where a particular issue was highly salient. One of the districts was the Arkansas Fifth District, which in 1958 was undergoing a hot contest between segregationist Dale Alford and moderate Brooks Hays, eventually won by Alford. *All* the respondents interviewed knew both candidates' stands on segregation.

[32] Miller and Stokes, "Constituency Influence in Congress," p. 56. See also Aage R. Clausen, *How Congressmen Decide: A Policy Focus* (New York: St. Martin's Press, Inc., 1973); Charles F. Cnudde and Donald J. McCrone, "The Linkage between Constituency Attitudes and Congressional Voting Behavior: A Causal Model," *American Political Science Review,* 60 (March 1966), 66–72.

and outside them whose help he needs to continue in office. He has a party to which he feels some loyalty and obligation, even though its leaders cannot "purge" him as in Great Britain. And he himself is not the mere plaything of external pressures; he is a human being with values, perceptions, and goals. Lacking the confining but simplifying all-powerful party cues of the MP, he has the freedom—and the necessity —to balance the many forces impinging on him and thus votes in ways that he and everyone important to him can live with.

## THE CHANGING ROLE OF MODERN DEMOCRATIC LEGISLATURES

### LOSS OF POLICY-MAKING INITIATIVE

The authors of the traditional conception of government mentioned at the beginning of this chapter believed that the legislature should be and in fact would be the main policy-making agency in any properly organized government. After all, they reasoned, statutes and public policy are identical; because the legislature will originate, amend, and pass all statutes, it will necessarily monopolize the making of public policy. In early debates on the new Constitution of the United States, most people thus agreed that the most powerful—and potentially the most dangerous—part of the government would be the House of Representatives; not only would it be a legislative body, which automatically made it very powerful, but it would also be the only body directly elected by the people and thus subject to popular passions, unrestrained by prudence and due consideration for minority interests.

**The executive proposes, the legislature disposes.** Source: UPI Photograph.

The Legislative Process

Contemporary political scientists agree that, setting aside the question of whether or not modern democratic legislatures *should* play such a role, the fact is that most do not. In almost every modern democratic nation during the past century the legislature has been increasingly losing the initiative in policy making to the executive and administrative agencies. The loss has perhaps been most precipitous and dramatic in France, where the national assembly dominated the executive and controlled policy making in the Fourth Republic (1945–1958) but has played only a minor role in the Fifth Republic.[33] In almost all the parliamentary democratic nations the prime ministers, cabinets, and ministries not only originate almost all major public bills but also control very tightly timing, agendas, and, in most instances, majorities of the legislative votes.[34]

Similar shifts have occurred in most of the presidential systems. In the United States, for example, an ever-larger proportion of major public bills is conceived, drafted, and pushed by the President and his executive and administrative associates —to the point that, as we shall see in the next chapter, he is commonly called our "chief legislator," as well as our "chief executive."[35] Somewhat the opposite development has apparently taken place in the Philippines: The authors of the Philippine Constitution deliberately made the presidency the most powerful agency of government. From World War II to the early 1970s the congress' role in policy-making grew noticeably,[36] but in 1972 President Ferdinand Marcos imposed martial law, pushed through a new Constitution creating a parliamentary form of government, but claimed for an indefinite time plenary powers for himself until the "time was ripe" for the new Constitution to go into effect.

## GROWTH AS CHECKERS, REVISERS, AND CRITICS

It would be a great mistake to conclude from the discussion above that the legislature plays *no* significant role in modern democratic government. It certainly does play a role, but a different one from that envisioned in traditional doctrine.

Although they have lost their power as initiators of policy to the executive and administrative agencies, democratic legislatures have greatly increased their power and activities as checkers, revisers, and critics of policies initiated by others. After all, they still retain their formal powers to make statutes, which means that, for a great many of his most cherished policies (for example, those relating to taxes, appropriations, treaties, and statutes of all types), the executive must obtain the consent of the legislature. Where, as in Great Britain and the dominions, the cabinets' control of the legislatures through the majority parties is at maximum strength, the executives appear able to ram through whatever policies they wish. Yet a rebellion within any

---

[33] Henry Ehrmann has entitled his chapter on this shift "The National Assembly—From Omnipotence to Impotence," in *Politics in France* (Boston: Little, Brown & Company, 1968), chap. 10.

[34] Wheare, *Legislatures*, chap 9.

[35] The point is well made by John S. Saloma III, who points out that, now as always, the President and Congress *share* power over policy making but that in recent years the President's share has increased; *Congress and the New Politics* (Boston: Little, Brown & Company, 1969), chap. 4.

[36] Jean Grossholtz, *Politics in the Philippines* (Boston: Little, Brown & Company, 1964), pp. 119–125.

**The popular stereotype of legislators is not flattering.** Source: (top) *Straight Herblock* (New York: Simon and Schuster, Inc., 1964). Source: (bottom) Editorial cartoon by Pat Oliphant. Copyright, The Denver Post. Reprinted with permission of Los Angeles Times Syndicate.

*"Leaving religion to private initiative is un-American!"*

*"Get those wheelchairs in a circle—he's comin' back!"*

majority party is always possible, and defeat by the voters at the next election is even more frequent. No British or dominion cabinet can or does totally ignore resentments and discontent within its own party or sharp criticisms by the opposition—especially those that appear to represent the feelings of substantial portions of the electorate or powerful pressure groups. In Great Britain and the dominions, though the objections and misgivings of legislators cannot force the executives to change their policies, they can and often do persuade them that a certain amount of trimming their sails and altering their courses will make for much smoother governmental passage.

**Congress is not totally helpless before the President.** Source: "Nixon Rated Cartoons" by Ranan Lurie, published by Quadrangle, the New York Times Book Co.

In countries like the United States and the democratic nations of Europe, where the executives' control over the legislatures is weaker than in Great Britain and the dominions, the legislatures' functions of revision and criticism are even more prominent. The President of the United States may initiate most major pieces of legislation, but he must expect most of them to emerge from Congress in somewhat altered form, and he will find that he cannot have some of them at all. He operates his administration, furthermore, in constant awareness of congressional investigations that draw public attention to the mistakes of executive officers and the peculations of administrators, object to various contracts and appointments, and in general resist the notion that he alone has a mandate to run the whole government and make whatever policy he wishes.

If there were ever any doubts about this, they were removed by the dramatic events of 1972–1974. Richard Nixon was reelected President in 1972 by a great landslide, but in less than two years Congress enacted legislation severely limiting presidential power to make war and substantially increasing its own budgetary powers. And in 1974 the certainty of impeachment by the House of Representatives and probable conviction by the Senate forced Nixon to become the first President in the nation's history to resign his office.

Henceforth, American Presidents, no less than British or dominion prime ministers and European premiers, will be vividly aware that there is always a legislature to deal with. And who, after all, is to say that the modern legislature's role of criticizing, revising, and checking the executive and the administration does not constitute as valuable a contribution to the health of democracy as did the monopoly of policy making originally assigned to it.

## OTHER SYSTEMS, OTHER LEGISLATURES

As we have seen, all the world's democratic systems have legislatures of some sort performing some kind of distinctive role in policy making. A number of nondemocratic nations apparently do not see any point in even going through the motions, and have no legislatures at all.[37] However, many nondemocratic regimes do have legislatures—of a sort. In many respects they resemble the democracies' legislatures: Their members are elected (usually without opposition) from districts; they meet periodically; they choose presiding officers, hear speeches, and vote on proposed legislation; and their acts constitute much of their nations' formal statutory law. But their roles in their political systems are actually very different from those of the democratic legislatures that we have been considering. Let us briefly examine a few of these other legislatures.

### THE SUPREME SOVIET OF THE USSR

The 1936 Constitution of the Soviet Union establishes a national bicameral legislature called the Supreme Soviet of the USSR. One house, the Soviet (council) of the Union

---

[37] According to *The Statesman's Year-Book,* in 1974 twenty-six nations had no legislatures of any kind at all: Algeria, Bahrain, Bolivia, Brunei, Burma, Burundi, Central African Republic, Cuba, Dahomey, Ecuador, Ghana, Greece, Iraq, Lesotho, Libya, Malagasy Republic, Mali, Nigeria, Oman, Peru, Philippines, Qatar, Saudi Arabia, Somalia, Togo, and Uganda; *The Statesman's Year-Book, 1973–1974* (New York: St. Martin's Press, 1974).

has 767 members, one for each 300,000 inhabitants, elected in the Soviet fashion (see Chap. 7) from single-member districts. The other house, the Soviet of Nationalities, has 750 members elected at large in varying proportions from the constituent republics, autonomous republics, autonomous regions, and national areas of the Soviet Union. Of the 1517 deputies to both houses elected in 1966, 1141 were members of the Communist Party of the Soviet Union, and 376 were not.[38]

The Constitution stipulates that the Supreme Soviet must meet at least twice a year, and since Stalin's death it has done so. But we obtain our first glimpse of its true nature when we learn that its sessions average only two to four days in length and that in any one year it never meets for as much as two weeks altogether. The only legislation considered is that sponsored by Communist party leaders, and these measures always pass without speeches or votes in opposition.

Each house appoints nine committees to consider proposed legislation in advance of the plenary sessions. Usually the committee discussions are carefully "guided" by the committees' party leaders, but occasionally freer discussion is permitted—either because of the leaders' indecision about what form of legislation will best accomplish their policy objectives or because they think that such discussion will help to arouse enthusiasm for the measure among the deputies and, through them, the masses.

The Supreme Soviet in joint session also elects a thirty-three-member presidium, which is empowered to issue decrees having the force of law in the intervals between the plenary sessions. These decrees are supposed to be ratified later by the full Supreme Soviet—and sometimes they are, always unanimously. Some decrees, however, are never brought before the Supreme Soviet at all; they have the force of law nevertheless.

The Soviet Union's national legislature thus has no real power whatever and cannot perform any of the legislative functions discussed earlier. What, then, *are* its functions? There are several, all desirable in the party leaders' view. Its existence makes the regime appear more democratic both at home and abroad. Its elections and meetings are useful occasions for rallying popular support behind party leaders and their policies. Its sessions serve as "briefing conferences" for minor and provincial party functionaries, who constitute most of the membership and serve as important conduits for transmitting the party "line" to the masses. Membership is generally considered an honor and therefore provides a reward for diligent party service in the boondocks. It even furnishes the leaders with an opportunity to identify promising individuals who may be future leadership material. Perhaps most important, according to one leading observer,

the Party utilizes the Supreme Soviet sessions as a device for testing public opinion. This is not accomplished through the "dangerous" procedures of uncontrolled debate and voting, but by more indirect sounding of the attitudes of

Governmental Authorities and Processes

[38] L. G. Churchward, *Contemporary Soviet Government* (London: Routledge & Kegan Paul Ltd., 1968), p. 119.

deputies who, after all, have been chosen to represent to some degree the extremely varied geographical, national, and social groups of the USSR.[39]

## OTHER LEGISLATURES

The legislatures in most other nondemocratic regimes play roles similar to that of the Supreme Soviet. The national people's congress of the People's Republic of China meets once a year, mainly to hear speeches by the party leaders and to roar its approval. Much the same may be said of the Albanian national assembly, the East German parliament, and (with some minor variations) the legislatures of the other Eastern European "people's democracies." Furthermore, ideology seems to make little difference in this regard, for the Reichstag under Adolf Hitler and the chambers of deputies and corporations under Benito Mussolini closely resembled the Supreme Soviet in both procedures and functions.

Even in Mexico, whose political system is considerably more democratic than is that of the Soviet Union, the bicameral *Congreso*—though more than 10 percent of its members belong to parties opposing the dominant Partido Revolucionario Institucional (PRI)—seems to resemble the Supreme Soviet more closely than it resembles the Congress of its northern neighbor. For, as one leading student has observed, decisions about public policy are "reached and appropriate legislative proposals prepared in the executive agencies before the matter is referred to Congress for rubber-stamp approval"; the Congress

> serves as little more than a convenient training ground for ambitious young politicians who wish to spend a few years in the national capital, as a kind of convenient patronage for certain political and functional interest association leaders, or as a quiet tapering-off appointment for older politicians who no longer are as efficient as they once were but are not quite ready to retire, or, perhaps more nearly correctly, to remove their names from the public payroll.[40]

In just about every modern government, democratic or nondemocratic, the executive agencies have thus come to play a considerably more powerful role in making public policy than does the legislature. In the next chapter we shall take a closer look at modern executives to see what kinds there are and how, under what handicaps, and with what success they shoulder their great burdens.

---

[39] John A. Armstrong, *Ideology, Politics, and Government in the Soviet Union* (3d ed.; New York: Frederick A. Praeger, Inc., 1974), p. 163.

[40] Robert E. Scott, *Mexican Government in Transition* (Urbana, Ill.: University of Illinois Press, 1959), pp. 265, 280.

# 16

# THE EXECUTIVE PROCESS

How many of the following can we name: the President of the United States, the senators from our state, the congressman from our district, the speaker of the House of Representatives, the majority and minority leaders in both houses of Congress, the governor of our state, the state legislators from our district, the majority and minority leaders of both houses of our state legislature?

If we are like most Americans we know who the President is, and we can probably also name our governor and perhaps one or both of our senators; but if we know the names of the other officials listed we can claim to be exceptionally well informed.

That we know more about top executives than about top legislators does not, however, mean that we are poor citizens; it means that for us, as for most Americans (and for most citizens of other democratic nations), executives are, so to speak, the "glamour boys" of government. The purveyors of news over the mass media talk far more about them than about individual legislators (with rare exceptions like Senators Edward Kennedy or Charles Percy) because they think that executives are more "newsworthy"—that is, we are presumed to be more interested in hearing about executives than about legislators.

That executives in most democratic systems normally receive more public attention than do other officials is both a result and a cause of the changing roles and positions of the executives and the legislatures. In Chapter 15 we noted that in most democratic nations the legislatures have largely lost their traditional policy-initiating role and have become checkers, revisers, and critics of policies initiated by the executives. In this chapter we shall take up the other side of this story: the general expansion of executive power and influence that has occurred in just about every democratic nation.

Before we begin this survey we must recognize that in the democratic nations officials generally called "executives" perform two distinct principal roles. The first is that of "chief of state," acting as the nation's official ceremonial head and spokesman for its whole people. The second is that of "head of government," acting as the leader of those officeholders who propose, direct, and enforce the nation's public policies. In the parliamentary democracies each role is performed by a distinctly different official or group of officials, whereas in the presidential systems both are performed by the same officials.

As the role of head of government has the greater impact on public policy in modern democratic systems, we shall devote most of our attention to it in this chapter. The role of chief of state is by no means insignificant, however, and we shall therefore begin by briefly summarizing what it involves, how it is performed, and who performs it.

## THE EXECUTIVE AS CHIEF OF STATE

### PRINCIPAL TYPES

#### Hereditary Monarchs

As Table 18 (Chap. 14) shows, the chiefs of state in sixteen democratic nations are hereditary monarchs—who inherit their positions by primogeniture[1] and who perform their functions either directly (as, for example, do the British queen, the Belgian and Scandinavian kings, and the Japanese emperor) or indirectly through personal representatives known as "governor-generals" (as, for example, in the British Commonwealth nations of Australia, Canada, and New Zealand).

As recently as the nineteenth century many hereditary monarchs not only were their nations' formal chiefs of state but also played prominent roles in policy making, and a few were close to being absolute dictators. Even today government in the "constitutional monarchies" is formally conducted in the monarchs' names: the British Queen, for example, opens and dissolves Parliament, gives her assent to all acts of Parliament before they become law, appoints all ministers, and awards all peerages and other honors. Yet the Queen, like her fellow sovereigns in the other nations considered here, does all these things only on the advice of her ministers, who are selected by Parliament and thus indirectly by the voters. Political scientists call these nations "constitutional monarchies" or "limited monarchies" and classify them near the democratic end of the spectrum. Only in a few "monarchical dictatorships" like Saudi Arabia and Bhutan do present-day monarchs play policy-making roles remotely approaching those of such "absolute monarchs" of yore as Elizabeth I of England or Louis XIV of France. Constitutional monarchs, then, are chiefs of state only; in this capacity they perform functions that we shall consider in a moment.

---

[1] The ancient rule of inheritance by which the firstborn has first claim on the deceased parent's estate.

## Elected "Monarchs"

In the nineteenth and twentieth centuries most absolute monarchs have been toppled from their hereditary pinnacles of power,[2] and many have been replaced with much more democratic regimes. In the constitutional monarchies this change has been accomplished by stripping the monarchs of all policy-making power and leaving them only ceremonial functions. Other nations have entirely abolished their monarchies and replaced them with republican regimes formally headed by elected officials, usually known as "presidents." These nations may be divided into two groups. The first includes those that, like Austria, West Germany, and India, have assigned to their presidents only the role of chief of state, thus making them "elected monarchs." Eight of the nations listed in Table 18 fall into this class.

## Elected Heads of Government

The nine presidential democracies listed in Table 18 vest the functions of chief of state in elected presidents who also act as heads of government. The outstanding instance of such an official is, of course, the President of the United States, but the same dual role is performed by the presidents of Argentina, Venezuela, Costa Rica, and Mexico, to mention some leading examples. In all these nations performance of these two quite different roles by single officials generates many complications, some of which we shall examine later.

## Collegial Executives

In only one modern democratic nation are the executive powers and functions not either divided between two officials, as in the parliamentary systems, or concentrated in one official, as in the presidential systems. In Switzerland they are performed by a seven-member federal council, selected every four years by the two houses of the national parliament meeting in joint session. The parliament also selects a member of the council to serve for one year as President of the Confederation, and the office rotates among the members of the council in order of seniority. Ceremonial functions are performed by the member who happens to be President at the moment, but the policy-directing functions are performed by the whole council.[3]

In Uruguay before 1967 the executive functions were vested in a nine-member national council—six members from the majority party and three from the largest minority party appointed for terms of four years by the two legislative houses in joint session. The presidency rotated annually among the members of the majority party in the council. In 1966, however, Uruguay's voters approved a proposal to replace their Swiss-style collegial executive with a one-man chief executive comparable to

---

[2] Most recently in Ethiopia, where in 1974 a coup by the revolutionary command council of army leaders overthrew the near-dictatorship of Emperor Haile Selassie and replaced it with a military junta.

[3] Christopher Hughes, *The Parliament of Switzerland* (London: Cassell & Co., Ltd., 1962), chaps. 7, 9; and George Arthur Codding, Jr., *The Federal Government of Switzerland* (Boston: Houghton Mifflin Company, 1961), chap. 6.

those in the other Latin American democracies; the first incumbent, President Jorge Pacheco Areco, took office in 1967.

## PRINCIPAL FUNCTIONS

### Symbolic and Ceremonial

In Chapters 2 and 3 we noted that one of the great problems facing the people of every modern democratic nation is maintaining a society and a government in which myriad interest groups can freely pursue their conflicting objectives yet continue to live together as one nation under one government. We observed that every such nation faces the ever-present possibility of civil war and disintegration and that it also contains certain social forces and institutions that encourage national unity and consensus. In the final analysis, we concluded, the citizens of the United States, like those of any democratic polity, will continue to live together in this fashion only as long as they think of themselves as *Americans* as well as blacks, rich people, workers, or whatever.

Every nation has symbols and ceremonies that help to remind its citizens of their national identity, their common achievements and aspirations. No American needs to be told of the significance of the Stars and Stripes, the Pledge of Allegiance, or the Fourth of July; every other nation has its own equivalents. Most citizens of every democratic nation evidently feel the need to include among these symbols a person who officially embodies their national identity and on certain great occasions speaks for the whole nation both to the nation itself and to the outside world.

This need is the main reason why every nation, democratic or dictatorial, has an official chief of state (usually, though not always, a single official), and it defines the functions the chief of state must perform. When, for example, a member of the armed forces is to receive the nation's highest decoration—the Congressional Medal of Honor or the Victoria Cross, for example—the President or the Queen pins it on. When the nation pays tribute to its war dead, it is the President or the Queen who lays the wreath on the unknown soldier's tomb. When the Red Cross, the boy scouts, or some other worthy enterprise needs a boost, the President or the Queen speaks in its behalf and is photographed subscribing to it. In these and many other ways the President and the Queen personalize and humanize that sometimes grim abstraction "the government" and remind the citizens of their common heritage and hopes.

### Reigning

Constitutional monarchs and elected "monarchs" perform largely but not exclusively ceremonial and symbolic functions. In addition to these duties they also "reign"— that is, provide the formal channel through which governmental power is passed in a peaceful and orderly way from one person or set of persons to another. In any of the parliamentary democracies, for example, when the prime minister leaves office and must be replaced by another, the chief of state formally accomplishes the transfer by "summoning" the new leader, who is then given the responsibility of forming a new government. On the great majority of such occasions in Great Britain and the

The Executive Process

The President as Chief of State: President Richard M. Nixon welcomes Jordan's King Hussein to the White House, April 8, 1969.
Source: UPI Photograph.

dominions the monarch has no option but must summon the leaders of the parties that control the lower houses of the legislatures. Yet British monarchs have occasionally made real choices: the clearest instance was in 1957, when Conservative party leader Prime Minister Sir Anthony Eden resigned. As the Conservatives held a majority in the House of Commons, Queen Elizabeth II had to replace Eden with another Conservative, but the party had never indicated whether it wished Eden's successor to be Harold Macmillan or R. A. Butler. After private consultations with her personal advisers, the Queen summoned Macmillan, and he became the new prime minister. She is widely believed to have played a similar role in the choice of Sir Alec Douglas-Home over Butler in 1963.

## SEPARATION AND COMBINATION OF ROLES

During the Korean war President Harry S Truman was scheduled to award a posthumous Congressional Medal of Honor to an American serviceman through his father, but the father refused to accept it, saying, "Harry Truman isn't fit to honor my son." This episode dramatized the disadvantages of combining in one executive officer the two quite separate roles of chief of state and head of government; obviously, the serviceman's father was not saying that the United States itself was unfit to honor his son but only that the individual Harry Truman—who was not only President of the United States but also head of the Democratic party, "that man who got us into the war," a Fair Dealer, and many other *political* things—was objectionable. In other words, the father objected to the head of government, not to the chief of state—but both officials came wrapped in the same package!

Radio and television networks face a similar problem. When an American President speaks free of charge over a national hookup on some public issue and the opposition party demands equal free time to reply, the networks must decide whether the President was speaking as chief of state or as leader of his party. If he was speaking in the former capacity, the opposition's demand can be denied, but if he was speaking as a partisan, fair play and the Federal Communications Commission's rules require that the opposition be given equal time.

It is illuminating to recall that when King Charles I and King George III sought active parts in policy making and strove to become the heads of their governments, they were widely and openly criticized—and, indeed, Charles I was executed. Now that such monarchs as Olav V and Elizabeth II are chiefs of state only, they are largely beyond public criticism and certainly are in no danger of losing their heads. Occasionally recent British monarchs and their consorts have been criticized for making "political speeches" (speeches in favor of certain policies), but such criticism means only that particular individuals may have stepped outside their proper roles, not that the roles themselves have become intermingled and confused, as in the United States. Herman Finer has summed up the advantages of assigning the two roles to different officials:

> As a father-image, or an impersonation of the romantic, says the psychoanalyst, king or queen stands scatheless, the noble father or mother, while the politicians may be vilified and scourged. This duality is politically comfortable. On the one hand, politics might be red in tooth and claw; on the other, royalty reminds the nation of its brotherhood amid their conflicts. The silk gloves are something to be thankful for.[4]

On the other hand, being chief of state is useful to the President of the United States in his role as head of government. As in all other modern democratic systems, the American executive's role most powerfully affects the making of public policy.

---

[4]Herman Finer, *Governments of Greater European Powers* (New York: Holt, Rinehart and Winston, Inc., 1956), pp. 189–190. See also Dermot Morrah, *The Work of the Queen* (London: William Kimber & Co., Ltd., 1958).

# THE EXECUTIVE AS HEAD OF GOVERNMENT

Every modern democracy except Switzerland has a single executive officer who assumes the demanding and key role of head of government. The manner in which he fills the role, however, is greatly affected by whether he heads a presidential or a parliamentary system (see Chap. 15). A useful way to describe the similarities and differences among modern democratic heads of government is to look first at the two principal types.

## THE PRESIDENT

In the nine presidential democracies listed in Table 18 the role of head of government is performed by chief executives officially called "president." These officers cannot be members of the legislatures and are elected either indirectly by an "electoral college," as in Finland and the United States, or directly by the voters, as in Argentina, Colombia, Costa Rica, Mexico, Panama, and Venezuela. A president holds office for a legally fixed term whether or not he commands the confidence of the legislature. The presidency of the United States is the oldest and best-known office of this type and is in many respects the prototype for the others.

## THE PRIME MINISTER

In every parliamentary democracy the role of head of government is performed by a leader formally designated by the chief of state for the post but actually selected by a majority of the legislature. He has no fixed term of office but depends upon his continuing ability to command the confidence of a legislative majority. When that majority votes "no confidence" in him, he must resign, and the chief of state must replace him with some other leader whom the legislature will support. In Great Britain, the dominions, and other parliamentary democracies with strong national two-party systems the prime ministers are normally leaders of the parties holding majorities or pluralities in the lower legislative houses.

Some European democratic polities, as we observed in Chapter 9, have rather highly fractionalized party systems, and no legislator can therefore hope to lead *the* majority party as the British prime minister usually does. In such democracies the heads of government are leaders formally designated by the chiefs of state and have such official titles as "chancellor" (West Germany) and "premier" (Italy). Each is chosen because he can head a coalition government, consisting of the leaders of several parties and supported by their members in the parliament. When one or two of the participating parties decide to withdraw their support, the premier's government falls, and he is replaced by another who has been able to put together a new party coalition constituting a legislative majority. Premiers in the more fractionalized party systems vary widely in the security of their tenure, their power, and their constitutional ability to direct public policy. Near one pole we can place the French premiers of the Third and Fourth Republics, whose terms in office averaged less than a year and who were widely regarded as much weaker than the prime ministers of most two-party nations. Near the other pole we can place not only the British prime ministers but also the premiers of several highly stable though fractionalized systems, like those of the Scandinavian nations, the Netherlands, and Israel.

We shall now examine in greater detail the nature, power, handicaps, and systemic roles of the presidential and prime-ministerial types of heads of government.

## THE PRESIDENT AS HEAD OF GOVERNMENT

### DEVELOPMENT OF THE OFFICE IN THE UNITED STATES

#### Intentions of the Founding Fathers

The members of the American Constitutional Convention in 1787 were well aware that many of their compatriots were extremely suspicious of executive power and that the weak governorships specified in many of the new state Constitutions reflected this suspicion. But the Founding Fathers, unlike some of their contemporaries, were equally suspicious of an all-powerful legislature and believed that a reasonably strong executive would be necessary to check Congress. Everyone knew, moreover, that George Washington, the most venerated American of his time, would occupy whatever executive office was created.

Accordingly, they intended the office of President of the United States to be something closely approaching what they understood the British monarchy to be—that is, the President was to be George III with the corruption and the hereditary principle removed. Clinton Rossiter has summed up their views: "The President was to be a strong, dignified, nonpolitical chief of state and government. In a word, he was to be George Washington."[5]

#### Expansion of the Presidency since 1789

The presidency of Gerald R. Ford in the 1970s is a radically different office from the presidency of George Washington and John Adams in the 1790s. The modern President is not only a partisan official but also the number-one leader of one of the nation's two great political parties. Rather than acting merely as an adviser to and restrainer of Congress, he is the principal initiator of the major public bills that Congress considers and is often called our "chief legislator." He and his advisers dominate the formulation and conduct of our foreign policy, and in times of national crisis the President becomes what some scholars have called a "constitutional dictator." Finally, what he does affects many more people than just Americans, for he is regarded as the leader of the free world in its struggle with its communist antagonists, and what goes on in the White House is of almost as much concern in London and Paris—and, for that matter, in Moscow and Peking—as it is in New York and Chicago.

The story of how and why the presidency of the 1970s is so much more

---

[5] Clinton Rossiter, *The American Presidency* (New York: Harcourt Brace Jovanovich, Inc., 1956), p. 60.

powerful than was the presidency of the 1790s is too long and complex to be related in its entirety here. Most political scientists believe that its expansion had two main causes.[6] First, the "democratization" of the office resulting from conversion of the Electoral College into a machine for the popular election of the President (see Chap. 11) has made him the only public official (except for the Vice-President, who is tied to the President) elected by all the nation's voters. (Gerald R. Ford is the first President in history to hold the office without having been popularly elected to it or to the vice presidency.) Every President since Andrew Jackson has to some degree regarded himself as holding a special mandate from the people to work in their behalf, and this view has greatly enhanced the powers of the presidency and inclined many occupants of the office to exercise them vigorously—for the most part with the full and enthusiastic approval of a majority of the voters. Second, the United States has grown from an agricultural nation of 4 million people to an industrial nation of more than 200 million, from a third-rate power to the most powerful nation in the world. This change has increasingly forced problems of foreign policy, international relations, and war and peace to the forefront of popular and governmental concern; as the President has always dominated the handling of such problems, their increased importance has greatly added to his power and prestige.

Some commentators have suggested that this expansion of presidential power reflects the greed for power of many of its custodians, who have not turned out to be the modest constitutional types envisioned by the Founding Fathers. The evidence suggests, however, that this explanation is highly superficial. For one thing, executive power has also expanded considerably in a great many local governments in the United States, and many mayors, city managers, and governors have increased their power in much the same manner as have the Presidents.[7] For another, as we shall observe at the end of this chapter, similar expansions of executive power have occurred in most other democratic nations. Increasing executive power is thus characteristic of most of the democratic world and not unique to the American presidency.

Whatever may be the causes there is no doubt that the American presidency has become the most powerful elective office in the world.

## AMERICAN PRESIDENTIAL ROLES[8]

### Chief of State

The first role of the President of the United States is that of chief of state, in which

---

[6] See George E. Reedy, *The Presidency in Flux* (New York: Columbia University Press, 1971); Arthur M. Schlesinger, Jr., *The Imperial Presidency* (Boston: Houghton Mifflin Company, 1974); and Nelson W. Polsby, *Congress and the Presidency* (Englewood Cliffs, N.J.: Prentice-Hall, Inc., 1964), pp. 12–14.

[7] See Leslie Lipson, *The American Governor: From Figurehead to Leader* (Chicago: University of Chicago Press, 1939); and Coleman B. Ransone, Jr., *The Office of Governor in the United States* (University, Ala.: University of Alabama Press, 1956).

[8] This enumeration of roles is drawn from Rossiter, *The American Presidency*. An unusually thoughtful and influential study of the presidency in action is Richard E. Neustadt, *Presidential Power* (New York: John Wiley & Sons, Inc., 1960).

The President as head of government: President Lyndon B. Johnson gives one of the 72 pens he used in signing the Civil Rights bill in the White House in 1964 to Roy Wilkins of the National Association for the Advancement of Colored People. Source: Wide World Photos.

capacity he performs symbolic and ceremonial functions similar to those of all chiefs of state. Although the combination of the roles of chief of state and head of government in the presidency generates a certain amount of confusion, it also lends the President a kind of majesty that assists him considerably in his second capacity. Sidney Hyman points out:

> Though he is sharply judged by the memories of his predecessors, his size seems to grow larger and clearer because he stands in their place.... Most important of all, he can lend his personal style to proud imitation by millions of people in private stations; he can bind the aspiration of the nation to the upward leap of his individual conscience, and infuse his own compassion into the national mind. He is, or can be, the essence of the nation's personality. In him, many things can flower—or decay.[9]

### Chief Executive

The President is formally responsible for most of the agencies charged with enforcing and administering acts of Congress and decisions of the national courts. In the mid 1970s President Ford was responsible in one way or another for the work of 11 major departments, more than 100 bureaus, 500 offices, 600 divisions, and a host of other

The Executive Process

[9] Sidney Hyman, *The American President* (New York: Harper & Row, Publishers, 1954), p. 13.

agencies. Together they employed a total of nearly 3 million people, not counting members of the armed forces. This figure includes approximately 1 out of every 60 civilians in the nation, in contrast to the ratio of 1 out of every 2000 in Washington's day.[10]

For many years the President's principal assistance in supervising administrative agencies came from the secretaries of his executive departments, of which there were once twelve: the Departments of State; the Treasury; Defense; Justice; the Post Office; Interior; Agriculture; Commerce; Labor; Health, Education and Welfare; Housing and Urban Development; and Transportation. Ever since the early 1790s these officers have regularly met with the President and advised him not only on matters of administration but on matters of legislation and other policy making as well. In their collective advisory capacity they are known as the Cabinet. Some Presidents have been strongly influenced by their Cabinets, whereas others have consigned theirs to a distinctly secondary role. Abraham Lincoln, for example, used his Cabinet as little more than a sounding board for his own ideas, whereas Dwight D. Eisenhower regarded his Cabinet as one of his most important advisory bodies.[11]

Over the years the Cabinet has increasingly become an advisory body on policy, rather than an administrative or supervisory agency, and recent Presidents have turned more and more to other agencies to assist them in their mammoth task of overseeing the administration. In 1939 Congress established the Executive Office of the President for this purpose. It now has more than 1200 full-time employees and includes such agencies as the White House Office, the National Security Council, the Council of Economic Advisers, the Office of Emergency Planning, and the Office of Management and Budget.

Probably even more important than these official aides is the President's "kitchen cabinet"—the small group of his most trusted advisers with whom he can talk most comfortably and whose candid advice he counts on whether they hold major or minor public offices or none. Any list of the men most influential in shaping recent Presidents' views on policy would include several who have held minor posts or none at all—Sherman Adams and Alfred Gruenther (Dwight D. Eisenhower), Theodore Sorensen and McGeorge Bundy (John F. Kennedy), Clark Clifford and Bill Moyers (Lyndon B. Johnson), and Henry Kissinger, H. R. Haldeman, and John Ehrlichman (Richard M. Nixon).

The presidency is thus no longer—if it ever was—something that the President carries around under his hat. It has become a large, complex network of public officials and private advisers performing in the President's name a wide variety of tasks, only a small fraction of which he can supervise personally. In Chapter 17 we shall consider further the consequences of this fact.

### Chief Diplomat

The President has always dominated the formulation and conduct of our foreign

---

[10] Hyman, *The American President*, pp. 9–10.

[11] See Richard F. Fenno, Jr., *The President's Cabinet* (Cambridge, Mass.: Harvard University Press, 1959). A 1970 law changed the Post Office to a non-Cabinet public corporation.

policy. He is the sole official channel of communication with foreign nations, and by receiving or refusing to receive official emissaries from foreign nations he alone determines whether or not the United States officially recognizes their governments. He and his representatives negotiate all international treaties and agreements. The Constitution requires that all treaties be approved by two-thirds of the Senate, but recent Presidents have concluded a great many "executive agreements"—international agreements made by the President on his own authority and not referred to the Senate for ratification. The importance of such agreements is shown by the Supreme Court's refusal to decide unequivocally whether or not they are equally binding and to be considered the "law of the land" within the meaning of the Constitution, equal to treaties ratified by the Senate.[12]

### Commander in Chief

The Constitution designates the President as commander in chief of all our armed forces. The framers of the Constitution wrote this clause mainly to establish the cherished principle of civilian supremacy and control over the military, and some wartime Presidents (like Abraham Lincoln and Franklin D. Roosevelt) have been very active in planning strategy and even directing troop movements, whereas others (like

---

The Executive Process

[12] See U.S. v. Belmont, 301 U.S. 324 (1937).

James Madison and Woodrow Wilson) have left such matters entirely to professional soldiers. The main significance of the designation lies in the power it gives the President to threaten or even wage war whether or not Congress has authorized it. In 1950 President Truman ordered American armed forces to resist the North Korean attack on South Korea. For two years we fought a "police action" in Korea that was not a "war" only because Congress had not formally declared it. A decade later, in 1962, President Kennedy ordered the armed forces to "quarantine" Cuba from further shipments of Russian missiles even if it meant sinking Russian ships and starting a thermonuclear war with the Soviet Union. A series of executive decisions by Presidents Eisenhower, Kennedy, and particularly Johnson increased American involvement in Vietnam from the supplying of advice and matériel to a full-scale war involving more than 500,000 American troops; only Congress' Tonkin Gulf Resolution of 1964 (repealed in 1970) served as a very broad authorization.

Up to the 1970s the Supreme Court consistently held that all these Presidents were acting properly under their powers as commander in chief.[13] In 1973, however, Congress took the first major step in over a century to limit the President's war-making powers. It passed a law setting a sixty-day limit on the President's power to commit troops abroad without a prior congressional declaration of war or specific authorization for the commitment of troops. The law also provides that Congress can at any time pass a concurrent resolution (a congressional act which requires no presidential signature to take effect) ending any unauthorized presidential commitment of combat troops. President Nixon vetoed the bill, arguing that it would imperil the nation's security by preventing him and future Presidents from acting swiftly in emergencies. But Congress was more concerned with recovering its constitutional power over war and peace, and both houses overrode the veto. The 1973 law thus constitutes one of the few major setbacks dealt to the growth of presidential power for a long time.

### Emergency Leader

In the spring of 1861, faced with the secession of a number of southern states and the imminent collapse of the Union, Abraham Lincoln ordered Fort Sumter to be provisioned and reinforced, knowing full well that his action would precipitate civil war. After Fort Sumter had been fired upon, Lincoln—on his own authority and without prior authorization from Congress—proclaimed a naval blockade of southern ports, summoned the South Carolina militia to active service, spent government money on war matériel, suspended the writ of habeas corpus, and in general simply ignored constitutional restraints on his power. Lincoln knew that he had violated the Constitution by these acts, but in a letter to one of his critics he explained why he had done so:

I felt that measures otherwise unconstitutional might become lawful by becoming indispensable to the preservation of the Constitution through the

---

[13] The leading case in point was Durand v. Hollins, 4 Blatch 451 (1860). For a discussion of the Court's position and an account of other episodes in which Presidents have used force abroad without prior authorization by Congress, see Edward S. Corwin, *The President: Office and Powers* (3d ed.; New York: New York University Press, 1948), pp. 241–249.

preservation of the nation. Right or wrong, I assumed this ground, and now avow it. I could not feel that, to the best of my ability, I had even tried to preserve the Constitution if, to save slavery or any minor matter, I should permit the wreck of the government, country, and Constitution all together.[14]

Lincoln believed that any government must have "emergency power"—the power to do whatever is necessary to save the nation in a time of crisis. As the President can act more swiftly than can Congress, this power must necessarily be his. Lincoln's reelection in 1864 and his subsequent elevation to something approaching national sainthood suggest that the American people in his time and since have not only approved his "taking over" in this crisis but have also expected his successors to do the same in other crises. Subsequent Presidents have at various times intervened in strikes, closed the banks, suspended stock-market operations, ordered troops to suppress domestic disorders, and in general acted as protectors of the nation's peace. There is no doubt that in any future crisis—a great depression or an atomic war—most Americans will look to the President, rather than to Congress, to lead them.

---

[14] Abraham Lincoln, letter to A. G. Hodges, April 4, 1864, quoted in Louis Brownlow, *The President and the Presidency* (Chicago: Public Administration Service, 1949), p. 58.

## Party Leader

The President is also either the chief Democrat or the chief Republican. The American national parties, as we observed in Chapter 9, are mainly devices for nominating and electing Presidents, to a lesser degree agencies for staffing the administrative agencies, and to a still lesser degree agencies for organizing Congress and guiding its activities. In all these operations the President is the leader of one of the two contesting parties. He names the chairman of his party's national committee and, if he is a candidate for reelection, dominates its national convention. Through his power of appointment he is the main dispenser of patronage. Through his appeals to party loyalty and his promise of support of his party's congressmen in their reelection campaigns he exerts some influence over Congress. In none of these capacities is he as powerful as are national party leaders in most other democratic nations, but he certainly comes much nearer to being the national leader of his party than does any other person. No matter how strongly he may wish to be "nonpartisan" and "the President of the whole people," he sooner or later finds himself forced to act in a partisan manner. For example, President Eisenhower at first wished to avoid any heavily partisan campaigning in the 1954 congressional elections, but the pleas of his fellow Republicans for help became so strong that he wound up not only issuing a public blanket endorsement of all Republican candidates against their Democratic opponents but also personally campaigning more actively than any President had ever done in an off-year election, at least up to President Nixon's efforts in 1970.[15]

## Chief Legislator

In his own executive capacity the President can make a great deal of "law," as the term is defined in this book: He can issue proclamations, directives, ordinances, regulations, and orders, all of which are at least legally binding on those to whom they apply and enforceable in the courts. He is generally also regarded as our chief legislator, however, mainly because he now has most of the initiative in the nation's statute-making process (see Chap. 15). Most of the major public bills passed by Congress are now conceived and drafted by the President's advisers in the Cabinet and the administrative agencies and are steered through Congress by the President's supporters there.

Congress does not, of course, supinely comply with the President's wishes—far from it. More often than not Congress revises his requests more or less drastically, and it not infrequently rejects them entirely. But to the extent that the American system provides a single source and supervisor of an overall legislative program, the President does the job.

Legislative relations between President and Congress are more often in the nature of a contest than of an effort at compromise. As Congress retains formal power to enact statutes and to make appropriations, it is far from helpless in this perennial

---

Governmental Authorities
and Processes

[15] See Robert J. Donovan, *Eisenhower: The Inside Story* (New York: Harper & Row, Publishers, 1956), chap. 20.

**Presidential leadership.**
Source: "Nixon Rated
Cartoons" by Ranan
Lurie, published by
Quadrangle, the New
York Times Book Co.

contest. Over the years, however, various Presidents have fashioned weapons to overcome Congress' constitutional advantages. Six of them are worthy of mention.[16]

**Convincing Congressmen**   During his service as floor leader of the Senate Democrats (1953–1960) Lyndon Johnson won a reputation as one of the most skilled legislative leaders in history. In his first years as President (1963–1966) he matched— many think excelled—Franklin Roosevelt's record of inducing Congress to adopt his

_____

[16] See Polsby, *Congress and the Presidency,* chap. 7.

programs, including such major and controversial measures as the Civil Rights Act of 1964, the Voting Rights Act of 1965, medicare, and the War on Poverty. Most observers believe that his basic method was to convince congressmen that it was in the nation's interest and their own to vote for his programs. He used direct conversation (the White House phone was in constant use), favors and reminders of past favors, and intimate knowledge of the politics and needs of congressmen's states and districts, which permitted him to know whom to press when, how hard, and how often. His phenomenal success suggests that the best way to win the legislative contest with Congress is to keep it from seeming a contest.

The personal touch, of course, does not always work—as is shown by this account of President Eisenhower's unsuccessful effort to pursuade Congressman Otto Passman (Democrat, Louisiana) to drop or modify his opposition to the 1957 foreign-aid bill:

> In 1957, as the foreign aid bill was getting its final touches, President Eisenhower and his advisers decided to try an advance talk with Otto. They gave him the full treatment, and he recalls it with a nice touch of sadness, even today.
>
> "It was kind of embarrassing, you understand," he told me in his musical southern voice. "I refer to it as the Passman trial. They sent for me in a long black Cadillac. I guess the first time I had ever been in one. I felt real important, which is not my usual way of feeling. When I got to the President's study at the White House, all the big shots were there. Admiral Radford and Secretary Dulles and the leaders of Congress. We had tea and little cakes, and they sat me right across from the President. They went around the room, asking for comments, one minute each. When they got to me, I said I would need more than one minute, maybe six or seven minutes, to tell what was wrong with their program. . . ."
>
> Passman's lecture was complete with footnotes and fine print, figures down to the last thin dime, unobligated balances in the various foreign aid accounts, carryover funds, re-obligated de-obligated obligations, supplies in the pipe-line, uncommitted balances, and so on—in that mysterious verbal shorthand that only a man who lives and breathes foreign aid could comprehend. . . . After . . . everyone left, the President turned to his staff and said,
>
> "Remind me never to invite that fellow down here again."[17]

When Congress refuses to be persuaded, the President has at least five other shots in the locker, however.

**The Veto and Threat of Veto** The Constitution provides that, if the President vetoes (refuses to assent to) an act of Congress, it can become law only if repassed by two-thirds of each house. Such majorities are usually very difficult to muster: From 1913 to 1973 a total of 1303 bills were vetoed; only 44 (3.4 percent) were overridden by Congress. The veto is thus a very powerful negative weapon.[18] It has also become a positive weapon, for many a President has let it be known through his

---

[17] Rowland Evans, Jr., "Louisiana's Passman: The Scourge of Foreign Aid," *Harper's Monthly,* January 1962, pp. 78–83.

[18] Polsby, *Congress and the Presidency,* p. 81; and *Congress and the Nation, 1965–1968,* Vol. 2 (Washington, D.C.: Congressional Quarterly Service, 1969), p. 92a. Figures for the period 1969–1973 are taken from various *Congressional Quarterly* weekly reports.

congressional spokesmen that, if a particular provision is retained in a particular bill, he will veto it and has thus often induced Congress to eliminate an objectionable provision. The effectiveness of the veto is limited, however, by the fact that it is not an "item veto" like that enjoyed by the governors of many American states; the President must either approve or veto a bill in its entirety and cannot veto only particular items while approving the rest. This rule has led to the practice of attaching "riders"; Congress includes items that the President opposes in a bill (especially an appropriations bill) that he cannot afford to veto. Even so, his veto power is a powerful weapon of legislative leadership.

**Patronage**   The President may, if he wishes, appoint to administrative positions people favored by his partisans in Congress; he can withhold such favors from his opponents. Franklin Roosevelt used this technique with great success early in his first term. His successors, however, have used it much less, mainly because they have had fewer patronage jobs at their disposal; merit-system regulations, to be described in Chapter 17, have reduced their number.

**Impoundment**[19]   Most government policies are implemented in large part by spending public funds, and so the appropriations process is a critical element in any policy making. The Constitution, however, leaves a certain ambiguity about just who controls the process, and recent Presidents, particularly Richard Nixon, have used the ambiguity to create the major new policy weapon of "impoundment." The Constitution locates in Congress the sole power to appropriate public funds (Article I, Section 7), and requires the President to "take care that the laws be faithfully executed" (Article II, Section 3). But it also makes the President chief executive and assigns him the power to direct the activities of most administrative agencies.

All Presidents since Franklin D. Roosevelt have occasionally used their powers as chief executive to "impound" funds—that is, to direct administrative agencies under their control not to spend certain funds that have been authorized and appropriated by Congress. Roosevelt began the practice in the early 1940s as a way of holding down nondefense spending in World War II, and his successors occasionally followed his lead. Richard Nixon, however, used this new weapon far more extensively than any previous President, and thereby precipitated something of a constitutional crisis. From 1969 to 1974 he "froze" somewhere between $9 billion and $18 billion per year (the amount depends on how one classifies various types of congressional authorizations). One of the most publicized instances was his refusal in 1973 to spend $6 billion of the $11 billion appropriated by Congress to build waste treatment plants for the control of water pollution.

This impoundment escalated the constitutional conflict. Nixon and his spokesmen argued that such impoundments are not only within the President's powers but are a necessary weapon for him to control inflation by holding down Federal spending. Many congressmen argued that the practice is both unconstitutional and dangerous: it is a direct violation of the President's constitutional duty to "take care that

---

[19] The most complete discussion is in Louis Fisher, *President and Congress: Power and Policy* (New York: The Free Press, 1972). See also Fisher, "The Politics of Impounded Funds," *Administrative Science Quarterly,* 15 (September 1970).

the laws be faithfully executed"; it allows the President to substitute his policy priorities for Congress'; it enables the President to punish or reward particular congressmen by freezing or releasing funds for projects in their districts; and it allows him to release frozen funds at a time when it will win him the greatest public favor.

By the end of 1973 over thirty cases had been brought in the lower Federal courts challenging the constitutionality of various presidential impoundments. All but a few were decided *against* the President,[20] but by early 1974 there still had been no authoritative ruling on the matter by the Supreme Court. If the Court makes such a ruling against the President, he will lose what has become one of the more potent weapons in his armory. If it does not, impoundment will continue to play a major role in the President's operations as the nation's chief policy maker.

**Party Leadership**  To some extent every President since William McKinley has used his position as party leader to induce Congress to follow his wishes; some, notably Woodrow Wilson, Franklin Roosevelt, and Lyndon Johnson, have used it with considerable success. As we noted in Chapter 9, however, the President can remove a recalcitrant congressman from his position only by defeating him in a state or local election. Only a few Presidents have tried to do so, and they have succeeded only on the rare occasions on which they were able to gain the support of the local party organizations.[21] Consequently, the President's party leadership is one of his weaker weapons.

**Appeal to Public Opinion**  Cleverly used, the President's most powerful weapon against balky legislators is a direct appeal to the people to pressure their congressmen to support the administration's program. Most Presidents have considered it a weapon of last resort, to be used only when all others have failed. If the President is more nearly in tune than is Congress with popular demands and if his appeal to the people is skillfully made, Congress can hardly resist him—for such an appeal hits congressmen where they are most vulnerable, in the ballot box. But, if congressmen have gauged the popular temper more closely than he has, if his appeal is inept, or if he makes too many appeals on too many issues, he loses his audience. The trick is knowing when, how, and on what issues to make such appeals.[22]

## POWER AND PROBLEMS OF THE AMERICAN PRESIDENT

In trying to be an effective head of government the President has several advantages over a prime minister. For one thing, he is not elected by or formally responsible to Congress (except for the twice-used device of impeachment). For another, he has a number of independent constitutional powers (as chief executive, as sole channel of

---

[20] See *Congressional Quarterly Weekly Report,* September 8, 1973, pp. 2395–2397.

[21] For a review of various presidential efforts to "purge" rebellious congressmen, see Austin Ranney and Willmoore Kendall, *Democracy and the American Party System* (New York: Harcourt Brace Jovanovich, Inc., 1956), pp. 286–289.

[22] See Pendleton Herring, *Presidential Leadership* (New York: Holt, Rinehart and Winston, Inc., 1940), pp. 68–69.

communications with foreign nations, and as commander in chief) that enable him to make and enforce many kinds of policy without even consulting Congress, let alone obtaining its approval. In addition, the succession to his office is regularized and *public,* which makes it seem more legitimate than are the secret processes by which British parties select their leaders and thus determine the succession to the prime ministership.[23] Perhaps most important, his many roles reinforce one another and strengthen his domination of the policy-making process, for as Rossiter has pointed out:

> He is a more exalted Chief of State because he is also Voice of the People, a more forceful Chief Diplomat because he commands the armed forces personally, a more effective Chief Legislator because the political system forces him to be Chief of Party, a more artful Manager of Prosperity because he is Chief Executive.[24]

**A view of presidential succession.** Source: Editorial cartoon by Pat Oliphant, copyright, The Denver *Post.* Reprinted with permission of *Los Angeles Times* Syndicate.

*The American Presidential Succession, 1969, as Michelangelo might have seen it.*

Yet there are many limitations on his power as head of government. As Richard Nixon learned the hard way in 1973–1974, the constitutional process of impeachment is still more than a quaint historical vestigial holdover. The Constitution limits him to two elected terms in office; Congress' and his fellow partisans' knowledge that he cannot be President after a certain date invariably weakens his legislative and party leadership. The Constitution also assigns large independent powers to Congress and the Supreme Court. When Congress denies him the legislation and appropriations that he seeks, he cannot, as can a prime minister, simply dissolve Congress and obtain one more to his liking. The Supreme Court can declare some of his actions unconstitu-

[23] Louis W. Koenig, *The Chief Executive* (New York: Harcourt Brace Jovanovich, Inc., 1964), pp. 389–391.

[24] Rossiter, *The American Presidency,* p. 25.

The Executive Process

tional (as it declared President Truman's seizure of the steel mills in 1952 unconstitutional), and, though he may threaten to "pack" the Court, the widespread belief in an independent judiciary may well frustrate his plans. He can never count upon either solid or energetic support for his policies among his partisans in Congress or elsewhere. Despite his formal position as chief executive, as we shall see in Chapter 17, he cannot even be sure that his orders to his administrative subordinates will be carried out as he wishes.

The presidency has become the key institution of the American government, but, although the system allows the President many opportunities to persuade, it offers him little opportunity to command. Here is testimony from one who knows:

> In the early summer of 1952, before the heat of the campaign, President Truman used to contemplate the problems of the General-become-President should Eisenhower win the forthcoming election. "He'll sit here," Truman would remark (tapping his desk for emphasis), "and he'll say, 'Do this! Do that!' *And nothing will happen.* Poor Ike—it won't be a bit like the Army. He'll find it very frustrating." . . . Long before he came to talk of Eisenhower he had put his own experience in other words: "I sit here all day trying to persuade people to do the things they ought to have sense enough to do without my persuading them. . . . That's all the powers of the President amount to."[25]

## THE PRESIDENCY OF FRANCE[26]

Before 1958 the President of France was an indirectly elected "monarch" of the type described earlier in this chapter, distinct in function and power from the premier, who served as head of government. The Constitution of the Fifth Republic, promulgated in that fateful year, converted the French presidency into a very different kind of office, and it has changed further in the years since.

The 1958 Constitution provided France with a form of government that does not fit easily into either the "presidential" or "parliamentary" categories that we have been using, though most observers originally thought it nearer to the latter than the former. The presidency of the Republic has been the regime's key office since 1958 and has, if anything, grown more powerful. Its incumbent is directly elected by the voters for a seven-year term, and there is no limit to how many terms he can serve. He appoints the premier, theoretically with a view to the distribution of party strength in the national assembly but actually as his personal choice. In 1958 President Charles de Gaulle chose as his first premier Michel Debré, a member of the Assembly, and second in command of the new Gaullist party, the Union pour la Nouvelle République (UNR). But in 1962 the two men disagreed about calling a

---

[25] Neustadt, *Presidential Power*, pp. 9–10.

[26] Useful discussions of this complex and changing institution include Maurice Duverger, *Institutions Politiques et Droit Constitutionnel* (Paris: Presses Universitaires de France, 1966); Henry W. Ehrmann, *Politics in France* (Boston: Little, Brown & Company, 1968), pp. 245–254; and Roy C. Macridis, "France," in Macridis and Ward (eds.), *Modern Political Systems: Europe* (2d ed.: Englewood Cliffs, N.J.: Prentice-Hall, Inc., 1968), pp. 254–259.

national election, and Debré resigned—not, be it noted, because the national assembly voted against him but because *le grand Charles* had decided to dismiss him. De Gaulle replaced him with Georges Pompidou, a businessman and long a loyal supporter, who had never been elected to any public office. This choice made it clear that the premier does not hold his position because he is the number-two leader of the largest party in the assembly; he is premier because the President wants him. He is, so to speak, the national commander's chief of staff. When Pompidou succeeded de Gaulle as President in 1969, he in turn selected his own man, Jacques Chaban-Delmas, rather than accepting someone picked for him by his party.

The French President has many other broad and significant powers. He can dissolve the National Assembly at his own discretion, whether the premier requests it or not. The famous Article 16 authorizes him, when the nation's independence or institutions are threatened, to suspend regular operations of the government and to take whatever other measures he sees fit—as de Gaulle actually did during the 1961 revolt by the French *colons* in Algiers. He can submit constitutional amendments directly to the voters for popular referenda without prior authorization by the national assembly—as, for example, in the referendum of 1962, in which de Gaulle's amendment providing for direct popular election of the President was approved.

Some observers thought that the Fifth Republic and its presidency were the personal creations of de Gaulle and that when (some said *if*) he left the scene both would change radically. The unexpected happened in 1969: De Gaulle resigned after the voters in a referendum rejected his proposals for constitutional reform. Pompidou won the ensuing election, and his presidency differed some in style and policy but very little in executive power from that of de Gaulle. The same has been true of the presidency of Giscard d'Estaing, who was elected in 1974.

What kind of government, then, *is* the Fifth Republic? The surest way to answer this question is to ask what would happen if the President and a majority of the national assembly had an irreconcilable difference on an important policy matter. In a pure presidential democracy each branch would nevertheless serve out its term in office. In a pure parliamentary democracy either the prime minister would resign, or a new election would be called. The new legislative majority would either reappoint the old prime minister or select a new one.

The national assembly has not yet flatly refused to take an action demanded by the President, but what would happen if it did? The President would presumably dissolve the assembly and call a legislative election. If that election returned a majority favorable to him, there would be no problem. But if it returned a hostile majority the Constitution would bar him from dissolving the new parliament until a year had elapsed. What would he do in that year?

No one can say with certainty. But whether the Fifth Republic is a presidential or a parliamentary system—or a hybrid—it is clear that "the President has emerged as the key policy-making organ" and that "the government headed by the Prime Minister has become essentially an organ of execution [whose] paramount function is to provide whatever is needed for the application of the policies conceived by the Chief of State."[27]

---

[27] Macridis, "France," p. 258; and Ehrmann, *Politics in France,* p. 255.

## OTHER PRESIDENCIES[28]

Although the presidencies of other democratic systems, unlike that of France, have been modeled on the office of President of the United States, most have become even more powerful than the prototype. Most have all the American President's formal powers—position as chief of state, power of appointment, direction of administration, dominance of foreign policy, command of the armed forces, the veto (most, indeed, have the item veto), and so on. Many also have some additional formal powers, notably the right to introduce bills directly in the legislature.

These other presidents are generally free of some of the American President's handicaps. For example, some have the power to make most or all administrative appointments without having to secure legislative approval, and no "senatorial courtesy" fences them in. Moreover, in none of these nations does a merit system (see Chap. 17) have anything like the coverage of that in the United States, and the president's appointment powers thus go far beyond those of his Washington counterpart. Furthermore, the legislatures of Colombia, Mexico, Venezuela, and the rest generally pass legislation couched in much more general and permissive language than is used by the United States Congress. As a result, their presidents' powers to issue *decretos con fuerza de ley* (decrees having the force of law) in specific application of general legislative instructions are far broader than is any comparable power of the President of the United States. In some nations, indeed, the president's *potestad reglamentaria* (ordinance power) applies to substantially more of the total policy-making process than does the legislature's statute-making power.

One striking recognition of executive power in the other presidential democracies is their long-standing limitations on presidential tenure; the United States has had such a limitation only since the adoption of the Twenty-Second Amendment in 1951, and France still has none at all. The most common form in the other democracies is a requirement that the president cannot be reelected until a specified period of time has elapsed after he leaves office (four years in Colombia, ten years in Venezuela).

The great formal powers of these other presidents are in every case substantially exceeded by their informal powers. The presidents are considerably stronger leaders of their national parties than is the man in the White House, and their control of very extensive patronage enables them to keep potential rebels in line far more effectively than he can. They are no more dictators than he is, for, with all their advantages, they still must persuade their legislatures to go along, and in some nations some of the time they are not very successful. Like the American President they have limited tenure in office and little or no influence over the choice of their successors. But while they are in office the Latin American presidents enjoy more weapons and fewer handicaps than does the President of the United States. When comparing presidents as a type with prime ministers as a type, it is well to keep this point in mind.

---

[28] For studies of Latin American presidencies see Martin C. Needler (ed.), *Political Systems of Latin America* (Princeton, N.J.: D. Van Nostrand Company, Inc., 1967). For the Philippine presidency, prior to the Marcos dictatorship, see Jean Grossholtz, *Politics in the Philippines* (Boston: Little, Brown & Company, 1964), chap. 5.

# THE PRIME MINISTER AS HEAD OF GOVERNMENT[29]

## FORMATION OF THE BRITISH EXECUTIVE

The British executive is composed of three interrelated but distinct sets of officials: the prime minister, the ministry, and the Cabinet. It is formed as follows.

First, the monarch summons one of her subjects and asks him to become prime minister and to form a government.[30] In most instances the monarch has no option but must pick the designated leader of the party holding a majority of the seats in the House of Commons, though, as we noted earlier, on a few occasions when the majority party has not designated a leader the monarch has exercised some real choice. The prime minister must be not only a member of Parliament but also, since 1902, a member of the House of Commons.

The prime minister automatically becomes First Lord of the Treasury (a sinecure with no administrative duties) and then proceeds to fill the other executive posts by making recommendations to the monarch, which are invariably accepted. These posts include the ministers—the heads of the twenty[31] executive departments, or ministries (for example, the Foreign Office, the Home Office, and the ministries of Defence and Education), and several additional ministers—some without departmental duties (the Lord Privy Seal and the Chancellor of the Duchy of Lancaster, for example) and some with (Economic Secretary to the Treasury, Minister of State in the Foreign Office, and the like); the parliamentary secretaries, who serve as deputies to the ministers of various departments; several law officers (like the Attorney General and the Solicitor General); and the whips (see Chap. 9). All these executives, amounting to about 100 officers in all, plus the prime minister, constitute the ministry, or government.

In making his recommendations to the monarch, however, the prime minister has by no means an absolutely free hand. In the first place, with rare exceptions every member of the ministry must be a member of Parliament, and most important ministers must be members of the House of Commons. Note that this rule is directly opposite to the rule in the presidential systems that prohibits anyone from holding both a seat in the legislature and an executive post at the same time. In the second place, most members of the ministry and all the important members must be leaders of the majority party—except in "coalition" or "national" (all-party) governments like those established during times of crisis (1895–1905, 1915–1922, 1940–1945). In

---

[29] Useful older accounts of the British executive include W. Ivor Jennings, *Cabinet Government* (New York: Cambridge University Press, 1959); and Herbert Morrison, *Government and Parliament* (New York: Oxford University Press, 1960). Still a useful analysis of the office of prime minister, though somewhat outdated, is Byrum E. Carter, *The Office of Prime Minister* (Princeton, N.J.: Princeton University Press, 1956). An excellent collection of recent discussions of the changing nature of the office is Anthony King (ed.), *The British Prime Minister* (New York: St. Martin's Press, Inc., 1969).

[30] In the technical parlance used in Great Britain, the dominions, and many other parliamentary democracies, the term "the government" is roughly synonymous with the American term "the administration" and encompasses all the officials in the ministry and Cabinet discussed in the text.

[31] The number has varied as new ministries have been established and old ones abolished from time to time.

**The Prime Minister.**
Source: Wide World
Photos.

the third place, the prime minister must find posts for the other top parliamentary leaders of his party regardless of how he feels about them personally, and he must also make sure that no major faction of his party feels left out.

The ministry rarely or never meets and deliberates as a body. This kind of activity is left to the Cabinet, which consists of those members of the ministry whom the prime minister regularly invites to consult with him as a group. Its size and composition change from time to time, in accordance with his desires, but normally it has between eighteen and twenty-three members (twenty in 1974) and includes all the top ministers both with and without departmental duties. It has thus been called "a select committee of Parliament" but could better be described as "a committee of the top leaders of the majority party."

## CABINET STATUS, FUNCTIONS, AND POWERS

Some commentators on the British system emphasize the convention according to which the Cabinet, like the ministry and the prime minister, remains in power only as long as it commands the confidence of the House of Commons—that is, as long as the House does not vote down any measure that the Cabinet regards as really important and does not pass a motion of no confidence in the whole Cabinet or any of its members. This emphasis, however, is misleading. Since 1894 only three prime ministers and cabinets have resigned because of adverse votes in the House (Lord Rosebery in 1895, Stanley Baldwin in 1924, and Neville Chamberlain in 1940), and the discipline and cohesion of British parties are so strong that such episodes, which can result only from rebellions within the majority party, are highly unlikely. The Cabinet cannot—and does not—totally ignore the feelings of the House, of course, but it can usually count on as much of its full statutory five-year tenure of office as it wishes.

Although a number of its members have administrative and supervisory duties, the Cabinet is almost exclusively a policy-making and legislation-designing body. Its members and their advisers conceive, draft, and introduce most of the major public bills in Parliament. They defend government policies in parliamentary debate, guide government legislation through the various parliamentary stages, decide which amendments to accept and reject, and generally control what Parliament does.

The dominance of the Cabinet over Parliament is far greater than that of the President over Congress. There are many reasons why, some of which, like the great cohesion and discipline of British parties, we have already noted. We should add one more: the prime minister's power to dissolve the House and force a general election. Although there is some doubt about the extent of this power, it is generally agreed that, when the prime minister asks the monarch to dissolve the House before its five-year term has expired, the monarch must do so. A general election for a new House must then be held forthwith. This requirement means, of course, that should the House kick over the traces and deny the prime minister and Cabinet some piece of legislation, the latter need not meekly resign. They can ask for a new election—which, after all, the opposition party may win. Therefore, a rebel MP's vote against his party leaders is tantamount to a vote to put the other side in power. And most MPs are unwilling to go quite *that* far in their occasional rebellions.[32] Most observers believe that these two powers of the party leaders—to withhold the party label from rebellious MPs and, even more, to dissolve Parliament—are the Cabinet's basic and nearly irresistible weapons in dealing with the House of Commons.

## THE ROLE OF THE BRITISH PRIME MINISTER

Not so long ago it was fashionable to say that the position of the prime minister in the Cabinet and the ministry is that of primus inter pares (first among equals), much like that of chairman of the board of directors of a business corporation. Most present-day commentators, however, believe that, though this description may have been valid years ago, the modern prime minister has become the dominant figure

---

[32] In a penetrating analysis of the causes of the varying degrees of party cohesion in the United States, Great Britain, and Canada, Leon D. Epstein concludes that this desire of MPs not to put the opposition party in power is the prime force not only in maintaining high cohesion but in cementing the power of the party leadership over votes in the House; "A Comparative Study of Canadian Parties," *American Political Science Review,* 58 (March 1964), 46–59.

within the Cabinet and the ministry and therefore within the whole British system of government. He and not the Cabinet has the power to ask the monarch to dissolve Parliament and to appoint and dismiss ministers, judges, and diplomatic representatives. He and not the Cabinet represents Britain at international "summit" conferences of heads of government. And it is he who determines who will sit in the Cabinet; the Cabinet does not determine who will be prime minister.

The present dominance of the prime minister is the result of three main factors. First, the increasing centralization, discipline, and cohesion of British political parties have given their leaders, one of whom is always prime minister, increasing control not only over the parties' rank and file but also over the second-echelon leaders who make up the Cabinet and the ministry.[33]

Second, the combination of universal suffrage and modern mass communications has increasingly converted British general elections into contests for the office of prime minister. The campaigns are centered mainly on the personalities and qualifications of the two rival party leaders, who do most of the campaigning for their respective parties. Most people vote for or against one of these two men, as well as for or against the party that he leads. As Lord Robert Cecil put it:

> I should say that if you really looked into the real principle of our constitution now, it is purely plebiscital, that you have really a plebiscite by which a particular man is selected as Prime Minister, he then selects the Ministry himself, and it is pretty much what he likes, subject to what affects the rule that he has to consider—namely, that he must not do anything that is very unpopular.[34]

Finally, the same kinds of economic and military crises that have, as we have noted, taken power away from the collegial body of Congress and given it to the President as "emergency leader" have also taken power away from the collegial body of the British Cabinet and given it to the prime minister as "emergency leader."

The prime minister is in some respects even more powerful than the President, particularly in his ability to lead his party and the legislature.[35] Such power is by no means enjoyed by the heads of government in all parliamentary democracies, however, as the following discussion will show.

## TENURE AND POWERS OF PREMIERS IN COALITION GOVERNMENTS

The British prime minister's power is firmly rooted in his leadership of a disciplined and cohesive political party that holds a majority of the seats in the House of

---

[33] This point is central in R. T. McKenzie's distinguished study of the internal power structures of the British parties, *British Political Parties* (2d ed.; New York: St.. Martin's Press. Inc., 1963), especially chaps. 2–3, 6.

[34] Quoted in Finer, *Theory and Practice of Modern Government* (rev. ed.; New York: Holt, Rinehart and Winston, Inc., 1949), p. 363.

[35] This picture of increased prime-ministerial power agrees with that presented by most British scholars, especially John P. Mackintosh, "The Position of the Prime Minister," in King, *The British Prime Minister,* pp. 3–43. For a contrary view, see G. W. Jones, "The Prime Minister's Power," in King, *The British Prime Minister,* pp. 168–190; and the rejoinder by Mackintosh, in King, *The British Prime Minister,* pp. 191–210.

Commons. As long as he commands its loyalty, he need not worry about how the opposition votes; he knows that it will usually vote against his program. His main political concern is that the voters approve his government's policies and renew its mandate to govern at the next election.

In the main democratic polities with more fractionalized party systems (see Chap. 9), however, one party rarely if ever comes even close to winning a majority of the legislative seats; the governments are necessarily coalitions of several parties. The premier of such a coalition cannot rely solely upon his own party's backing, for he needs the votes of the other coalition members to stay in office. His first (though not his only) concern must thus be what his coalition partners, rather than the voters, think of his actions and proposals.

TABLE 20
Party Fractionalization and Executive Tenure

| Nation | Fractionalization Ranking | Mean Legislative Party Fractionalization, 1945-1965 | Number of Changes in Party Leading Government, 1945-1973 |
|---|---|---|---|
| Israel | 1 | 0.80 | 2 |
| France | 2 | 0.77 | 25[a] |
| Denmark | 3 | 0.74 | 11 |
| Italy | 4 | 0.71 | 20 |
| West Germay | 5 | 0.69 | 1 |
| Norway | 6[b] | 0.67 | 5 |
| Ireland | 6[b] | 0.67 | 6 |
| Belgium | 8 | 0.62 | 19 |
| Austria | 9 | 0.56 | 2 |
| Canada | 10[b] | 0.52 | 2 |
| Great Britain | 10[b] | 0.52 | 5 |
| Australia | 12[b] | 0.49 | 2 |
| New Zealand | 12[b] | 0.49 | 3 |
| United States | 14 | 0.48 | 3 |

[a] All twenty-five changes occurred under the Fourth Republic (1946-1958).
[b] Ties.
Source: The fractionalization scores are taken from Table 16, Chap. 9. The data on changes in party control of government are taken from various political annuals.

How does this concern affect his power to stay in office—the first prerequisite for effective leadership? The answer evidently depends mainly upon the nature of the other parties in his coalition, rather than upon the degree of fractionalization in the party system as a whole. Evidence for this conclusion is presented in Table 20, which shows that executive tenure in modern democratic polities is far from a simple reflection of party fractionalization. To be sure, the six least fractionalized systems have had very low turnover rates among their chief executives. But Belgium, which ranks in the middle of the fractionalization scale, ranks third in the number of executive changes. On the other hand, Israel, with the most fractionalized party system of all, has had only six changes of government since 1949; only two of these changes have involved significant shifts in party strength within the coalitions, and the premier has always been a leader of the Mapai party.[36]

The undisputed champion regime for short executive tenure was the French Fourth Republic (1946–1958). In its thirteen-year existence there were no fewer than

[36] Leonard J. Fein, *Politics in Israel* (Boston: Little, Brown & Company, 1967), pp. 170–172.

twenty-five premiers. The longest tenure was sixteen months (Guy Mollet), the shortest was two days (Robert Schuman once and Henri Queuille once), and the average was just under six months.

Many Fourth Republic premiers were picked and approved by the national assembly because they were relatively obscure and inoffensive deputies and therefore less likely to be "dictatorial" than were top party leaders. As soon as a premier began to talk and act as if he intended to exert vigorous executive leadership, his days in office were numbered. Such was the fate of Pierre Mendès-France, Edgar Faure, René Pleven, and every other premier who refused to content himself with presiding and negotiating. Every change of premier did not, of course, mean a drastic change in the composition of the government. When a government fell, all its members resigned as the Constitution required, but a substantial number regularly turned up again in new governments. Indeed, no newly formed French government in the entire Fourth Republic was composed entirely of men who had not held posts in the outgoing government; more often than not, more than half the new ministers were carryovers from the old governments. The French called this process *replâtrage*—"replastering" the new government with materials carried over from the old. It meant, among other things, that the frequent and rapid changes in heads of French ministries and premiers did not produce equally frequent and rapid changes in ministerial personnel or public policy. Consequently there was somewhat greater continuity and stability in the Fourth Republic executive than appears at first glance but, of course, not nearly as much as there has been under the Fifth Republic.

By the 1970s Italy had won the dubious honor of succeeding France as the champion regime for short executive tenure. All postwar Italian premiers have been members of the Christian Democratic party, but that party is organizationally weak and permanently divided by strong ideological disagreements among its various factions. The result has been a "Byzantine maze of factional struggles within and between parties in the ruling coalition and the resultant rapid-fire succession of Premiers and Cabinets" typified by this course of events in the 1950s:

> Pella on the "right" wing of the [Christian Democrats] was succeeded by Fanfani on the "left" early in 1954, to be quickly followed by Scelba in the "right center," after which Segni in the center enjoyed power for two years, only to be replaced in July, 1958, by Fanfani, who again gave way to Segni, who after an interval was once again replaced by Fanfani, and so forth.[37]

The position of the premier in a coalition government seems to depend upon a few basic conditions. If the legislative seats are divided among many little parties instead of a few big ones, he will have that many more party leaders to find ministerial offices for and keep happy. If there are deep ideological divisions among the principal parties—and, even worse, among the factions of his own party, Italian-style—he will have to construct his program very carefully. If the party and factional

[37]Dante Germino and Stefano Passigli, *The Government and Politics of Contemporary Italy* (New York: Harper & Row, Publishers, 1968), p. 73.

Governmental Authorities
and Processes

leaders dislike one another personally, he will have to handle them with special tact.[38] Being premier of such a government is not the most desirable executive position in the world, though no nation seems to suffer any shortage of politicians trying to fill it.

## THE EXECUTIVE IN NONDEMOCRATIC SYSTEMS

We need not linger long over the similarities and differences of executive roles in democratic and nondemocratic political systems. In almost every Western democracy, as we have seen, the executive has become the single most powerful agency for making government policy. But we have also seen that he is far from omnipotent: Even the most powerful democratic chief executive (the president of France? of Venezuela? of Mexico?) must operate within very real limits set by legislatures, courts, opposition parties, factions in his own party, pressure groups, and ultimately the electorate.

The nondemocratic political systems have at least one trait in common, whether they be the communist systems of China and Eastern Europe or the one-party regimes or military dictatorships of Africa, Asia, and Latin America: In each the executive agency *is* the government. Indeed, as we have seen, no fewer than twenty-six nations in 1974 had no legislatures whatever. In this sense then, the core agency of *all* governments is the executive, not the legislature: for, while a number of nondemocratic regimes operate with no legislatures, *no* regime, democratic or undemocratic, operates without an executive. To be sure, the formal constitutional chief executives of some nondemocratic regimes may be only the chief errand boys of the all-powerful parties or ruling cliques. But the point is that, as we saw in Chapter 15, their legislatures are essentially sounding boards and cheering sections for the dictators, party leaders, or ruling juntas. And, as we shall see in Chapter 18, their courts of law operate as arms of the executives, not as checks upon them. Accordingly, Western political scientists simply do not bother much with questions of the power of executives relative to the legislatures and courts in the nondemocratic nations, nor shall we.

Perhaps the most interesting comparative observation is that in many modern governments, democratic and dictatorial alike, a great deal of government policy is made in the name of the executive or legislature—but often without its knowledge or approval—by "nonpolitical" public employees presumably hired to carry out the will of the "political" executives and legislatures. These employees have several labels: "civil servants," "apparatchiks," "bureaucrats," and the like. But, whatever they are called, they play a powerful—though usually obscure—role in determining what rules government in fact imposes upon the people under its jurisdiction. We shall examine their role in the following chapter.

---

[38] See Michael Taylor and V. M. Herman, "Party Systems and Government Stability," *American Political Science Review,* 65 (March 1971).

# 17

# THE ADMINISTRATIVE PROCESS

Let us approach the topic of this chapter by considering the following hypothetical situation. The leading issue in the 1980 American presidential election is foreign policy. The "outs" devote most of their campaign to denouncing the errors and pointing out the dangers of the policy followed by the "ins" and promise drastic changes if elected. After a hard-fought campaign, the "out" candidate is elected by a landslide.

On Inauguration Day, the incumbent secretary of state, the undersecretary, and all the assistant secretaries resign and are replaced by appointees of the new President. No one, not even the strongest partisan of the outgoing party, argues that the incumbents should be retained. Everyone takes for granted that the new President has the right to replace these top officials with appointees of his own party and beliefs.

The new President, however, is not satisfied. During the campaign he has promised a "top-to-bottom housecleaning of the whole State Department," and he believes in keeping his promises. He issues an order dismissing *every* employee of the department, from the director of the Office of Intelligence Research and the chief of the Telecommunications Division down to the last stenographer and messenger boy and announces that all positions will be filled with faithful members of *his* party.

Immediately a great shout of protest goes up all over the nation. Newspapers of all political complexions denounce "this crass return to the spoils system." The American Political Science Association protests "the destruction of the morale, professional security, and technical competence of the civil service." Thousands of people who voted for the new President wire him that they had no intention of giving him a mandate to pack the government service with his political henchmen.

Hypothetical though this situation may be, few of us would doubt that any such effort by a new president to force a complete turnover in government personnel would produce just such a popular uproar.[1]

For our purposes in this chapter, the interesting questions suggested by this imaginary episode are: Why the difference? Why do we permit a new President to fire some government employees but not others? Where do we draw the line and why?

The answers arise mainly from our acceptance of the propositions that "executive" and "political" officials differ significantly from "nonpolitical administrators" or "civil servants" and that the status and tenure of the latter are and should be quite different from those of the former.

Our task in this chapter is to examine the nature, status, functions, and role of administrative agencies and officials. We shall begin by considering why and in what respects such officials are generally regarded as significantly different from executives.

## THE DISTINCTION BETWEEN EXECUTIVES AND ADMINISTRATORS

### FUNCTIONS

During the formative period of the American Constitution most Americans adhered to the traditional conception of the governing process as consisting of three distinct kinds of activity: lawmaking, law enforcement, and adjudication. They also believed that power over the second of these activities should be assigned exclusively to the executive and that the executive should confine itself largely to the enforcement of policies initiated by the legislature.

In Chapter 16 we observed that since the nineteenth century the executives of most democratic nations have acquired ever-increasing influence over policy. Toward the end of the century a number of political scientists, notably Woodrow Wilson and Frank J. Goodnow, recognized that the traditional description of the executive as an enforcer rather than as an initiator of policy no longer fitted the facts. Yet they wished to make some kind of distinction between policy-making and policy-enforcing officials, and they also wished to reconcile the ideal of a permanent, professionalized civil service with the ideal of democracy. Consequently, they proposed a distinction between "political" (policy making) officials, including the President and other executives, and "administrative" (enforcement) officials. We shall return to their formula shortly.

### SELECTION AND TENURE

Although some present-day political scientists continue to distinguish between executives and administrators in the manner we have just observed, most believe that, because many administrators play major roles in policy making, this basis of distinc-

---

[1] Because of the wide application of the "merit system" to the federal civil service (as we shall see), when President Richard M. Nixon took office in January 1969, he actually had the power to fire and reappoint for political reasons only an estimated 6500 out of 3 million holders of government positions; *Congressional Quarterly,* January 3, 1969, pp. 15–31.

tion is meaningless. Few argue, however, that *all* public officials should be replaced whenever a majority of the voters transfer their favor from one political party or coalition to another. Most continue to believe, with Wilson and Goodnow, in a permanent, professionalized civil service under the direction and control of "political" executives and legislators.

Consequently, most contemporary political scientists distinguish between executives and administrators, or civil servants, mainly on grounds of selection and tenure. Executives, whether elected, as is the President, or appointed, as are his Cabinet members, hold the top positions in and ultimate control over the policy-making agencies outside the legislature; most are active party leaders, and their tenure in office depends directly upon whether their party or coalition currently commands a majority of the popular votes. All administrators, on the other hand, are appointed according to professional merit and technical competence, rather than because of partisan affiliations; their tenure in office is independent of changing party fortunes.[2]

## WHAT ABOUT BUREAUCRACY?

Many political scientists and political sociologists use the term "bureaucracy" as an approximate synonym for "administration" and "civil service." They follow the great German social theorist Max Weber in thinking of bureaucracy in this value-neutral sense of a government with fixed and official areas of jurisdiction for its officials, a graded system of centralized authority, a system of central files, and a body of officials with special professional skills who follow systematic general rules and procedures.[3]

For many other people, however, "bureaucracy" is value-laden: it means a kind of governmental sickness whose leading symptoms are the addiction of public officials to tortuous procedures, buck-passing, senseless rigid rules, and poor manners—everything summed up in the term "red tape."[4] We shall therefore stick to the more neutral terms "administration" and "civil service" to denote the parts of government with which we are concerned in this chapter.

## FORMAL STATUS OF ADMINISTRATIVE AGENCIES

### SIZE

In terms of the number of people employed, the administrative agencies constitute by far the largest element of any modern government. In 1973, for example, the

---

[2] For similar conceptions of administrators and civil servants, see Ira Sharkansky, *Public Administration: Policy-Making in Government Agencies* (Chicago: Markham Publishing Company, 1970), pp. 11–12; Ferrel Heady, "Civil Service," in David L. Sills (ed.), *International Encyclopedia of the Social Sciences,* Vol. 2 (New York: The Macmillan Company and The Free Press, 1968), pp. 495–501; and Leonard D. White, *Introduction to the Study of Public Administration* (4th ed.; New York: Crowell-Collier and Macmillan, Inc., 1955), pp. 1–2.

[3] H. H. Gerth and C. Wright Mills (eds.), *From Max Weber: Essays in Sociology* (New York: Oxford University Press, 1946), pp. 196–244.

[4] See Reinhard Bendix, "Bureaucracy," in Sills, *International Encyclopedia of the Social Sciences,* Vol. 2, pp. 206–219.

government of the United States employed a total of 2,768,000 civilians, 9,000 in the judicial branch, 33,000 in the legislative branch, and the remaining 2,726,000 in various executive and administrative agencies. The last figure represents only 3.71 percent of all civilians gainfully employed in the nation, but when state and local administrative employees are added the proportion is 18.3 percent.[5] Some democracies with less elaborate structures of regional and local government than the United States have (see Chap. 19) apparently employed smaller proportions of their labor forces in civil service; in the mid-1960s, for example, government employees constituted only 5.5 percent of the gainfully employed in Great Britain and 9.5 percent in France.[6]

## THE STRUCTURE OF ADMINISTRATIVE AGENCIES

### Principal Types

The most common type of administrative agency in modern democratic systems is the executive department, or ministry. Such an agency is formally headed by a member of the cabinet or ministry (see Chap. 16) and is established to formulate and administer government policy in such major areas as foreign affairs, fiscal affairs, agriculture, commerce, and labor. Each department has a number of subordinate agencies, variously called "bureaus," "divisions," or *directions;* many also maintain field offices to conduct business in particular parts of the nation under the direction of headquarters in the nation's capital.

In some democratic nations (for example, France) all administrative activities are formally conducted by these departments. Other nations, however, also have some "service-wide management agencies." Both the United States and Great Britain, for example, maintain civil-service commissions charged with overseeing examining, hiring, discharging, promoting, and working conditions of the employees of most of the departments and other agencies operating on the merit system.

Some democratic systems have also established "government corporations" more or less independent of the executive departments and charged with duties resembling those of privately owned business corporations. In the United States, for example, the Tennessee Valley Authority constructs dams and power plants and sells electric power to various state and local governments and private utilities. The United States Postal Service used to be an executive department, but is now a public corporation which collects and delivers the mail. The Federal Deposit Insurance Corporation insures the deposits of banks and savings-and-loan associations, and the National Capital Housing Authority reclaims slums and builds and rents low-cost housing in the District of Columbia. In Great Britain the British Broadcasting Corporation (BBC) sells licenses for radio receivers, prints a magazine, and uses the proceeds to prepare

---

[5] *The American Almanac, 1974* (The Statistical Abstract of the United States, prepared by the Bureau of the Census; New York: Grosset & Dunlap, Inc., 1974), pp. 229, 403.

[6] For Great Britain, see *Britain: An Official Handbook* (London: Central Office of Information, 1964), p. 449, Table 40; for France, see Henry W. Ehrmann, *Politics in France* (Boston: Little, Brown & Company, 1968), p. 265, Table VI.

and broadcast programs (see Chap. 6). Each of the nationalized industries—coal, electricity, gas, and the Bank of England—is operated by a government corporation organized much as is the BBC.

A few democratic countries, notably the United States, have established a fourth type of administrative agency known as "independent regulatory commissions." They include such bodies as the Interstate Commerce Commission, the Federal Communications Commission, and the Civil Aeronautics Board, each of which is charged with regulating a particular area of private business and all of which are formally responsible neither to the executive departments nor to the President.

### Formal Interrelations

Government corporations and regulatory commissions are independent in the sense that their heads are not generally required to report or to justify their decisions to the chief executive officer or to any other agency. Their members, however, are appointed by the chief executive, and he can thus exercise at least periodic control over their activities by granting or refusing reappointment. He also has the formal power, under certain circumstances, to set aside their orders, especially those of the civil-service commissions in the United States and Great Britain. Everywhere, however, the heads of the executive departments appointed by the chief executives are formally responsible to them and may be dismissed at any time. In a great many democratic systems by no means all administrative agencies are formally arranged in what many students of public administration believe to be the ideal fashion: a neat and consistent hierarchical structure of authority.

### Formal Internal Organization

A generation ago most students of public administration believed in certain principles of organization—certain correct ways of "interrelating the subdivisions of work by allotting them to men who are placed in a structure of authority, so that the work may be co-ordinated by orders of superiors to subordinates, reaching from the top to the bottom of the entire enterprise."[7] Today most political scientists are dubious about the universal scientific validity or practical applicability of these principles, but many continue to believe that most administrative agencies should be organized in accordance with the principles of hierarchy and separation of "staff" and "line" functions.

The principle of hierarchy, or, as some call it, "scalar organization," prescribes that the personnel of any administrative agency should be formally interrelated in pyramidal fashion, with a clear chain of command reaching from top to bottom and a line of responsibility from bottom to top. Each employee knows just who are his superiors, equals, and inferiors and therefore to whom he may give orders and from whom he must receive them. Often mentioned as models are the organization of any modern army and the clerical hierarchy of the Roman Catholic Church.

---

Governmental Authorities and Processes

[7] Luther Gulick, "Notes on the Theory of Organization," in Gulick and L. Urwick (eds.), *Papers on the Science of Administration* (New York: Institute of Public Administration, 1937), p. 6.

The principle of separation of staff and line functions is founded on the proposition that every agency performs two basic types of function. The Department of State, for example, negotiates treaties, exchanges official communications with foreign nations, and issues passports; all such activities are called its "line" functions. The department, if it is to be run efficiently, must also perform a number of "staff" or "housekeeping" functions: hiring and firing, determining promotions and pay increases, and budgeting. These two types of activities, many writers on public administration believe, should be performed by separate sets of agencies, each reporting to the agency's head but each independent of the other.

FIGURE 12
A model administrative
hierarchy.

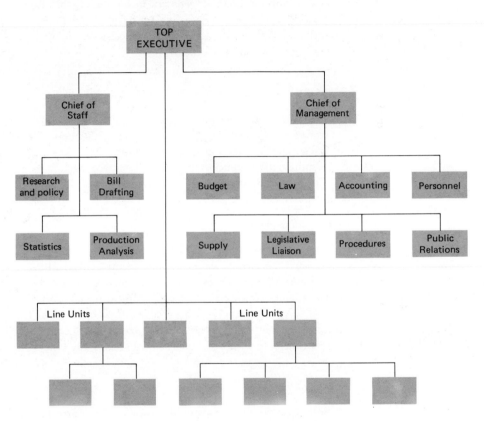

An agency organized in full accordance with both these principles could be represented graphically as in Figure 12. Few actual administrative agencies, however, are as neatly and consistently organized as is the model. Most students of public administration recognize that the practical problems of actual agencies usually necessitate deviations from the principles of hierarchy and separation of staff and line functions.

Many scholars, furthermore, agree with the statement of two recent commentators:

It can hardly escape the sharp-eyed observer that administrative bodies—and indeed all organizations, whether legislatures, political parties, labor unions,

The Administrative
Process

business enterprises, universities, churches, armies, or professional associations —respond in fact to a variety of informal patterns of influence among their membership. These are more or less at variance with the acknowledged structure of formal authority on which the organizations rest.[8]

An agency's formal organization is at most a rough guide to and a general limitation on its "informal," or "actual," organization—and it is the latter that gets things done. As this point has become more clearly perceived, a growing number of political scientists have chosen to study administrative agencies as a special aspect of the broad subject of behavior in human organizations. They focus not on legal powers and responsibilities but on networks of interpersonal communications and influence from which administrative decisions emerge and within which administrative functions are performed.[9]

## FORMAL ADMINISTRATIVE FUNCTIONS

From the point of view of subject matter, the functions formally assigned to administrative agencies are nearly coterminous with those of government itself, for every governmental function listed in Chapter 20 is performed mainly by one or more administrative agencies. Every administrative agency performs one or two but rarely all of the following principal activities.

### Providing Services

Some agencies mainly provide services for all who wish them. The Agricultural Research Service of the U.S. Department of Agriculture, for example, conducts an elaborate program of research on such matters as pest control, farm and land management, and breeding and raising livestock; it makes the results available at minimal cost to farmers who wish to improve their operations. The British National Health Service provides government-subsidized medical care and hospitalization for all who wish them. In Chapter 20 are listed a great many other activities of the service type.

### Regulating

Some agencies mainly regulate the operations of private individuals and organizations to keep them from engaging in certain forbidden practices. The outstanding example

---

[8] Harvey C. Mansfield and Fritz Morstein Marx, "Informal Organization," in Marx (ed.), *Elements of Public Administration* (2d ed.; Englewood Cliffs, N.J.: Prentice-Hall, Inc., 1959), p. 274. See also Herbert A. Simon, Donald W. Smithburg, and Victor A. Thompson, *Public Administration* (New York: Alfred A. Knopf, 1950), pp. 87–90.

[9] The leading studies include James G. March and Simon, *Organizations* (New York: John Wiley & Sons, Inc., 1958); Simon, *Administrative Behavior* (3d ed.; New York: Crowell-Collier and Macmillan, Inc., 1961); Charles E. Lindblom, *The Policy-Making Process* (Englewood Cliffs, N.J.: Prentice-Hall, Inc., 1968); and Aaron Wildavsky, *The Politics of the Budgetary Process* (Boston: Little, Brown & Company, 1964).

of such activity, of course, is the enforcement of criminal laws by the police, but there are many others. The American Federal Trade Commission, for example, issues "cease and desist" orders to private businesses engaging in such practices as misrepresenting or misbranding their products. The American Securities and Exchange Commission regulates the procedures of securities exchanges and determines what stocks may and may not be listed for sale. In Chapter 20 are also listed a great many other such regulatory activities.

### Licensing

In most democratic nations a private person or corporation can legally conduct certain kinds of business only after obtaining a license from some administrative agency. In one sense, then, licensing involves the performance of a service, but in another it also involves a considerable measure of regulation. This point is illustrated by the description in Chapter 6 of how the Federal Communications Commission uses its power to grant and renew licenses for radio and television stations to control certain aspects of broadcasters' activities. Similar regulatory power is involved in any agency's power to grant or withhold licenses.

### Adjudicating Disputes

The job of settling disputes by applying the law to particular situations (see Chap. 18) is assigned exclusively to the courts in the traditional allocation of government powers and functions. Yet in many democratic nations in recent decades administrative agencies have undertaken quasi-judicial functions—"quasi" only because they are performed by administrators instead of judges. When, for example, a worker or an employer complains to the National Labor Relations Board that an employer or union is engaging in an "unfair labor practice" in violation of the 1935 (Wagner) and 1947 (Taft-Hartley) labor-management relations acts, the NLRB is empowered to hold hearings, render a decision, and dismiss the complaint or order the challenged practice stopped. In Great Britain complaints by workers about the orders of their superiors in the nationalized coal industry, for example, are brought before the National Coal Board, which then decides who is in the right. This burgeoning type of administrative activity has drawn more and more attention to the problem of regular courts' power to review and reverse administrative decisions, and we shall return to this problem later in the chapter.

### Internal Management

An eminent student of public administration, Luther Gulick, coined a well-known catchword, POSDCORB, as a mnemonic device for recalling the internal-management functions that an administrative agency must perform if it is to carry on its external operations with maximum efficiency and economy. As he explained them, the letters in this word refer to the following functions: "P" is for planning, "O" for organization, "S" for staffing, "D" for directing, "CO" for coordinating, "R" for

*"Perhaps we didn't make it clear, Miss Jones, that
your job with the FBI is purely clerical."*

reporting, and "B" for budgeting.[10] They are mainly staff functions and, Gulick makes clear, the performance of any or all of them by staff and line agencies alike involves exercise of discretion by administrators.

In recent years another set of letters—PPBS—has almost crowded POSDCORB off the pages of most public-administration manuals. PPBS (Program Planning Budgeting System) is a system of budgeting in which computerized methods developed by economists for calculating relative benefits-for-cost ratios in existing and proposed programs are used to control, coordinate, and evaluate government programs. The methods were first developed in the 1950s and used in the Department of Defense under Secretary Robert McNamara in the 1960s. Their success there led President Lyndon B. Johnson in 1965 to direct that all Federal administrative units use them in the development of programs and budgets. The procedures and rationale of PPBS are far too complex to be discussed here,[11] but it is the latest and most technically advanced of many efforts to create a true "science of public administration."

## STATUS AND SELECTION OF ADMINISTRATIVE PERSONNEL

### Political Activity

Most modern democratic systems attempt to "keep politics out of administration"—that is, to remove civil servants in their professional capacities from the

---

[10] Gulick, "Notes on the Theory of Organization." p. 13.

[11] The most useful collection of details is David Novick (ed.), *Program Budgeting* (Cambridge, Mass.: Harvard University Press, 1965). For a shrewd review of PPBS' advantages and limitations, see Wildavsky, "The Political Economy of Efficiency: Cost-Benefit Analysis, Systems Analysis, and Program Budgeting," in Austin Ranney (ed.), *Political Science and Public Policy* (Chicago: Markham Publishing Company, 1968), pp. 55–82.

influence and control of political parties so that they may serve with equal faithfulness the leaders of *any* political party who may for the moment control the legislative and executive policy-making agencies. The most common means for achieving this end is to divorce civil servants' tenure from changes in party fortunes. A number of systems have added another: restricting civil servants' participation in partisan political activities. In the United States, for example, members of the national "classified" civil service and state and local employees of programs financed wholly or partly by the national government are forbidden by law from taking any active part in partisan activities. They may vote, privately voice their opinions, and even attend party rallies as spectators. But they may not solicit party funds, make partisan public speeches, hold party office, or work for a party in any other way. In Great Britain a number of rules promulgated by the Treasury and the various departments generally prohibit "policy-making" civil servants from engaging in such partisan activity as canvassing, making partisan public speeches, or standing as candidates, which might conflict with their roles as impartial servants of the whole nation and all parties; but in recent years civil servants with "routine" posts have been permitted increasing freedom of partisan activity. France is one of the few modern democracies that places no general restrictions upon such activities, but even in France the ministers and top administrators can and often do prevent, by means of administrative regulation, their employees' active support of extreme antigovernment parties.[12]

Administrative and political career lines coincide far more in Japan than in any other contemporary democratic system. Not only are civil servants allowed to engage freely in partisan and pressure politics there, but movement from the civil service into political leadership—very rare elsewhere—is quite common in Japan. Indeed, "parties have always recruited heavily from the bureaucracy both because of the great abilities and prestige of its administrators and the continued personal links such men have with former colleagues and the outside interests probably the surest route to highest political posts lies in a career with the bureaucracy."[13]

### Unions and Strikes

The classic weapons of industrial workers are forming unions and striking. Most modern democratic systems permit their civil servants to form unions but legally limit or deny altogether their right to strike. For example, employees like policemen, firemen, and postal workers are generally prohibited from striking on the ground that the continuous operation of their services is necessary to avoid national calamity. But these laws are difficult to enforce (it is impossible to jail, for example, hundreds of thousands of postal workers, as the United States found in 1970), and strikes or large-scale "sick-outs" by firemen, air-traffic controllers, police officers, sanitation

---

[12] For more detailed discussions, see James B. Christoph, "Political Rights and Administrative Impartiality in the British Civil Service," *American Political Science Review,* 51 (March 1957), pp. 67–87; Brian Chapman, *The Profession of Government* (London: George Allen & Unwin Ltd., 1959); and F. Ridley and J. Blondel, *Public Administration in France* (New York: Barnes & Noble, Inc., 1965).

[13] Frank Langdon, *Politics in Japan* (Boston: Little, Brown & Company, 1967), pp. 175–176, 228.

Legal prohibitions against strikes do not always keep public employees on the job: postal workers outside the main New York Post Office in the 1970 strike. Source: Wide World Photos.

workers, and others are by no means unknown. Public employees can also evade the prohibition of strikes in less risky ways. In the early 1960s, for example, British postal employees sought higher wages through a "work to rule" campaign, in which they rigidly enforced every last postal regulation, with the result that mail delivery was delayed so much that their discontents were very effectively brought to their superiors' attention. Employees of nationalized railways and coal mines, on the other hand, generally have the right to strike, although every effort is made to avoid such strikes by prior arbitration. The net effect of these rules in most democracies is that civil servants' right to organize unions is almost as well protected as that of nongovernmental workers but that their right to strike is greatly restricted.

### Selection

At some period in its history every modern democratic nation has selected its civil servants according to some standard other than technical competence. In Great Britain, for example, before the nineteenth century most government posts were filled by patronage—a system in which members of the nobility and of Parliament literally owned certain positions; as "patrons" they filled them with friends, retainers, or relatives, many of whom were too incompetent to hold any other kind of job. In France before the Revolution of 1789, all but the few highest offices in the kingdom were regarded as a species of private property, to be sold, bequeathed, or given away by their owners to whomever they pleased. In the United States before the late nineteenth century most civil-service posts were filled by the "spoils system," in which the political party replacing another in power dismissed from office as many adherents of the opposition party as it pleased and replaced them with its own supporters and contributors.

Prussia (and later Germany) was the first modern nation to select its civil servants by the "merit system." This system in its ideal form takes technical competence—the civil servants' ability to perform the functions of their posts with maximum efficiency—as the sole standard for selecting civil-service personnel and usually measures the competence of applicants by competitive examinations of knowledge and intelligence. Prussia instituted this system in the middle of the eighteenth century.

Beginning in the late eighteenth century civil-service reform movements arose in most of the democratic nations, aimed at abolition of patronage and spoils and replacement of them with merit systems on the Prussian model. The movement succeeded earliest in France, where revolutionary leaders and later Napoleon I installed a professionalized civil service. In Great Britain the reform began in the 1830s when the administrators of British India established a merit system for selecting members of the Indian civil service. It was extended to the whole British civil service after the publication and adoption in 1853 of the Trevelyan-Northcote Commission's report on the organization of the permanent civil service. In the United States general national reform began in 1883 with the passage of the Pendleton Act, which established the Civil Service Commission and provided for the progressive classification of members of the various administrative agencies.

In most democratic countries today all or nearly all civil-service employees are selected by some kind of examination, and their tenure is largely or entirely independent of their party affiliations. The United States' national civil service has been somewhat slower in this respect than most, but, as Figure 13 shows, it has come a long way since 1883. By 1970 about 99 percent of all American national civil-service employees were under the merit system, and in most other democratic nations the proportion was the same. Most or all civil servants in most democratic nations are thus "permanent" in the sense that they are not directly subject to the approval or disapproval of the voters through ordinary electoral processes.

FIGURE 13
Growth of the American
competitive civil service,
1883-1970.

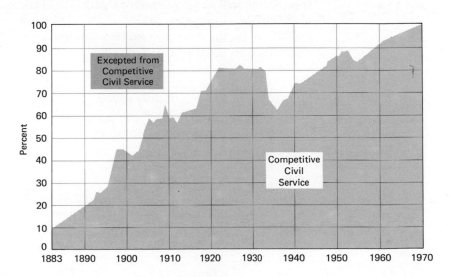

The selection systems of many modern democratic countries tend to produce a kind of distinct "administrative elite," or "administrative class," which mans and prepares to man the top posts. The procedures for recruitment, training, job assignment, promotion, and lateral movement are "career-directed": That is, they are deliberately designed to create a special elite corps of administrative supervisors with general managerial skills desirable for any supervisory post, rather than technical expertise suitable only for particular posts. These systems therefore recruit almost entirely from universities and professional schools with the highest prestige. In France, for example, it is next to impossible to enter the ranks of the young *hauts administrateurs* and eventually to become a *grand fonctionnaire* unless one is a graduate of either the École Polytechnique, the École Libre des Sciences Politiques, or the École Nationale d'Administration; more than two-thirds of the top administrators are themselves the children of high civil servants or comparable professionals.[14] In Great Britain examinations for admission to the administrative class of the civil service stress general cultural knowledge rather than technical expertise, and about 80 percent of the young recruits are graduates of the Universities of Oxford and Cambridge. Furthermore, more than half of the recruits have studied classics and history, whereas fewer than 5 percent have studied science or engineering.[15] Japan prescribes similar examinations for entrance to its top career-service line, and graduates of Tokyo University constitute about three-quarters of all higher civil servants.[16] The result is the establishment in these nations of distinct administrative elites, which have very little career exchange with private business or education: Few people who begin their careers outside the civil service ever enter it, and few civil servants ever leave for outside careers. The only major exception, as we have seen, is in Japan, where civil servants often go into partisan politics.

In the United States, on the other hand, the civil service is organized on much more "position-directed" lines. The examinations that must be taken to qualify for most positions are intended to test technical competence for particular positions, not general "cultural" or administrative ability. The "junior management" program and its qualifying examination come the closest to the British "administrative class" model, but for the most part position-direction standards prevail. One important result has been noted by Ira Sharkansky:

> The British generally appoint high-level administrators from within the ranks of the civil service. At both federal and state levels in the United States, however, many high-level administrative positions are filled with "outsiders." American executives in government and in the private sector believe that the

---

[14] Ehrmann, *Politics in France,* pp. 132–133.

[15] Anthony Sampson, *Anatomy of Britain* (London: Hodder & Stoughton, Ltd., 1962), pp. 224–226. For Continental European administrators, see John A. Armstrong, *The European Administrative Elite* (Princeton, N.J.: Princeton University Press, 1972).

[16] Heady, *Public Administration: A Comparative Perspective* (Englewood Cliffs, N.J.: Prentice-Hall, Inc., 1966), pp. 50–51.

"transient" business-government administrator can infuse the government bureaucracy with an innovative stimulus from outside.[17]

Despite these differences, however, the civil-service systems of all modern democratic countries furnish most of their employees, from bottom to top, with lifetime jobs as long as they perform with technical competence. The civil services are *professionalized.* But how can this professionalization be reconciled with the ideals of democracy? Those ideals, as we saw in Chapter 13, require that *all* public officials do what the people want them to do and refrain from doing what the people do not want them to do. And we noted in Chapters 7 and 14 that such responsiveness and responsibility are enforced upon legislators and executives by limitations on their terms of office and requirements that they periodically seek renewal of their mandates in popular elections. How, then, can a permanent, professionalized civil service possibly fit into a democratic system? This problem is one of the most often discussed of all administrative problems in democratic systems. Let us see what it involves.

## POLITICS, ADMINISTRATION, AND POLICY MAKING

### THE DICHOTOMY BETWEEN POLITICS AND ADMINISTRATION

Many nineteenth-century American reformers, as we have noted, valued highly the ideal of government efficiency and believed that a Prussian type of permanent, professionalized civil service would help to realize it in the United States. Most, however, also valued the ideal of democracy and had no wish to see the entire governmental structure "Prussianized." They were reluctant to choose between these two ideals, and for many the most urgent question was, How, if at all, can a permanent civil service be reconciled with the ideals and institutions of democracy?

Toward the end of the century some political scientists advanced a doctrine according to which these two ideals could be both reconciled and realized, and for several decades afterward most American students of government regarded this doctrine as having settled once and for all the problem of the proper place of professional administrators in a democratic government. Let us now examine its content, consequences, and current status.

### Origins and Content

Most students of public administration credit the first statement of the doctrine to an article published in 1887 by a young professor of politics at Princeton University named Woodrow Wilson. Briefly summarized, Wilson's argument ran as follows. The old classification of governmental powers and functions into legislative, executive, and judicial types does not fit the facts. All governments perform only two basic functions: "politics," the making of general policies and laws; and "administration," the application of policies and laws to particular individuals and situations. As

[17] Sharkansky, *Public Administration,* pp. 24–25.

administration is so different from politics, Wilson concluded, it must be kept non-political; for, in his words, "administrative questions are not political questions. Although politics sets the tasks for administration it should not be suffered to manipulate its offices. The field of administration is a field of business."[18]

Wilson's dichotomy between politics and administration was taken up by another eminent political scientist, Frank J. Goodnow, and elaborated into a broad doctrine of the proper place of administrators in a democracy, which he advanced in his book *Politics and Administration* (1900). Goodnow's position can be summarized briefly. All government activities are either politics ("operations necessary to the expression of [the state's] will") or administration ("operations necessary to the execution of that will"). Goodnow—unlike many of his self-proclaimed followers—believed that these two functions could not be completely separated or exclusively assigned to entirely separate agencies; he recommended, however, that as much as possible certain agencies be mainly political and others mainly administrative. He concluded that in a democracy the mainly administrative agencies must necessarily be subordinate to, controlled by, and in the service of the mainly political agencies. As he put it, "popular government requires that . . . the executing authority . . . shall be subordinate to the expressing authority, since the latter in the nature of things can be made much more representative of the people than can the executing authority."[19]

### Consequences

For four decades after 1900 the Wilson-Goodnow formula was almost universally accepted by American political scientists, and it deeply affected their thinking about the proper role of administrators in democratic government. As Dwight Waldo has summed it up: "Most subsequent students of administration, even when they have not read it and even when they arrive at quite opposite conclusions with respect to the application of politics and administration, have regarded *Politics and Administration* much as the eighteenth-century literati regarded Newton's *Principia.*"[20]

Among its specific effects three in particular should be mentioned. First, for most scholars and reformers it provided an eminently satisfactory theoretical justification for the presence of a permanent, professionalized civil service in a democracy. If administrators only carry out policies given to them by political agencies, they reasoned, there is no need to make them responsible to the voters.

Second, it provided the theoretical foundation for a new "science of public administration." which first emerged in the United States in the decade after publication of Goodnow's book. This new branch of political science concentrated upon such problems as how to organize administrative agencies and to recruit and train administrators so that administration can be conducted with maximum efficiency and econ-

---

[18] Woodrow Wilson, "The Study of Administration," *Political Science Quarterly,* 2 (June 1887), 197–222.

[19] Frank J. Goodnow, *Politics and Administration* (New York: Crowell-Collier and Macmillan, Inc., 1900), p. 24.

[20] Dwight Waldo, *The Administrative State: A Study of the Political Theory of Public Administration* (New York: The Ronald Press Company, 1948), p. 106.

omy—problems similar to those then being dealt with by the new and rising "scientific management" movement in private industry, headed by Frederick W. Taylor, the first of the modern "efficiency experts." Nor did the new specialists in public administration think that by concentrating on the values of efficiency and economy they were slighting the values of democracy. The latter, after all, seemed the concern of politics, not administration—and, as the two functions seemed distinct, students of public administration believed that civil servants can and should focus their attention on how to improve administration and leave to others the problems of maximizing democracy.

Third, it provided a clear and satisfying set of criteria for organizing governments: All policy-making officials were to be elected or appointed by elected officials, and all administrators were to be selected by the merit system and to hold office as long as they were technically competent—as illustrated by the hypothetical situation with which we began the present chapter. The city-manager form of municipal government, as we shall see in Chapter 19, is an effort to organize local governments in accordance with this principle.

### Present Eclipse

Since the late 1930s an ever-growing number of political scientists, led by such students of public administration as Luther Gulick, Robert A. Dahl, Charles S. Hyneman, and Carl J. Friedrich, have rejected both the dichotomy between politics and administration and the revised doctrine of separation of powers based on it. They have rejected the dichotomy because they believe it offers an inaccurate description of the governing process. The exercise of discretion, they argue, is the essence of policy determination; every public employee, whether he is called "political" or "administrative," exercises some discretion. If "politics" means policy making and not merely partisanship, they conclude, it cannot be "taken out of administration" as long as administrators exercise discretion—and there is no way to prevent this exercise, even if it were desirable to do so.

These scholars have been led to this conclusion mainly by their observation that administrative agencies, no matter how professionalized and formally "non-political," have a great deal to say about what policy is—and are by no means confined merely to carrying out policies laid down by legislatures and executives. These scholars are convinced, furthermore, that the policy-making powers of administrators do not result from any special hunger for power or contempt for democracy among the administrators themselves but are inevitable attributes of modern government. Let us briefly summarize the evidence on which they base these conclusions.

## POLICY MAKING BY ADMINISTRATORS[21]

### Administrative Influence on Legislative and Executive Policies

In almost any human decision-making organization the expert—the person who

---

[21] A useful general description and analysis is Harold Seidman, *Politics, Position, and Power* (New York: Oxford University Press, 1970).

knows the history of the organization's problems and has detailed technical information about the possibilities and practicality of the various proposed solutions—has an enormous advantage over the layman, who at best has only a general, partial, and probably shaky technical knowledge. The more complex and difficult the problems, furthermore, the greater the expert's advantage. As the problems of modern government are perhaps the most difficult ever faced by any human organization, the expert in government has a very great advantage indeed.

For a variety of reasons, an administrator has a much better chance than a legislator or an executive has to become an expert on the subject dealt with by a particular agency. For one thing, the administrator is a specialist in *one* subject, whether it be conservation, issuing passports, regulating railroad rates, or whatever. The legislator and the executive, on the other hand, necessarily deal with all these matters and many more besides. The "political" official cannot afford to specialize. What is more, the legislator or the executive is often an active leader of a political party and must therefore spend considerable time at party meetings, campaigning, and "politicking" in other ways. The administrator, however, is forbidden to engage in such activities and can therefore spend his full time and energy on the policy questions before his agency. Finally, most legislators and executives are considerably less "permanent" than are merit-system civil servants and do not have nearly such long periods in office during which to acquire the detailed technical knowledge and "feel" that constitute expertise.

In all modern democracies, accordingly, impermanent, part-time, and unspecialized political officials often ask advice from permanent, full-time, and specialized administrative experts on the relative merits of policies—and far more often than not they follow this advice. Administrators' own policy preferences inevitably enter into and affect their advice, for, as British scholar Harold J. Laski has written:

> You cannot ask an able man to concern himself with questions like education, public health, factory legislation, safety in mines, without two consequences following. To ask him to discover facts is to ask him to indicate conclusions; and the very fact that he reports conclusions necessarily indicates a theory of action.[22]

When such men are asked for advice they can hardly avoid making their views known, and when, as often happens, "political" officials and their constituents have no strong views of their own, civil servants' preferences are likely to become policy.

Occasionally, of course, a "political" official has strong views of his own that run sharply counter to those of the civil servants formally subordinate to him. The Goodnow doctrine requires that the administrator in such a situation subordinate his own preferences and loyally implement those of his superior. But government by no means always works this way, as the following episodes illustrate.

---

[22] Harold J. Laski, *Parliamentary Government in England* (London: George Allen & Unwin Ltd., 1938), pp. 260–261.

One of the "planks" on which the Labour party campaigned in the British general election of 1945 was reversal of the Conservative government's anti-Zionist policy in order to permit greater Jewish immigration into Palestine and to assist in the early formation of a Jewish state there. After Labour won the election and took office, Foreign Secretary Ernest Bevin discovered that experts in the Foreign Office were unanimously against supporting Zionism and maintained that only a pro-Arab policy could protect British interests in the Middle East. Their expert knowledge and forensic skill overcame Bevin's objections and "sold" him on continuing the previous anti-Zionist policy—which shortly became the official policy of the Labour government.[23]

In 1950 President Harry S. Truman, backed by a resolution of the United Nations General Assembly (see Chap. 24), ordered General Douglas MacArthur to take command of the American and other U.N. forces to repel the invasion of South Korea by the communist North Koreans. MacArthur not only drove the invaders back but occupied most of North Korea as well. This act brought the Chinese communists into the war, and MacArthur had to retreat. Truman and the United Nations were committed to a policy of limiting the war to Korea and seeking a negotiated peace on the basis of restoring the preinvasion boundaries and guaranteed independence for South Korea. But MacArthur did not agree. He issued a number of public statements calling for direct attacks on Red Chinese territory as a necessary step in reoccupying the entire peninsula. "There is no substitute for victory," he declared. In April 1951 Truman relieved him of his command on grounds of insubordination, but, after returning home, MacArthur continued to rally political support for his position, doing considerable damage to Truman's popularity.[24]

Less global in scope but equally instructive was the "Newburgh affair" of 1961. Joseph M. Mitchell became city manager of Newburgh, New York, in 1960—in which capacity, according to the code of ethics of the International City Managers Association, his job was to "submit policy proposals to the council with facts and advice on matters of policy to give the council a basis for making decisions on community goals." The council told him of its concern about rising costs of welfare aid, and Mitchell responded with a public speech to the effect that ever since the 1950s "criminal lawyers and all the mushy rabble of do-gooders and bleeding hearts in society and politics have marched under the Freudian flag toward the omnipotent state of Karl Marx." He then launched a campaign to prune the relief rolls of all "chiselers and freeloaders" deemed not to need or deserve aid. He ordered relief recipients to pick up their checks at the police station, where each was questioned by the police. The mayor opposed these practices and unsuccessfully tried to stop them. Before the November council election Mitchell publicly supported some candidates and opposed others. Furthermore, he offered to resign if the pro-Mitchell candidates were defeated and challenged the mayor to resign if they were elected.

---

[23] See Arthur Koestler, *Promise and Fulfilment: Palestine, 1917–1949* (New York: Crowell-Collier and Macmillan, Inc., 1949), chaps. 10–11.

[24] The episode is discussed at length in Richard E. Neustadt, *Presidential Power* (New York: John Wiley & Sons, Inc., 1960).

Mitchell was censured by the International City Managers Association for engaging in partisan politics, and most of his welfare rules were invalidated by court orders.[25] But the episode was another illustration—a particularly flamboyant one—of the fact that administrators sometimes do open battle for their policy preferences even when they run counter to those of their political superiors. In such battles the administrators are far from helpless.

## Administrative Legislation

Every statute and executive directive is necessarily general in expression, in the sense that its language must apply to many concrete situations yet cannot possibly describe each in detail. No concrete situation is exactly like any other, nor does any such situation exactly and in every detail fit the wording of the statute or directive. Consequently, no administrative agency can avoid developing its own body of rules for determining which specific instances do and do not fall within the terms of each statute or directive that it administers. This kind of derivative administrative rule making is generally known as "administrative legislation." Most students of government are convinced that the need for such rules necessarily involves administrators in policy making to some degree and that the broader and more general are the directives handed to the administrators, the more important "administrative legislation" becomes in shaping the policies that are actually applied.

Pressure groups have long known this political fact of life. The most successful and powerful of them, accordingly, have never regarded their work as finished when the legislature has passed a bill or the executive has issued a directive that they have sought. They have then shifted their attention to the appropriate administrative agencies, to ensure that the latter carry out the statute or directive as the pressure groups wish it carried out. For example, the "patriotic" groups supporting restrictive immigration laws have kept a close watch on the Immigration and Naturalization Service to make such that no "undesirable aliens" slip through the legal nets; and the National Cooperative Milk Producers' Federation once made sure that the Bureau of Internal Revenue diligently collected the special tax on oleomargarine (see Chap. 10). Recent studies of pressure politics in various democratic nations, indeed, have shown that administrative agencies are becoming targets of increasing importance for pressure groups.[26]

## The Role of Administrators in Developing Nations

There is no doubt, then, that career administrators play a significant role in the policy-making processes of the Western democratic nations. In most developing

---

[25] The Newburgh affair is recounted in Duane Lockard, *The Politics of State and Local Government* (New York: Crowell-Collier and Macmillan, Inc., 1963), pp. 445–447.

[26] L. Harmon Zeigler and G. Wayne Peak, *Interest Groups in American Society* (2d ed.; Englewood Cliffs, N.J.: Prentice-Hall, Inc. 1972); Robert H. Salisbury (ed.), *Interest Group Politics in America* (New York: Harper & Row, Publishers, 1970); Samuel E. Finer, *Anonymous Empire* (2d ed.; London: Pall Mall Press, 1966); and Joseph LaPalombara, *Interest Groups in Italian Politics* (Princeton, N.J.: Princeton University Press, 1964).

nations, however, their role is crucial. Economic development is the top-priority goal of most of these nations, and the planning and implementation of effective development programs require substantial technical expertise. Most of the expertise that these nations can mobilize belongs to their civil servants, rather than to their political leaders. As a result, some nations, for example Iran and other Middle Eastern countries, are trying to reverse the historical pattern of Western development: They are trying to develop competent civil services *before* they concentrate on economic development.[27]

This primacy of administration disturbs many sympathetic Western observers who believe that administrative dominance is a major barrier to balanced *political* development and makes any movement toward representative democracy particularly difficult.[28] It often prepares the way for the overthrow of "corrupt" civilian regimes by "clean" military juntas. And it perpetuates the psychological domination of the former colonial overlords:

> The organization of offices, the demeanor of the civil servants, even the general appearance of a *bureau,* strikingly mirror the national characteristics of the bureaucracies of the former colonial powers. The *fonctionnaire* slouched at his desk in Lomé or Cotonou, cigarette pasted to his underlip, has his counterpart in every provincial town in France; and the demeanor of an administrative officer in Accra or Lagos untying the red tape from his files would be recognizable to anyone familiar with Whitehall or, more specifically, with the Colonial Office.[29]

There is no escaping the conclusion that, whatever their formal status and powers may be, administrative agencies make policy in both established Western democracies and in new and developing nations. Whereas most democratic nations have emphasized, and to a large degree have succeeded in, "getting politics out of administration" in the sense of largely or entirely eliminating direct partisan control over the selection of administrative personnel, they have given far less attention to the significant fact that "administration has gotten into politics" in the sense of policy making.

This fact has not only made the Wilson-Goodnow dichotomy between politics and administration passé, but it has also caused a grave problem for those nations, Western or otherwise, that wish their governments to be democratic as well as efficient. We shall conclude this chapter by analyzing the problem and reviewing some of the efforts that have been made to solve it.

---

[27] See Heady, *Public Administration.* chap. 7; and Leonard Binder, *Iran: Political Development in a Changing Society* (Berkeley, Calif.: University of California Press, 1964).

[28] See especially LaPalombara, "An Overview of Bureaucracy and Political Development," and Riggs, "Bureaucrats and Political Development: A Paradoxical View," in LaPalombara (ed.), *Bureaucracy and Political Development* (Princeton, N.J.: Princeton University Press, 1963), pp. 3–44, 120–167.

[29] J. Donald Kingsley, "Bureaucracy and Political Development, with Particular Reference to Nigeria," in LaPalombara (ed.), *Bureaucracy and Political Development* (Princeton, N.J.: Princeton University Press, 1963), p. 303.

# "ADMINISTOCRACY" IN A DEMOCRACY:
# ATTEMPTED SOLUTIONS

## THE PROBLEM

The term "administocracy" was coined by Guy S. Claire to denote an "aristocracy of administrators"—a government effectively run by career civil servants.[30] The problem of administocracy may be stated as follows: Citizens of most democratic systems wish their governments to be efficient and are convinced that a permanent, professionalized civil service recruited and retained according to standards of technical competence is best calculated to produce efficiency; they have no wish to return to the bad old days of the patronage and spoils systems. Yet most of them also wish their governments to be democratic—committed to realizing the ideal of popular control of government and dedicated to doing what the people want and not what some elite thinks that the people ought to have. Most of us want both efficiency *and* democracy, and we do not wish to choose one ideal at the expense of slighting or ignoring the other.

Are these two ideals compatible? Can we pursue them both? These questions have long concerned political theorists. For several generations, as we have noted, most scholars believed that the dichotomy between politics and administration formulated by Wilson and Goodnow had solved the problem. Yet most present-day political scientists believe that this dichotomy is based upon a misconception of what administrators actually do and thus offers no solution at all.

Present-day political science, then, has rejected the Wilson-Goodnow solution. Has anything replaced it? Most contemporary political scientists believe that the solution to the problem of administocracy lies not in any futile attempt to prevent administrators from making policy but in ensuring that administrators are *responsible* in their policy-making activities. When we examine the relevant literature closely, however, we discover that its authors use the key word "responsibility" in two distinct senses; their proposals for making administrators responsible reflect different emphases on two meanings of the word.

### *"Responsibility" as Adherence to a Professional Code*

A number of political scientists, most notably Carl J. Friedrich, have argued that the political responsibility of administrators supposedly reflected in their accountability to elected officials can never be enforced completely. They argue that we must place at least equal reliance on developing "functional" or "objective" responsibility—that is, that we should select and train our administrators in such a way that they will operate according to certain professional standards and adhere to a professional code of ethics. Ideally, according to Friedrich, administrators should be responsible in the same sense and for similar reasons as are judges.

Judicial decisions are relatively responsible because judges have to account for their action in terms of a somewhat rationalized and previously established

---

[30] Guy S. Claire, *Administocracy* (New York: Crowell-Collier and Macmillan, Inc., 1934).

set of rules. Any deviation from these rules on the part of a judge will be subjected to extensive scrutiny by his colleagues and what is known as the "legal profession." Similarly, administrative officials seeking to apply scientific "standards" have to account for their action in terms of a somewhat rationalized and previously established set of hypotheses. Any deviation from these hypotheses will be subjected to thorough scrutiny by their colleagues in what is known as the "fellowship of science."[31]

### "Responsibility" as Accountability to Elected Officials

Other political scientists, notably Herman Finer and Charles S. Hyneman, have argued that, although administrative responsibility in Friedrich's sense is a fine thing, a democratic government must make its administrators responsible mainly by making them accountable to and subject to control by elected public officials. Only thus, they insist, can we establish the popular control of administrative policy making that democratic government—which, they agree, is not necessarily synonymous with "good" government—demands. As Hyneman puts it:

> Government has enormous power over us, and most of the acts of government are put into effect by the men and women who constitute the bureaucracy. It is in the power of these men and women to do us great injury, as it is in their power to advance our well-being. It is essential that they do what we want done, the way we want it done. Our concept of democratic government requires that these men and women be subject to direction and control that compel them to conform to the wishes of the people as a whole whether they wish to do so or not.[32]

Both the Friedrich and the Hyneman-Finer "schools" thus believe that some kind of external control of administrative policy making is necessary to solve the problem of administocracy, although they do not agree about how important this particular kind of control is. We shall conclude our discussion by examining briefly some of the principal methods of control currently employed by the democratic nations.

## SOLUTIONS

### Making Administrators Representative[33]

Some political scientists have suggested that one of the best ways to prevent adminis-

---

[31] Carl J. Friedrich, "Responsible Government Service under the American Constitution," in *Problems of the American Public Service* (New York: McGraw-Hill, Inc., 1935), pp. 36–37. See also Phillip Monypenny, "A Code of Ethics as a Means of Controlling Administrative Conduct," *Public Administration Review,* 13 (Summer 1953), 184–187.

[32] Charles Hyneman, *Bureaucracy in a Democracy* (New York: Harper & Row, Publishers, 1950), p. 38. See also Herman Finer, "Administrative Responsibility in a Democratic Government," *Public Administration Review,* 1 (Summer 1941), 335–350.

[33] A useful recent review of the arguments for and against this notion and an empirical study

tocracy is to have the administrative agencies themselves represent the population directly rather than to rely entirely upon elected representatives to keep an unrepresentative bureaucracy in line. By a "representative bureaucracy" they mean a civil service drawn from all the nation's social, racial, religious, and economic groups —though not necessarily in exactly the same proportions as they exist in the society at large. Such a bureaucracy, they argue, is likely to be responsive to the people's desires because it *is* the people, or at least a cross section of the people. Indeed, it may in some ways be *more* representative than are elected officials, for it will include members of some interests ignored by electoral majorities.[34] There is little hard evidence either to support or to refute this argument, but there is plenty of evidence that in most nations civil servants have primarily middle-class backgrounds. Where the society itself is largely middle class, as in the United States, the civil service can be said to be representative, but where only a small proportion of the society is middle class, as in India or Turkey, middle-class civil servants are bound to be very unrepresentative. It is far less clear, however, which, if any, of these bureaucracies is clearly the most *responsive,* and few political scientists believe that representativeness can be more than a minor feature of any system for keeping civil servants responsive.

### Control by Elected and Political Officials

**United States**  Political control of administrative agencies in the United States is exercised by Congress and the President, both jointly and separately. Jointly they approve legislation creating the administrative agencies, defining their objectives and powers, and establishing standards of performance; they provide the money that the administrative agencies spend; they collaborate on appointments to top administrative posts; they establish the procedures by which lesser appointments are made; and they review, criticize, and sometimes stop the actions of administrators.

In addition, the President, as chief executive, formally controls most civil servants. He appoints the heads and chief subordinates of most executive agencies, and they are responsible to him. They, in turn, formally control the employees of their agencies. It would seem then that, as can any commander in chief, the President can send orders down the administrative hierarchy, count on their being obeyed, and expect reports from his subordinates to keep him in touch with what is going on. But appearance is far from reality. Not only are the number of civil servants and the number and variety of their activities far too vast for any one man to keep an eye on, but the more conscientious employees are also likely to develop strong feelings

---

of the extent to which various civil services are actually representative is Samuel Krislov, *Representative Bureaucracy* (Englewood Cliffs, N.J.: Prentice-Hall, Inc., 1974). See also V. Subramaniam, "Representative Bureaucracy: A Reassessment," *American Political Science Review,* 61 (December 1967), 1010–1019.

[34] Norton E. Long, "Bureaucracy and Constitutionalism," *American Political Science Review,* 46 (September 1952), 808–818. See also Kingsley, *Representative Bureaucracy* (Yellow Springs, O.: The Antioch Press, 1944).

about what policies ought to be followed—feelings that do not always coincide with those of the President. Patriotic Americans can do no less than work for what they believe to be in the best interests of the nation, and losing a presidential order in the bureaucratic maze is not difficult. As Jonathan Daniels, a former presidential aide, wrote of Cabinet officers:

> Half of a President's suggestions, which theoretically carry the weight of orders, can be safely forgotten by a Cabinet member. And if the President asks about a suggestion a second time, he can be told that it is being investigated. If he asks a third time, a wise Cabinet officer will give him at least part of what he suggests. But only occasionally, except about the most important matters, do Presidents ever get around to asking three times.[35]

The most perceptive modern student of the presidency, Richard Neustadt, concludes that the President's power over his subordinates is less power to command than power to persuade—an opportunity "to induce them to believe that what he wants of them is what their own appraisal of their own responsibilities requires them to do in their own interest, not his."[36] Presidential control of administrators is thus not enough to keep them strictly obedient to the will of elected policy makers.

Congress, on the other hand, emphasizes reviewing and checking the activities of administrators. Most appropriations run for only a year or two, and when agency requests for new funds come before Congress the various subcommittees of the appropriations committee in each house use the occasion—when administrators are understandably in a very tractable mood—to review the agencies' past conduct and future plans and to offer whatever criticisms committee members think appropriate. Investigating committees, as we observed in Chapter 15, provide another useful means of making administrators toe the line. Congress frequently grants powers to administrative agencies for limited periods of time only and uses the occasions of renewing the grants to review not only policy but also the way that it has been carried out.

These examples are but a few of the many means that elected officials in the United States use to direct and control administrative agencies. If Congress and the President use them vigorously and intelligently with a clear understanding of what they are about and why, administocracy can be kept well within acceptable bounds. Hyneman has argued, however, that control of administration in the United States is made more difficult by the formal independence of Congress and the President from each other; because they are elected by different constituencies for different terms of office, more often than not they have conflicting views about what policies administrators should pursue and by what means. Many other students of this question are skeptical of the utility of Hyneman's proposed solution: a joint executive-legislative council to formulate policy and direct administration.[37] But most agree with his

---

[35] Jonathan Daniels, *Frontier on the Potomac* (New York: Crowell-Collier and Macmillan, Inc., 1946). pp. 31–32.

[36] Neustadt, *Presidential Power*, p. 46.

[37] Hyneman, *Bureaucracy in a Democracy*, chap. 25.

judgment that until the problem is solved the overall control of administrative agencies by elected officials in the United States will continue to be less effective than it should be.

**Parliamentary Systems** At first glance, the control of administrators by elected officials in the parliamentary systems appears to be much better organized and more effective than it is in the United States, for in most of them, as we learned in Chapter 16, the legislatures and executives usually speak with one voice. In such a nation the administrators in each executive department are directly responsible to and formally controlled by the minister, the minister is responsible to the cabinet, and the cabinet and the legislature are always in formal agreement about both policy ends and administrative means.

When we look a little closer, however, we learn that matters are not quite this simple or satisfactory. For one thing, as we have noted, many of these nations have established government corporations like the BBC, which are not subject to direct ministerial control. For another, members of the legislatures in many of these nations apparently think that ministerial control by itself is not sufficient to prevent administocracy. Consequently many parliamentary democracies have created such institutions as the British "question time" and the French *interpellation*.

On each of the first four days of every legislative week any member of the House of Commons may, after having given the government one or two days' notice, ask a question of any member of the ministry. The question, offered in both oral and written form, may simply be a request for information, or it may require the minister to explain and justify a specific action taken by his department. Furthermore, the questioner and other MPs may ask supplementary questions arising from the minister's oral answer to the initial question. Questions are asked not only by the opposition to embarrass the government but also by the back-benchers of the majority party. The question period thus not only offers an arena for conflict between government and opposition; it often also provides scope for contests between legislators and administrators. Asking questions, indeed, is the principal method by which rank-and-file MPs can review and criticize the actions of the civil service and one of the few areas in which they can participate in the governing process free of the shackles of party discipline and Cabinet control. An average of 70–100 oral questions are asked each day, a total of about 13,000 each year. Some observers believe that they have proved to be at least as effective as ministerial control in keeping civil servants in line.[38]

In the Third and Fourth Republics members of the French National Assembly also asked questions in a procedure similar to that of the House of Commons, though the questions were designed mainly to elicit information. Far more formidable was the practice of *interpellation*—requesting ministers to explain and justify the actions of their departments. After a minister had replied to a particular *interpellation*, a general debate was held, ending in a motion either censuring or approving the minister's reply

Governmental Authorities and Processes

[38] The definitive study is D. N. Chester and Nina Bowring, *Questions in Parliament* (New York: Oxford University Press, 1962).

and the action of his department. These practices constituted a powerful weapon for legislative control of administrators.

In the Fifth Republic, however, they have been severely limited. Question time is now restricted to one day a week, and the greater power of the executive (see Chap. 16) makes it extremely unlikely that a minister or the whole cabinet will be turned out because of unsatisfactory answers to legislators' questions.

**Communist Nations**   Whatever communist leaders may wish, the fact is that no authoritarian political system is a perfect hierarchy guided by omniscient and omnipotent leaders aware and in control of the lowliest subordinate's every move. As most enterprises in the Soviet Union, the People's Republic of China, and the Eastern European "people's democracies" are owned and operated by the state, their hordes of public employees are proportionately much larger than are those of the Western democratic nations. And, judging from what their own observers say, one of their most acute and recurring problems is controlling bureaucracy—how to establish and maintain a civil service that is efficient, incorruptible, and quickly responsive to the wishes of the rulers.[39]

The Soviet Union attacks the problem mainly by using the Communist party as the watchdog of the state administrative apparatus right down to the level of village governments and individual factories and collective farms. The central ministries customarily issue detailed instructions to regional and local units and enterprises, allowing them only small areas of discretion. Each unit and enterprise has some party members on its staff or overseeing it from local party headquarters—an updated version of the ancient Russian institution of "the inspector." Furthermore, the party uses *samokritika* (see Chap. 5) to encourage ordinary nonparty citizens to report and criticize lapses in zeal or performance by local administrators, factory managers, and collective-farm managers..[40]

The intensity of the party's scrutiny has varied from time to time (it was most intense under Joseph Stalin, was relaxed somewhat under Nikita Khrushchev, and has recently been tightened up again). One of its unanticipated consequences has been factory and farm managers' development of tricks for protecting themselves. Knowing that they will be in real trouble if they do not fulfill their assigned production quotas, they seek to have low quotas assigned—they underreport plant capacity and current output or maintain inventories of finished products or raw materials unknown to the central planners. In this way they can be confident of meeting their assigned quotas and hope to be praised for exceeding them.[41] Clearly, even in the Soviet Union public employees have ways of doing what they want to do rather than what their superiors want them to do.

The People's Republic of China has tried several different control systems, as outlined in Figure 14. Before the communist takeover in 1949 China had one of the

---

[39] See Heady, *Public Administration*, pp. 52–57.

[40] Frederick C. Barghoorn, *Politics in the USSR* (2d ed.; Boston: Little, Brown & Company, 1972), pp. 258–268, 279–282.

[41] Armstrong, *Ideology, Politics, and Government in the Soviet Union* (3d. ed.; New York: Frederick A. Praeger, Inc., 1974), pp. 143–145.

**FIGURE 14**
**Development of
command in Chinese
Communist industrial
management.** Source:
Franz Schurmann,
*Ideology and Organization
in Communist China* (2d
ed.; Berkeley and Los
Angeles, Calif.: University
of California Press), p. 308.
Originally published by
the University of Cali-
fornia Press, reprinted
by permission of The
Regents of the Univer-
sity of California.

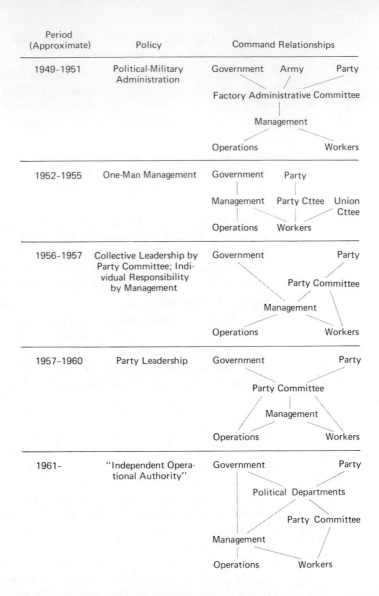

world's oldest traditions of professional bureaucracy and a distinct administrative
class with great prestige. To Mao Tse-tung and his followers these administrators
epitomized all that was wrong with the old regime, and as a result "few regimes in
the world have shown as much hostility to bureaucratic behavior as that of Communist China."[42] As Figure 14 shows, at the beginning the Peking regime followed the
Russian model of parallel party and management structures, with the party keeping
a close eye on the bureaucrats. In the early 1950s it turned to "one-man management"
of local enterprises. From then on and especially during the Great Leap Forward in

[42] Franz Schurmann, *Ideology and Organization in Communist China* (2d ed.; Berkeley, Calif.: University of California Press, 1968), p. 233.

the late 1950s party leaders sought to eliminate the evils of bureaucracy by weakening or eliminating all centralized bureaucratic structures and encouraging local enterprises and party cadres to carry out central directives without bureaucratic intermediaries. Whatever future changes may occur, it seems clear that any Chinese communist solution to the universal problem of administocracy will minimize the role of nonparty central administrative supervisors and local bureaucrats.[43]

## Control by Courts

In addition to legislative and executive methods of ensuring that administrative agencies adopt and enforce policies in accordance with popular desires, all democratic nations also provide various judicial restraints to prevent administrative agencies from encroaching upon the rights of individuals, as set forth in statutes, constitutions, and common law (see Chap. 18). If private citizens think that an administrative agency has used its power maliciously to harm them or their property, has stepped outside its jurisdiction in giving them an order, has exceeded its regulatory powers, or has unfairly denied them a license, they can go to some kind of court and seek redress. The remedy may take the form of damages, a writ of mandamus (that is, an order by a court to a public official ordering him to do his duty as the law requires), a writ of injunction (that is, a court order prohibiting an administrative official from performing a specific action), and so on.

Several democratic countries, including the United States and Great Britain, assign all such judicial review of and remedies for illegal administrative action to their ordinary courts, whereas others, like France, Italy, and Sweden, have established special sets of administrative courts to adjudicate such disputes. We shall examine both kinds of courts in greater detail in Chapter 18. The main purpose of judicial control of administration in most nations, whether exercised by regular or special courts, is not to prevent administocracy as the term is used here, however, but rather to protect the personal and property rights of individuals against administrative encroachment.

## Control by Ombudsman

For many private citizens suing an administrative agency in the courts is not attractive or even feasible: It is time-consuming, unpleasant, and costly—and there is no guarantee of winning. Judicial control, which leaves the initiative to the aggrieved, is thus more a last resort than a common device for keeping administrators in line.

Recognizing this difficulty as long ago as 1809, the government of Sweden established the special office of *ombudsman* (parliamentary commissioner) to act as the private citizens' watchdog over and advocate against administrative agencies. He is appointed by the Riksdag (parliament) to investigate and publicize any instance in which an administrator has used his powers wrongly or failed to act when he should. Any citizen may register a complaint with the *ombudsman*. He investigates each complaint and, on the basis of his findings, either publicly exonerates or publicly criticizes

---

[43] Schurmann, *Ideology and Organization in Communist China*, chap. 4.

the administrators involved. In most instances public criticism by the *ombudsman* is enough to make an erring administrator mend his ways in a hurry, but if he remains adamant the *ombudsman* is authorized to direct the public prosecutor to take the matter to court.

In this way most of the initiative and bother and all the cost of obtaining a remedy are born by the office of the *ombudsman* rather than by the private citizen, and many observers believe the institution to be one of the most effective devices in any modern democracy for keeping administrators acting as they should. It has therefore attracted increasing attention from political scientists and civic reformers around the world. Many smaller nations—Denmark, Norway, Finland, West Germany, New Zealand, and the Philippines among them—have adopted some version of the Swedish system, and a few larger ones, notably Great Britain, are considering it.[44]

## CONCLUSION

Their great numbers and power have elevated career civil servants to positions of enormous influence in all modern political systems, democratic and dictatorial alike, and their professionalization has given rise to problems of administocracy and bureaucracy. Some modern Cassandras, indeed, have cried that all is lost and that administocracy and "the new despotism" are already upon us.[45] The evidence presented in this chapter, however, strongly suggests that such lamentations are, to say the least, premature. That career administrators have great influence in the making of public policy does not mean that they have taken over the whole process and become absolute and unchecked despots. The democratic systems' various legislative, executive, and judicial controls over civil servants can fix very definite and firm limits upon what the latter can and cannot do. As long as those who exercise these controls continue to do so with the confidence that they are doing what their constituents want them to do, administrators will continue to be valuable servants, rather than the masters, of democratic regimes.

---

[44] The practices and problems of the *ombudsman* in various nations are analyzed in *University of Pennsylvania Law Review,* 109 (June 1961), 1057–1126.

[45] See Lord Hewart of Bury, *The New Despotism* (New York: Cosmopolitan Book Corp., 1929); James M. Beck, *Our Wonderland of Bureaucracy* (New York: Crowell-Collier and Macmillan, Inc., 1932); and Ludwig von Mises, *Bureaucracy* (New Haven, Conn.: Yale University Press, 1944).

# 18

# LAW AND THE JUDICIAL PROCESS

"The law," according to eighteenth-century playwright Charles Macklin, "is a sort of hocus-pocus science, that smiles in your face while it picks your pocket, and the glorious uncertainty of it is more use to the professors than the justice of it." But his contemporary Dr. Samuel Johnson declared, "The law is the last result of human wisdom acting upon human experience for the benefit of the public."

Some of us may sometimes be tempted to agree with Macklin—especially when we have just received a ticket for overparking or paid a lawyer's bill. But most of us believe, with Dr. Johnson, that law is one of the great achievements of human civilization and people's chances of living together happily and fruitfully in society depend largely upon their ability to live according to law. The famed hope of the framers of the Massachusetts Constitution that it might establish "a government of laws, and not of men" surely expresses a deep desire in most of us that our lives and fortunes be governed, not by the passing whims of a dictator, a ruling class, or even a popular majority, but by fundamental and changeless principles of right and reason. The actual laws that govern us at the moment may not measure up to this dream, to be sure, but in most of us the dream is strong.

Perhaps that is why the picture that many of us have of "the judge" is close to reverential, even though no actual judge may quite live up to it. He sits there on the bench, our ideal judge, listening courteously and impartially to the two litigants before him, seeing to it that each side receives its full rights under the law and deciding not to please this political party or that pressure group but to achieve what is *right* according to the law.

There is little doubt that law, and the judges and courts that interpret and apply it, occupy a place of high prestige in our attitudes toward government. To what extent do actual judges and courts live up to their ideal models? Perhaps we can discover some answers in this chapter, in which we investigate the structure and role of law and the courts as they currently operate in the democratic nations and contrast them with their counterparts in the Soviet Union.

## THE NATURE OF LAW

### THE MEANING OF "LAW"

Jurists—people who study the content and application of law—have long disagreed about the proper meaning of "law," and in their writings many different conceptions have been put forth.[1] Three of them are particularly relevant to our purposes.

### The Conception of Natural Law

Perhaps the basic issue on which jurists disagree is whether the essence of law—that is, the trait that distinguishes it from other rules affecting human conduct, like those described in Chapter 3—lies in its *content* or in the *procedures* by which it is made and enforced. Some argue that "the law" is a body of prescriptions for human behavior ordained by God or Nature, that the specific rules made and enforced by human agencies should approximate these eternal principles of right and wrong, and that people have no moral obligation to obey rules that contravene these eternal principles —which some jurists have called "the Higher Law" and others "the Law of Nature." Jurists who take this position are often called the "natural law" school, and their basic views are by no means heard only in academic ivory towers. When, for example, conscientious objectors refuse to obey government commands to join armies and kill their nations' enemies, they claim to be acting not lawlessly but rather in obedience to a higher law, "Thou shalt not kill." When civil-rights demonstrators lie in the streets in violation of ordinances prohibiting obstruction of traffic, they do so in the conviction that higher law prescribes that "all people of all races shall be treated equally." For that matter, when the leaders of the Committee to Reelect the President in 1972 decided to violate various campaign finance and corrupt practices laws, they were obeying (as they later explained in the Watergate hearings) the "higher necessity" of reelecting Richard Nixon—an end which, in their view, justified any means.

### The Positive Conception

Other jurists, sometimes called the "positive law" or "analytical" school, argue that, as people have no certain way of identifying or defining universal principles of right and wrong, the only meaningful definition of "law" is in terms of the particular human agencies that make and enforce its rules. The nineteenth-century English jurist John Austin, for example, defined law as the command of a political superior

---

[1] Useful summaries of the different definitions are presented in George Whitecross Paton, *A Textbook of Jurisprudence* (2d ed.; New York: Oxford University Press, 1948), chap. 3.

to inferiors backed by sanctions against those who disobey the commands. The twentieth-century American Supreme Court Justice Oliver Wendell Holmes, Jr., wrote that "the prophecies of what the courts will do in fact, and nothing more pretentious, are what I mean by law."[2]

### The Descriptive Conception

The first two schools of jurisprudence, then, have fundamentally different purposes in attempting to define "law." Adherents of natural law seek mainly to distinguish it from *wrong* principles of human conduct, whereas analytical jurists seek mainly to distinguish law from rules that emanate from nongovernmental sources. Several languages, significantly enough, have different words to denote these two conceptions of law: In Latin, for example, *ius* means eternal principles of right conduct, and *lex* means rules enforced by the state; in French their counterparts are *droit* and *loi,* in German *Recht* and *Gesetz,* in Italian *diritto* and *legge;* and in Spanish *derecho* and *ley.*[3]

In English, however, we have only the single word "law." And, as our purpose in this chapter is to examine the role of courts and judges in the governing process and to explain what most people in most nations ordinarily mean when they make statements like "that's against the law" and "that law should be changed," we shall use what may be called a "descriptive" definition.

Law in any nation is *the body of rules emanating from government agencies and applied by the courts.* We distinguish it from such other kinds of rules as moral precepts and customs (see Chap. 3). The reader should note that, according to this definition, no particular government agency is regarded as having a monopoly on lawmaking; the rules promulgated by any such agency achieve the full status of law only if the courts apply them. In Chapters 15–17 we have considered the lawmaking activities of legislators, executives, and administrators; in this chapter we shall examine both the lawmaking activities of judges and the procedures by which they apply laws made by themselves and other government agencies.

## SOME CLASSIFICATIONS

Because in any modern nation several different kinds of government agencies make law as defined here and because the courts of any nation apply several different kinds of legal rules, we shall conclude our brief survey of the nature of law by noting some of the most common classifications of legal rules.

### By Source

One familiar basis for classifying laws is the agency that promulgates them. There are six main types.

---

[2] Oliver Wendell Holmes, Jr., *Collected Legal Papers* (New York: Harcourt Brace Jovanovich, Inc., 1921), p. 173.

[3] See Roscoe Pound, *Outlines of Lectures on Jurisprudence* (Cambridge, Mass.: Harvard University Press, 1943), p. 60.

**Constitutional Law** Every nation, as we noted in Chapter 11, has a constitution—a body of fundamental rules, written and unwritten, according to which its government operates. We also noted that, though some of the rules consist of unwritten customs, most are, strictly speaking, "constitutional law" in the form of a basic written Constitution, a number of organic laws, and certain rules of interpretation laid down by the courts. Constitutional law is, furthermore, everywhere regarded as the most basic type of law, in the sense that any other type that contravenes a constitutional rule is superseded and canceled by that constitutional rule. Maintaining constitutional supremacy is the special prerogative of the courts in some nations; in others the job is done by the legislatures. The various processes by which constitutional law is made and changed and its supremacy maintained are described in Chapter 11.

**Statutory Law** Statutory law consists of all the rules commanding or prohibiting some form of human behavior *enacted by the legislature.* In most nations they are collected and published in "codes" or books of "statutes in force."

**Administrative Law** In Chapter 17 we noted that in all modern democratic systems many executive and administrative agencies are authorized by the Constitutions or the legislatures to make rules and regulations within certain specified limits. The total body of such rules is generally called "administrative law," and in most democratic nations it has grown to considerable size.

**Common Law** In twelfth-century England royal judges began to travel around the country to settle various local disputes according to their understanding of the prevailing "customs of the realm." During the ensuing centuries these judges and their successors generally followed the principle of stare decisis (let the decision stand), according to which judges are obligated to "follow precedent": when a judge considers a case to which a rule made in an earlier case applies, he must apply the old rule rather than formulating a new one. As a consequence of their general adherence to stare decisis these English judges over the centuries built up an elaborate body of legal rules that came to be known as "the common law," to distinguish it from rules laid down in acts of Parliament.[4] The common law was, of course, also applied by courts in the English colonies around the world; when some of these colonies became independent and sovereign nations—like the United States, Canada, New Zealand, and Australia—their courts continued to apply English common law, although in all these nations English principles have been revised to some degree. If any rule of common law contravenes a constitutional or statutory rule, the latter takes precedence. But in the nations mentioned common law continues to govern many matters on which the Constitutions and statutes are silent.

**Equity Law** During the long evolution of common law in medieval England an increasing number of British subjects demanded relief from injustices that they claimed resulted from it. The kings turned over all such complaints to their chief legal

[4] The story is told in detail in T.F.T. Plucknett, *A Concise History of the Common Law* (2d ed.; Rochester, N.Y.: The Lawyers Co-operative Publishing Co., 1936).

officers, the chancellors, who in turn appointed assistants known as "masters in chancery" to deal with them. Eventually these last-named officials came to constitute a regular court, the Court of Chancery. The rules developed by this court outside the common law have come to be known as "equity law," and they too were exported to the English colonies and revised after those colonies had won independence. Equity law, like common law, is superseded by constitutional and statutory law when there is conflict but still governs such matters as the administration of trusts, mortgages, and other fiduciary obligations on which the statutes are silent.

**Roman Law and Civil Law**   Every modern nation has constitutional law, statutory law, and administrative law, but common law and equity law operate mainly in the English-speaking nations. The nations of Western Europe and Latin America (as well as the state of Louisiana and the province of Quebec) supplement their constitutional, statutory, and administrative law with a system of jurisprudence commonly called "the civil law." It consists of a body of rules and procedures that, though differing somewhat from nation to nation, is based upon the *ius civile* of ancient Rome, which was rediscovered and adopted by European judges in the early Middle Ages. Its best-known and most influential codification is that made on the order of Napoleon I in 1804; it came to be known as the Code Napoléon or *Code civil*. Modern civil law differs from common law and equity not only in many specific rules and procedures but also in its general tone and manner of growth: Common and equity law is largely made by judges and remains pragmatic in tone, whereas civil law consists to a considerable degree of rules expounded by writers of books on jurisprudence and has a far more rationalistic and deductive tone than does common law.[5]

Various other kinds of law (for example, admiralty and maritime law and international law) are applied by the courts of modern nations, but the types that we have considered are the principal elements of modern democratic legal systems.

### By Subject Matter

One other classification of law is significant for our purposes—that which distinguishes between criminal and civil law.

**Criminal Law**   Criminal law, of course, deals with "crimes"; a "crime" is generally considered to be a wrong committed against the whole community—"any act done in violation of those duties which an individual owes to the community, and for the breach of which the law has provided that the offender shall make satisfaction to the public."[6] Crimes are usually classified as either "felonies" (more serious) or "misdemeanors" (less serious) and are punishable by death, imprisonment, fine, removal from office, or disqualification from holding office.

**Civil Law**   Civil law deals with wrongs committed against private individuals but

---

[5] A useful comparative study is W. W. Buckland and A. D. McNair, *Roman Law and Common Law* (New York: Oxford University Press, 1936).

[6] *Black's Law Dictionary* (4th ed.; St. Paul, Minn.: West Publishing Company, 1951), p. 445.

not considered damaging to the whole community, and the community's only stake is ensuring that the issue is settled fairly. For example, if A spreads malicious stories about B in the hope of ruining B's reputation, he is considered to have slandered B but not to have harmed the whole community; B's remedy is to sue A for damages. If A shoots and kills B, he is considered to have threatened the basic safety and security of the entire community, and the government will prosecute him for murder; if he is found guilty, he will be imprisoned or executed.

How are the courts that apply these principal types of law in modern democratic polities structured?

## COURT STRUCTURES IN DEMOCRATIC SYSTEMS

### THE SPECIALIZED JUDICIAL FUNCTION

#### Law Enforcement

Every law is a general rule made by a governmental agency either commanding or prohibiting a certain kind of human behavior. Every government from time immemorial has established certain official agencies to enforce the law—to detect instances in which "persons" (including both flesh-and-blood individuals and corporations, which are considered "legal persons") have violated these general rules and to punish the violators. Every agency performing this function must conduct a number of basic operations, which may be explained by a hypothetical example.

A nation has a law against murder, defined as one person's taking of another's life by deliberate intent and "with malice aforethought." One of its citizens, A, is found dead, and some of the people in the neighborhood tell the government that they think B shot A. The first thing that the government must do is to *ascertain the facts:* Is A really dead? Did he die from a gunshot wound? Did B fire the shot that killed A? Did B fire the shot with deliberate intent and malice aforethought? And so on. Second, the government must *interpret and apply the law:* It must decide whether or not what B did is an instance of the behavior prohibited by the law against murder. Third, if B is found to have committed murder, the government must *penalize the violator:* It must decide how grave a penalty is warranted by the facts and the law, pass sentence on B accordingly, and make sure that the sentence is carried out.

However they may be performed, these three basic operations constitute law enforcement.

#### Specialized Courts

During most of human history, as we noted in Chapter 15, societies did not make any theoretical distinction between lawmaking and law enforcement, nor did they establish governmental agencies clearly specializing in one kind of operation over the other. Kings, as well as their ministers and courts (a court was simply a king's whole retinue) made *and* enforced laws. In the late Middle Ages, however, the idea that justice is best served by having one kind of agency—which came to be called "the executive"—specialize in watching over the behavior of the king's subjects and prosecuting those it believes have violated the law and another kind of agency specialize in trying the people thus accused began to take hold. The latter agencies retained the ancient title of "courts," and by the eighteenth century in most nations they were clearly distinguished in both theory and organization from executive agencies and had largely taken over the functions of determining facts and interpreting and applying law described above.

### Anglo-American and French Prototypes

The legal-judicial structures in most modern democratic nations are patterned closely on the organization and procedures of one or the other of two great prototypes, the Anglo-American and the French. Although the two systems have many traits in common, they differ significantly in certain respects, some of which we shall consider in a moment. Before turning to specifics, however, we should note that the Anglo-American model predominates in Great Britain, the United States, and nations that have been British or American colonies (Canada, Australia, and the Philippines). The French model is followed by France, most other Western European democratic nations, and former colonies of France, Spain, and other Continental powers in Latin America, Africa, and Asia. Substantially more of the world's people thus live under Roman law administered through a French type of legal-judicial system than live under common and equity law administered by an Anglo-American type of legal-judicial system.

Later we shall consider some theories about the role that courts should perform in the total government process and shall observe some of the roles that they actually do perform in modern democratic systems. First, however, we shall review the principal types of courts, their formal interrelations, the selection and tenure of their judges, their procedures, and their formal relations with the other agencies of government.

## PRINCIPAL TYPES OF COURTS

### Regular and Administrative

We noted in Chapter 17 that in many democratic countries (for instance, the United States, Great Britain, the British dominions, the Scandinavian nations, and Switzerland) all legal controversies arising from the actions of administrative agencies are handled by the "regular" courts—that is, by the same courts that try other civil and criminal cases. A number of Continental European democratic countries (for example, Italy, West Germany, and Belgium), however, have followed the lead of France in establishing special administrative courts to provide their citizens with recourse against arbitrary and illegal administrative decisions. The first element of the French system, for example, consists of twenty-four regional *tribunaux administratifs* (administrative courts), which serve as trial courts for charges and claims against local administrative agencies. The second element is the Conseil d'État (council of state), which is composed of top career civil servants appointed by various ministers. The council advises the cabinet and ministry on matters of administrative policy, and its

Section du Contentieux (litigation section) of about eighty members acts as a court of appeal for decisions made by the lower administrative courts.[7]

## Civil and Criminal

In most democratic nations the same courts handle both civil and criminal cases, but some nations have established distinct sets of courts for each type of jurisdiction. In Great Britain, for example, civil cases are handled by a hierarchy of more than 400 county courts with the Supreme Court of Judicature at the top. The latter is divided into the High Court of Justice (which tries serious civil cases from any of its three divisions: Queen's Bench; Chancery; and Divorce, Probate, and Admiralty) and the Court of Appeal (which hears appeals from both the county courts and the High Court). Criminal cases in Great Britain are handled by a hierarchy consisting of the magistrates' courts, the quarter-sessions courts, the assize courts (each presided over by a single judge from the Queen's Bench), and a court of criminal appeal. The House of Lords (but, as we saw in Chapter 15, actually only about ten to fifteen of its members, including the Lord Chancellor, the nine Lords of Appeal in Ordinary, and other members who have held high judicial office) serves as the final court of appeal in *both* civil and criminal cases.[8] In West Germany each regular court at each level—local, district, appeal, and supreme—maintains one or more civil sections and one or more criminal sections. The two types of sections use somewhat different procedures, although they are not as clearly separated from each other as in Great Britain. But in most modern democratic systems both civil and criminal cases are handled by the same court hierarchies.

## National and Local

In the federal democracies, as we shall see in Chapter 19, there are two sets of sovereign governments, national and local, each with its own legislative, executive, and administrative agencies. It would seem that there should also be two complete parallel sets of courts, one national and one local, but only in the United States do they actually exist. Here there is a full set of national courts, consisting mainly of the Federal district courts, Federal courts of appeal, and the United States Supreme Court. In each of the states there are trial courts and a supreme court; many also have preliminary courts and intermediate courts of appeal. The Australian Constitution permits the establishment of a full set of national courts, but so far only a national High (supreme) Court and a few special courts have been set up, and most litigation is handled by the courts of the various states, which are authorized to supply national as well as state law. In Switzerland the only major national court is the federal

---

[7] A useful survey of the court systems of Great Britain, France, and the United States is Henry J. Abraham, *The Judicial Process* (3d ed.; New York: Oxford University Press, 1973). A more detailed study of the French system is Arthur T. von Mehren, *The Civil Law System* (Boston: Little, Brown & Company, 1957).

[8] The rather complicated structure of the British court system is lucidly described in Richard N. Jackson, *The Machinery of Justice in England* (New York: St. Martin's Press, Inc., 1960).

tribunal, and, as in Australia, most litigation is handled by the cantonal courts. Canada has a more nearly complete set of national courts than has either Australia or Switzerland, but in Canada too most litigation, even on matters of dominion law, is conducted in the provincial courts.[9] It is important to note, however, that in each of the federal democracies appeals can be made from the local courts to the national court or courts on questions involving interpretation of the national Constitution or national laws; on all such questions the national supreme courts, rather than any local supreme courts, have the final word. We shall return to this matter in Chapter 19.

In the unitary systems all courts are national in the sense that their judges are appointed by national authorities, although many have courts with only local jurisdictions. In Great Britain, for example, even the local justices of the peace and magistrates of the county courts are appointed by the crown on the advice of the Lord Chancellor. In France all judges are appointed by the President of the Republic on the advice of the Minister of Justice. In Italy the members of the Supreme Court of Cassation and the intermediate appeals courts are appointed by central authorities, and the judges of the appeals courts in turn appoint the judges of the lower courts in their particular regions. National appointment and control of all judges are the rule in the other unitary systems, and they therefore have no locally controlled courts like the American state courts.

HIERARCHIES OF APPEAL

*Hierarchy and the Appellate Process*

Every modern court system features provisions for appealing the decisions of some courts to others—usually only on points of proper interpretation of the law but not on findings of fact. In every nation the courts are arranged in a hierarchy of appeal, structured in pyramidal fashion from bottom to top. Such a structure is an obvious necessity for any court system, for if it were possible for the loser in any case to appeal the decision to any court in a circular fashion, then the process of appeal could go on indefinitely, no final decision could ever be made, and the litigants would grow poorer and poorer while the lawyers became richer and richer.

As it is, however, every court system provides some process of appeal from "inferior" to "superior" courts up to but not beyond a supreme court; when that court has rendered a decision, the only further judicial appeal possible is a request to the supreme court to reverse its own decision.

*General Structure*

Although the details of court names and jurisdictions vary considerably from nation to nation, most democratic court structures have four main levels.

---

[9] K. C. Wheare, *Federal Government* (4th ed.; New York: Oxford University Press, 1964), pp. 65–68.

**Preliminary Courts**  In many systems the lowest courts on the judicial ladder are what may be called "preliminary courts"—including justices of the peace (in Great Britain, Switzerland, and France), *conciliatores* and *praetors* (Italy), *Amtsgerichte* (West Germany), and so on. These bodies usually have the power to try only petty civil cases and misdemeanors and must refer all major cases to the next level of courts.

**General Trial Courts**  Every system has as the first major rung of its judicial ladder a number of courts authorized to try most major civil and criminal cases. In the American national system they are called "Federal district courts"; in Great Britain "county courts" for civil cases and "assize courts" for criminal cases; in France *tribunaux de première instance*; in West Germany *Landsgerichte*; and so on.

**Intermediate Courts of Appeal**  Most systems provide a series of intermediate courts mainly to hear appeals from the trial courts and rarely or never acting as trial courts themselves. In the American system there are regional Federal courts of appeal and one for the District of Columbia; in Great Britain there is the national Court of Appeal for civil cases and the national Court of Criminal Appeal for criminal cases; in France there are twenty-seven regional courts of appeal; in West Germany there are several *Oberlandesgerichte*; and so on.

**Supreme Courts**  Every system has a national supreme court. In each nation this court acts as the final court of appeal, and in some it also acts as a trial court in a few special types of cases. These bodies include the Supreme Court of the United States, the British House of Lords, French and Italian courts of cassation, the German Bundesgerichtshof, the Swiss federal tribunal, and so on.

A few democratic systems have established special national tribunals (like Italy's Corte Constituzionale) in addition to their regular supreme courts to pass upon the constitutionality of legislative and executive acts in the process known as "judicial review" (see Chap. 11). Most of the systems using judicial review, however, vest final reviewing power in their regular supreme courts.

## SELECTION AND TENURE OF JUDGES

### Lawyers and Judges in the Two Systems

Every modern democratic nation has a distinct legal profession whose members are specially trained in its legal principles and practices by law schools or as apprentices to established lawyers. Most are required to pass special examinations to become full-fledged members of the legal profession authorized to represent clients in dealings with police, prosecutors, courts, and other agencies of the legal-judicial structure. In the United States all such professionals are called "lawyers," and no formal distinctions are made because of their specializations within the profession. England, on the other hand, divides its lawyers into two groups: solicitors, the "office lawyers," who conduct about 95 percent of the nation's legal business, and barristers, the "trial lawyers," who do all the actual pleading before the higher courts. The French have three classes of lawyers: *avouets,* who are comparable to English solicitors; *avocats,* who are analagous to barristers; and *notaires,* who specialize in drafting and registering legal documents.[10]

The main difference between the Anglo-American and French systems is that in the former the legal profession is regarded as the source not only for legal advisers and advocates but also for all but the most minor judicial posts. All judges of the higher courts are former lawyers, all have had the same kind of legal training as have practicing lawyers, and lawyers and judges alike are regarded as members of one legal profession pursuing different aspects of a legal career.[11]

In France, however, a sharp distinction is made between the legal and judicial professions. A young Frenchman interested in the law decides early whether he wants to be a lawyer or a judge. If he decides on a legal career, he takes the appropriate training, passes examinations, and becomes an *avouet, avocat,* or *notaire.* But, if he chooses a judicial career, after he finishes legal training he must go on to the Centre National d'Études Judiciaires for four years. The successful graduate becomes, in effect, a civil servant under the Ministry of Justice. He is assigned to a court of first *instance* and works his way up to the higher judicial posts very much as a junior civil servant rises in any other ministry.[12]

### Appointment and Removal

With a few exceptions, which we shall note in a moment, most modern democratic nations select all their judges, from the lowest justice of the peace to the presiding judge of the supreme court, by appointment. The appointing officials vary somewhat from nation to nation, but in many nations all judges are appointed by the chief executive or by the minister of justice or his equivalent; in a few nations judges of some lower courts are appointed by judges of higher courts. Generally speaking, all appointed judges hold office during "good behavior," which means that they can be removed only by a special act of the legislature, called, for example, an "address of Parliament" in Great Britain and "impeachment" in the United States. This removal power is rarely exercised, however, and most judges in most democratic nations hold their offices for life.

### Election and Recall

In Switzerland some cantons choose some or all of their judges by popular election for limited terms of office, and the twenty-six members of the federal tribunal, the Swiss national supreme court, are elected by the federal assembly for six-year terms. The major exception to the general rule that judges are appointed for life, however, is to be found in the American states.

---

[10] For the United States, see Herbert Jacob, *Justice in America* (Boston: Little, Brown & Company, 1965), chaps. 4–5. For England and France, see Abraham, *The Judicial Process,* pp. 87–94.

[11] It is not surprising that American lawyers, through their main trade association, the American Bar Association, try hard and usually successfully to influence the selection of judges; see Joel B. Grossman, *Lawyers and Judges* (New York: John Wiley & Sons, Inc., 1965).

[12] Abraham, *The Judicial Process,* pp. 49–50, 93–94.

As of 1973 sixteen states elected all their judges; in thirteen states most judges were elected and a few minor ones appointed; in nine states higher judges were appointed initially but later had to win reelection by popular vote; and in twelve states all judges were appointed for "good behavior."[13] The great majority of state judges in the United States are thus elected rather than appointed.

In eight states, furthermore, judges are subject to "the recall." Under this procedure, if a designated number of voters sign a petition asking for the recall of a certain judge, a special election is held to determine whether or not he will remain in office. If a majority of the voters vote to recall him, he immediately leaves office, and his post is filled either by appointment or by a special election.

In the American states there is thus far more direct popular control over the selection and tenure of judges than in any democratic nation except possibly Switzerland; for, we should remember, all Federal judges in the United States are appointed by the President with the approval of a majority of the Senate.

Does it make any difference? Many political scientists, jurists, and lawyers in the United States argue that the popular election of judges is a serious weakness in the judicial systems of the states that use it. For many years they have pressed for replacement of elective systems with some version of appointment and permanent tenure. They argue that a judge who must worry about reelection must remain more a politician than a judge and cannot develop the calm, detached judicial temperament that every good judge must have. They also argue that popular election ensures frequent turnover among judges and that few stay in office long enough to acquire the judicial experience necessary to be a good judge.[14]

How valid are these arguments? No one can say with certainty, for careful and systematic empirical studies of the relative effects of election and appointment of judges upon the judicial process are just beginning to be made. No such study has been made of the relative "caliber" of the judges, however defined and measured, in the two types of legal systems. For some time to come this question is likely to be debated on the basis of hunches and general impressions rather than on systematic empirical knowledge, and there is no indication that many states presently using the elective system are likely to drop it.

## COURT PROCEDURES[15]

### Adversary and Inquisitorial

Most court proceedings in the Anglo-American legal systems arise from an underlying conviction that justice is best gained through "adversary proceedings." The main elements of this fundamental and pervasive notion are as follows. The task of the courts of law is to settle legal disputes. A legal dispute results from a plaintiff's

---

[13] *The Book of the States,* 1972–1973 (Chicago: Council of State Governments, 1972), pp. 130–132, Table 5.

[14] See Laurance M. Hyde, "Judges: Their Selection and Tenure," *Journal of the American Judicature Society,* 30 (February 1947), 153–159.

[15] This discussion is based on Abraham, *The Judicial Process,* pp. 98–137.

accusation that a defendant has in some way damaged him illegally. In a criminal case the government, through its official prosecutor, accuses the defendant of breaking the law; in a civil case one private party accuses another of illegally harming his person or property. The trial itself is a contest between the two adversaries. Each presents its arguments, supports them with testimony from witnesses and other evidence, and tries to discredit the other party's claims by cross-examining its witnesses, challenging its evidence, and refuting its arguments. The court's function is to umpire the contest and to declare the winner. It makes sure that each side, in presenting its case and attacking that of its adversary, stays within the established rules of the game—rules of proper evidence, argument, demeanor, and so on. And the court renders the decision according to its perception of the true facts and relevant law that emerge in the contest between plaintiff and defendant.

The criminal-law version of this pattern is the Anglo-American accusatorial system for determining the guilt or innocence of suspects. The police investigate the facts and report to the prosecutor. The prosecutor goes before a grand jury of ordinary citizens to convince them that there is enough evidence to justify "indicting" (formally accusing) a designated person in order that a full trial may take place. The person thus indicted is the defendant, and the prosecutor is the plaintiff in the ensuing trial. The court (a judge either acting alone or with a trial jury) listens to the arguments and evidence presented by the two adversaries and decides whether or not the defendant is guilty as charged. If the verdict is "innocent," the defendant goes free; if it is "guilty," the court fixes the penalty, within limits laid down by the legislature. But the court itself has little or no power to produce evidence, cross-examine witnesses, or act as other than a neutral umpire of the contest between adversaries. Hence the label "adversary system of justice."

### Inquisitorial

Under the French system of criminal justice the courts are not mere arbiters of adversary proceedings between government and citizen, as in the Anglo-American systems. Rather they are part of the government's machinery for enforcing the law, and their procedures in criminal trials are characterized by the "inquisitorial" approach.

The French procedure begins when the police notify the public prosecutor *(procureur)* that they believe a designated person likely to have committed a particular crime. If the prosecutor agrees, he notifies an examining magistrate *(juge d'instruction),* who proceeds to conduct the important preliminary investigation *(enquête).* This *enquête* goes a great deal farther than does a hearing before a grand jury. The magistrate examines the accused and the relevant witnesses in private. He is empowered to open mail, tap telephones, commission reports by experts, and take other steps to learn the facts. When faced with conflicting testimony by two or more witnesses he can call them into his office and "grill" them until he is satisfied that perjury has been eliminated and discrepancies in testimony reduced to a minimum. When the *enquête* is completed, the *juge d'instruction* decides whether or not to send the case to trial. And, as he does so only if he is convinced that the accused is guilty, the subsequent trial is usually little more than public verification of the record accumulated in the *enquête.*

(The award-winning French film Z provides a dramatic description of an *enquête* in which the original prosecutors end up as the accused.)

The French system differs from the Anglo-American system, then, in three main respects. First, the decision whether or not to try a person accused of a crime is made by a professional judge representing the Ministry of Justice, not by a grand jury of ordinary citizens. Second, the body of evidence and argument on which the fate of the accused is determined is controlled by the judges (both in the *enquête* and the later trial, if any,) rather than by the adversaries; the judge can take the initiative to find out anything that he thinks he must know to make a just decision. And, third, the result is less affected than in Anglo-American systems by the ability or inability of the defendant to hire an especially skilled lawyer to represent him.

On the available evidence we cannot say that either the Anglo-American accusatorial or the French inquisitorial system is clearly the more effective in punishing the guilty and protecting the innocent. It is important to note that there are two quite different systems to achieve the goals of justice sought by all democratic nations.

## FORMAL RELATIONS WITH LEGISLATURES AND EXECUTIVES

Many people and nations that do not subscribe to the doctrine of separation of powers in its entirety (see Chap. 15) nevertheless strongly support the ideal of an independent judiciary. This ideal calls for organizing the judiciary in accordance with two main precepts. First, its advocates believe that justice will not be served if the prosecutor and the judge are one and the same person or agency. They argue that the court would lose all semblance of impartiality and become merely an arm of the prosecution, a "star chamber" travesty on justice (the Star Chamber was a secret body established by the Tudor monarchs in sixteenth-century England to administer summary "justice" to their political opponents). This result can be avoided only by making the courts independent of the executive. Second, these jurists argue, if the judicial process is to be well performed, it must operate in an atmosphere of calmness, deliberation, and, above all, freedom from pressures by parties and pressure groups with axes to grind. The courts should thus also be free of the legislature. Many political theorists believe that an independent judiciary in both senses is the sine qua non of any governmental system intended to preserve human rights and freedoms.

### Separation of Judges from Prosecutors

The first aspect of the ideal of an independent judiciary, the formal separation of judges from prosecutors, is most clearly and firmly established in the English-speaking nations. At both national and state levels in the United States, for example, the prosecuting function is vested in an executive agency headed by an attorney general who supervises the work of a number of local U.S. attorneys (for the national government) and states' attorneys or district attorneys (for the state governments). In Great Britain the prosecuting function is vested mainly in the Director of Public Prosecutions, who, under the direction of the Attorney General, prepares the cases against those accused of crime and engages lawyers to prosecute the cases in court.

The Western European nations, on the other hand, treat judges and prosecutors as different sections of the same public service. In France, for example, there is a single profession—*la magistrature*—which includes three kinds of offices: the "sitting judges," who preside over the courts much as do English and American judges; the *parquets,* forming a kind of public prosecutor's office attached to each court; and the administrative staff of the Ministry of Justice. All are regarded as civil servants under the same ministry, and any member of the *magistrature* may serve in any of these three offices. It is not uncommon, indeed, for a particular *magistrat* to move from work on the bench in one court to work in the *parquet* of another, from there to a position in the ministry, and perhaps back again to a high judicial post. In any regular French court both the judge and the prosecutor are officers of the Ministry of Justice, and the two functions are much less clearly separated than in the English-speaking democracies.

### Insulation of Judges from Political Pressure

The second aspect of the ideal of an independent judiciary, the insulation of judges from political pressures, is generally established by securing the tenure of judges from partisan interferences. The Constitution of the United States, for example, provides that all Federal judges shall hold office "during good behavior" (until removed by impeachment) and that their salaries shall not be reduced during their terms of office; it also vests the judicial power in them alone. Judges can be removed from office only through impeachment by a majority of the House of Representatives and conviction by a two-thirds majority of the Senate. In Great Britain and the dominions, similarly, judges may be removed from office only by "an address" requiring a majority vote in both houses) of the parliaments.

In France and most Western European nations before World War II, tenure, salary, and promotion of judges depended mainly upon the determinations of the various ministries of justice. Since 1945, however, some nations have followed the lead of France in establishing special bodies to ensure that the status of judges will be somewhat better protected than by the ordinary procedures of the ministries. France has established a special judicial supervisory body, the Conseil Supérieur de la Magistrature, chosen partly by the national assembly and partly by the judicial profession itself, to supervise the corps of judges separately from that of the *parquets* and other civil servants. The ministry, however, retains the power of countersignature of the council's recommendations for appointment and promotion of judges.

On the basis of these facts, then, it seems that the English-speaking nations come nearer to realizing the ideal of an independent judiciary than do most Western European nations, but the latter appear to be moving in that direction.

However formally independent they may be, the actual freedom of judges from "politics" is a different matter, as we shall see.

## THE ROLE OF JUDGES IN GOVERNING

The 1960s and 1970s have produced a series of attacks on the American judiciary unlike any in this country since President Franklin D. Roosevelt proposed to "pack" the Supreme Court in 1937. These attacks, moreover, have come from both right and left. Right-wing critics have been outraged by the Supreme Court's decisions in the school-segregation cases in the 1950s, the cases on school prayers, legislative apportionment, and rights of defendants in the 1960s, and the cases on capital punishment, abortion, and bussing of school children in the 1970s. These critics charge that the Court is a bunch of politicians rather than a body of learned jurists, that it has been "brainwashed" with left-wing ideas, and, worst of all, that it has "legislated"—that is, written its own ideas of policy into the Constitution rather than interpreting that document "as it really is." Some right-wing critics propose impeaching the incumbent judges, others want Congress to withdraw much of the Court's appellate jurisdiction, others advocate enlarging the Court and appointing enough new judges to outvote the "radicals," and still others have proposed establishing a "court of the Union," consisting of the chief justices of all the state supreme courts, with power to overrule decisions by the national Supreme Court.

In the late 1960s and early 1970s left-wing critics have increasingly attacked the courts for the trials of black militants and anti-Vietnam-war protesters for illegal possession of weapons, draft evasion, and incitement to riot. The courts, these critics say, are not impartial arbiters of legal conflict between the government and the protesters; they are hired hands of the "establishment," working hand in glove with the police to preserve a corrupt system by stamping out all protest and dissent. Judges are really no different from policemen: They are all "pigs." Thus no less august a person than the president of Yale University, himself a lawyer, said in 1970 that no black militant like Bobby Seale could get a fair trial in any American court; and the black communist leader Angela Davis, after her acquittal on charges of aiding a conspiracy to murder a California judge, declared that the only fair trial would have been no trial at all.

The courts, of course, do not lack defenders. They reply to right-wing critics that any attack upon the integrity and independence of the judiciary will violate cherished American traditions and make us "a government of men, not of laws." And they reply to left-wing critics that the courts are not mere tools of a repressive system (after all, both Bobby Seale and Angela Davis were acquitted) but are the main defenders of the protesters' right to protest by peaceful means.

For our purposes the most interesting aspect of these debates is that in so many of them all sides adhere to a "mechanical" conception of the judicial process, which may be summarized as follows:

## THE MECHANICAL CONCEPTION[16]

### Judges as Technicians

According to the traditional conception of the proper distribution of governmental powers, as we noted earlier in this chapter, the function of the courts is to interpret and apply, in particular instances, the general rules formulated by lawmaking bodies. Judges do not *make* law; they *discover* it.

This view of the judicial function arises mainly from the views expressed in

---

[16] This point of view is well summarized and analyzed by Fred V. Cahill, Jr., *Judicial Legislation* (New York: The Ronald Press Company, 1952), chap. 1.

perhaps the most widely read and influential of all books among lawyers in the English-speaking nations for two centuries: the eighteenth-century English jurist Sir William Blackstone's *Commentaries on the Laws of England*. To Blackstone (and, apparently, to many of his readers) judges are "the living oracles . . . who are bound by an oath according to the law of the land"; even when they reverse earlier rulings on points of law, he wrote, "it is declared not that such a sentence was *bad law,* but that it was not *law*."[17]

This Blackstonian picture of judges as skilled technicians "declaring" rather than making law is well summed up in the following statement by the nineteenth-century American jurist James C. Carter:

> That judges *declare,* and do not *make,* the law is not a fiction or a pretense, but a profound truth. If courts really made the law, they would have and feel the freedom of legislators. They could and would make it in accordance with their own views of justice and expediency. . . . I need not say that the case is precisely contrary . . . they must decide it consistently with established rules. . . . Any judge who assumed to possess that measure of *arbitrary* power which a legislator really enjoys would clearly subject himself to impeachment.[18]

### The Independent, Nonpolitical Judiciary[19]

According to the traditional conception, then, judges "declare" law that others have made; they do not make it themselves. Finding out what the law *is* is thus a task for legal technicians, not politicians. It demands a high order of legal skill and training and a "judicial temperament"; therefore adherents of this conception insist that the courts should be organized in such a way as to ensure that these difficult technical tasks are performed most effectively and that the judiciary can consider each case strictly on its legal merits without being influenced by political considerations. For one thing, the judiciary should be made quite independent of both legislature and executive, which are necessarily political agencies. For another, it should be insulated from the selfish and noisy importunings of political parties and pressure groups. What is more, judges should be selected for their legal skill and judicial temperament rather than for their political preferences. Finally, judges should refrain from public statements of policy preference and should be careful to use only the technical language of the law in writing their decisions.

Judges, in short, should remain completely aloof from politics, and politics must not be permitted to begrime their deliberations. The strength of this general idea is indicated by the fact that until 1941 in the United States state and national judges were allowed to punish for "contempt of court" any person who sought to influence a judge while a case was in process—and even the Supreme Court decision that struck

---

[17] William Blackstone, *Commentaries on the Laws of England,* Vol. 1, ed. by Thomas M. Cooley (Chicago: Callaghan and Cockcroft, 1871), p. 69, italics added.

[18] James C. Carter, "The Province of the Written and Unwritten Law" (1890), quoted in Cahill, *Judicial Legislation,* p. 17, n. 26, italics added.

[19] This aspect of the traditional conception is perceptively described in Jack W. Peltason, *Federal Courts in the Political Process* (New York: Random House, Inc., 1955), chap. 3.

down this procedure was made by a bare majority.[20] And in Great Britain a newspaper can be fined heavily for even discussing a case in any but the vaguest terms while it is sub judice (under judicial consideration).

### Description or Ideal?

Many people who uphold this mechanical conception of the judicial process believe that many judges *do* behave in this fashion, although they usually disagree on *which* judges do. In 1937, for example, conservatives generally believed that the United States Supreme Court was acting quite properly in throwing out New Deal legislation, whereas the liberals accused the judges of writing their own social and economic views into the Constitution. Since 1954 the tables have been turned. Now liberals praise the Court for protecting our constitutional liberties, conservatives attack it for trying to foist judges' "left-wing political philosophy" on the nation, and radicals scorn it as a "front for the establishment."

The point is that in 1937, as today, a great many of *both* the Court's critics and defenders adhered to the traditional mechanical conception in the sense that they regarded it as the correct standard to apply to actual judges—not only morally right but also an attainable ideal if we can only get and keep the right kind of judges on the bench. In this sense, then, the traditional conception has had a powerful influence upon people's thinking about the role of judges in the governmental process.

## JUDICIAL LEGISLATION

### An Avoidable Deviation?

The present controversy over whether the Supreme Court is "legislating" its social and economic views or merely "declaring" the Constitution is not unique to our time. Such controversies have flared up over and over again ever since the birth of the Republic. The Jeffersonians, for example, bitterly accused John Marshall's Supreme Court and the rest of the Federalist-packed judiciary of trying to write Federalist party policies into the Constitution. Andrew Jackson and his Chief Justice, Roger B. Taney, were attacked by the Whigs on similar grounds, and the Taney Court's decision in the Dred Scott case in 1857 was condemned perhaps more violently than any other in history. The conservative judges of the late nineteenth and early twentieth centuries were often charged with trying to write their laissez-faire preferences into the Constitution; we have already noted the controversies over the Court in 1937 and since 1954.

Complaints about "judicial legislation" are thus endemic in the United States, and the scattered evidence available suggests that similar, though perhaps less noisy, complaints are perennial in every nation with a well-established tradition of an independent judiciary. When we examine the political views of those who attack and those who defend the courts on this score, we find, significantly, that with very few exceptions people who approve the political effects of a particular line of decisions

[20] Bridges v. California, 314 U.S. 252 (1941).

defend the courts for "enforcing the Constitution," whereas those who dislike those effects claim that the courts are improperly engaging in "judicial legislation." This curious paradox has inclined one observer of the American judicial process to conclude that "viewed *sub specie aeternitatis*, the basic principle of American constitutional interpretation, and of American politics, is 'whose ox is gored?' "[21]

The point is, however, that most of those who have charged the Court with engaging in judicial legislation have regarded such involvement as an *avoidable* deviation from the Court's true function of declaring the law and have believed that the right kind of judges—that is, jurists who are skilled technicians and who accept and will adhere to the proper mechanical function of declaring the law—can restore to the Court its proper role in the governmental process.

### Inherent in the Judicial Process?

By no means all observers of the judicial process regard judicial legislation as avoidable, however. A growing number of jurists, judges, and political scientists argue that it is an inherent and inescapable consequence of the very nature of the judicial process itself. Many start from a premise stated by the eighteenth-century jurist and Anglican bishop Benjamin Hoadly: "Whoever hath an *absolute authority to interpret* any written or spoken laws, it is *he* who is truly the *Law-Giver* to all interests and purposes, and not the person who first spoke or wrote them. . . ."[22] They reason that all Constitutions, statutes, executive and administrative ordinances, and other laws are necessarily to some degree general and must therefore be somewhat vague. They have to be interpreted in specific cases, but usually there is no one interpretation that can be agreed upon by all men of good will and high technical legal training and skill. Lawyers and judges disagree among themselves about what the law means in any particular situation. Previous court decisions rarely settle the question, for at least some precedent can be found for every possible interpretation—indeed, it is the duty of the lawyers for both sides to bring before the judge lists of such precedents, each list calling for an opposite interpretation from that of the other. Every judge is thus continually faced with different—but, judged by any human standard, equally reasonable—interpretations.

Each interpretation necessarily favors the interests of some groups and damages those of other groups. The judge cannot help choosing one of the several alternatives and therefore cannot avoid promoting the interests of some and hurting those of others. When we look behind the legal jargon, we cannot avoid recognizing that the process by which a judge chooses one interpretation over the others and makes his decision is *political* in nature, for whatever decision he makes necessarily satisfies some values and frustrates others.

This observation is true, these writers argue, not only of judges and courts that have the power of judicial review (see Chap. 11) but also of *every* court, because every court has the power to "interpret" if not to "override" a law. And it will continue

---

[21] John P. Roche, "Plessy v. Ferguson: Requiescat in Pace?" *University of Pennsylvania Law Review,* 103 (October 1954), p. 53.

[22] Quoted in Cahill, *Judicial Legislation,* p. 99.

Judges make policy too; the Supreme Court that outlawed capital punishment and antiabortion laws: (left to right, seated) Potter Stewart, William O. Douglas, Warren E. Burger; William J. Brennan, Jr., Byron R. White; (standing) Lewis F. Powell, Jr., Thurgood Marshall, Harry A. Blackmun, William H. Rehnquist. Source: UPI Photograph.

to be true until people perfect a machine like a cash register on which they can punch keys labeled "the facts," pull down a lever called "the law," and read "the decision" that pops out.

To illustrate this characterization of the policy-making functions of the judiciary, let us see what role the United States Supreme Court has played in the conflict over racial segregation.

### Equal Protection of the Laws and Racial Segregation

The Fourteenth Amendment to the Constitution of the United States declares that "no State shall . . . deny to any person within its jurisdiction the equal protection of the laws." Beginning late in the nineteenth century the southern and border states enacted a series of Jim Crow laws prohibiting Negroes from attending the same schools, riding in the same train cars, using the same public swimming pools and golf courses, and eating in the same restaurants as whites. A number of people, whom we may call the "antisegregation interest," thought that these laws violated the constitutional clause just quoted; on the other hand, most southern whites, whom we may call the "segregation interest," had no doubt that such laws were perfectly consonant with this clause. Certainly the wording of the clause is vague enough so that reasonable people can easily disagree about whether it prohibits or permits segregation laws.

In *Plessy v. Ferguson* (1896), the Supreme Court had to decide whether or not a state law requiring racial segregation on trains was constitutional; it found, under the "equal protection" clause, that segregation *in itself* was not unconstitutional as long as the accommodations provided for each race were substantially equal to those provided for the other. This ruling came to be known as the "separate-but-equal formula."

Governmental Authorities and Processes

From then until the late 1930s the Court, following the Plessy doctrine, upheld all state segregation laws and, indeed, was easily satisfied with what was defined as "equality" of accommodations. In the 1930s, however, the Court began to take a different line. It began to insist, for example, that states which would not admit blacks to their public universities must provide *really* equal facilities for them. In *Sweatt* v. *Painter* (1950) they insisted that Texas either admit a black applicant to the University of Texas law school or establish a separate law school for blacks that would be its equivalent in every respect—a multimillion dollar project. In effect, the Court was saying that *no* segregated black law school could be equal to the established university law school.

Finally, in the famous case of *Brown* v. *Board of Education* (1954) the Court overruled the Plessy decision and held that, no matter what relative accommodations are provided for the two races, segregation *in itself* is a denial of equal protection to blacks and that therefore all state laws requiring racial segregation in public schools are violations of the Fourteenth Amendment.

Many conservatives and most southern whites, as we have seen, have bitterly attacked the Court for this decision, and much of the present controversy about the role of the Court arises from it. The Court's critics charge it with making policy. So it did. But they also imply that such policy making is highly irregular and very wrong. What the critics forget, or at least do not wish to remember, is that the phrase "equal protection of the laws" is so vague that no single interpretation is clearly indicated to all persons of good will and legal expertise. The point is that the 1896 Court, which declared the separate-but-equal formula, was *also* making policy; in throwing out that formula the 1954 Court was not making policy de novo but was reversing a policy made earlier.

If present critics of the Court were given carte blanche to amend the Constitution and to alter the Court's personnel to their hearts' desire, they could very likely force it to make the kind of policy they prefer, but there is no conceivable way, short of total abolition, to prevent courts and judges from making *some* kind of policy.[23] Policy making is inherent in the nature of the judicial process itself.

## JUDGES IN THE POLITICAL PROCESS[24]

### The Approach of the Legal Realists

The arguments outlined in the preceding section are those of an increasing number of contemporary political scientists, although some still hold the traditional mechanical view of the judicial process as a desirable and attainable ideal, if not as an accurate description. In many law schools and among many contemporary jurists, however,

---

[23] For other illustrations of the inescapability of judicial legislation, see Victor G. Rosenblum, *Law as a Political Instrument* (New York: Random House, Inc., 1955); and Glendon Schubert, *Judicial Policy-Making* (Glenview, Ill.: Scott, Foresman and Company, 1965).

[24] For a useful general survey, see Sheldon Goldman and Thomas P. Jahnige, *The Federal Courts as a Political System* (New York: Harper & Row, Publishers, 1971)

these arguments are regarded as false and heretical, for the legal profession has ever been the great stronghold of the mechanical conception.

Yet lawyers, judges, and jurists have produced their own heretics. Perhaps the best known include a group of writers on legal theory, mainly Americans like Jerome Frank, Thurman Arnold, Fred Rodell, and Edward S. Robinson, who have come to be known as the "legal realists."[25] Taking their lead from the legal philosophies of men like Oliver Wendell Holmes, Jr., and John Dewey, these writers have discarded the mechanical conception as both an inaccurate description and an impossible ideal. They recognize that judges must make policy, and some of them have sought to analyze and predict the decisions of particular judges on the basis of their social backgrounds, social and economic values, political preferences, and internal thought processes. Legal realists have unquestionably had a considerable impact upon contemporary American jurisprudence and some upon jurisprudence in other nations.

### The Political-Process Approach

In recent years a number of political scientists, whose approach was pioneered by Jack W. Peltason in his monograph *Federal Courts in the Political Process* (1955), have gone well beyond the legal realists and have begun to explore the judicial process as simply one aspect of the total political-governmental process and to investigate it by means of the same techniques that political scientists use to examine the legislative, executive, and administrative processes. This approach to the judicial process has produced a growing number of systematic empirical explanations of how that process works. Peltason suggested a number of hypotheses that merit at least a brief review here.[26]

Peltason declared that the courts are as involved in political conflict (as the term is used in this book) as is any other government agency, for every case that comes before a court involves a conflict of interest between particular litigants, and many cases involve the interests of groups far broader than just the litigants themselves. In deciding each case—for example, ordering this man to go to jail for rioting or that corporation to end its control over other firms or that school board to admit blacks on an unsegregated basis—the courts lay down "authoritative value-allocations" in precisely the same sense that other government agencies do (see Chap. 3). Value allocations by the courts differ from those by legislatures, executives, and administrators only in form, not in substance.

Peltason further suggested that, for all the lip service paid to judicial independence, the interests most powerfully affected by court decisions have never refrained from trying to influence their outcome. Perhaps the main difference between political conflict centered upon the courts and that centered upon the other governmental agencies is that the former must be conducted within an atmosphere created by the general acceptance and respectability of the mechanical conception of the judicial process. If a pressure group announces quite frankly, "We intend to put pressure on Congress, the President, and the administrative agencies to get our poli-

---

[25] The main ideas of the legal realists are summarized in Cahill, *Judicial Legislation,* chaps. 5–7.

[26] See Peltason, *Federal Courts in the Political Process,* chaps. 4–6. For similar hypotheses and some verification, see Schubert (ed.), *Judicial Decision-Making* (New York: The Free Press, 1963); and Schubert, *Constitutional Politics* (New York: Holt, Rinehart and Winston, Inc., 1960).

cies adopted," few will think the worse of it. But let it announce with equal frankness, "We intend to put pressure on the judges so that their decisions will be made in our favor," and many potential allies will become enemies because of their disapproval of such "crass efforts to tamper with judicial independence and the Law." President Nixon and his aide John Ehrlichman flouted this norm in 1972 when, while the trial of Daniel Ellsberg for violations of security laws was going on, they approached the presiding judge, Matthew Byrne, to inquire about his interest in becoming the director of the FBI. Nixon and Ehrlichman later denied that they had done anything wrong, but many commentators condemned the approach as a highly improper effort to influence the rulings of a trial judge. Whereas a great many political interest groups, as we shall see, *do* try to influence judicial decisions, they rarely *talk* as if that is what they are doing. Rather, they talk in terms of "defending the integrity of the judiciary," "defending the Law against the depredations of political judges," "making sure that men with sound views of the Constitution get on the bench," and the like.

This kind of talk does not alter the *fact* of political conflict in the judicial process, but it does mean that such conflict is conducted in a rather special kind of atmosphere.

## POLITICAL CONFLICT IN THE JUDICIAL PROCESS

Peltason pointed out three main areas of political conflict in the judicial process.

### Selection of Judges

When selecting Federal judges in the United States, most Presidents and senators have *talked* as if they have been selecting only technicians of jurisprudence but have *acted* as if they have been selecting policy makers whose views they wished to accord with their own. "Since 1885 over 90 percent of all Federal judges have been filled by members—in most cases active members—of the same party as the President who chose them and most have been supporters of the senator who nominated them."[27] The American Bar Association has asked for a greater voice in the selection of judges (after all, it argues, who can determine the technical competence of a judge better than lawyers?), but the many other interests involved have been reluctant to turn over so much power to what is, in many instances, a rival interest.[28] On the other side of the fence, many judges have clung to their posts long after age and failing health have indicated the advisability of their retirement. Why? Because they have so strongly opposed the political views of the incumbent President and Senate majority that they have not wished the latter to name their successors. As Chief Justice William Howard Taft said (in 1929!), "As long as things continue as they are, and I am able to answer in my place, I must stay on the Court in order to prevent the Bolsheviki from getting control. . . ."[29]

---

[27] Peltason, *Federal Courts in the Political Process*, p. 31. See also David J. Danelski, *A Supreme Court Justice Is Appointed* (New York: Random House, Inc., 1964).

[28] See Grossman, *Lawyers and Judges.*

[29] Quoted in C. Herman Pritchett, *The Roosevelt Court* (New York: Crowell-Collier and Macmillan, Inc., 1948), p. 18.

## Decision Making

Interest groups try to influence the selection of judicial personnel whenever they can, but the relative stability of the bench means that for the most part they have to work with and through the judges who are in office. An interest group may only at great peril try to influence a judge in the same manner in which it might try to influence a congressman or an administrator. Most groups therefore exert direct influence only through such accepted channels as litigation, employing expensive and able lawyers, presenting the best possible "briefs," and so on. It is interesting to note that in recent decades it has become increasingly common for interest groups not directly party to a particular case that affects their interests to submit amicus curiae (friend of the court) briefs and to offer other legal help to litigants who represent legal principles that they want established or upheld. Many such briefs were submitted on both sides, for example, in the school-segregation cases of 1954. The ablest lawyers and the best-drawn briefs by no means always ensure victory, of course—but they help.

## Implementation of Decisions

In Chapter 17 we noted that just because a law has been enacted by the legislature and approved by the executive does not necessarily mean that it will be applied by the administrative agencies exactly, or in some instances even approximately, as its authors intended. The administrative process can be as significant a determinant of the policies that government actually follows as are the legislative and executive processes.

The same thing can be said of the judicial process. Just because the Supreme Court or any other judicial body has declared what the law is on a particular point does not necessarily mean that every other court and governmental agency will act accordingly. For one thing, the Court's decision is technically binding only upon the specific litigants in the particular case, and if interest groups similar to those represented by the losing litigants choose to ignore the decision, they can often get away with it. In 1947, for example, the Supreme Court declared that the Board of Education of Champaign County, Illinois, had violated the constitutional separation of church and state in its "released time" program by allowing religious teachers to hold classes in the public schools and requiring pupils either to attend the classes or to remain in study hall. After the decision the Champaign school board discontinued its program, but in many thousands of other school districts throughout the land similar "released time" programs were continued as if nothing had happened.[30] An even more dramatic illustration occurred in 1955, when the Supreme Court ordered the desegregation of all public schools "with all deliberate speed"; yet for over a decade the schools in many southern states remained almost as segregated as they were before the 1955 order.[31]

---

[30] Peltason, *Federal Courts in the Political Process,* p. 56.

[31] For many more examples of this sort, see Theodore L. Becker (ed.), *The Impact of Supreme Court Decisions* (2d ed.; New York: Oxford University Press, 1973).

Furthermore, the formal hierarchical structure of court systems is no guarantee that the lower courts will invariably interpret the law exactly as the higher courts wish. As Peltason pointed out:

> The subordinate judge's task of applying the Supreme Court's mandates is no more mechanical than is the Supreme Court's task of applying The Constitution's mandates. The high court decisions which are supposed to guide and control the subordinates are frequently just as ambiguous as is the Constitution or statute which is supposed to guide the Supreme Court, and they admit of many interpretations. Hence, just as it is said that the Constitution is what the judges say it is, so it can be said that a Supreme Court decision is what the subordinate judges who apply it say it is.[32]

Finally, groups whose interests are damaged by an adverse Court decision do not have to accept their defeat as final and rarely do. They can, for example, try to have the Constitution amended to prevent such rulings in the future (the purpose of the Eleventh and Sixteenth Amendments); to persuade the Court to reverse itself (as it did, for example, in the Brown case); to induce the lower courts to ignore the decisions; or to "pack" or threaten to "pack" the Court. Judicial decisions thus do not necessarily settle once and for all the political conflicts that they deal with, any more than do legislative acts or executive or administrative actions. But, because of the high prestige and officially nonpolitical atmosphere of the judicial process, a favorable court decision is an important victory for any interest group.

## THE COURTS AND THE DEMOCRATIC POLITICAL PROCESS

Some readers who may grant that I have presented a reasonably accurate picture of what the courts in the democracies actually do may nevertheless find it depressing. Perhaps they prefer to believe that somewhere in the political-governmental process issues are settled not through conflict between opposing selfish groups but by real statesmen who remain beyond such conflict and are guided only by eternal principles of right and wrong. Perhaps they at least hope that they will find such statesmen in the courts.

But there is no reason to be depressed by this picture of the political process. After all, democracy, as pictured here, is a process in which political conflict takes place among groups that are freely organized and at liberty to express their views: in which it takes the form of discussion and peaceful agitation in a spirit of respect for others' rights to live and "pursue happiness," that is, to try to achieve their goals; and in which value allocations result from government decisions intended both to hold the society together and to promote an abstract notion of perfect justice. If there is any validity in this view of democracy, then there is no reason to be either surprised or depressed by learning that judges and courts, like legislatures, executives, and administrators, are part of one pervasive democratic decision-making process.

---

[32] Peltason, *Federal Courts in the Political Process*, p. 14. For examples of "reversals by lower courts," see Becker, *The Impact of Supreme Court Decisions*, pp. 60–62.

We may be sure that most democrats would greatly prefer the kind of judicial process that we have described to those that operate in the Soviet Union and in the nations which govern themselves as the Soviets do.

## LAW AND COURTS IN THE SOVIET UNION

### THE COMMUNIST CONCEPTION OF LAW

According to communist political theory, as we saw in Chapters 5 and 13, all politics, and indeed all human activity, results from and reflects the basic struggle to the death between the bourgeoisie and the proletariet. Communist theorists therefore regard any government and all its agencies simply as instruments established by the dominant class to maintain its supremacy over the subject class. To them all democratic theories of law outlined earlier in this chapter are cynical or deluded claptrap, masking the naked reality of capitalist exploitation of the powerless workers.

A communist regime recognizes law as a weapon in class warfare and not only turns it to the advantage of the proletariat but also scorns any hypocritical attempt to conceal its true purposes. Article 590 of the Soviet penal code declares, for example, "Law is a system of social relationships which serves the interests of the ruling classes and hence is supported by their organized power, the state."[33]

Before we are too put off by this rhetoric, let us admit that in some respects—but with one crucial exception—this communist doctrine applies to the legal-judicial systems of the democracies. They too are committed to the preservation of their nations' independence and their constitutional regimes' basic institutions and values. They too sometimes abandon niceties of procedure and due process when national independence or basic constitutional structure is threatened. They too are more than mere neutral arbiters of conflict among others; sometimes they participate directly in political conflict and policy making. In this sense, at least, they *do* defend "the system" and refuse to become agencies for its overthrow.

There is, however, one fundamental difference. In the Soviet Union all questions about what measures will be taken to preserve the regime and accelerate its evolution toward true communism are settled by one all-powerful oligarchy: the leaders of the Communist Party of the Soviet Union. There is no room for policy dissent of any kind. Accordingly, it is inconceivable that any Soviet court would declare unconstitutional any act of the Supreme Soviet or refuse to convict anyone accused by CPSU leaders of being an "enemy of the state." In the Western democratic systems, on the other hand, there is no single agency that effectively determines for all the others what measures are in the nation's best interests. As we have seen, legislatures, executives, civil servants, and courts all have some say. Consequently, the courts are to some degree independent of the other government agencies. They do sometimes declare unconstitutional, set aside, ignore, or "interpret away" mea-

---

[33] Quoted in Kenneth Redden (ed.), *An Introductory Survey of the Place of Law in Our Civilization* (Charlottesville, Va.: The Michie Company, 1946), p. 14.

sures promulgated by other agencies. And they do sometimes refuse to convict people whom other agencies want put out of the way.

Thus the fact that the Soviet conception of law and court functions has something in common with Western democratic ideals and practices should not distract us from their basic differences.

## ROLES OF THE SOVIET COURTS

### Political

Most Western authorities agree that it is important to distinguish between the political and nonpolitical roles of the Soviet courts. When they are dealing with political matters—for example, trials of people accused of threatening the regime—they are simply administrative agents of the CPSU. Their task is not only to eliminate the subversives but also to help "educate" the masses. We noted in Chapter 5 that one major task of all Soviet institutions is to help arouse sufficient enthusiasm for party policies among the masses so that the policies can be executed with minimum physical coercion. As a leading Western student of the Soviet legal system has pointed out, the courts do their share as "teachers and parents" for the masses. When courts are hearing and deciding cases involving points on which the party thinks the masses need instruction, court sessions are arranged to permit maximum popular attendance, and the masses are encouraged to attend. Certainly all communist regimes have made considerable use of "purge trials" modeled on the Russian trials of 1936–1938, complete with public "confessions" of guilt and cooperation with the capitalist enemy. Communist leaders apparently believe that such trials are useful in educating the masses about the immorality and folly of opposing official policy.[34]

### Nonpolitical

As must any modern nation, the USSR must deal with many legal problems that have little or no political content: criminal acts like murder and rape and civil disputes like divorces and injuries to private citizens by other citizens. Most observers believe that the Soviet courts deal with such nonpolitical matters in ways very similar to those used by courts in the Western nations and that in such areas of concern "socialist justice" is not very different from "capitalist justice."

## THE COURT SYSTEM AND THE OFFICE OF PROCURATOR

The essentials of the formal structure of the Soviet court system are shown in Figure 15. Two aspects of that system are of special interest for our purposes.

---

[34] Harold J. Berman, *Justice in the USSR* (rev. ed.; New York: Vintage Books, 1963), chaps. 9–10.

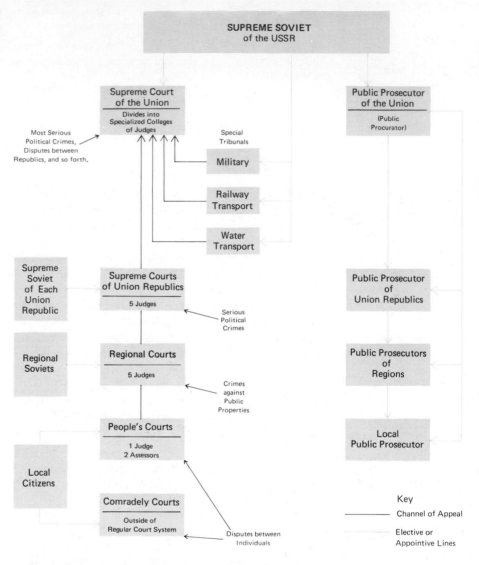

**FIGURE 15**
The Soviet court system and the public prosecutor.

SUPREME SOVIET
of the USSR

Supreme Court
of the Union

Divides into
Specialized Colleges
of Judges

Most Serious
Political Crimes,
Disputes between
Republics, and so forth.

Special
Tribunals

Military

Railway
Transport

Water
Transport

Public Prosecutor
of the Union

(Public
Procurator)

Supreme
Soviet
of Each
Union
Republic

Supreme Courts
of Union Republics

5 Judges

Serious
Political
Crimes

Public Prosecutor
of
Union Republics

Regional
Soviets

Regional Courts

5 Judges

Crimes
against
Public
Properties

Public Prosecutors
of
Regions

People's Courts

1 Judge
2 Assessors

Local
Public Prosecutor

Local
Citizens

Comradely Courts

Outside of
Regular Court System

Disputes between
Individuals

Key

Channel of Appeal

Elective or
Appointive Lines

## Selection of Judges and Assessors

The Soviet Constitution specifies that all judges are to be selected, but "election" has been interpreted to mean direct selection by the voters only of judges for the people's courts. The judges of all other courts are named for five-year terms by legislative assemblies at their respective levels, up to and including the supreme court of the USSR, the members of which are nominally selected by the Supreme Soviet (the national legislative assembly) but actually, of course, by the party politburo.

The judges of the people's courts are elected for five-year terms on the same kind of single-candidate-per-office slate prepared by the party for all other Soviet elections (see Chap. 7). Each people's court consists of one judge and two "assessors." The latter are elected every five years by the voters in the usual communist manner.

Governmental Authorities
and Processes

They are meant to act as lay assistants to the judges, as are Western juries, but complete party domination of the selection process makes any further analogy with Western institutions highly misleading.

### The Office of Procurator

The legal-judicial system of Russia under the czarist regime was closely modeled upon the French system. It followed the inquisitorial approach to the trial of people accused of crimes, and it gave a good deal of power to officials known as "procurators" who were very similar to the French *juges d' instruction.* After short-lived experimentation with other judicial structures, Nikolai Lenin revived these offices in 1922, and they have been an important element in the Soviet judicial system ever since.

As Figure 15 shows, procurators operate at all levels of the court system. They are headed by the public prosecutor of the USSR, who is selected for a seven-year term by the Supreme Soviet and works under the close instruction of the party presidium. He in turn selects a corps of local procurators and assigns each to a court at the local, regional, or republic level. They are strictly responsible to him and to no local authority.

Each procurator is charged with seeing to it that "no single decision of local authority deviates from the law" (from party policy). He is thus charged with protesting to higher authorities any illegal action by a local authority, with "ferreting out every single crime for punishment," with making sure that every arrest is legal, with prosecuting indicted criminals and ensuring that the court upholds the law, and with protesting to higher courts all lower court decisions and sentences rendered in violation of the law. It is not unknown for a procurator to ask that a guilty verdict be set aside or that a stiff penalty be reduced. He also supervises implementation of sentences and even intervenes to supervise the proceedings in civil cases.[35] He is thus all that a *juge d'instruction* is and more. He is one of the central party's most prominent local watchdogs not only over the behavior of individuals but also over the activities of the courts themselves. In every court proceeding he is unquestionably the dominant figure, for Soviet legal theory and practice assign to him even more than to the courts themselves the responsibility for ensuring that Soviet law and policies are carried out in the legal arena.

## SOVIET JUSTICE

Most Western observers agree that the Soviet system of justice works quite well by Western standards when no "political question" (that is, no question that the party regards as involving its ideals and policies) is involved; the treatment of ordinary crimes, family disputes, and the like by Soviet courts appears not to differ widely from its counterpart in the Western democracies.

When a "political question" is involved in a Soviet legal controversy, however,

---

[35] Merle Fainsod, *How Russia Is Ruled* (rev. ed.; Cambridge, Mass.: Harvard University Press, 1963), pp. 411–413.

justice and the will of the party are—as they are intended to be in communist doctrine—one and the same. Law and the courts in the USSR are like every other Soviet government agency: Both in communist theory and in Soviet practice they are instruments by which the party imposes its will upon the masses with minimum resistance from the latter and minimum expenditure of effort by the party.

# 19

---

# LOCAL GOVERNMENT AND FEDERALISM

Politics, as we have frequently observed in this book, is rarely a choice between perfect good and undiluted evil. If it were, life would be a great deal more simple and pleasant than it is. But the hard fact is that politics is nearly always a choice "between the lesser of two evils"—that is, between various mixtures of good and evil. Most of us have no trouble in realizing that our choices involve such mixtures, but we are seldom sure just what the proportions are, just how much of one good thing we shall have to give up to obtain another.

A particularly painful example of this confusion is the current dilemma over how to eliminate the pollution of air and water while preserving genuine local self-government. On one hand, there is no question that the sources of environmental pollution in any particular town, city, or even state extend well beyond local boundaries and can be dealt with effectively only through action by some higher authority. What good will it do Ohio, for example, to pass stern laws against pouring industrial wastes into Lake Erie, the "dead lake," if Michigan, Pennsylvania, and New York (and, for that matter, Ontario) let *their* factories do as they please? If Lake Erie is really to be cleaned up, all these states must agree upon common regulations. But if they refuse? Then the *national* government must clamp down on all of them.

Yet is there no value in letting each state experiment with different control methods? Do we really want to place all our reliance on the national government? What if it chooses a control system that does not work but declares no other system legally possible? And is there not some value in preserving the historic rights of Ohioans, Pennsylvanians, New Yorkers, and Michiganders to manage their own affairs as they see fit? Do we really want to dig up all our "grass roots" and become one huge, undifferentiated national mass with one gigantic all-powerful government? Is that the only way to end pollution? Even if it is, *is it worth it?*

These questions are not merely rhetorical or academic. They go right to the heart not only of the problem of ending pollution but also of the question of what, if any, role local governments have in a nation and a world in which most of the urgent problems are undeniably national and even international in scope.

To help us understand what is involved in these questions, let us begin by surveying the present status of local governments in modern nations.

## LOCAL COMMUNITIES AND LOCAL GOVERNMENTS

Under the modern state system, as we noted in Chapter 3, the earth's peoples are divided among 151 social-political-legal entities called "nations." These entities are the world's principal governing units, for each claims the exclusive right to make and enforce rules governing the behavior of the people within its territory, and none formally recognizes any superior rule-making authority.

That is why most of this book is devoted to describing government and politics in nations. Yet national communities and national governments are by no means the only communities and governments. Every nation contains subnational communities, each with its population, customs, attitudes, accent, dialect or language, and needs that differ to some extent from those of other local communities and of the nation as a whole.

Americans, for example, are well aware of the many significant differences among New Englanders, southerners, midwesterners, and westerners. Far too many of us are inclined to think of "the British" (no sense of humor) and "the French" (loose morals) as homogeneous national types. But, when we travel abroad or read British and French novels, we soon realize that the differences between the Highland Scots and the people of Devon and Cornwall are as great as those between Vermonters and Mississippians—and that those between the Normans and the Provençals are as great as those between New Yorkers and New Mexicans.

We also noted in Chapter 3 that for most people nationalism is the highest loyalty but not the *only* loyalty. Endemic in every modern nation is competition among local communities for industry, population, and largesse (in the form of veterans' hospitals, military bases, defense contracts, and the like) from the national government—and conflict between local communities and nations over the degree to which the former can manage their own affairs without direction from the latter. Not infrequently in the Western nations such loyalties have been strong enough to produce powerful "state's rights" and even secession movements. The revolt of the eleven Confederate States of America between 1860 and 1865 produced the bloodiest civil war in history, but many modern Western nations have had to contend with comparable, if less powerful, movements: for example, the Quebec separatist movement in Canada; the Irish, Scottish, and Welsh nationalist movements in Great Britain; and the bitter conflict between Flemings and Walloons in Belgium.

The problem is even more accute in many new and developing nations. A number of new African and Asian nations face the continuing problem of transforming traditional tribal loyalties into truly national loyalties, and finding a solution is not easy. India, for example, has been bedeviled from the beginning by demands for local autonomy by its many cultural-linguistic groups: the national government would like to make Hindi the official language, but millions of people speak the quite different Telugu, Marathi, Tamil, Bengali, Gujarati, and other languages, and these linguistic divisions must be taken into account in almost any national political effort.[1] Another example is the Democratic Republic of the Congo (Belgian Congo), racked from independence in 1960 until the late 1960s by civil war, in which the central government sought to prevent the secession of its wealthiest province, Katanga; the war, though it formally ended in 1967, has left many deep scars. The most recent and tragic example is the devastating 1967-1970 civil war in Nigeria resulting from the unsuccessful efforts of Ibo tribesmen to secede from the central government and form the independent nation of Biafra.

Local communities, then, are significant elements of every modern nation. Most have their own governments authorized, in various ways and within various limits, to make and enforce rules for their particular subnational jurisdictions. Our task in this chapter is to see what place these governments have in democratic theory and to examine the principal patterns of organization and problems in modern democratic nations.

## LOCAL GOVERNMENT IN DEMOCRATIC THEORY

### LOCAL COMMUNITIES IN THE NATIONAL COMMUNITY

Some theorists of democracy, notably Jean Jacques Rousseau and Thomas Jefferson in the eighteenth century and Baker Brownell in the twentieth, have argued that the health of democracy depends to a considerable degree upon preserving the special identities of local communities and that maintaining strong local self-government should therefore be a prime goal of government organization in any nation that wishes to be truly democratic. Arthur E. Morgan, former chairman of the Tennessee Valley Authority, spoke for these theorists when he wrote:

> For the preservation and transmission of the fundamentals of civilization, vigorous, wholesome [local] community life is imperative. Unless many people live and work in the intimate relationships of community life, there can never emerge a truly unified nation, or a community of mankind. If I do not love my neighbor whom I know, how can I love the human race, which is but an abstraction? If I have not learned to work with a few people, how can I be effective with many?[2]

### CONTRIBUTIONS OF LOCAL GOVERNMENT

Although some democratic theorists regard the local community as less crucial than do the writers just mentioned, almost all believe that properly organized local self-

---

[1] Richard L. Park, "India," in Robert E. Ward and Roy C. Macridis (eds.), *Modern Political Systems: Asia* (Englewood Cliffs, N.J.: Prentice-Hall, Inc., 1963), pp. 249–250.

[2] Arthur E. Morgan, *The Small Community: Foundation of Democratic Life* (New York: Harper & Row, Publishers, 1942), p. 19. See also Baker Brownell, *The Human Community* (New York: Harper & Row, Publishers, 1950).

government can contribute to the health of democracy. Five such contributions are most frequently mentioned.

First, although there is only one national government in each nation, there are many local governments, each of which has jurisdiction over far fewer people than has the national government. Many more people therefore can participate directly and continuously in local government than can participate in national government, and direct participation by a maximum number of citizens leads to healthy democracy and provides a strong barrier against tyranny. Thomas Jefferson put it thus:

> Where every man is a sharer in the direction of . . . and feels that he is a participator in, the government of affairs, not merely at an election one day in the year, but every day; where there shall be not a man in the State who will not be a member of some one of its councils, great or small, he will let the heart be torn out of his body sooner than his power be wrested from him by a Caesar or a Bonaparte.[3]

Second, in the words of the English political scientist Harold J. Laski, "all problems are not central problems, and . . . problems not central in their incidence require decision at the place, and by the persons, where and by whom the incidence is most deeply felt."[4] The zoning problems of Urbana, Illinois, concern mainly and are best understood by the residents of Urbana and not the residents of Chicago, New York, or Washington, D.C. Only the residents of Urbana should therefore have the power to make Urbana's zoning ordinances.

Third, "grass roots" participation in local government either as a public official or as a voter is excellent training for voting in national elections and holding national public office and thus provides an ever-fresh source of good citizens and leaders for the nation.

Fourth, local government is an invaluable sociopolitical laboratory for testing on a small scale various new proposals for government organization and social and economic policies. Local failures can be borne with far less social cost than can those of the national government, and local successes can and often do serve as models that the national government can follow with minimum risk.

Finally, a dead uniformity in all standards, policies, and organization imposed on all local areas by a national government is bound to stamp out the variety and local color that contribute so richly to the life of any nation; strong local self-government is the most effective barrier against such drab conformism.

## DISTRIBUTION OF FUNCTIONS

Few if any democratic theorists have argued that *all* government functions should be performed exclusively by either the national government or local governments. At the most general (and, therefore, perhaps not very useful) level of discussion, they all

---

[3] Thomas Jefferson, letter to Joseph C. Cabell, February 2, 1816, in Andrew A. Lipscomb (ed.), *The Writings of Thomas Jefferson,* Vol. 14 (Washington, D.C.: The Thomas Jefferson Memorial Association, 1903), p. 422.

[4] Harold J. Laski, *A Grammar of Politics* (New Haven, Conn.: Yale University Press, 1925), p. 411.

agree upon what might be called the "to each its own" standard: Let the national government deal with all problems that are mainly national in character, and let each local government deal with all problems that mainly concern its local community alone. As Jefferson put it:

> ... the way to have good and safe government, is not to trust it to one, but to divide it among the many, distributing to every one exactly the functions he is competent to. Let the national government be entrusted with the defense of the nation, and its foreign and federal relations; the State governments with the civil rights, laws, police, and administration of what concerns the State generally; the counties with the local concerns of the counties; and each ward direct the interests within itself.[5]

So general a standard unfortunately does not help us very much in the many concrete situations in which we have to decide which government should deal with specific problems. For example, both northern and southern whites in the United States believe that the national government should handle only national matters and that the states should control all purely state matters. But in the current controversy over the racial laws of the southern states (see Chap. 22) some southerners argue that each state's race relations are the rightful concern of that state alone and no business of the rest of the nation, whereas some northerners reply that, as southern blacks are citizens of the United States, as well as of the states in which they live, their rights are the proper concern of the whole nation. That both sides are sincere in their adherence to the "to each its own" standard and in their different applications of it has not made the settlement of this bitter dispute any easier.

In short, nearly every citizen of every democratic nation believes that both the national government and local governments have their proper place in the total scheme of things. Yet in every such nation—not just in the United States—there is a constant tug of war between national and local governments over which should have the power to perform which public functions.

## SALIENCE OF LOCAL GOVERNMENT

Advocates of maximum power for the "grass roots" have generally argued (or assumed) that, because local governments are much more immediately visible and accessible to ordinary citizens than are national governments, the citizens are bound to be much more interested in, informed about, and likely to participate in them than in the more remote national government.

Some political scientists have challenged this assumption. They remind us that in most modern democracies voting turnouts in national elections average from 60 to 90 percent (see Chap. 7) but that it is rare for more than half the eligible voters to vote in local elections, in which turnouts of 25 and 30 percent are quite common.

A recent study by two American political scientists has shaken the assumption even more. In their analysis of The University of Michigan Survey Research Center's

---

[5] Jefferson, letter to Joseph C. Cabell, February 2, 1816.

interviews with national samples of American voters in 1966 and 1968, M. Kent Jennings and Harmon Zeigler first eliminated the 17 percent who showed no interest in public affairs at any level and then asked the remainder to rank four levels of governmental affairs (international, national, state, and local) in order of their own interest and attention. The responses are arrayed in Table 21. The national government drew the most first choices (32 percent) but was followed closely by the local governments (30 percent), with the state governments bringing up the rear (17 percent). When the first- and second-place choices are averaged together, however, the rankings are: national, 32 percent; local, 25 percent; state, 25 percent; and international, 18 percent. And, when the national and international levels are combined and compared with the combined state and local levels, the high salience scores are divided fifty-fifty.

TABLE 21

Rank Ordering of Salience of Government Affairs at 4 Levels

| Level of Government Affairs | Attention Rank | | | | Total[a] | N |
|---|---|---|---|---|---|---|
| | First | Second | Third | Fourth | | |
| International | 20% | 16% | 22% | 42% | 100 | 983 |
| National | 32 | 31 | 26 | 10 | 99 | 983 |
| State | 17 | 33 | 27 | 22 | 99 | 983 |
| Local | 30 | 20 | 25 | 25 | 100 | 983 |
| | 99% | 100% | 100% | 99% | | |
| | N = 983 | 983 | 983 | 983 | | |

[a]Total percentages do not always equal 100% because of rounding. Cases involving tied ranks or missing data have been deleted from these data. Their inclusion in rows or columns would have a maximum effect of only 1 percent on any cell value. The total number of cases for analysis was 1008.
Source: M. Kent Jennings and Harmon Zeigler, "The Salience of American State Politics," American Political Science Review, 64 (June 1970), 525.

Jennings and Zeigler found some other intriguing associations. For example, compared with those most concerned with national and international affairs, the respondents for whom local and state politics were most salient included higher proportions of farmers, small-town residents, and southerners. The latter group also had on the average less formal education, lower voting rates, less trust in the honesty and reliability of others, and greater suspicion and dislike of larger and more remote environments.[6]

This record confirms findings by sociologists about differences in the socioeconomic characteristics and attitudes of "cosmopolitans" and "locals." Although the findings are not definitive, they all suggest that, as citizens become (as Americans are becoming) better educated and more concentrated in big cities, they are likely to grow even less interested in local affairs and more concerned with national and international matters. Henry Wadsworth Longfellow's village blacksmith may indeed have been the ideal citizen for a Jeffersonian grass-roots democracy, but his son who went to the big city and took a factory job was probably less interested in local politics than

[6] M. Kent Jennings and Harmon Zeigler, "The Salience of American State Politics," American Political Science Review, 64 (June 1970), 523–535.

his father had been. And the blacksmith's grandson who went to college and became an insurance executive with a home in the suburbs was probably even less concerned with what his local government was doing. How this kind of evolution affects the status of local government we shall consider later.

## LOCAL GOVERNMENT IN UNITARY SYSTEMS

In Chapter 12 a unitary system was defined as one in which the central government is legally supreme over all local governments within its borders. Most modern nations have unitary systems, and in each all local governments have been legally created by the national government and subjected to whatever degree of control and supervision the national authorities think best. Even in the few nations with federal governments, as we shall see, each of the "cosovereign" subnational governments (the states in the United States and Australia, the provinces in Canada, the *Länder* in West Germany, the cantons in Switzerland, and so on) is unitary within its boundaries. In this section we are interested in the local governments operating in unitary systems, and in the next section we shall consider local governments in federal systems.

There are, needless to say, apparently infinite variations in detail in the legal status, structure, and powers exercised by the hundreds of thousands of local governments operating in unitary systems the world over. Nevertheless, there are enough similarities to warrant at least a few general descriptive statements.

### LEVELS AND FORMS OF GOVERNMENT

#### *Territorial Levels*

Despite many variations in the ways in which modern nations divide and subdivide their territories and populations for purposes of local government, most have units at each of the following levels.

**Greater Regions**  Most nations first divide their territories and populations into large regional units. In the federal democracies these units are called "states," "provinces," "*Länder*," "cantons," and so on. The unitary democracies have comparable units, though, of course, with much less independent governing power. Great Britain, for example, has sixty-one administrative counties, the successors to the fifty-two shires (like Cornwall, Hampshire, and Shropshire) that were for many centuries the principal units of local government. It also has eighty-three county boroughs—cities with the same powers that counties have. France has ninety *départements* (for example, Côte d'Or, Gironde, Indre-et-Loire), which are also descended from but not identical with the nation's ancient provinces (like Burgundy, Provence, Gascony). The People's Republic of China maintains its ancient provinces (Hunan, Kwantung, Shantung, and others). India has states (Kerala, Madras, Punjab, Uttar Pradesh, and the rest). And so on.

**Lesser Regions**  Some nations also subdivide these greater regions into smaller regional units that still take in more territory than do cities. The United States, for example, has about 3000 counties, some of which—like Cook County in Illinois, Los

Local Government and Federalism

Angeles County in California, and Dade County in Florida—occasionally attract national attention. France divides its ninety *départements* into 450 *arrondissements*— which, alas, are given numbers rather than names. Japan has no intermediate regional units and is divided into forty-six prefectures. Most nations, however, omit lesser regional units and emphasize still a third level.

**Municipalities** Although some nations, like Israel, have no regional governments worth mentioning, every nation has municipal governments with legal jurisdiction over some kind of urban settlement. In socioeconomic terms an "urban settlement" consists of

> a collection of dwellings and other buildings plus a sizable resident population. The buildings are permanently situated, separated from other such settlements, and are compactly arranged with respect to each other—typically in blocks separated by streets or alleys. While there is no universal agreement as to how large the population must be before the settlement is classified as urban, the minimum is usually placed somewhere between 2500 and 10,000 people.[7]

Urban living is, of course, one of the most striking characteristics of social and economic modernization. In the United States, for example, the population has grown steadily more urban since we became an independent nation. In 1790 less than 10 percent of the population lived in urban settlements (defined as those with populations greater than 3000). In the 1970s more than 60 percent of all Americans live in urban settlements of more than 10,000 population, and nearly 30 percent live in settlements of more than 100,000 population. Many other Western democratic nations are even more urbanized; the United States ranks only thirteenth among Western nations in population per square mile.[8] The result is that urban living—with all its attendant special problems of transportation, water and air pollution, congestion, ethnic conflict, crime, and the like—is, for better or worse, increasingly the milieu of modern mankind.

The *legal* municipalities, it must be emphasized, often do not coincide with the *socioeconomic* urban settlements. A classic example is "Megalopolis"—the great sprawling urban settlement that begins in northeastern Massachusetts and continues almost without a break to northeastern Virginia. It runs through nine states and the District of Columbia and contains 20 municipalities of 100,000 or more population, as well as many smaller municipalities, sanitary districts, park districts, school districts, and other units of local government. Some political scientists regard Megalopolis as only the worst of many instances of the balkanization of American local government, a

---

[7] Theodore R. Anderson, "Comparative Urban Structure," in David L. Sills (ed.), *International Encyclopedia of the Social Sciences*, Vol. 2 (New York: The Macmillan Company and The Free Press, 1968), p. 466.

[8] The United States has 57 people per square mile, compared with the Netherlands' 840, Belgium's 824, Japan's 736, West Germany's 621, and Great Britain's 593. The most densely populated nations in the world are Singapore with 9,443, Malta with 2,678 and Barbados with 1,443; *The American Almanac, 1974* (The Statistical Abstract of the United States prepared by the Bureau of the Census; New York: Grosset & Dunlap, Inc., 1974), pp. 803–805, Table 1322.

problem to which we shall return in a moment. The point here is that, as more and more of the world's people move from rural areas to urban settlements and from smaller towns to bigger cities, the municipal level of government is increasingly and inescapably where the action—and the trouble—is.

*Forms of Government*

Regardless of territorial level and many differences in detail, most local governments in the Western democratic countries take one or another of the following three forms.

**Mayoral**   In Chapter 15 we noted that the national governments of most democratic countries can conveniently be classified as either "presidential" or "parliamentary." Many of their local governments can be fitted into quite similar categories. The "mayoral," or "mayor-council," form resembles presidential government in that the chief executive (the mayor) and the legislature (the council) are elected independently for fixed terms of office and serve them out regardless of disagreements and deadlocks between the two branches—which are by no means uncommon.

FIGURE 16
The weak-mayor-
council form of
municipal government.

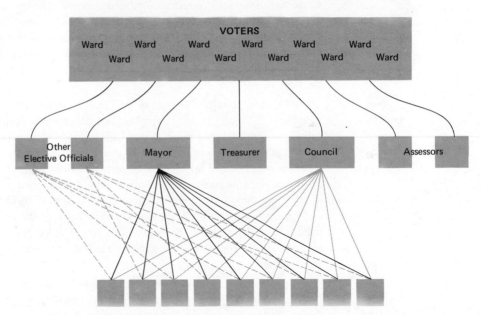

The mayoral form has two variations, "weak mayor" and "strong mayor." A model weak-mayor form is graphically represented in Figure 16. The weak-mayor-council structure is the most common form of municipal government in the United States, although in recent years it has been replaced in a number of municipalities by the strong-mayor and the council-manager forms. The weak mayor does not lack power to direct policy, for he usually presides over the council, has a veto over its actions, and is its main political leader. He is called "weak" because he is not the chief executive in the sense of having the sole formal power to appoint, remove, and supervise the municipality's administrative officers and employees. As Figure 16

Local Government and
Federalism

479

shows, some of these officials are elected by the voters, and the council shares with the mayor the power to appoint the others. Most political scientists believe this form of municipal government to be the worst, mainly because it fails to provide for administrative leadership and centralized control and responsibility, adds to the burdens of the local voters by giving them so many elective offices to fill, and violates many other "principles of public administration" (see Chap. 17). Nevertheless, it continues to be the most common form of municipal government, particularly in small towns, although cities as large as Minneapolis, Atlanta, and Providence also use it.

Many political scientists prefer the strong-mayor-council variation of this form, which resembles the structure of the American national government in that the mayor, like the President, is the only elected executive official, appoints and dismisses department heads, and shares policy-making functions with the council. This form is particularly successful in large cities and is currently used in New York, Philadelphia, Detroit, Cleveland, St. Louis, and elsewhere.[9]

**Conciliar**  In most Western European democratic nations the basic governing body at all levels of local government is an elected council. Great Britain adds a special twist by having the elected councillors also select a number of aldermen, either from among their own members or from outside the council, by a process known as "cooptation." The aldermen also sit on the council but have longer terms than do the directly elected councillors.

Whether it adds aldermen or not, each local council selects a presiding officer, usually from among its own members but occasionally from outside. This officer is called "mayor" or "chairman" (Great Britain), *maire* (France), *Bürgermeister* (Germany), *alcalde* (Spain), and so on. The whole council acts as the local legislature, and either its committees or the mayor acts as administrative supervisor. For each major type of service the unit performs the council establishes a committee of council members, distributed among the political parties according to their strength on the whole council. Each committee then supervises the work of the professional administrator heading the department for which it is responsible. The chairmen of the various committees act together as a sort of "cabinet" to guide both policy making and administration.

The mayor's power varies considerably among the various nations. In Great Britain he (often she) is almost entirely a ceremonial figure whose only specialized duties are to represent the local government at affairs honoring visiting dignitaries. In France, on the other hand, the *maire* is the most eminent local figure. Furthermore, most political careers begin with prominent local office and are based upon it; a number of *maires* also serve concurrently as national deputies or senators.[10] Most other

---

[9] A recent in-depth analysis of the interaction of government forms and political forces in local governments in the San Francisco Bay area is Heinz Eulau and Kenneth Prewitt, *Labyrinths of Democracy: Adaptations, Linkages, Representation, and Policies in Urban Politics* (Indianapolis, Ind.: The Bobbs-Merrill Company, Inc., 1973).

[10] See Mark Kesselman, *The Ambiguous Consensus: A Study of Local Government in France* (New York: Alfred A. Knopf, 1967), pp. 38–52.

Continental democracies seem to follow the French rather than the British model, making the mayor a figure of major local importance.

Typically, each unit of local government in a European democracy has a number of career administrative officials: the town or county clerk, who is the chief administrative officer; the treasurer, who presides over the collection of local taxes and the disbursement of local funds; the health officer; the sanitary inspector; the surveyor; and so on. These people also have high local standing, and where, as in much of Great Britain, the office of mayor is relatively weak the career civil servants come to resemble, in fact if not in legal form, the managers that govern some municipalities in the United States.

**FIGURE 17**
The council-manager
form of municipal
government.

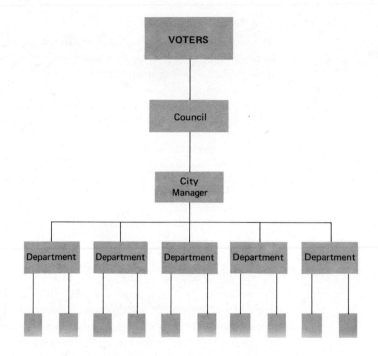

**Managerial**   The structure of a model managerial, or "council-manager," form of local government is shown in Figure 17. Many political scientists believe that for most municipalities the council-manager form is by far the best, and it is proposed in the "model city charter" of the National Municipal League. It has several principal virtues, they believe. It provides for the "short ballot," as only members of the council are elected. It clearly assigns policy-making and administrative functions to separate agencies (see Chap. 17). It not only centralizes in one person control of and responsibility for supervising administration, but it also requires him to be a *full-time,* trained career professional rather than a part-time amateur. Finally, as the manager is hired by the council and holds his job at the council's pleasure, he cannot become, as some critics charge, a "dictator."

As Charles R. Adrian has pointed out, however, the council-manager plan has its weaknesses: There is a shortage of able and well-trained professional managers; there is no institutional provision for policy leadership in the council; and the manag-

Local Government and
Federalism

er often participates actively in politics, dominates the council because of his greater expertise, and thus violates certain principles of democracy. Certainly the form is no panacea for the ills of all municipalities everywhere.[11] One measure of the popularity of the council-manager form in the five decades since it was first proposed is its adoption by a steadily increasing number of municipalities, and its abandonment by very few; it is now used in nearly 50 percent of American cities with populations of more than 25,000 and in more than 45 percent of those with populations of 10,000-25,000. The largest cities currently using it are Cincinnati, Kansas City (Missouri), Dallas, and San Antonio.

## FUNCTIONS

Although there are many variations in the functions of local government from nation to nation and from locality to locality within a particular nation, the most common include the following main types:

Protective functions: police, fire, and public health
Regulatory functions: zoning, licensing local businesses, parking regulations, and so on
Assistance functions: aid to the needy and sick
Service functions—free public education, building and maintaining roads, and providing such recreational facilities as libraries, parks, and swimming pools
Proprietary functions: operating municipally owned electric and gas utilities, waterworks, and transportation systems.

## DEGREES OF CENTRAL CONTROL

By definition, the legal powers of any local government in a unitary system are granted by the central government, which can exercise any degree and form of supervision and control that it prefers. There is, however, great variation in the degree of control that the central governments choose to exercise. Great Britain and the dominions, for example, generally treasure their long-standing traditions of vigorous local self-government, and their central governments allow a considerable degree of freedom, though various national ministries—particularly the Ministry of Housing and Local Government in Great Britain—do supervise many local activities. This kind of local freedom is also characteristic of the Scandinavian nations, especially Denmark, and of Switzerland, Belgium, and the Netherlands.

France and most other European democracies, on the other hand, prefer greater central control and exercise what is formally known as central "tutelage" (*tutelle*) of local governments. In the French system, which is generally regarded as the model for such centralization, the administrative head of each *departement* is the prefect. He

---

[11] Charles R. Adrian, *Governing Urban America* (New York: McGraw-Hill, Inc., 1955), pp. 201–204. See also the account of the Newburgh affair in Chap. 17.

is a national civil servant appointed by and responsible to the Minister of the Interior. He is responsible for the enforcement of all laws and executive orders in his jurisdiction. He designates another national civil servant, a subprefect, to represent him in supervising the government of each *arrondissement* in his *departement*. The prefect is authorized to suspend from office the mayor of any commune within his jurisdiction for a period of one month, and the Minister of the Interior can suspend any mayor for three months or, in unusually serious cases, dismiss him altogether. The prefect can also dismiss a municipal councillor from office for neglecting his duties or abusing his office for personal ends. All local budgets must be presented in a manner prescribed by the ministry, and any can be altered or set aside by the prefect and the ministry. Yet these tutelary powers, which seem rather extreme to English and American eyes, are rarely used; despite the high degree of formal central control local authorities, particularly the mayors, have considerable voice in what goes on. Local self-government is thus well established in France and some other European democratic nations, though it is perhaps not as strong as in Great Britain, Switzerland, and the Netherlands.

There is a great variation in the degrees of freedom that American state governments permit their local governments. Legally, of course, every local governing body is a "creature of the state," in the sense that the state creates it and grants its legal powers. A city, county, or township may legally do only what the state authorities permit it to do; any other action is ultra vires and will be stopped by the state's administrative authorities or courts. In deciding borderline cases, furthermore, most state courts follow the famous Dillon's Rule that cases of doubt about a local government's power should be resolved *against* the local government. ·

Important as judicial control of local governments in the American states remains, control by state administrative officers is increasingly the main method by which local governments are kept in line. These state officials use such noncoercive procedures as requiring reports, furnishing advice and information, and providing technical aid and such coercive procedures as withholding permits, issuing direct orders, and withholding state grants of money to local governments. Local governments in the American states are thus rather closely controlled by the state authorities, especially in the kinds and amounts of taxes they can levy, the amounts of indebtedness they can incur, the various functions they can perform, and the procedures they must follow in performing them.[12] Certainly Americans cannot boast that local self-government is stronger in the United States than in any other democratic nation.

## PROBLEMS

Judging by articles in scholarly journals, political debates, and newspaper editorials in various parts of the world, all modern democratic countries are concerned with a number of essentially similar problems relating to the status, organization, and operation of local governments. The main problems are as follows.

[12] See Adrian, *Governing Urban America,* chap. 12.

### Central Control and Local Freedom

Every nation, as we noted earlier in this chapter, is a collection of local communities with a national community, and every democratic nation is to some extent committed to the desirability of local self-government. Yet in every unitary system (and, as we shall see, in every federal situation as well) there is perpetual controversy over the amount of freedom from central control that should be allowed to local governments. Sometimes this question becomes a prominent issue in national elections. In the British general election of 1950, for example, the Conservatives charged that the Labour government had unduly interfered with the freedom of local government, and many observers believed that this charge cost the Labour party a substantial number of votes. The adherence of just about every citizen in every democratic country to the "to each its own" standard mentioned at the beginning of this chapter does not appear to have helped to settle this controversy anywhere, and no nation has yet found a perfect solution to it—if, indeed, such a solution can ever be found.

### Balkanization of Local Governments

In most democratic nations there are what many observers believe to be an unjustified proliferation and overlapping of local governing units, which have increased the cost and blurred the responsibility of local government in general. The most frequently discussed aspect of this problem is financial, service, and jurisdictional relations among the governing units within metropolitan areas. Most of the world's great cities are surrounded by suburbs whose inhabitants work in the "core cities" but are not governed by them and do not pay taxes to them. Particularly in the United States many core cities have to provide services to these commuting suburbanites without receiving commensurate tax funds from them or regulatory power over them. Political scientists in many nations have proposed the consolidation of overlapping local authorities as the best solution to the problem, but in most democratic countries as in the United States, the citizens and public officials concerned have shown relatively little disposition to accept these recommendations.

### Local Finance

In just about every democratic nation the increasing level of national taxation, the increasing costs of local services, and the many restrictions upon the levels and types of taxation permitted local governments have combined to intensify the desperation of local units seeking revenues adequate to support the services they are called upon to provide. Most central authorities, however, appear to be more reluctant to give local governments freedom in the fiscal area than in any other, and this problem too seems likely to plague local governments in many democracies for some time to come.

### Who Governs? Who Should Govern?

In recent years a growing number of social scientists have become concerned with the issue of "community power." This issue revolves partly around the factual question of what people and groups actually *do* run American local communities and governments and partly around the normative question of who *should* run them. One group of scholars, whom we may call the "power-elite" theorists, hold that American communities and their governments are typically run by small and stable power elites composed largely of local businessmen. These ruling elites, using suggestions here and threats there, not only control what local governments do but also what conflicts and disagreements will be permitted to surface as issues. They use their power to maintain the special economic and social status and privileges of their members, their friends, and others of their social class.[13]

Another group of scholars, whom we may call the "pluralist" theorists, hold that, though undoubtedly some local leaders always have more influence than others, in most communities there is no single tight little oligarchy that controls everything. Rather in every community there is a congeries of power groups, each concerned with and influential on some issues but unconcerned with and not influential on others. Most communities thus have plural elites, which often quarrel among themselves and whose power, whether singly or in combination, on any issue is limited by how much the others—*and* the general public—are concerned with the issue and are willing to accept.[14]

The dispute between adherents of the power-elite and pluralist views is primarily a scientific quarrel: It turns mainly on the factual question of who in fact *does* govern local communities. But it also has value overtones. Most of the power-elite writers seem to think that the present structure of American local community power is a highly effective device for maintaining the privileges of white middle-class business elements against the needs and demands of the poor and blacks. Most of the pluralist writers seem to think that the present structure enables *every* interest to have its say and provides a system for accommodating the conflicting demands of a wide variety of groups without resort to oppression or violence.[15] So far, however, neither

---

[13] The most general and influential exposition of this view, directed more at national than at local affairs, is C. Wright Mills, *The Power Elite* (New York: Oxford University Press, 1956). The best-known application of it in a local community-power study is Floyd Hunter's study of the distribution of influence in Atlanta, Georgia: *Community Power Structure* (Chapel Hill, N.C.: The University of North Carolina Press, 1953). Hunter's study was based on the "reputational method": He asked a sample of Atlanta's leading citizens who the most influential people in the community, and he defined the most often-mentioned names as constituting Atlanta's power elite, whose socioeconomic characteristics and methods he then studied.

[14] The best-known exposition and application of the pluralist view is Robert A. Dahl's study of decision-making in New Haven, Connecticut: *Who Governs? Democracy and Power in an American City* (New Haven, Conn.: Yale University Press, 1961). Dahl's study was based on the "decisional method": Rather than asking people who was influential, he observed who was active and who inactive in the making of a number of actual decisions, as well as who among the active won and lost and how often.

[15] A useful critique of the power-elite literature from the pluralist point of view is Nelson W. Polsby, *Community Power and Political Theory* (New Haven, Conn.: Yale University Press, 1963). The pluralists are criticized in Peter Bachrach and Morton S. Baratz, "Two Faces of Power," *American Political Science Review,* 56 (December 1962), pp. 947–952; and Bachrach and Baratz, "Decisions and Non-Decisions: An Analytical Framework," *American Political Science Review,* 62 (September 1968), pp. 632–642.

group has driven the other from the field on either scientific or normative grounds, nor has any genius stepped forward to combine the two positions in a higher synthesis.

The community-power problem arises, as do the others discussed in this chapter, in many unitary systems, in each of which the local governments legally have only those powers granted by the central authorities but in which there is also a general belief that central authorities should permit as much freedom to local governments as is consistent with national unity and welfare. How does the status of local governments differ when they stand in a *federal* relation to the national government? Let us see.

## LOCAL GOVERNMENT IN FEDERAL SYSTEMS

### FEDERALISM[16]

In Chapter 12 I defined a federal government as one in which power is constitutionally divided between the national government and certain local governments, each of which is legally supreme in its own sphere—in contrast to unitary governments, in which the national government is legally supreme over all local governments. I did not say that power must be divided equally—only that it must be divided to some degree. As political scientist William Riker has correctly pointed out, the theoretically possible divisions range from the minimum (the national government can make decisions in only one narrowly restricted category of action without obtaining approval of the local governments) to the maximum (the national government can make decisions without approval of the local governments in all but one narrowly restricted category of action).[17]

The general definition of federalism is thus relatively simple and generally agreed upon. But there is considerable disagreement among political scientists about which modern governments are truly federal. For instance, one well-known survey of modern Constitutions lists no fewer than twenty-one nations as having federal governments.[18] But most students of federalism agree that in some of these nations the *legal* federal structures are simply facades masking effective monopoly of power by the national governments. Accordingly, K. C. Wheare, for one, believes that only four nations are genuinely federal.[19] Riker disagrees. Federal government, he has

---

[16] The leading comparative studies include William H. Riker, *Federalism: Origin, Operation, Significance* (Boston: Little, Brown & Company, 1964): K. C. Wheare, *Federal Government* (4th ed.; New York: Oxford University Press, 1964); and Arthur W. MacMahon (ed.), *Federalism: Mature and Emergent* (New York: Columbia University Press, 1955).

[17] Riker, *Federalism,* pp. 5–6.

[18] Amos J. Peaslee (ed.), *Constitutions of Nations,* (2d ed.; The Hague: Martinus Nijhoff, 1956), pp. 3–4.

[19] Namely, Australia, Canada, Switzerland, and the United States; Wheare, *Federal Government,* chap. 22.

pointed out, is not necessarily the same thing as democratic government, and nations like the Soviet Union and Mexico demonstrate that it is possible to combine one-party dictatorship or domination with the forms of federalism. He has therefore listed eighteen nations deserving the label.[20]

The problem is not easy. To illustrate, let us take the example of India. Its 1950 Constitution allocates a number of powers to the states, as well as a number to the national government, and the states do in fact have considerable autonomy. But the Constitution also authorizes the national parliament to make by two-thirds vote laws that supersede *any* conflicting state law. Furthermore, the Constitution authorizes the president, in times of emergency, to suspend the Constitution and take over the administration of any state or states. This step has actually been taken twice in recent years. The first instance involved the state of Kerala in 1959: the Communists had formed the state government in 1957, but riots and disorders intensified, and in 1959 the national government proclaimed "president's rule," removed the Communist government, and ran things itself until the elections of 1960, in which Kerala voters returned a noncommunist government to power. The second episode was in the state of West Bengal in 1968. The Left (Maoist) Communists were the strongest of the fourteen parties in a coalition government, but in early 1968 the governing system broke down in a deadlock between the Communist-led coalition and the anticommunist state governor and his supporters. After some unsuccessful efforts to mediate the conflict, the national parliament, at the urging of Prime Minister Indira Gandhi, again declared "president's rule" and put the state's affairs in the hands of emissaries from New Delhi. Because of such episodes one authority has called India "a federal government in normal times, but a unitary government in times of emergency"; another has called it "a unitary state with subsidiary federal principles."[21]

The problem is further complicated by the fact that in such formally unitary nations as Great Britain the national government legally holds all the power but in fact permits its local governments a considerable area of freedom—more, indeed, than their counterparts enjoy in many formally federal nations. Perhaps we had best let others pick at this Gordian knot and confine our discussion to five nations in which, most political scientists agree, constitutional rules *and* actual practice give certain local governments powers that they can exercise as a matter of right without the national government's consent: Australia, Canada, West Germany, Switzerland, and the United States.

## WHY FEDERALISM?

In each of the five nations listed the federated subnational governments existed as independent sovereign governments before federation. Why did they join in national governments at all? And, having done so, why did they establish federal rather than

---

[20] Riker, *Federalism*, pp. 13–14.

[21] Norman D. Palmer, *The Indian Political System* (Boston: Houghton Mifflin Company, 1961), pp. 94–98, 208.

unitary governments? The answer to the first of these questions, according to Wheare, lies in a combination of factors present in all five instances:

> . . . in the modern federations some factors seem always to have been present. A sense of military insecurity and of the consequent need for common defense; a desire to be independent of foreign powers, and a realization that only through union could independence be secured; a hope of economic advantage from union; some political association of the communities concerned prior to their federal union . . . and similarity of political institutions. . . .[22]

The answer to the second question lies in the fact that in each of these five groups the previous independence of the federating units had instilled a habit of self-government and a tradition of local patriotism that they were unwilling to relinquish altogether; their mutual economic rivalries and traditional jealousies also precluded unitary organization. In Canada and the United States, furthermore, these particularist feelings were reinforced by differing social institutions that the federating governments were unwilling to submit to the mercy of an all-powerful national government: the splits between the French culture of Quebec and the British culture of the rest of Canada, and between the North and the South in the United States.

These elements were the main causes of federalism in each of the five instances that we are considering, but some political commentators, then and now, have also hailed federalism as a strong barrier against excessive government power in general. In Chapter 15 we noted that some writers have argued that unlimited government power is the mortal enemy of human liberties of conscience, expression, and property; they have proposed such devices as bills of rights and separation of powers to limit power. Some have also suggested that dividing power among two sets of governments in a nation will help to keep any one government from becoming powerful enough to crush civil rights. The eminent nineteenth-century British writer Lord Acton summed up this argument in these words:

> Of all checks on democracy, federation has been the most efficacious and the most congenial. . . . The federal system limits and restrains the sovereign power by dividing it and by assigning to Government only certain defined rights. It is the only method of curbing not only the majority but the power of whole people.[23]

However wide the appeal of such an argument, it is clear that in all five instances federalism was established mainly because the federating governments felt a need for the military, economic, and political advantages of a stronger union than "confederation" (see Chap. 12) yet were unwilling to surrender completely their identities and powers of independent action to unitary national governments. Federalism seemed to each an acceptable compromise between the equally undesirable extremes of confederation and centralism.

---

[22] Wheare, *Federal Government,* p. 37. See also Riker, *Federalism,* pp. 12–16.
[23] Lord Action, *Essays on Freedom and Power;* quoted in Herman Finer, *Theory and Practice of Modern Government* (rev. ed.; New York: Holt, Rinehart and Winston, Inc., 1949), p. 189.

## Constitutional Division of Powers

Each of the five federal governments we are considering has a written Constitution that allocates power to the national and local governments. In all the nations except Canada the Constitutions "enumerate" (list in fairly specific terms) the powers of the national government and assigns those left over ("reserved," or "residual," powers) to local governments. Only Canada enumerates the powers of the provinces and assigns the residual powers to the nation.

Some powers are granted exclusively to national governments, others exclusively to local governments, and still others "concurrently"—that is, to be exercised by both the national and local governments as long as they do not conflict. All five Constitutions have provisions for "national supremacy," according to which national law supersedes local law whenever national and local governments have passed conflicting laws in areas of concurrent jurisdiction. The Constitution of the United States, for example, declares,

> This Constitution, and the Laws of the United States which shall be made in Pursuance thereof; and all Treaties made, or which shall be made, under the Authority of the United States, shall be the supreme Law of the Land; and the Judges in every State shall be bound thereby, any Thing in the Constitution or Laws of any State to the Contrary notwithstanding. (Article VI, paragraph 2)

This paragraph states not that *any* national law supersedes *any* state law but only that any national law or treaty made "in pursuance" of the Constitution—that is, within the constitutionally assigned area of exclusive and concurrent powers—supersedes. Some such rule is included in each of the other federal Constitutions.

Among the most significant powers assigned to the national government, either exclusively or concurrently, in all five federal Constitutions are controlling relations with foreign nations; raising, supporting, and operating armed forces; declaring war and making peace; collecting taxes and levying import and export duties; regulating the movement of people and goods into, out of, and within the nation; and regulating economic matters that cross local boundaries.

Among the most significant powers generally assigned largely or exclusively to local governments are education, public health, criminal law, marriage and divorce, licensing of businesses, and regulation and administration of elections.[24]

## Representation of Local Governments in National Legislatures

Each of the five federal Constitutions makes some provisions for directly representing the local governments in the upper house of the national legislature. The United States, Switzerland, and Australia allow each "local" government, regardless of its

---

[24] See Wheare, *Federal Government,* chaps. 6–10, and H. R. G. Greaves, *Federal Union in Practice* (London: George Allen & Unwin Ltd., 1940), pp. 110–119.

size, an equal number of votes in the upper house; Canada and West Germany give the larger local governments more votes than they give the smaller ones. The United States, Switzerland (in most but not all cantons), and Australia are said to have "senate type" upper houses because their members are directly elected by the voters in each local unit. West Germany and Canada, on the other hand, are said to have "council type" upper houses, for their members are appointed—in West Germany by the governments of the various *Länder* and in Canada by the governor-general on the advice of the dominion prime minister. There is some reason to believe that a "council type" upper house strengthens the local governments more than does the "senate type."[25]

### Amending Processes

Because the Constitution establishes the legal division of powers, in an ideal or model federal government neither the national nor any local government should be able, by itself and over the objection of the other, to amend the Constitution to alter the division of powers. The amending procedures of the United States, Switzerland, and Australia approach this ideal fairly closely. The American Constitution has been amended only by joint actions by both sets of governments, in which the national Congress has passed by two-thirds votes of both houses amendments that have then been ratified by three-quarters of the states acting either through their legislatures (twenty-five times) or through special ratifying conventions (once). The other amending procedure, in which Congress, at the request of the legislatures of two-thirds of the states, calls a constitutional convention, which proposes amendments that are then ratified by three-quarters of the states, has never been used. In Australia and Switzerland the national legislatures propose amendments (in Switzerland an amendment may also be proposed by petition of 50,000 voters), which must be ratified in national popular referenda by "double majorities"—that is, both by majorities of all the voters voting in each nation *and* by majorities of the voters in each of a majority of the states or cantons.

Canada and West Germany, however, permit a kind of unilateral amendment by their national governments. In West Germany amendments become effective if approved by two-thirds votes in both houses of the national legislature, yet the Constitution prohibits any amendment affecting the status and powers of the *Länder*; in any case the members of the Bundesrat (the upper house) are appointed by and are responsible to the *Länder* governments, which gives the latter a substantial veto power over constitutional amendments.

Canada is farthest from the ideal of bilateral amendment. The British North America Act, which is the Canadian Constitution, is an act of the *British* Parliament and, for the most part, cannot be formally amended by any Canadian agency. The British Parliament, however, has always amended the act only by request of Canadian authorities and never on its own initiative. On most of the fourteen occasions on which it has amended the act since 1867, the British government has consulted the

[25] See Robert R. Bowie, "The Federal Legislature," in Bowie and Carl J. Friedrich (eds.), *Studies in Federalism* (Boston: Little, Brown & Company, 1954), pp. 8–10.

national authorities only and has not tried to determine the wishes of the provincial governments. The British government has made it clear that, if the Canadian governments can agree upon a method of amending the act, it will gladly turn the amending process entirely over to Canadians. As yet, however, Canada has been unable to agree upon the relative roles of the dominion and provincial governments in such amendments.[26]

## Umpiring National-Local Disputes

We noted in Chapter 18 that all laws are inescapably vague to some degree and therefore subject to differing interpretations by fallible human beings. This lesson certainly applies with full force to the clauses in federal Constitutions dividing powers between national and local governments; in all five nations there has been, and no doubt will continue to be, a great deal of controversy over questions of whether one government or the other has the constitutional power to engage in this or that activity.

Every federal nation has accordingly had to establish an "umpire" to decide all such disputes. In each of the five nations this "umpiring" function has been given to a national court: the Supreme Court of the United States, the Tribunal Fédéral of Switzerland, the Supreme Court of Canada (but not until 1949, previous to which the function was performed by the judicial committee of the British Privy Council), the Bundesverfassungsgericht (federal constitutional court) of West Germany, and the High Court of Australia. All five courts are empowered to overrule acts of local governments that they find in contravention of the national Constitutions, and four of the five are also authorized to overrule acts of the national government that they find ultra vires. Only in Switzerland is the Tribunal Fédéral required by the Constitution to uphold all acts of the *national* legislature and permitted to set aside only cantonal acts.

How impartial have these national umpires been? One may answer, As neutral and impartial as you could expect any umpire to be who is also a member of one of the competing teams! Although this quip may be an exaggeration, most political scientists agree that the settlement of national-local disputes by *national* judicial agencies in all five federal nations has had a great deal to do with shaping federalism in practice.

## FEDERALISM IN PRACTICE[27]

### Increasing National Power

Most students of federalism agree that in each of the five nations we are considering there has been considerable expansion of the national government's power from what

---

[26] See Edward McWhinney, "Amendment of the Constitution," in Bowie and Friedrich, *Studies in Federalism,* p. 793.

[27] The most thorough recent studies of American federalism in operation are Daniel J. Elazar, *American Federalism: A View from the States* (New York: Thomas Y. Crowell Company, 1966); and Michael D. Reagan, *The New Federalism* (New York: Oxford University Press, 1972).

was originally intended. In Switzerland this expansion has come about mainly through formal amendments to the Constitution, whereas in the other nations it has come about mainly through judicial interpretations favoring the national government. In all five nations the growth of national power has been a response to such developments as increasing national concern with wars and foreign affairs, nationalizing of economies and economic problems (as dramatized by great depressions), acceptance of the welfare state and insistence upon national minimum standards of social welfare, and the increasing importance of national over local patriotisms produced in part by technological improvement in communications and transportation.[28]

### Concern for State's Rights

By no means everyone in any of these nations has been entirely satisfied with the growth of national power, and in each there has always been and continues to be a substantial and vocal opinion that states' rights must be preserved against national encroachment.

This opinion, of course, can be partly accounted for as the perennial cry of the political party out of power in the national government, a handy stick with which to belabor the party in power; in the United States the Republicans, who from 1856 to 1933 were traditionally the strong centralist party, have since become the "states' rights" party during the long period as the minority party since 1933. It can also be explained as a convenient forensic gambit for those who believe in laissez-faire and wish *no* government to act in particular matters, fearing that the national government poses a greater threat than do local governments.

Yet, when "states' righters" of these two varieties are all accounted for, there unquestionably remains in each nation a number of people who fear that the increasing power of the national government will damage or destroy local self-govenment. In both Australia and Canada, accordingly, several royal commissions have been appointed to investigate the proper spheres of activity for the national and local governments. In the United States in recent years several prominent political scientists have written on this question,[29] and in 1953 Congress authorized and President Dwight D. Eisenhower appointed a commission on intergovernmental relations to determine which functions are proper for the nation and which for the states.

The reports of the commissions and the conclusions of the writers bear a striking similarity to the discussion, which we have noted, of local government problems in unitary systems. On one hand, they deplore local governments' loss of power and warn of the dangers of overcentralization, but, on the other hand, they are not prepared for any blanket reduction in national power, for such a move might fatally handicap the nation in dealing with the grave international and domestic problems it faces. The best answer they have come up with—perhaps the best answer there is—is a general solution based on the principle "to each government its own

---

[28] See Wheare, *Federal Government,* chap. 12.

[29] See Elazar, *American Federalism*; Reagan, *The New Federalism*; Leonard D. White, *The States and the Nation* (Baton Rouge, La.: Louisiana State University Press, 1953); and William Anderson, *The Nation and the States, Rivals or Partners?* (Minneapolis, Minn. University of Minnesota Press, 1955).

appropriate functions" and differing little, if at all, from Jefferson's beliefs quoted earlier in this chapter. The American commission's 1955 report rephrased this perennial standard:

> Leave to private initiative all the functions that citizens can perform privately; use the level of government closest to the community for all public functions it can handle; utilize cooperative intergovernmental arrangements where appropriate to attain economic performance and popular approval; reserve National action for residual participation where State and local governments are not fully adequate, and for the continuing responsibilities that only the National Government can undertake.[30]

Few Americans quarrel with any of these admirable propositions—but, unhappily, many Americans, like the commission itself, find them a great deal easier to state in general terms than to apply in concrete situations of national-state conflict.

The problem of intergovernmental relations in federal systems, then, is very much like that in unitary systems. As long as people continue to have loyalties to their local communities as well as to their national communities, neither problem is likely to be solved perfectly or permanently.

### Revenue Sharing

One reason why the national governments in the federal systems have grown more powerful vis-à-vis their subnational governments has been the former's greater financial resources. In the United States as in most of the other federations, the national Constitution has been much more permissive than the state Constitutions about the kinds and amounts of taxes that can be levied and funds that can be borrowed. As a result, the national governments have taxed more heavily, raised more money, and enjoyed greater freedom to raise even more. For example, in 1971 the national government of the United States collected $666 per capita in taxes, compared with a total of $460 for all state and local governments; and between 1950 and 1971 the national government collected 64 percent of all the nation's taxes and spent 55 percent of all government outlays. Part of the national government's expenditures was grants to the states: in 1971 Washington spent a total of $226 billion, of which $30 billion, or 13 percent, was allocated to the state and local governments as grants-in-aid.[31] But these grants had many different strings attached: they could be spent only for the purposes stipulated by the national government under standards laid down by the national government and enforced by national inspection. So in these grants the states served mainly as local paymasters for national programs rather than as developers and administrators of their own programs.

In 1972, however, the Nixon administration persuaded Congress to adopt a new "revenue sharing" program, which allocated $5.3 billion to the state and local governments with no strings attached, to spend as they wished, not as the national

---

[30] *Report of the Commission on Governmental Relations* (Washington, D.C.: U.S. Government Printing Office, 1955), p. 6.

[31] *The American Almanac, 1974*, pp. 410–413, 416–417.

**Revenue Sharing**
Source: "Nixon Rated
Cartoons" by Ranan
Lurie, published by
Quadrangle, the New
York Times Book Co.

Drawing by Ranan Lurie

Governmental Authorities
and Processes

government directed.[32] While some observers were skeptical about how wisely the states and localities would spend the money, most hailed the new program as an indispensable step toward the desired end of halting the steady growth of national power and beginning to restore a more even balance in the federal system.

## SOVIET NATIONALITIES AND FEDERALISM

The population of the USSR consists of seventeen different "nationalities," each with its distinctive homeland, language, history, and culture. They include Slavs, Turks, and Mongols; Russian Orthodox, Protestants, Jews, and Muslims; and many other cultural and ethnic groups. The "great Russian" nationality is the largest (129 million) and most powerful, but the others (perhaps those best known to outsiders are the 41 million Ukrainians, 9 million Belorussians, 9 million Uzbeks, 6 million Tatars, 3 million Georgians, 3 million Armenians, and 2 million Jews) play significant roles in the Soviet Union's national life.[33]

The 1936 Soviet Constitution established several levels of regional government: At the highest level and most analagous to the American states or German *Länder* are the fifteen union republics (for example, the Russian Soviet Federated Socialist Republic [RSFSR], the Ukraine, Belorussia, Kazakhstan, Uzbekistan). In addition there are nineteen autonomous republics (like the Tatar, Karelian, and Yakut republics); eight autonomous regions; and ten national areas (most of which are located within the RSFSR).[34] The Constitution lists the power of the national government (Article 14) and assigns the remainder to the union republics (Article 15). It also assigns to the latter the right to secede from the USSR (Article 17) and to enter into direct relations with foreign nations (Article 18a). The latter two provisions appear to make the Soviet Union even more decentralized than Switzerland is until we observe that the Constitution establishes no supreme court or other umpire to protect each level's assigned powers from encroachment by the other.

There is thus some doubt that the Soviet Union is even formally a federal state, as the term is used in this book. But there is no doubt of the realities. As one sympathetic Western observer has put it: "The USSR is not a federalism in the normal Western sense of the term. It is better described as a multi-national unitary state."[35] The Presidium of the Supreme Soviet has the formal power to annul any decree by a union republic's council of ministers. Each union republic's budget—including all provisions for taxation and appropriations—is drawn up by the Supreme Soviet, as are the budgets of the other subnational governments, and all are incorporated into one consolidated national budget. No union republic has its own source of revenue or the power to spend any funds except those authorized by the Supreme Soviet.[36]

---

[32] *Congressional Quarterly Weekly Report,* October 7, 1972, pp. 2630–2631.

[33] John A. Armstrong, *Ideology, Politics, and Government in the Soviet Union* (3d ed.; New York: Frederick A. Praeger, Inc., 1974), p. 188.

[34] See Randolph L. Braham (ed.), *Soviet Politics and Government: A Reader* (New York: Alfred A. Knopf, 1965), p. 269, Fig. 2.

[35] L. G. Churchward, *Contemporary Soviet Government* (London: Routledge & Kegan Paul Ltd., 1968), p. 167.

Far more important is the overriding fact that all effective power at all levels of government, regional and national alike, is held by the Communist Party of the Soviet Union. In its procedures for admission to membership and other organizational features the CPSU is highly centralized and closely controlled from Moscow; whatever may be the constitutional forms, the party holds a tight rein on government policy making at all levels.

During some periods the party has encouraged cultural autonomy and variety among the Soviet Union's nationalities, and during others it has followed a policy of linguistic, educational, and cultural "russification." But it has never allowed any significant local political or economic autonomy or variety. As a result, the government of the Soviet Union remains, despite its many nationalities, highly centralized in everything that matters politically.

## FEDERALISM: CURE FOR INTERNATIONAL ANARCHY?

In Chapters 23 and 24 we shall consider the international political system and political transactions *among* nations. International politics, as we shall see, resembles intranational politics in every major respect except one—but that one is of crucial importance. Unlike its national analogues, international politics has no government. In the vocabulary used in this book, it has no set of authorities capable of receiving the conflicting demands of its constituent actors (the world's independent sovereign nations) and converting them into authoritative allocations of values binding upon all the actors. The international political system is thus the clearest example we have of anarchy—politics without government.

Many political scientists, as we shall see, are convinced that international anarchy is the root cause of international wars and that war will never end until the United Nations becomes a true international government (which, for reasons that we shall explore, it is far from being at present). But the world's nations are endlessly varied in their cultures, languages, levels of political and economic development, and aspirations. Furthermore, most of them cherish national independence above all other political values and would not dream of surrendering it to a world government in whose power most would have only minor shares. How, then, can anyone seriously propose world government as the cure for international anarchy and war?

The answer, some believe, lies in adapting the domestic institution of federalism to the needs of the international political system. After all, they argue, the experience of nations like Canada, India, Switzerland, the Soviet Union, and the United States shows that it is possible to bring together peoples of substantially varied cultures, languages, and local loyalties in larger units whose federal governments combine central management of common problems and interests with high degrees of autonomy for local problems and interests. If they can do it, so can—and must—the world.[37]

---

[36] John N. Hazard, *The Soviet System of Government* (4th ed.; Chicago: University of Chicago Press, 1968), pp. 93–94.

[37] Two leading manifestos for world federalism are Clarence K. Streit, *Freedom against Itself* (New

We shall examine the "world federalists'" case and their critics' rejoinders in Chapter 24. It seems appropriate, however, to conclude this section of our survey of domestic political systems by noting that what we have learned about federalism; about other domestic political and governmental institutions, and about the economic, social, and psychological forces shaping them, provides the best intellectual basis that we have for understanding and dealing with the perils and possibilities of international politics.

York: Harper & Row, Publishers, 1954); and Norman Cousins, *In Place of Folly* (New York: Harper & Row, Publishers, 1961).

# VI

# POLICY OUTPUTS AND IMPACTS

# 20

# POLICY OUTPUTS: WHAT MODERN GOVERNMENTS DO

Most of us do not hold public office, buttonhole government officials in lobbies, or punch doorbells and lick envelopes in election campaigns. We thus have little or no firsthand knowledge of our political system's "conversion," or policy-making, processes, but know government mainly through the outputs of its various agencies as they impinge directly upon our lives. The school board builds primary and secondary schools, hires teachers and janitors, and directs truant officers to keep us in school until we are sixteen. Local clerks dispense marriage licenses, and perhaps local courts grant divorces. Other government officials license our automobiles, businesses, and dogs. And so on.

None of us, however, has been personally touched by *all* the policy outputs of all the governments with some jurisdiction over us. We may thus be tempted, like the blind men who examined the elephant, to think that the particular outputs we have experienced firsthand constitute everything—or at least everything important—that our governments do. No student of political systems should succumb to such a temptation, for one of the traits that make government such a uniquely pervasive and significant institution in modern life is the incredible variety and volume of its policy outputs. And in every modern nation one of the most durable and hotly disputed political issues is the perennial controversy over what government *should* do.

We noted in Chapter 2 that this book emphasizes political inputs and governmental "conversion processes" more than policy outputs and outcomes, for the former have been the focus of most political science research in recent years, and we simply know more about policy processes than about policy contents. Yet no survey of governing in the 1970s would be complete without some attention to what modern governments "produce." Furthermore, most citizens—unlike most political scientists, at least in their professional roles—are understandably and properly more concerned with the contents of public policies and their impacts than with the processes by which the policies are made.

In this chapter we shall survey some of the leading issues and points of view in the continuing dispute over what governments should do, outline what governments actually do, and consider the general role of government in modern life.

## WHAT SHOULD GOVERNMENT DO?

Some political controversy in any modern democratic system, as we have seen in previous chapters, is related to the forms and procedures of government. By far the largest proportion, however, centers on questions of what government should and should not do. Most of the political arguments that we hear and engage in at dinner parties and over back fences, read about in newspapers, and witness on television involve such matters as whether or not the government should deploy an antiballistic missile-defense system, force school desegregation by bussing pupils, outlaw cigarettes, and the like. To most of us this sort of controversy is the part of politics that really matters.

I shall not attempt anything so ambitious (and foolhardy) as offering a final disposition here of all arguments about the proper activities of government. I shall merely offer a few guideposts and warning signs that may assist readers to find their own way through the difficulties of this apparently permanent political dispute.

### SPECIFIC ISSUES AND GENERAL DEBATE

#### The Specific Nature of Government Outputs[1]

Every output produced by a modern government consists of a series of specific activities to which, for the sake of convenience, we customarily give a general label. When, for example, we speak of "government regulation of private motorists," we are referring to a series of episodes in which a policeman flags down a private motorist and gives him a ticket, after which a justice of the peace assesses a fine of so many dollars, which the motorist (usually) pays. When we speak of "foreign aid," we have in mind a series of episodes in which American government representatives in nations like Western Samoa, Brazil, and Turkey take money provided by American taxpayers and appropriated by Congress and give it to the officials of those foreign nations to buy food, tractors, lathes, and the like. Our mental picture of "policy outputs" is likely to be more accurate if we remember that each label pinned to an output refers to a series of specific actions.

#### The Specific Nature of Political Issues

As we noted in Chapter 3, everything that any government does—every policy it adopts and every action it takes—is a response to the demands of some political

---

[1] In this chapter, as in most of the book, we are interested mainly in domestic rather than foreign policy. The latter is considered in detail in Chaps. 23 and 24.

interest group over the objections of other such groups. Every government policy is controversial; simply because a particular policy is followed does not mean that everyone in the nation agrees that it should be followed. Some policies, of course, are more controversial than others. Far fewer people in the United States, for example, actively oppose free public education than actively oppose economic aid for foreign nations or racial integration of public schools. But some Americans—for instance, the publisher of a national chain of "freedom newspapers" with outlets in California, Colorado, and elsewhere—oppose even free public education.

Ultimately, therefore, all political conflict in the United States or any other nation revolves around *specific* issues: whether or not this particular person should go to jail, whether or not that particular corporation should be prosecuted for monopoly, whether or not that particular squadron of B-52s should drop bombs on Hanoi, and the like. We may customarily refer to these issues in general terms: "enforcement of law and order," "antitrust policy," "foreign policy," and so on. But it is well to remember that these general phrases refer to specific activities and issues and that the payoff in politics is what government actually does, not the general words that we use to describe what it does.

### Tangible and Symbolic Outcomes

In recent years political scientists have increasingly accepted Murray Edelman's thesis that government outputs produce outcomes of one of two quite distinct types, tangible and symbolic.[2] A tangible outcome, in Edelman's scheme, has mainly a visible impact upon some person or persons' material circumstances: It confers or confiscates economic wealth, prevents or encourages certain overt behavior, imprisons or frees, takes life, and so on. A symbolic outcome, on the other hand, has an impact mainly upon some person or persons' internal psychological state. It induces fear or reassurance, distrust or confidence, humiliation or pride, or the like.

It is common—and highly misleading—to think of politics as a struggle among people and groups competing exclusively for tangible benefits like higher wages, larger profits, government contracts, freedom from the draft, and so on. Such a view simply does not explain a great deal of human political behavior. For example, the Paris talks about ending the Vietnam war deadlocked for weeks in early 1969 over the issue of the shape of the negotiating table. The Americans and the South Vietnamese wanted a rectangular table, with their representatives seated on one side and those from North Vietnam and the National Liberation Front (Vietcong) on the other. The latter insisted on a circular table, with each of the four groups in its own position. Many observers, understandably eager for the parties to get on with negotiating peace, were disgusted by the long haggling over this issue. "What possible difference can it make?" they asked. "How silly can you get?" And, certainly, where the negotiators sat had no relevance to such pressing tangible issues as troop withdrawals, bombing halts, and elections. Nevertheless, the seating issue had great symbolic importance for all four parties: Sitting around a circular table would imply American and South Vietnamese recognition of the NLF as an independent body equal to each

---

[2] Murray Edelman, *The Symbolic Uses of Politics* (Urbana, Ill.: University of Illinois Press, 1964).

of the others in status and bargaining position. The argument continued until it was finally settled by a compromise: There would be a large circular table flanked by rectangular secretarial desks, creating one axis; the communists would sit on one side of that axis and the noncommunists on the other. As a logical arrangement it seemed a trivial solution to a trivial problem, but as a practical compromise it passed the critical test: All the parties agreed to it, and the negotiations turned to more tangible matters.

Another example of conflict over symbolic outcomes is the recurring clash in many states and municipalities over "loyalty oaths" as a condition of employment for teachers in public schools and universities. The patriotic groups who press for such requirements rarely argue that the oaths will be useful in detecting and rooting out subversives. After all, no one had advocated that everyone be required to take an oath that he has not and will not commit adultery, for example, and no one believes that such an oath would help to smoke out actual or potential adulterers. Yet the advocates of loyalty oaths feel strongly that teachers should be willing—indeed proud—to swear publicly that they are loyal to their country and do not advocate or favor its overthrow. If they are not willing, advocates of the oath feel, they are not fit to teach our children. The opponents of loyalty oaths are quite aware that signing them will not materially affect what or how teachers teach, but they feel strongly that requiring teachers to take oaths—while clergymen, businessmen, bartenders, operators of gambling casinos, and almost everyone else are not required to take them—singles out teachers as less reliable, less patriotic, and more in need of public confession of faith than are other citizens. The perennial struggles over loyalty oaths are fought fiercely by both sides—no less fiercely because they involve policies with symbolic rather than tangible outcomes.

People no doubt live by bread, but they certainly do not live by bread alone. Any policy output that affects them either tangibly or symbolically is bound to shape their lives. Therefore, as students of politics we must not be misled into thinking of either a tangible or a symbolic outcome as more "real" than the other.

### General Issues in Political Debate

Political debate in modern nations is to some degree conducted in general ideological terms. For example, advocates of progressive income taxes usually say something like "Such a tax makes for a more equitable distribution of income, and thus helps the nation avoid dangerous extremes of individual wealth and poverty." Its opponents usually reply in the vein of "Such a tax confiscates part of what a successful person earns and thus penalizes initiative and ability." Both groups may also argue about the proper size of surtaxes at upper-income levels, but they are likely to devote much of the debate to the more general question of whether or not *any* sort of income tax is desirable and just. So it is with just about all political debate—in fact, there is a danger that we may focus our attention on general issues so exclusively that we forget what really matters in politics: the specific, concrete activities that government does or does not undertake.

The most durable and frequently debated general issue was defined by British philosopher-politician Edmund Burke: "What the state ought to take upon itself to direct by public wisdom, and what it ought to leave, with as little interference as possible, to individual discretion."[3] In most of the democratic nations the debate over this perennial issue has revolved around the positions denoted by the terms "laissez-faire," "socialism," and "the welfare state." Each of these terms has two related but distinct meanings: Each is a descriptive label applied to a certain general pattern of government activity, and each refers to an ideology of how a government can best help its citizens achieve the good life. Let us examine both the descriptive and ideological aspects of each term.

## LAISSEZ-FAIRE

### "Laissez-Faire" as a Descriptive Term

It is said that Louis XIV's great finance minister, Jean Baptiste Colbert, once asked a meeting of French entrepreneurs what the state could do to help them. One answered, "Laissez-nous faire!" ("Let us alone!"). He thus gave a name, "laissez-faire," to both a condition and an ideology. Descriptively the term generally refers to situations in which there is minimum government interference in the lives and activities of private citizens, particularly in their economic activities. The government provides the basic conditions for free competition among its citizens by maintaining law and order, enforcing contracts, protecting private property, and defending the nation against attacks by other nations. Within these limits it allows competition to function freely and unregulated. *It neither holds back the successful nor helps the unsuccessful.*

### Laissez-Faire as an Ideology

The doctrine that "that government is best which governs least" was first enunciated in the seventeenth and early eighteenth centuries by such writers as the English philosopher John Locke and a group of French economists known as the Physiocrats (whose title meant something like "those who believe in rule according to nature"). Its most famous and influential exposition was *The Wealth of Nations,* a book published in 1776 by the Scottish professor Adam Smith. The case for laissez-faire may be summarized as follows. Society, like the physical universe, is a rationally designed, sensible, orderly mechanism governed by natural laws. These laws of social order are, like the laws of physical order, knowable by human reason, and some of them—for example, the law that prices in a freely competitive market are determined by the interplay of supply and demand and Gresham's law that bad money will drive good money out of the market—are already known. A nation that ignores or flouts these laws in shaping its economy will encounter disaster as surely as a person who ignores and flouts the law of gravity. If government attempts to regulate and restrict economic competition, hamper the efficient and successful, or help the inefficient and unsuccessful, it can only blunder and upset the delicate but perfectly adjusted balance of the natural economic system; the whole nation will suffer and be the poorer for it.

---

[3] *The Writings and Speeches of Edmund Burke,* Vol. 5 (Boston: Little, Brown & Company, 1901), p. 166.

The best economic policy that government can pursue, therefore, is to leave the economy strictly alone.

Some advocates of laissez-faire have carried the doctrine to its logical extreme, which is anarchy. After all, if that government is best which governs least, then the best government of all must be one which governs not at all. This position is, indeed, essentially that taken by the nineteenth-century English reformer Thomas Hodgskin and the twentieth-century American novelist and essayist Ayn Rand.

On the other hand, Adam Smith, like many other writers who have expounded the doctrine of laissez-faire, was perfectly willing to accept some deviations from the strict hands-off rule. He believed, for example, that government should not let any citizen, no matter how inefficient, starve. He also believed that government should regulate production and consumption in whatever ways necessary to ensure adequate defense against foreign attack. He added, however, that such deviations are justifiable only on humanitarian and nationalistic grounds; from the standpoint of strict *economic* efficiency, they are indefensible and should therefore be undertaken only when absolutely necessary.

## SOCIALISM

### *"Socialism" as a Descriptive Term*

The term "socialism" has been widely used in political discourse since the early nineteenth century. Unfortunately, it resembles terms like "democracy" and "freedom" in that, even in a purely descriptive sense, it means different things to different people and for most is highly charged with emotional connotations. To many people in many parts of the world it connotes equality, justice, the end of exploitation of the poor by the rich, and other equally noble traits. To many Americans, on the other hand, it connotes government confiscation of property, regimentation of individual life, red tape, inefficiency, coddling the lazy and incompetent, and a lot of other bad things. Its status as a "smear word" in the United States is well illustrated by one of the American Medical Association's more effective ploys in its long (but eventually losing) fight against proposals for compulsory health insurance (now called "medicare"): labeling them "socialized medicine."

In this book, however, the term is used as most political scientists use it, to denote a system in which most or all of a society's means of production, distribution, and exchange are owned by the society as a whole and administered in the interests of all.

### *Socialism as an Ideology*

There are many varieties of socialist doctrine, and some socialists devote a great deal more energy to pointing out the ideological errors and organizational sins of rival brands of socialism than to criticizing laissez-faire capitalism. Despite many and often bitter disagreements among themselves, however, all socialists have a sufficient number of beliefs in common that we may speak of socialism as a general ideology. John H. Hallowell defines those beliefs as follows:

There are many varieties of socialism but all socialists agree that the principal source of evil in the world is the institution of private property and all, although in varying degrees, advocate the common ownership of all the means of production as the cure. All advocate the transformation of private property into public property and the division of the income from such property in accordance with individual needs.[4]

### Socialists versus Communists

The main schism in modern socialism is between socialists and communists; the main disagreement between the two camps is over the question of *how* private property should be abolished and government ownership and operation of the economy established and maintained.

The socialists—including adherents of such groups as the British Labour party, the French and American Socialist parties, and the West German and Scandinavian Social Democratic parties—place a high value on democracy, as well as on socialism. They hold that socialism should be brought about only by such democratic and peaceful means as the organization of socialist political parties, their victory in elections and consequent capture of control of democratic governments, and the peaceful adoption and enforcement of socialist economic policies. In recent years, indeed, their fervor for the abolition of private property has generally yielded to less doctrinaire and more pragmatic programs of piecemeal social reform.

From its origins in the writings of Karl Marx and Friedrich Engels in the mid-nineteenth century to the death of Joseph Stalin in 1953, orthodox communist doctrine held, first, that true socialism can be established, as it was in Russia in 1917, only by violent revolution and the liquidation of unrepentant capitalists; second, that it can be maintained only through dictatorship of the proletariat and monopoly of power by Communist parties; and, third, that the Soviet Union must be the center and the Communist Party of the Soviet Union the commander of the world communist movement and all Communist parties and policies in other nations must unquestioningly follow the Soviet leaders' "line."

During that period, accordingly, socialists and communists occasionally collaborated with each other against a common enemy, as in the "popular front" against fascism in Western Europe in the 1930s. But most of the time they were in bitter conflict, for each saw the other as the betrayer of true socialism. Some of the communists' toughest opponents have been socialists like Chancellor Willy Brandt of West Germany, leader of the German Social Democratic party in the 1960s and early 1970s, and Hugh Gaitskell, leader of the British Labour party from 1955 to 1963.

### Schisms in Modern Communism

Since 1945 the monolithic, Moscow-commanded world communism of Lenin and Stalin has developed a number of deep, perhaps irreparable, fissures. In 1948 the

---

Policy Outputs: What
Modern Governments Do

[4] John H. Hallowell, *Main Currents in Modern Political Thought* (New York: Holt, Rinehart and Winston, Inc., 1950), pp. 368–369.

**Communist fragmenta-
tion near its borders
concerns the USSR.**
Source: *The Herblock
Gallery* (New York: Simon
and Shuster, Inc., 1968).

*"I don't care what 'the other kids' are doing—you can't
wear that outfit!"*

**World communism is no
longer monolithic: Sino-
Soviet confrontation on
the Ussuri River, 1969.**
Source: Wide World
Photos.

Policy Outputs and
Impacts

Communist dictator of Yugoslavia, Marshal Tito, refused to accept Moscow's over-lordship of Yugoslavian affairs, and Stalin expelled him and his party from the world movement. In 1949 the Chinese communists under Mao Tse-tung won complete control of mainland China and launched a policy of radical collectivization at home, aggressive expansion abroad, and war to the death with capitalism as the only proper course for communism. In 1953 Stalin died, and his eventual successor, Nikita Khrushchev, increasingly emphasized a policy of "peaceful coexistence" with the capitalist West. In the late 1950s and early 1960s the differences between the Chinese and Russian versions of communism sharpened and deepened, and the adherents of each began to attack each other more and more openly and virulently, finally breaking openly in 1963. The Chinese hailed Khrushchev's overthrow in 1964 as a great victory for their branch of the faith, but Russia's new leaders, Leonid I. Brezhnev and Alexei Kosygin, soon proved equally hostile to Maoism. The communists' internal cold war heated up considerably in early 1969, when Russian and Chinese troops fought several small but deadly battles for possession of an island in the Ussuri River, which marks their common border in one part of East Asia. In the early 1970s both sides sought advantage by cultivating good relations with the United States, long regarded by both as the arch-capitalist nation and therefore the archenemy of communism. By the mid-1970s it became quite clear that world communism had become something very different from the monolithic Moscow-commanded global movement of the period before 1948.[5]

## THE WELFARE STATE

### *"Welfare State" as a Descriptive Term*[6]

The term "welfare state" has been widely used in political discourse only since the early 1940s and is therefore much newer than either "laissez-faire" (which dates from the early 1700s) or "socialism" (which dates from about 1830). It generally denotes a government's guaranteeing to all its citizens certain minimum conditions of the good life: formal education, medical care, economic security in old age, housing, protection against loss of jobs or business, and so on.

A welfare state differs from a laissez-faire state mainly in that the latter guaran-

---

[5] For discussion of changes in the USSR since Stalin, see Carl A. Linden, *Khrushchev and the Soviet Leadership, 1957–1964* (Baltimore, Md.: The Johns Hopkins Press, 1966); and Alexander Dallin and Thomas B. Larson (eds.), *Soviet Politics since Khrushchev* (Englewood Cliffs, N.J.: Prentice-Hall, Inc., 1968). For analysis of the general fragmentation of world communism, see Zbigniew K. Brzezinski, *The Soviet Bloc: Unity and Conflict* (rev. ed.; Cambridge, Mass.: Harvard University Press, 1967); and Ghita Ionescu, *The Politics of the European Communist States* (New York: Frederick A. Praeger, Inc., 1967). For examination of the split between China and Russia, see William E. Griffith, *The Sino-Soviet Rift* (Cambridge, Mass.: M.I.T. Press, 1964).

[6] For useful general discussions, see Maurice Bruce, *The Coming of the Welfare State* (London: Batsford, 1961); Wayne Vasey, *Government and Social Welfare* (New York: Holt, Rinehart and Winston, Inc., 1958); Alfred de Grazia and Ted Gurr, *American Welfare* (New York: New York University Press, 1961). For a critical examination of the adequacy of American guarantees, see Gilbert Y. Steiner, *Social Insecurity: The Politics of Welfare* (Skokie, Ill.: Rand McNalley & Company, 1966).

*The laws of Moses and the laws of today*

tees to its citizens the opportunity to compete with one another for the good things of life but no guaranteed share in those good things. On the other hand, a welfare state, some of its opponents to the contrary, is not identical with socialism. It may provide some of the guaranteed minimums by socialistic means—free public schools, for instance—or it may provide them by such nonsocialistic (and also non-laissez-faire) means as government subsidies to war veterans for attendance at privately owned and operated schools, as in the G. I. Bill of Rights.

### The Welfare State as an Ideology

Advocates of the welfare state argue that every citizen is entitled to minimum conditions of the good life as a matter of right and justice and that no citizens should be denied them because they cannot finance them out of their own resources—even less because their parents cannot finance them. They do not all agree, of course, on the exact type and level of benefits that ought to be guaranteed. Some, for example, would include complete medical care "from the womb to the tomb," whereas others would include only hospitalization insurance. Some would include free public education for qualified students through the Ph.D. degree, whereas others would limit the guarantee to the high-school diploma. All welfare-state advocates agree, however, that the proper function of government is to provide every citizen with some degree

Policy Outputs and Impacts

of formal education and medical care even if it requires—as it usually does—that the rich be taxed to provide benefits for the poor.

In a sense, the welfare state represents a middle position on a scale with perfect socialism at the left extreme and perfect laissez-faire at the right. Perhaps it is not surprising, then, that government outputs in most developed nations add up to something more nearly resembling the welfare-state model than the socialist or laissez-faire model. The point to remember, however, is that no government's outputs constitute complete socialism or complete laissez-faire. All are mixtures of various models, mixtures in which the relative proportions vary, to be sure, but mixtures all the same. The ideological choice that nations face in fact (though perhaps not in rhetoric) is not "Shall we have socialism or laissez-faire?" It is, rather, "Shall we have *more* or *less* socialism or laissez-faire than we have now?" Recognizing this fact may not lower the political temperature of society, but it will certainly sharpen the political vision of its citizens.

## WHAT GOVERNMENTS DO IN THE UNITED STATES

Modern governments do a great deal. If we could compile a complete list of all the functions performed by all the world's governments today, it would undoubtedly include activities that directly and powerfully affect just about every conceivable aspect of human life—marriage, the rearing of children, education, the production and distribution of wealth, religion, art, sport, and so on ad infinitum.

Such assertions, however, are too general to mean very much. They do not provide a vivid sense of the enormous scale and seemingly endless variety of things that governments do. We shall therefore gather some sense of the scope of government operations from a brief listing and classification of the major activities now conducted in the United States by one or another of its local, state, and national governments. The United States makes a convenient case study, for its governments engage in fewer activities than do those of some developed nations (for example, Sweden, Great Britain, and Denmark) and more than do others (for example, Switzerland).

Government operations can be classified in several different ways, depending upon which aspects one is most interested in. As we are interested here mainly in the *content* of government outputs, we shall use three main categories: regulations, subsidies, and services.[7]

---

[7] Theodore Lowi has suggested classifying policy outputs according to their social impacts rather than their declared contents. He suggests three basic categories: *distributive* policies (those by which government gives goods to one part of the population without seriously depriving another part), *regulative* policies (those by which government restrains one segment of the community without directly aiding or hindering another), and *redistributive* policies (those that take goods away from one part of the community and give them to another part). Lowi believes that each "policy arena" has "its own characteristic political structure, political process, elites, and group relations"; see Theodore Lowi, "American Business, Public Policy, Case-Studies, and Political Theory," *World Politics,* 16 (July 1964), pp. 677–715. It is a stimulating idea, but his categories have not yet been much used for empirical research, and it is therefore difficult to say whether or not they are more useful than the policy-content categories presented in this text.

Policy Outputs: What
Modern Governments Do

# REGULATIONS

As the term is used in this book, a government regulation is a restraint or prohibition upon individual or group behavior that is disapproved by government. In the United States government regulations fall into two main subcategories.

## GOVERNING PRIVATE COMPETITION

1. Enforcement of contracts and the granting and protection of copyrights and patents
2. Control of the exchange of stocks and bonds
3. Prohibition of unfair competitive practices like false advertising
4. Prohibition of unfair labor practices by employers or unions
5. Enforcement of antimonopoly laws, corporation income taxes, excess-profits taxes, and the like, in an effort to prevent excessive concentration of economic power
6. Control of banking procedures, reserve funds, accounting, and so on
7. Control of the volume of currency, credit, and prices; initiation of public works; and the like, in an effort to prevent extreme fluctuations in the business cycle

## AFFECTING GENERAL SAFETY, WELFARE, AND MORALS

1. Detection, capture, trial, punishment, and rehabilitation of lawbreakers
2. Enforcement of safety standards in the construction of buildings, roads, bridges, harbors, airports, and the like
3. Enforcement of safety standards in the operation of all forms of public and most private transportation
4. Enforcement of health and sanitation standards in the production, labeling, and distribution of food and drugs
5. Enforcement of professional qualifications through the examination and licensing of doctors, nurses, pharmacists, lawyers, architects, teachers, pilots, and so on
6. Enforcement of rules governing private exploitation of mineral, forest, wildlife, and other natural resources
7. Prohibition of pollution of air, water, and other aspects of the environment
8. Enforcement of moral standards in production and distribution of liquor, drugs, gambling, movies, books, magazines, and television and radio programming
9. Prohibition of racial discrimination in education, registration and voting, employment, housing, use of public recreational facilities, and so on
10. Minimum-wage and maximum-hours laws
11. Limitation of aliens' access to professions and employment
12. Control of the spread of infectious and epidemic diseases by such means as quarantines
13. Zoning and antibillboard regulations to preserve the aesthetic qualities of parts of the environment

## SUBSIDIES

In this context a *subsidy* is a direct or indirect government subvention to a private person or group to enable him or it to purchase goods and services.

*Television, Radio Industry: Since cigarets are a menace to public health, I hereby propose to ban their advertising through your media.*

*Tobacco Industry: In keeping with our subsidy programs, the following is the money you will receive this year . . . in round millions, of course . . .*

## DIRECT

1. Gifts of land and facilities for construction of railroads, ships, aircraft, nuclear power plants, and the like
2. Crop loans and purchases to maintain "parity" price levels
3. "Fair trade" laws to maintain retail price levels
4. Construction and financing of rural electrification facilities
5. Payments to keep agricultural land out of production
6. Unemployment and workmen's compensation
7. Contributions to social-security old-age and survivors' insurance and to medical insurance for the elderly
8. Housing and income assistance for the elderly
9. Training and income assistance for the physically and mentally handicapped
10. Medical assistance for war veterans
11. Aid to dependent children
12. Scholarships and fellowships for students

## INDIRECT

1. Tariff charges on imported goods that compete with American goods
2. Research on materials, design, production, marketing, and so on, and dissemination of findings to private users
3. Construction and improvement of harbors, airports, navigable streams, canals, and highways
4. Construction and operation of air- and water-navigation aids
5. Public housing and rent subsidies
6. Guarantees of bank deposits and home-construction loans
7. Public works

Policy Outputs: What Modern Governments Do

8. Employment exchanges
9. Support of construction and operation of private schools and hospitals
10. Soil reclamation and leasing of reclaimed land to private users
11. Below-cost insurance for veterans, railroad employees, ships, and airlines
12. Support of medical research and dissemination of findings

## SERVICES

A *service* is an activity or benefit directly produced by a government agency and made available to the citizen free of charge, below cost, or at cost—but certainly more cheaply than its equivalent from a private firm.

1. Maintenance of armed forces to protect American lives and property from foreign invasion
2. Public schools at all levels from kindergarten through university postgraduate and professional studies
3. Fire prevention and fire fighting
4. Flood control and generation of hydroelectric power
5. Maintenance of libraries, museums, auditoriums, playgrounds, golf courses, public parks, monuments and historical sites, zoos, and other recreational facilities
6. Conciliation and mediation in labor-management disputes
7. Mail delivery
8. Maintenance and operation of machinery for popular control of government: registering voters, printing ballots, providing election officials, determining and announcing results in primary and general elections and referenda
9. Maintenance of standard uniform weights and measures
10. Free maternity and child-development clinics
11. Public hospitals for drug addiction, leprosy, tuberculosis, and so on
12. Weather forecasting
13. Support of basic and applied research in the physical, biological, and behavioral sciences
14. Support of creative work in the arts

## THE ROLE OF GOVERNMENTS IN WESTERN NATIONS

### THE PASSING OF LAISSEZ-FAIRE

Whatever may be the relative merits of the three ideologies summarized earlier, it is clear that the actual outputs of governments in Western nations add up to something far closer to the welfare state or socialism than to laissez-faire.[8] Indeed, in most European nations even the general ideology and slogans of laissez-faire have lost most of their support and are defended by only a few small right-wing political parties.

---

[8] For useful accounts of the rise of laissez-faire in Western nations in the eighteenth century, its heyday in the first half of the nineteenth century, and its steady and universal decline since then, see Karl Polanyi, *The Great Transformation* (New York: Holt, Rinehart and Winston, Inc., 1944); D. W. Brogan and Douglas V. Verney, *Political Patterns in Today's World* (New York: Harcourt Brace Jovanovich, Inc., 1963), chap. 4; and Harry K. Girvetz, *From Wealth to Welfare* (Stanford, Calif.: Stanford University Press, 1950).

Policy Outputs and
Impacts

*"Daddy's little baby must be kept warm."*

Even the Conservative party of Great Britain, despite its (to Americans) somewhat misleading name, espouses a program that fully accepts such socialist measures instituted by the Labour party between 1945 and 1951 as public ownership and operation of coal mines, railroads, and medical services. No major group or political party in Great Britain or any European nation advocates a return to laissez-faire.

The United States is one of the few modern nations in which the general ideology of laissez-faire still commands a good deal of support. We still hear many Americans speaking in favor of "free enterprise" and against government "regimentation" and "meddling" in business. These themes are central to the post-1945 conservative movement in the United States, which has had considerable political success, including the nomination (but not election) of Barry Goldwater as Republican candidate for president in 1964.[9]

---

[9] Among the leading statements of the conservative position are Frank S. Meyer, *In Defense of Freedom: A Conservative Credo* (Chicago: Henry Regnery Company, 1962); and William F. Buckley, Jr., *Up from Liberalism* (New York: Ivan Obolensky, Inc., 1959). But conservatism, like socialism, has schisms; for a different version see Willmoore Kendall, *The Conservative Affirmation* (Chicago: Henry Regnery Company, 1963).

When we look behind the ritual endorsements of "free enterprise" to see how Americans feel about the performance of specific functions by their government, however, we find that no major group in American politics seriously urges the sort of laissez-faire expounded by Adam Smith. Many American businessmen, for example, urge the elimination or sharp reduction of such governmental *regulations* of business as minimum-wage and maximum-hours laws, excess-profits taxes, and price controls. But very few advocate the elimination or reduction of such governmental *aids* to business as protective tariffs, direct subsidies of the sort given to airlines and the shipping industry, and the many research and marketing services of the Department of Commerce. Many American farmers strongly oppose government regulation and restriction of crop yields, but very few advocate total abolition of all such government aids to farmers as price supports, rural electrification, and the Department of Agriculture's research and marketing services. Few Americans *act* as if they long for genuine "free enterprise," in which each person tries for unlimited success and risks complete failure and the government neither restrains the successful nor helps the failures. One writer has suggested that, regardless of how most Americans *talk,* they *act* as if they believe in "safe enterprise" rather than "free enterprise"—that is, they seem to prefer reasonable and secure profit levels guaranteed by government subsidies and government regulation of "cutthroat competition" to being permitted to risk complete failure in the hope of unlimited success.[10]

The United States probably still has more "free enterprise" than does any other major developed nation. But even here the ideology of laissez-faire has lost its prestige to such an extent that few individuals and groups and no major political party argue that government should do *nothing* to prevent depressions, cushion business failures, put a floor under agricultural prices, or feed the unemployed. The actual functions that American governments perform, as we have seen, go far indeed beyond those that they should perform according to the classical doctrine of laissez-faire.

## THE OMNIPRESENCE OF GOVERNMENT

Most of us are primarily interested, understandably enough, in those aspects of society that appear to have the most direct and visible impacts upon our own personal lives and fortunes. Accordingly, most of us pay considerable attention to courtship, marriage, parent-child relations, schools, churches, businesses, and the like. We have all had a great deal of direct personal experience with these social institutions, and we know that they have powerful effects upon our lives.

By the same standard, most of us should find government downright fascinating, for what "they" do in Washington and in our state capitals and city halls profoundly affects even the most ordinary and uneventful life in all sorts of ways. Most of us are born in government-regulated hospitals and delivered by government-licensed doctors. Government protects us against certain kinds of treatment by our parents. We spend most of our childhood and youth in government-supported schools. Our marriages and divorces are contracted under close government supervi-

---

[10] See Nathan Robertson, "What Do You Mean, Free Enterprise?" *Harper's Monthly,* 97 (November 1948), pp. 70–75.

sion. We enter and leave business, engage in professions, buy and sell property, and retire in conformity with a considerable body of government regulations. We may be ordered by government to serve in the armed forces and even to kill or die at the orders of government officials known as "military officers." When we have finally filled out our last forms and paid our last tax bills, we are buried in government-licensed cemeteries, and our estates—minus portions retained by government as inheritance taxes—are handed on to our heirs by probate courts and government-licensed lawyers. Clearly, government plays a major role at just about every main juncture of our lives.

## REASONS FOR THE ROLE OF GOVERNMENT

### Impersonality of Life in Western Nations

Government has not always been as nearly omnipresent in men's lives as it is in our time. In the eighteenth and early nineteenth centuries a great many people in all nations lived out their lives with only occasional direct contacts with police magistrates and tax collectors and no contact whatever with draft boards and social security cards. Since the middle of the nineteenth century, however, the governments of all modern nations have steadily increased the volume and variety of their activities and have played a role of ever-growing significance in the lives of their citizens.

Most political scientists believe that the root of this universal expansion lies in the changing nature of society itself. The nations of the eighteenth and early nineteenth centuries were predominantly rural, and social relations were conducted mainly in direct personal fashion. Most of our great-great-grandfathers lived on farms or in small hamlets.[11] They had face-to-face acquaintance with most of the people who directly affected their lives: their neighbors; the people who bought their produce; those who sold them their equipment, seed, drugs, clothing; and so on. In protecting themselves against maltreatment by their associates they relied to a considerable extent upon self-help. If they had been cheated or injured, they often obtained redress through their own efforts rather than through appeals to government officials to intervene on their behalf.

The nations of our time, on the other hand, have become predominantly urban, and most social relations are indirect and impersonal. We never see face to face most of the people who directly affect our lives, and we often do not even know the names of the people in the next apartment. Many of the people who make our cars, compound our drugs, buy our products, and bank our money live hundreds and even

---

[11] The 1790 U.S. Census reported that no city in the nation had a population of more than 50,000 and that 95 percent of the people lived in areas of less than 2500 population. The 1970 Census, in sharp contrast, reported only 27 percent of the population living in rural areas and 28 percent living in cities of more than 100,000 population. Even so, the United States was far more thinly populated than are most Western European nations: As of 1971 we had 22 people per square kilometer, compared with the Netherlands' 323, Belgium's 319, Japan's 283, West Germany's 239, and Great Britain's 228. *The World Almanac & Book of Facts, 1974* (New York: Newspaper Enterprise Association, 1974), p. 620.

thousands of miles away, and most of them remain anonymous and faceless to us. The impersonality of modern life results not only from the sheer size of the communities in which most of us live but also from the complexity and high degree of labor specialization that characterize modern national societies.

To illustrate this point, let us consider an episode in the life of John Doe, a typical American living in 1830, and compare it with a similar episode in the life of his great-great-grandson, John Doe IV, living in 1970. John Doe feels a little out of sorts one day and decides that he needs a spring tonic to pick him up. He goes over to the next farm to see Ezra Roe, who makes and sells tonic, and buys a bottle. After a few swallows Doe becomes sick, however, and he knows that Roe has cheated him. He returns, demands his money, and, when Roe refuses, uses his fists to convince Roe that he had better return it after all. Doe sees no reason to ask Judge Solon down at the general store to intervene, for he is used to handling such matters himself.

Five generations later John Doe IV feels under par and goes to the corner drugstore to buy a bottle of Ezra Roe's Scientific Blood Reconditioner. He takes a couple of swallows, becomes sick, and learns from his doctor that he has a mild case of poisoning from impurities in the reconditioner. He feels like hitting the man who caused him this trouble, but the person who compounded this particular bottle of reconditioner is one of 4000 workers employed at the Roe Drug Corporation factory in a city 800 miles away. John Doe IV simply cannot gain redress purely through self-help, and it never occurs to him to try. Living as he does in an impersonal society, he turns instead to government: He sues the Roe Corporation for damages and writes to his congressman, urging that the pure-food-and-drug laws be tightened to prevent further damage.

### The Need to Bridge Gaps

This little story illustrates why government has come to play so pervasive a role in Western life. Few of us can ever see, identify, or know most of the persons whose activities bear directly upon our lives. We therefore customarily turn to government to bridge the gap between them and ourselves. We are so accustomed to the intervention of government between us and our fellows that we hardly give it a thought.

Take, for example, the act of faith that we all commit when we swallow aspirin. We ask the druggist for aspirin, pay our money, and take the pills. But how many of us are skilled enough at analytical chemistry to be sure merely by seeing and tasting the pills that they do in fact contain aspirin, as the label says they do, instead of arsenic or some other poison? How, then, do we dare to take the risks involved in swallowing them? The answer is that we know, without even bothering to think about it, that the people who make the tablets are checked by government inspectors and that the firms that manufacture and sell them are required by law, under threat of heavy penalties, to state on the label the contents of each pill and whether or not it is poisonous or dangerous. We do not have to be skilled analytical chemists to take aspirin safely, for the government protects us from our own ignorance and from the impersonality of life in our society.

Government is omnipresent in Western life because the conditions of Western

**FIGURE 18**
The wide and varied role of modern government in our daily lives. The documents represented above are (a)social security card, (b)New York State automobile registration, (c)New York State marriage license, (d)New York State death registry, and (e)Federal tax return for employers.

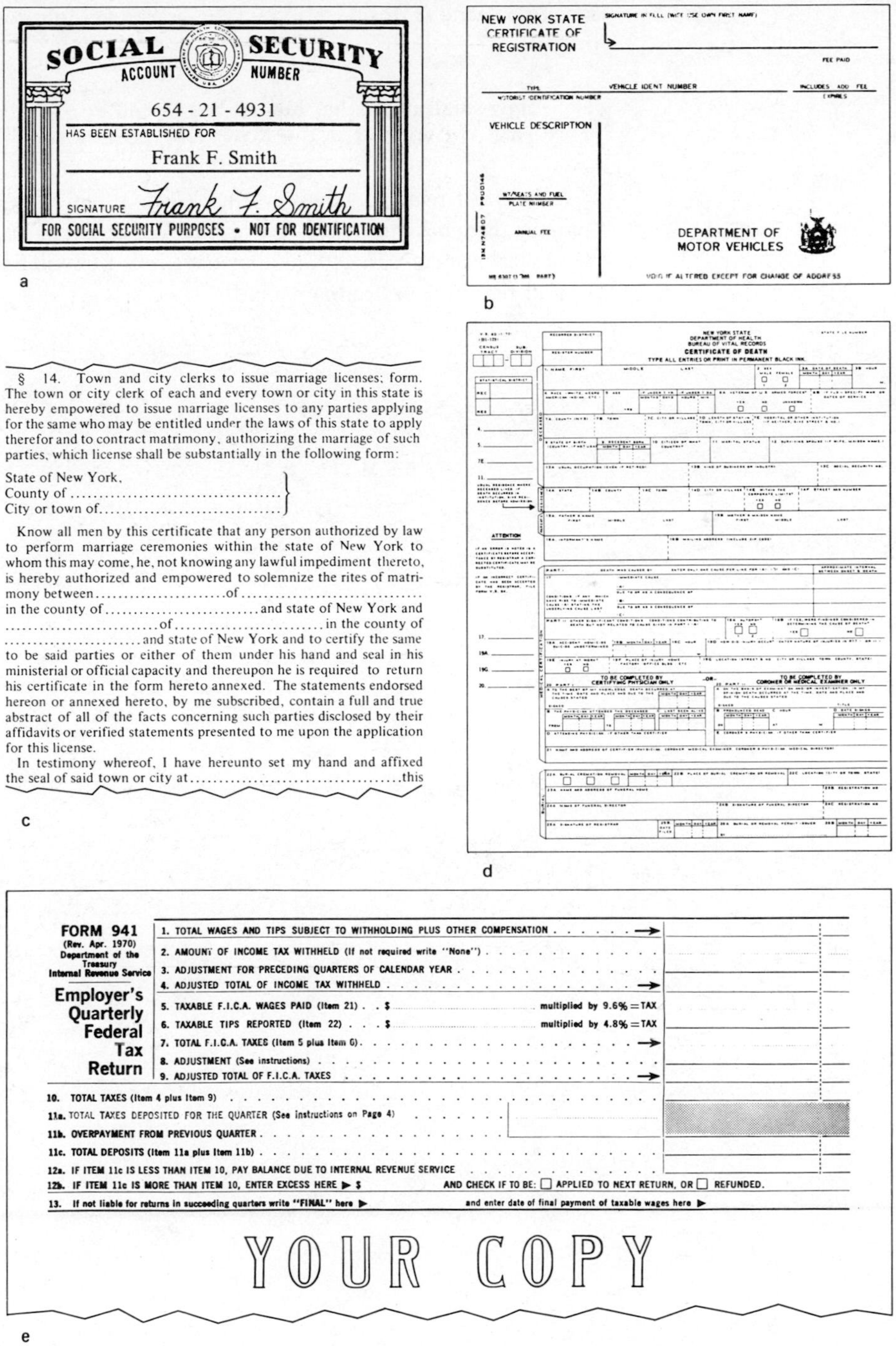

SOCIAL SECURITY
ACCOUNT NUMBER
654 - 21 - 4931
HAS BEEN ESTABLISHED FOR
Frank F. Smith
SIGNATURE *Frank F. Smith*
FOR SOCIAL SECURITY PURPOSES • NOT FOR IDENTIFICATION

a

NEW YORK STATE CERTIFICATE OF REGISTRATION
DEPARTMENT OF MOTOR VEHICLES

b

§ 14. Town and city clerks to issue marriage licenses; form. The town or city clerk of each and every town or city in this state is hereby empowered to issue marriage licenses to any parties applying for the same who may be entitled under the laws of this state to apply therefor and to contract matrimony, authorizing the marriage of such parties, which license shall be substantially in the following form:

State of New York,
County of ...................................
City or town of...............................

Know all men by this certificate that any person authorized by law to perform marriage ceremonies within the state of New York to whom this may come, he, not knowing any lawful impediment thereto, is hereby authorized and empowered to solemnize the rites of matrimony between.....................of...................................
in the county of...........................and state of New York and
..........................of...........................in the county of
.......................and state of New York and to certify the same to be said parties or either of them under his hand and seal in his ministerial or official capacity and thereupon he is required to return his certificate in the form hereto annexed. The statements endorsed hereon or annexed hereto, by me subscribed, contain a full and true abstract of all of the facts concerning such parties disclosed by their affidavits or verified statements presented to me upon the application for this license.

In testimony whereof, I have hereunto set my hand and affixed the seal of said town or city at.....................................this

c

NEW YORK STATE
DEPARTMENT OF HEALTH
BUREAU OF VITAL RECORDS
CERTIFICATE OF DEATH
TYPE ALL ENTRIES OR PRINT IN PERMANENT BLACK INK.

d

FORM 941
(Rev. Apr. 1970)
Department of the Treasury
Internal Revenue Service

**Employer's Quarterly Federal Tax Return**

1. TOTAL WAGES AND TIPS SUBJECT TO WITHHOLDING PLUS OTHER COMPENSATION . . . . . . ➤
2. AMOUNT OF INCOME TAX WITHHELD (If not required write "None") . . . . . . . . . . .
3. ADJUSTMENT FOR PRECEDING QUARTERS OF CALENDAR YEAR . . . . . . . . . . . . .
4. ADJUSTED TOTAL OF INCOME TAX WITHHELD . . . . . . . . . . . . . . . . . ➤
5. TAXABLE F.I.C.A. WAGES PAID (Item 21) . . . $ ............ multiplied by 9.6% = TAX
6. TAXABLE TIPS REPORTED (Item 22) . . . $ ............ multiplied by 4.8% = TAX
7. TOTAL F.I.C.A. TAXES (Item 5 plus Item 6). . . . . . . . . . . . . . . . . ➤
8. ADJUSTMENT (See instructions) . . . . . . . . . . . . . . . . . . . .
9. ADJUSTED TOTAL OF F.I.C.A. TAXES . . . . . . . . . . . . . . . . . . ➤
10. TOTAL TAXES (Item 4 plus Item 9) . . . . . . . . . . . . . . . . . . ➤
11a. TOTAL TAXES DEPOSITED FOR THE QUARTER (See instructions on Page 4) . . . . . . .
11b. OVERPAYMENT FROM PREVIOUS QUARTER . . . . . . . . . . . . . . .
11c. TOTAL DEPOSITS (Item 11a plus Item 11b) . . . . . . . . . . . . . . .
12a. IF ITEM 11c IS LESS THAN ITEM 10, PAY BALANCE DUE TO INTERNAL REVENUE SERVICE
12b. IF ITEM 11c IS MORE THAN ITEM 10, ENTER EXCESS HERE ➤ $ ...... AND CHECK IF TO BE: ☐ APPLIED TO NEXT RETURN, OR ☐ REFUNDED.
13. If not liable for returns in succeeding quarters write "FINAL" here ➤ ...... and enter date of final payment of taxable wages here ➤

YOUR COPY

e

The Rights of Man:
Principles and Problems

society demand it. It may still be true, as Samuel Johnson wrote two centuries ago, that

How small of all that human hearts endure
That part which Laws or Kings can cause or cure.

The fact remains, however, that Western nations and the human beings who compose them have turned to "Laws or Kings" as the principal means for putting into effect whatever cures they think they have found or will find in the foreseeable future for "all that human hearts endure."

# 21

# THE RIGHTS OF MAN: PRINCIPLES AND PROBLEMS

To begin with, you and I and everyone in the world have our own private selves. Whatever other people may tell us or we reveal to them, we know that we understand better than anyone else how we really feel about things. Indeed, the sum of our private beliefs and doubts, loves and hates, pleasures and pains, desires and fears *is* us. Most of us at some point in our lives, to be sure, undergo "crises of identity": We are unsure about how we really feel about things, about what is truly right and wrong, about who we really are. But that each of us has *some* identity that is truly ours alone is the very core of our existence.

Yet each of us lives in a world of other people and other identities—parents, siblings, teachers, schoolmates, employers, friends, opponents, compatriots, foreigners, and so on. We learn very early in life that a good deal of what they say and do impinges on and limits what we say and do—and vice versa. We may not like it, but there it is—and the only way out is the hermit's way.

As a result, the basic problem of people-in-society is how best to adjust the expressions and reticences of our identities with those of others' identities. How can a student square his passion to read straight through the novels of Albert Camus with his economics professor's assignment of 100 pages of Keynes for tomorrow's class? How can a man accommodate his wife's passion for a new sofa to his own longing for a case of La Tâche? How can a person square a longing to live a nonmaterialistic life with the necessities of making a living? How can one individual effectively express opposition to another's advocacy of laws prohibiting abortions without violating the latter's right to express those opinions?

This basic problem of people-in-society gives rise to a prime problem that every government confronts: How much, in what ways, and under what conditions may government legitimately limit the expressions and invade the privacy of individual identities in order to promote its conception of the general welfare? The world's governments deal with this problem in many different ways, most of which arise from one or another of the three general philosophies—liberalism, communism, and the New Left—on which we shall focus in this chapter.

## THE LIBERAL CONCEPTION OF HUMAN RIGHTS

### WHAT IS A CIVIL RIGHT?

Most people properly associate the terms "civil rights" and "freedom." What, then, is freedom? As Roger H. Soltau has pointed out:

> Originally to be free was not to be a slave, to have legal guaranteed control over one's person and this is still its essential meaning. To be free is not to be prevented from doing what one wants to do, and not being forced to do what one dislikes doing. Any limitation of this two-fold power is an interference with freedom, however excellent its motives, however necessary its action.[1]

Yet in every democracy, however constitutional or libertarian, everyone's freedoms are, by general agreement, subject to many limitations. Many parents spank small children for using profanity, but few consider the children's freedom of speech violated. Governments prohibit anyone from selling narcotics to high-school pupils, but no one says that the freedom to engage in the business of one's choosing has been wrongfully limited. Governments also prohibit devotees of one religion from murdering the followers of another, yet no one protests that freedom of religion has been abridged. Evidently a person's civil rights include only some freedoms; they are not a blank check to act as one pleases in all circumstances without any external restraint.

What kind of freedom, then, is a civil right? As the term is used in this book, it is *a constitutionally defined and governmentally protected area of freedom for individuals.* Civil rights fall into two general classes: *limitations on government,* things that government is forbidden to do to the individual, in order to preserve "those opportunities, the absence of which would deprive him of something essential," and *obligations of government,* a series of duties that government is pledged to perform for the individual, to preserve "those liberties without which man cannot be at his best or give of his best—what is needful to the adequate development and expression of his personality."[2] Before we consider the specific areas of freedom generally included in these two categories, however, we must first examine the principles underlying the liberal conception of the rights of man and take stock of some considerations that have impelled constitutional governments to establish and protect civil rights.

---

[1] Roger H. Soltau, *An Introduction to Politics* (London: Longmans, Green & Co., Ltd., 1951), p. 127.

[2] Soltau, *An Introduction to Politics,* p. 135.

Policy Outputs and Impacts

> We hold these truths to be self-evident, that all men are created equal, that they are endowed by their Creator with certain unalienable Rights, that among these are Life, Liberty and the Pursuit of Happiness.—That to secure these rights, Governmments are instituted among Men, deriving their just powers from the consent of the governed,—That whenever any Form of Government becomes destructive of these ends, it is the Right of the People to alter or to abolish it, and to institute new Government, laying its foundation on such principles and organizing its powers in such form, as to them shall seem most likely to effect their Safety and Happiness.

These winged words are, of course, taken from the opening sentences of the American Declaration of Independence. Drafted mainly by Thomas Jefferson and adopted by the Continental Congress of the rebel American colonies on July 4, 1776, this document is probably the most widely known, succinct, and eloquent statement of the liberal philosophy of the rights of man. Just about everyone who accepts this philosophy bases his conviction on one or a combination of two positions: First, civil rights are ends in themselves, and their preservation is the main function of government and the main reason for its existence; second, civil rights, though not necessarily ends in themselves, are indispensable means for the creation and maintenance of the good life and the good society. Let us briefly examine each position.

### Rights as Ends

Nearly all who argued and fought for civil rights in England and America in the seventeenth and eighteenth centuries did so out of deep commitment to the first of the two positions stated. Probably its most influential exponent was the English political philosopher John Locke. In the brilliant and widely read two treatises *Of Civil Government* (1690), Locke raised the central question, Under what circumstances and for what reasons should men obey the commands of government? The answer, he argued, must be based on the fact that men join together in civil societies and establish governments for only one reason: to secure more firmly the personal rights to life, liberty, and property that naturally belong equally to all men simply because they are human beings. As he put it, "The great and chief end . . . of men uniting into commonwealths, and putting themselves under government, is the preservation of their property [that is, their natural rights]."[3] When a government fails to preserve these rights and thus ceases to serve the end for which it was created, Locke continued, the citizens have the right—indeed, the duty—to overthrow it:

> Whenever the legislators endeavour to take away and destroy the [rights] of the people . . . they put themselves into a state of war with the people, who are thereupon absolved from any farther obedience, and . . . have a right to resume their original liberty, and by the establishment of a new legislative (such

The Rights of Man:
Principles and Problems

[3] John Locke, *Two Treatises of Civil Government* (London: J. M. Dent & Sons, Ltd., 1924), p. 180.

as they shall think fit) provide for their own safety and security, which is the end for which they are in society.[4]

Locke's convictions were known and shared by most of the American rebel leaders and became the basic justification of the Declaration of Independence. "Governments are instituted among Men," The Declaration proclaims, "to secure these rights . . . whenever any Form of Government becomes destructive of these ends, it is the Right of the People to alter or to abolish it."

Locke's position was also affirmed by the Declaration of the Rights of Man and of the Citizen proclaimed by the revolutionary French National Assembly on August 26, 1789:

> The aim of every political association is the preservation of the natural and imprescriptible rights of man. These rights are liberty, property, security, and resistance to oppression. . . . Any society in which the guarantee of the rights is not secured, or the separation of powers not determined, has no constitution at all.[5]

The most recent expression of Lockean ideas is the Universal Declaration of Human Rights adopted by the United Nations in 1948. Articles 1 and 2 of that document proclaim:

> All human beings are born free and equal in dignity and rights. They are endowed with reason and conscience and should act towards one another in a spirit of brotherhood. Everyone is entitled to all the rights and freedoms set forth in this Declaration, without distinction of any kind, such as race, color, sex, language, religion, political or other opinion, national or social origin, property, birth or other status. . . .[6]

But on what basis could Locke or anyone else assert that human rights are ends in themselves, that they morally precede government itself? The answer is that Locke and his disciples were committed to one of the oldest and most influential ideas in Western political philosophy: the doctrine of the law of nature. There have been several different versions of this doctrine. Philosophers of natural law have disagreed, for instance, about its source. Some have held that it consists of a series of more or less specific commands by God prescribing how individuals should behave and how societies and governments should be organized and operated. Others—notably Locke and his followers—have taken the view that God created nature and that the law of nature is in a general way implicit in His grand design rather than articulated in specific divine moral injunctions. Philosophers have also disagreed about the sanctions enforcing the law of nature. Some have held that a person or a society violating its commands will soon come to disaster on this earth as divine punishment for

---

[4] Locke, *Two Treatises of Civil Government,* p. 229.

[5] Reproduced in Herman Finer, *Governments of Greater European Powers* (New York: Holt, Rinehart and Winston, Inc., 1956), p. ix.

[6] "The Universal Declaration of Human Rights," *UNESCO Courier,* December 1963, pp. 16–17.

disobedience. Others have held that, though retribution may not come in this life, it will surely come in the Hereafter. Still others have regarded natural law as a matter of how individuals and societies *should* behave; consequently they have not dealt with the question of divine or other sanctions by which people may be forced to obey its commands.

Finally, liberal philosophers have not agreed on precisely what rules of political behavior the law of nature prescribes. In the seventeenth and eighteenth centuries, however, most of them did agree that natural law makes every human being the equal of every other human being at least in the sense that each has an "unalienable" right to the enjoyment of his or her own life, liberty, and property as his or her personal capacities permit. They also believed that people cannot satisfactorily secure their rights in a "state of nature" (anarchy), for when one must rely solely on one's own strength to preserve one's rights there is always the danger that the physically strong may abridge the rights of the weak. To secure their rights, therefore, people enter mutually into a "social contract" to form a society and erect a government that, by pooling the strength of many individuals, will better protect the rights of each against threats either from outside or from within the society.

Some philosophers believed that, in actual historical fact, all societies had been created by such "contracts" at some time in the past. They apparently assumed the existence of many ancient versions of the famous episode in November 1620, in which the Pilgrim fathers signed their compact in the cabin of the *Mayflower* anchored off the coast of New England. Others, however, used the "contract" as a rhetorical device for emphasizing their belief that the only rightful government is one based upon the free consent of its individual citizens and not upon any moral obligation of the living to perpetuate what has been passed on to them by the dead.

All these philosophers believed, however, that any government that, once established, abridges the people's rights thereby violates the law of nature and loses all moral claim to obedience from its citizens. Securing the rights of man, in short, is *the* purpose of government, because it is what God or the law of nature commands.

### Rights as Means

For better or worse the doctrine of the law of nature has far fewer adherents in our time than it had in 1776 and 1789. Under the influence of such more recent philosophies as utilitarianism, positivism, and pragmatism a great many philosophers and ordinary citizens have come to believe that such laws of nature as may exist are purely descriptive and not prescriptive or moral. These laws are only ways of describing certain recurring patterns of behavior; they tell us how physical phenomena—and perhaps human beings also—*do* behave, but they have and can have nothing to say about how people *should* behave. When modern mankind in bewilderment cries "What should I do?" the heavens do not reply.

If people can no longer rest the doctrine of the rights of man upon its original philosophical foundation, what have they left? Nothing, according to some philosophers. They argue that the only values and beliefs people will live by and, if need be, defend to the death are those they believe to be ordained by God or nature—that is, by some power greater than people's own conscience. Many people once believed that God and the law of nature command the protection of human rights, and they fought and died to secure these rights. But most moderns no longer believe that God or nature tells them clearly whether or not they should value human rights or anything else. They cannot be counted on to defend those rights, for they have no compelling philosophical or psychological motive for doing so. Unless free peoples revive their traditional belief in God and nature as the source of human rights, these philosophers conclude, the institutions and freedoms originally stemming from that belief may well follow it onto the ash heaps of history.

If this argument is correct, the future of civil rights in the free nations looks bleak indeed, for there seems little chance that many modern citizens will return to their forebears' belief in a law of nature as a guiding principle. Some modern writers, however, claim that declining belief in a moral natural law has not deprived the doctrine of human rights of all philosophical basis or stripped modern persons of reasons and motives to protect those rights. Instead they believe the doctrine can rest upon a new philosophical foundation at least as satisfactory as the old one. It consists mainly of three basic ideas.

**The Human Source of Human Values**   The crucial issue is whether or not people live by and fight for only those values and beliefs they believe are imposed upon them by some superhuman and extraworldly agency. Many modern philosophers argue (and many ordinary citizens believe) that nature does not tell us how we should behave and that we ourselves must therefore generate our own values and moral beliefs. Is that enough? These philosophers believe that it is. They argue that the important test of moral beliefs is, after all, whether or not we act consistently and courageously in accordance with them, whatever their source. Talk, however moral and elevated in tone, is cheap. The payoff is how we *act,* not how we talk. Judged by this standard, those who invoke no supernatural agency as the source of their moral beliefs are no less moral or courageous than those who do. In the particular instance of human rights, these writers submit, a great many modern citizens deeply believe in and fight for the preservation of such rights because they are human beings and because their personalities, life experiences, and instincts make unbearable the thought of living in a world or a society in which human beings are considered no more precious than cattle or gold. They believe in the supreme value of the individual.

**The Primacy of the Individual**   Many modern defenders of the rights of man rest their defense upon belief in the supreme value of the individual. Springing from such diverse sources as ancient Greco-Roman Stoicism (c. 300 B.C.) and more recent developments in the Jewish and Christian religions, this doctrine holds that all human beings, whatever their individual differences, are precious and that each has immense potential for good. A prime goal of all human societies should therefore be to permit and encourage the growth of each person and the realization of his or her potential to the fullest possible extent. All human institutions, including government, should be judged by the degree to which they help or hinder achievement of these goals. "People," in short, " are the measure of all things"—especially of society and government. The main purpose of the latter is to provide them with the most favorable environment possible for their full spiritual growth. Guarantees of the opportunity freely to form and express their own consciences are a prime element in such an environment.

But why should we believe in and act upon propositions that we do not believe ordained by nature? The only possible answer, these writers reply, is that we commit an act of faith. People who commit such an act give themselves up to a certain conviction not because they can scientifically, empirically, or even logically prove that it is correct but because they feel that it must be true and do not wish to live in a world where it is not true. After all, belief in the existence of God and in a moral natural law is also an act of faith, in the sense that there is no scientific or empirical proof that either exists. They conclude that the question for each individual is not one of choice between faith and certainty but one of *which* faith he or she finds easier to accept and live by. Many people today have found it easier to accept on faith the preciousness of the individual than to choose to believe in a moral law of nature.

**The Best Test of Truth**  Every nation, modern defenders of civil rights add, seeks to pursue policies best calculated to achieve whatever values it may hold. Discovering just which of the many policy proposals put forth are best is one of the greatest problems facing any government. Experience has shown that the most effective way to solve this problem is to permit advocates and critics of each proposal to argue their ideas freely, for in the long run good ideas and proposals will win public acceptance over bad ones.

The argument that the best test of truth is its ability to defeat falsehood in the competitive marketplace of ideas was first offered by the English poet and pamphleteer John Milton, in his famous pamphlet *Areopagitica* (1644). In his attack upon efforts by the English government to suppress the printing of subversive literature, Milton argued:

> And though all the winds of doctrine were let loose to play upon the earth, so Truth be in the field, we do injuriously, by licensing and prohibiting, to misdoubt her strength. Let her and Falsehood grapple; who ever knew Truth put to worse, in a free and open encounter? . . . She needs no policies, nor stratagems, nor licensings to make her victorious; those are but the shifts and defences that error uses against her power.[7]

A more recent but equally eloquent statement of this pragmatic argument for civil rights is the famous dissent by Justice Oliver Wendell Holmes, Jr., in *Abrams* v. *United States* (1919). In support of his view that Congress should suppress the advocacy of unpopular opinions only in conditions of extreme national danger, Justice Holmes wrote:

> But when men have realized that time has upset many fighting faiths, they may come to believe even more than they believe the very foundations of their

---

[7] John Milton, *Areopagitica and Other Prose Works* (London: J. M. Dent & Sons, Ltd., 1927), pp. 36–37.

own conduct that the ultimate good desired is better reached by free trade in ideas—that the best test of truth is the power of the thought to get itself accepted in the competition of the market; and that truth is the only ground upon which their wishes safety can be carried out. That, at any rate, is the theory of our Constitution. It is an experiment as all life is an experiment. Every year if not every day, we have to wager our salvation upon some prophecy based upon imperfect knowledge.[8]

### Which Position Is Correct?

Most present-day advocates of civil rights are convinced that the arguments just summarized are more than adequate and that one need not be committed to historic conceptions of natural law in order to believe in and vigorously defend the rights of man. The really difficult theoretical and practical problem of civil rights, they are convinced, is not their philosophical justification but the construction of sensible and reliable standards for determining how far such rights may extend when they conflict with the needs of modern governments to preserve internal order, protect the rights of one group of private citizens against the aggressions of other groups, and defend national institutions and independence against the onslaughts of other nations and ideologies that have only contempt for both the idea and the practice of civil rights. We shall return to these problems in the next chapter.

The debate that we have just reviewed is a single aspect of one of the oldest and most difficult problems in philosophy: What is and what should be the source of the ultimate moral values of individuals and societies? This problem has engaged the attention and energies of the greatest philosophical minds for centuries and continues to do so in our own time. As we have seen, no consensus, no single answer has yet emerged. It would therefore be highly presumptuous of me to label one of the two general positions outlined "correct." For the purposes of this book it is enough to recognize that they exist and that different people have at least somewhat different reasons for wishing to preserve human rights.

## THE FORMAL DESIGNATIONS

What *are* the rights of man? What specific areas of individual freedom are defined and guaranteed by the various constitutions of modern nations? We may begin to answer these questions by noting that every modern constitution contains at least some formal guarantees of civil rights. Needless to say, not every formal guarantee in each nation's constitution represents a genuinely protected right of the people living under the particular authority: But the mere presence of formally guaranteed rights in any nation's constitution means at least that the framers, for whatever reasons, deemed it desirable to pay at least lip service—and perhaps more—to the idea of the rights of man. I therefore list them here.

---

[8] Oliver Wendell Holmes, Jr., dissenting opinion in Abrams v. United States, 250 U.S. 616 (1919).

## LIMITATIONS ON GOVERNMENT

Protections of belief and expression[9]
> religious worship*
> speech*
> press*
> secrecy of correspondence*
> preservation of distinct subnational languages and cultures

Protections of action
> assembly*
> petition*
> suffrage*[10]
> secrecy of votes
> prohibition of slavery*
> practice of chosen profession
> privacy of domicile*
> movement within and to and from the nation
> organization of labor unions and trade associations
> strikes
> collective bargaining

Protections for those accused of crime
> prohibition of bills of attainder*
> ex post facto laws*
> guilt by association
> unreasonable searches and seizures*
> trial without indictment*
> double jeopardy for the same offense*
> coerced confessions*
> excessive bail and fines*
> cruel and unusual punishments*
> extradition for political crimes
> capital punishment
> imprisonment for debt

Guarantee of writ of habeas corpus*
> "due process of law"*

---

[9] This list is taken from my survey of the various Constitutions reproduced in Amos J. Peaslee (ed.), *Constitutions of Nations* (2d ed.; 3 vols.; The Hague: Martinus Nijhoff, 1956). The asterisks indicate rights formally guaranteed by the Constitution of the United States. To explore the full meaning of each of these formal guarantees is a task far beyond the scope of the present chapter. The reader who wishes to find out more about their interpretation and application in the United States is advised to consult such works as Henry J. Abraham, *Freedom and the Court* (2d ed.; New York: Oxford University Press, 1972); Thomas I. Emerson and David Haber, *Political and Civil Rights in the United States* (4th ed.; 2 vols.; Buffalo, N.Y.: Dennis & Co., Inc., 1967); and any description and analysis of the current American constitutional system.

[10] Some Constitutions guarantee universal suffrage. The American Constitution, through the Fifteenth and Nineteenth Amendments, prohibits the denial of the right to vote to any person on account of race, color, previous condition of servitude, or sex.

speedy and public trial*
trial by an impartial jury*
confrontation of hostile witnesses*
subpoena power for the defendant*
assistance of counsel*
equality before the law or equal protection of the laws*
Protections of property rights
just compensation for private property taken for public use*
patents and copyrights*


## OBLIGATIONS OF GOVERNMENT

To provide economic assistance
work
equal pay for equal work, regardless of sex, age, nationality, or caste
minimum wages
maximum hours
unemployment assistance
social security
To provide social assistance
education
prohibition of child labor
protection of families, children, and motherhood
preservation of historical monuments
recreation and culture


## CHALLENGERS AND CHAMPIONS

### THE CLASSIC LIBERAL VIEW: GOVERNMENT AS ENEMY

We noted previously that most of the Constitutions written before World War I guarantee only rights of the individual against government. Their "bills of rights" contain only lists of actions that government is prohibited from taking against the individual; abridging freedom of speech and religion, conducting unreasonable searches and seizures, coercing confessions, and the like. The classical meaning of "civil right," in short, is something that a government may not do to an individual person. Government was viewed as the only real enemy of liberty.

This conception of civil rights was rooted in the conviction of John Locke and his disciples among the constitution makers of the eighteenth and nineteenth centuries that human beings are naturally free and that all government authority, as an artificial creation of people rather than a universal creation of nature, is inherently hostile to human freedom and must be watched suspiciously and vigilantly guarded against.

Locke and his followers also recognized, however, that people's rights are unsafe in a state of anarchy, for when human aggressions are entirely unrestrained there is an ever-present danger that the strong will ride roughshod over the rights of the weak. Some kind of government, they believed, is indispensable to protection of the rights of *all* persons. They thus faced a dilemma: The rights of man cannot be preserved without government, but government itself is inherently hostile to those rights. The only way out of this dilemma, they believed, is to organize government so that it will maintain law and order without abridging human rights; and the only way to do that, they were convinced, is to organize it according to their version of the ancient doctrine of constitutionalism (see Chap. 13). All "rightful" governments, they held, must operate within limits specified by Constitutions. Each Constitution, in turn, must firmly restrain government power by listing what government may not do (as in a "bill of rights"), carefully defining the areas in which it is authorized to act (as in a list of "enumerated powers") and confining it strictly to such areas, and establishing "separation of powers"—distributing government power among three separate and mutually independent branches of government, the legislative, executive, and judicial. In this manner, the "constitutionalists" of the eighteenth century believed, the power of government could be restrained sufficiently to minimize its inherent danger to the rights of man.

It is not surprising that Locke and his followers should have regarded government as the sole enemy of human rights. The governments they lived under were of the ancien régime, founded on such principles as the divine right of kings and the privileges of royalty and nobility over peasants and yeomen. The actual violations of human rights they knew about—the suppression of antimonarchy speeches and pamphlets, jailing and torture of opponents of the regime by the star chamber, and the like—were all committed by agents of authoritarian governments in the name of royal prerogatives and reasons of state. The only serious and visible threat to human rights in Locke's time was government; as a result his belief in the rights of man led him logically to the antigovernment doctrine of constitutionalism.

In modern times, however, the liberal democratic nations have instituted governments whose decisions are made not by autocratic monarchs and their lackeys but by popular majorities and their representatives. Yet a great many citizens of the modern democratic systems fear that popular majorities may on occasion try to smash the rights of unpopular minorities and that such tyranny must be guarded against no less vigilantly than must tyranny by monarchs or aristocrats. They believe that constitutional government is quite as necessary to the preservation of human rights against modern popular majorities—"silent" or otherwise—as it ever was to preserve them against the authoritarian governments attacked by Locke and Paine.

The various Constitutions of the American states and the national government written after 1776 were the first in modern times to attempt to put the doctrine of constitutionalism into practice. It soon became apparent that the new systems needed "watchdogs"—that is, agencies whose special duty and prerogative are to determine, whenever a question arises, whether or not any branch of government is exceeding constitutional limits. In the United States the courts, rather than the legislatures or the executives, took over this role by assuming the power of judicial review. As noted in Chapter 11, however, some free nations with constitutional governments have assigned the watchdog function to their legislatures rather than to their courts, and some nations whose Constitutions formally establish judicial review actually have governments that are neither free nor constitutional.

Whether or not they have the power of judicial review, the courts in all the free nations have a special role in the protection of civil rights, for a great many (though not all) of the conflicts over such rights are fought in cases at law. When a person is being tried for a crime, for example, the court must not only determine the defendant's guilt or innocence but also decide whether or not the requirements of a fair trial and due process of law are being respected in the framing of charges, jury selection, admission of evidence, and proper provision for counsel. When a court is deciding a libel suit brought by plaintiff A against defendant B, it must determine whether or not in the particular circumstances A's right to his good name has been unduly infringed by what B has written about him—and whether or not punishing B would abridge B's freedom of speech and press. Whereas the courts of only some free nations have the power to set aside laws as unconstitutional, the courts of all free nations necessarily have the power to interpret and apply in specific cases the laws and constitutional provisions guaranteeing civil rights. Court decisions and judicial interpretations thus constitute a significant body of data in discovering the actual status of civil rights in any free nation, whether or not its courts have the power of judicial review.

## THE MODERN LIBERAL VIEW: GOVERNMENT AS BOTH ENEMY AND ALLY

Most citizens of the modern free nations agree with their eighteenth- and nineteenth-century ancestors that human rights must be protected against certain kinds of oppressive government action. Unlike their forebears, however, they do not regard government as the only serious threat to those rights. They have come to believe that there are at least three additional kinds of threats, each of which is no less dangerous than government oppression and each of which can be countered only by enlisting the power and authority of government to protect the individual.

The first is aggression against the rights of national citizens by local governments. A good deal of the conflict over civil rights in the United States in recent years has arisen from efforts by certain state and local governments to impose racial segregation and white supremacy on all blacks. The Fourteenth Amendment to the national Constitution renders blacks, along with other native-born or naturalized citizens, citizens of the United States first and citizens of the states in which they reside second; furthermore, it stipulates that "no State shall make or enforce any law which shall abridge the privileges or immunities of citizens of the United States. . . ." To secure their constitutional immunity against being forced to live as second-class citizens, blacks, particularly in the southern states, have often turned to the national government as their principal ally against oppression by state and local governments. In Chapter 22 we shall examine this conflict and its results in detail, but this brief mention should serve to illustrate the point that most people no longer view government in Lockean terms as a monolith threatening the civil rights of all; it has come to be viewed as an aggregation of many different levels and agencies, some of which

American blacks turned to the national government for protection of their rights against some state governments: Birmingham, Alabama, 1963. Source: Wide World Photos.

may well be the only instruments powerful enough to protect human rights against infringement by others.

The second kind of threat is aggression against the rights of private individuals by other private individuals. The rights of people accused of crime to fair trials have many times been threatened by lynch mobs; the only effective protection of their rights lies in the ability and determination of law-enforcement officials to save them from the mobs for trial by the courts. The rights of blacks and Jews to live in houses and neighborhoods that they like and can afford are widely violated by restrictive covenants—private agreements among property owners to sell only to white gentiles; the right to decent housing can often be protected only by the passage and enforcement of open-occupancy laws prohibiting such agreements. The rights of members of any sexual, racial, or ethnic group to opportunities for jobs and promotions according to ability and training equal to those of WASPMs (white Anglo-Saxon Protestant males) are often abridged by private employers' policies; such employment rights can be secured only by the enforcement of fair employment-practices laws forbidding such discrimination. The rights of black children to attend unsegregated schools may be violated—as in Boston, Massachusetts, in 1974—by white mobs trying to overturn the buses carrying them to school; only the intervention of the police can secure the children's rights and perhaps even save their lives. In all these situations government, far from being the enemy of human rights, is their chief defender.

In Chapter 20 we noted the nearly universal acceptance in modern nations of the idea that all people have a right to at least the minimum conditions of a decent life for themselves and their families; the third kind of threat includes such ancient

The Rights of Man: Principles and Problems

Police as protectors of civil rights: South Carolina state troopers just after rescuing black children from a school bus tipped over by white supremacists, March 1970. Source: UPI Photograph.

hazards as unemployment, poverty, old age, illness, and, above all, ignorance. Here, too, most modern citizens look to government, not as their enemy, but as their main hope of overcoming these hazards.

Whether or not they have formally enshrined in their Constitutions this new conception of government as the protector of human rights, all modern democracies have clearly accepted the principle for many years and from time to time have brought new rights under government protection. We have noted that in the third category the principle of the welfare state and such of its guarantees as universal free public education and protection against starvation are so firmly established in all free nations that any effort to remove them is likely to be considered about as drastic an attack on the rights of man as would a proposal to repeal the constitutional guarantees of freedom of speech or fair trial.

Similar developments have occurred in the first two categories as well. In the United States as early as 1866 and 1870, for example, Congress enacted laws penalizing any individual who "willfully subjects any person to a deprivation of any rights or privileges secured by the Constitution or laws of the United States." For many years the enforcement of these laws was left in the hands of U.S. attorneys in various localities, and few people were prosecuted for violating them. In 1939, however, Attorney General Frank Murphy established the Civil Rights Section in the Criminal Division of the Department of Justice and charged it with undertaking more vigorous enforcement of the 1866 and 1870 laws. Since then the national government has played a far more active part in protecting human rights. The greatest single leap forward came when Congress passed the Civil Rights Act of 1964, which commits the national government to positive action to secure for all citizens full equality in

Policy Outputs and Impacts

their rights to register and vote, to be served by private businesses offering public accommodations, to use public facilities, and to enjoy equal job opportunities. We shall examine the act and its impact further in Chapter 22, but it should be noted here as the greatest triumph for liberalism in the United States since the ratification of the Bill of Rights.

## CHALLENGERS TO LIBERALISM

Since the rise of liberalism in the seventeenth century its ideas have often been challenged, and institutions designed to establish liberal systems have been undermined or overthrown. Many fascist regimes of the twentieth century—Francisco Franco's Spain, Antonio Salazar's Portugal, Benito Mussolini's Italy, Adolf Hitler's Germany, and François Duvalier's Haiti—have been explicitly antiliberal in philosophy and totalitarian in fact. In the last third of the twentieth century, however, the main challengers in thought and action are communism and the New Left. Let us breifly examine the ideas of each.

### Communism

The sixteen separate articles of Chapter X of the Soviet Constitution of 1936 enumerate "Fundamental Rights and Duties of the Citizen," which include many of the same rights dear to liberals: separation of church and state and religious freedom (Article CXXIV); freedom of speech, press, and assembly (Article CXXV); immunity from arbitrary arrest (Article CXXVII); and so on.[11] Yet everyone knows what Nikita Khrushchev himself revealed in his famous speech to the Twentieth Party Congress in 1956: For thirty years under Joseph Stalin's dictatorship secret arrests, torture, and execution without trial were the lot of anyone even suspected of harboring rebellious thoughts against the regime. Even in the post-Stalin "thaw" many novelists, poets, and pamphleteers have been exiled to "corrective labor camps" or committed to mental hospitals because of their alleged antiparty or antisocialist ideas. And when in 1968 the liberal-leaning communist leaders of Czechoslovakia allowed "dangerous" freedom of expression, resulting in "provocative" criticism of the Soviet leaders and system, Soviet troops and tanks invaded and effectively crushed the Czechs' nascent liberalism.

What, then, are we to make of the Soviet Constitution's guarantees of freedom? Are they mere verbal smoke screens to mask Russian leaders' naked and unrestrained power from ordinary Russians and the outside world? Or are they sincere but misleading expressions of what a liberal would regard as very illiberal ideas about human rights?

The answer is suggested by the following passage from a leading official exegesis of the Soviet "bill of rights":

> The fundamental rights of Soviet citizens are constitutional rights conforming to the interests of the working people of town and country. . . . When Soviet power was coming into being, not a single Soviet institution restricted any citizen

[11] An English translation is available in Randolph L. Braham (ed.), *Soviet Politics and Government: A Reader* (New York: Alfred A. Knopf, 1965), pp. 555–579.

*"Prison? This is an asylum, comrade, and that's Occupational Therapy."*

in his democratic rights. The bourgeoisie and the landlords took advantage of this and utilized the freedoms of speech, assembly and the press, together with all other political rights gained as a result of the October Revolution, for their counter-revolutionary ends. In their speeches and newspapers the enemies of the working people slandered the October Revolution and the Soviet Government. They interpreted the right to free association to mean freedom for all exploiters and traitors to set up their counter-revolutionary organizations. Similarly, the bourgeoisie and the landlords utilized the electoral rights for their anti-Soviet activity. They fraudulently infiltrated into the organs of the Soviet state, trying to undermine and corrupt them from within. The Soviet Government detected these criminal machinations of the enemies of the working people in good time and deprived them of political rights.[12]

Policy Outputs and Impacts

[12] A. Denisov and M. Kirichenko, *Soviet State Law* (1960), quoted in Braham, *Soviet Politics and Government,* p. 393.

Clearly the Soviets do *not* regard their guarantees of civil rights as protections of the individual's private and personal self against invasion by other individuals or by government. Like all other communist political institutions, they are regarded as tools for sustaining the Soviet regime at home and overthrowing anti-Soviet regimes abroad. For example, Article CXXV prefaces its guarantees of free speech, press, and assembly with this statement of their purpose: "In conformity with the interests of the working people, and in order to strengthen the socialist system, the citizens of the U.S.S.R. are guaranteed. . . ." As a leading Western scholar observes, "these 'liberties' are reserved for adherents and denied to opponents of the regime. Freedom, in the Soviet constitutional lexicon, is the duty to ratify the policies of the ruling group and not the right to criticize them."[13]

### The New Left

Most political science professors—especially those more than forty years old—are liberals of the old school in matters of human rights. Accordingly, many were surprised, upset, and often overwhelmed by such tactics of student protest movements of the 1960s as howling down speakers expressing "Establishment clichés," disrupting classes, occupying buildings, and destroying professors' files. They were even more upset when they realized that the protesters' New Left leaders openly denounced the traditional ideas and institutions of liberalism as hypocritical, irrelevant, or both. The New Left, then and now, make no bones about being antiliberal. The reasons for their contempt have been most carefully and thoroughly set forth by one of their favorite philosophers, Herbert Marcuse, essentially as follows.

Freedom of expression, he says, is not an end in itself but merely a means for achieving the "good society." Ideas that promote social progress therefore deserve expression, but those which block progress should be suppressed. Marcuse rejects Holmes's notion that the best way to discover the truth value of ideas is to let all be heard and undergo the test of competition with contrary ideas. After all, Marcuse says, we already know that war, racism, and poverty are evil. Yet the police, the courts, the mass media, the universities, and all the other Establishment institutions of our present society have so corrupted the masses that they are incapable of knowing and choosing what is right over what is wrong. In such a situation old-fashioned equal tolerance for all ideas inevitably means the victory of the worst.

What we need instead, Marcuse declares, is "repressive tolerance," or "liberating tolerance," which he defines as

> . . . intolerance against movements from the Right, and toleration of movements from the Left. . . . [which] would extend to the stage of action as well as of discussion and propaganda, of deed as well as of word.[14] . . . tolerance cannot be indiscriminate and equal with respect to the contents of expression, neither in word nor in deed; it cannot protect false words and wrong deeds which

---

[13] Merle Fainsod, *How Russia Is Ruled* (rev. ed.; Cambridge, Mass.: Harvard University Press, 1963), p. 378.

[14] Herbert Marcuse, "Repressive Tolerance," in Robert Paul Wolff, Barrington Moore, Jr., and Herbert Marcuse (eds.), *A Critique of Pure Tolerance* (Boston: The Beacon Press, 1969), p. 109.

demonstrate that they contradict and counteract the possibilities of liberation. Such indiscriminate tolerance is justified in harmless debates, in conversation, in academic discussion; it is indispensable in the scientific enterprise, in private religion. But society cannot be indiscriminate where the pacification of existence, where freedom and happiness themselves are at stake; here, certain things cannot be said, certain ideas cannot be expressed, certain policies cannot be proposed, certain behavior cannot be permitted without making tolerance an instrument for the continuation of servitude.[15]

A professor himself, Marcuse recognizes that restoring *true* freedom of thought (in his sense) "may necessitate new and rigid restrictions on teachings and practices in the educational institutions which, by their very methods and concepts, serve to enclose the mind within the established universe of discourse and behavior. . . ."[16] He ends by making clear how the new "liberating tolerance" can—and cannot—come to prevail:

The tolerance which is the life element, the token of a free society, will never be the gift of the powers that be; it can, under the prevailing conditions of

---

[15] Marcuse, "Repressive Tolerance," p. 88.
[16] Marcuse, "Repressive Tolerance," pp. 100–101.

tyranny by the majority, only be won in the sustained effort of radical minorities, willing to break this tyranny and to work for the emergence of a free and sovereign majority—minorities intolerant, militantly intolerant and disobedient to the rules of behavior which tolerate destruction and suppression.[17]

## CHOICES

There is no divine command or historical inevitability that liberalism will survive in the United States or anywhere else. Nor are its communist and New Left enemies the only problems that liberalism faces. Even if every fascist, communist, and Weatherman were to become a devoted liberal, liberalism would still face enormously complex and difficult problems in preserving human rights in modern industrial society. We cannot begin to understand these problems until we recognize that they all involve making painful choices among cherished—but competing—values.

The point may be illuminated by considering the two main kinds of choices that any government must make when dealing with human rights.

### FREEDOM VERSUS SECURITY

#### *The Problem*

One ever-recurring dilemma of government in a free nation arises from two facts: First, most citizens value both freedom and security—freedom for reasons outlined earlier in this chapter and security (governmental preservation of law and order) for reasons outlined in Chapter 3. Second, freedom and security are always in conflict, and whatever government does to promote one is likely to jeopardize the other.

Let us consider the conflicting claims of freedom and security in an example. A child is kidnapped and later found brutally tortured and murdered. The outraged townspeople demand that the murderer be arrested and punished immediately. The police turn up enough evidence to convince them that a tramp named John Doe is the murderer—but not enough to guarantee his conviction under the stringent rules of evidence used in American courts. So they arrest Doe "on suspicion" and "grill" him in an effort to make him confess, knowing that a confession added to the evidence that they already have will be sufficient to convict him. But Doe refuses to confess. The police are convinced that he is lying, and they know that giving him the "third degree"—beating him with a rubber truncheon, shining bright lights in his eyes while they question him until he breaks down, pressing lighted cigarettes on parts of his body—may force him to confess. The townspeople, meanwhile, fear that Doe will go free because of some "legal technicality" and that the hideous crime will go unpunished. Someone suggests taking a rope, dragging him out of jail, and hanging him to the nearest lamp post.

Now if security—punishing the guilty and deterring potential criminals—were the *only* value held by the townspeople and police, the question of what to do would be easily answered: Beat a confession out of Doe, or just string him up without a trial.

---

[17] Marcuse, "Repressive Tolerance," p. 123.

Even a person accused of the most heinous crime deserves a fair trial: Dallas, Texas, November 24, 1963. Source: Wide World Photos.

This course of action is, sad to say, no mere theoretical extreme dreamed up to make a point. In Brazil, for example, capital punishment was not legal until recently, and no convicted criminal ever served more than thirty years in jail. The police of Rio de Janeiro evidently felt that this practice amounted to unendurable coddling of the guilty, so they formed small secret bands (Esquadrão de Morte), which tracked down, tortured, and executed criminals who they thought had cheated the law.[18] Nor should North Americans feel self-righteous about such Latin barbarism. Not long ago in many parts of the South lynching was the accepted form of instant trial and punishment for blacks accused of capital crimes against whites. In the North there have been all too many cases in which prosecutors—despite their sworn duty to

Policy Outputs and
Impacts

[18] *Time,* April 25, 1969, p. 61.

protect the innocent as well as to prosecute the accused—have concealed and distorted evidence to build up their "conviction scores."[19] And the ugly, though still unproved, suspicions that some police departments have assassinated leaders of the militant Black Panther party are all too reminiscent of the Esquadrão de Morte.

In a nation with liberal traditions like the United States, however, punishing the guilty is only one of the values that people hold. The townspeople and police in our example have no wish to hang Doe if he is innocent. They must therefore choose which they value more: punishing the guilty or protecting the innocent. If they choose the former and torture or lynch Doe, they run the risk of punishing an innocent man; and if they choose the latter and give Doe all his constitutional rights to a fair trial, they run the risk of letting a murderer go unpunished. They cannot have it both ways; they have to take one risk or the other.

Most citizens of the liberal nations, then, are willing neither to sacrifice all security for absolute freedom nor to abandon all freedom for absolute security. In the free nations, accordingly, one ever-present problem is that of determining in specific instances just where the line should be drawn between the conflicting claims of freedom and security—for conflicting they will always be.

### Some American Standards for Drawing the Line

Recognizing that this kind of decision must be made in every concrete instance in which the question of government restraining human activity is involved, most of us would agree that it should be made according to the most just and sensible general standards we can devise. We certainly do not want to leave it entirely to the personal preferences of whatever law-enforcement officer happens to be around or whatever judge happens to be assigned to the case.

Yet we should recognize that such decisions are not and cannot be made in social vacuums in which the decision makers operate entirely free from any kind of political or psychological pressures for particular decisions. As we shall see in a moment, they are made by fallible human beings often operating under great and conflicting pressures. That being the case, we can learn a good deal about how civil rights decisions are made—and with what consequences—by focusing on some of the leading decisions made and issues pending in one such environment, the United States in recent years. That we shall do in the remainder of this chapter.

We may begin by noting that the U.S. Supreme Court has evolved several general standards for drawing the line between freedom and security. The best known are applicable to circumstances in which speech and writing may be suppressed without violating the First Amendment injunction that "Congress shall make no law . . . abridging the freedom of speech or of the press." The principal tests may be briefly summarized.[20]

---

[19] *Time,* March 31, 1967, pp. 72–73.

[20] The reader who wishes more information about the nature and application of these standards than can be presented in these short text summaries is advised to consult the lucid short description in James M. Burns and Jack W. Peltason, *Government by the People* (7th ed.; Englewood Cliffs, N.J.: Prentice-Hall, Inc., 1969), pp. 114–116.

**Clear and Present Danger** The decision in *Schenck v. U.S.* (1919) first ruled that speech and writing can be suppressed only when "the words are used in circumstances and are of such a nature as to create a clear and present danger that they will bring about the substantive evils that Congress has a right to prevent."[21] More specifically, speech may be suppressed only when it clearly has the potential of inciting to riot, assassination, subversion, or the like and when it is uttered in circumstances in which such eventualities are likely as a direct result of the utterance. The presumption is clearly against suppressing speech, and the burden of proof rests with those who would suppress it. This test, with occasional departures, has been generally followed by the Court in free-speech cases since 1919.

**FIGURE 19**
The "gravity of evil" test: when to allow and when to prohibit potentially dangerous speech and writing.

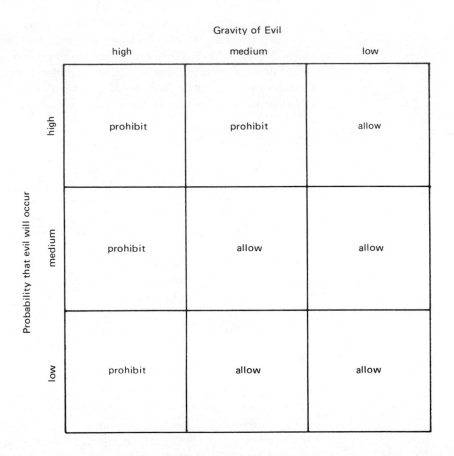

**Gravity of Evil** In its 1951 opinion (*Dennis v. U.S.*) upholding the conviction of eleven Communist party leaders for conspiring to advocate violent overthrow of the government, the Court took a somewhat different position. It held that freedom of speech can be invaded whenever "the gravity of evil, discounted by its improbability,

[21] Schenck v. U.S., 249 U.S. 47 (1919).

justifies such invasion . . . as is necessary to avoid the danger."[22] That is, if the evil that authority is trying to prevent would be very grave if it did come to pass, then words that *might* lead to it—even if the possibility is relatively slight—may be suppressed. This rather complicated judicial calculus may become clearer when presented graphically, as in Figure 19. Under the "gravity of evil" standard the presumption is far more in favor of suppressing speech than it is under the "clear and present danger" rule. The Dennis standard has been used by the courts in some post–World War II cases involving the advocacy of communist doctrines. In cases involving speech by people other than communists, however, the Court has sometimes followed one standard, sometimes the other. We shall inspect some of the details in Chapter 22.

## GROUP VERSUS GROUP, RIGHT VERSUS RIGHT

Some people try to resolve the dilemmas and escape the hard choices that liberty demands by declaring that "we all should be free to exercise our rights so long as we do not interfere with anyone else's rights." This aphorism has a comfortingly plausible air of sweet reasonableness about it, and its popularity is not surprising. The only thing wrong with it is that it seldom works. Why? Because, in most real-life situations, securing the rights of one group of citizens inevitably abridges the rights of other groups.

Consider, for example, one of the most difficult and acerbic civil-rights issues of the 1970s: the clash between the right of a woman to have an abortion to avoid having an unwanted baby, and the right to life of the fetus (or unborn child—even which term is proper is very much in dispute). Until the early 1970s most states had laws prohibiting abortions except when deemed necessary by physicians to save mothers' lives. However, in the 1960s and 1970s members of one wing of the women's rights movement (see Chap. 22) pressed with increasing vigor for the repeal of these laws. They insisted that every woman has a fundamental right to the control of her own body and that that right entitles her to terminate any unwanted pregnancy just as much as it entitles her to refuse any unwanted sexual intercourse. Their opponents argued, with equal moral fervor, that every human being has just as much right to life between conception and birth as after birth, and that legalized abortion is therefore tantamount to legalized murder.

It is a tough and painful issue, but one aspect of it, at least, is quite clear: it cannot be resolved by any pat formula that a pregnant woman's rights leave off where her fetus's begin—or vice versa. If we protect the fetus's right to birth we cannot avoid abridging the woman's right to control her own body; and if we protect the latter right we cannot avoid abridging the former. We cannot, sad to say, have it both ways.

Whatever may be the merits of the issue, it was resolved by a 1973 Supreme Court ruling that the decision to have an abortion in the first three months of pregnancy must be left strictly up to the woman and her physician, and their freedom

The Rights of Man:
Principles and Problems

[22] Dennis v. U.S., 341 U.S. 494 (1951).

to make the decision may not be restricted by any state or national law. The Court added that governments may exert some limited control over abortions in the second three months of pregnancy, but they may constitutionally prohibit abortions altogether only in the final three months.[23]

Some Americans hailed the Court's decision as a great victory for women's rights; others denounced it as a grievous blow to everyone's right to life. It is no business of a book like this to say who was right. But it is this book's business to point out that there was no way on earth *either* right could be fully protected and freely exercised without to some extent abridging the other. The Supreme Court—like the state legislatures whose laws it overrode—had to choose, and choose it did. We may agree or disagree with that choice; we may even question the Court's power to have the final word; but we cannot blink the fact that a choice had to be made.

## CIVIL RIGHTS IN THE POLITICAL PROCESS

### CIVIL-RIGHTS CONFLICTS AS POLITICAL CONFLICTS[24]

We are likely to understand better what is involved in conflicts over civil rights if we remember that they are political in nature. To be sure, they are often fought out largely (though never entirely) in courts of law and some people mistakenly regard the judicial process as somehow not political in the same sense that legislative and executive processes are political. This may obscure their political nature. Yet, according to the analytical framework used in this book, these conflicts cannot be other than political. Every conflict over civil rights involves the question of government policy: Should government restrict this person's or that group's freedom of action? And, as we saw in Chapters 2 and 3, every government action promotes some people's goals and damages the interests of others.

If, for example, government enforces a policy of racial integration in public schools, it promotes some blacks' and whites' goal of equal status and frustrates some other blacks' and whites' desire for segregation. If government bans the sale of "obscene" magazines or comic books, it promotes the cause of certain religious sects and groups of parents and damages the authors, artists, and publishers concerned. When government enforces open-occupancy laws, it furthers the claims of blacks and Jews to equal housing opportunities and thwarts efforts by certain whites and gentiles to keep their neighborhoods "exclusive."

Decisions on what government will do in these and all similar situations are thus, in our sense of the term, political. We should expect, therefore, that they will be made as all other political decisions are made; as the result of conflict among competing political actors. Most of these actors will, of course, publicly defend their positions in terms of constitutional rights rather than of self-interest, and most will

---

[23] Roe v. Wade, 410 U.S. 113 (1973).

[24] The point of view expressed here is a special application of the general position so ably presented in Jack W. Peltason, *Federal Courts in the Political Process* (New York: Random House, Inc., 1955).

genuinely believe that freedom of speech and due process of law—quite apart from crass considerations of self-interest—require decisions favorable to their points of view. This tendency should not, however, conceal the fact that in civil-rights matters, as in all other matters of government policy, somebody stands to gain and somebody stands to lose. Students of politics and government will better understand any particular conflict over civil rights if they explore, in addition to the ideological aspects of the conflict, the question of who stands to win what and who stands to lose what.

## SOME CONSEQUENCES

Viewing civil-rights conflicts as political conflicts may suggest that the processes by which they are conducted and the government decisions affecting them are essentially the same as the processes by which all other political conflicts are conducted and all other government decisions made. This approach to civil-rights conflicts may well provide understanding otherwise absent. Some people, for example, think that government policies (including court decisions) on civil-rights questions should always be made in conformity with a set of clear and mutually consistent logical principles, and they are disturbed that such decisions often seem instead to shift logical grounds according to time and circumstances. Perhaps they would be less disturbed if they recognized the political nature of civil-rights conflicts, for then they would start with the assumption that particular decisions are the products, not of ill will or temporary aberrations from sanity by judges and legislators, but rather of the variations in the nature and fluctuations in the strength of the competing interests involved.

Another consequence of this view is awareness that in any political system the particular processes by which conflicts are conducted and the civil rights of individuals determined are shaped by the same forces that shape the system's other political conflicts and government policies. The general condition of civil rights in a particular system depends largely upon such matters as the number and variety of its competing interests, the issues that separate them and bring them into conflict, the degree of overlapping membership, the degree to which the competing groups are mobilized, the number and strength of common interests and other unifying forces, the general level of material wealth and its distribution, the degree of security from foreign attack, and all those other general factors affecting politics and government that we have previously examined.

Even for those groups and nations that wish to "buy," the "price of liberty" varies from issue to issue and from time to time. What "prices" are the free nations and their competing groups currently willing to pay? We shall find some of the answers in the following chapter, in which we consider some principal challenges to civil rights in modern nations and some ways in which various nations have responded to them.

# 22

# THE RIGHTS OF MAN: CHALLENGES AND RESPONSES

In every nation that values liberty the problem of preserving human rights in a world of international conflict and intranational protest and backlash is both perennial and grave. In the United States and most other such nations it has, in recent years, broken out of the relative quiet of the scholar's study and the judge's chambers into the forefront of political struggle.

"Clergymen Denounce Supreme Court's Ban on School Prayers." "Senator Blasts Witnesses for Hiding behind Fifth Amendment." "Three Civil Rights Workers Murdered in Mississippi." "Draft Card Burners Sentenced to Jail." Such headlines have been prominent in American newspapers since the end of World War II, and current disputes over civil rights and "law and order" are among the most acute problems with which the nation must deal.

The dilemmas faced by every free nation in preserving human rights, as we observed in Chapter 21, unhappily cannot be solved by the simplistic formula that we all should be free to do what we wish as long as we do not abridge the freedom of others. Let us never forget every government action involves coercing some people to do something or to refrain from doing something else. Unavoidably, every such action restricts someone's freedom to some extent. Guaranteeing a pregnant woman's right to an abortion abridges her fetus's right to life. Protecting Jehovah's Witnesses' rights to seek converts by door-to-door canvassing abridges the "heathens'" right to privacy. Protecting a suspected criminal's privacy by prohibiting the tapping of his telephone handicaps police efforts to protect other people's rights to security of life and property. Preserving freedom forces all free nations to make choices—hard choices, *political* choices.

Political conflict over human rights is between group and group, not between

Policy Outputs and
Impacts

546

"the individual" and "the government." Every time a particular group calls upon government to engage in some action or inaction, it challenges the civil rights of some other group. It is clearly impossible in the limited space of this chapter to describe all challenges to human rights and all government responses to those challenges in all modern free nations. The discussion will be limited to a survey of three areas of present-day political conflict over civil rights in certain free nations that have received the most attention: police powers and defendants' rights, sexual status, and racial status.

## CONFLICT OVER POLICE POWERS AND DEFENDANTS' RIGHTS

### CRIME AND THE POLICE

#### Crime, Organized and Unorganized[1]

We noted in Chapter 2 that any political system differs from all other social systems mainly in that it makes authoritative rules, intended to be binding on all people living in the society and taking precedence over the rules of all other social organizations. As people are people and not angels, no government's rules are obeyed by all of the people all of the time. The most serious violations are called "crimes"—that is, acts generally considered to be wrongs committed against the whole community. They include "any act done in violation of those duties which an individual owes to the community, and for the breach of which the law has provided that the offender shall make satisfaction to the public."[2] Crimes are usually classified as either felonies (the more serious) or misdemeanors (the less serious) and are punishable by disqualification from holding public office, removal from office, a fine, imprisonment, or death.

Crimes are usually distinguished from "civil wrongs," which are offenses committed against private individuals but not considered damaging to the whole community. If A spreads malicious stories intended to ruin B's reputation, he is considered to have slandered B but not to have injured the whole community. Hence B's remedy is to sue A for damages, and the community's interest is solely to see that the dispute is conducted fairly and settled equitably. But if A shoots and kills B, he is considered to have damaged not merely B alone but also the basic security of the whole community. Therefore, the government will prosecute A for murder, and if he is found guilty he will be imprisoned or executed.

No one knows precisely how many crimes are committed in each year in any modern nation, for some are always undetected and others unreported. Reasonable estimates can be and are made, however, and they suggest that crime rates are rising in many Western democracies, especially the United States. The most authoritative

---

[1] A recent authoritative study of this vast and complex subject in the United States is the 1967 report of the President's Commission on Law Enforcement and Administration of Justice, *The Challenge of Crime in a Free Society* (Washington, D.C.: U.S. Government Printing Office, 1967).

[2] *Black's Law Dictionary* (4th ed.; St. Paul, Minn.: West Publishing Company, 1951), p. 445.

annual estimates of American crime rates are made by the Federal Bureau of Investigation, and its figures reveal the depressing story summarized in Table 22.

TABLE 22

Crime Rates in the United States, 1962-1972

| Year | Violent Crimes | Property Crimes | Total Crimes Index[a] |
|---|---|---|---|
| 1962 | 160.9 | 1,103.3 | 1,194.2 |
| 1964 | 188.7 | 1,254.7 | 1,443.4 |
| 1966 | 217.7 | 1,452.9 | 1,670.7 |
| 1968 | 295.3 | 1,944.9 | 2,240.2 |
| 1970 | 360.7 | 2,386.1 | 2,746.9 |
| 1972 | 397.7 | 2,431.8 | 2,829.5 |
| Rate of increase, 1962-72 | 147.2% | 135.3% | 136.9% |
| Rate of population increase, 1962-72: 13.3% | | | |

[a] Figures are number of crimes per 100,000 population for the year.
*Source:* FBI Annual Reports, summarized in *Associated Press Almanac, 1974* (Maplewood, N.J.: Hammond Almanac, Inc., 1974), p. 236.

A majority of the crimes reported in Table 22 were "unorganized"; that is, they were committed by individuals acting alone or in small ad hoc groups, as in the muggings that have made the streets and parks of so many American cities unsafe at night. But a good many offenses are committed by "organized crime," by large and well-organized criminal "corporations" like Cosa Nostra, which operate for profit both illegal enterprises (gambling, narcotics, loan-sharking, extortion, "protection," and so on) and legal businesses (real estate, restaurants, bars and taverns, vending machines, and the like).

Crime ranges from crimes of passion in families through adolescent "joy-riding" in stolen automobiles to such highly organized and profitable businesses as selling narcotics and running the numbers game. Organized or unorganized, it is growing in the United States and many other nations, and it presents a serious threat to everyone living in society, as well as a massive challenge to the police forces, which bear the main government responsibility for preventing crime and capturing criminals.

### The Policeman's Job

To ensure that its laws are obeyed, every political system must rely mainly on the willingness of its citizens to obey the law—yes, even when they do not believe that a particular law is just. After all, it simply is not possible to put half or three-quarters of the population in jail or shoot or exile them. Consequently, as we noted in Chapter 3, any political community in which a substantial portion of the people deny the legitimacy of the rule makers' powers and refuse to obey the laws is no longer a community but an arena for civil war.

Yet no political system depends *entirely* upon faith that all its citizens are law-abiding. Every system has a corps of police to deal with lawbreakers. There is wide variation among (and within) modern nations in the organization, specialization, training, methods, and effectiveness of police, but in all nations they are charged with detecting and arresting lawbreakers and delivering them to the executive and judicial agencies for determination of their guilt or innocence (see Chap. 18). Many totalitarian systems have relied heavily upon special secret police mainly concerned with such "crimes against the state and the people" as speaking and working against the regime; the best-known examples in recent years have been the Nazi Gestapo and the Soviet agency known successively as the Cheka, GPU, NKVD, MGB, MVD, and KGB.[3]

We are interested here only in tasks generally assigned to unspecialized, nonsecret "regular" police. They include preventing violations of law from taking place (patrolling streets and checking stores to discourage burglars), stopping law violations that do take place (removing political protesters who are blocking a public highway), determining who has committed particular crimes, arresting suspects and delivering them to the prosecuting authorities, and providing evidence at the ensuing trials. In a free nation the police have at least one other major duty: to protect the legal and constitutional rights of all persons, whether they are lawbreakers or innocent bystanders.

### The Policeman's Lot[4]

The policeman's job is to enforce the law—but only by the means and within the limits allowed by the law. In many nations, especially the United States, the policeman's lot indeed is "not a happy one." His duties are always demanding, and he often risks physical injury and even death. All too often he is underpaid, undereducated, poorly trained, and overworked. Furthermore, he frequently must work among people who distrust and hate him, particularly in urban slum and ghetto areas where crime rates are high. The most common epithets applied to him—"pig," "flatfoot," "cossack," "the fuzz"—do not encourage him to feel that he serves in a proud profession respected by all: even the occasional "Support Your Local Police" bumper sticker does not help his morale very much.

At bottom, however, the policeman's lot is unhappy because, more than most public officials, he operates on the front lines of the conflict between his society's widely held but antagonistic values of security and freedom. We can sit in our classrooms and strongly endorse both "law and order" and "civil rights" without having to adjust one to the other more than verbally. But the policeman is charged with fighting crime and with protecting the rights of everyone, including lawbreakers. Depending upon what kind of trouble he has in resolving this conflict, he may be charged with brutality, incompetence, or corruption.

To understand the policeman's dilemma better let us briefly survey some of the rights he is charged with protecting while fighting crime.

---

[3] See Carl J. Friedrich and Zbigniew K. Brzezinski, *Totalitarian Dictatorship and Autocracy* (2d ed.; Cambridge, Mass.: Harvard University Press, 1965), chap. 14.

[4] A leading study of the problems, attitudes, and behavior of police in the United States is James Q. Wilson, *Varieties of Police Behavior* (Cambridge, Mass.: Harvard University Press, 1968).

HEY, BROTHER, YOU DON'T WANT TO RIP ME OFF...    FREE HUEY...    FREE ANGELA...    FREE ATTICA...

**Views of the police may depend on one's situation.** © 1971 Jules Feiffer. Courtesy Publishers-Hall Syndicate.

## THE RIGHTS OF DEFENDANTS[5]

### The Law

Although there are many variations in detail from one nation to another, the main rights of defendants most commonly guaranteed by law in the Western democratic systems include the following.

**Pretrial Rights**   The law guarantees every person *immunity from arbitrary arrest;* he may be arrested only in pursuance of a warrant issued by a judge or upon a police officer's belief, supported by some valid evidence, that he may have committed a crime. If his arrest satisfies neither requirement, he can collect damages by suing the arresting officer for false arrest. Shortly after his detention, the suspect has the right to the *assistance of counsel,* and if he cannot afford a lawyer the government is obligated to provide one for him. During his interrogation by the police he has the *right of silence* and the guarantee that his silence cannot later be used as evidence against him. The *prohibition of coerced confessions* means he cannot in any way be forced to give testimony that might help to convict him. Perhaps most important of all, he has the right to a *writ of habeas corpus:* If the police arrest him, jail him, but refuse to charge him formally before a court, he or his agent can petition a judge for a court order commanding the jailer to produce the prisoner and show cause why he is being held. If the judge decides that the detention is unlawful—that the charges are unspecified or the evidence insufficient—he orders the prisoner's immediate release. More than any other legal device, the writ of habeas corpus is a safeguard against preventive detention and imprisonment without trial—devices which are so prevalent in totalitarian methods of law enforcement.

**Rights during Trial**   The law seeks to guarantee a fair trial to every person accused of crime. It requires that *advance knowledge of the specific charges* be given to the accused so that he may prepare his best defense. His right to the *assistance of counsel* continues There must be an *impartial judge,* an *impartial jury,* or both to decide the case on the basis

---

[5] There is a large body of scholarly literature on this topic. Some useful comparative studies are David Fellman, *The Defendant's Rights* (New York: Holt, Rinehart and Winston, Inc., 1958); Fellman, *The Defendant's Rights under English Law* (Madison, Wis.: University of Wisconsin Press, 1966); and Ronald F. Bunn and William G. Andrews (eds.), *Politics and Civil Liberties in Europe* (Princeton, N.J.: D. Van Nostrand Company, Inc., 1967).

Policy Outputs and Impacts

550

FREE ALL POLITICAL PRISONERS...

RIGHT ON!

ALL POWER TO THE—

POLICE!

©1971 Bill Sanders

Dist. Publishers-Hall Syndicate

of law and evidence, without prejudice against the defendant. He can obtain a *change of venue* if he can convince the judge that the climate of opinion at the trial site is prejudicial to his defense. He has the same power as does the prosecution to *subpoena witnesses.* He (or his counsel) has the right to *confront and cross-examine hostile witnesses.* His *immunity from double jeopardy* means that if, in a valid trial, he is found innocent of a particular charge, he can never again be tried on that same charge. *No ex post facto law* can be applied to him; that is, he cannot be convicted of a crime that was not a crime when he committed it. If convicted, he has the *right of appeal* to a higher court, and if he can convince the appellate court that he has not been allowed full exercise of his rights, his conviction will be set aside. If his conviction stands, *no cruel and unusual punishment* can be inflicted upon him.[6]

In sum, the law in most Western democratic systems presumes the defendant's innocence and places the burden of proof upon the prosecution. Insufficient or inconclusive evidence and reasonable doubt are to be resolved in his favor.[7] This legal premise reflects the conviction that it is better to be sure that the innocent go free at the cost of letting some of the guilty escape than to punish all the guilty at the cost of unjustly punishing some of the innocent.

### The Conflict

Each of the defendant's rights just listed places one more handicap on the police in their efforts to detect and arrest suspected criminals and on prosecutors in their efforts to amass the evidence necessary to convict those who are apprehended and charged. In every democratic system, accordingly, there is always some pressure to attack crime more effectively by giving police and prosecutors more freedom of action. There is also some countervailing pressure to make defendants' rights a little more secure by tightening the restraints on law-enforcement officers. In the United States this perennial conflict between the claims of "law and order" and the claims of "individual rights" has grown more intense and rancorous in recent years. It has involved mainly the following issues.

---

[6] In a landmark 1972 decision the Supreme Court held that existing state laws providing for capital punishment were cruel and unusual punishments within the meaning of the Constitution, and were therefore unconstitutional: Furman v. Georgia, 408 U.S. 238 (1972).

[7] There are, however, important differences in procedures and underlying assumptions between nations (like the United States) using the "adversary system" of criminal justice and those (like France) using the "accusatorial system." For details, see Chap. 18.

The Rights of Man:
Challenges and Responses

*'Quick! While I Keep 'Em Pinned Down, Run
And Bring Each Of Them A Lawyer —
And Don't Forget Ours!'*

**Electronic Eavesdropping**   Modern electronics has developed a wide range of easily
hidden "bugging" devices capable of eavesdropping on private telephone conversations and even on private conversations in offices and homes. Police naturally find
these devices very useful in gathering information about the activities, associations,
and plans of suspected criminals, and the width of their electronic net was dramatized
by the revelation in the 1973 Watergate hearings that the private telephones of many
high officials in the Department of State had been tapped on the orders of the
President. Many citizens strongly object to the use of these devices, arguing that they
allow government to invade every area of private life in the nightmare totalitarian
fashion of George Orwell's *1984.* Many law-enforcement officials argue with equal
vehemence that depriving the police of this tool will benefit only criminals.

The legal phase of the conflict centers upon the constitutional prohibition of
"unreasonable searches and seizures"; search warrants "particularly describing the
place to be searched, and the persons or things to be seized" are required (Fourth
Amendment). A generation ago the Supreme Court ruled that wiretapping in itself
does not violate this rule.[8] A series of recent Court decisions, however, has greatly
restricted the circumstances in which police may constitutionally use electronic

[8] Olmstead v. United States, 227 U.S. 438 (1928).

**"Bugging" has increased in recent years.** Source: Copyright © 1969 The Chicago Sun-Times. Reproduced by courtesy of Wil-Jo Associates, Inc. and Bill Mauldin.

eavesdropping devices, mainly by requiring that investigators must first have a warrant from a judge, thus satisfying the requirement that the places to be searched and the things to be seized be specified in advance.[9]

After intense pressure to sidestep—and counterpressure to support—the Court's restrictions, Congress included in the Omnibus Crime Control and Safe Streets Act of 1968 an authorization of police wiretapping and "bugging" in investigations of a wide variety of specified crimes. In most instances the police are required to obtain warrants first, but in investigations of organized crime or national-security cases, if they find that an emergency exists, they can intercept private communications for forty-eight hours without a warrant.

This law was a major victory for the police-powers side, but it did not end the war. Most observers believe that the next round will be fought in the courts.

The Rights of Man: Challenges and Responses

[9] Katz v. United States, 389 U.S. 347 (1967); and Berger v. State of New York, 388 U.S. 41 (1967).

**Voluntary Confessions**   A defendant's confession, unsupported or contradicted by other evidence, is not sufficient to convict him. On the other hand, if the prosecution has some evidence pointing to his guilt but not enough to convince the judge or jury beyond a reasonable doubt, his confession usually provides the clincher. It is therefore not surprising that police and prosecutors try hard to make defendants confess— or that defendants, both guilty and innocent, resist.

As in most constitutional democracies, courts in the United States will admit confessions as evidence only if they are voluntarily given, for, in the famous phrase from the Fifth Amendment, "no person . . . shall be compelled in any criminal case to be a witness against himself." "Taking the Fifth" refers to a defendant's exercise of his constitutional right to refuse to answer any question put to him by public authorities if he can convince a court that his answers "may tend to incriminate" him—that is, be used to convict him in the present or some future criminal case. He has a right to remain silent, and the courts have ruled that his silence may not be used by the prosecution as an indication that he has something guilty to hide. But there is no way of keeping a jury from drawing its own conclusions, and if the defendant voluntarily takes the witness stand he cannot claim immunity from cross-examination by the prosecution.

In another recent series of controversial opinions the Supreme Court has gone far to ensure that confessions used as evidence in criminal cases are truly voluntary. The culmination was the decision in *Miranda* v. *Arizona* (1966), which stipulated that any evidence, including material obtained by the police in pretrial "custodial interrogation," would be admissible only if the police had told the defendant that he had a right to remain silent, that anything he said could be used against him, that he had a right to have his attorney present during the questioning, that if he could not afford an attorney one would be provided for him, and that he had the right to terminate the police interrogation at any time.[10]

The Miranda decision evoked a storm of protest from law-enforcement officials. They noted that about 90 percent of all criminal convictions result from guilty pleas, which, they argued, means that pretrial interrogation and investigation are the critical stages in law enforcement. The Court's restrictions, they declared, would make convicting criminals enormously difficult and thus seriously cripple the police in their war against crime. Congress agreed. The 1968 Crime Control Act authorized the trial judge to investigate the circumstances in which a confession is made, determine whether or not it is voluntary, and instruct the jury to decide what weight should be given to it. In making his determination, the judge need not be bound by any single factor of those stipulated in the Miranda decision but can take the whole situation into account.

This law was also a major victory for the police-powers side, but in the United States, as in other constitutional democracies, the courts, and especially the Supreme Court, have the last word about whether any particular defendant has or has not been coerced into confessing and unjustly convicted as a result. It therefore seems likely that the perennial conflict between proponents of police powers and defendants'

[10] Miranda v. Arizona, 384 U.S. 436 (1966).

rights will continue without a total victory for either side as long as the people and their public officials continue to value both law and order and civil rights.

## CONFLICT OVER THE STATUS OF WOMEN[11]

### "SEXISM": MEANING AND MANIFESTATIONS

With the dubious exception of the legendary Amazons, in almost all societies in almost all periods of history women have been treated in most ways as men's inferiors. Typically, women have been barred from owning property, from employment in any but menial service jobs, from holding public office, even from voting. This discrimination has often been embodied in laws and even more often enforced by rigid social customs. It has been rooted in most men's—and many women's—views about the proper consequences of women's unique biological function of bearing and nursing children and of men's generally greater physical size and strength. The former trait has inclined societies to impose—and women to accept—the prime obligation of caring for children from birth to adulthood. The latter trait has helped men to keep in their inferior roles even those few, women who have rebelled against it.

Sex discrimination has been particularly evident in politics. History tells of a few powerful queens—Elizabeth I, Anne, and Victoria of England, Catherine the Great of Russia, Christina of Sweden. But in most nations of the ancien régime the Salic law excluded women from succeeding to the throne, and so women could play political roles only as wives and mothers (Catherine de Medici, Anne of Austria) or mistresses (Diane de Poitiers, Nell Gwyn) of kings.

The twentieth century has thus far seen more improvement in the status of women, at least in the developed nations, than in all previous history. Most Western nations, including the United States, gave women the right to vote around the time of World War I. In the 1920s the new Soviet regime placed women in many jobs (for example, bus drivers, airline pilots, even combat soldiers) they had never held before, and in the 1950s the new Communist regime in China followed suit. In both communist systems, however, women are still very far from achieving political parity: for example, only about 10 to 20 percent of the members of the ruling Communist parties are women, and no woman has yet led either nation.[12] And in the noncommunist nations of the West this century's modest social and political gains for women seem to many to illuminate not so much how far they have come as how far they have yet to go. We shall therefore examine their present economic and political status in the United States, where the movement for women's rights is now probably the strongest in the noncommunist world.

---

[11] Many scholarly and polemical works on the status of women have been published in the United States in recent years. A useful annotated bibliography of them is Marie B. Rosenberg and Len V. Bergstrom, *Women and Society* (Beverly Hills, Calif.: Sage Publications, Inc., 1974).

[12] See John A. Armstrong, *Ideology, Politics, and Government in the Soviet Union* (rev. ed.; New York: Frederick A. Praeger, Inc., 1967), p. 54; and John W. Lewis, *Leadership in Communist China* (Ithaca, N.Y.: Cornell University Press, 1963), p. 109.

**"Women's Lib" in the USSR?** Source: Reprinted by permission of *National Review*.

*"A People's Democracy that needs its women in the fields, on the docks and in the factories may take a dim view of your idea of Women's Liberation, Anna Petrovna."*

### In Employment and Pay[13]

In 1972, women constituted 51.5 percent of America's population, but only 38.0 percent of its fulltime workers. Even so, this proportion had increased markedly in the preceding decade: of the 11.9 million new jobs added to the labor force from 1960 to 1970, 65 percent went to women (for example, 75 percent of the new bus drivers were women, as were over 50 percent of the new newspaper reporters and editors). But women's continuing underrepresentation in the labor force doubtless reflected in part their special responsibilities for rearing children: In 1970, of all women with

---

[13] The most comprehensive summary is taken from hearings before congressional committees: Catherine R. Stimpson (ed.), *Discrimination against Women* (Washington, D.C.: R. R. Bowker, 1973). See also Vivian Gornick and Barbara K. Moran (eds.), *Women in Sexist Society* (New York: Basic Books, Inc., 1971).

children under the age of six (when most children start attending school full time) only 30 percent were employed, compared with nearly half of the women with older children or no children.

But the proportion of women with jobs of some kind tells only the lesser part of the story; the greater part is the inferior status of women in types of jobs and rates of pay. In 1971, the median pay of all women working full time was only 59.5 percent as high as that of men working full time. Seventy-five percent of such women were paid less than $6,000 per year, compared with only 33 percent of the comparable men. College-educated women working full time had a median income of $7,400, compared with $12,000 for college-educated men working full time. In the field of education, 88 percent of elementary school teachers—but only 22 percent of the principals—were women; and the comparable figures for women high school teachers and principals were 48 percent and 4 percent respectively. My own field of political science was certainly no exception: in college and university departments of political science in 1972, 82 percent of the men were on "tenure track" appointments, compared to 63 percent of the women; the average salary of fulltime male professors was $15,200 compared with $12,720 for their female colleagues.[14] It is not surprising, therefore, that the women's rights movement puts a high priority on the goals of equal job opportunities and equal pay for equal work.

### In Politics and Government[15]

In 1972, women constituted 53.8 percent of the voting-age population in the United States, but a far smaller proportion of the political elite. Neither major political party, of course, nominated a woman for the presidency or vice-presidency, and none ever has.[16] Perhaps more striking is the fact that of the 66 major-party candidates for the U.S. Senate, 2 were women (3.0 percent); and of the 870 major-party candidates for the House of Representatives, 32 were women (3.7 percent). Both women senatorial candidates (including incumbent Margaret Chase Smith of Maine) were defeated, but 14 women were elected to the lower chamber.[17] This was the largest number in history, but women still constituted only 3.2 percent of the members of the House and 2.6 percent of all members of Congress.

The main political advancement for women in recent years has resulted from the efforts of both major parties to increase the proportions of women among the delegates to their national nominating conventions. The Democrats used a quota

---

[14] Ada W. Finifter, "The Professional Status of Women in Political Science: Some Current Data," *PS,* 6 (Fall 1973), pp. 406–419.

[15] For an attack on political discrimination against women, see Kirsten Amundsen, *The Silenced Majority* (Englewood Cliffs, N.J.: Prentice-Hall, Inc., 1971). A most instructive scholarly work is Jeane J. Kilpatrick's analysis of the personality traits and political experiences of some leading women legislators, *Political Woman* (New York: Basic Books, Inc., 1974).

[16] Some minor parties did, however. The Socialist Workers party candidate for President was Linda Jenness in some states and Evelyn Reed in others. The Libertarian party nominated Theodora Nathan for Vice-President.

[17] This result prompted an unfortunate and possibly male-chauvinist observation by one observer: "The 1972 results show that a woman's place is in the House."

system, the Republicans used an "affirmative action" program, and the results are shown in Table 23.

**TABLE 23**

**Women Delegates in National Nominating Conventions, 1968-1972**

| Party | Percent of Women among All Delegates | |
| --- | --- | --- |
| | 1968 | 1972 |
| Democratic | 13 | 40 |
| Republican | 17 | 30 |

*Source:* Austin Ranney, *Curing the Mischiefs of Faction: Party Reform in America* (Berkeley, Calif.: University of California Press, 1974). Originally published by the University of California Press; reprinted by permission of The Regents of the University of California.

In 1974 the Democrats dropped their quotas for women in favor of "affirmative action programs" to encourage participation by women. But it was clear that for some time to come women would continue to hold a higher proportion of official positions in the major parties' national conventions than in any other comparably powerful level of American politics and government.

### THE WOMEN'S RIGHTS MOVEMENT[18]

Ever since the eighteenth century there have been occasional "feminist" movements to improve the status of women by political action. Among the most successful were the "suffragette" movements of the early 1900s, which played major roles in securing women's rights to vote in a number of Western nations.[19] The American women's rights (or "women's liberation" or "women's lib") movement of the 1970s, however, has succeeded and perhaps surpassed the suffragettes as the most active and powerful feminist movement the world has yet seen.

Like most protest movements (see, for example, the black civil-rights movement discussed below), the women's rights movement has no universally agreed list of demands or monolithic dogma. It has its radicals (men are incurably hostile and oppressive, and women should have as little to do with them as possible), its moderates (women should have the same basic rights and opportunities as men, and right-thinking men can and will help women achieve them), and its conservatives (women will and should always be mainly wives and mothers, though perhaps they deserve a somewhat better break politically and socially than they have had).

The women's movement also has no one dominant organization. Among its leading pressure groups are the National Organization for Women (NOW), the Wom-

---

[18] One of the more extreme statements of modern feminism, which has played a major catalytic role in the women's rights movement, is Betty Friedan, *The Feminine Mystique* (New York: W. W. Norton & Company, 1968). The strongest statement against radical feminism is Midge Decter, *The New Chastity* (New York: Coward, McCann & Geoghegan, Inc., 1972). Somewhere between these two views is Jessie Bernard, *Women and the Public Interest* (Chicago: Aldine-Atherton, 1971).

[19] The United States, which adopted the woman's suffrage (Nineteenth) amendment in 1920, was neither the earliest nor the last to give women the vote. New Zealand did so as early as 1893, Norway in 1913, and Great Britain in 1918. France and Italy, on the other hand, did not adopt woman suffrage until 1946, and Switzerland—that model democracy—did not do so until 1971!

**One response to the Women's Rights movement.** Source: UPI Photograph.

The Rights of Man: Challenges and Responses

en's Equity Action League, the Women's National Abortion Action Coalition, and the Women's Political Caucus. The prime objectives sought by these and other organizations include: the elimination of all sexual discrimination in employment opportunities, pay, and advancement; liberalized birth-control and abortion laws; expanded children's day-care programs; liberalized tax deductions for child-care expenses; more women candidates and public officeholders; and the repeal of all laws which in any way give women a legal status inferior to men's.

The women's organizations, with some help from male allies, have used most of the broad range of pressure-group tactics (see Chapter 10) to persuade or force the national and state governments to adopt policies promoting these goals. Like other protest movements, they have won a few and lost a few; but, compared with most such movements, they have done well and are likely to do even better, as is evident from the following brief survey of recent developments.

## RECENT POLITICAL AND LEGAL DEVELOPMENTS

### *"Affirmative Action"*

Since the early 1960s there have been three main political and legal developments in the drive for women's rights. In Chapter 21 we noted one, the Supreme Court's 1973 decision voiding all laws prohibiting abortions in the first three months of pregnancy, and we shall examine another, the effort to secure ratification of an equal-rights amendment to the Constitution, in the next section. The third began with the back-handed adoption of an amendment to the Civil Rights Act of 1964. That act, as we shall see below, was intended mainly to secure equal rights for black Americans. Its congressional opponents, mainly southerners, argued that the equal-rights sword could cut northern liberals as well as southern conservatives. To dramatize their point they half-jokingly introduced an amendment to the act's employment section prohibiting job discrimination on grounds of sex as well as on grounds of race or national origin. Some of the bill's proponents opposed the amendment as a cute trick to defeat the whole bill, but others voted for it on its own merits. It ultimately passed with the support of a curious coalition of northern liberals and southern conservatives.

For several years this section of the act lay dormant while enforcement efforts were concentrated on upgrading the status of blacks. In 1971, however, the Department of Health, Education, and Welfare (HEW) announced that it would henceforth require all colleges and universities supported by Federal funds to file "affirmative action" programs for ending sex discrimination in their hiring and promotion practices. The penalty for noncompliance would be the withdrawal of all Federal support, which in many cases amounted to half or more of the institution's total funds. Moreover, this threat proved to be no paper tiger: HEW sent examiners to many campuses to review plans and check on their implementation, and when Columbia University failed to submit a satisfactory plan its funds were actually stopped for five months until it finally complied.

Progress toward true sexual equality in university staffs has so far been detectable but slow. Many problems remain, but two stand out. The first is the fact that for most colleges and universities the period since 1971 has been one of static or declining enrollments and funds, and there simply have been too few new jobs to hire substantial numbers of blacks, chicanos, and other minorities *or* women. The second is the fact that many young white male teachers feel that, with so few jobs available for anyone, giving preference without proper regard for professional qualifications to women or blacks amounts to rank discrimination against white men, and some have begun to challenge HEW's affirmative-action orders in the courts. Their fight against what they call "reverse discrimination" is likely to remain a hot issue until (if ever) academic jobs again become plentiful, and it may not be resolved even then.

### The Equal-Rights Amendment

Many leaders of the women's movement have concluded that their cause must rest on firmer ground than the vagaries of administrators' plans and judges' interpretations. They have therefore put high priority on amending the Constitution to prohibit sexual discrimination once and for all. The first of several such amendments was introduced in Congress way back in 1923, but none passed until nearly a half-century later. In 1971 Congress finally approved and sent to the states for ratification an equal-rights amendment (if adopted, it would be the Twenty-Seventh) which reads as follows:

> Equality of rights under the law shall not be denied or abridged by the United States or by any state on account of sex.

Not surprisingly, the ratification of the equal-rights amendment has touched off a major political battle. It has been hotly opposed by a number of groups including an antifeminist women's organization led by the noted conservative activist Phyllis Schlafly. They have argued that the amendment would deprive women of all the protections they now enjoy, force them to be drafted for combat military service, outlaw all segregated sanitary facilities, leave divorced mothers with no alimony for feeding their children, and so on. After all, they avow, women are by nature primarily wives and mothers; they should be specially protected as such, and the necessary and just price for that protection is to preserve the special role of men as husbands, fathers, and breadwinners. The amendment's supporters reply that these alleged protections have helped women very little, that they have mainly served as a mask and justification for discrimination, and that reasonable legal distinctions in sexual status—as opposed to the sexist discrimination they claim now prevails—could still be made.

Under the Constitution's three-quarters rule, the amendment needs the approval of thirty-eight of the fifty state legislatures. By the spring of 1974 twenty-eight had ratified it, twelve had rejected it, and ten had not yet acted. While it was possible for some of the rejecting legislatures to change their minds, it was clear that the amendment needed the approval of almost all of the undecided states to be ratified.

Clearly the amendment had an uphill fight the rest of the way. Win or lose, however, the women's rights movement had every intention of continuing to fight not only for the amendment but also for other measures in Congress, the administrative agencies, the courts, and all branches of the state and local governments. This strategy is dictated by the great number and wide dispersion of power nodes in the American governmental system, and it has also been pursued by both sides in another

The Rights of Man:
Challenges and Responses

and even more bitter American civil-rights conflict: the struggle over the status of blacks. To that struggle we now turn our attention.

## CONFLICT OVER THE STATUS OF BLACKS[20]

### BLACK AMERICA YESTERDAY AND TODAY

Racial discrimination imposes a handicap on all members of a particular racial group solely because of their race and without regard to their individual characteristics: barring any black, no matter how intelligent or well prepared, from attending a particular school or prohibiting any Jew, no matter how pleasant or cooperative, from buying a house in a "restricted" neighborhood, for example. It is one of the oldest and most often encountered aspects of man's inhumanity to man. Wherever people of different ethnic groups have been thrown together in the same society, at least some members of the dominant group have attempted to discriminate against members of another group or groups—gentiles against Jews, whites against blacks, Africans against Indians, Anglo-Saxons against Latins, Occidentals against Orientals, and so on. In most societies such conflicts over discrimination sooner or later become political; groups favoring discrimination try to have their views incorporated into government policy, whereas antidiscrimination groups try to secure prohibition of discrimination.

The United States, as we shall see, certainly has no monopoly on racial discrimination, public or private. But discrimination against blacks in this country has, justly or not, received more attention and comment both here and abroad than has discrimination in any other nation, with the possible exception of the Republic of South Africa.

The problem of the status of blacks has plagued American society and government for more than three centuries. By the 1780s enough African slaves had been imported so that questions of what to do about slavery and how to count slaves for purposes of congressional representation sharply divided the Constitutional Convention of 1787. The question of whether slavery should be extended, maintained, or abolished was the proximate cause of our Civil War, the bloodiest war in American history. The war resulted in legal emancipation of the slaves, but for a century after Appomattox, blacks remained second-class citizens in every way.

Since 1945 the struggle over the status of blacks has greatly intensified. With the various spinoff clashes it has generated, it has become one of the most divisive domestic political issues of our time, and there is no end in sight. It involves the status

---

[20] Two influential black authors have written: "There is growing resentment of the word 'Negro' . . . because the term is the invention of our oppressor; it is *his* image of us that he describes. Many blacks are now calling themselves African-Americans, Afro-Americans, or black people because that is *our* image of ourselves." Stokely Carmichael and Charles V. Hamilton, *Black Power: The Politics of Liberation in America* (New York: Vintage Books, 1967), p. 37. Whatever may be the merits of this argument—and many members of the authors' race disagree with it—the fact is that a growing number of the most active politically do agree; therefore in this book the term "black" is used instead of "Negro" except in quotations.

of only 11 percent of our population—but that means more than 22 million human beings. By far the most numerous and visible of the nation's depressed minorities, the blacks are also the most significant politically. They differ sharply from the white majority in appearance, history, culture, and other respects, some of which are shown in Table 24.

TABLE 24

Blacks and Whites in the United States, 1970-1972

| Characteristic | Black | White |
|---|---|---|
| Head of family | | |
| Male | 71.1% | 90.6% |
| Female | 28.9 | 9.4 |
| | 100.0% | 100.0% |
| | | |
| Residence | | |
| Metropolitan central cities | 56.5% | 27.9% |
| Metropolitan suburbs | 12.2 | 28.8 |
| Outside urban areas | 12.0 | 15.7 |
| Rural | 19.3 | 27.6 |
| | 100.0% | 100.0% |
| | | |
| Life expectancy in years at birth | | |
| Male | 60.5 | 67.8 |
| Female | 68.4 | 75.1 |
| | | |
| Median school years completed by persons twenty-five years of age and older | 9.9 | 12.2 |
| | | |
| Occupation | | |
| Professional | 9.0% | 14.6% |
| Managerial | 4.1 | 11.8 |
| Sales and clerical | 16.0 | 24.3 |
| Blue collar | 39.9 | 33.7 |
| Service | 27.6 | 11.8 |
| Farmworkers | 3.4 | 3.8 |
| | 100.0% | 100.0% |
| | | |
| Median family income | $6,516 | $10,236 |
| | | |
| Unemployment rate (April 1972) | 9.0% | 5.1% |
| | | |
| Proportion of persons below poverty level | 32.1% | 9.9% |
| | | |
| Voting turnout | | |
| 1970 congressional elections | 43.5% | 56.0% |
| 1972 presidential election | 64.0 | 72.0 |

Source: The 1972 presidential election data are from the Survey Research Center, University of Michigan. The other data are from *The American Almanac, 1973* (The Statistical Abstract of the United States, prepared by the Bureau of the Census; New York: Grosset & Dunlap, Inc., 1973).

Table 24 makes it clear that, compared with whites, American blacks today are more concentrated in the inner cities of our large metropolitan areas, have a higher proportion of matriarchal families, have lower life expectancies, have substantially less formal education, work disproportionately in the lower-status and lower-paid occupations, make substantially less money, have more unemployment and more persons below the poverty line, and vote in substantially smaller proportions. Indeed, if we look past their surface manifestations, a good many of the toughest problems American government faces—the "urban problem," poverty, undereducation, unemployment, and so on—are largely indications of the underlying problem of the status of blacks. Let us begin our examination of that problem be reviewing the three principal forces in the conflict and the different objectives sought by each.


## THE THREE SIDES

### White Supremacists

Until the 1950s the status of blacks in the United States was determined largely by a powerful group of whites whom we can designate "white supremacists," and they are still very much to be reckoned with. They believe, first, in racial segregation, the doctrine that whites and blacks should carry on most of their activities in all-white and all-black situations. There must be racially segregated schools, housing areas, transportation, athletic contests, public accommodations, recreation facilities, churches, jobs, and so on. Above all, there should be no interracial marriage. These people believe, second, that whites should dominate both parts of the segregated society, should decide what areas of life will be segregated and what facilities will be enjoyed by each race. And they believe, third, that racial segregation and white supremacy should be embodied in law, as, indeed, they were in the "Jim Crow" laws prevalent before the 1950s.

Up to the 1970s the most visible, vocal, and powerful white supremacists have been concentrated and overwhelmingly dominant in the Deep South: Alabama, Georgia, Louisiana, Mississippi, and South Carolina. Their most prominent official spokesmen have included Senator Strom Thurmond (South Carolina), Governor Lester Maddox (Georgia), Governor John Bell Williams (Mississippi), and, above all, Governor George C. Wallace (Alabama). Their main formal organizations have been the white citizens' councils, the Society for the Preservation of the White Race, and the less "respectable" but active Ku Klux Klan.

When the struggle over desegregating schools, housing, jobs, and unions spread from the South to the northern big cities, however, it became clear that a good many northern whites, particularly blue-collar workers and lower middle-class people, are no more eager for racial integration and equality than are their southern counterparts. "White backlash"—a term coined for the resistance of northern whites to forced desegregation and black militancy—became a major factor in the politics of New York, Chicago, Los Angeles, Minneapolis, and many other northern cities. In the 1968 presidential election segregationist George Wallace carried only Alabama, Arkansas, Georgia, Louisiana, and Mississippi, but he won more than 10 percent of the vote in eight northern states as well. Many observers think that white backlash has played a major role in many recent municipal elections and is likely to become increasingly powerful in northern politics generally.

Briefly, the white supremacists' underlying belief is that blacks are *inherently* inferior to whites in intelligence, morality, civic-mindedness, emotional stability, and so on. This inferiority is no fault of theirs; they are simply born that way, as a horse is born a horse and a monkey is born a monkey. As long as blacks are "kept in their

Some say whites are inherently superior: a white-supremacy counterdemonstration in Louisiana. Source: Wide World Photos.

place," they can play useful roles in society by performing many of its menial jobs; furthermore, they themselves will be happiest playing only these roles. But if blacks are not kept in their place—if, for instance, they are permitted to vote, to hold public office, to attend the same schools as whites, and to hold the same jobs as whites—their inherent inferiority will drag down the whole community, blacks and whites alike, to their own low level. The worst catastrophe that can occur is racial intermarriage, for the children produced by such alliances will "mongrelize" the whole population with disastrous consequences for the nation. If blacks will not voluntarily keep their places therefore, they must be forcibly kept there. Any effort by black or white integrationists to raise blacks to a higher place must be vigilantly guarded against. To this end the white supremacists have employed various devices, some of which we shall consider later.

The Rights of Man: Challenges and Responses

565

"I have a dream..." Martin Luther King, Jr., addressing a crowd at the Lincoln Memorial during the August 1963 March on Washington. Source: Pictorial Parade Inc.

*Integrationists*

Until recently the white supremacists' most visible opponents have been both black and white integrationists. They have fought for a society most eloquently described by the martyred black leader, Rev. Martin Luther King, Jr., in his famous speech at the Lincoln Memorial during the March on Washington in 1963:

> The marvelous new militancy which has engulfed the Negro community must not lead us to a distrust of all white people, for many of our white brothers, as evidenced by their presence here today, have come to realize that their destiny is tied up with our destiny. They have come to realize that their freedom is inextricably bound to our freedom. We cannot walk alone. . . . I have a dream that my four little children will one day live in a nation where they will not be judged by the color of their skin but by the content of their character.[21]

Integrationists seek a society in which blacks and whites intermingle as much or as little as they wish, enjoy the same welfare-state guarantees, and are denied no

[21] This speech has been reproduced in many books, including John Hope Franklin and Isidore Starr (eds.), *The Negro in Twentieth Century America* (New York: Vintage Books, 1967), pp. 145–146.

opportunity because of skin color. Many integrationist organizations have been formed, but the most influential have been the following.[22]

**The National Association for the Advancement of Colored People (NAACP)**
The oldest of the integrationist groups, the National Association for the Advancement of Colored People, founded in 1909, has consistently emphasized pressure on Congress and constitutional challenges to discrimination in the Federal courts and has won many notable legislative and judicial victories, some of which we shall consider in a moment. Its emphasis on acting within the system, its occasional acceptance of whites in positions of leadership, and its strong resistance to the movement toward black autonomy and separatism have given it the reputation of being the conservative wing of the black movement.

**The National Urban League**    The National Urban League, founded in 1910, stresses interracial educational programs in local communities, aimed at breaking down segregation and discrimination, particularly in housing and employment. It operates as actively in the North as in the South, and its long-time Executive Director, Whitney M. Young, Jr., was generally regarded as one of the leading moderates in the movement.

**The Southern Christian Leadership Conference (SCLC)**    The Southern Christian Leadership Conference was founded by Dr. King in 1957 and headed by him until his murder in 1968. It pioneered the use of Gandhian nonviolent resistance and has won not only a number of victories over segregation in southern cities but also the 1965 Nobel Peace Prize for Dr. King. In recent years, under the leadership of Dr. King's successor, Ralph D. Abernathy, it has joined with impoverished whites and Mexican-Americans to press for greater government efforts to end poverty.

**The Congress of Racial Equality (CORE)**    Probably the most militant of the integrationist organizations has been the Congress of Racial Equality, founded in 1941 by James Farmer. CORE at first operated mainly in the North, but since the early 1950s it has operated in the South as well. It pioneered the use of such direct-action techniques as picketing, demonstrations, "sit-ins," and boycotts. It has not, however, committed itself to the black-autonomy movement; indeed, in 1969 Farmer accepted an appointment as Assistant Secretary for Administration of the Department of Health, Education and Welfare in the new Nixon administration, though he later resigned.

These four organizations have been in the forefront of the post-1945 battles over desegregation, which we shall survey briefly later. First, however, we must note a highly significant new development in black politics: the rise of a group that rejects integration as a goal for blacks and works instead for an autonomous black community, segregated from whites and run by blacks for blacks.

---

[22] For more detailed descriptions of these organizations see Arnold M. Rose (ed.), "The Negro Protest," *Annals of the American Academy of Political and Social Science,* 357 (January 1965); and Matthew Holden, Jr., *The Politics of the Black "Nation"* (San Francisco: Chandler Publishing Company, 1973).

Integrationists want blacks and whites to work together for a better future: VISTA worker in a North Carolina school. Source: Bruce Roberts, Rapho Guillumette.

### Black Autonomists

During black Americans' long struggle to climb out of slavery and second-class citizenship a few leaders have flatly rejected racial integration as a goal. They have urged that, rather than swallowing white values and clawing for places in the white man's world, blacks should take pride in their blackness and rejoice in their differences from whites. And they have insisted that blacks should demand a society in which they can preserve their own cultural heritage, live by their own values, and control their own politics, government, and economy. There are variations on this position: black nationalism, black separatism, Black Power. But the theme of black autonomy—of black control of black affairs—is basic to all.

The best known of the early black autonomists was Marcus Garvey, an immigrant from Jamaica, who founded and led the Universal Negro Improvement Association in the 1920s. Presaging the ideas of many of today's black autonomists, Garvey

**Marcus Garvey.** Source:
Culver Pictures, Inc.

denounced the NAACP's quest for integration as submission to the white oppressor's values, gloried in American blacks' African roots, preached black pride in black distinctiveness, and proclaimed that the future for all blacks lies in Africa rather than in white society.[23] Establishing an independent all-black nation in Africa, declared Garvey, is the only answer:

> Nationhood is the strongest security of any people and it is for that the Universal Negro Improvement Association strives at this time. With the clamor of other peoples for a similar purpose, we raise a noise even to high heaven for the admission of the Negro into the plan of autonomy.[24]

In our time the main exponents of black autonomy have been the Black Muslims and the exponents of Black Power. Their somewhat different positions may be characterized as follows.

---

[23] The leading account of Garvey's life and ideas is E. David Cronon, *Black Moses: The Story of Marcus Garvey and the Universal Negro Improvement Association* (Madison, Wis.: University of Wisconsin Press, 1968).

[24] Marcus Garvey, ''The Negro's Place in World Reorganization,'' in Franklin and Starr, *The Negro in Twentieth Century America,* p. 109.

**The Black Muslims**[25]    The Black Muslim political-religious movement was founded early in the twentieth century and since 1934 has been led by a former Baptist minister, Elijah Poole, who has taken the name Elijah Muhammed.[26] The movement proceeds from the premise that the black man is the true descendant of the original man created by Allah the Supreme Being. A white is not really a man at all but rather a kind of devil created by an antigod to test Allah's people—hence the Black Muslims' talk of "white devils." Palaver about the possibility or desirability of equality between whites and blacks is all dishonest, for blacks are historically and by destiny the superior race. Christianity is a false religion worshiping a false god, and blacks must be free of its lies before they can achieve their true destiny. The idea of racial integration is an insult to blackness and a dangerous chimera for blacks; for, in the words of Malcolm X, Elijah Muhammed's chief spokesman before his defection and murder:

> We believe that the earth will become all Muslim, all Islam, and because we are in a Christian country we believe that this Christian country will have to accept Allah as God, accept the religion of Islam as God's religion, or otherwise God will come in and wipe it out. And we don't want to be wiped out with the American white man, we don't want to integrate with him, we want to separate from him.[27]

The only acceptable goal for American blacks, according to Elijah Muhammed, is complete separation of the races and the resettlement of all blacks in their own nation, run by blacks for blacks, though initially supported by whites as token compensation for three centuries of unpaid black toil:

> We want our people in America whose parents or grandparents were descendants from slaves, to be allowed to establish a separate state or territory of their own—either on this continent or elsewhere. We believe that our former slave masters are obligated to provide such land and that the area must be fertile and minerally rich. We believe that our former slave masters are obligated to maintain and supply our needs in this separate territory for the next 20 to 25 years—until we are able to produce and supply our own needs.[28]

The Black Muslims remain a very small proportion of American blacks (membership is estimated at no more than 100,000). But the acerbic brilliance of Malcom

---

[25] The most thorough study is C. Eric Lincoln, *The Black Muslims in America* (Boston: The Beacon Press, 1961).

[26] All Black Muslims take new names upon joining the movement: Malcolm Little thus became Malcolm X, and Cassius Clay became Muhammed Ali. The reason is that, as blacks are descended from slaves and slaves were given the surnames of their white owners, clinging to those names is a form of submission to white racism; see the explanation by Malcolm X in Francis L. Broderick and August Meier (eds.), *Negro Protest Thought in the Twentieth Century* (Indianapolis, Ind.: The Bobbs-Merrill Company, Inc., 1965), p. 358.

[27] Broderick and Meier, *Negro Protest Thought in the Twentieth Century,* p. 365.

[28] Elijah Muhammed, "What the Muslims Want," *Muhammed Speaks* [the Black Muslims' official newspaper], July 2, 1965, quoted in Franklin and Starr, *The Negro in Twentieth Century America,* p. 121.

Leaders of the Black Muslim movement: (left) Elijah Muhammed, 1965; (right) Malcolm X, 1963. Source: Wide World Photos.

X[29] and the pugilistic success and legal and religious difficulties of Muhammed Ali have brought considerable attention to the movement and its views. And it is among the most extreme of the black autonomist movements—at a time when today's militant may well be tomorrow's Uncle Tom. As such it exerts considerable ideological pressure on other black movements.

**Black Power: Doctrine and Organization**   The Student Nonviolent Coordinating Committee (SNCC) was organized in 1960 by black and white college students to coordinate student "sit-ins." It soon shifted its emphasis to organizing voter-registration and -education drives for southern blacks and to protesting the Vietnam war. In the mid-1960s SNCC was dominated by dynamic young black leaders—notably Stokely Carmichael, H. Rap Brown, and James Forman—who converted it into an organization to press for their version of black autonomy, which they dubbed "Black Power."[30]

As set forth in the clearest and most authoritative exposition,[31] the first main tenet of Black Power is that all blacks must develop a strong sense of their community in blackness; pride in their African, slave, and ghetto heritage; full acceptance of black values; and a deep conviction that they are fundamentally different from whites, that "black is beautiful." The first job for blacks is "to redefine ourselves. Our basic need is to reclaim our history and our identity from what must be called cultural terrorism, from the depredation of self-justifying white guilt."[32]

---

[29] As vividly apparent in his absorbing *Autobiography* (New York: Grove Press, Inc., 1966).

[30] A brief sympathetic account of SNCC's evolution is presented in Paul Jacobs and Saul Landau, *The New Radicals* (New York: Vintage Books 1966), chap. 3.

[31] Carmichael and Hamilton, *Black Power*.

[32] Carmichael and Hamilton, *Black Power*, pp. 34–35.

Second, although organizations like SNCC that work for black causes may be willing to accept financial and work support from whites, they should be led by blacks only; any white who wishes to help must clearly understand his subordinate role. For, the authors say, "no matter how 'liberal' a white person might be, he cannot ultimately escape the overpowering influence—on himself and on black people—of his whiteness in a racist society."[33] This statement, they make clear, applies to *all* whites, no matter how young or liberal or anti-Establishment:

> All too frequently ... many young, middle-class, white Americans, like some sort of Pepsi generation, have wanted to "come alive" through the black community and black groups. They have wanted to be where the action is—and the action has been in those places. They have sought refuge among blacks from a sterile, meaningless, irrelevant life in middle-class America. They have been unable to deal with the stifling, racist, parochial, split-level mentality of their parents, teachers, preachers and friends. Many have come seeing "no difference in color," they have come "color blind." But at this time and in this land, color *is* a factor and we should not overlook or deny this. The black organizations do not need this kind of idealism, which borders on paternalism.[34]

Third, blacks must abandon all delusions that they can make real progress through the voluntary surrender of domination by whites, liberal or not. They must *make* whites meet black demands in the only way possible: by organizing and mobilizing black votes and black economic power so as to make it impossible for whites to ignore black demands or fob them off with "tokenism." Black Power must do in the twentieth century what Irish power, Italian power, and Jewish power did in the nineteenth to overcome oppression by the WASPs.[35]

Fourth, blacks will never advance by working within the white man's parties or playing them off against one another. Blacks can never be more than small minorities perpetually manipulated by white party leaders. They must therefore organize their own, entirely new, all-black parties; elect militant blacks to office wherever black voters are in the majority; demand a fair share of the offices where black voters are less than a majority; and, above all, keep up such unremitting, uncompromising, militant pressure that whites will have no choice but to yield.[36]

The Black Panther party was organized by SNCC in Lowndes County, Alabama, in 1966 in accordance with these ideas, and branches have been established in several other places since. During its early years it was less a political party than a kind of defense arm for protecting—with arms, if necessary—blacks from white violence. For a time it served for many whites as the embodiment of the idea of war-to-the-death between blacks and whites; some of its leaders (for example, Fred Hampton) were killed in clashes with white police; others (Eldridge Cleaver) left the country completely to escape prosecution; and still others (Bobby Seale) were tried for violent crimes but acquitted. In the mid-1970s, however, it moved away from

---

[33] Carmichael and Hamilton, *Black Power,* p. 61.

[34] Carmichael and Hamilton, *Black Power,* p. 83; italics in the original.

[35] Carmichael and Hamilton, *Black Power,* pp. 51–52.

[36] Carmichael and Hamilton, *Black Power,* chaps. 5, 8.

**Black Panthers, berets, and salutes.** Source: Black Star—Claus Meyer.

violent action to become more of a social-service organization for impoverished blacks and a party operating inside the regular bounds of the American electoral system. This was dramatized by Bobby Seale's race for mayor of Oakland, California, in 1973, in which he abandoned most militant rhetoric and finished second in the election.

It seems clear that, until now at least, only a small fraction of American blacks support Black Power in its most extreme version. For example, a sample survey of the nation's blacks taken for *Newsweek* in 1969 found that 78 percent preferred integrated schools and 74 percent favored integrated neighborhoods, whereas only 21 percent favored a separate black nation.[37] However, "only" 21 percent of American blacks is nearly 5 million people, and later surveys suggest that the proportion of black separatists may be getting larger.

The Rights of Man: Challenges and Responses

[37] *Newsweek,* June 30, 1969, p. 20.

But, as does any militant minority of *enragés* burning with a sense of injustice and an impatience to end it, Black Power advocates have had a great deal of influence and are likely to have more. For one thing, they put heavy pressure on integrationist organizations to produce real and visible gains soon. For another, blacks under thirty are significantly more militant than are those over thirty: more of them are attracted to Black Power doctrines, believe that ghetto riots are justified, think that blacks will gain by violence, approve of the ideas of Malcolm X, and favor militant black organizations. That the "under thirties" constitute a much higher proportion of blacks than of whites (the median age of blacks is twenty-one, compared with twenty-nine for whites) suggests that black militancy and some version of Black Power are likely to grow stronger, rather than weaker, in the years to come.[38]

For the moment, however, the political goal of perhaps three-fourths of America's blacks is integration, not autonomy. Their struggle for integration began in earnest in the 1940s, accelerated in the 1950s, and accelerated even more in the 1960s and early 1970s. We shall conclude this survey by briefly noting the current status of the struggle in each of its most important arenas.

## THE STRUGGLE FOR INTEGRATION

### Voting

Since the Reconstruction period immediately following the Civil War, southern white supremacists have attempted, by means of one device or another—poll taxes, literacy tests, "grandfather clauses," and "white primaries"—to keep blacks from exercising the voting rights granted them by the Fifteenth Amendment. But the Twenty-Fourth Amendment, ratified in 1964, outlaws state requirements of poll taxes for voting in Federal elections, and the Supreme Court has held unconstitutional all legal devices intended to keep blacks from voting because of their race.

Most important of all is the Voting Rights Act passed by Congress in 1965. This act instructs the U.S. Attorney General to determine whether or not an unusually low voting turnout in any of the nation's counties results from racial discrimination. If he determines that it does, he is empowered to send Federal registrars into any such county with the authority and duty to register all qualified voters, regardless of local officials. Furthermore, the Federal representatives must ignore any local rules used to discriminate against blacks and must supervise the conduct of elections to make sure that no registered voter is in any way inhibited from voting. Such registrars have been sent into a number of southern counties; in other areas local registrars have voluntarily given up trying to disfranchise blacks. As a result, over 60 percent of the eligible blacks are now registered voters in the eleven southern (former Confederate) states, compared with an estimated 12 percent in 1947! In the 1968 presidential election, the Census Bureau estimates, 51.4 percent of voting-age blacks in the South actually voted, compared with 44.0 percent in 1964 and 28.0 percent in 1960.[39]

---

[38] Richard Scammon in *Newsweek*, June 30, 1969, p. 18, and the poll results, p. 21.

[39] U.S. Bureau of the Census, *Current Population Reports* (Washington, D.C.: U.S. Government Printing Office, 1968), Series P-20, No. 177.

It is unlikely that increased voting power will by itself enable southern blacks to win all their objectives;[40] but winning the full *right* to vote is surely a major step toward equal rights, integration, Black Power, or any other black goal.[41]

## Education[42]

For many years white supremacists have insisted that under no conditions must blacks be permitted to attend the same schools as whites, arguing that the blacks' intellectual inferiority will be a drag on the educational development of white pupils. Immediately after the Civil War most states, southern and northern alike, adopted constitutional or statutory prohibitions on racial integration in public schools.[43] In the succeeding decades, however, most states outside the South repealed them, and twenty-two states adopted constitutional or statutory provisions specifically prohibiting such segregation.

The present crisis in this long-standing conflict began in 1954. In that year a total of nineteen states (four of them outside the South) and the District of Columbia legally required racial segregation in their public schools. On several occasions these laws had been challenged in the Supreme Court as violations of the clause in the Fourteenth Amendment that provides, "No State shall . . . deny to any person within its jurisdiction the equal protection of the laws"; but the Court had consistently upheld them, following the "separate but equal" rule first laid down in 1896 on grounds that segregation in itself was not a denial of equal protection as long as equal facilities were afforded to both races.[44] In the early 1950s, however, the NAACP under the leadership of its principal constitutional lawyer, Thurgood Marshall (now serving as the first black Justice of the U.S. Supreme Court), again challenged the constitutionality of state school-segregation laws, asking the Court to abandon the old "separate but equal" formula. In a unanimous opinion written by Chief Justice Earl Warren in *Brown* v. *Board of Education* the Court did just that, holding that racial segregation is in itself a denial of equal protection, regardless of the facilities provided; in 1955 the Court ordered the Federal district courts to proceed "with all deliberate speed" to see that local school boards complied with the ruling.[45]

---

[40] This conclusion is shared by William R. Keech, *The Impact of Negro Voting: The Role of the Vote in the Quest for Equality* (Skokie, Ill.: Rand McNally & Company, 1968).

[41] For a study in depth of factors affecting southern blacks' political attitudes and participation levels, see Donald R. Matthews and James W. Prothro, *Negroes and The New Southern Politics* (New York: Harcourt Brace Jovanovich, Inc., 1966).

[42] An excellent account of the background of the Brown decision is Robert J. Harris, *The Quest for Equality* (Baton Rouge, La.: Louisiana State University Press, 1960). The Southern Education Reporting Service provides the most up-to-date information on the progress of school desegregation.

[43] These prohibitions were embodied in Jim Crow laws requiring racial segregation in a number of areas; see C. Vann Woodward, *The Strange Career of Jim Crow* (New York: Oxford University Press, 1957).

[44] Plessy v. Ferguson, 163 U.S. 537 (1896).

[45] Brown v. Board of Education, 347 U.S. 483 (1954); and the implementation decision, 349 U.S. 294 (1955).

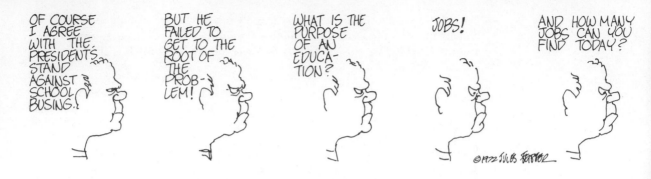

OF COURSE I AGREE WITH THE PRESIDENT'S STAND AGAINST SCHOOL BUSING!

BUT HE FAILED TO GET TO THE ROOT OF THE PROBLEM!

WHAT IS THE PURPOSE OF AN EDUCATION?

JOBS!

AND HOW MANY JOBS CAN YOU FIND TODAY?

©1972 JULES FEIFFER

**A liberal's view of a conservative's view of busing.** Source: ©1972 Jules Feiffer. Courtesy Publishers-Hall Syndicate.

The border states (Delaware, Kentucky, Maryland, Missouri, Oklahoma, and West Virginia) quickly complied with the Court's ruling. The upper southern states (Arkansas, Florida, North Carolina, Tennessee, Texas, and Virginia) also complied, though more slowly and less completely. The Deep South states complied very little, and ten years after the Brown decision their schools were almost as segregated as they had been before.

Then in 1964 Congress—under the leadership of Senator Hubert Humphrey and the relentless prodding, ironically, of the first southern President since 1869, Lyndon B. Johnson of Texas—passed the most far-reaching Federal civil-rights legislation since Reconstruction. We shall observe the impact of the Civil Rights Act of 1964 in several areas. Title VI authorizes the Office of Education to cut off Federal financial aid to any school district that refuses to initiate an acceptable program of desegregation. There has been a great deal of controversy over the Office's use of its powers. Many southern whites protest that they are being strong-armed into premature and ill-advised desegregation, and many integrationist leaders charge that the government has been far too prone to accept "tokenism" as satisfying desegregation requirements.

The problem and the controversy have, furthermore, become as acute in many northern big cities as in the South. The concentration of blacks in the cities' ghetto areas plus the traditional practice of drawing school-district boundaries to serve local neighborhoods has resulted in de facto segregation: Although no black children are now *legally* prohibited from attending white schools, most live in all-black neighborhoods and consequently attend all-black schools. Some cities have attempted to overcome de facto segregation by bussing children from black neighborhoods to white schools and vice versa, but many white parents strongly object, and the conflict has spread more and more among northern as well as southern schools.[46]

The conflict escalated sharply in January 1972 when Federal district judge Robert Merhige ordered all the school districts, both urban and suburban, of Richmond, Virginia, consolidated into one, and directed that every school in the new district must have from 20 to 40 percent black pupils. This could only be accomplished by bussing children from the white suburbs to mainly black schools in the

Policy Outputs and Impacts

---

[46] See the summary in *Congressional Quarterly Weekly Report,* July 29, 1972, pp. 1882–1885.

central city and vice versa, and the decision touched off a major political storm. In March President Nixon called for a moratorium on all court-ordered bussing intended to produce arithmetic racial balance in public schools, and proposed increased Federal expenditures to upgrade the schools in poor (that is, mainly black, center-city) schools. George Wallace made opposition to bussing one of the main themes in his campaign for the Democratic presidential nomination, and won a good deal of support in the North as well as the South (for example, he swept the Michigan primary with 51 percent of the votes compared to McGovern's 27 percent and Humphrey's 16 percent). The two major parties were sharply opposed on the bussing issue in the 1972 campaign: the Democratic platform declared that bussing "must continue to be available to eliminate legally imposed segregation and improve the quality of education for all children"; the Republican platform endorsed Nixon's moratorium plan and declared, "We are unequivocally opposed to bussing for racial balance. . . . We regard it as unnecessary, counter-productive and wrong."

In June 1972 a court of appeals overruled Judge Merhige's decision, and in May 1973 the Supreme Court split four to four in its review of the case. This had the effect of upholding the ruling of the court of appeals, but provided no authoritative Supreme Court decision on the basic issue of whether de facto school segregation may—or must—be overcome by legally-imposed racial balance in all schools, through bussing or any other means. Such a decision is likely to come soon, and when it does it will constitute another milestone in the long and difficult path toward (or away from?) the racial integration of the nation's schools. In short, the 1954 Brown decision constituted a single—but far from total—victory for the forces of integration.

### Housing

For many years blacks (and, to a lesser extent, Jews) have been denied equal opportunities for housing by means of "restrictive convenants," agreements among white property owners that they will not sell their houses to black buyers, thus preserving all-white neighborhoods. These covenants used to be inserted in formal contracts among property owners; an owner who violated such a covenant by selling to a black could be sued in the courts for breach of contract. In 1948, however, the Supreme Court struck a powerful (though not mortal) blow at restrictive covenants by ruling that, though they are not in themselves unlawful, they cannot be enforced by any court of law, state or Federal, for such enforcement would make the courts parties to the covenants, in violation of the Fourteenth Amendment.[47]

But this decision was at best a negative sanction, and many restrictive covenants continued to be made and effectively enforced as unwritten "gentlemen's agreements." Finally, in 1968, after years of battle over the issue, Congress passed a major open-housing law. The 1968 act prohibits racial discrimination in the sale or rental of most of the nation's housing. It applies to all public housing and urban-renewal projects, all private multiple-unit dwellings except those of no more than four units and occupied by their owners, all single-family houses not owned by private individuals, and all privately owned single-family houses sold or rented by real-estate agents or brokers. About the only exemptions are privately owned homes whose owners sell or rent them without the services of real-estate agents or brokers. The act is thus estimated to apply to about 80 percent of all the nation's dwelling units.

The passage of such an act was certainly a great victory for the integrationists. How effectively and faithfully it is enforced (the act places enforcement responsibility upon the Secretary of Housing and Urban Development) will determine how great the victory was.

### Public Accommodations

White supremacists have long sought to keep blacks from using the same public services and accommodations that whites use—riding in the same parts of trains and buses; sitting in the same parts of theaters; using the same restaurants, golf courses, swimming pools, barbershops, public rest rooms, and public drinking fountains. For a time more than twenty states had Jim Crow laws requiring such segregation, but they were deemed unconstitutional after the Brown decision had thrown out the old "separate but equal" formula. Another twenty states adopted laws prohibiting racial discrimination by private businesses offering public accommodations or by any publicly owned and operated facility. But many of these laws were enforced little or not at all, blacks were commonly refused service, and integrationist leaders came to believe that only action by the Federal government could guarantee equal rights in this area.

They achieved their goal in the Civil Rights Act of 1964. Title II forbids racial discrimination in all publicly owned or operated facilities. It also prohibits racial discrimination in serving customers of all private businesses that provide public accommodations—hotels, motels, restaurants, gasoline stations, theaters, sports arenas, and the like. Most of the larger businesses in this category in most southern medium-sized and large cities have evidently concluded that resistance to the law is hopeless and have opened their doors to blacks on an equal footing with whites. A number of small and rural communities in the South still exclude blacks from municipal and private accommodations, but nevertheless this area is one in which integrationists have won their most solid victories.

[47] Shelley v. Kraemer, 334 U.S. 1 (1948).

*Employment*

Blacks have long been and still are the most economically depressed ethnic group in America. The data in Table 24 show that the median income of black families in 1970 was only about 64 percent of that of white families—not by chance. White employers and white-dominated unions have long arranged that the only jobs open to most blacks have been the lowest-paying, especially in unskilled agricultural and industrial labor and domestic service. Most black leaders, whatever their differences on other issues, give top priority to making sure that a qualified black has as good a chance at a desirable job as does an equally qualified white. Some militant leaders, indeed, argue that blacks should be given preferential treatment over whites if their qualifications are anywhere near equal; for it is only simple justice, they argue, to reverse the racial advantages that whites have enjoyed for so long. Other black leaders, however, emphasize the right to equal opportunity along with provision of genuinely equal job opportunities; they urge that the nation also provide massive programs for educating and training blacks in knowledge and skills that will enable them to perform well in demanding and well-paying jobs.

Before 1964 some states had adopted fair employment-practices laws, but many had not. Again the Civil Rights Act was a major turning point. Title VII forbids private employers to practice racial discrimination in hiring or promotion. It also prohibits labor unions from excluding any applicant for membership because of his race. The rules are enforced by a five-man Equal Employment Opportunity Commission, which is empowered to hear and investigate charges of discrimination against employers or unions and to ask the U.S. Attorney General to force compliance when efforts at persuasion fail.

In the first few years after the 1964 act went into effect the Commission averaged around 6500 complaints a year; race was the basis of three out of five. In 1967 Secretary of Labor W. Willard Wirtz reported that, as a result of the act, "the great majority" of employers had abandoned or reduced discriminatory hiring policies at the "entry" level but that "when it comes to upgrading promotions, and hiring in higher level jobs, hardly a dent has been made."[48] Since Secretary Wirtz wrote those words, the evidence is that at least a small dent has been made: in the period 1967-1968 the median income of black families was only about 58 percent of that of white families, while, as we have seen, in 1970 it had risen to 64 percent.

This, then, is progress for the cause of equal employment rights for black Americans, but it is slow progress. Many black leaders are impatient with its slowness, and many believe that the success or failure of the integrationist appeal to blacks will ultimately turn upon developments in this area more than upon any other single factor. Title VII of the 1964 Civil Rights Act is less a victory than a step that makes possible the greatest victory of all—but one that has so far been only partially achieved.

---

[48] Quoted in *Revolution in Civil Rights* (4th ed.; Washington, D.C.: Congressional Quarterly Service, 1968), p. 31.

## RACIAL SEPARATION AND DISCRIMINATION
## IN THE REPUBLIC OF SOUTH AFRICA[49]

The United States is by no means the only democratic country in which a major political group is pressing for a government policy of white supremacy. Most Australians, for example, have long regarded their nation as "a white island in a colored sea," and since its origins as a nation Australia has consistently followed a "white Australia" policy supported by all parties. This policy has prevented racial conflict by simply prohibiting nonwhite immigration and thus restricting the nonwhite population to a tiny fraction of the total.[50]

Even Great Britain, long considered a model of racial equality, has had its troubles. The great influx of Pakistanis and black West Indians in the 1950s led to the formation of racial ghettos in several big cities, race riots in the Notting Hill Gate area of London, and such ugly political slogans as "If you want a nigger neighbour, vote Labour," which is supposed to have cost Labour's prospective foreign secretary, Patrick Gordon Walker, his seat at Smethwick in the 1964 general election. It also led to the passage in 1961 of the Commonwealth Immigrants Act, which ended the free entry of West Indians and Pakistanis.

The drive for governmentally enforced white supremacy has come closest to total victory in the Republic of South Africa, which presently has a population of nearly 23 million, of whom 3,750,000 are of pure European descent, 2,000,000 are "colored" (of mixed native and European descent), and 17,000,000 are of pure native, or Bantu, descent. Most of the Europeans are highly conscious of their status as a small white minority among a large native majority, and their consciousness is reinforced by the knowledge that on the whole continent of Africa there are only about 5 million Europeans, compared with nearly 300 million natives.

From the time of the earliest white settlements, most Europeans in South Africa—the Afrikaners (settlers of Dutch descent) and the British-descended settlers alike—have been acutely conscious of the *swart gevaar* ("black menace" in Afrikaans, the language of the Dutch-descended South Africans) and have resolved to maintain the *baaskap* (literally "boss-ship") of white men over black. Their fears and resolution were clearly expressed in a 1955 statement by Eric H. Louw, then South African Foreign Minister:

> If we were to give [the natives] equality of franchise, then eventually the white man would be outvoted, and the non-Europeans would have control. The present laws which are for the purpose of keeping the races separate, allowing each race to develop along its own lines in its own areas—those laws would all be swept away. European and Bantu would live together. There would be mis-

---

[49] Among the best discussions are Gwendolen M. Carter, *The Politics of Inequality* (2d ed.; New York: Frederick A. Praeger, Inc., 1959); Edward Roux, *Time Longer than Rope* (2d ed.; Madison, Wis.: University of Wisconsin Press, 1964); and Leonard M. Thompson, *Politics in the Republic of South Africa* (Boston: Little, Brown & Company, 1966).

[50] See Alexander Brady, *Democracy in the Dominions* (2d ed.; Toronto: University of Toronto Press, 1952), pp. 143–147.

cegenation, and in another 100 years, or even earlier, South Africa would become a country with a large mixed population.[51]

### The Policy of Apartheid

For many years the white rulers of South Africa have pursued the policy of apartheid ("separateness"). The long-range goal of this policy is complete separation of the natives from the Europeans, with each race living in its own special areas but with ultimate governmental power over all areas and races remaining exclusively in white hands. Most white South Africans, however, regard the achievement of this goal as 200–300 years away; as a short-range policy apartheid generally means as nearly complete segregation of the races as possible and white supremacy in all aspects of life. Among its leading legal manifestations are the following.

**Separation**   The Population Registration Act of 1950 provides for the classification and registration of the entire South African population in three categories: European, native, and colored. Each person must be ticketed and photographed and must carry an identity card showing to which of the three races he belongs. The ultimate goal is the compilation of a complete "Book of Life" containing the racial classification of every South African. The Group Areas Act of 1950 empowers the government to designate particular areas for exclusive occupancy by particular races, and the Native Resettlement Act authorizes the forcible relocation of natives from their present living areas to native "reserves." Every native must carry an identity card, and if he wishes to travel or live outside his reserve he must show on demand a pass authorizing him to do so. Since 1950 the government has actually moved several hundred thousand natives in accordance with this legislation, but at present fewer than half the natives live in reserves. Those who do are required by the government to follow their ancient forms of tribal government and chieftainship, even though many believe that these forms are outmoded and wish to adopt more modern procedures.

**Education**   The South African government now controls all native education and for the most part teaches only what it finds appropriate to the traditionally primitive culture and technology of the Bantus. Before 1957 a few coloreds and natives attended South Africa's universities. The Separate Universities Education Act of 1957 ended that; all nonwhites are barred from attending any of the regular universities, and a Bantu college has been established for each nonwhite ethnic group: one for the Xhosa, another for the Zulus, another for the Sotho, another for the coloreds, and so on. None of these colleges is independent; all are administered directly by government departments to make sure that the "right" things are taught.

**Political Participation**   In only one of the five provinces, Cape Province, have natives and coloreds ever been allowed to vote for members of the national Parliament. The Representation of Natives Act of 1936 confined the natives to voting for only

[51] From a copyrighted interview in *U.S. News & World Report,* 39 (July 22, 1955), pp. 58–63.

seven members of Parliament, each of whom had to be a European. In 1956 the coloreds were deprived of the right to vote for members of Parliament other than the seven "native representatives." And in 1960 Cape Province natives and colored were deprived of even these rights, and the native representatives were abolished.

**Occupations**   Natives in South Africa have long been informally barred from engaging in any occupation higher or better paid than domestic service and unskilled labor. The Industrial Conciliation Act of 1954 placed the power of the government behind this discrimination by authorizing the Minister of Labor to determine at his own discretion what occupations will be open to members of the various races.

**Public Services and Accommodations**   Complete racial segregation in such areas as transportation, hospitals, cemeteries, restaurants, and theaters has long been practiced by the private individuals who manage them. The Separate Amenities Act of 1953 made such segregation compulsory.

### Political Conflict and Constitutional Revision

Only a few South African whites (including the well-known novelist Alan Paton) support the tiny Liberal party, which advocates a policy of gradual racial integration and equality. The great bulk of the European population and the parties they support believe in some form of apartheid, although there has been sharp conflict over the pace and proper means of achieving it. This conflict has centered mainly on the two leading political parties: the Nationalist party, now led by Prime Minister B. J. Vorster, and the United party, formerly led by Field Marshal Jan Christiaan Smuts and now headed by Sir de Villiers Graaff.

The Nationalists replaced the United party in power in the general election of 1948 and since then have pressed for drastic apartheid at a pace more rapid than their opponents have thought proper. They have controlled Parliament ever since, and in their resolute effort to establish apartheid and to stamp out all effective opposition to it they have pushed the nation well along the road to totalitarianism, although not yet quite all the way. There have been several major milestones in this movement.

In 1951 the Nationalist Government forced through the Suppression of Communism Act, which not only empowers the government to jail all "communists" and suppress all "communist" doctrines but also defines "communism" as any doctrine or scheme "which aims at bringing about any political, industrial, or economic change within the [Republic] by the promotion of disturbance or by the threat of such acts" or "which aims at the encouragement of feelings of hostility between the European and non-European races in the [Republic]."[52]

In 1951 the Nationalist Government pushed through Parliament a bill to strike the coloreds from the common roll of voters in Cape Province, but the five-man Supreme Court of Appeals unanimously declared it unconstitutional. The Nationalists then adopted a bill making Parliament itself the high court with final authority to interpret the Constitution; the Supreme Court also declared this law unconstitu-

---

[52] Quoted in John Gunther, *Inside Africa* (New York: Harper & Row, Publishers, 1955), p. 540.

tional. After three years of searching for ways of circumventing the Court, the Nationalists found one: In 1955 they passed a bill enlarging the Court from five to eleven members; the Nationalist Prime Minister appointed as the six new judges men known to be faithful supporters of the Nationalist program. Thereafter the Court caused no trouble.

In the years following, the Nationalists passed the "ninety-day law," which empowers the government to arrest anyone it wishes and to hold him in house or village arrest without having to bring him to trial. Under this provision Chief Albert Luthuli, who won the 1960 Nobel Peace Prize, was confined to his village in Natal for years, and some white as well as black dissenters have been jailed under it. In 1962 the Nationalists also enacted the General Law Amendment (Sabotage) Act, which gives a very broad definition of sabotage and makes it punishable by death. Most observers now believe that there is no legal or political barrier in the path of any policy of apartheid that the Nationalists may wish to enact.

### The Future of Apartheid

In 1955 the Nationalist Government appointed a special commission, headed by F. R. Tomlinson, to study the problem of implementing apartheid more rapidly. In 1956 the government accepted the commission's report as the basis of its future policy, which has come to be known as the "Bantustan policy." It proposes to press on with the development of four exclusively native areas and to spend money to develop them for mass relocation of the natives. The Promotion of Bantu Self-Government Act of 1959 established the first Bantustan under the new policy. The government has announced, however, that it will not spend its funds for development of these areas and that any development funds must come from the natives themselves. An American commentator, Gwendolen M. Carter, has suggested that, as there is no possibility that the natives can ever provide from their own resources anything remotely approaching what is needed, it is unlikely that the Bantustan policy will be fully implemented in the foreseeable future.[53] If she is correct, for some time to come apartheid in South Africa will continue to mean government policies of segregation and white supremacy, rather than complete separation of the two races.

## THE RIGHTS OF MAN: A SUMMARY

In this and the preceding chapter I have tried to portray the problem of the rights of man in the modern world in its philosophical and legal and in its political aspects as well. Specifically, I have made the following observations.

First, the term "civil rights" refers both to certain things that governments are constitutionally prohibited from doing to individuals and to certain duties that governments are constitutionally obligated to perform for individuals.

Second, although every present-day Constitution contains at least some formal guarantees of civil rights, modern nations can be divided into two classes: the "free nations," in which most people value highly the protection of these rights and insist

---

The Rights of Man:
Challenges and Responses

[53] Carter, "The Consequences of *Apartheid," Annals of the American Academy of Political and Social Science,* 306 (July 1956), pp. 38–42.

that their governments preserve them, and the "authoritarian nations," in which the preservation of civil rights is far outranked by other, conflicting values.

Third, in the free nations most people are committed to the idea that civil rights should be preserved either as ends in themselves or as indispensable means for creating and maintaining the good society.

Fourth, the problem of preserving civil rights in the free nations is best understood when we recognize that conflict over human freedom occurs between group and group, not between "the individual" and "the government." Guaranteeing the freedom of one group usually means abridging the freedom of another. The basic question of freedom is not whether or not there will be any but rather what kind of freedom will be preserved and for whom.

Fifth, one great problem in the free nations is fighting crime effectively without abridging the right of every citizen to privacy and a fair trial. Rising crime rates and increasing demands that government "take the handcuffs off the police" have been countered in the United States in recent years by the Supreme Court's decision prohibiting certain police practices. The conflict is still unresolved, and no universally satisfactory resolution is possible in the United States or any nation whose people value both law and order *and* the rights of man.

Sixth, another great problem is grappling with the many changes—social, economic, legal, political, and above all psychological—involved in the current drive of women in many Western nations, especially the United States, to achieve a status of full equality with men. The cause of women's rights has made major advances in the past few years, but full equality is still far from being achieved. It continues to be one of the nation's most pressing conflicts.

Seventh, some free nations are faced with another challenge to civil rights: the conflict over the status of blacks. In the United States the groups pressing for equal rights for blacks have recently won a series of impressive victories but are still far from having achieved their ultimate goal of complete equality. At the same time white-supremacy groups in the Republic of South Africa, with ever-increasing vigor and success, have smashed all efforts to secure anything approaching equal rights with whites for people classified as natives or coloreds.

What does it all add up to? Essentially the question eternally facing all free nations is not whether they will guarantee absolute freedom and equality for all or none whatever but rather *which* freedoms and equalities they will guarantee to which groups and at what social costs. No free nation has resolved this problem perfectly, if indeed it can be resolved perfectly. But seeking more satisfactory solutions, to benefit ever-increasing proportions of their citizens, is surely one of the most crucial and difficult tasks facing all free nations.

# VII

# THE INTERNATIONAL POLITICAL SYSTEM

# 23

# POLITICS
# AMONG
# NATIONS

After World War I the German novelist Erich Maria Remarque wrote a scene in *All Quiet on the Western Front* that must strike a responsive chord in anyone who has ever crouched in a slit trench, peered out of a bomber at bursting flak, or huddled in a bomb shelter during a raid—or in anyone who thinks that one day he may have to do so. In this scene a group of German soldiers are in a rest area behind the lines, and the following conversation ensues after one of them, Tjaden, has asked what causes wars. His comrade Albert Kropp replies:

"Mostly by one country badly offending another," . . .

Then Tjaden pretends to be obtuse. "A country? I don't follow. A mountain in Germany cannot offend a mountain in France. Or a river, or a wood, or a field of wheat."

"Are you really as stupid as that, or are you just pulling my leg?" growls Kropp. "I don't mean that at all. One people offends the other—"

"Then I haven't any business here at all," replies Tjaden. "I don't feel myself offended."

"Well, let me tell you," says Albert sourly, "it doesn't apply to tramps like you."

"Then I can be going home right away," retorts Tjaden, and we all laugh.

"Ach, man! he means the people as a whole, the State—" exclaims Müller.

"State, State—" Tjaden snaps his fingers contemptuously. "Gendarmes, police, taxes, that's your State;—if that's what you are talking about, no thank you."

"That's right," says Kat, "you've said something for once, Tjaden. State and home-country, there's a big difference."

"But they go together," insists Kropp, "without the State there wouldn't be any home-country."

"True, but just you consider, almost all of us are simple folk. And in France, too, the majority of men are labourers, workmen, or poor clerks. Now just why would a French blacksmith or a French shoemaker want to attack us? No, it is merely the rulers. I had never seen a Frenchman before I came here, and it will be just the same with the majority of Frenchmen as regards us. They weren't asked about it any more than we were."

And one of the soldiers proposes a solution that would surely be endorsed by a great many GIs, Tommies, *poilus,* and Ivans:

Kropp on the other hand is a thinker. He proposes that a declaration of war should be a kind of popular festival with entrance-tickets and bands, like a bull fight. Then in the arena the ministers and generals of the two countries, dressed in bathing-drawers and armed with clubs, can have it out among themselves. Whoever survives, his country wins. That would be much simpler and more just than this arrangement, where the wrong people do the fighting.[1]

The questions these fictional soldiers—and so many real soldiers and their sweethearts, parents, and friends—have asked are among the most difficult and urgent facing anyone concerned with the impact of politics on modern life: What causes wars? How, if at all, can they be prevented?

In this and the following chapter I cannot hope to answer either of these questions fully and satisfactorily. I can, however, identify and explain some of the more prominent factors which political scientists believe must be taken into account in the search for answers.

## THE NATURE OF INTERNATIONAL POLITICS[2]

International war is part of the pathology of international politics just as civil war and domestic violence are part of the pathology of domestic politics. Up to this point in our inquiry we have considered mainly the latter and some of the factors that affect a nation's ability to conduct and resolve its internal political conflicts with minimum

---

[1] Erich Maria Remarque, *All Quiet on the Western Front,* trans. by A. W. Wheen (Boston: Little, Brown & Company, 1929), pp. 206–209, 40. Reprinted by permission of Little, Brown & Company, and of Putnam & Co., Ltd.

[2] Among the more thoughtful and suggestive, though not necessarily concurring, discussions of this basic question are Richard Rosecrance, *International Politics* (New York: McGraw-Hill, Inc., 1973); Robert Art and Robert Jervis, *International Politics* (Boston: Little, Brown & Company, 1973); Inis L. Claude, Jr., *Power and International Relations* (New York: Random House, Inc., 1963); Morton A. Kaplan, *System and Process in International Politics* (New York: John Wiley & Sons, Inc., 1964); and Raymond Aron, *Peace and War* (New York: Doubleday & Company, Inc., 1967).

domestic violence. What we have learned about domestic politics can greatly assist us in our effort to understand international politics, particularly if we begin by recognizing the principal similarities and differences between the two kinds of politics.

## SIMILARITIES

International politics is like domestic politics in many ways. For one, it consists of conflict among human groups whose values—the objectives of their members' collective desires—differ and are incompatible to some extent. If some groups' values are satisfied, the values of other groups must go unsatisfied, and it is impossible to satisfy *all* groups equally.

For another, each group to some extent and in some manner *acts* to achieve its values as fully as possible, which inevitably brings it into conflict with other groups holding contrary values. In international as in domestic politics *conflict* among human groups is thus not an unfortunate but avoidable aberration from the political norm; it is rather the very essence of politics and human life itself. International no less than domestic politics is a perpetual struggle over "who gets what, when, and how."

For a third, in some respects international conflict is not much more cumulative than domestic conflict. We observed in Chapter 2 that conflict in domestic politics tends to be "noncumulative" in that the replacement of one issue by another in the center of the political stage is accompanied by a reshuffling of the conflicting individuals: Some "pros" and "cons" on issue A remain associated on issue B, but some find themselves on opposite sides, and some are indifferent; some who were indifferent on issue A, on the other hand, become partisans on issue B. The hatreds generated by one issue are thus not fully reinforced by every other issue; they are to some extent redirected and moderated by the succession of new issues.

The actors in international politics are generally defined as whole nations. And international conflict is thus also noncumulative, for the shuffling and reshuffling of allies and enemies is as normal as in domestic politics. From 1941 to 1945, for example, Great Britain and the United States fought with the Soviet Union and China against Germany and Japan. Since 1945 Great Britain and the United States have relied heavily on the support of their former enemies, West Germany and Japan, in their "cold war" with their former allies, the Soviet Union and China. From 1949 to the late 1950s the Soviet Union and the People's Republic of China (PRC) stood shoulder to shoulder in a worldwide struggle against the Western powers. Since then, however, the two communist giants have come close to war with each other, whereas both the Soviet Union's and the PRC's cold wars with the West have thawed a bit. There is nothing particularly cumulative about these great struggles. Some onlookers may regard this kind of shifting about as evidence of the mendacity and hypocrisy of the great powers, but others may find it merely an indication that politics is politics, whatever the arena. In fact, unless we long for an Armageddon in which the good nations wipe out the bad ones once and for all, we can perhaps view this shifting, however repulsive morally, as fortunate.

Finally, in both international and domestic politics competing groups sometimes use violence to achieve their goals (see Chap. 10). The horrors of international warfare sometimes cause us to forget that, until the 1960s at least, more people had

*"Baby play with nice ball?"*

been killed in civil wars than in international wars.[3] For Americans the most dramatic evidence is that more *Americans* were killed in our Civil War than in all our international wars put together, including the undeclared wars in Korea in the 1950s and Vietnam in the 1960s and 1970s. Yet in the early 1970s domestic political conflict poses a far smaller threat to any nation than does international escalation into full-scale thermonuclear war and extermination of large parts of the human race. Domestic conflicts like those between the white supremacists and the racial egalitarians in the United States or the Flemings and Walloons in Belgium, bitter and sometimes violent though they be, are not likely to be settled by one side's dropping a hydrogen bomb on the other. But no one can predict with confidence that the disagreements between the United States and the Soviet Union or the PRC will not be settled in precisely this manner. The differences between international and domestic politics, therefore, are at least as significant as are the similarities.

## DIFFERENCES

International politics differs from domestic politics mainly in the kinds of groups among which conflicts take place and the legal, social, and political framework in which it takes place.

[3] See Lewis F. Richardson, *Statistics of Deadly Quarrels* (Pittsburgh, Pa.: The Boxwood Press, 1960), pp. 32–50.

### Nations as Contestants

The main contestants in international politics are nations, or nation-states,[4] which differ from the subnational political interest groups we have considered mainly in that overlapping membership is far less frequent. Within any nation, as we noted in Chapter 2, each person is a member, formally or not, of many different groups; he can, for example, be simultaneously a white person of Irish extraction, a Roman Catholic, a Democrat, a graduate of Fordham University, and an officer of a union. Among nations, however, the situation is quite different. Although a few people have "dual citizenship" (two or more nations claim them as citizens) and a few others are "stateless" (no nation claims them as citizens), nearly every one of the world's 3.7 billion inhabitants[5] is legally a citizen of one nation only; very few indeed think of themselves as equally Americans and Russians or as equally Israelis and Egyptians—or, for that matter, as both citizens of their nations and "citizens of the world."

### Absence of an Authoritative Allocator of Values

In domestic politics, as we have seen, political interest groups try to achieve their ends solely or mainly by inducing the government to make and enforce policies the groups favor. Every government makes authoritative allocations of values, and domestic politics is a contest among the nation's groups to determine those allocations.

There is, however, no world government with the power to make and enforce policies binding upon all nations—no global "authoritative allocator of values." Each nation therefore seeks to achieve its goals by inducing other nations, both allies and enemies, to act as it wishes. Its power, as we shall see, is measured by its success in this effort and not by its success in influencing the policy outputs of a nonexistent world government.

International politics is thus like domestic politics in that the essence of both is the conflict among human groups to determine whose values will be more nearly achieved and whose will be less fully achieved. It differs from domestic politics mainly in that its contesting groups are nations with little or no overlapping membership and in the lack of an authoritative allocator of values. These differences arise from the state system in which international politics is conducted.

## THE STATE SYSTEM

The state system, as we learned in Chapter 3, is the present organization of the world's population into a number of "independent, sovereign nation-states." This organi-

---

[4] As noted in Chap. 3, some writers distinguish between a "nation," as a group of people sharing feelings of nationalism, and a "nation-state," as a nation possessing a legally sovereign government; the terms are used interchangeably here.

[5] The United Nations estimate as of June 1969, taken from *The American Almanac, 1974* (The Statistical Abstract of the United States, prepared by the Bureau of the Census; New York: Grosset & Dunlap, Inc., 1974), p. 802.

zation emerged at the end of the Middle Ages as the result of three main developments. The first was the splintering of medieval Christendom into many different denominations after the Protestant Reformation, which ended the spiritual dominance and ideological universalism of the Roman Catholic Church in the Western world. The second was the parallel disintegration of the Holy Roman Empire into a series of independent sovereign nations. The third was the displacement within most of these new political units of the decentralized and contractual medieval structure of feudalism by highly centralized and powerful national monarchies like those of France under Henri IV and England under Henry VIII.[6]

Because the state system provides the basic framework within which international politics is conducted in our time, we should have at least a general understanding of its legal, political, and psychological structure. Particularly important features for our purposes are nationalism, sovereignty, and anarchy, which we shall now examine in some detail.

## PSYCHOLOGICAL NATIONALISM

The state system rests upon the psychological base of nationalism, and all its other characteristics—indeed, the whole nature of modern world politics—arise from the basic loyalty of most human beings to nations rather than to churches, races, economic classes, or any other group. As Vernon Van Dyke has correctly put it:

> If men thought of themselves primarily as farmers or factory workers or businessmen or clergymen, and identified themselves primarily with their counterparts all over the world, nations could not exist. To constitute a nation, they must think of themselves primarily as Americans, Frenchmen, Germans, and regard the bonds that tie them to the country as more important than any bonds that they have with people in other countries.[7]

In Chapter 3 we noted some of the elements—common territory, language, government—that help to generate and reinforce feelings of nationalism among groups of people. Yet we should remember that nationalism itself exists in people's minds. The French thinker Joseph Ernest Renan put it this way: "What constitutes a nation is not speaking the same tongue or belonging to the same ethnic group, but having accomplished great things in the past and having the wish to accomplish them in the future."[8]

Having a common territory or language may help to make a people feel this way, yet Englishmen and Americans speak (approximately) the same language and

---

[6] For a more detailed historical account of how the state system arose, see Carlton J. H. Hayes, *The Historical Evolution of Modern Nationalism* (New York: Crowell-Collier and Macmillan, Inc., 1931); and Hans Kohn, *Nationalism: Its Meaning and History* (New York: Crowell-Collier and Macmillan, Inc., 1955).

[7] Vernon Van Dyke, *International Politics* (New York: Appleton-Century-Crofts, 1957), p. 44. See also Karl W. Deutsch, *Nationalism and Social Communication: An Inquiry into the Foundations of Nationality* (Cambridge, Mass.: M.I.T. Press, 1953).

[8] Quoted in Frederick H. Hartmann, *The Relations of Nations* (New York: Crowell-Collier and Macmillan, Inc., 1957), p. 28.

are friends and allies rather than conationals, whereas the Swiss have no fewer than four official languages yet are one of the most tightly knit nations in the world. For many centuries the Jews were scattered all over the earth, yet Zionism—Jewish nationalism—became a strong enough force to bring about the establishment of a Jewish nation in Israel. We should therefore think of nationalism as a psychological attitude (expressed by such various slogans as "God bless America," "Rule Britannia," " *Vive la France*," and " *Deutschland über Alles*") shared by a large group of people who also often, but by no means always, share some of the "objective" features of nationalism noted in Chapter 3. It is thus the psychological base of the state system.

Is nationalism weakening in our time? Is the psychological base for a new system of world politics emerging? The answer to both questions appears to be no. Perhaps the most powerful political movement in the world since 1945 has been the drive of colonial peoples everywhere to throw off their legal subjugation by Western masters and to win national independence. The result, as we noted in Chapter 3, has been the greatest proliferation of new nations in history: Of 151 nations generally recognized in 1970, no fewer than 81 (54 percent) had achieved formal independence after 1945! To be sure, many nations, new and old, have joined such international organizations as the United Nations and various regional associations, but we shall see in Chapter 24 that most have done so to advance their particular national interests, rather than to submerge them in a more general interest. The many fissures in supposedly monolithic world communism (see Chap. 20) have arisen mainly from the insistence of leaders in various nations on practicing communism in ways best for *their* nations and not necessarily best for the Soviet Union or the PRC. And the United States has found it impossible to convince its friends and allies that the version of anticommunism that is best suited to the United States' interests is totally and exactly right for their somewhat differently viewed national interests.

Nationalism and the state system that has grown from it thus appear to be at least as strong today as at any time since they first emerged at the end of the Middle Ages.

## LEGAL SOVEREIGNTY

The main legal expression of nationalism in the modern state system is the concept of sovereignty. The Charter of the United Nations declares the first principle on which the organization is based: "the principle of the sovereign equality of all its Members" (Article 2, section 1), which is also the basic legal principle of the state system. A nation's sovereignty may be defined as its *legal* power to make and enforce whatever internal laws it sees fit and to be subjected only to those external limitations to which it has voluntarily agreed.

Hans J. Morgenthau has explained national sovereignty by offering three "synonyms" for it. The first is *independence*. Each sovereign nation's authority over its own area is exclusive, and no nation has a legal right to interfere in the affairs of any other nation. The only limitations that are *legally* binding upon a nation are those that it imposes upon itself. The second is *equality*. If each sovereign state has supreme authority over its own territory, then all sovereign states must be equal in this respect, for logically there cannot be degrees of supremacy. In the legislative aspect of international law (see Chap. 24) each nation's vote thus counts for as much as, but no more than, every other nation's vote. Third is *unanimity*. As a logical consequence of the first two principles, any rule of international law must be unanimously accepted by all the nations to which it applies; otherwise some nations could make law for others, in which event the latter could not be called truly "sovereign."[9]

A warning: *National sovereignty is a legal concept only*, not a description of actual relations among nations. If, for example, the Republic of Panama wanted to permit Soviet troops to establish bases just outside the Canal Zone, we may be sure that, one way or another, the United States would prevent it—although *legally* Panama is as sovereign in its right to conclude agreements with other nations as is the United States. Sovereignty is a formal standard of how nations *should* treat one another, not a scientific description of how they *do* treat one another. It is just like any other legal concept in this regard, for, as we noted in Chapter 18, legal *shoulds* and actual *dos* are never identical even within nations. In Chapter 24, we shall observe how great is the disparity between the two in international law.

A second warning: Even in strictly legal terms "the sovereign equality of nations" does not mean that every nation has exactly the same legal rights and privileges as every other nation; many nations have incurred legal burdens not imposed on others, like the reparations that losing nations agree to pay to the victors after a war. Nor, in strictly legal terms, does the principle mean that any nation can legally divest itself of any and all of its legal obligations whenever it wishes. The principle does imply that no basic *change* can be made in the legal rights, privileges, and obligations of a nation without its consent. In what sense and to what degree the rules of international law are binding upon the nations that agree to them are questions we shall take up in Chapter 24.

## POLITICAL ANARCHY

Some political theorists, like Thomas Hodgskin, Josiah Warren, Michael Bakunin, and Prince Peter Kropotkin, have argued that the ideal political organization of human society is anarchy—a system in which there is no government or other agency with the legal right or physical power to force people to do what they do not wish to do. Under anarchy people would participate in cooperative activities only by the free and independent consent of each, never by orders from a popular majority or a ruling class or a monarch. We noted in Chapter 3 that no human community has ever formally adopted anarchy as its organizing principle, although governments have from time to time broken down and lost their power to make authoritative value allocations—but usually for only brief periods of time.

Yet the state system, both in legal principle and in political practice, comes very close to constituting a genuinely anarchical world political system. The principle of sovereignty, as we have seen, provides that no international law which a nation has not accepted is legally binding upon it. Such cooperative activities as nations may engage in are undertaken because each participating government has decided to par-

---

[9] Hans J. Morgenthau, *Politics among Nations* (4th ed.; New York: Alfred A. Knopf, 1967), chap. 19.

*The fight for a Better Environment...*

**The International Political
System as Anarchy.**
Source: Behrendt—
Het Parool, Amsterdam
(Rothco).

ticipate. There is no world legislature to make laws binding upon all nations, no world executive and police force to make sure that world laws are obeyed, and no world judiciary to adjudicate violations of the law and to punish the violators. The United Nations General Assembly, is, to be sure, a sort of pseudolegislature, the United Nations Security Council a sort of pseudoexecutive, and the International Court of Justice a sort of pseudosupreme court. But, as we shall see in Chapter 24, none of these institutions has any real power beyond what the individual nations give them—and can withhold or withdraw whenever they desire.

The state system, in sum, means that international politics is conducted within a framework of both legal and political anarchy, which is the basic determinant of the nature of international political conflict.

## CHARACTERISTICS OF INTERNATIONAL CONFLICT

For years after 1945 many Americans thought that the only international conflict that amounted to anything was the cold war between the "free world" and "international communism." But, as we have sometimes been pained to learn, some other nations rarely see things this way. India and Pakistan, for example, have been much more concerned with the status of the Bengalis, and went to war over the independence of Bangladesh. The Arab nations of the Middle East and Israel have had no doubt that their hot-and-cold war is the crucial contest. And so on.

In the early 1970s many Americans are no longer sure that there is a *single* international conflict dividing the whole world into two great camps. There seem, instead, to be many divisions cutting across one another. Americans are currently involved in no shooting war with any nation, but there are other conflicts aplenty: Arabs versus Israelis, Greece versus Turkey, El Salvador versus Honduras, and—potentially the most important of all—the PRC versus the Soviet Union. Each of these conflicts has its own particular constellation of issues, contestants, and techniques and is in some ways different from all other international conflicts past and present. Yet most political scientists are convinced that all past and present international conflicts under the state system are to some degree alike and that understanding their common denominator will greatly help us to understand what is involved in the conflicts with which we are most vitally concerned.

In this section, accordingly, we shall examine what political scientists generally believe to be the enduring characteristics of all international conflict under the state system.

## SOME GOALS OF FOREIGN POLICY[10]

Every nation's foreign policy is the product of its policy makers' answers to these questions: What should be our national goals? If some are incompatible with others, which are the most important—which are our "vital interests"? What kinds of actions are we capable of? Which are best calculated to achieve the goals we hold most dear?

National foreign policies thus originate in national goals; although these goals vary considerably from nation to nation, the most common types can be classified under five headings.

### Security

Probably the prime goal of every nation and the one to which all other goals will be sacrificed if necessary is security. It has two main aspects: first, the preservation of the nation's legal status as an independent sovereign nation and its practical ability to rule its own affairs; and, second, creation of an atmosphere in which the nation can be relatively free of fear for its survival and independence. There is no such thing as absolute security or complete freedom from fear for any nation, of course, and each therefore strives for the degree of security that its governors think is most reasonably attainable. Even this minimum security is by no means the only goal of the nation, however, and may often conflict with some of the others.

---

[10] See A. F. K. Organski, *World Politics* (New York: Alfred A. Knopf, 1961), chaps. 3–4; and Ernst B. Haas and Allen S. Whiting, *Dynamics of International Relations* (New York: McGraw-Hill, Inc., 1956), chap. 4.

Oil: a new weapon in foreign policy: Arab oil ministers, meeting in Kuwait, announce a large increase in the price of their crude oil, October 1973. Source: UPI photograph.

### Markets and Prosperity

Every nation wishes to maintain and improve its citizens' standard of living. In foreign policy this goal affects a wide variety of matters, including tariffs and trade agreements, currency-exchange rates, giving or receiving economic aid·and technical assistance, and so on. One illustration all too vivid for most Americans is the high priority our foreign policy gives in the mid-1970's to ending the Arab nations' embargo on oil exports to us. Japan and most Western European nations, with much fewer domestic oil resources than the United States, give even higher priority to preserving their supplies from the Arabs.

Some recent analysts from the New Left[11] have refurbished a dogma of the "old Left" to the effect that aggression, imperialism, and war are inevitable products of capitalism and can be eliminated only by overthrowing capitalism and adopting worldwide socialism.[12] Capitalism, according to this argument, produces surplus capital and goods; domestic markets are not enough to absorb such surpluses; the capitalists therefore direct the government, which of course they "own," to embark on imperialist ventures for the purpose of gaining control of new markets; these ventures involve nations in wars with natives of the areas to be conquered and with other capitalist-imperialist nations trying to conquer the same areas for the same reasons. The United States is thus believed to have involved itself in World War II to save its European markets, the Korean war in the 1950s and the civil wars in Vietnam and the Dominican Republic in the 1960s to protect old markets and to gain

---

[11] The most extended and influential statement of the New Left version is C. Wright Mills, *The Causes of World War III* (New York: Simon and Schuster, Inc., 1958).

[12] The classic statement is N. Lenin, *Imperialism: The Highest Stage of Capitalism* (New York: International Publishers Co., Inc., 1940).

new ones; Israel is believed to have invaded Egypt in 1956 and 1967 for the same reasons; and so on.

This analysis is appealing in its simplicity and its clear identification of heroes and villains, but most political scientists believe that it "won't wash," for it does not explain aggressive activity by socialist nations. For example, what about the Soviet Union's conquest of Estonia, Latvia, and Lithuania in the 1930s and its invasion of Czechoslovakia in 1968? Irrelevant, reply the spokesmen of the New Left: The Soviet Union is not a truly socialist nation. But then, counter their critics, Mao Tse-Tung's China, regarded by the New Left as the very model of a socialist nation, conquered Tibet in 1951 and encroached on India's northern borders in 1962. Here the New Leftists' response is a bit less clear, but it involves "wars of liberation" or "preventive action for self-defense." Evidently, then, the capitalist drive for markets is not the *only* drive that leads some nations to invade others.[13] Most political scientists therefore continue to regard gaining markets and enhancing economic prosperity as only two of several foreign-policy goals.

### Territorial Expansion

Relatively few diplomats think it politic to admit that their nations want more territory, but just about every nation at one time or another has pursued such a goal. They have followed expansionist—or, as they are sometimes called, "Imperialist"—policies for one or more reasons: to obtain more *lebensraum* for overcrowded national populations; to obtain economic advantages expected from controlling new mineral and other resources and opening up new "captive markets"; and to realize the sheer expansive force of "manifest destiny" to rule (which characterized American western expansion in the nineteenth century).

### Defending and Spreading Ideology

In recent years a number of political scientists have argued about the proper role of political and moral ideals in the formation of foreign policy.[14] Some have contended that the real goal of any nation's foreign policy is to defend and promote its "national interests," conceived mainly as the most advantageous "power position" for preserving and improving the nation's military, territorial, and economic security. All talk about "political ideals" and "moral values," these commentators argue, is at best a way of disguising and promoting the nation's underlying *real* interests, but if the policy makers forget the true nature and purpose of such talk and begin to take it at

---

[13] Leading critiques of the Leninist argument include Eugene Staley, *War and the Private Investor* (New York: Doubleday & Company, Inc., 1935); and Jacob Viner, "International Relations between State-Controlled National Economies," in *International Economics* (New York: The Free Press, 1951), pp. 216–231.

[14] The "realists" include Morgenthau, *In Defense of the National Interest* (New York: Alfred A. Knopf, 1951); and George F. Kennan, *Realities of American Foreign Policy* (Princeton, N.J.: Princeton University Press, 1954). The "idealists" include Thomas I. Cook and Malcolm Moos, *Power through Purpose: The Realism of Idealism as a Basis for Foreign Policy* (Baltimore, Md.: The Johns Hopkins Press, 1955); and Frank Tannenbaum, *The American Tradition in Foreign Policy* (Norman, Okla.: University of Oklahoma Press, 1955).

its own face value, their naiveté will only plunge the nation into serious trouble. The opposing argument is that the main purpose, at least of a democratic nation's foreign policy, is—or should be—to promote such moral values as freedom, democracy, and equality for all people everywhere; otherwise foreign policy and international politics become merely a global chess game, hideous because played with human lives and meaningless because lacking any higher purpose.

In my opinion this debate centers upon a false issue, that of ideology *versus* other national interests, as if the two were incompatible and one or the other had to be totally sacrificed. There is every reason to believe that both ideology *and* other national interests are goals of every nation's foreign policy. We have already noted some of the other goals. Let us examine ideology for a moment.

Most Americans wish to preserve the independence and security of the United States and to defend and promote this "national interest," but let us ask ourselves *why* preserving the United States is important enough to justify risking even thermonuclear war for. Some people will reply, "It isn't!" Others will insist that it is necessary to "secure the blessings of liberty to ourselves and our posterity" or to "preserve the American way of life." That way of life includes not only a high standard of physical comfort but also several ideals: free elections, popular control of public officials, due process of law, religious freedom, and so on.

The same is true of other peoples in other nations. After 1933 many Germans left Germany because they could not bear to live under the regime of Adolf Hitler. Most of them later fought with the Allies in the war against Germany. To many Germans, therefore, the Germany of Hitler did not seem worth preserving. How many of us would feel the same about the United States if it came to be ruled by a native dictator?

Such attitudes among the people—who, let us remember, constitute the nation —help to account for some, though by no means all, the foreign policies pursued by nations. In 1939, for example, a strong argument could be made that the clash of American and British interests in the western hemisphere made Great Britain a far more formidable rival of the United States than was Germany. Yet we lined up with and ultimately fought beside Great Britain against Germany. Why? Surely one powerful reason was that the British, like ourselves, are committed to democratic institutions and ideals and were therefore defending values that we also held dear, whereas aggressively fascist Germany was seeking to destroy them.

The argument offered here is not that a democratic nation does or should always support all other democratic nations and oppose all dictatorial regimes. After all, from 1941 to 1945 we gladly accepted the Soviet Union's help against the Germans, we now accept fascist Spain as an ally against the Soviets, and we did nothing to help a democratic regime in Czechoslovakia in 1938 or an anticommunist rebellion in Hungary in 1956. The point is that defending and spreading its ideology constitute *one* of the goals of every nation, and, like every other goal, it is sometimes in conflict with other goals and must compete with them for priority in foreign policy. To overlook or slight the observable significance of ideology as a factor in foreign policy and international politics is therefore highly "unrealistic."

*Peace*

Judging by what their spokesmen say, all nations and all peoples of the world cherish peace, regard war as the greatest of evils, and condemn those who cause wars as the greatest of villains. The Charter of the United Nations declares that the organization's first purpose is "to maintain international peace and security," requires its members to "settle their international disputes by peaceful means," and opens membership to "all other peace-loving states." In most international conflicts all sides strive constantly to paint themselves as the true lovers and defenders of peace and their antagonists as aggressors and warmongers.

Individuals feel the same. If we take a poll among our friends on the question, "Do you want us to go to war with China?" the nearly unanimous negative replies could certainly be matched by a similar poll in Peking.

Just about every person and every nation, then, wants peace—and, we should add, sincerely wants it. Yet hardly a person or a nation in the world does not believe that thermonuclear World War III is a serious possibility. We are faced with this great paradox: Everyone wants peace, yet, as the Bible says, there have always been "wars and rumors of wars." How can this be?

Perhaps the following catechism will provide the answer: Peace is the absence of war, and it takes at least two to make a fight. If the United States really wants peace, let it announce to all the world that under no conditions whatever will it fight another war and that it is dumping all its weapons into the ocean. This policy is absolutely guaranteed to bring peace, and anyone who *really* wants peace should urge it upon the President and Congress.

But some would say, that is ridiculous: if we disarmed ourselves, the communists would simply move in and take over. Others would say that unilateral disarmament would render us helpless to support our friends against their enemies—for example, Israel against the Arabs. Either or both may be true—but do we or do we not want peace? The answer, I think, is that we do—but not at any price. For we agree, as do most people, with General Emiliano Zapata's famous maxim, "It is better to die on your feet than to live on your knees."

The solution to this paradox is that people and nations genuinely desire peace—but peace is only one of several things they desire. Sometimes the desire for peace comes into sharp conflict with other desires, like that for preservation of national independence. When that happens, people and nations must choose which goals they want most and be prepared to sacrifice those that they want less. Such choices are the very essence of making foreign policy.

## MAKING FOREIGN POLICY[15]

### Choosing Goals, Techniques, and Capabilities

Making foreign policy for any nation involves making at least three kinds of choices. Logically first is the choice of goals—deciding what should be the nation's general

---

[15] Useful discussions include Francis O. Wilcox, *Congress, the Executive, and Foreign Policy* (New York: Harper & Row, Publishers, 1971); Robert L. Rothstein, *Planning, Prediction, and Policy Making in Foreign Affairs* (Boston: Little, Brown & Company, 1972); Roger Hilsman, *The Politics of Policy Making in Defense and Foreign Affairs* (New York: Harper & Row, Publishers, 1971); and Bernard C. Cohen, *The Political Process and Foreign Policy: The Making of the Japanese Peace Settlement* (Princeton, N.J.: Princeton University Press, 1957).

*Teamwork*

objectives in international politics and its specific objectives in particular situations. As we have noted, this choice often involves sacrificing or risking some goals in order to pursue other, more cherished ones.

Second, once the goals and their order of priority are set, the next step is to select and put into operation the techniques most likely to achieve the goals  We shall survey the most commonly used techniques shortly.

Third, capabilities must be assessed. Both of the first two types of choices must necessarily be influenced by the policy makers' judgment of what the nation can and cannot do relative to the capabilities of the other nations directly involved. For example, Cuba is a small and not very powerful nation. Even if Fidel Castro dreamed of dominating the whole western hemisphere, he would be well advised not to pursue his goal by launching a military attack on the United States. Like any other nation, Cuba can successfully pursue those goals and employ only those techniques within its powers and capabilities. If it ventures beyond them, it is likely to end up worse off than it began. Even the world's "superpowers," the United States and the Soviet Union, have learned that being "global policemen" is beyond their capacities.

Some political scientists have sought to understand national strategies and their mutual effects by applying the "theory of games" to international politics. This elaborate mathematical theory gauges the probable success or failure of various strategies devised by individual "players" in model conflict situations involving $n$ players in "zero-sum games" (those in which the losers' losses equal the winner's gains) or "non-zero-sum games" (those in which the total losses and gains do not equal each other). This mode of analysis was developed by mathematician John von Neumann and was first applied to economic behavior.[16] In recent years Morton

---

[16] John von Neumann and Oskar Morgenstern, *The Theory of Games and Economic Behavior* (Princeton, N.J.: Princeton University Press, 1944).

Kaplan has led political scientists in applying it to international conflict and William Riker in applying it to political conflict in general.[17] Their analyses are far too complex to summarize here, but both have created mathematical models of rational choices among strategies and formation of coalitions and countercoalitions that can (as do our models of democracy and dictatorship in Chap. 13) serve to measure and help to explain the deviations of actual strategies from the models.

We should not, however, picture any nation's foreign-policy making as a process in which steel-nerved and far-seeing diplomats cooly survey an infinite range of possibilities and choose those unmistakably calculated to promote the national interest. As many foreign-office officials who have actually engaged in making policy have testified, the process is like that of any other policy making: The decisions are made by fallible human beings subject to a variety of external pressures from pressure groups, public opinion, and other government agencies.[18] In a democratic system foreign policy can never be made in complete isolation from the demands of domestic policy. The makers of foreign policy are also subject to many internal doubts and hesitations, for they are caught up in actual situations, in which the possibilities do not seem nearly as close to infinite as they may appear to critics in college seminars and opposition parties. They have to make the best choices possible within limits imposed by their individual abilities and the concrete situations in which they find themselves. The eminent British diplomat and historian Sir Harold Nicolson, who knew firsthand the intricacies of foreign-policy formulation, has given us something of the "feel" in this illuminating passage:

> Nobody who has not watched "policy" expressing itself in day-to-day action can realize how seldom is the course of events determined by deliberately planned purpose, or how often what in retrospect appears to have been a fully conscious intention was at the time governed and directed by that most potent of all factors—"the chain of circumstance." Few indeed are the occasions on which any statesman sees his objective clearly before him and marches towards it with undeviating stride; numerous indeed are the occasions when a decision or an event, which at the time seemed wholly unimportant, leads almost fortuitously to another decision which is no less incidental, until, little link by link, the chain of circumstances is forged.[19]

---

[17] Kaplan, *System and Process in International Politics*; and William H. Riker, *The Theory of Political Coalitions* (New Haven, Conn.: Yale University Press, 1962). See also Thomas C. Schelling, *The Strategy of Conflict* (Cambridge, Mass.: Harvard University Press, 1960); and Richard C. Snyder, "Game Theory and the Analysis of Political Behavior," in James N. Rosenau (ed.), *International Politics and Foreign Policy* (New York: The Free Press, 1961).

[18] Graham T. Allison offers an absorbing illustration of this point by telling the story of the Cuban missile crisis of 1962 from three different basic perspectives: the "rational-policy model," the "organizational-process model," and the "bureaucratic-politics model"; Allison, "Conceptual Models and the Cuban Missile Crisis," *American Political Science Review*, 63 (September 1969), pp. 689–718.

[19] Harold Nicolson, *The Congress of Vienna* (New York: Harcourt Brace Jovanovich, Inc., 1946), pp. 19–20.

Moreover, as Bernard C. Cohen has shown so convincingly, those who make foreign policy in the democratic nations do so within very real limits imposed by public opinion.[20]

### *Agencies and Officers*[21]

In almost every modern nation the government agencies most directly and exclusively concerned with the making and conduct of foreign policy are headed by the political chief executive, or head of government, although in none of the democracies does the executive have an unrestrained monopoly over such policy (see Chap. 16). The principal agency working under his direction is a department specializing in foreign affairs, called variously the Department of State (United States), the Foreign Office (Great Britain), the Ministere des Affaires Étrangères (foreign ministry) (France), the Minindel (Soviet Union), and so on. The head of this department—secretary of state or foreign minister—is generally regarded as the number-two man in the executive group and often succeeds to the top position.

The officers and top employees under his direction are generally known as "the foreign service," which, in most nations, was one of the first administrative agencies to be put under the merit system (see Chap. 17). Foreign-service officers perform one of two general types of activities, consular and diplomatic. The consular activities are the older but today the less important. Consuls in various foreign cities concentrate mainly on reporting economic information about their host countries and promoting the sale of the home country's goods, although they also perform some services for fellow nationals traveling abroad.

Diplomatic officials, whether stationed in the foreign-affairs office at home or in the nation's various legations abroad (most nations rotate their foreign-service officers from home duty to foreign duty and the reverse), have four main types of functions.

1. Communications and negotiation, including transmission and reception of all official communications with foreign nations and negotiation of international treaties and agreements.
2. Intelligence, including the study of current and probable future events in foreign nations likely to affect their foreign policies and reporting conclusions to the home office. In many nations military services also conduct intelligence operations, and in the United States we have a third major group performing this function, the Central Intelligence Agency.
3. Policy recommendations; although ultimate foreign-policy decisions belong to the foreign secretary, the chief executive, and the legislature, subordinate officers and some employees of the foreign-affairs department are expected to make recommenda-

---

[20] Cohen, *The Public's Impact on Foreign Policy* (Boston: Little, Brown & Company, 1973).

[21] A useful general description is Philip W. Buck and Martin B. Travis, Jr. (eds.), *Control of Foreign Relations in Modern Nations* (New York: W. W. Norton & Company, 1957). For American practice, see James L. McCamy, *Conduct of the New Diplomacy* (New York: Harper & Row, Publishers, 1964).

tions in their particular special areas of concern. For reasons discussed in Chapter 17, these recommendations more often than not become policy.

4. Services, including issuing passports and visas, assisting citizens who have encountered legal trouble in foreign nations, and so on.

### Some Techniques of Foreign Policy

**Diplomacy and Recognition** "Diplomacy" means the conduct of international relations by negotiation among official envoys generally called "diplomats." Basic formal relations between any two nations are established through the exchange of official diplomatic "missions"—composed of a top envoy known as an "ambassador," "minister," or "chargé d'affaires," and a number of subordinate aides—secretaries, attachés, and so on. In deciding whether or not to receive officially some particular foreign diplomatic mission, each nation determines whether or not it formally "recognizes" those who send the emissaries as the foreign nation's legitimate rulers. A nation or a set of rulers whose envoys are not recognized by any other nation is in great trouble, for it cannot conclude any formal international treaty or agreement, provide any legal protection for its citizens traveling abroad, or engage in any of the legal relations that are basic to an independent, sovereign nation.

The decision whether or not to recognize a particular foreign nation can thus become a major question in any nation's foreign policy. The basic question is whether to recognize all governments that are actually in full control of their particular nations or only those that pass certain minimum standards of moral and political respectability. Some nations have attempted to answer these questions by extending de jure recognition to governments of which they approve and de facto recognition to those of which they disapprove. The United States, however, has occasionally refused formal recognition to regimes that were in full control. Notable instances include the communist governments of China (since 1949) and Cuba (since 1961), as well as the white-supremacy government of Rhodesia (since 1970).[22]

Perhaps the most extreme way in which a nation can show its displeasure with a foreign nation short of going to war is to "sever diplomatic relations" by withdrawing its diplomatic mission and ordering the other nation's mission to leave, as Egypt did to the United States in 1967 in protest of American support of Israel in the six-day war.

From the beginning of the state system until the outbreak of World War I in 1914, professional diplomats in foreign missions played significant parts in the formation and conduct of foreign policy. Their official titles as "ambassadors and ministers plenipotentiary" were accurate descriptions of their powers, for the difficulty and loss of time involved in communicating with officials at home necessarily gave them very wide discretion in negotiating and concluding agreements with their host na-

---

[22] See Hersch Lauterpacht, *Recognition in International Law* (Cambridge, Mass.: Harvard University Press, 1947); and Donald M. Dozer, "Recognition in Contemporary Inter-American Relations," *Journal of Inter-American Studies,* 8 (April 1966), pp. 318–335.

tions. Since World War I, however, professional diplomats have lost much of their power of independent negotiation and agreement and have become mainly cultivators of good will and reporters of developments in their host nations. Most important negotiations are conducted by foreign secretaries, special envoys like Henry Kissinger, or even by the heads of government themselves "at the summit," as at Teheran, Yalta, and Potsdam during World War II and at Moscow and Peking since then. "Diplomacy by conference" has, in fact, become a principal method of conducting international relations.

Whoever may conduct it, the technique of diplomacy can be used for different purposes, each of which can be illustrated from cold-war diplomatic relations since 1945. First, it can be used to seek genuine agreements, as when the Americans and British in 1963 negotiated an agreement with the Soviet Union to end the atmospheric testing of nuclear weapons. Second, it can be used as a propaganda device to embarrass the nation's opponents. An example is the Soviet Union's many dramatic—and impossible—proposals for disarmament and banning nuclear weapons since 1945, all intended not to secure genuine and workable disarmament but simply to preempt the title "peace lover" for itself while pinning the odious label "warmonger" on the Western allies. Finally, diplomacy can be used to stall for time while awaiting improvement in the military situation. An example is the lengthy "peace talks" between the Chinese communists and U.N. representatives in Korea in 1952 and 1953, in which the Chinese threw up one forensic roadblock after another for more than a year while continuing intermittent military offensives. Only when the communists became convinced that their military situation would not markedly improve did they begin to negotiate a truce seriously; the truce was concluded in a mere two months.

For these reasons, then, diplomacy can be considered a technique of foreign policy, as well as the formal conduct of all international relations under the state system.[23]

**Propaganda and Subversion**[24]    Any nation's efforts to achieve its goals through diplomacy are, by definition, direct and external attempts to induce the public officials of other nations to act in the desired manner. Propaganda and subversion, on the other hand, are intended to bring about certain internal developments in the target nations that will indirectly force their public officials to adopt the desired policies.

"Propaganda" in this context means the use of various forms of mass communications to create a climate of opinion among the target nation's general public that will induce its officials to act as the propagandizing nation wishes. Most major powers use propaganda for these purposes. The United States, for example, maintains

---

[23] The leading studies of modern diplomacy include Schelling, *The Strategy of Conflict;* Nicolson, *Diplomacy* (New York: Oxford University Press, 1964); Fred C. Ikle, *How Nations Negotiate* (New York: Harper & Row, Publishers, 1964); and Arthur Lall, *Modern International Negotiation* (New York: Columbia University Press, 1966). For a fascinating account of some of the difficulties of diplomacy even between strong allies like the United States and Great Britain, written by a political scientist who participated in the events, see Richard E. Neustadt, *Alliance Politics* (New York: Columbia University Press, 1970).

[24] See Haas and Whiting, *Dynamics of International Relations*, chap. 9.

the U.S. Information Agency to organize broadcasts, libraries, film showings, and other programs in friendly and neutral foreign nations, in order to present the American point of view in the most favorable light. The Voice of America beams radio broadcasts to the other side of the iron curtain. Radio Cairo beams Egyptian broadcasts all over the Middle East and North Africa, denouncing Israel and the Western powers and calling for all Arabs to drive out the "foreign imperialists." The Soviet Union made great use of the Stockholm Peace Petition to paint itself as the great defender of peace against the warmongering Western nations and used posters, films, and radio broadcasts to spread the accusation that the inhuman and bestial Americans had used germ warfare in Korea. The technological improvement of mass communications and the increasing importance of public opinion have made propaganda of this sort far more common than it was before World War I.

Sometimes nations try to influence the policies of others by subversion—clandestine support of sympathetic or pliable leaders and forces in the target nation or efforts to weaken hostile and intransigent forces. The built-in secrecy of these operations makes it very difficult to obtain accurate data and analyze them in a scholarly way, and most of what is written on current subversion efforts is journalistic, often sensational, and impossible to verify or disprove. Some commentators, for example, allege that the American CIA has tried to bolster anticommunist elements in many African, Asian, and Latin American nations; others contend that the International Telephone and Telegraph Company (ITT) engineered the military coup against Chile's President Salvadore Allende in 1973; still others assert that the PRC, Cuba, and the Soviet Union have tried to foment communist revolutions in these same nations. Movements of a generation earlier are much easier to document. It is now well established that in the 1920s and 1930s the Soviet Union, operating through the Communist International (Comintern), carried on a program of espionage, sabotage, infiltration of other nations' governments, and even assassination in order to promote Soviet foreign-policy objectives. It has equally been confirmed that the Nazis in the 1930s sought to weaken resistance to Hitler's foreign policies—and ultimately to his armies—by organizing "fifth columns" of Nazi sympathizers in the target nations: for example, France's Pierre Laval and the man whose name has become synonymous with "collaborator," Norway's Vidkun Quisling. Distasteful though subversion may be, compared with the older technique of diplomacy, it seems likely that it is still being used by many nations as a technique of foreign policy.

**Trade Policies and Foreign Aid**[25]  Most nations use trade restrictions like tariffs, import quotas and licenses, export controls, regulations of rates and conditions of international currency exchange, and even barter to control their economic relations. Many have also entered into agreements, like the American reciprocal-trade

---

[25] Some useful analyses are Robert S. Wallace, *American and Soviet Aid* (Pittsburgh, Pa.: University of Pittsburgh Press, 1971); John D. Montgomery, *Foreign Aid in International Politics* (Englewood Cliffs, N.J.: Prentice-Hall, Inc., 1967); Joan Nelson, *Aid, Influence, and Foreign Policy* (New York: Crowell-Collier and Macmillan, Inc., 1968); and Marshall Goldman, *Soviet Foreign Aid* (New York: Frederick A. Praeger, Inc., 1967).

**American foreign aid does not guarantee friendship: Panama university students demonstrating for "Yankees" to get out of the country.** Source: Wide World Photos.

agreements and the European Economic Community, to give one another preferential treatment under such controls. For a long time the main purpose of such policies was to promote the economic prosperity of the nation pursuing them, but since World War I increasing numbers of nations have used them for political purposes as well: to promote the economic health of friendly nations or to damage that of unfriendly nations. In many nations, indeed, the economic and political purposes of trade policies often conflict. For example, for many years the United States, in response to pressure by American beef producers, prohibited the importation of all Argentine beef, on the official ground that it might carry hoof-and-mouth disease. Not only did Argentinians lose a lucrative market for their beef, but their pride was also considerably damaged; anti-American feeling was prevalent in Argentina until World War II. During and since the war the State Department has been able to secure permission for the importation of limited amounts of Argentine beef, and, although such imports have been vigorously opposed by the American Meat Institute, relations between the two nations have improved, partly as a result of this change in a foreign trade policy.

Politics Among Nations

Foreign aid is largely a post-1945 development. The United States launched it in 1947 with the creation of the famous Marshall Plan to assist the economic recovery of the European nations, and it has subsequently become a major foreign-policy weapon not only for the United States but also for the Soviet Union, Great Britain, France, and other nations. Foreign aid is generally intended to accomplish two main goals: to strengthen the economies and ensure the political support of friendly nations and to strengthen the economies and increase the good will and support of neutral nations. These goals are pursued through outright grants of money, food, machinery, and other goods; through "technical assistance," mainly in the form of expertise and information on how to increase productivity; and through supplying military weapons, matériel, and military advisers. From 1945 to 1968 the United States gave a total of $78 billion in economic aid and another $38 billion in military aid.[26] From 1954 to 1962 the Soviet Union gave the equivalent of $3 billion to noncommunist nations and another $6 billion to other communist nations.[27] There has never been general agreement on how effective foreign aid is as a device for winning friends among the neutral nations,[28] and it seems that in the United States each year the requested appropriation for foreign aid grows smaller—and harder to steer through Congress. Still, as long as the "other side" is dispensing aid, it seems unlikely that the United States or any other major power will abandon it altogether; it also seems likely to remain a major weapon of foreign policy—largely for relatively rich nations—for some time to come.

**War**[29]    War has long been regarded by most people as perhaps the worst disease in the whole grim pathology of human affairs—and for good reason. Even before the discovery of nuclear power wars exacted a price in human death and suffering too enormous for the imagination to grasp. It is estimated, for example, that in World War I an incomprehensible total of 37 million human beings died either on the battlefield or as a direct result of the famine and disease brought on by the conflict. In World War II another 22 million perished. Wars have damaged the human race in other ways: Not only have they taken as soldiers some of the finest elements of the nations' populations, but the moral, social, and economic deterioration that infects both winners and losers alike after most wars has also left the world considerably poorer.[30] Paying for past, present, and future wars is by far the greatest single economic burden borne by any large modern nation. All these things were true of war before men had

---

[26] *The 1970 World Almanac* (New York: Newspaper Enterprise Association, Inc., 1970), p. 744.

[27] Fred Greene, *Dynamics of International Relations* (New York: Holt, Rinehart and Winston, Inc., 1964), pp. 475–477.

[28] For an instructive analysis of the relationship between the amount of U.S. foreign aid and the tendency of recipient nations to support U.S. policies in the United Nations, see Eugene R. Wittkopf, "Foreign Aid and United Nations Votes," *American Political Science Review,* 67 (September 1973), pp. 868–888.

[29] The most comprehensive study in English of past wars is Quincy Wright, *A Study of War* (2 vols.; Chicago: University of Chicago Press, 1942). A stimulating—and frightening—contemplation of possible future wars is Herman Kahn, *On Thermonuclear War* (Princeton, N.J.: Princeton University Press, 1961).

[30] See the many illustrations given in Wright, *A Study of War.*

discovered nuclear power; what the costs of war are likely to be now that thermonuclear weapons are functional we can only guess.

Yet scarcely any generation in the history of any modern nation has lived out its time in peace, and many generations in many nations have endured as many as two or three major wars. Terrible though they may be, then, wars are a recurring general phenomenon in international society. One of the most baffling and increasingly urgent questions before the student of human affairs is, How can something so terrible happen so regularly?

Some philosophers and theologians believe war to be a divine punishment laid upon mankind for its sins, and so it may be. Social scientists, however, must proceed from the assumption that war is not imposed on people by forces entirely outside themselves but is rather an activity they engage in voluntarily for purposes of their own. Political scientists in particular regard war much as did the great Prussian student of war Karl von Clausewitz, who declared, "War is a political instrument, a continuation of political relations, a carrying out the same by other means."[31]

To the political scientist, then, war is one of the techniques that nations use to achieve their ends: For most nations it is the weapon of last resort because of its tremendous cost and the risk to the nation's very existence. For these reasons a nation turns to war only when one of its most cherished goals—like preserving its independence or protecting its basic ideology—appears to be in mortal danger and all other means of achieving it seem to have failed. Only such a goal in such circumstances can justify the costs and risks of war.

Yet we cannot talk only of the costs and risks of war without discussing what wars have achieved for nations in the past; the fact is that many nations have won highly valued goals through war, as they might not have done by other means. The United States and Israel, for example, established their very national existence by fighting and winning wars. Great Britain and the United States may not have "made the world safe for democracy" by fighting World War II, but at least they preserved their own sovereignty and helped to save the world from Hitler's "thousand-year Reich." Many of the world's great religions—notably Christianity and Islam—have been spread among the heathen and defended against infidels and heretics largely by the sword. We are clearly not justified in calling *all* wars "futile" and "barren of accomplishment." One of the most eminent students of war sums it up:

> War, then, has been the instrument by which most of the great facts of political national history have been established and maintained. . . . The map of the world today has been largely determined upon the battlefield. The maintenance of civilization itself has been, and still continues to be, underwritten by the insurance of an army and navy ready to strike at any time where danger threatens.[32]

The great questions that face nations in this atomic age are the following: Is war still a thinkable instrument of national policy, or has weapons technology ad-

---

[31] Karl von Clausewitz, *On War,* Vol. 3 (London: Routledge and Kegan Paul Ltd., 1940), p. 122.

[32] James T. Shotwell, *War as an Instrument of National Policy* (New York: Harcourt Brace Jovanovich, Inc., 1929), p. 15.

vanced so far that war will destroy everything and achieve nothing for any nation? Can it be totally avoided or limited? We shall return to these questions in Chapter 24.

## POWER: THE INDISPENSABLE MEANS TO NATIONAL ENDS

### THE MEANING OF POWER[33]

#### As a Relationship

"Power" is one of the concepts most widely used in the discussion and analysis not only of international politics but of domestic politics as well. It is therefore not surprising that there is no general agreement upon its precise meaning or role in human affairs.

In this discussion of international relations "power" refers to the relations of subordination and superordination that exist among nations pursuing conflicting goals. For example, everyone would say that the United States is more powerful than the Dominican Republic. Why? Not merely because the United States is richer and larger and has more modern weapons—for these advantages in themselves have no political significance until they are brought to bear in some kind of international political conflict. We say that the United States is more powerful than the Dominican Republic because we observe that in just about every instance in which a goal or policy of the latter comes into clear and direct conflict with a goal or policy of the former, Santo Domingan desires will be less fully satisfied than will American desires. The superiority of American over Santo Domingan power may *result* from the Latin republic's fear of military conquest by the United States, from its knowledge of economic sanctions that the United States can apply, from the greater cleverness of our diplomats, or from any of hundreds of other factors. But in this situation the power of the United States consists of the fact that it does regularly have its way, by whatever means, when its desires clash with those of the Dominican Republic. The utility of this conception of national power, in my opinion, is that it does not automatically exclude any factor that produces particular power relationships.

#### As a Means

Some writers suggest that maximizing power—maneuvering into positions in which all relations with other nations resemble those between the United States and the Dominican Republic—becomes an end in itself for at least some nations. Yet "power," as the term is used here, can be detected only in the *conflict* of specific nations over

---

[33] Leading analyses of the general concept of power include Harold D. Lasswell, *Power and Personality* (New York: W. W. Norton & Company, Inc., 1948); Lasswell and Abraham Kaplan, *Power and Society* (New Haven, Conn.: Yale University Press, 1950); Robert A. Dahl, *Modern Political Analysis* (Englewood Cliffs, N.J.: Prentice-Hall, Inc., 1963), chap. 5; and Riker, "Some Ambiguities in the Notion of Power," *American Political Science Review,* 58 (June 1964), pp. 341–349.

specific conflicting goals, and it therefore seems more useful to think of it as an indispensable *means* to achieve any national goal. Nation A may seek to spread communism throughout the world, B to preserve its democratic system against A's aggressions, C to annex islands belonging to D, E to exterminate F, and F to preserve its national existence against E—but each nation must seek sufficient power to achieve its ends against its antagonists and must attempt whatever social, economic, military, and governmental changes will help to achieve the necessary power. Seeking power is thus not a particular kind of national policy; it is essential to following *any* policy successfully, except perhaps one of total surrender and national self-abnegation.

Power may be, as a former State Department official has written, "the capacity to achieve intended results."[34] But any nation's capacity can be measured only in specific conflicts with specific foreign nations and only after the results have actually been achieved. When we try to guess beforehand what a nation's power will be in a given situation, we must see where it and its opponents and allies stand in respect to a number of factors that have been correlated with success in past power conflicts.

## FACTORS CORRELATED WITH NATIONAL POWER[35]

Political analysts have found many different kinds of factors to be correlated with national power, and we shall briefly survey the main types. The reader should remember however, that no one of these factors by itself is enough to make a nation powerful in all circumstances and that no nation has ever been well situated relative to all factors at once. Although we cannot say which single factor offers the most important index of power, we can say that the most powerful nations are those that score the highest—*always relative to their opponents*—in the largest number of factors.

### Physical

Political analysts have found that several physical characteristics are correlated with national power. A favorable *geographic location,* like that of the United States (separated from its main rivals by great oceans) or even that of Great Britain (separated from Europe by the English Channel), makes a nation less vulnerable to invasion and thus offers it several advantages over nations like France or Poland, which have no natural barriers against invasion. Also significant is the possession of *natural resources,* including such necessary elements as food, fuel, minerals, and other industrial raw materials. For example, Great Britain has never produced enough food to feed its own citizens or any oil at all and has thus been forced to import these basic materials from abroad; it has therefore been more vulnerable than have nations with enough of such materials. On the other hand, the enormous oil resources of such otherwise minor

[34] Charles B. Marshall, "The Nature of Foreign Policy," *Department of State Bulletin,* March 17, 1952, p. 418.

[35] See Harold and Margaret Sprout (eds.), *Foundations of National Power* (Princeton, N.J.: D. Van Nostrand Company, Inc., 1951); Klaus Knorr, *The War Potential of Nations* (Princeton, N.J.: Princeton University Press, 1956); Morgenthau, *Politics among Nations,* chaps. 3, 8–10; and Van Dyke, *International Politics,* chap. 10.

Arab nations as Saudi Arabia and Kuwait have given them a powerful policy weapon, as was shown dramatically by the diplomatic results of their oil embargo against the United States in 1973-1974.

### Demographic

The sheer *size* of a nation's population, though never enough in itself to make a nation powerful, is nevertheless an important factor in power. The Soviet Union and the United States, generally considered to be the two most powerful nations in the world today, rank third and fourth respectively in total populations; significantly, China and India, the largest and second largest respectively, are becoming increasingly powerful in international politics. A powerful nation, it seems, needs a plentiful supply of manpower to man its armies and operate its industry. The *distribution* of a nation's population among various age groups is also a significant factor, for the "working-fighting" part of a population consists mainly of people between the ages of sixteen and sixty-five, and people over sixty-five are mainly pensioners and burdens on the productive groups. The younger the average population, the more valuable it is from the point of view of power.

### Psychological

A well-situated, rich, and populous nation may still be ineffective in international conflicts if it is seriously deficient in various psychological factors. The *kinds and degrees of social tension and consensus* may sometimes be decisive. In France in the 1930s, for example, the internal struggle among various economic classes and ideologies was so venomous that France became, in effect, several nations instead of one and was increasingly helpless both diplomatically and militarily against the German onslaught. In Great Britain during the same period, social and political conflict never grew so bitter that the contestants forgot they were all Britons; perhaps more than any other factor this unity helped them make of 1940, not the tragic time of national collapse that it was for France, but "their finest hour."

An illustration closer to home is the unhappy experience of the United States during two recent "limited wars." American combat forces were sent to Korea from 1950 to 1953 and to South Vietnam from 1965 to 1973 to prevent noncommunist governments from being overthrown by combined invasion by neighboring communist governments and insurrection by local communists. There are many striking parallels between the two instances. In each the American President (Harry S. Truman and Lyndon B. Johnson, respectively) tried to limit the war: The objective was to preserve the noncommunist government, not to conquer the communist neighbor and occupy its territory. Each relied on limited numbers of troops, limited types of weapons (no nuclear devices were employed), and very limited mobilization at home. The result in each instance was neither defeat nor victory but stalemate—stalemate that nevertheless continued to produce American casualties. Each President came under increasingly sharp attack at home from two different directions: from those who thought the war immoral and illegal and demanded total withdrawal and from those who demanded an all-out effort for total victory. Each President withdrew from candidacy for reelection after an unexpected electoral setback in the New Hampshire presidential primary. Some observers have concluded from these two episodes that, although most of the American people will strongly support total effort for total victory (as in World War II) or substantial withdrawal from international involvement (as in the 1920s and 1930s), they will not support a limited war for very long—certainly not a war that costs more and more American lives and treasure without even the announced aim of victory. If this picture of American attitudes is indeed a true one, it certainly sets very real limits on what those who make our foreign policy can attempt.

Even more basic, though harder to assess, is national character—the common popular attitudes and behavior patterns that make of the labels American, British, French, Russian, German, and so on more than merely legal designations of citizenship. The "character" of a nation's people is admittedly the most elusive of all the factors mentioned here, but most students of international politics are convinced that it exists and that differing national characters significantly affect the distribution of power among nations.

### Organizational

Several times in preceding chapters we have observed that effective organization is highly desirable, if not indispensable, for success in domestic politics, for it is the principal means by which any human group's latent resources and strength are brought to bear upon the decision points in the political process. The same is true in international politics. For example, no matter how large a nation's population or how rich its natural resources, it is not likely to translate those advantages into political power unless they are organized into *an effective economic and productive system* convertible into military power by *an advanced technology.* By the same token, a nation must have *an effective governmental system* if it is to mobilize its geographic, economic, and other resources so as to advance its international ends. Most scholars believe that China's long-time failure to become a major power, despite its huge population and plentiful natural resources, resulted largely from its ineffective economic system and government structure; these scholars are watching—many with apprehension—to see whether or not Mao Tse-tung will succeed where Chiang Kai-shek, Sun Yat-sen, and the mandarins failed: in welding China into a full-fledged world power. As the ability to wage war with maximum skill and success adds greatly to any nation's ability to succeed by war—and having a reputation as a nation skilled in war is almost equally helpful in time of peace—*an effective military establishment* considerably enhances a nation's power both in peace and war. Finally, the *skill of its diplomats* will determine how effectively a nation can bring all its other advantages to bear in conflicts with other nations.

### ASSESSING POWER

We have noted that one question the makers of foreign policy must answer is, What are the nation's capabilities in the situation at hand relative to those of the other nations involved? What is the present and potential power of the nation itself, its allies, and its antagonists? Such questions are so crucial in making foreign policy that a considerable part of the intelligence activities of any foreign office or military service

National power requires ever more demanding technology: loaded, cocked, and aimed at a strategic target sits one of the United States' 54 Titan II missiles, sheltered deep inside an underground silo hardened to protect it from nuclear attack. Source: Wide World Photos.

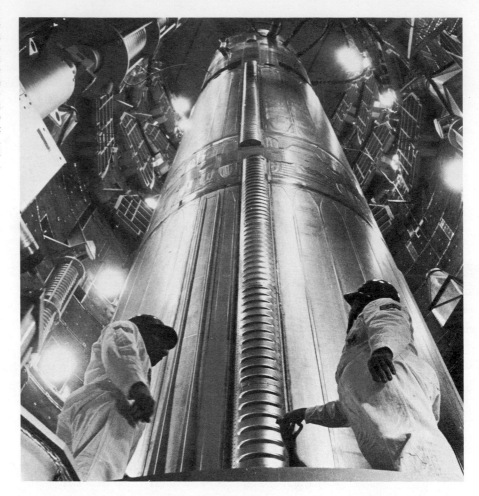

is devoted to investigating and attempting to measure the ever-shifting power relations among the various nations, friends and foes alike, with which the policy makers are concerned.

The task is far too difficult to be handled perfectly by any set of analytical tools presently available to any nation's intelligence specialists. The analysts would have to know, to begin with, not only what all the factors of power are but how they relate to one another. They would also have to know exactly where each foreign nation and their own stood at any moment in relation to every significant factor. Finally, they would have to be able to project present trends into the future. People's present skills in these matters permit at best only "educated guesses" and often only the most general, approximate, and tentative ones. The analysts can adopt Hans Morgenthau's advice—to avoid such errors as thinking of power as absolute and permanent instead of as relative and changing and trying to explain all power in terms of a single factor like geographical position or military might.[36] But at best their guesses will only be

[36] Morgenthau, *Politics among Nations,* chap. 10.

more "educated"; they certainly will not produce precise descriptions, accurate predictions, or infallible policies.

Foreign-policy makers clearly cannot avoid continually assessing their nations' power relative to that of other nations and designing policies to fit their assessments, but the wise ones are likely to keep their fingers permanently crossed while going about their jobs.

## POLITICS AMONG NATIONS: A SUMMARY

International politics, like domestic politics, is basically a struggle among human groups to realize different and conflicting group values. International politics, however, differs significantly from domestic politics in several respects. First, its contestants are nations, whose memberships legally and psychologically overlap far less than do those of the contesting groups in domestic politics. Second, nations seek their ends mainly by trying to affect the actions of other nations, rather than, as in domestic politics, by trying to influence the actions of an "authoritative allocator."

International politics since the late Middle Ages has been conducted within the framework of the state system. This system rests on the psychological foundation of nationalism, in which most people's primary loyalties are given to their nations rather than to other social and political groups. Its legal basis is "the sovereign equality of nations," which results in international anarchy: political conflict conducted in the absence of a common government.

For each nation within the state system peace is a goal, but only one among a number of goals, with some of which it is always in conflict. By the same token, war is one of several techniques that a nation may choose to pursue its ends—a technique so costly and risky, to be sure, that almost all nations regard it as a weapon of last resort yet one that most nations have occasionally felt compelled to use to preserve deeply cherished values or to pursue highly valued goals.

In our time, however, military technology is advancing at so frightening a pace that citizens of many nations are reassessing the utility of war as an instrument of national policy and as a method of conducting international conflict. When the United States and the Soviet Union developed thermonuclear bombs in the early 1950s, they created weapons of previously unimagined destructiveness. When they sent their Sputniks and Explorers whirling into outer space in the winter of 1957–1958, they served notice that mankind now has a means of delivering thermonuclear bombs against which there is no known defense.

Is it not therefore possible that these technological developments have made the cost of war so insupportable and the risk of war so unbearable that war is unthinkable as a technique of foreign policy? May it not also be true that most people and most nations do not see the problem this way and that World War III continues to be all too real and imminent a possibility?

To these grave and perplexing questions we turn in Chapter 24.

# 24

# THE QUEST FOR PEACE IN THE THERMO NUCLEAR AGE

If it comes, what will World War III be like? Figure 20, which shows the damage range of a hypothetical thermonuclear bomb detonated over the center of Washington, D.C., suggests part of the answer. According to data from official tests, on which Figure 20 is based, *one* 20-megaton thermonuclear bomb[1] is more powerful than *all* the bombs dropped on Germany and Japan in World War II put together. One 10-megaton bomb obliterates everything within a radius of 5 miles around the blast point and leaves only a poisonously radioactive crater more than 500 feet deep. The blast sets off a suffocating fire storm for a radius of 25 miles or more. More than 200 different radioactive species are created and attached to particles of debris, which are swept into the air and form the familiar mushroom cloud. These deadly particles float back to earth at varying speeds, depending upon their weight and, if spread uniformly, produce lethal levels of radioactivity over about 5000 square miles.[2]

But that is only what one bomb can do. What about the 150 or so bombs that might be delivered in a massive attack? In 1959 the Special Subcommittee on Radiation of the Joint Congressional Committee on Atomic Energy tried to answer this question. Its members heard testimony from military, scientific, and medical experts about the probable effects of a 1500-megaton attack on the United States. They concluded that 25 million people would die the first day, another 25 million would be fatally injured, and still another 20 million would be injured but not fatally. A 20,000-megaton attack with "dirty" bombs (those with high-fission yield) would,

---

[1] One megaton equals the destructive force of 1 million tons of TNT.

[2] The authoritative public account is Samuel Glasstone (ed.), *The Effects of Nuclear Weapons* (rev. ed.; Washington, D.C.: U.S. Atomic Energy Commission, 1962).

**FIGURE 20**
The damage range of a
thermonuclear bomb.

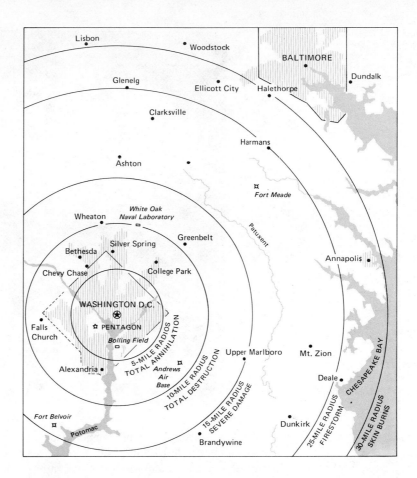

within 60 days, kill by fallout every American who had survived the original blasts and fire storms.[3]

At present the United States and the Soviet Union have each a stock of bombs that totals far more than 20,000 megatons; indeed, the experts often use the term "overkill" to denote nuclear capability beyond what is necessary to exterminate an enemy nation's entire population. If thermonuclear bombs are delivered as the war-heads of intercontinental ballistic missiles (ICBMs) launched from deep and inde-structible concrete "silos," there is no known way of preventing them from reaching their targets. No nation can hope to defend itself against thermonuclear attack; it can only retaliate by sending its own ICBMs against the aggressor—and hope that the fear of such retaliation and reciprocal annihilation will deter any potential aggressor from launching an attack. That is why a nation's nuclear arsenal and delivery system are often called its "deterrent."[4]

---

[3] Harrison Brown and James Real, *Community of Fear* (Santa Barbara, Calif.: Center for the Study of Democratic Institutions, 1960), pp. 14–20.

[4] For critical analyses of the theory and practice of deterrence, see Glenn H. Snyder, *Deterrence and Defense: Toward a Theory of National Security* (Princeton, N.J.: Princeton University Press, 1961);

**Fireball and fallout.**
Source: Wide World
Photos.

For these reasons, then, no one doubts that in the ICBM with a thermonuclear warhead we have at last found "the absolute weapon" with which we can literally exterminate mankind and most other living things on the planet. Everyone recognizes that the thermonuclear age may very well be our last twilight—if we decide to fight World War III and to fight it with thermonuclear weapons. The grim fact dominating our time is that the quest for peace has become a quest for the means of sheer physical survival for all people in all nations.

It is further complicated by the "*n*th-country problem." Although at present the United States and the Soviet Union are by far the biggest nuclear powers, at least four other nations—Great Britain, France, the PRC, and India—also have thermonuclear weapons and some means of delivering them. And many other nations (like West Germany, Japan, Israel, and Sweden) have the scientific knowledge and the engineering capabilities necessary to make nuclear weapons. If the possession of such weapons by the United States and the Soviet Union makes us a bit nervous, how about their possession by, say, Syria and Israel, or West Germany and East Germany? For World War III might be touched off, not by the original nuclear powers, but by the *n*th country to possess the Bomb.

---

The International Political
System

and Evan Luard, "Conciliation and Deterrence: A Comparison of Political Strategies in the Interwar and Postwar Years," *World Politics,* 19 (1967), pp. 167–189.

Precisely this apprehension induced the Soviet Union and the United States to take the lead in drawing up and pressing for adoption of the general Nuclear Nonproliferation Treaty in 1968. The treaty provides, first, that nations now possessing nuclear weapons will not transfer them to any other nation; second, that "nonnuclear" nations will not manufacture or acquire nuclear weapons; third, that the International Atomic Energy Authority is to conduct inspections in the various nations to ensure compliance; and, fourth, that all signatory nations will have access to information about peaceful uses of atomic energy. By early 1970 a total of ninety-seven nations had signed the treaty. They included only three of the six members of the "nuclear club," for France, the PRC, and India refused to sign. Israel, a potential nuclear power, also refused to sign, and the treaty is thus far from a complete solution to the $n$th-country problem. But at least it gives us some hope that the problem will eventually be brought under control.

What, then, are our chances of survival? Some observers believe that they depend upon our ability to keep World War III from being fought with thermonuclear weapons and to confine nations to the use of old-fashioned weapons, which, however destructive, do not have the capacity to wipe out the whole race; these writers believe that there is a strong possibility that nations will refrain by mutual consent from using thermonuclear weapons. Most commentators, however, agree with the late Sir Winston Churchill that "it would be folly to suppose . . . if war should come, these weapons would [not] be used."[5] Other analysts argue that our best chance lies in keeping all future wars limited, in geographic area as well as in the number of nations involved, as those in Korea, Indochina, and the Middle East have been since 1945. Still others insist that, because limiting wars is at best chancy—we need fail only once to lose the whole game—our only real chance for survival is to find a way to prevent *all* international wars, limited or general.

Whatever may be the directions in which they think we should look, however, all present-day students of international affairs believe that the thermonuclear age has transformed the ancient quest for peace from a search for a utopia of tranquility into a hunt for the minimum conditions of human survival. This hunt, moreover, must take place in an age when nuclear power makes it urgent while the political fission characteristic of the state system may prevent—as it always prevented—people from finding a way to eliminate war.

War, as we noted in Chapter 23, has always been both costly and risky for any nation, and few nations' leaders have ever engaged in it for its own sake. Yet under the state system just about every nation has fought wars when its leaders and people came to believe that not fighting would bring even greater disasters than the horrors of war. We have no a priori reason to suppose that the enormously greater costs of thermonuclear war have basically altered this historic approach to international violence.

---

[5] Quoted in Vernon Van Dyke, *International Politics* (New York: Appleton-Century-Crofts, 1957), p. 332. Van Dyke presents a thoughtful assessment of the probable costs of thermonuclear World War III and the possibilities of lessening or avoiding them. *International Politics*, pp. 323–335.

If peace is to reign in our time, it will come either because modern nations desire no national goal strongly enough to resort to war in order to achieve it or because they believe that they can achieve any national goal by means other than war. The quest for peace in our age is thus a search for a world political structure that will incline peoples and leaders to adopt either or both attitudes toward war as a means of gaining their ends.

In this chapter, accordingly, we shall examine the nature and record of some of the more prominent approaches to international political conflict without war that have already been tried or considered.

## APPROACHES TO PEACE WITHIN THE STATE SYSTEM[6]

The state system, as we learned in Chapter 23, is deeply rooted in the universal hold of nationalism, that is, in the fact that most people's basic loyalties are to their nations rather than to their churches, races, economic classes, or other groups to which they belong. Although their leaders have long sought ways of resolving international conflict without resorting to war, most have had no desire to eliminate—and even more have despaired of the possibility of eliminating—such basic features of the state system as the legal right of each nation to govern its own internal and external affairs. Our first general category of approaches to peace therefore includes those which do not involve negation of the basic principles of the state system but that rely instead on the voluntary actions of the independent sovereign nations.

Each of these approaches, moreover, rests upon a set of ideas about what causes wars and is intended to alleviate or eliminate such irritants from international relations. We shall, accordingly, consider the rationale as well as the record of each of these approaches to peace.

### BALANCE OF POWER

#### A Description and an Approach to Peace

The term "balance of power" is used in several different senses by students of international affairs. In a purely descriptive sense it simply means the distribution of power among nations at any given moment and carries no necessary connotation of equal shares. As a method for maintaining peace, however, "balance of power" means a sufficiently even distribution of power among antagonistic nations to prevent any one of them from feeling strong enough to threaten the independence of any other. Following a "balance of power" policy means striving for such a distribution of power. The balance of power approach to peace is based on the assumption that war results when a particular nation feels enough stronger than its antagonists to believe that it can threaten or attack them with full assurance of success. The adher-

---

[6] The theories of the causes of war underlying the various approaches to peace are perceptively identified and analyzed in Inis L. Claude, Jr., *Swords into Plowshares* (3d ed.; New York: Random House, Inc., 1964). The account in this text generally follows Claude's analysis. See also Robert F. Randle, *Origins of Peace* (New York: The Free Press, 1973).

*This is the house that diplomacy built*

ents of this approach propose to keep the peace by preventing any nation from feeling that much stronger than any of its rivals.[7]

## Methods

Many nations have sought both to protect their national interests and to avoid war by pursuing balance-of-power policies calculated to keep opposing nations or combinations of nations from becoming too strong. Among the traditional methods have been *domestic measures* like building up their armaments and strengthening their military organizations; *alliances,* including both acquiring allies for themselves and splitting off their opponents' allies in the ancient strategy of "divide and conquer";[8] *compensations,* including dividing up non-self-governing colonial areas among the great powers so that the latter will be diverted from aggression toward the other great powers; and *war,* used as a last resort to prevent the opposing nation or nations from becoming too powerful. The classic illustration of a balance-of-power policy is that followed by Great Britain since the sixteenth century, in which it lends its weight

---

[7] For the various meanings of "balance of power," see Hans J. Morgenthau, *Politics among Nations* (3d ed.; New York: Alfred A. Knopf, 1962), chap. 2.

[8] A stimulating analysis of why and how alliances are formed and dissolved is George Liska, *Nations in Alliance* (Baltimore, Md.: The Johns Hopkins Press, 1962). For an illuminating case study of the stresses and strains in one such alliance (that between the United States and Great Britain), see Richard E. Neustadt, *Alliance Politics* (New York: Columbia University Press, 1970).

against whatever is the single most powerful nation in Europe—first Spain, then the Netherlands, then France, then Germany, and now the Soviet Union.

### Evaluation

Most political scientists believe that, whatever balance-of-power policies may have done for the interests of individual nations, they have signally failed to keep the peace. Their failure results partly from the impossibility, noted in Chapter 23, of measuring accurately what the distribution of power *is* at any given moment. This means that no nation can ever be sure when power is "balanced" and when it is not. Another reason is that most nations are convinced that prudence requires them to leave a margin for error in their calculations; they therefore build up their armaments and their alliances to a level higher than what they guess to be the necessary minimum. Their antagonists, however, feel the same need for a margin of safety, and they in turn build their armaments up to a level beyond that of the first group of nations. And so on in a process familiarly known as an "arms race."

The whole idea of a balance of power thus rests upon an oversimplified and mechanical conception of international relations and assumes a calculability of national power and motives that does not exist. It has never succeeded in keeping the peace in the past, and it seems likely that its modern version, called by some commentators "the balance of terror," will not succeed either, despite the possibility that fear of thermonuclear weapons may make nations more hesitant to resort to war than in the past. Always before some nation or group of nations has sooner or later come to believe that the only way to "restore the balance" is to go to war before it is too late. There is no reason to suppose that the present balance of power will work any better.[9]

## COLLECTIVE SECURITY

### Meaning and Rationale

Those who seek peace through balance-of-power methods, as we have seen, assume that no nation will launch a military attack upon any other nation unless it is confident that it has the preponderance of power necessary for victory. Peace can be maintained, they reason, by keeping any nation from acquiring enough extra power to feel this kind of confidence.

"Collective security" is a major extension and reorientation of this point of view. Its adherents seek to preserve peace through agreement among a large number of nations that each will treat a military attack upon any of the others as an attack upon itself and that all will participate fully in a defensive war against aggression toward any one of them. They seek peace by making it clear *in advance* to any would-be aggressor that the contemplated aggression will be met with overwhelming force and therefore cannot possibly succeed. It has been one of the most widely

[9] See Morgenthau, *Politics among Nations*, chap. 14; and Van Dyke, *International Politics,* chap. 11.

approved of all approaches to peace within the state system and, as we shall see, is now one of the basic elements in the United Nations approach to peace.

Inis Claude has pointed out that collective security is often confused with defensive military alliances like the North Atlantic Treaty Organization (NATO) and the communist nations' Warsaw Pact. These treaties, however, differ from true collective-security agreements mainly in that they are not intended to be universal in their membership; universality is at least one major goal of all genuine collective-security agreements. The NATO and Warsaw alliances are examples of a type of defensive military alliance within what is basically a balance-of-power framework; the nearest approximations to a genuine collective-security system in the twentieth century have been embodied in certain articles in the Covenant of the League of Nations and the Charter of the United Nations.[10] We shall consider these provisions later.

### Preconditions

The theory of collective security does not propose any alteration in the formal structure of the state system, in the sense of establishing a global government with the legal and physical power to *make* nations come to one another's defense whether they want to or not. Rather, it depends upon their willingness, even eagerness, to do so voluntarily. It does, however, require a number of drastic changes in the attitudes of nations and the makers of their foreign policies. For, if collective security is to work as intended, most people in most nations must fully accept at least the idea of "the indivisibility of peace"—the notion that their destinies are deeply involved in the security and welfare of all nations, not just of their own. Furthermore, the people and the policy makers of each nation must put the general requirements and obligations of collective security before their own national interests. Finally, each nation must voluntarily surrender to some kind of international body a considerable portion of its power over its own foreign policy.

To illustrate the differences between balance-of-power and collective-security arrangements for meeting aggression, let us consider the case of American policy toward Korea in the 1950s. When the North Koreans attacked the South Koreans in 1950, the United Nations under American leadership declared the North Koreans the aggressors and called for all member nations to come to South Korea's defense. The United States, which had already started to fight the North Koreans, complied with the resolution by sending large numbers of troops into Korea, although many other members did not. The United States thus acted just as a nation should in a collective-security system.

But let us suppose that the South Koreans had attacked the North Koreans. Let us suppose, further, that the United Nations had branded South Korea the aggressor and had called upon all member nations to go to the communists' defense. What would we have done? What *should* we have done? On one hand, many of us feel that any aggression *by* communists is dangerous to American security whereas any aggression *against* communists is helpful to American interests. Yet under a collective-security agreement we would have been bound to help the communists just as

[10] Claude, *Swords into Plowshares,* pp. 234–252.

diligently as we did help the anticommunists in 1950–1952; if we were to honor our commitments American troops would then be in the hills of Korea, aiming their rifles south. If such a situation were actually to arise, it is not likely that the United States would join in any collective-security defense of communism any more than the Soviet Union joined in a collective-security defense against communism in 1950.

Hans Morgenthau has neatly summed up the difference between the national attitudes required by genuine collective security and those that actually prevail under the state system:

> Collective security as an ideal is directed against all aggression in the abstract; foreign policy can only operate against a particular concrete aggressor. The only question collective security is allowed to ask is: "Who has committed aggression?" Foreign policy cannot help asking: "What interest do I have in opposing this particular aggressor, and what power do I have with which to oppose him?"[11]

Until such time as the United States can be counted upon to rush to the defense of communists against anticommunist aggression, no global collective-security system in the strict sense can exist, for the good and sufficient reason that what Claude calls the "subjective requirements" for it do not presently exist. We shall return to this problem in our discussion of the United Nations.

## DISARMAMENT[12]

### Rationale

Since the end of the Napoleonic wars in 1815 every major nation has occasionally publicly declared itself in favor of some kind of disarmament—that is, of some kind of agreement among nations to reduce mutually and simultaneously the general quantities of all their armed forces and weapons or to limit or eliminate particular weapons. Nations advance such proposals for various reasons, including their desire to reduce the heavy economic burdens of large military establishments, their longing to reduce the destructiveness of war if it should come, their wish to improve their own power positions, and even their hope of achieving propaganda victories over their antagonists by donning the mantle of peace lover. The motive for disarmament proposals with which we are concerned here, however, is the desire to prevent war.

The theory of disarmament as an approach to peace is based upon the assumption that, if there is no restriction on the level of armaments of the major powers, they will inevitably engage in arms races; and, as people simply cannot be trusted not to use huge military establishments if they have them, sooner or later arms races bring on wars. According to Claude's vivid summary of this theory, "men are not gods, and

---

[11] Morgenthau, *Politics among Nations,* p. 415.

[12] Recent analyses include Bernhard G. Bechhoefer, *Postwar Negotiations for Arms Control* (Washington, D.C.: The Brookings Institution, 1961); John W. Spanier and Joseph L. Nogee, *The Politics of Disarmament* (New York: Frederick A. Praeger, Inc., 1962); and David V. Edwards, *Arms Control in International Politics* (New York: Holt, Rinehart and Winston, Inc., 1969).

when they gather the power of the gods in their hands they come to behave like beasts."[13] One way of approaching peace, not necessarily an exclusive way but often complementary to other ways, is to persuade all nations either to agree to limit the total quantities of their weapons, to forswear the use of certain weapons (for example, poison gas, bacterial bombs, atomic bombs), or both.

### Record

Since 1815 many attempts have been made at both general and localized disarmament. There have been a few successes with the latter, the best known being the Rush-Bagot Agreement of 1817 between the United States and Canada, which limits naval forces on the Great Lakes and has come by informal extension to mean the demilitarization of the entire Canadian-American border.

The most notable efforts at general disarmament have been the Holy Alliance of the immediate post-Waterloo period, the Hague peace conferences of 1899 and 1907, the Washington naval conference of 1922, the world disarmament conference of 1932, and the various efforts made in the disarmament commissions of the League of Nations and the United Nations. Generally speaking, such efforts have failed to accomplish anything remotely approaching their stated objectives, for reasons that we shall review in a moment.

### Atomic Disarmament and Control

We noted earlier in this chapter that the development of thermonuclear weapons has cast the age-old quest for peace into a brand-new atmosphere of very great urgency; much the same can be said for the problem of disarmament, which since 1945 has centered mainly upon the problem of the reduction or abolition of atomic weapons and the control of materials and facilities for nuclear fission. A brief review of these negotiations should illuminate not only the special difficulties in atomic disarmament but also the continuing difficulties in any effort at general disarmament under the state system.

In 1946 the United States—which at that time had a world monopoly on nuclear weapons—laid before the Atomic Energy Commission of the United Nations its Acheson-Lilienthal-Baruch Plan, which proposed that an international atomic-development authority be created as a body affiliated with but independent of the United Nations. This agency would be given a worldwide monopoly of the ownership and operation of all mines and plants producing fissionable materials and of all research and testing of atomic weapons. It would also be empowered to license nations to use nuclear materials for peaceful purposes and would make uninhibited inspections of all nations' scientific and industrial establishments to detect illicit supplies of fissionable materials and misuse of licenses for their peaceful employment. When such an authority was established and working to American satisfaction, the United States would surrender to the authority our national stockpiles of atomic bombs and fissionable materials.

[13] Claude, *Swords into Plowshares,* p. 262.

The Soviet Union, however, found the proposal unacceptable. It insisted that the establishment of any international control of atomic energy be preceded by the legal prohibition of all nuclear weapons and by the United States' destruction of its stocks of such weapons; it also insisted that the proposed international authority should have no power to own, operate, or license atomic facilities and that even in the authority's rather vague inspecting functions it should operate in clear subordination to the Security Council, over whose operations the great powers have a veto.

In 1948 the General Assembly approved a somewhat revised version of the American plan, but the Soviets were so hostile to it that no serious attempt has ever been made to implement it. Since 1948 there have been many sessions of haggling in the Disarmament Commission and the Atomic Energy Commission, and many dramatic speeches before the General Assembly—but little effective agreement.

Several small rays of hope have appeared in the 1960s and early 1970s. The first came in 1963, when the United States and the Soviet Union signed a treaty to end the testing of nuclear weapons in the atmosphere, outer space, and under water, in which they were joined by more than 100 other nations. But the treaty provided for no system of inspection (which was considered unnecessary because the development of sensitive detection devices has made it almost impossible to conduct such tests without the other signatories' knowledge), and the two newest members of the "nuclear club," France and the PRC, refused to sign it. The second hopeful development was the 1968 launching of the Nuclear Nonproliferation Treaty, also boycotted by France and the PRC. A third was the opening of the strategic-arms limitations talks (SALT) between the Soviet Union and the United States in 1970.

There are a few other bright spots in the picture. The two nuclear superpowers have concluded that a nuclear arms race is not only dangerous but is also extremely costly and damages too many other programs.[14] The SALT talks have shown that both nations are searching for some way of limiting and reducing their own stocks of nuclear weapons and of preventing the spread of such weapons to the nonnuclear powers. The Soviet Union, indeed, shows some signs of being prepared to accept some form of inspection to ensure that the treaty terms are observed. Nevertheless, few analysts are optimistic about the long-run prospects for serious nuclear disarmament and arms control under the state system. Why? For basically the same reasons that most general efforts at disarmament under the state system have failed. First, there are many technical difficulties even with traditional weapons—determining the proper ratios of strength among nations and implementing whatever agreements can be achieved on this point. Most atomic scientists believe that it is now so easy for any nation to hide lethal amounts of fissionable materials from any kind of inspection that no system of atomic disarmament can depend upon inspection for enforcement.[15] Second, even if the technical difficulties could be solved, nations are unwilling to give up their weapons—especially such powerful ones—as long as they think that doing

---

[14] For an analysis of American defense expenditures and their consequences for domestic programs, see Bruce M. Russett, *What Price Vigilance? The Burdens of National Defense* (New Haven, Conn.: Yale University Press, 1970).

[15] See Eugene Rabinowitch, "Living with H-Bombs," *Bulletin of the Atomic Scientists,* January 1955, p. 6.

so might make them vulnerable to attack by other, less scrupulous nations. Atomic disarmament has failed, as so many earlier attempts at general disarmament have failed, basically because nations—particularly powerful nations—simply are not willing to trust their ways of life, ideologies, and national independence to the official good will and public promises of other nations.

Most political scientists would agree with Claude that the failure of attempts at atomic disarmament and control surely underscore what has been learned from comparable failures in the past: "No means have been discovered for evading the requirement that states participating in an arms regulation system be imbued with mutual trust."[16]

## PEACEFUL SETTLEMENT OF DISPUTES

### Rationale

The idea of peaceful settlement rests upon the assumption that wars are mainly a technique for settling international disputes. Nations continually dispute with one another, and their disputes are sooner or later settled one way or another. Nations usually fight wars when there seems to be no other way to settle a dispute and when national tempers have grown hot enough in the negotiating process. Warfare often results from the failure of the disputants to understand all the facts and from the inability of either side to endure the blow to its national pride involved in "making concessions." As international disputes themselves cannot be eliminated, proponents of peaceful settlement favor providing a series of techniques for settling them peacefully—techniques that will permit hot tempers to cool, acquaint the disputing parties with all the facts, and introduce a neutral party as judge, arbitrator, or conciliator to settle disputes without loss of "face" to any nation.

### Techniques

A number of techniques for peaceful settlement have been introduced. One is *direct negotiation,* in which the disputants try to iron out their disagreements by mutual give-and-take, often accepting the "good offices" of a neutral nation as mediator and conciliator—as in 1973–1974, when the American Secretary of State, Henry Kissinger, brought about a cease-fire agreement between Egypt and Israel and effectively ended the "Yom Kippur war."

More often discussed but less often used than direct negotiation is *arbitration.* Although there are many variations in details, arbitration generally involves an agreement—either by general treaty or ad hoc for a specific dispute—between two or more quarreling nations to establish an arbitration tribunal. Usually each nation appoints two members to the tribunal, only one of whom may be one of its own citizens. The four arbitrators thus chosen pick a fifth. The five-member tribunal hears the arguments on both sides and makes a decision, which both sides have previously agreed

[16] Claude, *Swords into Plowshares,* p. 315.

to accept. Substantial numbers of nations have concluded bilateral (between two nations) and multilateral (among three or more nations) arbitration agreements in which they have consented to submit all disputes to such arbitration. Many of these agreements were made in the early twentieth century, when people believed that arbitration was the best way to prevent war. As William Wordsworth said of early French Revolutionary days, "Bliss in that dawn it was to be alive, but to be young was very heaven." The machinery, however, has been used relatively little, for reasons that we shall examine shortly.

A third general technique of peaceful settlement is *adjudication*—taking disputes to the International Court of Justice for settlement. We shall examine the nature and handicaps of this method in our consideration of international law.

### Record

Arbitration machinery has been used relatively little. Most of the disputes it has dealt with have been of a primarily nonpolitical character—that is, not involving what the disputants have regarded as vital interests or power. Almost every nation has refused to submit to arbitration or adjudication anything it has regarded as a major political dispute. For example, Indian leaders from Jawaharlal Nehru to Indira Gandhi have certainly been among the world's most prolific sources of praise for peaceful settlement and international rectitude, as well as tart critics of other nations' failure to meet India's high standards. Yet they themselves have consistently refused to submit the India-Pakistan dispute over the ownership of Kashmir to any kind of international arbitration or adjudication. As Nehru said, "great political questions ... are not handed over in this way to arbitrators from foreign countries or any country."[17]

That is why the record of compliance with arbitration and adjudication is so good—and why it is very misleading. As we have seen, no nation will submit a dispute to this kind of machinery at all unless it has previously decided that it is prepared to accept and abide by an adverse ruling of the deciding tribunal. On the record, no nation will accept a ruling that it believes affects its vital interests and power position adversely; and no nation will therefore submit to peaceful settlement any dispute that seems to involve these matters at all directly. Yet it is precisely such disputes that cause wars, and therefore peaceful settlement alone has never prevented wars in the past and is clearly incapable of doing so in the future.

### INTERNATIONAL LAW[18]

### Approach to Peace

The peculiar nature and problems of international law are suggested by the disagree-

---

[17] Quoted in Morgenthau, *Politics among Nations,* p. 431.

[18] A leading summary and exegesis of the formal rules is J. L. Brierly, *The Law of Nations* (6th ed.; New York: Oxford University Press, 1963). Stimulating discussions of the nature of international law compared with other forms of law include Charles de Visscher, *Theory and Reality in Public International Law* (Princeton, N.J.: Princeton University Press, 1957); and Morton A. Kaplan and Nicholas de B. Katzenbach, *The Political Foundations of International Law* (New York: John Wiley & Sons, Inc., 1961).

ment between jurists and political scientists over whether or not it really is law. As this debate turns upon the question whether or not "real law" must emanate from an authoritative legislative source, be enforced by an authoritative executive, and be applied by authoritative judicial agencies, we need not linger over it. Certainly international law is not law in exactly the same sense as is domestic law (see Chap. 18), yet it certainly plays a significant role in international relations. It may be defined as the body of rules and principles of action that civilized states usually accept as binding in their relations with one another.

Before World War I war was entirely legal under these rules, and international law was useful as an approach to establishing peace only in the sense that it provided a body of rules and principles for the settlement of international disputes and therefore helped to avoid or limit war. Since 1918, however, war—at least war waged for purposes other than "self-defense"—has become "illegal" according to these rules: The Covenant of the League of Nations severely restricted the circumstances in which member nations could go to war: nearly all the nations in the world ratified the Kellogg-Briand Pact of 1928, which declared that all the parties "condemn recourse to war for the solution of international controversies, and renounce it as an instrument of national policy"; and the United Nations Charter requires that all its members "shall settle their international disputes by peaceful means" and "refrain . . . from the threat or use of force against the territorial integrity or political independence of any other state" (Article 2). International law now seeks to prevent war by making it illegal as well as by providing rules and procedures for settling the disputes that lead to it. How effective these legal rules are and why we shall consider shortly.

### Scope and Content

Vernon Van Dyke offers a convenient classification of the rules of international law into four main categories.[19]

The law of peace includes rules like those affecting the legal birth of sovereign states and their recognition by other states, the definition of national boundaries, the extent of nations' legal jurisdiction over their territories, the status of alien persons and property, and so on. The law of war regulates the declaration and termination of war; the conduct of hostilities; treatment of enemy civilians and their property, prisoners of war, and spies; exclusion of certain weapons (like poison gas); and so on. The law of neutrality includes the definition and protection of the rights and obligations of neutrals and belligerents in their interrelations. The laws concerning resort to war, as we have noted, now consist of prohibitions against war except for "self-defense."

### Structure

The differences between domestic and international law, all of which relate to the utility of the latter as an approach to peace, are mostly clearly shown by examining the legislative, judicial, and executive structure of international law.

[19] Van Dyke, *International Politics,* pp. 293–296.

*"He started a Preventive War and I'm fightin' to End War."*

**Legislation** The rules of international law arise from two principal sources. Some arise from "customs," which are regular ways of handling certain types of situations, usually followed by nations from a sense of obligation over a long period of time (like the custom that no nation will exercise its police powers in other nations without

The International Political System

630

permission). Other rules arise from "treaties"—formal international agreements between two or more nations. It is important to note that *no* rule of international law is even formally binding upon any nation that has not voluntarily accepted it: No custom is binding unless the nation adheres to it (for example, the Israelis did not let the police-power rule prevent their agents from capturing Adolf Eichmann in Argentina in 1961), and no treaty is binding unless the nation formally ratifies it. No new rule of international law can thus legally be forced upon a nation by any outside agency—for that would violate its sovereignty (see Chap. 23).[20] The legislative process in international law is thus extremely decentralized in comparison with domestic legislative processes (see Chap. 15).

Once a nation has accepted a custom or ratified a treaty, how binding are its rules *legally?* Two equally valid but quite contradictory legal maxims apply: *pacta sunt servanda* (agreements are to be observed), which means that a nation cannot legally free itself at will from treaty obligations, and *rebus sic stantibus* (at this point of affairs), meaning that treaties legally cease to be obligatory as soon as the facts and conditions upon which they were founded have substantially changed. Who, then, is to say which treaty obligations are binding upon a nation and which are not? Who is authorized to interpret international law? The answer is that each nation interprets such law for itself; if it wishes, it may submit questions of disputed interpretation to an international judicial body.

**Adjudication**  Although some nations, as we have noted, may sometimes submit legal questions to arbitration in a sort of quasi-judicial procedure, the only body that can be regarded as a permanent international court is the International Court of Justice (ICJ). This body, which sits at the Hague, in the Netherlands, consists of fifteen judges, each from a different nation and each selected for a nine-year term by concurrent action of the United Nations Security Council and General Assembly.

The ICJ, however, is a pale image of a "world supreme court." For all practical purposes it has no compulsory jurisdiction—that is, there is no legal way in which it can compel a nation to come before it. The Statute of the Court declares in Article 36 that its jurisdiction comprises "all cases which the parties refer it." The oft-mentioned "optional clause" of the statute, to be sure, permits the parties to make unilateral declarations "that they recognize as compulsory *ipso facto* and without special agreement, in relation to any other state accepting the same obligation, the jurisdiction of the Court" in certain kinds of cases.[21] Yet almost half the members of the United Nations (including the USSR) have not made such declarations, and many

---

[20] The United Nations Charter does, however, provide that "the Organization shall ensure that states which are not Members of the United Nations act in accordance with these Principles so far as may be necessary for the maintenance of international peace and security" (Article 2, Section 6). Some jurists have argued that this provision is an effort to "legislate" for nonmember nations without their consent.

[21] The statute is reproduced in *Yearbook of the United Nations* (New York: United Nations, annual).

that have (including the United States and Great Britain) have included so many qualifications and reservations that they are legally quite free to refuse to take any kind of dispute to the Court. The ICJ cannot legally compel any nation to appear before it, nor can any nation legally "arraign" another against its desires. This lack of any effective compulsory jurisdiction sharply differentiates it from any domestic court.

The judicial function in international law is accordingly as decentralized as is its legislative function. Each nation has the legal power to interpret the rules of international law that it considers binding upon itself, and there is no clear and authoritative legal procedure by which any nation's interpretation can be overridden without its consent by another nation or by an international judicial body.

**Execution** The execution of international law is also very decentralized. For the most part the rules are enforced through the voluntary compliance of the nations themselves. Before World War I the only way in which a nation could legally be compelled to obey international law was through severance of diplomatic relations, boycotts and embargoes, blockades, and even military intervention. The collective-security provisions of the League of Nations Covenant and the United Nations Charter permit the use of collective sanctions for the enforcement of international law, but, as we have seen, they have been little used for this purpose. For the most part, accordingly, the enforcement of international law depends upon the willingness of nations to abide by it, rather than upon compulsion by any international police force.

### Record

There is a widespread popular impression that international law is a kind of feeble political joke and that nations ignore it all the time as a matter of course. This belief, however, is far from true, for, as J. L. Brierly has pointed out:

> [International] law is normally observed because ... the demands that it makes on states are generally not exacting, and on the whole states find it convenient to observe it; but this fact receives little notice because the interest of most people in international law is not in the ordinary routine of international legal business, but in the occasions, rare but generally sensational, on which it is flagrantly broken. Such breaches generally occur either when some great political issue has arisen between states, or in that part of the system which professes to regulate the conduct of war.[22]

The rules of international law that apply to technical and nonpolitical matters are thus faithfully observed by nations for the excellent reason that they all find such observance in their self-interest; these rules constitute the great bulk of international law. This service to mankind, as Brierly has correctly noted, should not be overlooked or undervalued.

[22] Brierly, *The Law of Nations*, pp. 71–72.

By the same token, however, the few areas in which international law is largely impotent are precisely those in which conflicts generally lead to war. International law in the current state of world politics thus makes many valuable contributions but is of little use as a barrier against war. The value and limitations of its general role have been well summed up by Gaetano Anzilotti, a former member of the ICJ:

> The interests protected by international law are not those which are of major weight in the life of states. It is sufficient to think of the great political and economic rivalries to which no juridical formula applies, in order to realize the truth of this statement. International law develops its true function in a sphere considerably circumscribed and modest, not in that in which there move the great conflicts of interests which induce states to stake their very existence in order to make them prevail.[23]

Perhaps that is why the often-heard charge that America's participation in the Vietnam war was "illegal" had so little effect on ending it—and why at the same time America's alleged violations of international law in its border disputes with Mexico were settled so amicably "out of court."

## APPROACHES TO PEACE THROUGH THE UNITED NATIONS

The United Nations, like its predecessor, the League of Nations,[24] was not intended to achieve world peace by abolishing the state system; indeed, its Charter specifically states that "the Organization is based on the principle of the sovereign equality of all its Members" (Article 2), which, as we noted in Chapter 23, is the basic legal principle of the state system. The United Nations is not, as the term is used in this book, a "world government" in any sense.

What is it, then? Perhaps the most accurate answer is that the United Nations represents an effort to do two things. The first is to draw together in one world organization the various instruments for seeking peace within the state system outlined in the preceding section, so that they may be used with maximum effectiveness. The second is to encourage and administer international cooperation on many largely nonpolitical matters. The United Nations is not committed to any one approach to peace but attempts to further all approaches that do not involve basic alterations of the state system. Claude has accurately summed up its eclectic nature and purposes in these words:

> However dogmatic and monistic certain thinkers may be in explaining the

---

[23] Quoted in H. Lauterpacht, *The Function of Law in the International Community* (New York: Oxford University Press, 1933), p. 169.

[24] Limitations of space preclude any discussion of the League of Nations, an organization whose structure, problems, and history offer many significant similarities to and contrasts with the United Nations. The reader who wishes to explore these matters may well consult F. P. Walters, *A History of the League of Nations* (New York: Oxford University Press, 1952); and Alfred E. Zimmern, *The League of Nations and the Rule of Law* (New York: Crowell-Collier and Macmillan, Inc., 1939).

cause of war and the means to peace, the founding fathers of the United Nations have clearly been prepared to try every device which shows promise of contributing to the conditions of peace, and to reject exclusive reliance upon any single device. Our present institutional structure is analogous to a shotgun rather than a rifle, inasmuch as it reflects distrust of the accuracy of anyone's aim at a solution and preference for releasing a shower of shots in the general direction of the problem; we do not know which approach to peace is valid, so we try them all, hoping that not all the shots will be wasted.[25]

The United Nations is thus an international organization, not a world government. In this discussion we shall not attempt to examine all its many and varied organs and activities but shall concentrate mainly on the nature and results of those Charter provisions and organs most directly related to the maintenance of peace and security.

## ESTABLISHMENT

The label "united nations" was first applied to a loose association of the nations fighting against Germany and Japan in World War II, all of which, on or after January 1, 1942, signed the Declaration of the United Nations in favor of certain general war aims and against concluding any separate peace with the Axis powers. Preliminary plans for a permanent peacetime organization of such powers were drawn up at the two Dumbarton Oaks conferences of August and September 1944. The Charter of the United Nations was written at the United Nations conference on international organization in San Francisco in April-June 1945. The United Nations was born in January 1946, when the first General Assembly and Security Council met in London. Since 1950 the organization has had its permanent headquarters in New York City.

## STRUCTURE

### Membership

The United Nations consists of the fifty-one nations that originally signed the Charter and the nations that have subsequently applied and been admitted by votes of the General Assembly upon recommendations by the Security Council. As of 1973 there were 135 members, including almost all the nations of the world and a few regions (for example, the Ukraine and Byelorussia) that are not full-fledged nations. Only one nation (Indonesia) has withdrawn (it later rejoined), and one (the Chinese Nationalist government of Taiwan) has been expelled.

### Organs

According to the Charter (Article 7) the United Nations has six principal organs: the General Assembly, Security Council, Secretariat, Economic and Social Council, Inter-

[25] Claude, *Swords into Plowshares,* p. 199.

national Court of Justice, and Trusteeship Council (see Figure 21). We shall consider only the first three here.

**General Assembly**   The General Assembly is the only organ of the United Nations that includes all its members, and it holds annual sessions. Each nation has one vote in its deliberations, although each can send a delegation of up to five members. The body exercises powers and functions that may be categorized as "deliberative" (discussing any and all matters within the scope of the Charter); "supervisory" (controlling and regulating other organs—receiving annual reports from them and establishing certain administrative procedures for them to follow); "financial" (making up the United Nations budget and apportioning expenses among the members); "elective" (admitting new members and choosing members for the other organs); and "constituent" (proposing amendments to the Charter). Several of these powers, as we shall see, are exercised jointly with the Security Council. The "uniting for peace" resolution of 1950 has given the General Assembly an even more prominent role in the organization's affairs than it was originally intended to have. On "important questions" (defined in Article 18) it decides by two-thirds majorities of the members present and voting and on all other matters by simple majorities.

**Security Council**   The Security Council consists of fifteen members of the United Nations, divided into two classes: five permanent members (the PRC, France, the Soviet Union, Great Britain, and the United States); and ten nonpermanent members, which are elected for two-year terms by the General Assembly. The terms of the elected members are staggered so that five new members are elected each year, and no nonpermanent member may serve two consecutive terms. The Security Council was originally intended to bear the main responsibility for and control over U.N. machinery for maintaining peace and security, but it has lost much of its preeminence in this area to the General Assembly.

The most noteworthy feature of the Security Council is its voting procedure, which provides for the famous veto by any of the five permanent members. Article 27 of the Charter stipulates:

> 1. Each member of the Security Council shall have one vote. 2. Decisions of the Security Council on procedural matters shall be made by an affirmative vote of nine members. 3. Decisions of the Security Council on all other matters shall be made by an affirmative vote of nine members *including the concurring votes of the permanent members. . . .* (italics added)

The Security Council, which is supposed to be the United Nation's main acting body, thus cannot act unless the five permanent members unanimously agree that it should act. This veto provision and its frequent use by the Soviet Union (which has registered more than 100 vetoes since 1946) are often blamed for the failure of the organization to live up to its promise, but the fact is that the United States, though it has used the veto only once, opposes its elimination quite as strongly as the Soviets do. The veto reflects and to some extent influences current international politics, but it certainly did not create them nor is it alone preventing the United Nations from becoming a world government. We shall return to this point.

FIGURE 21
The structure of the
United Nations.

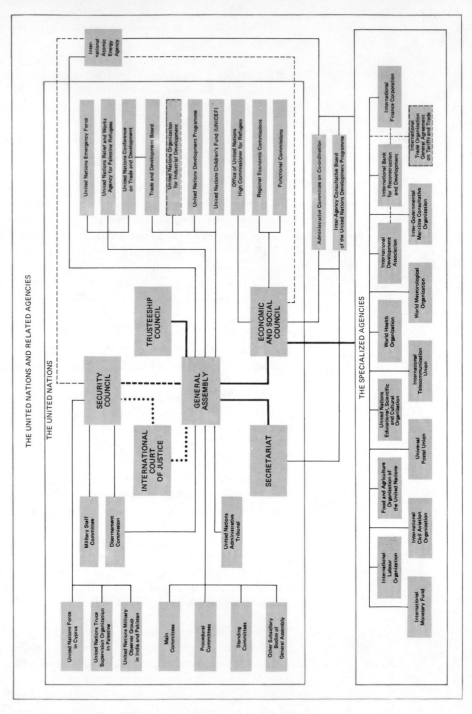

THE UNITED NATIONS AND RELATED AGENCIES

THE UNITED NATIONS

THE SPECIALIZED AGENCIES

International Atomic Energy Agency

United Nations Emergency Force

United Nations Relief and Works Agency for Palestine Refugees

United Nations Conference on Trade and Development

Trade and Development Board

United Nations Organization for Industrial Development

United Nations Development Programme

United Nations Children's Fund (UNICEF)

Office of United Nations High Commissioner for Refugees

Regional Economic Commissions

Functional Commissions

Administrative Committee on Co-ordination

Inter-Agency Consultative Board of the United Nations Development Programme

TRUSTEESHIP COUNCIL

SECURITY COUNCIL

GENERAL ASSEMBLY

ECONOMIC AND SOCIAL COUNCIL

INTERNATIONAL COURT OF JUSTICE

SECRETARIAT

Military Staff Committee

Disarmament Commission

United Nations Administrative Tribunal

United Nations Force in Cyprus

United Nations Truce Supervision Organization in Palestine

United Nations Military Observer Group in India and Pakistan

Main Committees

Procedural Committees

Standing Committees

Other Subsidiary Bodies of General Assembly

International Finance Corporation

International Trade Organization General Agreement on Tariffs and Trade

International Bank for Reconstruction and Development

Inter-Governmental Maritime Consultative Organization

International Development Association

World Meteorological Organization

World Health Organization

International Telecommunication Union

United Nations Educational, Scientific and Cultural Organization

Universal Postal Union

Food and Agriculture Organization of the United Nations

International Civil Aviation Organization

International Labour Organization

International Monetary Fund

**Secretariat and Secretary-General**    The United Nations Secretariat is the organization's civil service and performs many secretarial, research, and other administrative chores for the various agencies. It is headed by the Secretary-General, who is appointed by the General Assembly on the recommendation of the Security Council. In addition to acting as the organization's chief administrative officer, the Secretary-General plays a significant political role. Article 99 of the Charter authorizes him to "bring to the attention of the Security Council any matter which in his opinion may threaten international peace and security." All occupants of the office to date—Trygve Lie from 1946 to 1954, Dag Hammarskjöld from 1954 to 1961, U Thant from 1961 to 1972, and Kurt Waldheim since 1972—have made full use of this power, and the office of Secretary-General has thus come to be one of the most powerful agencies in the whole U.N. structure, exercising a notable influence upon its decisions.[26]

These organs, then, are the principal ones for maintaining international peace and security. Let us now examine the Charter's provisions for handling such matters and how they have worked out in practice.

## MAINTAINING INTERNATIONAL PEACE AND SECURITY

The United Nations Charter incorporates many "approaches" to peace. In the General Assembly and Security Council it provides forums in which international issues can be discussed, "world public opinion" can be influenced and expressed, and negotiations can be conducted among disputing nations. The Economic and Social Council and affiliated specialized agencies provide opportunities for many kinds of cooperation on nonpolitical and technical matters so that a "world community" may eventually come into being. The Trusteeship Council not only provides a means for the enlightened administration of non-self-governing territories by its members but also seeks to eliminate quarrels over colonies as a cause of war.[27] The United Nations also has agencies for the mediation and conciliation of disputes, the adjudication of legal controversies (the ICJ), and the reduction and regulation of armaments.

The central approach to peace embodied in the Charter, however, is collective security. The relevant provisions are stated mainly in Chapter VII, Articles 39–51, and may be briefly summarized. The Security Council is charged with determining "the existence of any threat to the peace, breach of the peace, or act of aggression" and with deciding what measures will be taken when such situations are deemed to exist (Article 39). It may decide to adopt measures not involving the use of armed force and may call upon the members to apply any and all such measures. "These may include complete or partial interruption of economic relations and of rail, sea, air, postal, telegraphic, radio, and other means of communication, and the severance of diplomatic relations" (Article 41). If the Security Council decides that these measures

---

[26] The Secretary-General's role is examined in Dag Hammarskjöld, *The International Civil Servant in Law and in Fact* (New York: Oxford University Press, 1961); and Howard H. Lentner, "Political Responsibility and Accountability of the United Nations Secretary-General," *Journal of Politics,* 27 (November 1965), pp. 818–838.

[27] See James N. Murray, *The United Nations Trusteeship System* (Urbana, Ill.: University of Illinois Press, 1957).

*History doesn't repeat itself.*

are inadequate, it may adopt others "to maintain or restore international peace and security. Such action may include demonstrations, blockades, and other operations by air, sea, or land forces of Members of the United Nations" (Article 42). And the members are obligated to respond to the Security Council's requests that they take such action (Articles 48–50).

These Charter provisions are clearly intended to create a strong collective-security system centered upon the Security Council as the decision-making body. How have they worked out in practice?

## THE CHANGING UNITED NATIONS

During much of the time since the United Nations began functioning in 1946 the basic fact of international politics has been the cold war between the United States and its allies, on one hand, and the Soviet Union and its allies, on the other. The fundamental prerequisite for the successful operation of the U.N. collective-security system—unanimity among the great powers in the Security Council—has thus rarely been present. In those instances of aggression or breaches of the peace in which the Soviet Union and the United States have favored different combatants, the Security Council has been unable to act at all because the Soviets have used or threatened to use the veto. They have done so in the clashes between communists and anticommunists in Greece in the late 1940s, the war in Indochina and the Hungarian revolt in the 1950s, and the war between North and South Vietnam in the 1960s.

The one notable exception to this generalization was the Korean crisis of 1950. In June of that year the communist North Koreans attacked the noncommunist South

Koreans in a clear instance of aggression. By a strange twist of fate the Soviets at that moment were boycotting the United Nations in protest against its failure to admit the PRC, and the American-proposed resolution in the Security Council to invoke Article 42 against the North Koreans was therefore passed. The Soviets returned too late to veto it. The response of the member nations to the Security Council's call, however, was somewhat less than unanimous, enthusiastic cooperation. Of the sixty members, only sixteen sent armed forces of any kind, and only the United States, Great Britain, and Canada sent more than token forces. Most nations sat on the sidelines, some of them (like the Latin American nations) cheering the U.N. "team" on, others (like India) wringing their hands over the whole unfortunate affair, and still others (the communist bloc) denouncing the action as illegal, imperialistic, warmon-gering, and so on. The Korean episode, accordingly, represented neither a complete collapse nor a great success for the collective-security system. Certainly it was made possible at all only because the Soviet Union was boycotting the United Nations when the communist aggression took place. Otherwise the Security Council would have been prevented from taking action just as it has been in other instances of aggression since 1946.

On several other occasions the United Nations has sent "peace-keeping forces" or "truce-supervisory teams" into some of the world's trouble spots to observe, report, and try to prevent violations of truce agreements among warring factions or nations. The General Assembly, operating under the uniting-for-peace resolution, sent about 23,000 troops to the Congo in 1960 to prevent expansion of the civil war in that newly independent nation. The communist bloc strongly opposed the inter-vention, however, and Secretary-General Dag Hammarskjöld was killed in the crash of a U.N. plane flying a reconnaissance mission over the fighting area. In 1964 the Security Council, this time with Soviet concurrence, sent a force of 6000 to Cyprus to prevent the clash between Greek and Turkish Cypriots from escalating into a full-scale civil war that might well have brought on a Turkish invasion. Perhaps the best-known such force is the U.N. emergency force of 6000 sent to the Middle East in 1956 to supervise the armistice demarcation lines established after the Egypt-Israel war.[28] The force continued to operate in the area for years afterward but was unable to prevent the outbreak in 1967 of the six-day war between Israel and the Arab nations and later was unable to prevent violations of the postwar cease-fire agreements and a new war in 1973. The U.N. peace-keeping operations have thus had only modest success.[29]

### Decline of the Security Council, Rise of the General Assembly

The greatest change in the United Nations has been the steady decline in the significance of the Security Council and the concomitant increase in the significance of the General Assembly. The principal formal evidence of this change is the uniting-for-peace resolution passed by the General Assembly in 1950 under the following circumstances.

Shortly after the Security Council had adopted resolutions calling for U.N. intervention against the North Koreans, the Soviets returned to the organization in an effort to make up lost ground. They argued that, although abstention from voting in the Security Council is not tantamount to a veto, absence is—and that therefore the intervention in Korea was "unconstitutional." They were unable to persuade most other nations to accept this view, but they were able to prevent the Council from taking further action.

The United States therefore determined to counter the Soviet tactics, which were paralyzing U.N. action against communist aggression. In November 1950 the General Assembly, under the leadership of the United States, resolved that in instances in which there appear to be threats to peace or acts of aggression and in which the Security Council, because of a veto by one of the permanent members, fails to recommend action under Articles 41 and 42, the General Assembly will immediately consider the matter. If it deems necessary, the General Assembly will recommend that the member nations use whatever measures, including armed force, seem appropriate to maintain or restore international peace and security.[30]

The changing relative positions of the Security Council and the General Assembly dramatized by this resolution are also indicated by several other facts: Since 1950

---

[28] The Security Council sought to keep great-power rivalries out of the operation by using troops only from nations that are not permanent members of the Security Council. The force included military units from Brazil, Canada, Colombia, Denmark, Finland, India, Indonesia, Norway, Sweden, and Yugoslavia and for much of the time was commanded by Norwegian General Odd Bull.

[29] See Larry L. Fabian, *Soldiers without Enemies* (Washington, D.C.: The Brookings Institution, 1971).

[30] The text is given in Jack E. Vincent, *A Handbook of the United Nations* (Woodbury, N.Y.: Barron's Educational Series, Inc., 1969), pp. 55–56.

the Security Council has met far less frequently than before, whereas the General Assembly's annual sessions have grown longer and longer; also since 1950 the Security Council has been considering fewer and fewer political issues, whereas the General Assembly has been considering substantially more.[31] The result is that the "vetoless" General Assembly has unquestionably become the main *political,* as well as deliberative and supervisory, organ of the United Nations.

### Increased Power of the Afro-Asian Nations

The founders of the United Nations intended that the permanent members of the Security Council would dominate its political activities. The post-1950 shift in decision making from the Security Council to the General Assembly has produced a shift in power from the Big Five to the other member nations, particularly to the developing nations of Africa and Asia. Table 25 shows how this shift has come about. Before 1950 the Afro-Asian nations were the second biggest group in the General Assembly but still had only 28 percent of the votes. Since the uniting-for-peace resolution was adopted, however, more than two-thirds of the United Nations' new members have come from Africa and Asia. As a result, this bloc now controls almost a majority of votes in the General Assembly and far outnumbers all other blocs.

TABLE 25

**Changing Membership of the United Nations**

| Blocs of Member Nations | By Period of Admission | | | | Total, 1973 | Percentage of Total Votes |
|---|---|---|---|---|---|---|
| | Before 1950 | Percentage of Votes | Since 1950 | Percentage of Votes | | |
| Afro-Asian | 17 | 28% | 46 | 62% | 63 | 47% |
| Communist | 7 | 12 | 6 | 8 | 13 | 10 |
| Western Europe[a] | 10 | 16 | 7 | 10 | 17 | 12 |
| British Commonwealth | 5 | 8 | 7 | 10 | 12 | 9 |
| Latin America | 20 | 33 | 1 | 1 | 21 | 15 |
| Other | 2 | 3 | 7 | 10 | 9 | 7 |
| | 61 | 100% | 74 | 101% | 135 | 100% |

[a] Includes the United States and Canada.
*Source: The World Almanac & Book of Facts, 1974* (New York: Newspaper Enterprise Association, Inc., 1974), pp. 621–622. Reprinted by permission of Newspaper Enterprise Association, Inc.

But has this shift made any substantive difference? Several studies of voting in the General Assembly show that it has.[32] On issues of "colonialism" (for example, resolutions condemning Portuguese suppression of Angolan struggles for independence) and "racism" (resolutions condemning apartheid in South Africa) the Afro-Asian nations vote together as a solid bloc. But on cold-war issues (like the admission of the PRC) they divide among themselves; some (Egypt, Ghana, Guinea)

---

[31] Claude, *Swords into Plowshares,* pp. 159–164.

[32] See Hayward R. Alker, Jr., and Russett, *World Politics in the General Assembly* (New Haven, Conn.: Yale University Press, 1965); Thomas Hovet, Jr., *Bloc Politics in the United Nations* (Cambridge Mass.: Harvard University Press, 1960); and Robert O. Keohane, "Political Influence in the General Assembly," *International Conciliation,* 557 (March 1966), pp. 5–64.

usually support the Soviet Union, and others (Japan, Thailand, the Philippines) usually support the United States. But the point is that, whereas before 1957 the United States customarily won majorities for its positions on cold-war issues with relative ease, since then it has had an increasingly difficult time lining up enough Afro-Asian nations to win. For better or worse, the latter, and not the Big Five, have come to dominate the General Assembly and therefore the United Nations.

EVALUATION[33]

Any evaluation of the United Nations' record in dealing with the political problems of preventing war should be based upon a recognition of the fact noted at the beginning of this section: The United Nations does *not* represent an effort to abandon the state system and to strike out in an entirely new direction. This point was made painfully clear in the growing financial crisis of the mid-1960s. The United Nations is financed by contributions apportioned among its members according to a formula determined by the General Assembly. In 1973 it assigned the largest share to the United States (31.44 percent), the second largest to the Soviet Union (14.15 percent), and the third largest to France (6.00 percent).[34] Article 19 of the Charter provides that any member nation more than two years in arrears in its contributions will have no vote in the General Assembly.

After 1956 the United Nations incurred heavy expenses from its peace-keeping operations in the Middle East and the Congo, and the General Assembly attempted to finance them by levying special assessments on all the members. But the communist bloc, led by the USSR, refused to pay, arguing that these operations were in violation of the Charter. In 1962 the ICJ ruled that the operations were lawful and that all members were obligated to pay. The communist bloc continued to refuse, however. France joined it, arguing that only Security Council decisions are binding on all members and that it is for members who agree with General Assembly recommendations—not their opponents—to find means to finance them. At this point the United States demanded that Article 19 be invoked and that all nonpayers be deprived of their votes—but it did not press its position, recognizing that a showdown would mean secession of the communist nations and France and the probable ruin of the United Nations. In the 1964 session of the General Assembly, accordingly, no formal votes were taken at all,[35] and the members adjourned early in the hope that some compromise could be worked out. In 1965 the United States finally abandoned

---

[33] Of the many evaluations of the United Nations' record the most laudatory is Clark M. Eichelberger, *UN: The First Twenty Years* (New York: Harper & Row, Publishers, 1965); the most denunciatory is Chesly Manly. *The UN Record* (Chicago: Henry Regnery Company, 1955). Somewhat less forensic are H.G. Nicholas, *The United Nations as a Political Institution* (4th ed.; New York: Oxford University Press, 1972); and Leon Gordenker (ed.), *The United Nations in International Politics* (Princeton, N.J.: Princeton University Press, 1971).

[34] *The American Almanac, 1974* (The Statistical Abstract of the United States, prepared by the Bureau of the Census; New York: Grosset & Dunlap, Inc., 1974), pp. 833–834, Table 1350.

[35] When an issue had to be decided, General Assembly President Alex Quaison-Sackley of Ghana would invite the members to give him their "opinions" privately, after which he would "announce the consensus" of the Assembly.

its insistence that Article 19 be enforced, on the ground that only thus could the United Nations be held together. This resolution of the problem made even clearer than before the organization's basic character as a league of independent sovereign nations rather than a world government.[36]

The United Nations, then, represents an effort to provide a worldwide centralized organization for various approaches to peace within the state system. It cannot escape the limitations inherent in each of these approaches, but it can, and in many instances has, made it possible to pursue them more effectively than would be possible in complete organizational isolation from one another: for example, in preventing the Congolese civil war from becoming an international war.

As long as nations and their citizens continue to prefer national independence and self-determination to supranational government, the United Nations cannot become significantly "stronger" than it now is: eliminating the veto from the Security Council or any other institutional tinkering cannot change this fact. As long as powerful nations like the United States, the Soviet Union, and France continue to clash over issues that they regard as basic to their national interests, the United Nations cannot be expected to bring world peace.

Yet, despite these handicaps, the organization has already achieved a far better record than the League of Nations did. In 1950 it authorized military action that stopped communist aggression in Korea. In 1956 it sent a truce team to patrol the frontiers between Israel and its Arab enemies and for more than a decade prevented major violations of the truce. In 1960 it sent another military force to the former Belgian Congo to prevent secession from and maintain order in the newly independent nation—and, with Dag Hammarskjöld's death in the course of duty, gained its first hero. In 1964 it sent yet another military force to Cyprus to prevent the civil war between the Greek and Turkish Cypriots from becoming an international war between Greece and Turkey. Any of these local crises could have escalated into a major war involving the great powers, but U.N. intervention prevented it. These achievements are not negligible.

The United Nations was not intended to alter any basic trait of the state system, nor can it do so. If the state system is the basic cause of international violence, the United Nations is powerless to prevent it. But, if even within the state system there is some real hope of preventing World War III, then the organization has made a major contribution to keeping that hope alive.

## APPROACHES TO PEACE THROUGH WORLD GOVERNMENT

### THE WORLD-GOVERNMENT MOVEMENT

World government has long been a dream of some philosophers and poets who have seen it as signaling people's triumph over their base, quarrelsome, and chauvinist tendencies to create a truly human race. The best-known expression of this dream is

---

[36] For a review of the crisis and its implications, see Norman J. Padelford, "Financing Peacekeeping: Politics and Crisis," *International Organization,* 19 (Summer 1965), pp. 444–462.

**The U.N. polices a cease-fire along the Suez Canal, July 1967.** Source: UPI Photograph.

the prophetic poem "Locksley Hall" (1842) by Alfred, Lord Tennyson, in which, he foresaw the day when

> . . . the war drum throbbed no longer
>   and the battle flags were furled
> In the Parliament of Man, the Federation
>   of the world.

Since World War II, however, world government has been graduated from the status of poet's dream to that of reform movement. Mainly in Western Europe and the English-speaking nations such writers as Clarence K. Streit, Cord Meyer, Emery Reeves, Norman Cousins, and Stringfellow Barr have advocated world government, not as the fulfillment of man's highest nature, but as the minimum condition for his physical survival.[37] Several organizations have been established to hasten the achievement of this goal, and, though they differ somewhat in the details of their

---

[37] See Clarence K. Streit, *Freedom against Itself* (New York: Harper & Row, Publishers, 1954); Cord Meyer, *Peace or Anarchy* (Boston: Little, Brown & Company, 1947); Emery Reeves, *The Anatomy of Peace* (New York: Pocket Books, Inc., 1946); Stringfellow Barr, *Citizens of the World* (New York: Doubleday & Company, Inc., 1953); and Norman Cousins, *In Place of Folly* (New York: Harper & Row, Publishers, 1961).

The International Political System

proposals, they are sufficiently similar that we shall consider them together as one "world government" movement.

## THE CASE FOR WORLD GOVERNMENT

Although there are a few minor differences among them, the "world governmentalists" (or "world federalists," as they are often called) generally base their case upon the following propositions.

Thermonuclear World War III will exterminate most human beings and annihilate civilization. This limitless disaster is almost upon us; the clock of human destiny stands at one minute to midnight. There is thus no time for dallying with palliatives; we must immediately start the basic cure for the ills of international society, or we shall perish.

The basic disease that has caused past wars and will, if left unremedied, bring World War III is the international anarchy of the state system itself. War is the inevitable result of anarchy, and the only possible alternative to either is world government. No effort to achieve peace within the state system, including establishment of the United Nations, can prevent war because none can touch the basic cause of wars.

If we are to survive, therefore, we have no choice but to establish a world federal government, modeled more or less closely upon the American or Swiss system, one that will have all power over international political affairs while leaving to each nation control of its own purely domestic affairs. This goal can perhaps best be achieved by revising the United Nations Charter to make the United Nations into such a supernational government; but, however it is achieved, it must be achieved soon, or mankind will die.

How can we achieve this goal? As the peoples of the various nations are far more ready for world government than are their shortsighted, timid, and confused statesmen, we must launch a worldwide propaganda (or "educational") campaign to stimulate and activate latent popular enthusiasm for this plan. When the people are aroused, the statesmen will soon be converted.

These reasons and methods are why and how world federalists hope to achieve world government.

## CRITICISMS OF THE WORLD-GOVERNMENT POSITION

The world-government movement has won support from many intellectuals and even from a few public officials—all of them, needless to say, on this side of the iron curtain. Most political scientists who specialize in international affairs have not been converted, however. Generally speaking, they object to the world-federalist doctrine on grounds of desirability, practicality, or both.

### Desirability

Some political scientists, notably Claude, have raised questions about whether or not a world federal government would prevent war, as its advocates promise. Claude has pointed out that government *within* nations has never been a magic cure for violence and civil war and that federal governments in particular have experienced much internecine strife—one outstanding example being the American Civil War. It may well be that in the kind of violent and fragmented world in which we live only the most ruthless kind of world dictatorship could possibly prevent war. Should we, Claude has asked, pay so great a price even for world peace?[38]

*Practicality*

Most political scientists, however, agree with the world federalists on the desirability of world government to prevent war. But they believe that world government simply is not possible in the present state of international society.

In essence, their criticism is based on the fact that governments, wherever they have been successfully established and have kept domestic peace, have reflected the prior existence of *communities.* That is, the people who have established them and accepted their rule have consciously shared certain common values, loyalties, and attitudes the preservation of which has seemed to require the services of government. As we noted in Chapter 3, where no such consensus, or feeling of community, exists or where it is less important to the community's major groups than are their own special interests, government cannot prevent domestic violence or even maintain its own existence.

The evidence, most political scientists are convinced, overwhelmingly indicates that no such world community exists at the present time. Contrary to the assumptions of world federalists, the peoples of most nations are more nationalistic and parochial than their leaders are. Foreign offices and diplomats are far more often criticized for being too "internationalistic" than for being too "nationalistic." As long as national loyalties continue deeply rooted in people's minds, no world community can exist, and no world government can be established or sustained.

Even granting the argument that only world government can prevent World War III, most political scientists thus agree with Claude's judgment that political science "grimly reminds man that he must do what he can; world federalism more sanguinely asserts that man can do what he must" and that "the dilemma of the world federalist is that there is no necessary correlation between human need and human capacity."[39]

## APPROACHES TO PEACE THROUGH REGIONAL ORGANIZATIONS

The preceding discussion suggests that, if humanity's only alternatives are world government tomorrow or World War III next week, our prospects are bleak indeed. But many nations' policy makers have refused to accept these alternatives as the only ones. They have joined in creating regional international organizations, which some analysts believe are valuable supplements to the Uniteds Nations and perhaps even halfway stations between the perilous anarchy of the state system and the distant

---

[38] Claude, *Swords into Plowshares,* pp. 380–391.

[39] Claude, *Swords into Plowshares,* pp. 374, 379. See also Van Dyke, *International Politics,* chap. 21; Morgenthau, *Politics among Nations,* chap. 29.

utopia of world government. The United Nations Charter recognizes both the existence and the desirability of regional organizations:

> 1. Nothing in the present Charter precludes the existence of regional arrangements or agencies for dealing with such matters relating to the maintenance of international peace and security as are appropriate for regional action, provided that such arrangements or agencies and their activities are consistent with the Purposes and Principles of the United Nations.

> 2. The Members of the United Nations entering into such arrangements or constituting such agencies shall make every effort to achieve pacific settlement of local disputes through such regional arrangements or by such regional agencies before referring them to the Security Council. (Chapter VIII, Article 52)

A considerable variety of regional international organizations now exists, and the leading types and examples deserve much more than the brief survey that can be offered here.[40]

## MAINLY MILITARY

Although multilateral military alliances have long been a feature of international politics, the tensions of the cold war have produced some of the largest and most powerful in history. One of the two most powerful is the North Atlantic Treaty Organization (NATO), established in 1949 on American initiative and designed to mobilize Western European military strength against possible invasion from the east. Its members include not only nine Continental and Scandinavian nations but also Canada, Greece, Iceland, Turkey, and the United States. NATO forces include ground, air, and sea units, all under one supreme commander, who has until recently always been an American general. The easing of cold-war tensions in the 1960s led to some reduction of commitments by some members: France withdrew altogether in 1966 and forced the removal of NATO headquarters from Paris to Brussels; Canada reduced its contribution to NATO forces in the early 1970s. NATO's future depends mainly upon how much the Western European nations continue to fear armed attack from the communist bloc. Many observers, however, believe that NATO played a significant role in stabilizing the European balance of power in the 1950s and 1960s and thus helped to prevent any major clash between East and West that might have escalated into World War III.[41]

NATO's opposite number is the Warsaw Treaty Organization, an alliance of eight Eastern European communist nations established under Soviet direction in 1955 as a counterweight to NATO—indeed with formal pledges of mutual support in case of attack very much like those in the North Atlantic Treaty. Albania has subsequently withdrawn, in support of the PRC against the Soviet Union in the schism within world communism. The organization's most notable action occurred in 1968, when

---

[40] The most comprehensive discussion is Ernst B. Haas, *Beyond the Nation-State: Functionalism and International Organization* (Stanford, Calif.: Stanford University Press, 1965).

[41] See Karl W. Deutsch *et al., Political Community and the North Atlantic Area* (Princeton, N.J.: Princeton University Press, 1957); and Charles O. Lerche, Jr., *Last Chance in Europe* (Chicago: Quadrangle Books, 1967).

the Soviets led troops from all the Warsaw pact nations except Romania into Czechoslovakia to suppress that nation's accelerating pro-Western policies. The Warsaw pact's role has never been as important as that of NATO's, and it too will probably decline as and if the cold war eases.[42]

## MAINLY ECONOMIC

Perhaps the best known and most successful of all post-1945 regional international organizations is the European Economic Community (EEC), established in 1958 by a treaty among Belgium, France, West Germany, Italy, Luxembourg, and the Netherlands. Denmark, Ireland, and the United Kingdom joined in 1972. EEC's basic purpose is to create a free trading market among its members and a common tariff for trade with nonmembers. It has a European parliament composed of delegates from the nine members' parliaments, a council of ministers composed of one minister from each member nation, and a commission of economic experts ("Eurocrats") drawn from the member nations. Although the final word on policy rests with the individual governments, commission headquarters in Brussels has had a great deal of influence on EEC development. Generally the commission's members have been more committed to increasing economic and political integration than have the EEC's political leaders, and many observers credit to the commission's leadership much of the organization's great success in raising member nations' gross national products and standards of living.[43] Some, indeed, believe that EEC offers the most promising basis yet for establishing the United States of Europe long dreamed of by such men as Sir Winston Churchill and Jean Monnet, founder of EEC.

Various other regional economic organizations are also in operation. The European Free Trade Association (EFTA) was established in 1960 by the "outer seven" (Austria, Denmark, Norway, Portugal, Sweden, Switzerland, and the United Kingdom) to achieve goals comparable to those of EEC, but its failure is apparent in recent applications by EFTA nations to become full or associate members of EEC. Another instance is the Latin American Common Market, formed in 1967 by the United States and all Latin American nations except Bolivia, Cuba, Ecuador, and Haiti; its purpose is to develop free trade among Latin American nations and to modernize their economies. The communist-bloc version is the Council of Mutual Economic Assistance (COMECON), created in 1949 by nine nations to promote trade, stabilize currency, and provide mutual economic assistance. Albania was expelled in 1962, and Yugoslavia entered into a "cooperative relationship" with COMECON in 1964. None of these organizations, communist or otherwise, has had anything like the success of EEC.

## COLLECTIVE SECURITY PLUS

At least two regional organizations have goals mainly associated with collective security, but they have also tried to develop political and cultural ties as well. The

---

[42] See Kazimierz Grzybowski, *The Socialist Commonwealth of Nations* (New Haven, Conn.: Yale University Press, 1964).

[43] See Leon N. Lindberg, *The Political Dynamics of European Economic Integration* (Stanford, Calif.: Stanford University Press, 1963); and Lindberg and Stuart A. Scheingold, *Europe's Would-Be Polity* (Englewood Cliffs, N.J.: Prentice-Hall, Inc., 1970).

more successful of the two is the Organization of American States (OAS), founded in 1948 and now composed of the United States and twenty-one South and Central American nations. Unlike NATO, which is mainly an arrangement for defense against outside attack, the OAS seeks also to provide collective security *within* the hemisphere. It has intervened in several intrahemisphere disputes over such matters as borders and treatment of exiles. Not all these interventions have been successful, but the OAS is generally credited with having significantly reduced the incidence of wars among American nations.[44]

The Arab League was established in 1945 and now includes thirteen Arabic-speaking nations of North Africa and the Middle East. Its primary purpose, of course, has been to mobilize member nations' collective strength against Israel, but it also has the secondary purpose of promoting trade among and economic development within the member nations. The United Arab Republic (Egypt) has dominated the League from its beginnings, but there have been frequent disputes among the members—like the "cold war" between the UAR and Saudi Arabia in the late 1960s over the civil war in Yemen. Even so, the member nations have developed one of the most cohesive voting records among all the caucuses in the United Nations General Assembly, and the League has undoubtedly strengthened the Arab alliance against Israel. What it might achieve beyond that goal remains in doubt.[45]

## THE RECORD

The mainly military regional organizations are, as we have seen, essentially updated versions of traditional collective-security arrangements. NATO and the Warsaw Treaty Organization have served their respective members' limited purposes rather well, at least as long as cold-war issues and fears have dominated their thinking and policies. Furthermore, each camp has deprived the other of the chance to increase its power and territory through the use of nonnuclear weapons alone. And, as neither the United States nor the Soviet Union has yet shown much inclination to use nuclear weapons in regional conflicts, many observers believe that the two regional organizations have made a substantial contribution—much greater than that of U.N. mediation—to preventing the outbreak of war in Europe.

The most spectacular successes have been scored by the mainly economic regional organizations, particularly the EEC. The Common Market's contribution to maintaining peace in Europe is less clear, but its economic aid to developing nations in Africa and Asia has undoubtedly helped to reduce tensions and conflict in those areas. The other economic associations have been less successful, but they remain in existence and at least offer hope and opportunity for better things. Although its associated economic development and free-trade programs have yet to show much result, the OAS has on several occasions dampened or resolved conflict among nations in the western hemisphere and has made a modest but undeniable contribution to peace.

---

[44] See O. C. Stoetzer, *The OAS: An Introduction* (New York: Frederick A. Praeger, Inc., 1967); and J. Drier, *The OAS and Hemispheric Crisis* (New York: Council on Foreign Relations, 1962).

[45] See R. W. Macdonald, *The League of Arab States* (Princeton, N.J.: Princeton University press, 1965).

It seems that the regional organizations have done things that the United Nations could not do, both in cooling conflict and promoting economic development. Perhaps one day the United Nations will become a world government and render the regional organizations unnecessary. Until that day, however, it seems likely that they will continue to carry at least part of the peace-keeping burden that the United Nations in its present form cannot carry alone.

## HAS HUMANITY A FUTURE?

In the present state of political science, as we saw in Chapter 1, there are many questions that cannot be answered with any degree of probability beyond that of the educated guess. The question of humanity's future is certainly an example.

Political scientists usually regret their inability to make reliable predictions on such matters, but perhaps in this instance we should be glad. For, if the answer is that humanity has no future, most of us prefer not to know it until we have to. In any case the political scientist—or anyone else—can answer only "maybe."

Political scientists can predict with considerable confidence, however, at least the short-term prospects for many variables that affect this question. Most students of international affairs agree that the immediate future will include certain elements. The essential features of the state system will remain unchanged for some time to come, although the atomistic nationalism and independent action characteristic of world politics before 1914 will be increasingly shaped into regional associations of nations with common interests and similar ideologies like NATO, EEC, and OAS. The United Nations will continue to have its greatest successes in nonpolitical and technical activities like combating illiteracy and disease and its greatest failures in political efforts to prevent aggression and maintain peace through collective security, disarmament, and peaceful settlement of disputes. Thermonuclear weapons will continue to be made, stockpiled, and held in readiness by the United States, the Soviet Union, the PRC, and the other nuclear powers; the means of delivering them over intercontinental distances with no possibility of successful defense will become technically more and more effective.

We must accept the fact that for an indefinite number of years we shall live in a world in which the possibility of thermonuclear warfare is ever present and in which smaller, less devastating wars will occur from time to time, posing the danger of becoming general and unlimited wars. Neither physical security nor psychic ease can be expected by any alert and intelligent person for some time to come. We can expect to live for many decades in what some writers have called—with grim accuracy —"the age of anxiety."

That much the political scientist can foretell. Has humanity a future? Perhaps fortunately neither we nor anyone else can tell. As thermonuclear-age humor has it, "An optimist is one who believes the future is uncertain."

# ANNOTATED BIBLIOGRAPHY

In this book I have not attempted the impossible task of trying to tell readers everything they may ever want to know about governing. I have tried to furnish an *introduction* to political science, and one of my main hopes is that readers' intellectual appetites will be whetted, rather than sated or killed. What follows is a list of some of the leading works in each of the areas we have considered. Readers eager for more may turn to them with profit. Needless to say, the list is far from exhaustive. It is intended as a sampling of the rich literature on politics and government in today's world and as a starting point for further exploration. Limitations on space have necessitated excluding all but a few items from the voluminous and useful periodical literature available.

## PART I POLITICAL SCIENCE: DISCIPLINE AND PROFESSION

### THE EMERGENCE AND PRESENT STATUS OF POLITICAL SCIENCE

Anderson, William. *Man's Quest for Political Knowledge: The Study and Teaching of Politics in Ancient Times.* Minneapolis, Minn.: University of Minnesota Press, 1964. Survey of empirical analyses of politics from the ancient Greeks to the Middle Ages.

*Contemporary Political Science.* Paris: Unesco Publication No. 426, 1950. Essays describing status of political science in various nations in the immediate postwar period, now out of date in many respects.

Duverger, Maurice. *An Introduction to the Social Sciences.* New York: Frederick A. Praeger, Inc., 1964. Contains useful history of the emergence of political science as a distinct discipline.

Haddow, Anna. *Political Science in American Colleges and Universities, 1636–1900.* New York: Appleton-Century-Crofts, 1939.

Robson, William A. *The University Teaching of Social Sciences: Political Science.* Leiden: A. W. Sijthoff, 1954. Useful short survey of the academic status of political science in various nations.

Somit, Albert, and Joseph Tanenhaus. *American Political Science: A Profile of a Discipline.* New York: Atherton Press, 1964. A careful and instructive sample survey of political scientists' attitudes toward the discipline.

————. *The Development of American Political Science: From Burgess to Behavioralism.* Boston: Allyn and Bacon, Inc., 1967. Takes up the story where Anderson and Haddow leave off.

## RESEARCH METHODS IN POLITICAL SCIENCE

*Buchanan, William. *Understanding Political Variables.* New York: Charles Scribner's Sons, 1969. An introduction to behavioral-research methods.

*Conway, M. Margaret, and Frank B. Feigert. *Political Analysis: An Introduction.* Boston: Allyn and Bacon, Inc., 1972. Same.

*Leege, David C., and Wayne, L. Francis *Political Research.* New York: Basic Books, Inc., 1974. Same.

*Merritt, Richard L., and Gloria J. Pyszka. *The Student Political Scientist's Handbook.* Cambridge, Mass.: Schenkman Publishing Company, Inc., 1969. Same, although with more attention to nonquantitative methods.

*Payne, James L. *Foundations of Empirical Political Analysis.* Chicago: Markham Publishing Company, 1973. Same.

*Shiveley, W. Phillips. *The Craft of Political Research: A Primer.* Englewood Cliffs, N.J.: Prentice-Hall, Inc., 1974. Same.

## ISSUES OF THE SCOPE, METHODS, AND USES OF POLITICAL SCIENCE

*Alker, Hayward R., Jr. *Mathematics and Politics.* New York: Crowell-Collier and Macmillan, Inc., 1965. Introductory survey of uses of mathematical methods in analysis of political behavior.

Beck, Lewis White. *Philosophic Inquiry.* Englewood Cliffs, N.J.: Prentice-Hall, Inc., 1952. Analysis of the presuppositions and techniques of various forms of human inquiry.

Catlin, George E. G. *The Science and Method of Politics.* New York: Alfred A. Knopf, 1927. Pioneer systematic analysis of politics, emphasizing power as the orienting concept.

————. *Systematic Politics: Elementa Politica et Sociologica.* Toronto: University of Toronto Press, 1962. Recent reflections.

Charlesworth, James C. *Contemporary Political Analysis* New York: The Free Press, 1967. Essays on various methodological issues in contemporary political science.

*———— (ed.). *The Limits of Behavioralism in Political Science.* Philadelphia: American Academy of Political and Social Science, 1962. Essays by both behavioralists and antibehavioralists.

Cohen, Morris R. *Reason and Nature.* New York: Harcourt Brace Jovanovich, Inc., 1931. Influential discussion of scientific method in physical and social sciences.

---

Annotated Bibliography

*Books listed with an asterisk are available in paperback editions.

652

Crick, Bernard. *The American Science of Politics.* Berkeley, Calif.: University of California Press, 1959. Attack upon the behavioralist approach.

Easton, David. *A Framework for Political Analysis.* Englewood Cliffs, N.J.: Prentice-Hall, Inc., 1965. General scheme for understanding politics, based on systems theory.

———. *The Political System.* New York: Alfred A. Knopf, 1953. Survey of contemporary political science, emphasizing the need for and lack of broad systematic theory.

*Eulau, Heinz. *The Behavioral Persuasion.* New York: Random House, Inc., 1963. Urbane introduction to the behavioral point of view.

———. *Micro-Macro Political Analysis.* Chicago: Aldine Publishing Company, 1969. Collection of substantive and methodological essays by a leading behavioralist.

*Eulau, Heinz, and James G. March (eds.). *Political Science.* Englewood Cliffs, N.J.: Prentice-Hall, Inc., 1969. Report of the political science panel of the Behavioral and Social Sciences Survey, intended as a survey of the field for laymen.

Golembiewski, Robert T., William A. Welsh, and William J. Crotty. *A Methodological Primer for Political Scientists.* Skokie, Ill.: Rand McNally & Company, 1969. Critical analysis of the literature in various fields from a behavioral point of view.

Graham, George J., Jr., and George W. Carey. *The Post-Behavioral Era.* New York: David McKay Company, Inc., 1972. Essays on the current state of political science.

Hyneman, Charles S. *The Study of Politics.* Urbana, Ill.: University of Illinois Press, 1959. Comprehensive description of intellectual concerns of American political scientists.

Irish, Marian D. (ed.). *Political Science: Advance of the Discipline.* Englewood Cliffs, N.J.: Prentice-Hall, Inc., 1968. Collection of critical essays, evaluating the state of knowledge in the discipline's principal fields.

*Kaplan, Abraham. *The Conduct of Inquiry.* San Francisco: Chandler Publishing Company, 1964. Leading recent survey of the behavioral framework for the study of social affairs.

Landau, Martin. *Political Theory and Political Science.* New York: Crowell-Collier and Macmillan, Inc., 1972. Critical examination of concepts underlying behavioral and nonbehavioral methodologies.

Lasswell, Harold D. *The Future of Political Science.* New York: Atherton Press, 1963. Survey of the present state and future possibilities of political science by one of its most distinguished practitioners.

McCoy, Charles, and John Playford (eds.). *Apolitical Politics: A Critique of Behavioralism.* New York: Thomas Y. Crowell Company, 1967. Accuses behavioralists of obsession with quantification and behavioralism of irrelevance to current political issues.

Northrop, F. S. C. *The Logic of the Sciences and the Humanities.* New York: Crowell-Collier and Macmillan, Inc., 1947. Analysis of the presuppositions and techniques of various forms of human inquiry.

Ranney, Austin. *Political Science and Public Policy.* Chicago: Markham Publishing Company, 1968. Essays on possibilities and problems in further study of policy contents and impacts.

——— (ed.). *Essays in the Behavioral Study of Politics.* Urbana, Ill.: University of Illinois Press, 1962. Essays on the achievements and problems of behavioral analysis in various fields of political science.

Schaar, John H., and Sheldon S. Wolin. "Essays on the Scientific Study of Politics: A Critique." *American Political Science Review,* 57 (March 1963), pp. 125–150. A sharp attack on Storing's volume of essays. Replies by Herbert Storing, Leo Strauss, Walter Berns, Leo Weinstein, and Robert Horwitz appear in the same issue, pp. 151–160.

Annotated Bibliography

*Somit, Albert (ed.). *Political Science and the Study of the Future.* Hinsdale, Ill.: The Dryden Press, 1974. Essays on "futuristics" as a way of understanding politics.

*Sorauf, Frank J. *Political Science: An Informal Overview.* Columbus O.: Charles E. Merrill Books Inc., 1965. A judicious survey of the strength and weaknesses of contemporary political science.

Storing, Herbert J. (ed.). *Essays on the Scientific Study of Politics.* New York: Holt, Rinehart and Winston, Inc., 1962. Most concentrated attack upon the behavioral point of view.

Surkin, Marvin, and Alan Wolfe (eds.). *An End to Political Science: The Caucus Papers.* New York: Basic Books, Inc., 1970. Accompanies McCoy and Playford as one of two major published collections of essays presenting the views of the Caucus for a New Political Science.

Van Dyke, Vernon. *Political Science: A Philosophical Analysis.* Stanford, Calif.: Stanford University Press, 1960. Appraisal of political science methodology from a moderate behavioral point of view.

Voegelin, Eric. *The New Science of Politics.* Chicago: University of Chicago Press, 1952. Attack on positivism, "scientism," and moral relativism in current political science.

Young, Roland (ed.). *Approaches to the Study of Politics.* Evanston, Ill.: Northwestern University Press, 1958. Essays on various aspects of the study of politics, mostly from a behavioral point of view.

## PART II  POLITICAL SYSTEMS AND THEIR ENVIRONMENTS

### THE GENERAL NATURE OF POLITICS AND GOVERNMENT

Almond, Gabriel A., and James S. Coleman (eds.), *The Politics of Developing Areas.* Princeton, N.J.: Princeton University Press, 1957. Influential study of comparative political institutions, especially notable for the theoretical scheme presented in the first and last chapters.

*Almond, Gabriel A., and G. Bingham Powell, Jr. *Comparative Politics: A Developmental Approach.* Boston: Little, Brown & Company, 1966. Short general analysis of politics, using systems theory and structural-functional theory.

Bailey, F. G. *Strategems and Spoils: A Social Anthropology of Politics.* New York: Schocken Books, 1972. The political process as viewed by a social anthropologist.

Bentley, Arthur F. *The Process of Government.* Chicago: University of Chicago Press, 1908. Reprinted Evanston, Ill.: Principia Press, 1935. The classic statement of the group structure of politics, one of the most influential works of twentieth-century political science.

*Dahl, Robert A., *Modern Political Analysis.* Englewood Cliffs, N.J.: Prentice-Hall, Inc., 1963. A short but rich introduction to the study of politics by a distinguished political scientist.

*Deutsch, Karl W., and William J. Foltz (eds.). *Nation-Building.* New York: Atherton Press, 1966. Essays on the formation and development of political societies.

*Dewey, John. *The Public and Its Problems.* New York: Holt, Rinehart and Winston, Inc., 1927. Difficult but influential analysis of the nature of politics and government.

Downs, Anthony. *An Economic Theory of Democracy.* New York: Harper & Row, Publishers, 1957. An original and provocative model of decision making in a democracy drawn from economic theories of perfect competition.

Annotated Bibliography

Easton, David. *A Systems Analysis of Political Life.* New York: John Wiley & Sons, Inc., 1965. A major effort to conceptualize politics and government in terms of systems theory.

Edelman, Murray. *The Symbolic Uses of Politics.* Urbana, Ill.: University of Illinois Press, 1964. Stimulating analysis of the role of symbols in political conflict and resolution.

Emerson, Rupert. *From Empire to Nation.* Cambridge, Mass.: Harvard University Press, 1960. A useful analysis of the emergence and problems of the developing nations.

Finer, Herman. *Theory and Practice of Modern Government.* Rev. ed. New York: Holt, Rinehart and Winston, Inc., 1949. Comprehensive survey of political problems and government institutions in various modern nations, both democratic and dictatorial.

Friedrich, Carl J. *The Pathology of Politics.* New York: Harper & Row, Publishers, 1972. A distinguished political scientist's argument that certain ethical violations in politics are not only common but essential to political growth and change.

Gurr, Ted Robert. *Why Men Rebel.* Princeton, N.J.: Princeton University Press, 1970. Prize-winning study of nature, conditions, and consequences of political violence.

Huntington, Samuel P. *Political Order in Changing Societies.* New Haven, Conn.: Yale University Press, 1968. Analysis of political change from a view other than the "developmental" one.

*Lasswell, Harold D. *Politics: Who Gets What, When, How.* New York: McGraw-Hill, Inc., 1936. A theory of politics emphasizing value conflicts.

*Lasswell, Harold D., and Abraham Kaplan. *Power and Society.* New Haven, Conn.: Yale University Press, 1950. Abstract and difficult but important and influential theory of politics based on power as the key concept.

MacIver, Robert M. *The Web of Government.* New York: Crowell-Collier and Macmillan, Inc., 1947. A distinguished sociologist considers government in its social setting.

*Millikan, Max F., and Donald L. M. Blackmer. *The Emerging Nations.* Boston: Little, Brown & Company, 1961. Useful general survey of political problems and institutions in the developing nations.

*Plato. *The Republic and The Laws.* Many editions have been published. These and Aristotle's works were the first systematic studies of the ideal and the actual in politics and government, and they continue to hold more than historical interest for students.

*Pye, Lucian W. *Aspects of Political Development.* Boston: Little, Brown & Company, 1966. Succinct statement of the developmental approach to study of non-Western nations.

Truman, David B. *The Governmental Process,* 2d ed. New York: Alfred A. Knopf, 1971. An updating of Bentley's thesis, with particular attention to the operations of American pressure groups.

*Von der Mehden, Fred R. *Politics of the Developing Nations.* Englewood Cliffs, N.J.: Prentice-Hall, Inc., 1964. Short but useful comparative study of politics and government in developing nations.

Waldman, Sidney R. *Foundations of Political Action: An Exchange Theory of Politics.* Boston: Little, Brown & Company, 1972. A general conceptual framework alternative to Easton's type of systems theory.

*Wallas, Graham. *Human Nature in Politics.* Boston: Houghton Mifflin Company, 1908. Pioneer application of modern psychology to analysis of politics.

Weber, Max. *The Theory of Social and Economic Organization,* trans. by A. M. Henderson and Talcott Parsons. New York: Oxford University Press, 1947. Useful collection of much of the work on society and politics by one of the most influential modern social thinkers.

## POLITICAL NOVELS

One of the best ways to acquire a "feel" for politics is by vicarious participation, reading novels focused on political conflict. Here is a short list of novels dealing with politics in various settings.

*Burdick, Eugene L., *The Ninth Wave.* Boston: Houghton Mifflin Company, 1956.

Camus, Albert. *The Plague,* trans. by Stuart Gilbert. New York: Alfred A. Knopf, 1948.

*Dostoyevsky, Fyodor. *The Possessed,* trans. by Constance Garnett. New York: Modern Library, Inc., 1936.

Fienburgh, Wilfred. *No Love for Johnnie.* London: Hutchinson & Co. (Publishers), Ltd., 1959.

Forster, E. M. *A Passage to India.* New York: Modern Library, Inc., 1940.

*Koestler, Arthur, *Darkness at Noon,* trans. by Daphne Hardy. New York: Modern Library, Inc., 1941.

*O'Connor, Edwin. *The Last Hurrah.* Boston: Little, Brown & Company, 1955.

*Orwell, George. *1984.* New York: New American Library of World Literature, Inc., 1951.

*Paton, Alan. *Cry, the Beloved Country.* New York: Charles Scribner's Sons, 1948.

*Silone, Ignazio. *Bread and Wine,* trans. by Gwenda David and Eric Mosbacher. New York: Harper & Row, Publishers, 1937.

*Snow, C. P. *The Masters.* New York: Crowell-Collier and Macmillan, Inc., 1951.

Spring, Howard. *Fame Is the Spur.* New York: The Viking Press, Inc., 1949.

*Trollope, Anthony. *Barchester Towers.* New York: Modern Library, Inc., 1950.

_____. *Phineas Finn.* New York: Oxford University Press, 1949.

_____. *The Prime Minister.* New York: Oxford University Press, 1951.

*Warren, Robert Penn. *All the King's Men.* New York: Bantam Books, 1950.

## POLITICAL CULTURE

*Almond, Gabriel A., and Sidney Verba. *The Civic Culture.* Boston: Little, Brown & Company, 1965. Comparative sample survey of political attitudes in the United States, Great Britain, West Germany, Italy, and Mexico.

Devine, Donald J. *The Political Culture of the United States.* Boston: Little, Brown & Company, 1972. Summary based mainly on survey data.

DiPalma, Giuseppe. *Apathy and Participation: Mass Politics in Western Societies.* New York: The Free Press, 1970. Comparative study of major aspects of political cultures in Western democracies.

Eckstein, Harry. *A Theory of Stable Democracy.* Princeton, N.J.: Center of International Studies, 1961. General theory of the impact of political culture on political stability, based on data from Norway.

*Finifter, Ada W. (ed.). *Alienation and the Social System.* New York: John Wiley & Sons, Inc., 1972. Collection of essays on aspects of one important dimension of political culture.

McClelland, David C. *The Achieving Society.* Princeton, N.J.: D. Van Nostrand Company, Inc., 1961. A social psychologist's analysis of Western societies in terms of attitudes toward work derived from the Protestant Ethic.

*Milbrath, Lester W. *Political Participation.* Skokie, Ill.: Rand McNally & Company, 1965. Summary of leading findings about causes and levels of political activity.

Pye, Lucian W. *Politics, Personality, and Nation-Building.* New Haven, Conn.: Yale University Press, 1962. Theory of role of "identity crises" in political development.

Pye, Lucian, and Sidney Verba (eds.). *Political Culture and Political Development.* Princeton, N.J.: Princeton University Press, 1965. Fullest statement of the concept of political culture and examination of its role in ten nations.

Rose, Richard. *People in Politics: Observations across the Atlantic.* New York: Basic Books, Inc., 1970. Comparative analysis of political cultures of the United States and Great Britain.

Scott, James C. *Comparative Political Corruption.* Englewood Cliffs, N.J.: Prentice-Hall, Inc., 1971. Study of role of corruption in political development in the United States and some developing nations.

Verba, Sidney, and Norman H. Nie. *Participation in America.* New York: Harper & Row, Publishers, 1972. Prize-winning analysis of ways in which Americans participate in political life.

*Wylie, Laurence. *Village in the Vaucluse.* New York: Harper Colophon Books, 1964. Classic study of political culture and politics in a small French village.

## POLITICAL SOCIALIZATION

Coleman, James S. *The Adolescent Society.* New York: The Free Press, 1961. Study of developing political attitudes in teen-agers.

*Dawson, Richard E., and Kenneth Prewitt. *Political Socialization.* Boston: Little, Brown & Company, 1969. General survey of socialization literature and theories.

Easton, David, and Jack Dennis. *Children in the Political System.* New York: McGraw-Hill, Inc., 1969. Report of a major survey of the development of children's political attitudes in the United States.

Golembiewski, Robert T. *The Small Group.* Chicago: University of Chicago Press, 1963. Study of the impact of primary-group memberships on attitudes.

*Greenstein, Fred I. *Children and Politics.* New Haven, Conn.: Yale University Press, 1965. Describes development of children's political attitudes in New Haven.

———. *Personality and Politics.* Chicago: Markham Publishing Company, 1969. A critical review of the literature explaining politics in terms of individual personality factors.

*Hess, Robert, and Judith Torney. *The Development of Political Attitudes in Children.* Chicago: Aldine Publishing Company, 1967. One of the leading socialization studies.

Hyman, Herbert H. *Political Socialization.* New York: The Free Press, 1959. One of the earliest surveys of research and theory in the field of socialization.

*Verba, Sidney. *Small Groups and Political Behavior.* Princeton, N.J.: Princeton University Press, 1961. Examines political influence of primary-group membership.

Weissberg, Robert. *Political Learning, Political Choice, and Political Leadership.* Englewood Cliffs, N.J.: Prentice-Hall, Inc., 1974. Relates political socialization to U.S. political processes.

## PART III   POLITICAL INPUTS

## NATURE AND DETERMINANTS OF PUBLIC OPINION

Centers, Richard. *The Psychology of Social Classes.* Princeton, N.J.: Princeton University Press, 1949. A social psychologist's analysis of the influence of class on political attitudes.

Davies, James C. *Human Nature in Politics.* New York: John Wiley & Sons, Inc., 1963. Focuses on individual psychological structure as it bears on political behavior.

Festinger, Leon. *A Theory of Cognitive Dissonance.* New York: Harper & Row, Publishers, 1957. Leading exposition of the theory that people's reality perceptions are affected by what they want to perceive.

Hennessy, Bernard C. *Public Opinion.* Belmont, Calif.: Wadsworth Publishing Company, Inc., 1965. A useful introduction to the subject, incorporating much recent research.

Homans, George C. *The Human Group.* New York: Harcourt Brace Jovanovich, Inc., 1950. Summary of conclusions reached in various studies of primary-group leadership and opinion formation.

Hyman, Herbert H. *Political Socialization.* New York: The Free Press, 1959. Summary of conclusions reached in various studies of how people acquire their political attitudes from childhood on.

Inkeles, Alex. *Public Opinion in Soviet Russia.* Cambridge, Mass.: Harvard University Press, 1950. Illuminating description of meaning and manipulation of public opinion in the USSR.

Key, V. O., Jr. *Public Opinion and American Democracy.* New York: Alfred A. Knopf, 1961. A distinguished political scientist's analysis of public opinion.

*Lane, Robert E. *Political Ideology.* New York: The Free Press, 1962. In-depth analysis of the political attitudes of a few selected adult respondents.

————. *Political Thinking and Consciousness.* Chicago: Markham Publishing Company, 1969. Comparable analysis of the political attitudes of a few selected college students.

*Lane, Robert E. and David O. Sears. *Public Opinion.* Englewood Cliffs, N.J.: Prentice-Hall, Inc., 1964. Useful short introduction to the subject.


## COMMUNICATIONS AND POLITICS

*Cohen, Bernard C. *The Press and Foreign Policy.* Princeton, N.J.: Princeton University Press, 1963. Analysis of the role of the press in shaping opinions affecting foreign policy.

*Deutsch, Karl W. *The Nerves of Government: Models of Political Communication and Control.* New York: The Free Press, 1963. Stimulating general theory about government as a series of interconnected communications processes.

Dexter, Lewis Anthony, and David Manning White. *People, Society and Mass Communications.* New York: The Free Press, 1964. Good collection of essays on the role of communications.

*Fagen, Richard R. *Politics and Communication.* Boston: Little, Brown & Company, 1966. Careful study of the role of communications, particularly in political development.

Hollander, Gayle Durham. *Soviet Political Indoctrination.* New York: Frederick A. Praeger, Inc., 1972. Analysis of "agitprop" operations since Stalin's death.

*Katz, Elihu, and Paul F. Lazarsfeld. *Personal Influence.* New York: The Free Press, 1955. Leading analysis of the "opinion leader."

Klapper, Joseph T. *The Effects of Mass Communications.* New York: The Free Press, 1960. Leading study of the impact of mass media on opinion formation.

Mazrui, Ali A. *Cultural Engineering and Nation-Building in East Africa.* Evanston, Ill.: Northwestern University Press, 1972. Distinguished African political scientist's study of role of communications in integrating some developing nations.

*McGinniss, Joe. *The Selling of the President, 1968.* New York: Trident Press, 1969. A reporter's account of advertising agencies' handling of the Nixon campaign in 1968.

Peterson, Theodore, Jay W. Jensen, and William L. Rivers. *The Mass Media and Modern Society.* New York: Holt, Rinehart and Winston, Inc., 1965. Useful account of the organization of mass media in the modern world.

*Pye, Lucian W. (ed.). *Communications and Political Development.* Princeton, N.J.: Princeton University Press, 1963. Comprehensive statement of the role of communications in developing nations, with several studies of specific nations.

Schramm, Wilbur (ed.). *The Process and Effects of Mass Communications.* Urbana, Ill.: University of Illinois Press, 1954. Selected readings.

Siepmann, Charles A. *Radio, Television, and Society.* New York: Oxford University Press, 1950. Special emphasis on the role of broadcasting in opinion formation.

Thomson, Charles A. H. *Television and Presidential Politics.* Washington, D.C.: The Brookings Institution, 1956. Evaluation of impact on political campaigns.

## PUBLIC OPINION POLLS

*Backstrom, Charles H., and Gerald D. Hursh. *Survey Research.* Evanston, Ill.: Northwestern University Press, 1963. Useful elementary how-to-do-it manual.

Bogart, Leo. *Silent Politics.* New York: John Wiley & Sons, Inc., 1972. Description of role of opinion polls, public and private, in American politics.

Gallup, George. *A Guide to Public Opinion Polls.* 2d ed. Princeton, N.J.: Princeton University Press, 1948. Description and defense of polls by a leading commercial practitioner.

Remmers, H. H. *Introduction to Opinion and Attitude Measurement.* New York: Harper & Row, Publishers, 1954. Detailed description of sample-survey problems and techniques.

Robinson, Claude E. *Straw Votes: A Study in Political Prediction.* New York: Columbia University Press, 1932. Description of the sample surveys' predecessors.

Rogers, Lindsay. *The Pollsters.* New York: Alfred A. Knopf, 1949. Attack on the polls' validity and utility.

Roll, Charles W., Jr., and Bert H. Cantril. *Polls: Their Use and Misuse in Politics.* New York: Basic Books, Inc., 1973. Covers same ground as Bogart.

*Stephan, Frederick F., and Philip J. McCarthy. *Sampling Opinions: An Analysis of Survey Procedure.* New York: John Wiley & Sons, Inc., 1958. Detailed description of sample-survey problems and techniques.

## SUFFRAGE

Abraham, Henry J. *Compulsory Voting.* Washington, D.C.: Public Affairs Press, 1955. Description and evaluation of voting.

Gosnell, Harold F. *Democracy, the Threshold of Freedom.* New York: The Ronald Press Company, 1948. Analyzes theories of the right to vote.

Porter, Kirk H. *A History of Suffrage in the United States.* Chicago: University of Chicago Press, 1918. Standard history of events leading up to the Nineteenth Amendment.

* *Report of the President's Commission on Registration and Voting Participation.* Washington, D.C.: U.S. Government Printing Office, 1963. Summary of registration and voting procedures in the United States and recommendations for simplifying voting.

## NOMINATIONS AND CANDIDATE SELECTION

Dallinger, Frederick W. *Nominations for Elective Office in the United States.* New York: David McKay Company, Inc., 1897. Standard history of methods used before the advent of the direct primary.

*David, Paul T., Ralph M. Goldman, and Richard C. Bain. *The Politics of National Party Conventions.* Washington, D.C.: The Brookings Institution, 1960. Comprehensive description and analysis of nominations of presidential candidates. An abridged paperback edition is also available.

*Davis, James W. *Presidential Primaries: Road to the White House.* New York: Thomas Y. Crowell Company, 1967. The most complete account of presidential primary elections.

Harris, Joseph P. *A Model Direct Primary System.* New York: National Municipal League, 1951. Defense of the direct-primary system and suggestions for improving it.

Merriam, Charles E., and Louise Overacker. *Primary Elections.* Rev. ed. Chicago: University of Chicago Press, 1928. Standard history and description of American direct-primary system.

Meyer, Ernst C. *Nominating Systems.* Madison, Wis.: The author, 1902. Historical survey covering various nations.

Parris, Judith H. *The Convention Problem.* Washington, D.C.: The Brookings Institution, 1972. Analysis of issues in the reform of the national conventions.

Prewitt, Kenneth. *The Recruitment of Political Leaders.* Indianapolis, Ind.: The Bobbs Merrill Company, Inc., 1970. Theoretically sophisticated study of recruitment patterns among city councils in the San Francisco Bay area.

Ranney, Austin. *Pathways to Parliament.* Madison, Wis.: University of Wisconsin Press, 1965. Detailed study of selection of British parliamentary candidates since 1945.

Seligman, Lester G. *Leadership in a New Nation.* New York: Atherton Press, 1964. Contains the best account of candidate selection in Israel.

*White, Theodore H. *The Making of the President, 1960.* New York: Atheneum Publishers, 1961. Presents an outstanding account of John F. Kennedy's successful drive for the Democratic nomination.

## ELECTIONS

*Adamany, David W. *Campaign Finance in America.* North Scituate, Mass.: Duxbury Press, 1972. Analysis of campaign finance regulation with proposal for public support of campaigns.

*Alexander, Herbert. *Political Financing.* Minneapolis, Minn.: Burgess Publishing Company, 1973. Succinct review of political finance in America.

Butler, David E. *Elections Abroad.* London: New York: St. Martin's Press, Inc., 1959. Detailed studies of elections in France, Ireland, Poland, and South Africa, 1957–1958.

———. *The Electoral System in Britain since 1918.* 2d ed. Oxford, Eng.: Clarendon Press, 1963. Useful analysis of the development of legal machinery and its effects on party fortunes.

Butler, David E., and Anthony King. *The British General Election of 1966.* New York: St. Martin's Press, Inc., 1967. One of the "Nuffield Studies" of successive general elections.

———. *The British General Election of 1964.* New York: St. Martin's Press, Inc., 1965. One of the "Nuffield Studies" of successive general elections.

Butler, David E., and Michael Pinto-Duschinsky. *The British General Election of 1970.*

New York: St. Martin's Press, Inc., 1971. One of the "Nuffield Studies" of successive general elections.

Campbell, Peter. *French Electoral Systems and Elections, 1789–1957.* New York: Frederick A. Praeger, Inc., 1958. Useful historical analysis of changing French systems and their effects on distribution of power.

Harris, Joseph P. *Election Administration in the United States.* Washington, D.C.: The Brookings Institution, 1934. Outdated in several respects but still the most comprehensive survey.

Lakeman, Enid. *How Democracies Vote.* London: Faber & Faber, Ltd. 1970. Survey of various electoral systems by a strong advocate of proportional representation.

Leonard, Richard L. *Elections in Britain.* Princeton, N.J.: D. Van Nostrand Company, Inc., 1968. Good popular outline of British election procedures.

Mackenzie, W. J. M. *Free Elections.* New York: Holt, Rinehart and Winston, Inc., 1958. A short and well-written introduction to institutions and problems connected with elections in democratic nations.

*Polsby, Nelson W., and Aaron B. Wildavsky. *Presidential Elections.* 3d ed. New York: Charles Scribner's Sons, 1971. Analysis of Campaign strategies and strategic situations.

*Rae, Douglas W. *The Political Consequences of Electoral Laws.* Rev. ed. New Haven, Conn.: Yale University Press, 1971. A lucid and well-documented analysis of how various electoral systems affect the number and strength of parties.

*Sayre, Wallace S., and Judith H. Parris. *Voting for President.* Washington, D.C.: The Brookings Institution, 1970. Analysis of various proposals for replacing the electoral college.

Schofield, A. N. *Parliamentary Elections.* 2d ed. London: Shaw & Sons, Ltd. 1955. Authoritative detailed exposition of British election laws.

Smith. T. E. *Elections in Developing Countries.* New York: St. Martin's Press, Inc., 1960. General survey of procedures and problems of elections in development nations.

Van den Bergh, George. *Unity in Diversity: A Systematic Critical Analysis of All Electoral Systems.* London: B. T. Batsford, 1956. Takes a different point of view from that of Lakeman and Lambert.

Wiatr, Jerzy J. "Elections and Voting Behavior in Poland," in Austin Ranney (ed.), *Essays on the Behavioral Study of Politics.* Urbana, Ill.: University of Illinois Press, 1962, pp. 235–251. Ingenious argument about the role of elections as opinion indicators in a communist system.

## CAMPAIGN STRATEGY, TACTICS, AND IMPACTS

*Agranoff, Robert (ed.). *The New Style in Election Campaigns.* Boston: Holbrook Press, Inc., 1972. Collection of essays on the professionalization of campaigning in America.

Curtis, Gerald L. *Election Campaigning Japanese Style.* New York: Columbia University Press, 1971. Detailed description of campaign strategy and tactics used by a candidate for the Japanese parliament.

Kingdon, John W. *Candidates for Office: Beliefs and Strategies.* New York: Random House, Inc., 1968. Analysis of the campaign strategies of candidates for the legislature of Wisconsin.

Lamb, Karl A., and Paul A. Smith. *Campaign Decision-Making: The Presidential Election of 1964.* Belmont, Calif.: Wadsworth Publishing Company, Inc., 1968. Analysis of the 1964 national campaigns by political scientists who worked in the parties' headquarters during the campaign.

Leuthold, David A. *Electioneering in a Democracy.* New York: John Wiley & Sons, Inc., 1968. Campaign strategy and tactics of candidates for United States House of Representatives.

*Nimmo, Dan. *The Political Persuaders.* Englewood Cliffs, N.J.: Prentice-Hall, Inc., 1970. Description of nature and consequences of "campaign consultants" operations in modern campaigns.

Rose, Richard. *Influencing Voters: A Study of Campaign Rationality.* New York: St. Martin's Press, Inc., 1967. A study of British national campaigning and an attempt to develop a broad general theory.


## VOTING BEHAVIOR

Alford, Robert R. *Party and Society.* Skokie, Ill.: Rand McNally & Company, 1963. Comparative survey of voting patterns in the United States, Great Britain, Canada, and Australia, based on polling data.

Allardt, Erik, and Yrjö Littunen (eds.). *Cleavages, Ideologies, and Party Systems.* Turku: The Westermarck Society, Vol. 10, 1964. Essays on voting behavior in the United States, Scandinavia, and Continental Europe.

Benney, Mark, A. P. Gray, and R. H. Pear. *How People Vote.* London: Routledge & Kegan Paul Ltd., 1956. Sample survey of English voters in Greenwich constituency.

Berelson, Bernard, Paul F. Lazarsfeld, and William N. McPhee. *Voting.* Chicago: University of Chicago Press, 1954. Sample survey of the 1948 presidential election in Elmira, New York, and summary of findings from other studies of determinants of voting behavior.

*Blondel, Jean. *Voters, Parties, and Leaders.* Baltimore, Md.: Penguin Books, Inc., 1963. Perceptive survey of British voting patterns.

*Butler, David, and Donald Stokes. *Political Change in Britain.* New York: St. Martin's Press, Inc., 1969. By far the most authoritative study of British voting behavior.

*Campbell, Angus, Philip E. Converse, Warren E. Miller, and Donald E. Stokes. *The American Voter.* New York: John Wiley & Sons, Inc., 1960. Generally regarded as the leading work on American voting behavior, based on sample surveys for the 1952 and 1956 presidential elections. Abridged paperback edition also available.

_____. *Elections and the Political Order.* New York: John Wiley & Sons, Inc., 1966. Collection of essays, many with even more direct application to politics than the same authors' classic *The American Voter* has.

*DeVries, Walter and V. Lance Tarrance. *The Ticket-Splitter: A New Force in American Politics.* Grand Rapids, Mich.: William B. Eerdmans Publishing Company, 1972. Analysis of increase and impact of split-ticket voting in the United States.

Key, V. O., Jr. *American State Politics: An Introduction.* New York: Alfred A. Knopf, 1956. Analysis of election patterns at the state level, using aggregate data.

Kitzinger, Uwe W. *German Electoral Politics: A Study of the 1957 Campaign.* New York: Oxford University Press, 1960. Study of recent German voting patterns.

*Lane, Robert E. *Political Life.* New York: The Free Press, 1959. General survey of factors influencing high and low participation in politics.

*Levy, Mark R., and Michael S. Kramer. *The Ethnic Factor: How America's Minorities Decide Elections.* New York: Simon and Schuster, Inc., 1973. Stimulating, though overstated, case for the crucial role of the "ethnics" in American elections.

*Lipset, Seymour Martin. *Political Man.* New York: Doubleday & Company, Inc., 1960. Broad comparative survey of preferences and participation patterns in many countries.

*Matthews, Donald R., and James W. Prothro. *Negroes and the New Southern Politics.* New York: Harcourt Brace Jovanovich, Inc., 1966. Massive empirical study of the rise of voting participation among southern blacks.

Merriam, Charles E., and Harold F. Gosnell. *Non-Voting.* Chicago: University of Chicago Press, 1924. Pioneer study of one aspect of voting behavior.

Rokkan, Stein. *Citizens, Elections, Parties.* New York: David McKay Company, Inc., 1970. Studies by a distinguished scholar of comparative politics, analyzing the social bases of party divisions in Western nations.

Rose, Richard (ed.). *Electoral Behavior.* New York: The Free Press, 1973. Essays on elections and voting behavior in twelve Western nations.

Thompson, Dennis F. *The Democratic Citizen: Social Science and Democratic Theory in the Twentieth Century.* New York: Cambridge University Press, 1970. Reconsideration of democratic theory in the light of empirical studies showing low participation in Great Britain and the United States.

Tingsten, Herbert. *Political Behavior.* London: P. S. King & Staples, Ltd., 1937. Pioneer aggregate-data study of voting patterns in various nations by a Swedish political scientist.

## DEMOCRATIC POLITICAL PARTIES

Broder, David S. *The Party's Over.* New York: Harper & Row, Publishers, 1971. Distinguished journalist's plea for more disciplined and programmatic American parties.

*Burns, James MacGregor. *The Deadlock of Democracy.* Englewood Cliffs, N.J.: Prentice-Hall, Inc., 1963. Plea for greater centralization and discipline in American parties.

Committee on Political Parties of the American Political Science Association. *Toward a More Responsible Two-Party System.* New York: Holt, Rinehart and Winston, Inc., 1950. Criticisms of American parties, based on a responsible-parties model, and proposal for reform.

*Duverger, Maurice. *Political Parties.* New York: John Wiley & Sons, Inc., 1954. Influential work by a French political scientist, outlining a general theory of political parties applying to many nations.

Eldersveld, Samuel J. *Political Parties: A Behavioral Analysis.* Skokie, Ill.: Rand McNally & Company, 1964. Development of a general empirical theory about local party organization, based on intensive study of the Detroit area.

*Epstein, Leon D. *Political Parties in Western Democracies.* New York: Frederick A. Praeger, Inc., 1967. Covers much the same ground as Duverger but in a more empirical and pragmatic manner—a useful corrective.

Guttsman, W. L. *The British Political Elite.* London: MacGibbon & Kee, 1963. Sociological analysis of British party leadership.

Harrison, Martin. *Trade Unions and the Labour Party since 1945.* London: George Allen & Unwin Ltd., 1960. Authoritative account of the special role of unions in the Labour party's structure and policies.

Herring, Pendleton. *The Politics of Democracy.* New York: Holt, Rinehart and Winston, Inc., 1940. Classic defense of the decentralized American party system.

Key, V. O., Jr. *Politics, Parties, and Pressure Groups.* 5th ed. New York: Thomas Y. Crowell Company, 1964. The most comprehensive and influential general description of the American party system.

Kochanek, Stanley A. *The Congress Party of India.* Princeton, N.J.: Princeton University Press, 1968. Detailed description of a major democratic party in an Asian setting.

Leiserson, Avery. *Parties and Politics: An Institutional and Behavioral Approach.* New York: Alfred A. Knopf, 1958. General survey of political parties with special attention to the American system.

Lipset, Seymour M., and Stein Rokkan (eds.). *Party Systems and Voter Alignments: Cross-National Perspectives.* New York: The Free Press, 1967. Collection of essays on interaction between party organizations and voting alignments in the electorate.

*McDonald, Neil A. *The Study of Political Parties.* New York: Random House, Inc., 1955. Critical survey of scholarly literature on parties, mostly American.

*McKenzie, Robert T. *British Political Parties.* 2d ed. London: Mercury Books, 1963. Principal study of the British party system, with special attention to distribution of power within each.

*Michels, Robert. *Political Parties.* New York: The Free Press, 1949. First published in 1915. Development of the influential "iron law of oligarchy," based on study of European socialist parties in the early twentieth century.

Neumann, Sigmund (ed.). *Modern Political Parties.* Chicago: University of Chicago Press, 1956. Useful descriptions of various party systems throughout the world.

*Ostrogorski, M. I. *Democracy and the Organization of Political Parties.* 2 vols. New York: Crowell-Collier and Macmillan, Inc., 1902. Classic study of the history and organization of British and American Parties up to 1900 and an attack on "permanent parties." Also available in abridged paperback edition.

*Ranney, Austin. *The Doctrine of Responsible Party Government.* Urbana, Ill.: University of Illinois Press, 1954. Description of the origins of the responsible-parties model and criticism of present versions.

———. *Curing the Mischiefs of Faction: Party Reform in America.* Berkeley, Calif.: University of California Press, 1974. Analysis of theory, practice, and consequences of party reform from the 1820s to the present.

Ranney, Austin, and Willmoore Kendall. *Democracy and the American Party System.* New York: Harcourt Brace Jovanovich, Inc., 1956. General survey of American parties, with special attention to their viability as agencies of democratic government.

Rose, Richard, and Arnold J. Heidenheimer (eds.) "Comparative Party Finance," *Journal of Politics.* 25 (August 1963). Series of essays constituting the most comprehensive survey of the subject yet done.

Schattschneider, E. E. *Party Government.* New York: Holt, Rinehart and Winston, Inc., 1942. Influential exposition of the responsible-parties model and criticism of American parties.

———. *The Semisovereign People.* New York: Holt, Rinehart and Winston, Inc., 1960. A further explication of the responsible-parties point of view.

*Sorauf, Frank J. *Political Parties in the American System.* Boston: Little, Brown & Company, 1964. A brief but provocative analysis of American parties with reference to democratic theory.

*Valen, Henry, and Daniel Katz. *Political Parties in Norway.* London: Tavistock Publications, 1964. A general survey of the Norwegian system with an exploration in depth of voters, party leaders, and party organization in the Stavanger area.

*Weiner, Myron. *Party Politics in India.* Princeton, N.J.: Princeton University Press, 1957. Skillful account of India's fascinating and significant party system.

Williams, Philip. *Politics in Post-War France.* 2d ed. New York: David McKay Company, Inc., 1958. The best account of parties in the Fourth Republic.

## SEMI- AND NONDEMOCRATIC PARTIES

Armstrong, John A. *The Politics of Totalitarianism.* New York: Random House, Inc., 1961. History and contemporary operation of the Communist party of the Soviet Union.

Carter, Gwendolen M. (ed.). *African One-Party States.* Ithaca, N.Y.: Cornell University Press, 1962. Essays on one-party systems in some of Africa's new nations.

Einaudi, Mario, Jean-Marie Domenach, and Aldo Garosci. *Communism in Western Europe.* Ithaca, N.Y.: Cornell University Press, 1951. Description of Communist parties in European democracies.

Gehlen, Michael P. *The Communist Party of the Soviet Union.* Bloomington, Ind.: Indiana University Press, 1969. Detailed analysis of the structure, activities, and role of the CPSU.

*Hodgkin, Thomas. *African Political Parties.* Baltimore, Md.: Penguin Books, Inc., 1961. General analysis of African party regimes.

Huntington, Samuel P., and Clement H. Moore (eds.). *Authoritarian Politics in Modern Society.* New York: Basic Books, Inc., 1970. Essays on the nature and problems of leading contemporary one-party regimes.

Kautsky, John H. *Moscow and the Communist Party of India.* New York: John Wiley & Sons, Inc., 1956. Emphasis on methods of direction from Moscow.

*LaPalombara, Joseph, and Myron Weiner (eds.). *Political Parties and Political Development.* Princeton, N.J.: Princeton University Press, 1966. Comprehensive survey of the role of parties in developing nations.

*Scott, Robert E. *Mexican Government in Transition.* Urbana, Ill.: University of Illinois Press, 1959. Illuminating description of Mexico's one-party dominant system.

*Zolberg, Aristide R. *Creating Political Order: The One-Party States of West Africa.* Skokie, Ill.: Rand McNally & Company, 1966. Sophisticated analysis of monoparty states with general theoretical applications.

## PRESSURE GROUPS IN GENERAL

Bondurant, Joan V. *Conquest of Violence: The Gandhian Philosophy of Conflict.* Princeton, N.J.: Princeton University Press, 1958. Description of the development of the philosophy and tactics of nonviolent resistance that have become increasingly important in pressure-group politics.

Dexter, Lewis Anthony. *How Organizations are Represented in Washington.* Indianapolis, Ind.: The Bobbs Merrill Company, Inc., 1969. Perceptive account of nature and consequences of lobbying in America.

*Ehrmann, Henry W. (ed.). *Interest Groups on Four Continents.* Pittsburgh, Pa.: University of Pittsburgh Press, 1958. Essays on pressure-group objectives and tactics in a number of nations.

Finer, Samuel E. *Anonymous Empire.* London: Pall Mall Press, 1958. Pressure-group objectives and tactics in Britain.

*Graham, Hugh Davis, and Ted Robert Gurr. *Violence in America: Historical and Comparative Perspectives.* New York: Bantam Books, 1969. Study of violence in the United States and other Western nations.

Hibbs, Douglas A., Jr. *Mass Political Violence.* New York: John Wiley & Sons, Inc., 1973. Comparative study of internal violence in over 100 nations.

Latham, Earl. *The Group Basis of Politics.* Ithaca, N.Y.: Cornell University Press, 1952. General discussion of pressure politics illustrated by a case study.

Meynaud, Jean. *Les Groupes de Pression en France*. Paris: Librairie Armond Colin, 1959. Objectives and tactics of pressure groups in France.

Milbrath, Lester W. *The Washington Lobbyists*. Skokie, Ill.: Rand McNally & Company, 1963. Detailed study of pressure tactics.

*Nieburg, H. L. *Political Violence: The Behavioral Process*. New York: St. Martin's Press, Inc., 1969. Study of causes and consequences of political violence in the United States.

Potter, Allen. *Organized Groups in British National Politics*. London: Faber & Faber, Ltd., 1961. Detailed study of British pressure tactics.

Skilling, H. Gordon, and Franklin Griffiths (eds.). *Interest Groups in Soviet Politics*. Princeton, N.J.: Princeton University Press, 1971. Essays and case studies on contending groups in the politics of the USSR.

Wilson, James Q. *Political Organizations*. New York: Basic Books, Inc., 1974. Analysis of pressure politics in terms of organization theory.

*Wooton, Graham. *Interest Groups*. Englewood Cliffs, N.J.: Prentice-Hall, Inc., 1970. Schematic theoretical analysis of the nature and role of interest groups in modern political systems.

*Zeigler, L. Harmon, and G. Wayne Peake. *Interest Groups in American Society*. 2d ed. Englewood Cliffs, N.J.: Prentice-Hall, Inc., 1972. Emphasizes general theory.

## PARTICULAR PRESSURE AND PROTEST GROUPS

Baker, Roscoe. *The American Legion and American Foreign Policy*. New York: Bookman Associates, 1954.

*Bauer, Raymond A., Ithiel de Sola Pool, and Lewis Anthony Dexter. *American Business and Public Policy: The Politics of Foreign Trade*. New York: Atherton Press, 1963.

Bell, Daniel (ed.). *The Radical Right*. New York: Doubleday & Company, Inc., 1963.

Bunzel, John H. *The American Small Businessman*. New York: Alfred A. Knopf, 1962.

Eckstein, Harry. *Pressure Group Politics: The Case of the British Medical Association*. London: George Allen & Unwin Ltd., 1960.

Ehrmann, Henry W. *Organized Business in France*. Princeton, N.J.: Princeton University Press, 1957.

Garfinkel, Herbert. *When Negroes March*. New York: The Free Press, 1959.

Gerberding, William P., and Duane E. Smith (eds). *The Radical Left: Abuse of Discontent*. Boston: Houghton Mifflin Company, 1970. Essays on the costs and limits of protest politics.

*Greenstone, J. David. *Labor in American Politics*. New York: Alfred A. Knopf, 1969.

Grossman, Joel B. *Lawyers and Judges: The American Bar Association and the Politics of Judicial Selection*. New York: John Wiley & Sons, Inc., 1965.

Hyman, Sidney. *Youth in Politics*. New York: Basic Books, Inc., 1972. Analysis of current and potential impact of young people in American politics.

*Jacobs, Paul, and Saul Landau. *The New Radicals*. New York: Vintage Books, 1966. Sympathetic account of student and militant black-protest groups.

Keech, William R. *The Impact of Negro Voting: The Role of the Vote in the Quest for Equality*. Skokie, Ill.: Rand McNally & Company, 1968. Case study of blacks' use of political organization in southern communities.

LaPalombara, Joseph. *Interest Groups in Italian Politics*. Princeton, N.J.: Princeton University Press, 1964. Illuminating study of Italian pressure groups in action.

Odegard, Peter H. *Pressure Politics: The Story of the Anti-Saloon League*. New York: Columbia University Press, 1928.

*Skolnick, Jerome H. *The Politics of Protest.* New York: Simon and Schuster, Inc., 1969. Study of tactics, successes, and failures of current American protest groups.

Wilson, H. H. *Pressure Group: The Campaign for Commercial Television in England.* New Brunswick, N.J.: Rutgers University Press, 1961.

*Wilson, James Q. *Negro Politics.* New York: The Free Press, 1960.

Zeigler, Harmon. *The Politics of Small Business.* Washington, D.C.: Public Affairs Press, 1961.

## PART IV  GOVERNMENTAL STRUCTURES

### THE NATURE OF CONSTITUTIONS

Bagehot, Walter. *The English Constitution.* New York: Oxford University Press, 1936. First published in 1867. Classic study of the "real" and "literary" constitutions of England.

Blaustein, Albert P., and Gisbert Flanz (eds.). *Constitutions of the Countries of the World.* 12 vols. Dobbs Ferry, N.Y.: Oceana Publications, 1971. Massive compilation of chronology, texts, and bibliographies of world's written Constitutions.

Chapman, Brian. *Police State.* New York: Frederick A. Praeger, Inc., 1970. Detailed description of totalitarianism as practiced in Hitler's Third Reich.

Jennings, Ivor. *The British Constitution.* 3d ed. New York: Cambridge University Press, 1950. Leading modern study of written and unwritten aspects of the British constitution.

Marshall, Geoffrey. *Constitutional Theory.* Oxford, Eng.: Clarendon Press, 1971. Philosophical analysis of nature, development, and role of constitutions in Great Britain and the United States.

Peaslee, Amos J. (ed.). *Constitutions of Nations.* 2d ed. 3 vols. The Hague: Martinus Nijhoff, 1956. Compilation of written Constitutions of modern nations, with tables summarizing incidence of various institutions.

Wheare, K. C. *Modern Constitutions.* New York: Oxford University Press, 1951. Useful brief discussion of the nature, role, and variations of the constitutions of modern nations.

### THE DOCTRINE OF CONSTITUTIONALISM

Friedrich, Carl J. *Constitutional Government and Democracy.* Rev. ed. Boston: Ginn & Company, 1950. Description of theory and practice of constitutionalism in modern Europe and the United States.

————. *Limited Government.* Englewood Cliffs, N.J.: Prentice-Hall, Inc., 1974. Concise analysis of doctrine of constitutionalism and role of constitutions.

*McIlwain, Charles H. *Constitutionalism, Ancient and Modern.* Ithaca, N.Y.: Cornell University Press, 1940. Standard history of meaning and development of constitutionalism.

Vose, Clement E. *Constitutional Change.* Lexington, Mass.: D. C. Heath and Company, 1972. Analysis of roles of formal amendments and court decisions in American constitutional change since 1900.

*Wheare, K. C. *Modern Constitutions.* New York: Oxford University Press, 1951. Broad survey of the main similarities and differences in modern constitutions.

Wormuth, Francis D. *The Origins of Modern Constitutionalism.* New York: Harper & Row, Publishers, 1949. History and meaning of constitutionalism.

Annotated Bibliography

# FORMS OF GOVERNMENT

*Arendt, Hannah. *The Origins of Totalitarianism.* New York: Harcourt Brace Jovanovich, Inc., 1954. Imaginative analysis of psychological and philosophical sources of totalitarian regimes.

*Bachrach, Peter. *The Theory of Democratic Elitism.* Boston: Little, Brown & Company, 1967. Attack on social scientists' acceptance of low political participation, and advocacy of participatory democracy.

*Brzezinski, Zbigniew, and Samuel P. Huntington. *Political Power: USA/USSR.* New York: The Viking Press, Inc., 1965. Stimulating discussion of how the American and Soviet systems work, with comparisons and contrasts noted at many points.

Cnudde, Charles F., and Deane E. Neubauer (eds.). *Empirical Democratic Theory.* Chicago: Markham Publishing Company, 1969. Collection of essays on democratic theory in the light of modern social science research.

*Friedrich, Carl J., and Zbigniew Brzezinski. *Totalitarian Dictatorship and Autocracy.* 2d ed. Cambridge, Mass.: Harvard University Press, 1965. Analysis of fascist and communist systems.

Gregor, A. James. *The Ideology of Fascism.* New York: The Free Press, 1969. Analysis of the rationale underlying Mussolini's version of totalitarianism.

Mayo, H. B. *Democracy and Marxism.* New York: Oxford University Press, 1955. Comparative analysis of democratic and Marxist political ideas.

*Mills, C. Wright. *The Power Elite.* New York: Oxford University Press, 1956. Offers the much-discussed thesis that a small military-industrial oligarchy rules the United States.

*Moore, Barrington, Jr. *Social Origins of Dictatorship and Democracy.* Boston: The Beacon Press, 1966. Broad historical analysis of social conditions producing different kinds of political systems.

# MODELS OF DEMOCRACY AND DICTATORSHIP

*Armstrong, John A. *Ideology, Politics, and Government in the Soviet Union.* 3d ed. New York: Frederick A. Praeger, Inc., 1974. Useful short analysis of essentials of the Soviet regime.

*Barghoorn, Frederick C. *Politics in the USSR.* 2d ed. Boston: Little, Brown & Company, 1972. Similar to Armstrong.

*Cook, Terrence E., and Patrick M. Morgan (eds.). *Participatory Democracy.* San Francisco: Canfield Press, 1971. Collection of essays on the theory of participatory democracy by writers of different persuasions.

Dahl, Robert A. *Pluralist Democracy in the United States.* Skokie, Ill.: Rand McNally & Company, 1967. General survey of American institutions, based on an approach contrary to the "power elite" thesis.

*_____. *Polyarchy.* New Haven, Conn.: Yale University Press, 1972. View of democracy as competition among different elites.

*_____. *A Preface to Democratic Theory.* Chicago: University of Chicago Press, 1956. Develops the "polyarchy' model of democracy and analyzes alternative models.

Dallin, Alexander and George W. Breslauer. *Political Terror in Communist Systems.* Stanford, Calif.: Stanford University Press, 1970. Comparative study of methods used by Communist parties to consolidate power in communist nations.

Fainsod, Merle. *How Russia is Ruled.* Rev. ed. Cambridge, Mass.: Harvard University Press, 1962. Comprehensive account of government and politics in the USSR.

Hattersley, A. N. *A Short History of Democracy.* New York: Cambridge University Press,

1930. Describes development of democratic ideas and institutions since the time of Periclean Athens.

*Hsiung, James C. *Ideology and Practice: Evolution of Chinese Communism.* New York: Frederick A. Praeger, Inc., 1970. Brief analysis of Maoist ideology and government practice in the PRC.

Kendall, Willmoore. *John Locke and the Doctrine of Majority Rule.* Urbana, Ill.: University of Illinois Press, 1941. Explanation of origins and content of "absolute majority rule" position.

*Lewis, John Wilson. *Leadership in Communist China.* Ithaca, N.Y.: Cornell University Press, 1963. A leading analysis of politics in the PRC.

Lindsay, A. D. *The Essentials of Democracy.* 2d ed. New York: Oxford University Press, 1942. Emphasizes the role of discussion and consensus.

*————. *The Modern Democratic State.* New York: Oxford University Press, 1947. Description of some of modern democracy's leading institutions and problems.

*Mayo, H. B. *Introduction to Democratic Theory.* New York: Oxford University Press, 1960. Takes a moderate position between limited and absolute majority-rule positions.

Pateman, Carole. *Participation and Democratic Theory.* New York: Cambridge University Press, 1970. Most thoughtful defense of participatory-democracy model.

Pennock, J. Roland. *Liberal Democracy: Its Merits and Prospects.* New York: Holt, Rinehart and Winston, Inc., 1950. Emphasizes civil rights and restraints on majority rule as essentials of democracy.

Ranney, Austin, and Willmoore Kendall. *Democracy and the American Party System.* New York: Harcourt Brace Jovanovich, Inc., 1956. Chapters 1–3 present the conception of democracy employed in this book.

*Sartori, Giovanni. *Democratic Theory.* New York: Frederick A. Praeger, Inc. 1965. Perhaps the most exhaustive discussion of the various meanings of "democracy."

*Schumpeter, Joseph. *Capitalism, Socialism, and Democracy.* 3d ed. New York: Harper Torchbooks, 1950. Influential analytical discussion of democracy as choosing between competing elites.

*Schurmann, Franz. *Ideology and Organization in Communist China.* Rev. ed. Berkeley, Calif.: University of California Press, 1968. A leading analysis of the PRC's political system.

*Thorson, Thomas Landon. *The Logic of Democracy.* New York: Holt, Rinehart and Winston, Inc., 1962. Stimulating analysis of problems in definition and implementation of democracy.

## REPRESENTATION

Burke, Edmund, "Address to the Electors of Bristol," in *The Works of Edmund Burke,* Vol. 1. New York: Harper & Brothers, 1855, pp. 219–222. Classic exposition of the "independence" theory of representative-constituent relations.

Clarke, Maude V. *Medieval Representation and Consent.* London: Longmans, Green & Co., Ltd., 1936. Description of predemocratic theories and institutions.

Cole, G. D. H. *Guild Socialism Re-stated.* Philadelphia: J. B. Lippincott Company, 1920. Leading exposition of the functional-representation position.

De Grazia, Alfred. *Public and Republic.* New York: Alfred A. Knopf, 1951. Summary and analysis of various theories of representation.

Dixon, Robert G., Jr. *Democratic Representation.* New York: Oxford University Press, 1968. Summary and analysis of theories of representation, with detailed examination of American reapportionment controversies.

Field, G. Lowell, *The Syndical and Corporative Institutions of Italian Fascism.* New York:

Columbia University Press, 1938. Description of the fascist version of functional representation.

Ford, Henry Jones. *Representative Government.* New York: Holt, Rinehart and Winston, Inc., 1924. Historical description of the development of democratic representation.

Hayward, J. E. S. *Private Interests and Public Policy: The Experience of the French Economic and Social Council.* New York: Barnes & Noble, Inc., 1966. Authoritative study of interest representation under the Fifth Republic.

Hogan, James. *Election and Representation.* Cork, Ire.: Cork University Press, 1945. Summary and analysis of various theories of representation.

Leiserson, Avery. *Administrative Regulation: A Study in the Representation of Interests.* Chicago: University of Chicago Press, 1942. Leading study of de facto functional representation in the United States.

*Mill, John Stuart. *Considerations on Representative Government* (1861). Many editions have been published. Classic statement of democratic theory of representation.

Nova, Fritz. *Functional Representation.* Dubuque, Ia.: William C. Brown Company, 1950. Latest exposition of the functional-representation view.

O'Sullivan, Donal. *The Irish Free State and Its Senate.* London: Faber & Faber, Ltd., 1940. Description of a democratic attempt to incorporate functional representation in a legislative body.

Pennock, J. Roland, and John W. Chapman (eds.). *Representation.* New York: Atherton Press, 1968. Good collection of essays on theories of representation.

Pitkin, Hanna Fenichel (ed.). *The Concept of Representation.* Berkeley, Calif.: University of California Press, 1966. The most comprehensive and illuminating analysis of the leading theories of representation.

————. *Representation.* New York: Atherton Press, 1969. Collection of essays on theories of representation, with a useful introductory paper by the editor.

Rousseau, Jean Jacques. *Considerations on the Government of Poland* (1778). Several editions have been published. Classic exposition of the "mandate" theory of representative-constituent relations.


## PROPORTIONAL REPRESENTATION

Hermens, Ferdinand A. *Democracy or Anarchy?* Notre Dame, Ind.: The Review of Politics, 1941. Leading attack on proportional representation.

Hoag, Clarence G., and George H. Hallett. *Proportional Representation.* New York: Crowell-Collier and Macmillan, Inc., 1926. For many years the standard exposition of the case for PR.

Ross, J. F. S. *Elections and Electors.* London: Eyre & Spottiswoode, Ltd., 1955. Attack on single-member plurality systems and advocacy of the single-transferable-vote system of PR.


## DIRECT LEGISLATION

Bonjour, Felix. *Real Democracy in Action.* Philadelphia: J. B. Lippincott Company, 1920. Description and praise of Swiss direct-legislation system.

Gosnell, Harold R., and Margaret J. Schmidt. "Popular Law-Making in the United States, 1924–1936," in *Proceedings of the New York State Constitutional Convention, 1938,* vol. 7. Summary of American experience with direct legislation.

Munro, William B. (ed.). *The Initiative, Referendum, and Recall.* New York: Appleton-Century-Crofts, 1912. Leading American exposition of direct legislation.

# PART V  GOVERNMENTAL AUTHORITIES AND PROCESSES

## THE LEGISLATIVE PROCESS

Adams, John Clarke, *The Quest for Democratic Law: The Role of Parliament in the Legislative Process.* New York: Thomas Y. Crowell Company, 1970. Comparative analysis of role of legislatures in policy-making processes of Western democracies.

Barber, James David. *The Lawmakers.* New Haven, Conn.: Yale University Press, 1965. Study of the role perceptions of freshman legislators in Connecticut.

Campion, Gilbert, *et al. Parliament: A Survey.* London: George Allen & Unwin Ltd., 1955. Detailed description of procedures.

*Clapp, Charles L. *The Congressman: His Work as He Sees It.* Washington, D.C.: The Brookings Institution, 1963. Perceptions of members of the United States House of Representatives.

*Clausen, Aage R. *How Congressmen Decide.* New York: St. Martin's Press, Inc., 1973. Careful study of congressional voting patterns based on roll-call analysis.

Davidson, Roger H. *The Role of the Congressman.* New York: Pegasus, 1969. Description of the "independent operator" role based on extensive interviews.

Debuyst, Frédéric. *La fonction parlementaire en Belgique: Mécanismes d'accès et images.* Brussels: Centre de Recherche et d'Information Socio-Politique, 1966. Detailed study of the political lives of Belgian deputies.

*Dexter, Lewis Anthony. *The Sociology and Politics of Congress.* Skokie, Ill.: Rand McNally & Company, 1969. Original and stimulating essays on aspects of congressional behavior.

Fenno, Richard F., Jr. *Congressmen in Committees.* Boston: Little, Brown & Company, 1973. Perceptive analysis of nature and role of congressional committees.

*_____. *The Power of the Purse.* Boston: Little, Brown & Company, 1966. A massive, sophisticated study of relations among appropriations committee members and between the committees and their respective legislative chambers.

Froman, Lewis A., Jr. *The Congressional Process: Strategies, Rules, and Procedures.* Boston: Little, Brown & Company, 1967. Study of formal rules and their impact on decision making.

Goodwin, George, Jr. *The Little Legislatures: Committees of Congress.* Amherst, Mass.: University of Massachusetts Press, 1970. General description and analysis.

Huitt, Ralph K., and Robert L. Peabody. *Congress: Two Decades of Analysis.* New York: Harper & Row, Publishers, 1969. Collection of essays by two leading students of Congress.

Inter-Parliamentary Union. *Parliaments.* New York: Frederick A. Praeger, Inc., 1961. Useful summary of formal procedures in most of the world's legislatures.

Keefe, William J., and Morris S. Ogul. *The American Legislative Process: Congress and the States.* 2d ed. Englewood Cliffs, N.J.: Prentice-Hall, Inc., 1968. Comprehensive survey of American legislative processes at both national and state levels.

King, Anthony, and Anne Sloman. *Westminster and Beyond.* London: Macmillan and Co., Ltd., 1973. Survey of the life of MPs based on extensive interviews.

Kornberg, Allan, and Lloyd D. Musolf (eds.). *Legislatures in Developmental Perspective.* Durham, N.C.: Duke University Press, 1970. Collection of essays analyzing structure and role of legislatures in eight American, European, African, and Asian nations.

Leonard, Dick, and Valentine Herman (eds.). *The Backbencher and Parliament.* New York: St. Martin's Press, 1972. Essays on activities and role of rank-and-file MPs.

Annotated Bibliography

Loewenberg, Gerhard. *Parliament in the German Political System.* Ithaca, N.Y.: Cornell University Press, 1967. One of the best studies of a Western European parliament in action.

Manley, John F. *The House Committee on Ways and Means, 1947–1966.* Boston: Little, Brown & Company, 1970. A perceptive study in depth of one of Congress' most powerful committees.

*Matthews, Donald R. *U.S. Senators and Their World.* Chapel Hill, N.C.: The University of North Carolina Press, 1960. Useful study of role perceptions of members of the "most exclusive club in the world."

Richards, Peter G. *Honourable Members.* London: Faber & Faber, Ltd., 1959. Description of the role of British backbenchers.

Rieselbach, LeRoy N. *Congressional Politics.* New York: McGraw-Hill, Inc., 1973. Study of congressional politics using systems-analysis framework.

*Ripley, Randall B. *Party Leaders in the House of Representatives.* Washington, D.C.: The Brookings Institution, 1967. One of the most thorough studies of party machinery in Congress.

*Saloma, John S., III. *Congress and the New Politics.* Boston: Little, Brown & Company, 1969. An effort to analyze the changing role of Congress vis-à-vis the President.

Tacheron, Donald G., and Morris K. Udall. *The Job of the Congressman.* Indianapolis, Ind.: The Bobbs-Merrill Company, Inc., 1966. Manual by a political scientist and a congressman, intended for the use of freshmen congressmen.

Vogler, David J. *The Third House.* Evanston, Ill.: Northwestern University Press, 1971. Analysis of operation and impact of congressional conference committees.

Wahlke, John C., Heinz Eulau, William Buchanan, and Leroy C. Ferguson. *The Legislative System.* New York: John Wiley & Sons, Inc., 1962. Massive and influential study of legislative roles and attitudes in four states, based on extensive interviewing.

*Wheare, K. C. *Legislatures.* New York: Oxford University Press, 1963. Introductory survey of principal features of legislatures in democratic nations.


THE EXECUTIVE PROCESS

Carter, Byrum E. *The Office of Prime Minister.* Princeton, N.J.: Princeton University Press, 1956. Analysis of government powers and political position.

*Corwin, Edward S. *The President: Office and Powers.* 3d ed. New York: New York University Press, 1948. Comprehensive and authoritative legal analysis of the office.

*Fenno, Richard F., Jr. *The President's Cabinet.* Cambridge, Mass.: Harvard University Press, 1959. Authoritative study of the Cabinet's varying importance in different administrations.

Fisher, Louis. *President and Congress: Power and Policy.* New York: The Free Press, 1972. Historical-analytical study of struggles between Congress and the President, with an especially good discussion of impoundment.

Herring, E. Pendleton. *Presidential Leadership.* New York: Holt, Rinehart and Winston, Inc., 1940. Still a useful analysis of the President's weapons and handicaps in policy leadership.

Holtzman, Abraham. *Legislative Liaison: Executive Leadership in Congress.* Skokie, Ill.: Rand McNally & Company, 1970. Detailed study of the President's strategies and tactics as "chief legislator."

Hyman, Sidney. *The American President.* New York: Harper & Row, Publishers, 1954. Well-written discussion of the place of the executive in the American system.

Jennings, Ivor. *Cabinet Government.* New York: Cambridge University Press, 1947. Long the leading British study of the British executive.

King, Anthony (ed.). *The British Prime Minister.* New York: St. Martin's Press, Inc., 1969. Best and most recent collection of essays on the British executive.

Koenig, Louis W. *The Chief Executive.* New York: Harcourt Brace Jovanovich, Inc., 1964. Comprehensive study of law and politics of the presidency.

*Neustadt, Richard E. *Presidential Power.* New York: John Wiley & Sons, Inc., 1960. Perceptive and influential study of the President's relations with his subordinates, illustrated by three case studies.

*Polsby, Nelson W. *Congress and the Presidency.* 2d ed. Englewood Cliffs, N.J.: Prentice-Hall, Inc., 1971. Shrewd and succinct study of advantages and handicaps of both branches in their continuing contest over public policy.

Ransone, Coleman B., Jr. *The Office of Governor in the United States.* University, Ala.: University of Alabama Press, 1956. Useful for comparisons with the presidency.

Reedy, George E. *The Presidency in Flux.* New York: Columbia University Press, 1971. Discussion of the "overloaded" modern presidency by a former presidential press secretary.

*Rossiter, Clinton. *The American Presidency.* New York: Harcourt Brace Jovanovich, Inc., 1956. Sprightly popular discussion.

Schlesinger, Arthur M., Jr. *The Imperial Presidency.* Boston: Houghton Mifflin Company, 1974. Discussion of how and with what consequences the President has become so powerful.

## THE ADMINISTRATIVE PROCESS

Armstrong, John A. *The European Administrative Elite.* Princeton, N.J.: Princeton University Press, 1972. Comparative study of Western European bureaucrats.

Brewer, Garry D. *Politicians, Bureaucrats, and Consultants.* New York: Basic Books, Inc., 1973. Two case studies of pitfalls and possibilities in applying technical expertise to urban-renewal problems.

Chapman, Brian. *The Profession of Government.* London: George Allen & Unwin Ltd., 1959. Comparative analysis of the status and tenure of civil servants.

Chester, D. N., and Nina Bowring. *Questions in Parliament.* New York: Oxford University Press, 1962. Authoritative study of a significant institution.

Goodnow, Frank J. *Politics and Administration.* New York: Crowell-Collier and Macmillan, Inc., 1900. Classic statement of the "politics-administration" formula.

Gulick, Luther, and L. Urwick (eds.). *Papers on the Science of Administration.* New York: Institute of Public Administration, 1937. Leading essays on the "principles of public administration," now questioned by political scientists.

Heady, Ferrel, *Public Administration: A Comparative Perspective.* Englewood Cliffs, N.J.: Prentice-Hall, Inc., 1966. Broad comparative analysis, covering both Western and non-Western nations.

Hyneman, Charles S. *Bureaucracy in a Democracy.* New York: Harper & Row, Publishers, 1950. Influential discussion of the problem and methods of democratic control over permanent civil servants.

*Krislov, Samuel. *Representative Bureaucracy.* Englewood Cliffs, N.J.: Prentice-Hall, Inc., 1974. Theoretical and empirical examination of the idea of a representative bureaucracy.

LaPalombara, Joseph, and Fred W. Riggs (eds.). *Bureaucracy and Political Development.* Princeton, N.J.: Princeton University Press, 1963. Collection of essays on the role of civil servants in developing nations.

Annotated Bibliography

*Lindblom, Charles E. *The Policy-Making Process.* Englewood Cliffs, N.J.: Prentice-Hall, Inc., 1968. Short theoretical analysis, emphasizing the role of administrative experts.

Mackenzie, W. J. M., and J. W. Grove. *Central Administration in Great Britain.* London: Longmans, Green & Co., Ltd., 1957. The most comprehensive description of the British civil service.

March, James G., and Herbert A. Simon. *Organizations.* New York: John Wiley & Sons, Inc., 1958. General theory of organizational behavior with special attention to government administrative agencies.

Novick, David (ed.). *Program Budgeting.* Cambridge, Mass.: Harvard University Press, 1965. Collection of essays describing and evaluating the Program Planning Budgeting System.

Ridley, F., and Jean Blondel. *Public Administration in France.* New York: Barnes & Noble, Inc., 1965. Leading study of this subject in English.

Robson, William A. (ed.). *The Civil Service in Britain and France.* London: Hogarth Press, Ltd., 1956. Collection of essays useful for comparisons.

Seidman, Harold. *Politics, Position, and Power.* New York: Oxford University Press, 1970. Perceptive study of American administrative agencies' position and role in policy making.

Selznick, Philip. *Leadership in Administration.* New York: Harper & Row, Publishers, 1957. Study of administration by a political sociologist.

Sharkansky, Ira. *Public Administration: Policy-Making in Government Agencies.* Chicago: Markham Publishing Company, 1970. Recent general analysis stressing policy-making roles of career civil servants.

Simon, Herbert A. *Administrative Behavior.* 2d ed. New York: Crowell-Collier and Macmillan, Inc., 1957. Influential study of administrative decision making from the point of view of organization theory and social psychology.

Simon, Herbert A., Donald W. Smithburg, and Victor A. Thompson. *Public Administration.* New York: Alfred A. Knopf, 1950. Pioneering analysis of public administration from the behavioral point of view.

White, Leonard D. *Introduction to the Study of Public Administration.* 4th ed. New York: Crowell-Collier and Macmillan, Inc., 1955. The most influential of the traditional textbook descriptions of the American administrative system.

Wildavsky, Aaron. *The Politics of the Budgetary Process.* Boston: Little, Brown & Company, 1964. Behavioral analysis of key administrative activity, emphasizing the "incremental" nature of changes.

## LAW AND COURT STRUCTURES

*Abraham, Henry J. *The Judicial Process.* 3d ed. New York: Oxford University Press, 1973. Clear and informative description of court structures and procedures in the United States, France, and Great Britain.

Allen, Carleton Kemp. *Law in the Making.* 6th ed. New York: Oxford University Press, 1958. Analysis of the development of principal legal systems.

Beck, F., and E. Goodin. *Russian Purges and the Extraction of Confession.* New York: The Viking Press, Inc., 1951. Description of the "educative" functions of communist justice.

*Berman, Harold J. *Justice in the USSR.* Rev. ed. New York: Vintage Books, 1963. Analysis of the communist system of justice.

Jackson, Richard N. *The Machinery of Justice in England.* London: Macmillan & Co., Ltd., 1960. Survey of court organization and administration of justice in England.

*Jacob, Herbert. *Justice in America.* Boston: Little, Brown & Company, 1965. Survey of court structures and legal systems in the United States.

Kelsen, Hans. *The Communist Theory of Law.* New York: Frederick A. Praeger, Inc., 1955. Emphasis on theories of Marx and Engels.

Richardson, Richard J., and Kenneth N. Vines. *The Politics of Federal Courts: Lower Courts in the United States.* Boston: Little, Brown & Company, 1970. Emphasizes the semiautonomy of Federal district and appellate courts.

Sieghart, Marguerite A. *Government by Decree: A Comparative History of the Ordinance in English and French Law.* New York: Frederick A. Praeger, Inc., 1950. Study of administrative law in the two nations.

Von Mehren, Arthur T. *The Civil Law System,* Boston: Little, Brown & Company, 1957. Comparative study of French and German legal systems.

Vyshinsky, Andrei Y. *The Law of the Soviet State.* New York: Crowell-Collier and Macmillan, Inc., 1948. Exposition of the communist conception of law and justice.

## THE JUDICIAL PROCESS

*Becker, Theodore L. (ed.). *The Impact of Supreme Court Decisions.* 2d ed. New York: Oxford University Press, 1973. Illuminating collection of studies of what happens *after* the Supreme Court has presumably decided a question.

Cahill, Fred V., Jr. *Judicial Legislation.* New York: The Ronald Press Company, 1952. Description of judges' policy-making role and analysis of "mechanical" and "legal realist" schools of jurisprudence.

Cappaletti, Mauro. *Judicial Review in the Contemporary World.* Indianapolis, Ind.: The Bobbs Merrill Company, Inc., 1971. Comparative analysis of judicial review by an Italian jurist.

Cardozo, Benjamin N. *The Nature of the Judicial Process.* New Haven, Conn.: Yale University Press, 1921. Early anticipation of "legal realism" by a distinguished American judge and jurist.

Corwin, Edward S. *Court over Constitution.* 2d ed. New York: Peter Smith, 1950. Description and evaluation of judicial review.

*Danelski, David J. *A Supreme Court Justice Is Appointed.* New York: Random House, Inc., 1964. Study of the politics of judicial appointments.

Frank, Jerome. *Law and the Modern Mind.* New York: Brentano's, 1930. Leading exposition of "legal realism."

*Goldman, Sheldon, and Thomas P. Jahnige. *The Federal Courts as a Political System.* New York: Harper & Row, Publishers, 1971. Survey of court structures and practices from judicial-legislation point of view.

Haines, Charles Grove. *The American Doctrine of Judicial Supremacy.* 2d ed. 2 vols. Berkeley, Calif.: University of California Press, 1932. Analysis and evaluation of the American system of judicial review.

*Peltason, Jack W. *Federal Courts in the Political Process.* New York: Doubleday & Company, Inc., 1955. Influential exposition of the conception of judicial process as part of political process.

*Rosenblum, Victor G. *Law as a Political Instrument.* New York: Doubleday & Company, Inc., 1955. Case studies of the policy-making role of judges.

Schubert, Glendon. *Constitutional Politics.* New York: Holt, Rinehart and Winston, Inc., 1960. The most comprehensive behavioral analysis of judicial process.

―――― (ed.). *Judicial Decision-Making.* New York: The Free Press, 1963. Collection of essays on behavioral analysis of judicial process.

___. *Judicial Policy-Making.* Glenview, Ill.: Scott, Foresman and Company, 1965. Study of judicial legislation.

Wasby, Stephen L. *The Impact of the United States Supreme Court: Some Perspectives.* Homewood, Ill.: Dorsey Press, 1970. General analysis of impact of Supreme Court decisions.

## LOCAL GOVERNMENT

Adrian, Charles R. *Governing Urban Armerica.* New York: McGraw-Hill, Inc., 1955. General description.

Brownell, Baker. *The Human Community.* New York: Harper & Row, Publishers, 1950. Theory of local government as a key institution in a healthy democracy.

Chapman, Brian. *Introduction to French Local Government.* London: George Allen & Unwin Ltd., 1953. Major study in English.

Clarke, John J. *The Local Government of the United Kingdom.* 15th ed. London: Sir Isacc Pitman & Sons, Ltd., 1956. Most comprehensive description.

*Dahl, Robert A. *Who Governs? Democracy and Power in an American City.* New Haven, Conn.: Yale University Press, 1961. Leading statement of "pluralist" position on community power, based on study of key decisions in New Haven.

*Eulau, Heinz, and Kenneth Prewitt. *Labyrinths of Democracy: Adaptations, Linkages, Representation, and Policies in Urban Politics.* Indianapolis, Ind.: The Bobbs Merrill Company, Inc., 1973. Massive study of the interaction of institutions and political forces in local governments in the San Francisco Bay area.

Harris, G. Montagu. *Comparative Local Government.* London: Hutchinson & Co. (Publishers), 1948. Description of structure and problems of local government in various nations.

*Hunter, Floyd. *Community Power Structure.* Chapel Hill, N.C.: The University of North Carolina Press, 1953. Leading statement of the power-elite theory of community power, based on interviews with leaders in Atlanta.

Jacob, Herbert, and Kenneth N. Vines (eds.). *Politics in the American States.* 2d ed. Boston: Little, Brown & Company, 1971. Comparative analysis of various aspects of state government.

*Kaufman, Herbert. *Politics and Policies in State and Local Governments.* Englewood Cliffs, N.J.: Prentice-Hall, Inc., 1963. Imaginative and well-written introductory survey.

Kneier, Charles M. *City Government in the United States.* 3d ed. New York: Harper & Row, Publishers, 1957. General description.

Lockard, Duane. *The Politics of State and Local Government.* New York: Crowell-Collier and Macmillan, Inc., 1963. General description with emphasis on politics.

Loveridge, Ronald O. *City Managers in Legislative Politics.* Indianapolis, Ind.: The Bobbs Merrill Company, Inc., 1971. Analysis of policy-making roles of city managers in the San Francisco Bay area cities.

Maddick, Henry. *Panchayati Raj: A Study of Rural Local Government in India.* London: Longmans Group, Ltd., 1970. Detailed study of local government in an Asian democracy.

Morgan, Arthur E. *The Small Community: Foundation of Democratic Life.* New York: Harper & Row, Publishers, 1942. Importance of local self-government for democracy.

*Polsby, Nelson W. *Community Power and Political Theory.* New Haven, Conn.: Yale University Press, 1963. Analysis of theories of community power from a "pluralist" point of view.

Robson, William A. (ed.). *Great Cities of the World: Their Government, Politics, and Planning.* New York: Crowell-Collier and Macmillan, Inc., 1954. Description of various metropolitan governments in various nations.

Snider, Clyde F. *American State and Local Government.* 2d ed. New York: Appleton-Century-Crofts, 1965. Most complete structural survey.

## FEDERALISM

Anderson, William. *The Nation and the States: Rivals or Partners?* Minneapolis, Minn.: University of Minnesota Press, 1955. Argument by a distinguished political scientist that the two levels need not be in competition.

Barghoorn, Frederick C. *Soviet Russian Nationalism.* New York: Oxford University Press, 1956. Study of federalism in the USSR.

Elazar, Daniel J. *American Federalism: A View from the States.* New York: Thomas Y. Crowell Company, 1966. Thorough recent analysis of relative powers and functions of states and national government in the United States.

Friedrich, Carl J., and Robert R. Bowie (eds.). *Studies in Federalism.* Boston: Little, Brown & Company, 1954. Essays on various aspects of federalism.

Macmahon, Arthur W. (ed.). *Federalism: Mature and Emergent.* New York: Doubleday & Company, Inc., 1955. Essays on practice and problems of federalism in old and new nations.

Reagan, Michael D. *The New Federalism.* New York: Oxford University Press, 1972. Analysis of current problems in federal-state relations.

*Report of the Commission on Governmental Relations.* Washington, D.C.: U.S. Government Printing Office, 1955. Report on the proper distribution of functions between the national and state governments.

*Riker, William H. *Federalism: Origin, Operation, Significance.* Boston: Little, Brown & Company, 1964. A fresh look at the nature and consequences ·of federalism.

*Wheare, K. C. *Federal Government.* 4th ed. New York: Oxford University Press, 1964. More formal description and analysis by a leading British scholar.

## PART VI  POLICY OUTPUTS AND IMPACTS

## MODERN POLICY OUTPUTS

Bruce, Maurice. *The Coming of the Welfare State.* London: B. T. Batsford, 1961. Comparative analysis of passing of laissez-faire and the rise of the welfare state.

Buckley, William F., Jr. *Up from Liberalism.* New York: Ivan Obolensky, Inc., 1959. Popular exposition of conservative laissez-faire.

*Dahl, Robert A., and Charles E. Lindblom. *Politics, Economics and Welfare.* New York: Harper & Row, Publishers, 1953. Explores interrelated patterns of political and economic power and the role of government in modern economies.

Davis, James W., Jr., and Kenneth M. Dolbeare, *Little Groups of Neighbors: The Selective Service System.* Chicago: Markham Publishing Company, 1968. Influential analysis of selective-service system.

De Grazia, Alfred, and Ted Gurr. *American Welfare.* New York: New York University Press, 1961. Analysis of American welfare-state programs.

*Finer, Herman. *The Road to Reaction.* Boston: Little, Brown & Company, 1945. Defense of the welfare state and attack on Friedrich A. Hayek and laissez-faire.

Girvetz, Harry K. *From Wealth to Welfare.* Stanford, Calif.: Stanford University Press, 1950. History of the rise of the welfare state.

Hall, P. *The Social Services of Modern England.* London: Routledge & Kegan Paul Ltd., 1959. Description of English socialism.

*Hayek, Friedrich A. *The Road to Serfdom.* Chicago: University of Chicago Press, 1944. Defense of laissez-faire and attack on the welfare state.

Kendall, Willmoore. *The Conservative Affirmation.* Chicago: Henry Regnery Company, 1963. Exposition of conservative philosophy with only minor stress on laissez-faire.

*Lowi, Theodore J. *The End of Liberalism.* New York: W. W. Norton & Company, Inc., 1969. Attack on "interest-group liberalism" and the resulting American version of the welfare state.

Meyer, Frank S. *In Defense of Freedom: A Conservative Credo.* Chicago: Henry Regnery Company, 1962. Exposition of laissez-faire conservatism.

Pierce, Lawrence C. *The Politics of Fiscal Policy Formation.* Pacific Palisades, Calif.: Goodyear Publishing Co., Inc., 1971. Analysis of issues and forces involved in making American tax and budget policies.

Polanyi, Karl. *The Great Transformation.* New York: Holt, Rinehart and Winston, Inc., 1944. Classic description of social factors causing the rise and fall of laissez-faire.

Roos, Leslie L., Jr. (ed.). *The Politics of Ecosuicide.* New York: Holt, Rinehart and Winston, Inc., 1971. Essays on environmental policies.

Sharkansky, Ira. *The Politics of Taxing and Spending.* Indianapolis, Ind.: The Bobbs Merrill Company, Inc., 1969. Budget policies.

*Steiner, Gilbert Y. *The State of Welfare.* Washington, D.C.: The Brookings Institution, 1971. Critical analysis of American welfare programs.

## THEORIES OF CIVIL LIBERTIES

*Abraham, Henry J. *Freedom and the Court.* 2d ed. New York: Oxford University Press, 1972. Comprehensive review of current status of First Amendment freedoms.

*Becker, Carl L. *The Declaration of Independence.* New York: Alfred A. Knopf, 1951. First published in 1922. Historical study of the natural-law theories underlying this famous document.

*_____. *Freedom and Responsibility in the American Way of Life.* New York: Alfred A. Knopf, 1945. History and analysis of American concepts of civil liberties.

Carr, Robert K. *Federal Protection of Civil Rights.* Ithaca, N.Y.: Cornell University Press, 1947. Emphasizes the role of government as a protector of rights.

Chafee, Zechariah, Jr. *Free Speech in the United States.* Cambridge, Mass.: Harvard University Press, 1941. Influential defense of the idea of free speech.

Gellhorn, Walter. *American Rights.* New York: Crowell-Collier and Macmillan, Inc., 1960. Survey of the law of civil rights.

Hocking, William E. *Freedom of the Press: A Framework of Principle.* Chicago: University of Chicago Press, 1947. A distinguished philosopher's theory of civil liberties.

Holcombe, Arthur H. *Human Rights in the Modern World.* New York: New York University Press, 1947. Survey of the legal and actual status of civil liberties in various modern nations.

Hook, Sidney. *Heresy, Yes—Conspiracy, No!* New York: The John Day Company, Inc., 1953. Analysis of the limits of free speech in the face of communist subversion.

Hyneman, Charles S. "Free Speech: At What Price?" *American Political Science Review,* 56 (December 1962), pp. 847–852. Presidential address to the American Political Science Association, emphasizing the necessity of limiting free speech to preserve other values.

Meiklejohn, Alexander. *Free Speech and Its Relation to Self-Government.* New York: Harper & Row, Publishers, 1948. The best modern exposition of "absolute free speech" doctrine.

*Mill, John Stuart. *On Liberty* (1859). Many editions have been published. Classic defense of free speech.

Milton, John. *Areopagitica* (1644). Many editions have been published. One of the earliest and still influential arguments for free speech.

Reddaway, Peter (ed.). *Uncensored Russia: Protest and Dissent in the Soviet Union.* New York: American Heritage Press, 1972. Documentary account of current libertarian movement in the USSR.

*Street, Harry. *Freedom, the Individual, and the Law.* Baltimore, Md.: Penguin Books, Inc., 1963. The most comprehensive survey of civil rights in Great Britain.

*Wolff, Robert Paul, Barrington Moore, Jr., and Herbert Marcuse (eds.). *A Critique of Pure Tolerance.* Boston: The Beacon Press, 1969. New Left attack on liberal ideas of free speech for all, especially interesting for Marcuse's views.

## POLICE POWER AND THE RIGHTS OF DEFENDANTS

*Bunn, Ronald F., and William G. Andrews (eds.). *Politics and Civil Liberties in Europe.* Princeton, N.J.: D. Van Nostrand Company, Inc., 1967. Comparative survey of guarantees of due process of law in European nations.

Casper, Jonathan O. *Lawyers before the Warren Court.* Urbana, Ill.: University of Illinois Press, 1972. Innovative study of lawyer-client relations in civil-rights cases in period 1957–1966.

*The Challenge of Crime in a Free Society: Report of the President's Commission on Law Enforcement and Administration of Justice.* Washington, D.C.: U.S. Government Printing Office, 1967. Discussion of police responsibilities and handicaps.

Fellman, David. *The Defendant's rights.* New York: Holt, Rinehart, and Winston, Inc., 1958. Comprehensive survey of American guarantees of due process of law.

———. *The Defendant's Rights under English Law.* Madison, Wis.: University of Wisconsin Press, 1966. Comprehensive survey of English guarantees of due process of law.

*Jacob, Herbert. *Courts, Lawyers, and the Judicial Process.* 2d ed. Boston: Little, Brown & Company, 1972. Analysis of administration of American criminal justice and civil rights.

Kaplan, John. *Criminal Justice.* New York: The Foundation Press, 1973. Survey of structure and procedures of America's criminal justice system.

*Lewis, Anthony. *Gideon's Trumpet.* New York: Random House, Inc., 1964. Dramatic account of a famous Supreme Court decision on defendant's right to counsel.

Murphy, Walter F. *Wiretapping on Trial.* New York: Random House, Inc., 1965. Lucid analysis of conflict between police needs and defendants' rights in use of electronic surveillance.

Trebach, Arnold S. *The Rationing of Justice: Constitutional Rights and the Criminal Process.* New Brunswick, N.J.: Rutgers University Press, 1964. Analysis of handicaps of the poor in American adversary system of criminal justice.

## CIVIL LIBERTIES AND THE STATUS OF WOMEN

Amundsen, Kirsten. *The Silenced Majority.* Englewood Cliffs, N.J.: Prentice-Hall, Inc., 1971. Attack on political discrimination against women.

Bernard, Jessie. *Women and the Public Interest.* Chicago: Aldine-Atherton, 1971. A middle-position statement of the feminist case.

Decter, Midge. *The New Chastity.* New York: Coward, McCann & Geoghegan, Inc., 1972. Strongest attack by a woman on radical feminist position.

*Friedan, Betty. *The Feminine Mystique.* New York: W. W. Norton & Company, Inc., 1968. The book which, more than any other, stimulated the contemporary women's rights movement.

Gornick, Vivian, and Barbara K. Moran (eds.). *Women in Sexist Society.* New York: Basic Books, Inc., 1971. Survey of various forms of discrimination against women.

Kirkpatrick, Jeane J. *Political Woman.* New York: Basic Books, Inc., 1974. Instructive empirical study of women successful in politics, prominent state legislators.

Rosenberg, Marie B., and Len V. Bergstrom. *Women and Society.* Beverly Hills, Calif.: Sage Publications, Inc., 1974. Comprehensive annotated bibliography of works on the status of women.

Stimpson, Catherine R. (ed.). *Discrimination against Women.* Washington, D.C.: R. R. Bowker Company, 1973. Summary of hearings before congressional committees, the most comprehensive statement of the legal and economic status of women.

## CIVIL LIBERTIES AND RACE RELATIONS

Adam, Herbert. *Modernizing Racial Domination: The Dynamics of South African Politics.* Berkeley, Calif.: University of California Press, 1971. Analysis of impact of "Bantustan" program on status of black natives and apartheid.

Broderick, Francis L., and August Meier (eds.). *Negro Protest Thought in the Twentieth Century.* Indianapolis, Ind.: The Bobbs-Merrill Company, Inc., 1965. Collection of articles and speeches by militant black leaders.

*Carmichael, Stokely, and Charles V. Hamilton. *Black Power: The Politics of Liberation in America.* New York: Vintage Books, 1967. The leading statement of the Black Power position by a militant black leader and a black political scientist.

Carter, Gwendolen M. *The Politics of Inequality.* 2d ed. New York: Frederick A. Praeger, Inc., 1959. Analysis of South African apartheid.

*Franklin, John Hope, and Isidore Starr (eds.). *The Negro in Twentieth Century America.* New York: Vintage Books, 1967. Selection of essays and speeches by black leaders of various degrees of militancy.

Hamilton, Charles V. *The Bench and the Ballot.* New York: Oxford University Press, 1973. Study of impact of congressional legislation and court decisions on black voting in the South.

*Holden, Matthew H., Jr. *The Politics of the Black "Nation."* San Francisco: Chandler Publishing Company, 1973. Analysis of the internal politics of the black community.

*———. *The White Man's Burden.* San Francisco: Chandler Publishing Company, 1973. Political scientist's analysis of racial conflict in the United States, with recommendations for their accommodation.

Lincoln, C. Eric. *The Black Muslims in America.* Boston: The Beacon Press, 1961. Most authoritative analysis of one black separatist organization.

McEntire, Davis. *Residence and Race.* Berkeley, Calif.: University of California Press, 1960. Describes discrimination in housing in the United States.

*Malcolm X. *Autobiography.* New York: Grove Press, Inc., 1966. Brilliantly written thoughts and recollections of one of the most influential black militant leaders.

Marquand, Leopold. *The Peoples and Policies of South Africa.* 3d ed. New York: Oxford University Press, 1962. A thorough examination of apartheid.

Newby, I.A. *Jim Crow's Defense: Anti-Negro Thought in America, 1900–1930.* Baton Rouge, La.: Louisiana State University Press, 1965. Useful description of white-supremacy views underlying racial segregation laws.

Peltason, Jack W. *Fifty-Eight Lonely Men*. New York: Harcourt Brace Jovanovich, Inc., 1961. Study of desegregation of southern schools, focused on the role of Federal district judges.

Walton, Hanes Jr. *Black Politics*. Philadelphia: J. B. Lippincott Company, 1972. Study of origins, strategy, and tactics of various black political groups in America.

## PART VII   THE INTERNATIONAL POLITICAL SYSTEM

### INTERNATIONAL POLITICS

Art, Robert, and Robert Jervis. *International Politics*. Boston: Little, Brown & Company, 1973. Analysis of anarchy, force, and imperialism as basic concepts in understanding international politics.

Claude, Inis L., Jr. *Power and International Relations*. New York: Random House, Inc., 1963. Analysis of the basic structure of international politics as it affects chances for maintaining peace.

Deutsch, Karl W. *Nationalism and Its Alternatives*. New York: Alfred A. Knopf, 1969. Assessment of the prospects for developing international loyalties and community.

*_____. *Nationalism and Social Communication*. New York: John Wiley & Sons, Inc., 1953. Analysis of effects of nationalism on attitudes and communication.

Haas, Ernst B., and Allen S. Whiting. *Dynamics of International Relations*. New York: McGraw-Hill, Inc., 1956. Emphasizes social-psychological categories for explaining international politics.

Hayes, Carlton J. H. *The Historical Evolution of Modern Nationalism*. New York: Crowell-Collier and Macmillan, Inc., 1931. Describes origins of the state system.

*Kaplan, Morton A. *System and Process in International Relations*. New York: John Wiley & Sons, Inc., 1964. Highly abstract theorizing about international relations, using the theory of games as an explanatory tool.

Kohn, Hans. *Nationalsim: Its Meaning and History*. New York: Crowell-Collier and Macmillan, Inc., 1955. Analysis of the psychological basis of the state system.

Manning, C. W. *The Nature of International Society*. New York: John Wiley & Sons, Inc., 1962. General survey from a behavioral point of view.

Morgenthau, Hans J. *Politics among Nations*. 5th ed. New York: Alfred A. Knopf, 1972. Description and explanation in terms of "power" as a basic orienting concept.

Northedge, F. S., and M. D. Donelan. *International Disputes: The Political Aspects*. New York: St. Martin's Press, Inc., 1972. Accounts of 50 international disputes from 1945 to 1970, with analyses of why some were settled by force and others peacefully.

Organski, A. F. K. *World Politics*. New York: Alfred A. Knopf, 1961. General survey based on the power concept.

Rosecrance, Richard. *International Politics*. New York: McGraw-Hill, Inc., 1973. General survey focusing on causes of international conflicts.

Schelling, Thomas C. *The Strategy of Conflict*. Cambridge, Mass.: Harvard University Press, 1960. Stimulating analysis of international conflict based on game theory.

Singer, J. David (ed.). *Human Behavior and International Politics*. Skokie, Ill.: Rand McNally & Company, 1965. Collection of essays analyzing international politics from a behavioral point of view.

Van Dyke, Vernon. *International Politics*. New York: Appleton-Century-Crofts, 1957. General description.

*Almond, Gabriel A. The American People and Foreign Policy.* New York: Harcourt Brace Jovanovich, Inc., 1950. Description of pressures on the foreign-policy process in the United States.

Beloff, Max. *Foreign Policy and the Democratic Process.* Baltimore, Md.: The Johns Hopkins Press, 1955. Discussion of problems of making foreign policy in a democracy.

Brecher, Michael. *The Foreign Policy System of Israel.* New Haven, Conn.: Yale University Press, 1972. Prize-winning analysis in depth of factors and processes shaping foreign policy in a democracy under siege.

Buck, Phillip W., and Martin B. Travis, Jr. *Control of Foreign Relations in Modern Nations.* New York: W. W. Norton & Company, Inc., 1957. Description of government machinery for making and administering foreign policy in various nations.

Cohen, Bernard C. *The Political Process and Foreign Policy: The Making of the Japanese Peace Settlement.* Princeton, N.J.: Princeton University Press, 1957. A carefully analyzed case study illuminating the general process.

————. *The Public's Impact on Foreign Policy.* Boston: Little, Brown & Company, 1973. Authoritative analysis of impact of public opinion on making of American foreign policy.

Cook, Thomas I., and Malcolm Moos. *Power through Purpose: The Realism of Idealism as a Basis for Foreign Policy.* Baltimore, Md.: The Johns Hopkins Press, 1955. Exposition of the "idealist" view.

*Dahl, Robert A. *Congress and Foreign Policy.* New York: Harcourt Brace Jovanovich, Inc., 1950. Roles of Congress, the President, and civil servants in making foreign policy.

Hilsman, Roger. *The Politics of Policy Making in Defense and Foreign Affairs.* New York: Harper & Row, Publishers, 1971. By a political scientist who formerly served in the Department of State.

Iklé, Fred C. *How Nations Negotiate.* New York: Harper & Row, Publishers, 1964. Analysis of diplomatic methods and results.

Kennan, George F. *Realities of American Foreign Policy.* Princeton, N.J.: Princeton University Press, 1954. Exposition of the "realist" view.

Knorr, Klaus. *The War Potential of Nations.* Princeton, N.J.: Princeton University Press, 1956. Analysis of elements and evaluation of national power.

Lall, Arthur. *Modern International Negotiations.* New York: Columbia University Press, 1966. Analysis of diplomatic methods and the general role of diplomacy.

Liska, George. *Nations in Alliance.* Baltimore, Md.: The Johns Hopkins Press, 1962. A theory of international relations focused on factors involved in forming and dissolving alliances.

London, Kurt. *The Making of Foreign Policy, East and West.* Philadelphia: J. B. Lippincott Company, 1965. Study of foreign-policy-making machinery in Western nations and the USSR.

McCamy, James L. *Conduct of the New Diplomacy.* New York: Harper & Row, Publishers, 1964. Describes administration of foreign policy.

Macridis, Roy C. *Foreign Policy in World Politics.* 2d ed. Englewood Cliffs, N.J.: Prentice-Hall, Inc., 1962. The process of making foreign policy in various nations.

Marshall, Charles B. *The Limits of Foreign Policy.* New York: Holt, Rinehart and Winston, Inc., 1954. Analysis of problems of making foreign policy.

Montgomery, John D. *Foreign Aid in International Politics.* Englewood Cliffs, N.J.: Prentice-Hall, Inc., 1967. Useful analysis of foreign aid as a weapon of foreign policy.

Annotated Bibliography

Morgenthau, Hans J. *In Defense of the National Interest.* New York: Alfred A. Knopf, 1951. Exposition of the "realist" view.

Neustadt, Richard E. *Alliance Politics.* New York: Columbia University Press, 1970. Perceptively analyzed case study of process of reaching agreement between two close allies.

*Riker, William H. *The Theory of Political Coalitions.* New Haven, Conn.: Yale University Press, 1962. Application of game theory to political conflict.

Rosenau, James N. (ed.). *International Politics and Foreign Policy.* New York: The Free Press, 1961. Collection of essays stressing interchange between international politics and domestic foreign-policy making.

Rothstein, Robert L. *Planning, Prediction, and Policy Making in Foreign Affairs.* Boston: Little, Brown & Company, 1972. Analysis of processes involved in making foreign policy.

Snyder, Richard C., H. W. Bruck, and Burton Sapin (eds.). *Foreign Policy Decision Making: An Approach to the Study of International Politics.* New York: The Free Press, 1962. Essays on process and problems of making foreign policy.

Sprout, Harold, and Margaret Sprout (eds.). *Foundations of National Power.* Princeton, N.J.: D. Van Nostrand Company, Inc., 1951. Essays on elements and evaluation of national power.

Wallace, Robert S. *American and Soviet Aid.* Pittsburgh, Pa.: University of Pittsburgh Press, 1971. Study of changing levels and types of foreign aid in foreign policies of the two superpowers.

Westerfield, H. B. *Foreign Policy and Party Politics.* New Haven, Conn.: Yale University Press, 1956. Analyzes problems of maintaining a "bipartisan" foreign policy after World War II.

Wilcox, Francis O. *Congress, the Executive, and Foreign Policy.* New York: Harper & Row, Publishers, 1971. Reflections on current problems by a distinguished analyst of foreign-policy processes.

Wolfers, Arnold, and Lawrence W. Martin. *The Anglo-American Tradition in Foreign Policy.* New Haven, Conn.: Yale University Press, 1956. Historical comparative analysis.

## THE COSTS AND CAUSES OF WAR

Aron, Raymond. *Peace and War.* New York: Doubleday & Company, Inc., 1967. Thoughtful discussion by a leading French political analyst.

*Brown, Harrison, and James Real. *Community of Fear.* Santa Barbara, Calif.: Center for the Study of Democratic Institutions, 1960. Popular short discussion of probable effects of thermonuclear war.

Cantril, Hadley (ed.). *Tensions That Cause Wars.* Urbana, Ill.: University of Illinois Press, 1951. Essays emphasizing social-psychological causes of war.

Glasstone, Samuel (ed.). *The Effects of Nuclear Weapons.* Rev. ed. Washington, D.C.: U.S. Atomic Energy Commission, 1962. Authoritative description of effects of thermonuclear weapons.

Kahn, Herman. *On Thermonuclear War.* Princeton, N.J.: Princeton University Press, 1961. "Thinking about the unthinkable."

Lenin, V.I. *Imperialism: The Highest Stage of Capitalism.* New York: International Publishers Co., Inc., 1940. The classic statement of the Marxist-Leninist theory of war.

Mills, C. Wright. *The Causes of World War III.* New York: Simon and Schuster, Inc., 1958. Influential New Left statement of American capitalism as the basic cause of wars.

Nef, John U. *War and Human Progress.* Cambridge, Mass.: Harvard University Press, 1950. Analysis of effects of past wars on human welfare.

Richardson, Lewis F. *Statistics of Deadly Quarrels.* Pittsburgh, Pa.: The Boxwood Press, 1960. Pioneering effort to count civil and international wars and resulting casualties exactly.

Robbins, Lionel. *The Economic Causes of War.* London: Jonathan Cape, Ltd., 1939.

Russett, Bruce M. *What Price Vigilance? The Burdens of National Defense.* New Haven, Conn.: Yale University Press, 1970. Examination of United States defense expenditures and their consequences for domestic programs.

Shotwell, James T. *War as an Instrument of National Policy.* New York: Harcourt Brace Jovanovich, Inc., 1929. Political analysis of causes of war.

Wright, Quincy. *A Study of War.* 2 vols. Chicago: University of Chicago Press, 1942. Most comprehensive study.


## APPROACHES TO PEACE

Alker, Hayward R., and Bruce M. Russett, *World Politics in the General Assembly.* New Haven, Conn.: Yale University Press, 1965. Voting patterns in the United Nations.

Barr, Stringfellow. *Citizens of the World.* New York: Doubleday & Company, Inc. 1953. Exposition of the world-government view.

Bechhoefer, Bernhard. *Postwar Negotiations for Arms Control.* Washington, D.C.: The Brookings Institution, 1961. Discussion of disarmament problems.

Brierly, J. L. *The Law of Nations.* 6th ed. New York: Oxford University Press, 1963. Contains both summaries of rules and description of the general nature and role of international law.

Claude, Inis L., Jr. *Swords into Plowshares.* 3d ed. New York: Random House, Inc., 1964. Analysis of theories and results of various approaches to peace within the state system.

*Cousins, Norman. *In Place of Folly.* New York: Harper & Row, Publishers, 1961. Exposition of the world-government position.

*Deutsch, Karl W. *Political Community at the International Level: Problems of Definition and Measurement.* New York: Doubleday & Company, Inc., 1954. Analysis of methodological problems involved in assessing the preconditions for world government.

Edwards, David V. *Arms Control in International Politics.* New York: Holt, Rinehart, and Winston, Inc., 1969. Analysis of efforts at international disarmament treaties.

Fabian, Larry L. *Soldiers without Enemies.* Washington, D.C.: The Brookings Institution, 1971. Thorough account of United Nations efforts at peacekeeping by use of military forces.

Gordenker, Leon (ed.). *The United Nations in International Politics.* Princeton, N.J.: Princeton University Press, 1971. Essays on current operations and problems of UN.

Grzybowski, Kazimierz. *The Socialist Commonwealth of Nations.* New Haven, Conn.: Yale University Press, 1964. Leading analysis of the Warsaw pact.

Haas, Ernst B. *Beyond the Nation-State: Functionalism and International Organization.* Stanford, Calif.: Stanford University Press, 1965. General theoretical analysis of factors and forms in international integration.

Hammarskjöld, Dag. *The International Civil Servant in Law and in Fact.* New York: Oxford University Press, 1961. Analysis of the United Nations Secretariat's role by the late Secretary-General.

Hovet, Thomas, Jr. *Bloc Politics in the United Nations.* Cambridge, Mass.: Harvard University Press, 1960. Voting patterns in the United Nations General Assembly.

Kaplan, Morton A., and Nicholas De B. Katzenbach. *The Political Foundations of International Law.* New York: John Wiley & Sons, Inc., 1961. Analyzes origins and limitations.

Lindberg, Leon N. *The Political Dynamics of European Economic Integration.* Stanford, Calif.: Stanford University Press, 1963. Leading analysis of political and economic forces affecting the European Economic Community.

Lindberg, Leon N., and Stuart A. Scheingold. *Europe's Would-Be Polity.* Englewood Cliffs, N.J.: Prentice-Hall, Inc., 1970. Study of problems, achievements, and possibilities of the European Economic Community.

Macdonald, R. W. *The League of Arab States.* Princeton, N.J.: Princeton University Press, 1965. Leading analysis of a potentially important regional organization.

Mangone, Gerard A. *The Idea and Practice of World Government.* New York: Columbia University Press, 1951. General analysis.

———. *A Short History of International Organization.* New York: McGraw-Hill, Inc., 1954. Useful introduction.

Manly, Chesly. *The UN Record.* Chicago: Henry Regnery Company, 1955. Denunciation of the United Nations as a subversive force.

Nicholas, H. G. *The United Nations as a Political Institution.* 4th ed. New York: Oxford University Press, 1972. Study and evaluation of achievements and limitations of the United Nations.

Randle, Robert F. *Origins of Peace.* New York: The Free Press, 1973. Analysis of factors in peacemaking process.

Spanier, John W., and Joseph L. Nogee. *The Politics of Disarmament.* New York: Frederick A. Praeger, Inc., 1962. Analysis of postwar disarmament problems.

Stoetzer, O.C. *The OAS: An Introduction.* New York: Frederick A. Praeger, Inc., 1967.

Streit, Clarence K. *Freedom against Itself.* New York: Harper & Row, Publishers, 1954. Exposition of the world-federalist position.

Walters, F.P. *A History of the League of Nations.* 2 vols. New York: Oxford University Press, 1952. The most comprehensive description.

Zimmern, Alfred E. *The League of Nations and the Rule of Law.* New York: Crowell-Collier and Macmillan, Inc., 1939. Sympathetic evaluation.

Annotated Bibliography

# INDEX

Abernathy, Ralph D., 567
Abortion, 543–544, 560
Abraham, Henry J., 151n, 448n, 451n, 452n, 529n
*Abrams* v. *United States,* 527
Accusatorial court procedures, 452–453
Action, political, 240–249; boycotts, 245–246; demonstrations, 243–245; electioneering, 242–243: lobbying, 240–241; mass propaganda, 243; nonviolent civil disobedience, 246; organization, 240; strikes, 245–246; violence, 247–249; working inside political parties, 241–242
Activities, government, 501–514
Acton, Lord, 488n
Adamany, David, 206n
Adams, John, 389
Adams, Sherman, 392
Adelson, Joseph, 91n
Adjudication of international disputes, 628–629
Administration, 412–440; status of, 404–425. *See also* Administrative agencies
Administrative agencies: court control of, 439; foreign policy and, 603–604; internal organization of, 416–418; personnel number of, 414–415; political activity and, 420–421; political control

Administrative agencies (*cont.*)
of, 434–439; as pressure groups, 238–239; selection of, 422–425; strikes and, 421–422; status of, 420–425; structure of, 415–418; types of, 415–416; unions and, 421–422
Administrative law, 444
Administrators: executives distinguished from, 413–414; functions of, 413, 418–420; role of, in developing nations, 430–431; selection of, 413–414; tenure of, 413–414
Adrian, Charles R., 481, 482n, 483n
Adversary court procedures, 452–453
Advertising, 126, 138; institutional, 243
Advisors, presidential, 392
Advisory bodies, 341
Affective responses, 81–82
Affirmative action program, 557, 560–561
Age, voting patterns and, 192
Age groups, influence on individuals, 76
Agnew, Spiro T., 184, 185
Agricultural pressure groups, 234
Agricultural Research Service, 418
Air pollution, 471
Akzin, Benjamin, 58n
Alexander, Herbert E., 206n
Alford, Dale, 374n
Alford, Robert R., 78n, 187n

Cohen, Morris R., 17n
Colbert, Jean Baptiste, 505
Cold war, 595, 638
Cole, G. D. H., 327
Coleman, James S., 62n, 97n, 197n, 210n, 232n
Collective security, 622–624, 648–649
Committee for Draft Resistance, 238
Committee on Political Education (COPE), 242, 252
Committee to Reelect the President, 33, 86, 127, 442
Committees: executive, 368; joint, 364; legislative, 363–365; policy, 368; select, 364; standing, 363, steering, 368
Common law, 444
Communications: effects of environment on, 137–138; effects on political opinion and behavior, 138–141
Communications, political, 125–142; audiences and, 138; developing nations and, 141–142; elements of, 127–128; face-to-face, 135–137; media of, 128–142; nature of, 126–128; opinion leaders and, 136–137; two-step flow of, 136–137
Communism, 217; civil rights under, 535–537; constitutions and, 277–278; as model of democracy, 301–303; modern, schisms in, 507–509; representation theory of, 329–330. *See also* People's Republic of China; Union of Soviet Socialist Republics
Communist nations, administrative process in, 437–439
Communist Party of the Soviet Union, 222–224
Communities, local government and, 472–473
"Community power," 484–485
Compromise, government and, 66–68
Compte, Auguste, 8
Conceptualization, 71; levels of, 72–73
Confederate States of America, 472
Confédération Française des Travailleurs Chrétiens, 233, 234
Confédération Générale de l'Agriculture, 234
Confédération Générale des Viniculteurs, 233
Confédération Générale du Travail, 232, 234, 245
Confédération Nationale du Patronat Français, 232
Confessions, voluntary, 544–555
Conflicts: civil rights, as political, 544–545; defendants' rights, 550–554; human life

Conflicts (*cont.*)
and, 36–37; police powers, 547–549; politics as, 35–44; status of blacks, 562–583; status of women, 555–562
Conflicts, international: characteristics of, 595–610; peaceful settlement of, 627–628
Congregations, influence on individuals, 76
Congress, President and, 396–400
Congress of Racial Equality (CORE), 236, 567
Consensus, influence on form of government, 292–293
Conservatism, 515
Constitutional law, 444
Constitutionalism, 263–264, 286, 531; democracy and, 313–314
Constitutional rules, 264–274; customary, 268; provisions of, 270–274; status of, 264–266; where found, 266–270
Constitutions, 266–279; amendment of, 273–274, 274, 490–491; changes in, 274–277; civil rights and, 528–530; communist concept of, 277–278; constitutionalism and, 263–264; definitions of, 262–264; democratic systems and, 264–277; dictatorial systems and, 277–279; and distribution of powers, 272; judicial revision of, 275–277; provisions of, 270–274; Soviet, 278–279; statutory revisions of, 274–275; substituting, 274; written, 266–267
Consultation, popular, 309
Contents, policy, 32–35
Conservatism: antidemocratic, 218; democratic, 218–219
Conventions, nominating, 155
Converse, Philip E., 73n, 78n, 83n, 93n, 94n, 95, 110n, 111n, 176n, 177n, 178n, 179n, 180n, 191n, 192n, 194n, 195n, 293n, 325n
Conway, M. Margaret, 18n
Cook, Thomas I., 598n
Cooley, Thomas M., 457n
COPE. *See* Committee on Political Education
Corwin, Edward S., 394n
Cosa Nostra, 548
Cotter, Cornelius P., 203n
Council of Economic Advisers, 392
Council of Mutual Economic Assistance (COMECON), 648
Council for Social Action of the Congregational Churches, 236
Council-manager form of local government, 481–482

Councilar form of municipal government, 480–481

Courts: civil, 448; control of administrative agencies by, 439; criminal, 448; democratic nations and, 446–455; democratic political process and, 465–466; function of, 456–457; general trial, 450; hierarchies of appeal, 449–450; intermediate, of appeal, 450; local, 448–449; national, 448–449; origin of, 446–447; preliminary, 450; procedures of, 452–454; Soviet Union and, 466–469; types of, 447–449; supreme, 450. *See also* International Court of Justice; Judicial branch of government; judicial review; Supreme Court (US)

Cousins, Norman, 497n, 644

Cree, Nathan, 342n

Crime, 285; defined, 547; organized, 547–548; police and, 547–549; unorganized, 547–548

Criminal courts, 448

Criminal law, 445

Cronon, E. David, 569n

Crossley, Archibald, 114, 118n

Crossley, Helen M., 118n

Crowe, Robert W., 320n

Culture: concept of, 80–82; nationalism and, 61

Culture, political, 69–89; components of, 80–82; definition of, 79–80, 293; influence on form of government, 293

Customs: behavior and, 47; constitutional, 268–270

Cutright, Phillips, 290n

Dahl, Robert A., 16, 17n, 29n, 106n, 258n, 285n, 287n, 304n, 305n, 427, 485n, 610n

Daley, Richard J., 83, 205, 324

Dallin, Alexander, 509n

Danelski, David J., 463n

Daniels, Jonathan, 435

Daughters of the American Revolution, 250

David, Paul T., 155n, 211n

Davies, James C., 70n

Davies, S. O., 213n

Davis, Angela, 456

Davis, James W., Jr., 14n

Davis, Lane, 288n

Dawson, Richard E., 90n

Dawson, Robert M., 340n

Dayan, Moshe, 28

Debate, political, general issues in, 504–505

Debré, Michel, 402

Debuyst, Frederic, 370n

Decatur, Stephen, 81

Declaration of Independence, 280, 283, 523–524

Declaration of the Rights of Man and of the Citizen, 524

Decter, Midge, 558n

Deener, David, 265n

Defendants' rights, 550–554

de Gaulle, Charles, 28, 131, 185, 203, 325, 365, 402–403

de Grazia, Alfred, 322n, 509n

de Jouvenel, Bertrand, 295

de Medici, Catherine, 555

Democracy, 280, 281, 286, 287, 293; areas of agreement and disagreement about, 305–306; aristocracy in, 423–440, characteristics of, 305–306, Chinese model of, 302–303; Christian, 218; communist models of, 301–303; constitutionalism and, 313–314; constitutions and, 264–277; definition of, 306–312; direct (participatory) model of, 288, 303–304; desire for, 294; indirect (elitist) model of, 304–305; legislative process in, 351–353; local government in, 473–477; majoritarian concept of, 312–313; models of, 301–314; nations ranked according to degree of, 300; noncommunist models of, 303–306; parliamentary, legislative process in, 352–353; participatory, 288, 303–304; political parties and, 196–221; presidential, 351–352; pressure groups in, 255–258; public opinion and, 103–119; representation and, 319–345; Soviet model of, 301–302; suffrage and, 147–151

Democratic conservatism, 218

Democratic socialism, 217

Demonstrations, 243–245

Denisov, A., 278n, 536n

Dennis, Jack, 81n, 83n, 89n

*Dennis* v. *United States,* 542, 543n

Dependend variable, defined, 33n

de Poitiers, Diane, 555

*De Rerum Novarum,* 218

de Ruggiero, Guido, 218n

Desegregation, 564, 566–567

Deutsch, Karl W., 58n, 60n, 62n, 127n, 592n, 647n

de Valera, Eamon, 327–328

Developing nations, 61–63, 284; administrators in, role of, 430–431; party system in, 227–228; political communication and, 141–142

Devine, Donald J., 292n
de Visscher, Charles, 628n
DeVries, Walter, 189n
Dewey, Thomas E., 72
Dexter, Lewis Anthony, 114n, 129n, 371n
*Dharna,* 246
Dictatorship, 280, 281, 285, 287, 293;
    constitutions and, 277–279; definition
    of, 315; essentials of, 314–317; models
    of, 314–317; origin of term, 314;
    political parties and, 221–228; public
    opinion and, 104; totalitarianism
    distinguished from, 315–317; varieties
    of, 315
Dillon's Rule (John F. Dillon), 483
Diplomacy, as foreign policy technique,
    604–605
Diplomats, functions of, 603–604
Disarmament, 624–627; atomic, 625–627
Discrimination, racial, 55–56, 562–563; by
    sex, 555–558; South Africa and,
    580–583
Disputes: international, peaceful settlement
    of, 627–628; national-local, settling,
    491
Dixon, Robert G., Jr., 322n, 332n
Dolbeare, Kenneth M., 14n
Donovan, Robert J., 396n
Douglas, William O., 460
Douglas-Home, Sir Alec, 185, 386
Downs, Anthony, 220n
Dozer, Donald M., 604n
Dred Scott case, 458
Drier, J., 649n
Drury, Allen, 373n
Duclos, Jacques, 162
Dupeux, Georges, 95n, 177n, 178n, 325n
*Durand* v. *Hollins,* 394n
Duvalier, François, 316, 535
Duverger, Maurice, 9n, 196n, 201n, 208n,
    212, 402n

Eagleton, Thomas, 185
Easton, David, 17n, 21n, 24n, 30, 63, 64n,
    89n, 90, 290
Eastland, James, 369
Eavesdropping, electronic, 552–553
Eckstein, Harry, 99n
École Libre des Sciences Politiques, 9
Economic and Social Council (UN), 637
Economy: free market, 296; influence on
    form of government, 291
Edelman, Murray, 131n, 503n
Eden, Anthony, 158, 386
Edinger, Lewis J., 86n, 187n
Edison Electric Institute, 233

Education: blacks and, 575–577; propaganda
    versus, 128; purposes of, 77
Educational groups, influence on individual,
    77
Edwards, David V., 624n
Efficacy, political, perceived, 88–89
Ehrlichman, John, 392, 463
Ehrmann, Henry W., 131n, 203n, 232n,
    376n, 402n, 415n, 424n
Eichelberger, Clark M., 642n
Eichmann, Adolf, 631
Eisenhower, Dwight D., 184n, 195, 238, 252,
    325, 392, 394, 398, 402, 492
*Ekklesia,* 319–320, 350
Elazar, Daniel J., 491n, 492n
Eldersveld, Samuel J., 200n
Electioneering, 242–243
Elections, 156–171; administering, 156–159,
    fraud and, 159; free democratic model
    of, 144–146; frequency of, 156–158;
    problems in, 159–160; representation
    and, 160; timing of, 156–158; in USSR,
    168–171
Electoral process, 142–171; democratic,
    160–168; majority, 161–162; party-list,
    164–166; policial effects of, 166–168;
    proportional, 162–166
Elijah Muhammed (Elijah Poole), 570–571
Elitism, 286, 287–288
Elizabeth I, Queen (England), 555
Elizabeth II, Queen (England), 386, 387
Ellsberg, Daniel, 463
Emergency Planning, Office of, 392
Emerson, Rupert, 62n
Emerson, Thomas I., 529n
Empirical beliefs, 80–81
Employees, civil service. *See* Civil service
    employees
Employment, blacks, and, 579
Energy crisis. *See* Arab oil embargo
Engels, Friedrich, 507
Environment, physical, political opinions
    and, 73
Environments, of political systems, 288–291
Epstein, Leon D., 146n, 155n, 197n, 198n,
    200n, 204, 208n, 213n, 407n
Equal Employment Opportunity
    Commission, 579
Equal Rights Amendment, 561–562
Equality, political, 308–309
Equity law, 444–445
Ervin, Sam, 356
Eskimos, political system of, 48, 57, 284
Esquadrão de Morte (Brazil), 540
Ethnic groups: influence on individuals,
    75–76; as pressure groups, 236

International law, 628–633
International Political Science Association, 10, 11
International politics. *See* Politics, international
International Telephone and Telegraph, 606
Ionescu, Ghita, 509n
Irish, Marian D., 12n
Irwin, Henry D., 268n
Issue orientation, voting behavior and, 180–182
Izaak Walton League of America, 250

Jackson, Andrew, 390, 458
Jackson, Henry "Scoop," 185
Jackson, Jesse, 324
Jackson, Richard N., 448n
Jacob, Herbert, 451n
Jacobs, Paul, 571n
Jahnige, Thomas P., 461n
Javits, Jacob, 369
"Jawboning," 32
Jefferson, Thomas, 28, 150, 350, 473, 474, 475
Jenness, Linda, 557n
Jennings, M. Kent, 97n, 476
Jennings, W. Ivor, 359n, 404n
Jensen, Jay W., 130n, 134n, 137, 138n
Jervis, Robert, 588n
Jewish Defense League, 236
Johnson, Andrew, 355
Johnson, Lyndon B., 72, 184n, 203, 213, 247, 344, 391, 392, 394, 397, 420, 575
Johnson, Samuel, 441, 520
Joint committees, 364
Jones, A. H. M., 303n
Jones, Charles O., 367n
Jones, G. W., 408n
Jones, W. B., 268n
Judges, 340; appointment of, 451; election of, 451–452; insulation from political pressure, 455; political process and, 461–463; recall of, 451–452; removal of, 451; selection of, 450–452, 463; separation from prosecutors, 454–455; tenure of, 450–452
Judicial branch of government, 441–470; decision making and, 464; formal relations with legislatures and executives, 454–455; implementation of decisions, 464–465; policy-making and, 459–460
Judicial decisions, 267–268. *See also* Supreme Court (US)
Judicial legislation, 458–461

Judicial process, political conflict in, 463–465
Judicial review, 265–266, 267–268; defined, 265
Justice, Soviet concept of, 469–470

Kahn, Herman, 608n
Kalinin, M. I., 169
Kaplan, Abraham, 17n, 21n, 29n, 295, 610n
Kaplan, Morton A., 588n, 602, 628
Kariel, Henry S., 258n
Karlsson, Georg, 97n
Katz, Elihu, 136n
*Katz* v. *United States*, 553n
Katzenbach, Nicholas de B., 628n
Kautsky, John H., 62n
Keech, William R., 575n
Keefe, William J., 197n, 214n, 360n, 369n
Kefauver, Estes, 268n
Kellog-Briand Pact, 629
Kendall, Willmoore, 3n, 44n, 106n, 211n, 306n, 400n, 515n
Keniston, Kenneth, 95n
Kennan, George, 598n
Kennedy, Edward, 184, 185, 382
Kennedy, John F., 86, 114, 188, 193, 194, 247, 249, 270, 392, 394, 395
Kennedy, Robert F., 54, 86, 247, 352
Keohane, Robert O., 641n
Kessel, John L., 73n
Kesselman, Mark, 480n
Key, V. O., Jr., 73n, 103n, 105, 111, 138n, 155n, 160n, 198n, 235
Khruschev, Nikita, 437, 509, 535
Kibbutzim, 94n
Kilpatrick, Jeane J., 557n
King, Anthony, 132n, 185n, 197n, 368n, 370n, 405n, 408n
King, Martin Luther, Jr., 54, 86, 245, 246, 247, 566, 567
Kingdon, John W., 173n
Kingsley, J. Donald, 431n, 434n
Kirichenko, M., 278n, 536n
Kirkpatrick, Evron M., 17n
Kirkpatrick, Jeane J., 73n, 325, 371n
Kissinger, Henry, 392, 627
"Kitchen cabinet," President's, 392
Klapper, Joseph, T., 137n, 139n, 141n
Knights of Labor, 233
Knorr, Klaus, 611n
Koenig, Louis W., 401n
Koestler, Arthur, 429n
Kohn, Hans, 58n, 592n
Korean War, 638–639
Kosygin, Alexei, 509
Kotler, Milton, 304n, 322n

Marshall, Charles B., 611n
Marshall, John, 265, 458
Marshall Plan, 245, 608
Marshall, Thurgood, 3, 460, 575
Marx, Fritz Morstein, 418n
Marx, Karl, 78, 291, 301, 429, 507
Marxism, 208
Mass media: political communication and, 129–135; political socialization and, 98
Matthews, Donald R., 371n, 575n
May, John D., 299n
Mayo, Henry B., 305n
Mayoral form of municipal government, 479–480
Media: political communication, 128–137; various, effects of, 139–141. *See also* Mass media
Medicare, 238, 398
Meier, August, 570n
Meisel, John, 212n
Mendés-France, Pierre, 233, 410
Meredith, James, 249
Merhige, Robert, 576, 577
Merit system, 423. *See also* Civil service
Merriam, Charles E., 173
Meyer, Alfred G., 277n, 279n, 302n
Meyer, Cord, 644
Meyer, Frank S., 515n
Meynaud, Jean, 232n
Michels, Robert, 200
Middleton, John, 48n
Milbrath, Lester W., 82n, 174n, 191n, 240n, 256n
Mill, John Stuart, 158, 159n
Miller, Arthur H., 73n, 83n, 87, 185
Miller, Warren E., 73n, 78n, 83n, 93n, 94n, 95, 97n, 110, 111n, 176n, 177n, 179n, 180n, 185, 189n, 191n, 192n, 194n, 195n, 293n, 373n, 374
Mills, C. Wright, 258n, 288, 414n, 285n, 597n
Milne, Edward, 213n
Milton, John, 527
Minority leader, 368
Minutemen, 238
*Miranda* v. *Arizona,* 554
Misdemeanors, 547
Mississippi White Knights, 238, 247–248
Mitchell, Joseph M., 429–430
Models, 294–318; comparing reality with, 297–298; of democracy, 301–314; of dictatorship, 314–317; of government, 297; nature and uses of, in social sciences, 295–301; normative versus descriptive, 296–297
Mollet, Guy, 410

Monarchs: elected, 384; hereditary, 383
Monarchy, 286
Montesquieu, 350–351, 353
Montgomery, John D., 606n
Monypenny, Phillip, 433n
Moore, Barrington, Jr., 292n, 537n
Moore, Clement, 221n
Moos, Malcolm, 598n
Moral precepts, behavior and, 46
Moran, Barbara, 556n
Morgan, Arthur E., 473
Morgenstern, Oskar, 602n
Morgenthau, Hans J., 593, 594n, 598n, 611n, 614n, 621n, 622n, 624, 628n, 646n
Morrah, Dermot, 387n
Morrison, Herbert, 404n
Motion pictures, as political communication media, 123, 134–135
Moyers, Bill, 392
Mueller, John E., 344n
Muhammed Ali (Cassius Clay), 570n, 571
Muhammed, Elijah. *See* Elijah Muhammed
Munger, Frank J., 200n
Municipal government, 478–479; forms of, 479–482. *See also* Local government
Munro, William B., 342n
Murphy, Frank, 534
Murphy, George, 70n
Murray, James N., 637n
Muskie, Edmund, 126, 185
Mussolini, Benito, 219, 224, 294, 325, 328, 381, 535

Nader, Ralph, 231
Nassar, Gamal Abdel, 295
Nathan, Theodore, 557n
National Association for the Advancement of Colored People (NAACP), 3, 55–56, 236, 567, 575
National Association of Manufacturers, 232, 240, 242
National Capitol Housing Authority, 415
National Catholic Welfare Conference, 236
National Coal Board (England), 419
National Commission on the Causes and Prevention of Violence, 247
National Cooperative Milk Producer's Federation, 234
National Council against Conscription, 232
National courts, 448–449
National Farmer's Union, 234, 250
National Labor Relations Board, 419
National Mobilization Committee to End the War in Vietnam, 238
National Municipal League, 236, 481

Index

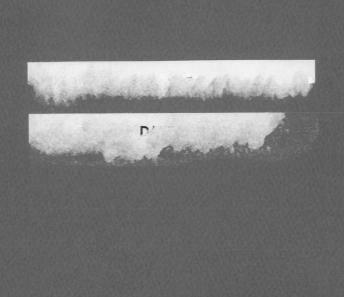